W9-CLZ-232

SPARKNOTES™
101

Short Stories

SPARK PUBLISHING

© 2007 by Spark Publishing

All rights reserved. No part of this publication may be reproduced, stored in a retrieval system, or transmitted, in any form or by any means, electronic, mechanical, photocopying, recording, or otherwise, without prior written permission from the publisher.

SPARKNOTES is a registered trademark of SparkNotes LLC

Spark Publishing
A Division of Barnes & Noble
120 Fifth Avenue
New York, NY 10011
www.sparknotes.com

Library of Congress Cataloging-in-Publication Data

SparkNotes 101–short stories.
    p. cm.
  Includes bibliographical references.
  ISBN-13: 978-1-4114-9865-5
  ISBN-10: 1-4114-9865-8
  1. Short stories, American–Stories, plots, etc. 2. Short stories, English—Stories, plots, etc.
3. Short stories—Stories, plots, etc. 4. Literature–Examinations–Study guides. I. Title: Short stories.

PS648.S5S685 2006
823'.0108–dc22

                                                                                    2006028152

Please submit changes or report errors to www.sparknotes.com/errors.

Printed and bound in the United States.

1 3 5 7 9 10 8 6 4 2

Contents

A+ Student Essays

A Note from SparkNotes

Welcome to the *SparkNotes 101* series! This book covers the fifty-five short stories that have had the greatest impact on American literature and are studied most often in literature classes.

Every component of this study guide has been designed to help you process the material more quickly. Below are some quick tips and explanations to help you get the most out of this book.

INTRODUCTION

Before diving into the notes, you may want to get an overview of the short story genre. The Introduction will discuss the nature of the short story, the history of the form, and some of the most important short story writers in the literary canon.

THE NOTES

To make navigation easy, the fifty-five entries are arranged alphabetically by title. If you want to see the stories listed alphabetically by author, turn to page 491 and consult the Appendix. Each story's note contains the following sections:

- **Context:** An overview of the author, the circumstances surrounding the writing of the story, and how the story and the author have affected short story writing in general.
- **Plot Overview:** A concise summary of the story to refresh your memory and help you understand major plot points.
- **Character List:** A list of characters in order of importance, along with a brief explanation of the role each character plays in the story.
- **Analysis of Major Characters:** In-depth studies of what makes the most important characters tick.
- **Themes, Motifs, and Symbols:** The most important ideas of the story, all in one place. Themes are the fundamental and often universal ideas explored in a literary work. Motifs are recurring structures, contrasts, or literary devices that can help develop and inform the text's major themes. Symbols are objects, characters, figures, or colors used to represent abstract ideas or concepts.
- **Short Story Analysis:** Critical discussions that explore what makes each story remarkable.
- **Important Quotations Explained:** The most important lines from the story with explanations of why they're significant.

A+ STUDENT ESSAYS

They're the real thing. At the end of the book, we give you ten essays of A+ quality so you can see how students have responded to questions similar to those you might find on an exam.

These essays will show you how to pull together the ideas of the story and use them in a compelling argument.

We hope *SparkNotes 101: Short Stories* helps you, gives you confidence, and occasionally saves your butt! We also hope this book helps you discover the pleasure that comes from reading and understanding short stories. Your input makes us better. Let us know what you think or how we can improve this book at **sparknotes.com/comments**.

Introduction

The authors we've included in *SparkNotes 101: Short Stories* range from the earliest pioneers of the genre to some of today's most exciting and important writers. What links them all is a masterful exploration of the possibilities of the short story and a willingness to experiment with new ideas and new ways of conveying human experience through writing. These are the writers and the stories that readers turn to in order to get a brief but unforgettable look at life in the modern world.

The huge number of short stories available to read means that there is great diversity within the form, not only in subject matter and style but in length. Ernest Hemingway's story "Hills Like White Elephants," for example, is not much longer than an average high-school term paper—about 1,500 words. James Joyce's story "The Dead," on the other hand, is about ten times that long. Despite this wide variation, scholars generally agree that a short story is any piece of fiction that can be comfortably read in a single sitting and that usually focuses on one incident featuring a small number of characters. Short stories are remarkable for being fast and to the point.

Many people think that because short stories are so brief and narrow in focus, they are easier to understand than novels, plays, or poems and must therefore be easier to write. In truth, it requires great skill and subtlety on a writer's part to achieve powerful intellectual and emotional effects in such a small amount of space. Even writing a short story that makes sense, let alone one that people would care to read, is a difficult task, as writers do not have the luxury of lengthy exposition, scene setting, and character development in a short story as they do in a novel. The short story is a difficult form to master, and many writers spend years reworking a single story before they are willing to publish it.

A small number of stories, such as Shirley Jackson's "The Lottery" and works by Edgar Allen Poe and Arthur Conan Doyle, have become cultural touchstones and achieved the ultimate contemporary honor: they have appeared in episodes of *The Simpsons*. More important for the history of literature, short stories as a whole have had a profound impact on the form of the novel. Compared to earlier novels by the likes of Henry James or Virginia Woolf, more recent novels favor shorter scenes with fewer internal monologues and less exposition, a sign that the short story is melding with and transforming the novel. In fact, a growing trend is the publication of novels that are a collection of short stories about the same characters. The influence of short stories, as well as their continued popularity, has made them the quintessential literary form of our fast-paced modern life.

Although the ancestry of the short story can be traced back to the myths and fables of antiquity, the form began to take on its modern shape only in the eighteenth century with the emergence of the literary genre known as the sketch. Similar to myths and fables, sketches are very short pieces that provide character studies or give brief overviews of some event, usually comical in nature. Sketches were important because writers paid greater attention to realism than they had in previous short pieces. Unlike fables, however, sketches explored social, emotional, and intellectual life, rather than merely teaching moral lessons. The popularity of sketches lasted for a considerable time, and several of the nineteenth century's most famous novelists, Charles Dickens in particular, got their start writing sketches. Sketches were also the inspiration for the men many consider to be the first modern short story writers, Edgar Allen Poe and Nathaniel Hawthorne, who wrote several canonical short stories in the 1830s and 1840s. The works of these two writers marked not only the beginning of the modern short story but also the beginning of a long trend of American dominance of the form, a trend that still persists today.

Although short stories have been most popular in the United States, some of the form's most important innovators hailed from around the globe. In the late nineteenth century, French writer Guy de Maupassant and Russian writer Anton Chekhov developed new techniques for writing short stories that have had considerable influence. Guy de Maupassant took techniques that had previously only appeared in melodramatic novels, such as sudden plot twists and ironic developments, and incorporated them into his short stories. Many subsequent stories by numerous other writers use these methods, which fit well with the fast pace of short stories. Anton Chekhov, on the other hand, wrote stories that are remarkable for focusing on the brief moments in which characters' inner lives are revealed, rather than on exciting action or clear climaxes. Although this technique is quite different from de Maupassant's, it has been similarly influential.

By the end of the nineteenth century, the mass production of magazines had become cheap and easy, and the short story blossomed because magazine editors needed to fill space and attract readers with engaging but brief fiction. In Britain, the *Strand* magazine rose to unprecedented popularity on the strength of the Sherlock Holmes stories of Arthur Conan Doyle, and in the United States, the *Saturday Evening Post* and *Atlantic Monthly* both became prime forums for short story writers such as John Steinbeck and Ernest Hemingway.

The first issue of the *New Yorker* was published in 1925, and the magazine quickly became the most prestigious venue for short fiction in the English language. The list of writers published in the *New Yorker* is great in length and quality, and the magazine's tendency to favor sophistication and cleverness in its fiction led writer Dorothy Parker to suggest that there is a distinct literary genre known as "a *New Yorker* story." For better or worse, the *New Yorker* is still seen as the standard-bearer for short stories today, but there are countless magazines and literary journals where readers can find short stories that are as numerous and various as the people who read them.

A&P

John Updike
(1932–)

CONTEXT

John Updike was born in Shillington, Pennsylvania, in 1932. His mother was a writer, and she encouraged her precocious son's writing. Updike attended Harvard University, where he was editor of the *Harvard Lampoon*, and did postgraduate work at Oxford. In the mid-1950s, Updike was hired by the *New Yorker* as a staff writer. *The New Yorker* was then, as now, a prestigious venue for new short fiction, and Updike's work fit in well with the magazine's urbane, witty style. "A&P," published in 1961 and appearing in the 1962 collection *Pigeon Feathers and Other Stories*, is in many ways a prototypical *New Yorker* story: a short, realistic, first-person narrative written in a distinctive voice and focusing on character study. The master of such fiction and Updike's acknowledged early role model was J. D. Salinger, whom Updike has praised for his ability to capture life in all its messy shapelessness. Updike has long since moved out of Salinger's shadow, however, and is renowned for his polished, descriptive prose that captures both the natural world and the cultural environment of our times. As Updike puts it, his short fiction is intended to "give the mundane its beautiful due."

Updike has been a consistently popular and highly prolific author since 1959, when he published both his first collection of short fiction, *The Same Door*, and his first novel, *The Poorhouse Fair*. Since then, he has continued to produce novels, short stories, poems, memoirs, essays, art criticism, and book reviews at an impressive clip. Updike has the unusual distinction of combining serious critical acclaim (although this has not been universal) and scholarly appreciation with a steady popularity with the reading public. Among his best-known novels are *Couples* (1968); *The Witches of Eastwick* (1984), which was made into a popular movie; and the "Rabbit" series: *Rabbit, Run* (1960), *Rabbit Redux* (1971), *Rabbit Is Rich* (1981), and *Rabbit at Rest* (1990). Much of Updike's fiction focuses on upper-middle-class suburban life, usually in New England or the Northeast, and often centers on a marriage under stress owing to the affairs of one or both of the partners. Updike has described his primary fictional concern as "the American small town, Protestant middle class"; the "Rabbit" series perfectly highlights this concern, as it traces the life of Harry "Rabbit" Angstrom, a suburban Pennsylvanian, from adolescence though old age, one decade at a time. The series has been celebrated for its evocation of America in the 1960s, 1970s, and 1980s. Updike's work has been shaped by his Christian faith and especially by the work of the Protestant theologians Karl Barth and Søren Kierkegaard.

Although he has had one of the most successful careers of any American writers, Updike has always had his detractors and enjoyed his fair share of controversy. He has feuded publicly with the famously touchy essayist and novelist Gore Vidal, as well as with the novelist John Gardner, who described Updike's work as "bourgeois-pornographic" fiction that glorifies adultery. Similar criticism has often been aimed at Updike's more sexually explicit work, particularly *Couples*, and even the early story "A&P," in which Updike's interest in the

A

dynamics of sexual attraction is clear. More recently, Updike's negative review of a novel by Tom Wolfe drew a withering reply from Wolfe, and the subsequent war of words, waged in the pages and letters columns of several magazines, was gleefully followed by the literary world. Still producing novels, stories, and criticism regularly, Updike remains one of the most visible figures in American letters, a perennial candidate for the Nobel Prize, and the rare writer who can combine literary merit with popular success.

PLOT OVERVIEW

Three teenage girls, wearing only their bathing suits, walk into an A&P grocery store in a small New England town. Sammy, a young man working the checkout line, watches them closely. He appraises their looks and notes even minute details about the way they carry themselves. He also speculates about their personalities and their motivation for entering the store dressed the way they are. Sammy is particularly interested in the most attractive girl, who appears to be the leader of the group. This girl, whom Sammy dubs "Queenie," has a natural grace and confidence, in addition to her beauty. As the girls roam the aisles of the A&P, they create a stir. As Sammy points out, the store is in the center of town, nowhere near the beach, where the girls' attire would attract less notice. Sammy's coworker Stokesie ogles the girls as well, joking around with Sammy as he does so. Sammy jokes along with him, but he feels the contrast between himself, still single, and the married Stokesie. Stokesie is resigned to a life of working at the A&P, whereas Sammy, although admitting that he and Stokesie are much alike, seems to feel that such a future is beneath him. As yet another of his coworkers begins to admire the girls, Sammy feels a twinge of pity for them for having compromised themselves this way, most likely without realizing it. This feeling is quickly supplanted by pure excitement as the girls choose Sammy's checkout line to make their purchase.

Lengel, the store manager, approaches Sammy's checkout lane. Lengel chastises the girls for entering the store in bathing suits, citing store policy. The girls are embarrassed, and Queenie protests that her mother wanted her to come in and buy some herring snacks. In this statement, Sammy gleans insight into Queenie's life. He imagines her parents at a party, everyone dressed nicely and sipping "drinks the color of water." He thinks about his own parents' parties, where people drink lemonade or cheap beer.

As the girls begin to leave the store, Sammy suddenly turns to Lengel and quits his job, protesting the way Lengel has embarrassed the girls. Sammy hopes the girls are watching him. Lengel tries to talk Sammy out of quitting, telling him that he will regret the decision later and that his quitting will disappoint his parents. Sammy, however, feels that he must see the gesture through to its conclusion, and he exits the A&P. When he reaches the parking lot, he sees that the girls are long gone. Sammy is left alone with his ambiguous feelings and a growing sense of foreboding about what life has in store for him.

CHARACTER LIST

Sammy   The narrator. Sammy is a nineteen-year-old boy working the checkout line at an A&P in a small New England town. When three girls come into the store wearing only bathing suits and are chastised by the store manager, Sammy quits his job, hoping to impress them, and is then filled with foreboding about the future.

Queenie A teenage girl who enters the A&P in her bathing suit and is nicknamed "Queenie" by Sammy. Queenie, the attractive leader of the three girls, rouses Sammy's desire from the minute he sees her. When the store manager reprimands her for wearing only a bathing suit in the store, she defends herself by saying she needs to buy herring snacks for her mother. Her response suggests to Sammy a sophisticated world very different from the one in which his own family lives.

Lengel The manager of the A&P. Lengel is a by-the-books manager, as well as a Sunday-school teacher. Stuffy and uptight, Lengel is, to Sammy, a prisoner of the system as well as an authority figure. Lengel confronts the girls about their skimpy attire, embarrassing them and angering Sammy.

Stokesie A checkout clerk at the A&P. Although Stokesie is only a few years older than Sammy, he is already married and has two children. Sammy condescends to Stokesie, who intends to make a career out of working at the A&P. However, Sammy also identifies with Stokesie in some ways and sees him as a cautionary example of how he himself might end up.

The First Friend ("Plaid") One of the three girls who wear bathing suits into the A&P. The first friend is somewhat attractive, but she is overshadowed by the girl Sammy calls Queenie.

The Second Friend ("Big Tall Goony Goony") One of the three girls who wear bathing suits into the A&P. The second friend serves as a contrast to the most attractive girl, whom Sammy calls Queenie.

ANALYSIS OF MAJOR CHARACTERS

SAMMY Sammy, the narrator of "A&P," is an opinionated, sarcastic, disaffected teenager with a healthy interest in the opposite sex and a keen observational sense. Sammy notices everything around him, and he drinks in every detail of the girls' physical appearance, from the texture and patterns of their bathing suits to the different boundaries of their tan lines. Sammy goes beyond the surface details to glean insights about the people he observes. For example, Queenie's dangling bra straps are intensely interesting in a purely sensual way, but they are also clues from which he begins to construct an image of her inner life. Once he hears the girls speak, his image becomes even more detailed, as he is able to get an impression of Queenie's social status. Sammy's focused observations and descriptions reveal his own prejudices and blind spots. For example, Sammy's frankly lustful ogling of the girls reveals a certain immaturity, and he is dismissive and contemptuous of the A&P customers, seeing them as "sheep" and "houseslaves." He is equally dismissive of his coworker Stokesie, whom Sammy sarcastically presents as an unimaginative drone.

The irony of Sammy's sense of superiority is that he realizes that, in the eyes of the rich, carefree Queenie, he must seem just like Stokesie and the straight-laced Lengel. His desire to set himself apart from them—to prove that he is different—compels him to quit his job. However, he announces, "I quit" primarily because he wants the girls to overhear him, and the gesture loses resonance when he realizes they didn't notice it. It seems less wise when he is left not with admiration but with a vague guilt and doubt about his rash action. Sammy's desire for Queenie, which begins merely as a young man's interest in a pretty girl, ends up as a desire for escape from the A&P and, in effect his own life. The world he imagines through Queenie—a world of sophisticated parents, summer vacations, and the freedom to disregard the social norms of places like the A&P—makes him hunger for opportunities beyond his limited experience. In resigning his position, Sammy is trying to signal his desired membership in this glamorous alternate world and exercise his desire to make a new life.

QUEENIE   Queenie is a mixture of precocity and innocence, testing the boundaries of allowable behavior without fully grasping the implications of her actions until she is confronted and embarrassed by Lengel. Queenie is the leader of her group of friends, and she has clearly induced the other two girls into making a spectacle of themselves by walking into the A&P wearing only their bathing suits. While the other girls seem awkward and abashed, Queenie is undaunted by the disapproving glances of the other shoppers and the eager gazes of the male employees. Although she simply goes about the task of finding her herring snacks, her confident stride reveals her awareness of being observed: she seems to be putting on a performance of both independence and sexual power. When Lengel challenges her behavior, however, her self-confidence weakens slightly. Called to task for her skimpy garments, she hovers between her desire to be sexually provocative and her knowledge of the vulnerable position in which she has put herself. No longer a self-assured sexual being, her response—that she is buying something for her mother—reveals that she has not yet quite reached adulthood. The combination of her brazenness and vulnerability ultimately spurs Sammy to shun the rules that bind him.

THEMES, MOTIFS, AND SYMBOLS

THEMES

THE POWER OF DESIRE   From the moment the girls walk into the A&P, they attract the gaze of every man in the store, which demonstrates the power their sexuality gives them over the opposite sex. Although they make a point of acting nonchalant (Queenie more successfully than the other two), the girls are well aware of the eyes tracking their every move. As long as the girls do not acknowledge the men's interest, they are in a position of power—inspiring desire but not subject to it. Their strategy works well, and the A&P's male employees—even the unyielding Lengel—show some degree of sexual interest. However, Lengel ultimately undermines this strategy and tries to lessen their power. By confronting the girls so bluntly, Lengel calls the girls on their behavior, embarrassing them by suggesting that they are well aware of the inappropriateness of their attire. Queenie's claim—"We *are* decent"—is an attempt to reestablish their superior position, implying that it is Lengel who is being inappropriate.

The girls have a profound transformative effect on the men in the A&P, especially Sammy. They inspire the men to act piggishly, as they stare at the girls while making lewd comments to one another. For these men, their response seems rooted in hormones, and Lengel's attempt to get the girls to respect social norms is an effort both to control the desire of such young men and to protect the girls from it. In Sammy, however, the girls inspire a more profound reaction. Under the influence of his desire for Queenie, Sammy's imagination is awakened, and he takes a dramatic step to change his life. Sammy's actions are not purely motivated by his desire, but they are inseparable from it.

THE MYSTERY OF OTHER MINDS Throughout the story, Sammy exhibits prowess in both observing others and gleaning insights from those observations, but the girls suggest to him the true mystery of other minds. When a customer reprimands Sammy for a mistake, Sammy characterizes the woman as a witch straight out of Salem and thinks, "I know it made her day to trip me up." For Sammy, the customers at the A&P are all too easy to understand. The same holds true for Stokesie and Lengel, who Sammy believes he has thoroughly figured out. When the girls enter the store, however, Sammy wonders what on earth they're thinking. Although Sammy makes an effort to understand the girls, especially Queenie, and believes that he is successful, his confidence is undermined by his actions at the end of the story. His grand gesture of sympathy for the girls—his quitting—goes unnoticed, and his motivations are muddled and confused. He is left with a sense that, for all his ability to observe and understand others, he must now turn his inquisitive eye on himself.

MOTIFS

GIRL-WATCHING Girl-watching is what sets "A&P" in motion, and Sammy provides copious details of the three girls as he watches them walk around the store. Sammy describes each of the girls in turn, noticing the details of their bathing suits, their hairstyles, and their bodies. His interest is explicitly sexual. Sammy appraises the first friend's "can" and almost becomes faint over Queenie's breasts. He notices the varied shades of their skin and even analyzes Queenie's gait. Such detailed observations suggest the extent of Sammy's rapturous appreciation of beauty as well as the underlying aggression in the male gaze. Sammy's girl-watching leads to both a warm, imaginative interest in the object of his desire and a darker, more possessive feeling (at one point, Sammy refers to "my girls"). In the end, any possession of the girls Sammy has experienced is revealed to be an illusion. He has watched them, and that is all.

BRAND NAMES Brand names appear throughout "A&P," setting the story firmly in the postwar period of American prosperity, when a flood of consumer goods hit the markets and advertising became a pervasive force. Updike tries to capture the sense of plenitude in a well-stocked market by referring to "the cat-and-dog-food-breakfast-cereal-macaroni-rice-raisins-seasonings-spreads-spaghetti-soft-drinks-crackers-and-cookies aisle." But he also tries to convey some of the artificiality inherent in an environment dominated by marketing and branding by focusing on the cheesy labels on all the merchandise. He repeatedly invokes the brand names: Hiho crackers, Diet Delight peaches, Kingfish Fancy Herring Snacks in Pure Sour Cream, and so on. They are all unified under the A&P logo and surrounded by cars such as the Ford Falcon. For better or worse, brands and labels are an important part of the cultural landscape, and their artificiality is one of the things against which Sammy ultimately rebels.

SYMBOLS

BATHING SUITS The bathing suits that the girls wear into the A&P are an emblem of the girls' casual disregard of the social rules of the small town. They also represent the girls' deliberate provocation, an attempt to attract the eye of every man they encounter. Sammy is initially drawn to the girls simply because they are scantily clad, young, and attractive.

However, for Sammy, the bathing suits come to symbolize freedom and escape from the world in which he finds himself. What he ultimately finds compelling about the girls in their bathing suits is that they have disrupted the system of rules that he has been forced to observe, an observation that Lengel, the authority figure, underscores by trying to enforce the rules the girls have violated. When Sammy quits his job, he significantly removes the corporate uniform (apron and bowtie) that establishes his place in the system. However, the freedom of the bathing-suited girls remains unavailable to him. Sammy ends up alone, in a white shirt his mother ironed for him, wondering what to do next.

HERRING SNACKS The Kingfish Fancy Herring Snacks in Pure Sour Cream purchased by Queenie take on a symbolic value in Sammy's eyes when he hears Queenie explain that she is buying them for her mother. Instantly, Sammy has a vision of the kind of party at which such herring snacks would be served, and it is a world away from the parties his own parents throw. Sammy mentally contrasts the white jackets, herring snacks, and sophisticated cocktails of Queenie's social set with the lemonade, Schlitz beer (a working-class brew), and novelty glasses of his own parents' group. Sammy understands that from Queenie's perspective, "the crowd that runs the A&P must look pretty crummy." Sammy's sense of his own superiority to his surroundings is both heightened and humbled by this realization. But rather than resent Queenie for her social advantages, Sammy envies her freedom from the constraints he himself feels. Quitting his job, then, is both a doomed attempt to impress the girl and a gesture of self-liberation.

SHORT STORY ANALYSIS

FIRST-PERSON NARRATION AND THE UNRELIABLE NARRATOR The voice that Updike creates for Sammy is both deliberately casual and poetically descriptive, alternating between common slang and sharp wit. Sammy is clearly intelligent, although still uneducated at nineteen, and capable of creating striking images, such as calling a girl's hair "oaky" and describing the sunlight as "skating around" the parking lot. Updike keeps Sammy's language colloquial, beginning sentences with "You know" and "Really" and including asides and hesitations in an attempt to keep the language natural. The effect of Updike's technique in handling the first-person narration in "A&P" is to ensure that the reader will not mistake Sammy's voice for Updike's. That is, Sammy is not meant to function as a stand-in for Updike or as a spokesman for the "authorial" point of view.

Sammy is a classic example of an "unreliable" narrator—that is, a narrator who is a full-fledged character in the story and whose opinions must be analyzed rather than simply accepted. For example, Sammy's comment on the unknowability of the female mind should be taken as a statement in a character's voice and not as a statement of Updike's feelings on the topic. A more significant example is Sammy's statement that "once you begin a gesture it's fatal not to go through with it." This is by no means a message statement by Updike. Rather, it is a highly debatable proposition by an impulsive young man who may have reason to regret the gesture he completes. An understanding of Updike's subtle handling of his narrator is key to grasping the true action of the plot of "A&P": the slow revelation of a young man's character.

CONFORMITY AND REBELLION   One of the things Sammy comes to understand during the course of "A&P" is how close he is to being assimilated into the corporate structure represented by the A&P. At the beginning of the story, Sammy is quite clear that he is unlike the "sheep" and "houseslaves" milling about the aisles of the store. Sammy is equally confident that he is neither a chump like Stokesie, who wants to climb the management ladder, nor a flunky like Lengel, who haggles over cabbages and hides behind his office door all day. As he surveys the scene, Sammy is comfortable behind his wised-up, sarcastic attitude. However, all this self-confidence is shaken by the three girls who enter the store in their bathing suits, and especially by the beautiful leader of the group. From the start, Updike emphasizes the disruptive effect the girls have on the usual order of the store. They immediately cause Sammy to make an error at his register, which he hardly ever does. They move against the usual traffic flow of the store, disturbing the other shoppers. And of course they completely distract all the male employees and eventually draw the disapproving attention of Lengel.

Although Sammy's attention is riveted by the sexual display the girls make, their casual defiance of the standards of the community ultimately affects Sammy more strongly. Sammy is used to being a sarcastic, ironic observer of the rules, whereas Queenie and her friends simply ignore those rules. When Queenie defends herself against Lengel by insisting, "We *are* decent," she is only trying to get out of an embarrassing situation. Sammy, however, decides that she is simply correct: youth and beauty are always decent, and natural grace should trump the world of brand names and money every time. Sammy quits because he is infatuated with the glamour and sophistication he imagines in Queenie's life and wants to impress her. He also quits because he realizes that in a quarrel between rebellious beauty and stifling order, he wants beauty to win (even if that stifling order provides him with a paycheck).

HISTORICAL CONTEXT   "A&P" was published in 1961 and is an early version of what would become the defining narrative of the 1960s in popular mythology—the youthful rebels taking on the soulless system. The story includes the key elements of the myth, including the backdrop of postwar prosperity and the attendant consumer culture, a hint of the Cold War (Sammy imagines the Russians controlling the A&P in 1990), and the requisite opposition of youth and authority in the confrontation between Sammy, the girls, and Lengel. An important indicator of the seismic social upheavals of the 1960s that lay ahead is the story's focus on the inappropriate dress of the girls. The ultimate symbol of the generational conflict of the 1960s was the contrast between long-haired, freewheeling hippies and their parents in traditional suits and dresses. The immodesty of the girls walking around the A&P in revealing bathing suits is a harbinger of the many confrontations over public decency that would come in the ensuing decade.

Sammy seems already to be on the side of those who favor the "natural" approach over the "uptight" buttoned-down style of the older generation, although what he really wants from life is still defined mostly in terms of what he *doesn't* want: he doesn't want to be stuck at the A&P like Stokesie, he doesn't want to be buttoned up like Lengel, and he doesn't want the kind of life his parents have. The vague desires he does have seem to be mirrored in the brazen, scantily clad girls. This sort of conflict between the "establishment" and the "rebels" would soon become a favorite Hollywood device, recycled endlessly from *Easy Rider* to *American Beauty*. In the case of "A&P," the ultimate result of Sammy's act of defiance is not some glorious liberation but only a young man at loose ends, struggling to redefine himself just as the country faced its own changing identity in the 1960s.

IMPORTANT QUOTATIONS EXPLAINED

---

1. *You never know for sure how girls' minds work (do you really think it's a mind in there or just a little buzz like a bee in a glass jar?).*

Sammy speculates on the mental processes of girls early in the story, at the height of his confidence. Condescending and arrogant, he assumes that if he cannot understand the workings of a girl's mind, it is because there is no mind there to understand. The opposite possibility—that it is his understanding that is limited—does not occur to him. Sammy's male chauvinist attitude is mostly a pose, however, part of his idea of himself as the smart, sarcastic observer. This observation is actually linked to a close reading by Sammy of the body language and interaction of the three girls. Despite Sammy's posing, he is deeply interested in women, both physically and mentally, although he is not as worldly or wise as he supposes.

---

2. *But it seems to me that once you begin a gesture it's fatal not to go through with it.*

Sammy makes this resolution near the end of the story, as Lengel tries to dissuade him from quitting his job. The issue here for Sammy is one of authenticity. Sammy thinks that it would be "fatal" for him not to complete the gesture of quitting over Lengel's treatment of the girls because the gesture in question has become a matter of self-definition. By quitting, Sammy intends to align himself with Queenie's world, a world of sophistication, youth, and beauty, whose values seem opposite to those of the A&P. If he doesn't go through with quitting, he feels he'll be accepting the values he has come to associate with the A&P: conformity, authority, and shallow materialism. The problem for Sammy is that he discovers that going through with such a self-defining gesture is just as "fatal" as not going through with it—fatal in the sense of determining one's fate. Sammy makes his dramatic gesture, but he must now live with the consequences.

---

3. *His face was dark gray and his back stiff, as if he'd just had an injection of iron, and my stomach kind of fell as I felt how hard the world was going to be to me hereafter.*

In this, the last sentence of the story, Sammy looks back through the window of the store at Lengel taking his place behind the register. Through the window, Lengel appears as cold and hard as metal, as inflexible physically as he was in his actions. Sammy connects the "hardness" of Lengel's appearance with the hardness that awaits him in his future dealings with the world—there are a lot of Lengels out there, and they tend to do the hiring. In another sense, Sammy has discovered that the world can be "hard" in same way that a math problem can be hard. Sammy's self-satisfaction has been deflated, and he has learned that he is not able to negotiate every difficulty successfully. Sammy has learned a little bit about the kind of person he is and the specific way in which the world will always be "hard" for and to him.

Araby

James Joyce
(1882–1941)

CONTEXT

James Joyce was born to a middle-class Catholic family in 1882 in Rathagar, a suburb of Dublin, Ireland. The family's prosperity dwindled soon after Joyce's birth, however, and his parents were forced to move from their comfortable home to an unfashionable and impoverished area of North Dublin. Despite the family's difficulties, Joyce was well educated. After attending a prestigious Jesuit school, he studied philosophy and languages at University College, Dublin. Intent on becoming a doctor, he moved to Paris after graduating in 1902, where he instead turned his attention to writing. He returned to Dublin after just a year and met his future wife, a chambermaid named Nora Barnacle, in 1904. They lived together as common-law partners for twenty-eight years before getting married in 1931.

Joyce and his wife traveled widely and made their home in other countries. They lived in Rome and Trieste, Italy, from 1905 to 1915. While there, Joyce published a collection of poetry called *Chamber Music* (1907) when he was just twenty-five years old. He'd previously written a short story collection entitled *Dubliners*, but it wasn't published in 1914 because it was so controversial. The stories contained characters and settings that were alarmingly similar to real people and places, raising concerns about libel. Joyce indeed based many of the characters in *Dubliners* on real people, and such suggestive details, coupled with the book's historical and geographical precision and piercing examination of relationships, worried potential publishers. The Joyces had two children while living in Italy: a son named George and a daughter named Lucia, who in the 1920s was institutionalized for schizophrenia.

The Joyces moved to Zurich, Switzerland, in 1915, where they stayed for four years. Joyce and Nora had many difficult years in Italy and Zurich before Joyce won literary acclaim. In Italy, they were nearly destitute, supported by loans and Joyce's meager teaching salary. His fortune changed when he met Harriet Stow Weaver, a publisher who would become his financial supporter for the next two decades. In Zurich, Joyce published an autobiographical novel, *A Portrait of the Artist as a Young Man*, in 1916 and a play, *Exiles*, in 1918.

Between World War I and World War II, the Joyces lived in Paris, where Joyce wrote *Ulysses* (1922) and *Finnegans Wake* (1939), the experimental novels that made him famous. In Paris, Joyce was among one of the many so-called Lost Generation writers, a term coined by the writer Gertrude Stein to describe the writers and artists whose young adulthood was defined by World War I. This group of writers, including Ernest Hemingway and F. Scott Fitzgerald, frequently gathered at the famous Left Bank bookshop, Shakespeare and Company, and the bookshop's owner, Sylvia Beach, published Joyce's two landmark novels. In 1940, Joyce and his wife returned to Zurich, where he died in 1941.

Joyce wrote "Araby" when he was just twenty-two years old. "Araby" is the third story in the fifteen-story collection *Dubliners* and the final story in the collection to be narrated by a child; the remaining stories have adult narrators and protagonists. As with the other stories in the collection, "Araby" depicts disappointment, disillusionment, and the inability to change the circumstances of one's life. In 1904, Joyce wrote that he chose the title *Dubliners* to "betray the soul of that hemiplegia or paralysis which many consider a city."

PLOT OVERVIEW

The narrator, an unnamed boy, describes the street in North Dublin where his house is located. He thinks about the priest who died in the house before his family moved in and the games that he and his friends played in the street. He recalls how they would run through the back lanes of the houses and hide in the shadows when they reached the street again, hoping to avoid people in the neighborhood, particularly the boy's uncle and his friend Mangan's sister. The sister often comes to the front of their house to call Mangan, a moment that the narrator savors.

Every day begins for this narrator with glimpses of Mangan's sister. He places himself in the front room of his house so that he can see her leave her house, and then he rushes out to walk behind her quietly until finally passing her. The narrator and Mangan's sister talk little, but she is always in his thoughts. He thinks about her when he accompanies his aunt to shop for food on Saturday evenings in the busy marketplace and when he sits alone in the back room of his house. The narrator's infatuation is so intense that he fears he will never gather the courage to speak with the girl and express his feelings.

One morning, Mangan's sister asks the narrator if he plans to go to Araby, a Dublin bazaar. She tells him that she can't go herself because she has already committed to go on a school retreat at the same time. After recovering from the shock of the conversation, the narrator offers to bring her something from the bazaar. This brief meeting launches the narrator into a period of eager, restless waiting in anticipation of the bazaar. He can't focus in school and finds the lessons tedious because they distract him from thinking about Mangan's sister.

On the morning that he plans to go to the bazaar, the narrator reminds his uncle that he wants to go so that his uncle will return home early and give him money to take the train. Dinner passes and a guest visits that evening, but the uncle doesn't return. The narrator waits impatiently until the uncle finally returns at 9 P.M., unbothered that he has forgotten about the narrator's plans. Reciting the epigram "All work and no play makes Jack a dull boy," the uncle gives the narrator some money for the train and asks him if he knows the poem "The Arab's Farewell to His Steed." The narrator leaves just as his uncle begins to recite the lines and barely manages to arrive at the bazaar before it closes at 10 P.M. He approaches one stall that's still open but buys nothing, feeling unwanted by the woman watching over the goods. Not having purchased anything for Mangan's sister, the narrator stands angrily in the deserted bazaar as the lights go out.

CHARACTER LIST

The Narrator   The amorous boy who has feelings for Mangan's sister. Images and thoughts of the girl subsume the narrator's days, but the moment when he finally speaks to her is brief and awkward. When Mangan's sister tells the narrator about a bazaar called Araby, the narrator decides to go there and buy something for her. He arrives at the bazaar too late, however, and doesn't buy anything. The narrator feels the joys and frustrations of young love, and his inability to pursue his desires angers him.

Mangan's Sister   The love interest in "Araby." Mangan's sister tells the narrator that she wishes she could go to the Araby bazaar, prompting him to travel there. She suggests the familiarity of Dublin as well as the hope of love and the exotic appeal of new places.

The Narrator's Uncle   The narrator's apparent guardian. The narrator's uncle promises to come home from work early to give the narrator money to ride the train to the bazaar, but he forgets and arrives late. Although he eventually gives the narrator the money, he first tries to delay him by reciting a poem.

ANALYSIS OF MAJOR CHARACTERS

THE NARRATOR   The narrator's love for Mangan's sister moves him from being carefree to feeling elation and then frustrated loneliness as he explores the threshold between childhood and adulthood. When his infatuation with Mangan's sister begins, he is fully childlike, playing in the street with his friends and standing shyly by her railing when she emerges from her house. But the infatuation also leads him to act more pensively, a sign of adulthood. He spends great quantities of time at his window hoping to see Mangan's sister, and he sinks deep into his own thoughts of her and his romantic yearnings. The bazaar serves as a symbol for the young narrator, a place that holds the promise to push him fully into the adult world by allowing him to express his feelings for Mangan's sister. The bazaar is exotic, and the narrator's youthfulness fires a yearning to experience new places and things. When he thinks about the bazaar, he feels overcome by an "Eastern enchantment." However, his burgeoning adulthood forces him to grapple with the conflict between everyday life and the promise of love. Striving to see himself as an adult, he dismisses his distracting schoolwork as "child's play" and expresses his intense emotions in dramatic, romantic gestures. His inability to actively pursue what he desires traps him in a child's world. He must rely on his uncle for train fare and is rendered powerless when his uncle carelessly forgets his promise to return home early. The narrator's dilemma highlights the hope of youth stymied by the unavoidable realities of Dublin life.

THEMES, MOTIFS, AND SYMBOLS

THEMES

THE PRISON OF ROUTINE   Restrictive routines and the repetitive, mundane details of everyday life mark the narrator's life and trap him in a circle of frustration, restraint, and despair. The most significant consequences of following mundane routines are loneliness and unrequited love. The narrator wants to go to the bazaar to buy a gift for the girl he loves; for him, the bazaar seems to promise not only success in love but also the granting of full adult status. The bazaar, a rare event, stands outside the narrator's ordinary life, and its novelty is what gives it so much power for the narrator. However, the narrator is late to the bazaar because his uncle becomes mired in the routine of his workday. Even after the uncle returns home, he engages in the routines of the home—taking off his coat, sitting down to dinner. The uncle, utterly trapped in the prison of his routines, is so immune to the possibility of transformation that he seems entirely unaware of how important the bazaar is to the narrator, and he even tries to delay the narrator further by reciting a poem. The narrator is not only trapped in the routine of his own life, with his yearnings and unrequited love, but he is also trapped by the routines of those around him. The circularity of the Dubliners' lives in "Araby" effectively traps them, preventing them from being receptive to new experiences and happiness.

THE FRUSTRATED SEARCH FOR LOVE   The tedious events that delay the narrator's trip indicate that no room exists for love in the daily lives of Dubliners, and the absence of love renders the characters in the story anonymous. Although the narrator might imagine himself to be carrying thoughts of Mangan's sister through his day as a priest would carry a Eucharistic chalice to an altar, the minutes tick away through school, dinner, and his uncle's boring poetic recitation. Time does not adhere to the narrator's visions of his relationship. The story presents this frustration as universal: the narrator is nameless, the girl is always "Mangan's sister" as though she is any girl next door, and the story closes with the narrator imagining himself to be a creature. In "Araby," Joyce suggests that all people experience frustrated desire for love and new experiences.

The narrator's change of heart concludes the story on a moment of epiphany, but not a positive one. Instead of reaffirming his love or realizing that he doesn't need gifts to express his feelings for Mangan's sister, the narrator simply gives up. He seems to interpret his arrival at the bazaar as it fades into darkness as a sign that any relationship with Mangan's sister will also remain just wishful thinking and that his infatuation was as misguided as his fantasies about the bazaar. What might have been a story of happy, youthful love becomes a tragic story of defeat. The narrator's failure at the bazaar suggests that fulfillment and contentedness remain foreign to Dubliners.

MOTIFS

RELIGION   References to religious figures, beliefs, and accoutrements appear throughout "Araby" and suggest both the depth and futility of the narrator's infatuation. The narrator is literally surrounded by religion. His house is on the same street as a Christian school, and a priest once lived in the narrator's house. Both the school and the priest suggest futility because the priest has died and the narrator mentions the school only to describe the noise the boys make when the school day ends. Mangan's sister seems to be an almost religious figure, radiantly lit by the light from the door. When she emerges into that light, the narrator is overwhelmed by intense feelings. He even compares those feelings to a Eucharistic chalice and calls his quiet admirations "prayers and praises." Despite the narrator's desire and devotion, he is ultimately left empty and unfulfilled. The things he most believed in—his love for Mangan's sister and the bazaar's transformative quality—have proven to be hollow and disappointing.

SYMBOLS

THE BAZAAR   The "Araby" bazaar represents the promise of transformation: from childhood to adulthood, from unrequited love to returned love, from numbing routine to excitement and change. The narrator, living day in and day out with his secret infatuation with Mangan's sister, sees the bazaar as his chance to impress her. Because she is unable to go, he promises to go and buy her something, feeling empowered by the idea of giving her a gift. The narrator never questions the outcome and seems to think that attending the bazaar and buying the gift will somehow fulfill all his desires. As he anticipates the bazaar, he attributes so much potential to it that he can no longer focus on his daily life. He has no patience for the pastimes of his childhood, even though he is not yet sure what adulthood will hold for him. When he is late getting there because of his uncle, the narrator is almost literally "escaping" to the bazaar—fleeing the house before his uncle can trap him again. The exotic, Eastern aura of the bazaar seems like a beacon to him because it is vastly different from his normal life.

All the promise of the bazaar ultimately remains unfulfilled, however. Even though he manages to make it to the bazaar before it closes, the narrator discovers that nothing has changed. He's still more of a child than an adult, standing awkwardly among things he can't afford and doesn't even want. He is still lonely, perhaps even more so now that the impossibility of Mangan's sister ever returning his feelings is now clear. And he is still mired in familiar routines of disappointment and frustration, despite his attempt to overcome them. The bazaar is ultimately a false promise, which leaves the narrator stunned and angry.

SHORT STORY ANALYSIS

DUBLINERS: JOYCE'S VIEW OF THE CITY *Dubliners*, the collection in which "Araby" appears, contains fifteen portraits of life in the Irish capital. Joyce focuses on children and adults who skirt the middle class, such as housemaids, office clerks, music teachers, students, shop girls, swindlers, and out-of-luck businessmen. Joyce envisioned his collection to be a looking glass through which the Irish could observe and study themselves. In most of the stories, Joyce uses a detached but highly perceptive narrative voice to convey these lives to readers in precise detail. Rather than present intricate dramas with complex plots, these stories sketch daily situations in which not much seems to happen—a boy visits a bazaar, a woman buys sweets for holiday festivities, a man reunites with an old friend over a few drinks. Although these events may not appear profound, his characters nevertheless come to intensely personal and often tragic revelations. The stories in *Dubliners* peer into the homes, hearts, and minds of people whose lives connect and intermingle through the shared space and spirit of Dublin. Such subtle connections create a sense of shared experience and evoke a map of Dublin life that Joyce would return to again in his later works.

"Araby" is firmly entrenched in Dublin and Dublin life. We know "Araby" takes place in Dublin by virtue of its being included in *Dubliners*, but in the first paragraph, Joyce provides an even more exact location of where the story takes place: the narrator lives on North Richmond Street. When the narrator walks through the market with his aunt, Dublin life surrounds him. He hears the street singers' rendition of a song about O'Donovan Rossa, an Irishman from the 1840s who supported independence for Ireland. They also sing about the "troubles in our native land," which refers to the political and cultural uncertainty occurring in Ireland at the time, as Ireland sought independence from Great Britain and strived to reinvigorate its national identity. When the narrator finally goes to the bazaar, Joyce again provides specific locations: he walks down Buckingham Street and takes the train to Westland Row Station. All of these details place "Araby" firmly in the Dublin world that Joyce explored so completely in his collection.

IMPORTANT QUOTATIONS EXPLAINED

---

1. *I had never spoken to her, except for a few casual words, and yet her name was like a summons to all my foolish blood.*

This quotation appears at the end of the fourth paragraph. The narrator has just described how he peers through his window every morning until he sees Mangan's sister emerge from her house, then he follows her. His infatuation with her is intense, but even here, when he describes the effect her name has on him, he doesn't actually tell readers her name. Throughout the story, he refers to her exclusively as "Mangan's sister," naming his friend but not the girl. The only other character he names is Mrs. Mercer, a guest of his aunt's. The narrator, his aunt, his uncle, and Mangan's sister all remain nameless. "Araby" is filled with specifics, such as the street names and song topics the narrator observes, but these unnamed characters play a role in defining Dublin life as well. By not naming his characters, Joyce suggests that they are universal figures—that all Dubliners face the same kinds of struggles, routines, and futile infatuations. The unnamed narrator, in particular, represents every adolescent who straddles the threshold between childhood and adulthood.

---

2. *I watched my master's face pass from amiability to sternness; he hoped I was not beginning to idle. I could not call my wandering thoughts together. I had hardly any patience with the serious work of life which, now that it stood between me and my desire, seemed to me child's play, ugly monotonous child's play.*

In this quote, the young narrator has just spoken with Mangan's sister and now finds himself entirely uninterested and bored by the demands of the classroom. Instead, he thinks of Mangan's sister, the upcoming bazaar, and anything except what's right in front of him. This scene forecasts the boy's future frustration with the tedious details that foil his desires, and it also illustrates the boy's struggle to define himself as an adult, even in the space of the classroom, which is structured as a hierarchy between master and student. Just as mundane lessons obstruct the boy's thoughts, by the end of the story everyday delays undermine his hopes to purchase something for Mangan's sister at the bazaar. In both cases, monotony prevents the boy from fulfilling his desires.

Babylon Revisited

F. Scott Fitzgerald
(1896–1940)

CONTEXT

F. Scott Fitzgerald was born in 1896 in St. Paul, Minnesota. His given name, Francis Scott Key Fitzgerald, was a tribute to his relative Francis Scott Key, who wrote "The Star Spangled Banner." Fitzgerald grew up in Buffalo, New York, and Minnesota. His family, Roman Catholics of Irish descent, didn't have much money, but Fitzgerald still managed to attend prep school in New Jersey thanks to financial help from an aunt. He then went to Princeton University for three years but dropped out and enlisted in the army in 1917 when the United States entered World War I. He wrote his first novel while training to be an officer and submitted it to an editor at Scribner's, who turned it down. While still in training, Fitzgerald also met Zelda Sayre, a high-society girl from Alabama whom he would eventually marry in 1920. Fortunately, the war ended before he could be deployed to Europe.

While living at his parents' house in St. Paul, Fitzgerald revised the novel he had written in training camp and changed its title from *The Romantic Egoist* to *This Side of Paradise*. Finally published in 1920, his first novel was a great success and made Fitzgerald famous. To capitalize on the popularity of *This Side of Paradise*, Fitzgerald's publishers rushed to publish *Flappers and Philosophers* (1920), his first collection of short stories. In 1922, Fitzgerald came out with a second collection, *Tales of the Jazz Age*, followed by *The Beautiful and Damned* (1922) and *The Great Gatsby* (1925), which is widely considered Fitzgerald's finest work. Nine years passed before the publication of Fitzgerald's next novel, *Tender Is the Night* (1934), the story of a psychiatrist and his mentally ill wife.

Many of the recurring themes in Fitzgerald's work—money, class, ambition, alcoholism, mental illness—have their roots in his personal life. He had a tumultuous and passionate relationship with Zelda, with whom he had one daughter, Frances Scott. Despite the success of his novels, Fitzgerald was often short of the money necessary to pay for his glamorous, fast-paced lifestyle in New York. His agent and editor loaned him funds, and he supplemented his income by writing for such magazines as *Esquire* and the *Saturday Evening Post*. He also earned money by selling the film rights to his work. Poor health plagued him and his family: Fitzgerald was an alcoholic, and Zelda was hospitalized for schizophrenia in 1932, a disaster that likely inspired *Tender Is the Night*, which Fitzgerald wrote while living in a rented house near Zelda's hospital.

In the 1930s, Fitzgerald left Zelda and moved to Hollywood. Even though the couple never filed for divorce, they never lived together again. In Hollywood, Fitzgerald moved in with a movie columnist named Sheilah Graham and worked on scripts, short stories, and a fifth novel. Fitzgerald hated his work in Hollywood and believed he was wasting his talent, but he didn't quit because he needed the money. In 1940, Fitzgerald suffered two heart attacks and died later that year at age forty-four, leaving his last novel unfinished. Edmund Wilson, a well-known writer and critic and a friend of Fitzgerald's since their days together at Princeton, edited the manuscript and notes that Fitzgerald left behind. The result was published in 1940 as *The Last Tycoon*.

Fitzgerald is considered the voice of the Lost Generation, the generation that came of age during World War I. He's also considered the ultimate explicator of the Jazz Age of the 1920s, a period characterized by individualism and decadence. Although he is best known for his novels, he wrote about 160 short stories. The number is difficult to pin down precisely because many of his pieces blur the lines between story, essay, and article. "Babylon Revisited" was written in 1930 and published in 1931 in the *Saturday Evening Post*. Fitzgerald's editor, Malcolm Cowley, wrote that in comparison with other stories of Fitzgerald's, "Babylon Revisited" evidences "less regret for the past and more dignity in the face of real sorrow."

PLOT OVERVIEW

Part I opens in the middle of a conversation between Charlie Wales and Alix, a bartender at the Ritz. Charlie asks Alix to pass along his brother-in-law's address to Duncan Schaeffer. The narrator says that Paris and the Ritz bar feel deserted. Charlie says he has been sober for a year and a half and that he is now a businessman living in Prague. He and Alix gossip about old acquaintances. Charlie says he's in town to see his daughter.

Charlie gets in a taxi. The Left Bank looks provincial to him, and he wonders whether he's ruined the city for himself. The narrator tells us that Charlie is a handsome thirty-five-year-old. Charlie goes to his brother-in-law's house, where his daughter, Honoria, jumps into his arms. Marion Peters, his sister-in-law, greets him without warmth, although his brother-in-law, Lincoln Peters, is friendlier. In a calculated remark, Charlie boasts about how good his finances are these days. Lincoln looks restless, so Charlie changes the subject. Marion says she's glad there aren't many Americans left in Paris, and it's clear that she doesn't like Charlie.

After eating dinner with the Peters family, Charlie goes to see a famous dancer named Josephine Baker, then to Montmartre, where he passes nightclubs that he recognizes. He sees a few scared tourists go into one club. He thinks about the meaning of dissipation and remembers the vast sums of money he threw away. After ignoring a woman's advances, he goes home.

Part II begins the following morning. Charlie takes Honoria to lunch. He suggests going to a toy store and then to a vaudeville show. Honoria doesn't want to go to the toy store because she's worried they're no longer rich. Charlie playfully introduces himself to her as if they are strangers. He pretends that her doll is her child, and she goes along with the joke. She says she prefers Lincoln to Marion and asks why she can't live with Charlie.

Leaving the restaurant, they run into Duncan Schaeffer and Lorraine Quarrles, two of Charlie's friends from the old days. Lorraine says she and her husband are poor now and that she is alone in Paris. They ask Charlie to join them for dinner, but he brushes them off and refuses to tell them where he's staying. They see each other again at the vaudeville, and he has a drink with them. In the cab on the way home, Honoria says she wants to live with him, which thrills Charlie. She blows him a kiss when she is safely inside the house.

In Part III, Charlie meets with Marion and Lincoln. He says that he wants Honoria to live with him and that he has changed. He says he drinks one drink per day on purpose so that he doesn't obsess about it ever again. Marion doesn't understand this, but Lincoln claims that he understands Charlie. Charlie settles in for a long fight, reminding himself that his objective isn't to justify his behavior but to win Honoria back. Marion says that Charlie hasn't existed for her since he locked Helen, her sister and Charlie's wife, out of their apartment. Charlie says Marion can trust him. As it becomes increasingly clear that Marion simply doesn't like Charlie, he begins to worry that she will turn Honoria against him. He stresses that he will be able to give Honoria a good life and then realizes that Marion and Lincoln don't want to hear about how much wealthier he is than they are. He craves a drink.

The narrator says that Marion understands Charlie's wish to be with his daughter but needs to see him as the villain. She implies that Charlie was responsible for Helen's death. Lincoln objects. Charlie says that heart trouble killed Helen, and Marion sarcastically agrees with him. Suddenly giving up the fight, she leaves the room. Lincoln tells Charlie that he can take Honoria. Back in his hotel room, Charlie thinks of the way he and Helen destroyed their love for no good reason. He remembers the night they fought and she kissed another man; he got home before her and locked her out. There was a snowstorm later, and Helen wandered around in the cold. The incident marked the "beginning of the end." Charlie falls asleep and dreams of Helen, who says that she wants him and Honoria to be together.

Part IV begins the next morning. Charlie interviews two potential governesses and then eats lunch with Lincoln. He says Marion resents the fact that Charlie and Helen were spending a fortune while she and Lincoln were just scraping along. In his hotel room, Charlie gets a *pneumatique* (a letter delivered by pneumatic tube) from Lorraine, who reminisces about their drunken pranks and asks to see him at the Ritz bar. The adventures that Lorraine looks back on with fondness strike Charlie as nightmarish.

Charlie goes to Marion and Lincoln's house in the afternoon. Honoria has been told of the decision and is delighted. The room feels safe and warm. The doorbell rings—it is Lorraine and Duncan, who are drunk. Slurring their words, they ask Charlie to dinner. He refuses twice and they leave angry. Furious, Marion leaves the room. The children eat dinner, and Lincoln goes to check on Marion. When he comes back, he tells Charlie that the plans have changed.

In Part V, Charlie goes to the Ritz bar. He sees Paul, a bartender he knew in the old days. He thinks of the fights that he and Helen had, the people out of their minds on alcohol and drugs, and the way he locked Helen out in the snow. He calls Lincoln, who says that for six months, they have to drop the question of Honoria living with Charlie. Charlie goes back to the bar. He realizes that the only thing he can do for Honoria is buy her things, which he knows is inadequate. He plans to come back and try again.

CHARACTER LIST

Charlie Wales   The handsome, thirty-five-year-old protagonist of the story. Once worth a small fortune, Charlie spent all his money in Paris during the mid-1920s. An alcoholic, he collapsed along with the stock market in 1929. Since regaining his sobriety and financial footing as a businessman in Prague, Charlie has become ashamed of his past recklessness. He adores his daughter, Honoria, and misses his wife, Helen, for whose death he may bear partial responsibility.

Honoria Wales   Charlie's daughter. Honoria is a sunny, smart nine-year-old. She loves her father dearly and, although she is happy enough with Marion and Lincoln, wants to live with Charlie. A smart girl, she has a rich inner life and thinks about difficult subjects such as money and love. Honoria claims that she misses her mother, but she doesn't seem to remember her well.

Marion Peters   Charlie's sister-in-law. Marion resents Charlie both because of his former recklessness and because she believes he mistreated her sister, Helen. Marion fixates on the night Charlie locked Helen out of the house during a snowstorm and believes he's responsible for her death. Marion understands why Charlie wants Honoria to live with him, but she worries that he will lapse back into his old ways.

Lincoln Peters   Marion's husband and Charlie's brother-in-law. Lincoln lacks Charlie's knack for business, but he is a solid, responsible father and husband. He is quieter than his wife and more sympathetic to Charlie's desire to live with Honoria. Still, his primary loyalty is to Marion, whom he truly loves. He takes Marion's side whenever he believes that Charlie's actions are hurting her.

Helen   Charlie's deceased wife. Helen passed away many years before and appears in the story only as a figure in Charlie's dream. She and Charlie loved each other deeply, and it seems they destroyed their relationship for no real reason. Even though their marriage ended badly, they did love each other, which is why Helen appears encouraging and loving in Charlie's dream.

Lorraine Quarrles   A thirty-year-old blonde American woman. Lorraine is a figure from Charlie's debauched past. She too has lost her fortune but hasn't stopped trying to live the way she did when she had money. Now a sad, almost pathetic figure, she chases after Charlie, whose newfound sobriety both amuses her and makes her jealous.

Duncan Schaeffer   Lorraine's companion and an American who attended college with Charlie. Duncan, who doesn't say much, amplifies Lorraine's recklessness. He accompanies Lorraine wherever she goes, drinks when she drinks, and unexpectedly arrives at Marion and Lincoln's house with her.

Elsie and Richard Peters   Marion and Lincoln's children. Elsie and Richard are about Honoria's age, well behaved, but don't perform as well in school as Honoria.

Paul   A bartender at the Ritz. In the days of great wealth, he drove a fancy car to work.

Alix   A bartender at the Ritz. Alix gives Charlie updates on the Americans who used to live in Paris.

ANALYSIS OF MAJOR CHARACTERS

CHARLIE WALES   Despite his many flaws, Charlie is a man whom almost everyone can't help but like. It's surprising that Charlie's so likeable considering his wild past of uncontrollable alcoholism, his possible complicity in his wife's death, and the fact that he essentially abandoned his child. Charlie is hard to dislike in part because he seems so earnest in his efforts to turn over a new leaf. If we're wary of him in the beginning of the story, we increasingly trust him as he rebuffs his former friends and sticks to just one drink a day. Fitzgerald also conveys Charlie's great personal charm. Charlie is a physically attractive man, a quality that clearly affects Lorraine and possibly even Marion. He is also a winning, persuasive speaker, able to manipulate listeners without seeming to try.

If we can't help but like Charlie, however, neither can we help feeling slightly suspicious of him. His justification for taking one drink per day makes sense when he explains it—he implies that he doesn't want to give alcohol undue power over him by avoiding it altogether—but seems nonsensical later. We wonder if he has hoodwinked us and worry that he'll slip back into drinking heavily. When Charlie disavows his former friends, we think back to the beginning of the story when he gives Lincoln and Marion's address to Alix, knowing that it'll land in Duncan Schaeffer's hands. As a result, we wonder whether some part of him actually wants to return to the old days. Although we're naturally inclined to take Charlie's side because of his good intentions, Fitzgerald doesn't allow us to root for him unrestrainedly.

MARION PETERS   Marion acts both as a stand-in and a foil for the reader. On the one hand, we likely share all her reservations about Charlie. On the other hand, her off-putting personal qualities set us against her. We want to dismiss her reservations, even if we know we shouldn't, which puts us even more firmly in Charlie's camp. Marion is the mirror image of Charlie: although logic demands that we approve of her actions, her prickly personality masks her essential goodness and makes her difficult to like. Marion is unhappy with her own life and focuses her frustrations on Charlie, but there's no doubt that she is a good woman. She has taken Honoria in, treated her as her own child, and brought her up to be a happy, self-sufficient girl. She also loves her husband. Her marriage to him is the most successful romantic adult relationship in the story, a stark contrast to Charlie's disastrous marriage, which ended in senseless destruction. Still, Marion's judgmental tone and slight air of irrationality make her an unsympathetic character. Because we see Marion from Charlie's perspective, we focus only on her frustrations rather than her good motivations.

THEMES, MOTIFS, AND SYMBOLS

THEMES

THE INESCAPABILITY OF THE PAST   Even though Charlie's wilder days have long since passed, he'll never be able to truly escape them. Although he actively tries to avoid reminders of the Paris he used to know, they nevertheless follow him everywhere. When he goes to lunch with Honoria, for example, he can find only one restaurant that doesn't remind him of drunken meals that lasted for hours. When he walks through Montmartre, old haunts surround him. Even the things that have changed remind him of his past, simply because the newness of them strikes him as odd. The scared tourists heading into cafés are pale imitations of the partiers he and his friends once were, and the once-bustling places that these tourists frequent are now nearly empty. Charlie would like to put his failed marriage behind him, but he cannot. Marion constantly reminds him of his mistakes, which she clings to almost obsessively. The past informs the present: because of what Charlie did to Helen, he is prevented from living with Honoria. Perhaps the most ominous figures from the past are Duncan and Lorraine, living reminders of the bad old days, who still try to follow him wherever he goes.

If Charlie wants to shake off the past, however, some part of him simultaneously can't let it go. He asks his cabbie to drive to the Avenue de l'Opera, he goes to Montmartre and visits the places he used to frequent, and he begins and ends the story in the familiar Ritz bar. While these incidents suggest that the past still haunts Charlie, we can't help thinking that Charlie is actually looking to be haunted. He must know, consciously or subconsciously, that visiting the scenes of his former life will fill him with regret and possibly even longing. Perhaps most damning of all is the fact that Charlie gives Lincoln and Marion's address to Alix, asking him to pass it along to Duncan. He later ignores Lorraine and refuses to give his hotel address to them, but his protestations mean nothing because he's already told them where they can find him. We know that some part of him must want the debauchery of the old days back in his life, thereby planting the seeds of his own failure.

THE PURITY OF PATERNAL LOVE Fitzgerald characterizes the love that fathers and daughters feel for each other as the only pure, unadulterated kind of love in the world. Other types of love, however passionate or intense they may be, are always complicated by dislike or mistrust. Charlie and Helen loved each other, for example, but they tormented and abused each other: Helen kissed other men, they fought, and Charlie locked her out in a snowstorm. Lincoln and Marion demonstrate another type of marital love, one that's genuine but strained by financial and familial difficulties. To some degree, Charlie loves Lincoln and Marion, whom he still considers family. At the same time, however, he thinks of them as adversaries, and their mutual distrust of each other makes their love less than pure. Only Honoria and Charlie love each other in an unadulterated way. They often speak of their love for each other, and she asks him whether he loves her more than anyone in the world. Marital and familial love may fall apart with regularity, but the love between children and parents is the most pure.

MOTIFS

THE OUTDOORS Many scenes in "Babylon Revisited" take place on the streets of Paris, where people go when they're lonely or angry. Charlie forces Lorraine and Duncan out onto the street, for example, when they surprise him at Marion and Lincoln's house, and they leave in a fit of anger. When Charlie wanders through Montmartre, the nervous tourists and overeager nightclub employees only make him feel more solitary. Most obviously abandoned to the dangerous streets is Helen, whom Charlie had locked out after fighting with her. The fact that Charlie locked her outside during a snowstorm is a particularly cruel gesture in this story, which characterizes the outdoors as a place of sadness and danger. Fitzgerald emphasizes the melancholy quality of the outdoors by contrasting it with the indoors, which he portrays as warm, cozy, and safe. All the scenes that take place in Marion and Lincoln's house, for example, connote a happy family atmosphere created by responsible adults. When Charlie finally leaves their house toward the end of the story, he is appropriately cast back into the lonely streets.

SYMBOLS

THE RITZ BAR The bar at the Ritz Hotel symbolizes Charlie's spiritual home. Charlie is a wanderer: he no longer lives in America, his birthplace, and we never see him in Prague, his new home. He visits Marion and Lincoln's house as an interloper, more of a resented outsider than a member of the family. The place that closest resembles his home, however, is the bar at the Ritz, and the story begins and ends there, emphasizing its importance to Charlie. Like a real home, the walls of the Ritz bar have witnessed the changes that have happened to him. Whereas he once spent many late, drunken nights at the bar in his wilder days, he now sits there to consume his one customary drink every day. Charlie and Alix, the bartender, gossip about the people they both once knew, drinkers and ex-drinkers who have fallen on hard times, just as two family members might gossip about wayward relatives. One the other hand, the bar could never be a fulfilling substitute for a real home. As Charlie sits with Alix at the end of the story, he thinks about how terribly alone he is. The bar may be the closest thing Charlie has to a home, but its comforts are inferior in every way to those of an actual household.

SHORT STORY ANALYSIS

DIALOGUE "Babylon Revisited" conveys strong and painful feelings, principally through the use of dialogue. Some of the most fraught exchanges in the story occur between Charlie and Marion. Charlie's words make it clear that he is desperate to get Honoria back, enough to plan almost every phrase he utters and pause he takes. He stresses his healthy income to prove that he can provide for his daughter, but he drops the topic the moment he senses that Lincoln is growing annoyed with it. He coaches himself through the emotional conversation about Honoria's future, silently reminding himself that he has to control his temper in front of Marion if he wants Honoria. The care with which he chooses his words and his self-control demonstrate how desperately he wants to be with his daughter. These conversations are not one-sided, however. Through Marion's curt and cutting responses, we know that she loved her sister, Helen, very much, strongly dislikes Charlie, but only wants the best for Honoria.

Charlie's conversations with Honoria are equally emotional, albeit much happier. Honoria repeats the word *dad* when saying hello or goodbye to Charlie, a kind of incantation that conveys how much she loves him. Their conversations can be serious at times, such as when Honoria says that she doesn't want to go to the toy store because she's worried about the family's finances. Their conversations can also be comical, and a few moments later, Charlie asks her whether she's married or single, to which she playfully replies that she's single. Their dialogue is realistic and entertaining, but it also reveals the characteristics of their relationship. They don't know each other well, but they like and respect each other and enjoy spending time together. Fitzgerald's portrayal of this father-daughter relationship is extremely memorable, vivid, and true to life, and it is accomplished largely through the use of dialogue.

STRUCTURE Fitzgerald structures "Babylon Revisited" in a way that allows him to emphasize different events by altering the pace of the story. The story is divided into five sections, each consisting of a different set of events and period of time. Section I is wide-ranging and introduces us to Paris, Charlie, and the basic details of Charlie's life. In one line, Alix, the bartender, asks him about his daughter, but a few lines later, Charlie is abruptly back on the street, having left the bar. By leaping from place to place without mentioning the passage of time, Fitzgerald gives us the background information we need and suggests that we're getting to know Charlie just as Charlie is getting to know Paris once again. Section II slows down considerably, focusing entirely on Charlie's lunch with Honoria to highlight their relationship. Fitzgerald's placement of the scene just after the opening section emphasizes how dearly Charlie loves Honoria.

Section III also focuses solely on just one scene, namely Charlie's conversation with Marion and Lincoln about Honoria's future. Even though less time passes in this section than in the first, Fitzgerald devotes roughly the same number of pages to each to emphasize how important this conversation is to Charlie. The placement of the conversation is important too; section III ends happily, with Charlie securing a promise from Lincoln that Honoria will return to him. But because we know the story isn't over, we begin to worry about a reversal, an effect that Fitzgerald uses intentionally to heighten the tension. Section IV puts that reversal in motion. Its sped-up pace, which rushes us from interviews with nannies to Lorraine's *pneumatique* to the disastrous evening at Marion and Lincoln's house, mirrors the increasing desperation Charlie feels as events spiral out of control. Section V is an embittered conclusion, and its brevity suggests that Charlie can hardly bear to dwell on the loss of his daughter once again.

HISTORICAL CONTEXT   The melancholy mood of "Babylon Revisited" comes partly from the historical period in which it is set. Fitzgerald is often identified as the voice of the Jazz Age, but in this story he portrays the post–Jazz Age world, which is sober and full of regret. Charlie returns to a Paris that has changed dramatically. In the old days, before the story's action takes place, Americans like Charlie and Helen "were a sort of royalty, almost infallible" because they had money to burn. Like drunken children, rich Americans ran wild all over the city in the 1920s. Then the American stock market crashed in 1929, an event mentioned only briefly in the story but one that casts a pall over its characters. Charlie's personal history runs parallel to the course of history itself. During the Jazz Age, he lived lavishly, giving hundreds of francs to doormen and thousands of francs to orchestras. He was blindingly drunk most of the time and pulled childish pranks. He lived a dissipated, crazed life that epitomized the hedonism of wealthy Americans living in the mid-1920s. Then, just as the stock market crashed, Charlie's alcoholism landed him in a sanitarium. By drawing parallels between history and Charlie's life, Fitzgerald makes Charlie representative of an entire age.

IMPORTANT QUOTATIONS EXPLAINED

1. *Again the memory of those days swept over him like a nightmare . . . The men who locked their wives out in the snow, because the snow of twenty-nine wasn't real snow. If you didn't want it to be snow, you just paid some money.*

These sentences, which come near the end of the story, complicate our understanding of Helen's death. Marion strongly implies that Charlie was responsible for his wife's demise, and she scoffs at his explanation that Helen died of heart trouble. Her scornful reaction affects Charlie strongly, but it isn't clear whether the accusation fills him with anger or guilt. This passage gives the impression that Charlie blames himself, at least to some degree. At the zenith of those wild days in 1929, men like Charlie felt like gods. They imagined that they controlled the entire world, even the weather itself. Thoughtless actions didn't seem to have real consequences, and it was inconceivable that someone could be hurt by the cold. You could pay for everything else, Charlie thinks sarcastically, so of course you could pay to make real snow imaginary. The bitter tone of this passage, with its angry repetition of the word *snow*, suggests that only now does Charlie realize that such ideas were dangerous.

Barn Burning
William Faulkner
(1897–1962)

CONTEXT

Born in New Albany, Mississippi, in 1897, William Faulkner became famous for a series of novels that explore the South's historical legacy, its fraught and often tensely violent present, and its uncertain future. This grouping of major works includes *The Sound and the Fury* (1929), *As I Lay Dying* (1930), *Light in August* (1931), and *Absalom, Absalom!* (1936), all firmly rooted in the fictional Mississippi county of Yoknapatawpha. By creating an imaginary setting, Faulkner allows his characters to inhabit a fully realized world that serves as a mirror to and microcosm of the South that the novelist knew so well and explored so deeply. Faulkner's legendary milieu serves as a safe and distant—albeit magnifying—lens through which he could examine the practices, folkways, and attitudes that have united and divided the people of the South.

Faulkner was particularly interested in the moral implications of history. As the South emerged from the Civil War and Reconstruction and attempted to shake off the stigma of slavery, its residents were often portrayed as being caught in competing and evolving modes, torn between a new and an older, more tenaciously rooted world order. Religion and politics frequently fell short of their implied goals of providing order and guidance and served only to complicate and divide. Society, with its gossip, judgment, and harsh pronouncements, conspired to thwart the desires and ambitions of individuals struggling to unearth and embrace their identities. Across Faulkner's fictive landscapes, individual characters often stage epic struggles, prevented from realizing their potential or establishing and asserting a firm sense of their place in the world.

"Barn Burning," in its examination of a boy's struggle with family loyalty and a higher sense of justice, fits firmly in Faulkner's familiar fictional mode. Poverty and irrational, criminal behavior divide a family and, in the end, leave them more indigent and dependent than ever. The story first appeared in the June 1939 issue of *Harper's* magazine and received the O. Henry Award for the year's best work of short fiction. The story, a critical and popular favorite, was included in Faulkner's *Collected Stories* (1950) and later reprinted in the *Selected Short Stories of William Faulkner* (1961). In his portrayal of the Snopes clan, an underprivileged family with few economic prospects, Faulkner examines the deep-rooted classism and systems that rigidly divided southern society along racial, economic, and familial lines. The Snopeses and their struggle, in particular, symbolize the falling away of an old order, as the agrarian South slowly shifted to embrace a new era of industrialization and modernization. Although Faulkner's merciless portrayal of Abner Snopes precludes any sympathy for his peculiar brand of vigilante justice, the harsh reality the family faced was little more than institutionalized slavery and a life sentence of poverty and subsistence living.

Abner Snopes represents a common trope in Faulkner's fiction—the dispossessed male, shorn of power and lashing out at a world that he perceives as habitually wronging him and thwarting his felonious desires. Faulkner examines the sway that such menacing figures have over family and community by portraying the individuals caught up in the shadows of these savage personalities, individuals who are powerless and often culpable. Freedom comes only for Sartoris, the youngest Snopes boy, but, as is frequently the case in Faulkner's works, emancipation comes at a price. Sartoris has defended his sense of honor and attempted to restore the family name, but he ultimately faces an uncertain future alone.

Faulkner won the Nobel Prize for Literature in 1949, and he donated half the prize money to a fund that supports new writers. His gift takes the form today of the PEN/Faulkner Award. He died in 1962.

PLOT OVERVIEW

Young Colonel Sartoris Snopes crouches on a keg in the back of the store that doubles for the town court. He cannot see the table where his father and his father's opponent, Mr. Harris, are seated. The justice of the peace asks Mr. Harris for proof that Mr. Snopes burned his barn. Mr. Harris describes the numerous times Snopes's hog broke through the fence and got into his cornfields. The final time, when Mr. Harris demanded a dollar for the animal's return, the black man who was sent to fetch the hog gave Mr. Harris an ominous warning that wood and hay are combustible. Later that night, fire claimed Mr. Harris's barn. While the judge claims that that by itself isn't proof, Mr. Harris has Sartoris called to testify before the court. The boy knows his father is expecting him to lie on his behalf. After doing so, the judge asks Mr. Harris whether he wants the child cross-examined, but Mr. Harris snarls to have the boy removed.

The judge dismisses the charges against Snopes but warns him to leave the county for good, and Snopes agrees to comply. Snopes and his two sons then leave the store and head to their wagon. A child in the crowd accuses them of being barn burners and strikes Sartoris, knocking him down. Snopes orders Sartoris into the wagon, which is laden with their possessions and where his two sisters, mother, and aunt are waiting. Snopes prevents his crying wife from cleaning Sartoris's bloodied face. That night, the family camps around the father's typically small fire. Snopes wakes Sartoris and takes him onto the dark road, where he accuses him of planning to inform the judge of his guilt in the arson case. Snopes strikes Sartoris on the head and tells him he must always remain loyal to his family.

The next day, the family arrives at its new home and begins unloading the wagon. Snopes takes Sartoris to the house of Major de Spain, the owner on whose land the family will work. Despite the servant's protests, Snopes tracks horse manure into the opulent house, leaving only when Miss Lula asks him to. He resentfully remarks that the home was built by slave labor. Two hours later, the servant drops off the rug that Snopes had soiled and instructs him to clean and return it. Snopes supervises as the two sisters reluctantly clean the carpet with lye, and he uses a jagged stone to work the surface of the expensive rug. After dinner, the family retires to their sleeping areas. Snopes forces Sartoris to fetch the mule and ride along with him to return the cleaned rug. At the house, Snopes flings the rug onto the floor after loudly kicking at the door several times.

The next morning, as Sartoris and Snopes prepare the mules for plowing, de Spain arrives on horseback to inform them that the rug was ruined from improper cleaning. In lieu of the hundred-dollar replacement fee, the major says Snopes will be charged twenty additional bushels of corn. Sartoris defends Snopes's actions, telling him that he did the best he could with the soiled carpet and that they will refuse to supply the extra crops. Snopes puts Sartoris back to work, and the following days are consumed with the constant labor of working their acreage. Sartoris hopes that Snopes will turn once and for all from his destructive impulses.

The next weekend, Snopes and his two sons head once again to a court appearance at the country store, where the well-dressed de Spain is in attendance. Sartoris attempts to defend Snopes, saying that he never burned the barn, but Snopes orders him back to the wagon. The judge mistakenly thinks the rug was burned in addition to being soiled and destroyed. He rules that Snopes must pay ten extra bushels of corn when the crop comes due, and court is adjourned. After a trip to the blacksmith's shop for wagon repairs, a light meal in front of the general store, and a trip to a corral where horses are displayed and sold, Snopes and his sons return home after sundown.

Despite his wife's protests, Snopes empties the kerosene from the lamp back into its five-gallon container and secures a lit candle stub in the neck of a bottle. Snopes orders Sartoris to fetch the oil. He obeys but fantasizes about running away. He tries to dissuade Snopes, but Snopes grabs Sartoris by the collar and orders his wife to restrain him. Sartoris escapes his mother's clutches and runs to the de Spain house, bursting in on the startled servant. Breathlessly, he blurts out the word *Barn!* Sartoris runs desperately down the road, moving aside as the major's horse comes thundering by him. Three shots ring out and Snope is killed, his plan to burn de Spain's barn thwarted. At midnight, Sartoris sits on a hill. Stiff and cold, he hears the whippoorwills and heads down the hill to the dark woods, not pausing to look back.

CHARACTER LIST

Colonel Sartoris Snopes (Sarty)   A ten-year-old boy and the story's protagonist. Small and wiry, with wild, gray eyes and uncombed brown hair, Sartoris wears patched and faded jeans that are too small for him. He has inherited his innocence and morality from his mother, but his father's influence has made Sartoris old beyond his years. He is forced to confront an ethical quandary that pits his loyalty to his family against the higher concepts of justice and morality.

Abner Snopes   Sartoris's father and a serial arsonist. Cold and violent, Snopes has a harsh, emotionless voice, shaggy gray eyebrows, and pebble-colored eyes. Stiff-bodied, he walks with a limp he acquired from being shot by a Confederate's provost thirty years earlier while stealing a horse during the Civil War. Known for his wolflike independence and anger, he is convinced of his right to unleash his destructive revenge on anyone whom he believes has wronged him.

Lennie Snopes   Sartoris's mother. Sad, emotional, and caring, Lennie futilely attempts to stem her husband's destructive impulses. She is beaten down by the family's endless cycle of flight and resettlement and the pall of criminality that has stained her clan. Nervous in the presence of her irascible, unpredictable husband, she is a slim source of comfort for Sartoris in the violence-tinged world of the Snopes family.

Major de Spain   A well-dressed and affluent landowner. De Spain brings the soiled rug to the Snopeses' cabin and insists that they clean it and return it. Snopes's unpredictable nature unsettles de Spain, and he uneasily answers Snopes's charges in court.

Mr. Harris   A landowner for whom the Snopeses were short-term tenants. The plaintiff in the first court case, Harris had attempted to resolve the conflict over the Snopeses' hog. In the end, he is left with a burned barn and no legal recourse, as his case is dismissed for lack of evidence.

Colonel John Snopes   Sartoris's older brother. Although his name is not given in the story, Faulkner's other works of fiction feature the same character and identify him. A silent, brooding version of his father, John is slightly thicker, with muddy eyes and a habit of chewing tobacco.

Net and an Unnamed Sister   Sartoris's twin sisters. In his brief description of the two women, Faulkner focuses on their physicality and corpulence. They are described as large, bovine, and lethargic, with flat loud voices. They are cheaply dressed in calico and ribbons.

Lizzie   Lennie's sister and Sartoris's aunt. Lizzie supplies a voice of justice and morality when she boldly asserts, at the end of the story, that if Sartoris does not warn the de Spains that their barn is about to be burned, then she will.

Lula de Spain   Major de Spain's wife. Lula wears a smooth, gray gown with lace at the throat, with rolled-up sleeves and an apron tied around her. Assertive but intimidated by the imposing presence of Snopes, she resents having her home violated.

The Servant   A man in livery who works in the de Spain mansion. When Snopes bursts in and damages the rug, he calls the servant a racist epithet, viewing his presence as a mere extension of the slavery that dominated the South until the Civil War.

ANALYSIS OF MAJOR CHARACTERS

COLONEL SARTORIS SNOPES   "Barn Burning" explores the coming of age of Sartoris Snopes, as he is forced to grapple with issues of right and wrong that require a maturity and insight beyond his years. "You're getting to be a man," Snopes tells his ten-year-old son after delivering a blow to the side of his head. In Sartoris's world, violence is a fundamental element of manhood, something he knows all too well from living with his father. Sartoris is impressionable, inarticulate, and subject to his father's potentially corrupting influence, but he is also infused with a sense of justice. Sartoris is in many ways a raw, unformed creature of nature, untouched by education, the refining influences of civilization, or the stability of a permanent home. The sight of the de Spain house gives him an instinctive feeling of peace and joy, but, as Faulkner notes, the child could not have translated such a reaction into words. Later, Sartoris reacts instinctively again when he prevents his father from burning de Spain's barn. He cannot articulate why he warns de Spain or ultimately runs away, but his actions suggest that Sartoris's core consists of goodness and morality rather than the corruption that his father attempts to teach him.

Sartoris's worldview and morality may exist beyond the adult world of precise language and articulation, but he displays an insight that is far more developed than many of the adults who surround him. He sees through his father's attempts to manipulate him by harping on the importance of family loyalty as a means of guaranteeing Sartoris's silence. Sartoris's brother, John, lacks Sartoris's insight, and he is an example of what young Sartoris could easily become. Snopes has successfully taught John his ideas of family loyalty, and John blindly follows Snopes's criminal lead. Sartoris, far from silently obeying, instigates the climactic end of Snopes's reign of terror. At the end of the story, Sartoris betrays the family "honor" and must persevere on his own. As his father warned, if Sartoris failed to support his family, support would not be offered to him. As frightening as the unknown future might be, Sartoris has decided that the kind of "support" his family can offer is something he can do without. His flight marks an end to the legacy of bitterness and shame that he stood to inherit.

ABNER SNOPES   Snopes is an influential, towering presence in Sartoris's eyes, but he himself is simply a primitive, thoughtless force of violence and destruction. With his family he is stiff, without depth, emotion, or complexity. This stiffness makes him seem almost less than human, and Faulkner often characterizes Snopes in metallic terms, portraying him as ironlike, cut from tin, a mechanical presence whose lack of emotion underscores his compromised sense of morality. Snopes's physical presence fully reflects the inner corruption and love of revenge that he embodies. His leg, shot in the war when he was stealing Confederate horses for personal profit, drags lamely behind him, an external manifestation of his warped inner life. Because Snopes is wholly unable to express himself articulately or intelligently, his sole recourses for self-expression are violence and cruelty. These tactics have overtaken his worldview so completely that they have infused his sense of who he is.

Not satisfied with confining his deep unhappiness to his personal realm, Snopes seems to befoul everything he touches, and he becomes almost bestial in his lack of regard for others. In the de Spain home, Snopes intentionally steps in horse manure and tracks it throughout the house. Later, Faulkner compares Snopes to a stinging wasp or housefly, and Snopes lifts his hand "like a curled claw." These images suggest that Snopes is not actually human but instead simply resembles the form of a man. Fed by jealousy and rage, Snopes's need for revenge is borne of his sense of inferiority, lack of power, and gradual emasculation by the dismal sharecropping system. He compensates for these shortcomings by being a silent tyrant, ruling his family with threats and the promise of violence, as well as by destroying the livelihood of those individuals he believes have slighted him.

LENNIE SNOPES   Opposite Abner Snopes, with his penchant for revenge and destruction, is Lennie Snopes, a voice of reason and morality in the family. Because her morals are so different from her husband's, Lennie sharpens the conflict that Sartoris faces as he attempts to form his own ideas of right and wrong. The fact that Lennie has not simply succumbed to her domineering, violent husband makes her character remarkable. Surely, her spirit has been wounded by the grinding cycle of poverty, crime, and rootlessness to which Snopes has subjected the family. She has also endured physical violence throughout her married life. Lennie's spirit has not been broken completely, however. She repeatedly attempts to stop Snopes from lashing out at the landowners who provide the family's livelihood, even though her attempts are unsuccessful. Her unbroken spirit is perhaps most evident in the way she has influenced Sartoris. Although Lennie is forced into a quiet, inferior position in the family, she has managed to instill her values in Sartoris, despite the overwhelming, corrupting influence that Snopes tries to enforce. Although Lennie is abandoned by Sartoris in the end, he leaves because she has quietly taught him that it is the right thing to do.

THEMES, MOTIFS, AND SYMBOLS

THEMES

LOYALTY TO FAMILY VERSUS LOYALTY TO THE LAW   In "Barn Burning," Sartoris must decide whether loyalty to family or loyalty to the law is the moral imperative. For the Snopes family, particularly for Sartoris's father, family loyalty is valued above all else. The family seems to exist outside of society and even outside the law, and their moral code is based on family loyalty rather than traditional notions of right or wrong. Snopes tells Sartoris that he should remain loyal to his "blood," or family, or he will find himself alone. This threat suggests how isolated the family really is and how fully they rely on one another for protection, even when their faith in this protection is unfounded.

Blood in a literal sense appears as well, underscoring the intensity of the ties among family. For example, when the Snopeses are leaving the makeshift courthouse at the beginning of the story, a local boy accuses Snopes of being a barn burner, and, when Sartoris whirls around to confront him, the boy hits Sartoris and bloodies his face. The blood, dried and caked on his face during the ride out of town, is, in a way, a mark of pride: Sartoris had defended the family name. However, after Snopes once again plans to burn a barn, Sartoris understands that family loyalty comes at too great a cost and is too heavy a burden. He rejects family loyalty and instead betrays his father, warning de Spain that his barn is about to be burned. Only when Snopes is killed—presumably shot to death by de Spain at the end of the story—is the family free. They were loyal, but they still wind up alone.

THE SEARCH FOR PEACE   Surrounded by violence and conflict, Sartoris is constantly overwhelmed by fear, grief, and despair, and he knows that he must search for peace if he ever wants to be free from these tumultuous emotions. Sartoris specifically refers to fear, grief, and despair throughout the story, revealing the depth of his struggle to find his place among the demands of his family and his own developing ideas of morality. To Sartoris, peace, joy, and dignity are the alluring promises of a different kind of life, one that seems very far away from life in the Snopes household. His sense that a different kind of life exists grows particularly acute when he and Snopes approach de Spain's house. Sartoris is enamored with the grounds and the imposing house, and the domestic bliss that seems to emanate from the estate gives Sartoris a temporary comfort. The "spell of the house" seems to change everything, and Sartoris foolishly hopes that it has the power to turn his father from his criminal ways. For the first time, Sartoris has glimpsed a peaceful future.

Although Sartoris eventually frees himself from his father and his oppressive family life, he does not immediately find the peace and dignity that he expected would await him. Perhaps the happiness he seeks does exist for him in the future, as he leaves his family and old life behind without looking back. However, Sartoris has found a quieter, more subtle form of happiness. Life under his father was lived in a heightened state of extreme fear, grief, and despair. Now, the extreme emotions that loomed over Sartoris's young life have eased. His life may not have undergone a radical transformation, but "grief and despair [were] now no longer terror and fear but just grief and despair." Sartoris can't escape entirely, but he has already achieved a kind of peace.

MOTIFS

DARKNESS   The pervasive darkness in "Barn Burning" gestures to the lack of clarity that prevails in Snopes's thoughts and actions as well as the bleakness into which Snopes drags his family. Several significant episodes in the family's life occur under cover of darkness. For example, when the family camps by the roadside on their way to their new sharecroppers' cabin on the de Spain property, Snopes beats Sartoris and scolds him for planning to reveal his guilt at the courthouse. Sartoris can't see his father in the darkness, which reveals the alienation that is at the heart of their relationship. In the final portion of the story, darkness changes from being suffocating to suggesting freedom and escape. Snopes's plan to burn yet another barn is hatched in the darkness, and the night seems to promise nothing but more crime and despair. However, Sartoris rallies his own sense of morality during this night as well, finally standing up for what he believes in. Sartoris embarks on his new life just as the darkness ends and dawn approaches.

THE WORD RAVENING   The word *ravening*, which means devouring greedily, destroying, or preying on, appears several times in the story, and every time it highlights Snopes's malicious character. In its first sense, "devouring greedily," the word resembles "ravenous," which gestures to the poverty the family must endure. When the family does eat, the meal is makeshift and cold. For example, when Snopes and his sons are in town to pursue their case again de Spain, Snopes buys a small portion of cheese, which he divides into three even smaller pieces. Faulkner also uses the word to link Snopes and fire. Snopes's "latent ravening ferocity" and his "ravening and jealous rage" are expressed in the fire, which hungrily destroys the beams and dry hay bales of his employers' barns. Finally, Faulkner's use of the word also suggests the overpowering destructive impulse that defines Snopes. He is a parasite, preying on others to his own advantage, gleefully seeking the destruction of others' livelihood and property in his own hunger for revenge.

SYMBOLS

FIRE   Fire is a constant threat in "Barn Burning," and it represents both Snopes's inherent powerlessness and his quest for power and self-expression. After the family has been run out of town because Snopes burned a barn, Snopes steals a split rail from a fence and builds a small fire by the roadside, barely functional and hardly suited to the large family's needs on a cold evening. He'd committed his fiery crime in a desperate grasp at power, but now he reveals how utterly powerless he is to adequately care for his family. When Snopes turns the fire on others' property, however, his power increases, albeit criminally. Snopes has grown adept at committing crimes and escaping undetected, and his entire family is drawn in to this pattern of lying and evasion. Unlike the small, inadequate fire Snopes built for his family, the criminal fire that Snopes set in Mr. Harris's barn sent Confederate patrols out for many nights of searching for the rogue and horse thief. For Snopes, fire is a means of preserving his integrity and avenging the slights he believes have been ceaselessly meted out to him throughout his life. Powerless and poor, Snopes turns to fire to tilt the balance in his favor, even if it is only for one brief, blazing moment.

THE SOILED RUG   The rug that Snopes soils with horse manure in the de Spain home indicates a critical shift in his typical method of operating, because this is the first time that Snopes has intruded into and violated a home. Snopes's destruction is a swipe at the financial security that de Spain has and that Snopes lacks, as well as a clear statement of his unhappiness at being subservient to de Spain for his livelihood. Without even knowing the de Spains, Snopes resents them simply for being prosperous landowners and in a superior position. A barn holds a farmer's livelihood, including crops, livestock, and machinery, and this is Snopes's usual target. Extending his criminal reach to the rug signals that Snopes's resentment now encompasses the domestic sphere as well. The shocking act of smearing the rug with excrement eventually leads to the rug's complete destruction, which then leads to another court hearing, another act of revenge, and ultimately Snopes's death. The expensive rug represents for Snopes every comfort, opportunity, and privilege he feels he has been unfairly denied, and in destroying it, he renounces all regard for his life and family's future.

SHORT STORY ANALYSIS

STRUCTURE AND STYLE   Faulkner is known for his distinctive style, especially his use of long sentences that are frequently interrupted by clauses. For example, the lengthy second sentence of "Barn Burning" would be considered typical Faulkner. This unique style lends Faulkner's work a sense of scope and continuity. Faulkner seems to suggest that human understanding and perception are unstable and always changing, subject to the environment and other people. This style also suggests a lack of clear resolution to the action. For example, at the end of "Barn Burning," Sartoris has finally escaped his father's clutches, but we are left with an unresolved sense of the impact that Sartoris's escape will ultimately have on him and his family. Faulkner's syntax (the way a sentence is put together) helps contribute to this lack of a definitive conclusion, because many of his sentences meander and digress before ending—sometimes to the extent that we forget how the sentence began. This technique adds complexity to Faulkner's fiction, which he intended to reflect the struggles faced in everyday world—struggles that usually don't have clear resolutions.

Faulkner's long, looping sentences form a stream-of-consciousness style in which a character's roving thoughts and associations are reproduced on the page. The opening paragraph is a key example of this style. The second sentence spills out, each subsequent clause modifying the observations and thoughts that have come before it, ultimately forming a chain of loosely connected impressions and ideas. In real life, thoughts are not linear, and Faulkner represents the chaotic quality of private thought by interrupting the flow of the sentence with clauses. The sentence thus gives us a peek into Sartoris's swirling sensory impressions, revealing much more than simply his observations of what's around him. Sartoris's impressions reflect the hunger, fear, and guilt he feels, an impoverished child watching his father's hearing from the back of a general store. The sight and smell of the foods surrounding Sartoris remind him of his empty stomach, which then leads him to consider more abstract concerns, such as his sadness and struggle to sustain his family loyalty.

SETTING   Faulkner uses setting to evoke the class distinctions that fuel Snopes's deep resentment. The Snopes family lives in dire circumstances that are vastly different from the lifestyles of the landowning families for whom they work as sharecroppers, and the story hinges on Snopes's destruction of property and violation of the home. Once content with avenging perceived injustices by burning a landowner's barn, thus compromising his liveli-hood, Snopes begins avenging the vaguer wrongs that he feels he has endured simply by virtue of his poverty. At the de Spains' opulent home, for example, he rudely forces his way inside, staining the rug with manure and then destroying it when he is ordered to clean it. He is avenging nothing: the de Spains were strangers when he walked into the house, strang-ers who had chosen to allow Snopes to reside on their property and sharecrop on their land. The story's setting, including the Snopeses' packed wagon and the expansive de Spain estate, highlights the outsider status of the Snopes family and ignites Snopes's rage.

Another unique aspect of setting in "Barn Burning" is the courthouse, which is simply a general store that is used for legal proceedings. This is the place where justice is meted out to Snopes, where he is punished for avenging the injustices he believes he has endured. The fact that the courthouse isn't a real courthouse just augments Snopes's perception that he isn't treated fairly, and it highlights his status as a rogue outsider—his own vigilante justice is punished in a haphazard fashion, within the law but also outside it. The idea of a courthouse that isn't a courthouse appears again when Sartoris first sees the de Spains' home. "Hit's big as a courthouse," he thinks to himself as the house comes fully into view. Because the only courthouse Sartoris has seen is likely the inside of the general store, the courthouse to which he compares the house is simply an image he has created in his imagination. His compari-son suggests how removed Sartoris is from the world beyond the small sharecropping com-munity in which the Snopes family lives.

DIALECT AND DICTION In "Barn Burning," Faulkner mimics the dialect (regional speech patterns) of the simple agrarian family he is portraying, which adds realism and immediacy to the story. For example, during Snopes's hearing at the beginning of the story, Sartoris looks at Mr. Harris and concludes that he is his family's enemy for attempting to bring charges against Snopes, thinking, "ourn! mine and hisn both!" When Lennie asks her youngest son whether he was hurt after his scuffle with another boy, Sartoris replies, "Naw, . . . Hit don't hurt. Lemme be." Through the words the characters use, Faulkner re-veals much about the education and background of this farm family, and he stays true to their actual way of speaking.

The agrarian life that was only beginning to disappear in the turn-of-the-century South also provides the story with a rich lexicon of specialized diction. As Major de Spain rides up to confront Snopes about the ruined rug, Snopes is stooped over the plow, buckling the hame, one of the two curved pieces, usually made of metal or wood, on a harness. Later, during the course of the tense exchange, Snopes asks Sartoris whether he has put "the cut-ter back in that straight stock," referring respectively to the blade and frame of a plow. Later, before the second hearing in the rural store, Sartoris dreams of his father reforming while "running a middle buster," a special kind of plow used to break up the tough clods of earth in the center of a field row. Faulkner knew well the trappings and lingo of southern plantation and farm life, and he also meticulously researched his stories. The specific language choices that Faulkner makes give his tale the ring of authenticity, bringing the hardscrabble, labor-intensive lifestyle of the Snopeses vividly and memorably to life.

IMPORTANT QUOTATIONS EXPLAINED

1. *Maybe he will feel it too. Maybe it will even change him now from what maybe he couldn't help but be.*

This quotation occurs as Snopes and Sartoris slowly approach the de Spain house and Sartoris, overwhelmed by the peace and joy he feels in the presence of the large home, wishes for the eradication of sorrow, envy, jealousy, and rage from his family life. Similar sentiments are echoed later, during the incident with the rug. Sartoris hopes that his father will learn a lesson from having to pay for the carpet's replacement and will finally "stop forever and always from being what he used to be." Both of these statements reveal that Sartoris has a core of morality that is separate from Snopes's influence. Although Sartoris's loyalties are divided through most of the story, Faulkner makes it clear where his wavering sympathies ultimately lie: Sartoris desires to conform to a generalized sense of justice that applies equally to all, not the moral relativism of his scoundrel father who expects the family to lie on one another's behalf. Sartoris believes in the capacity for change, even in his father's case. His journey in the story involves his gradual acceptance that some individuals are unwilling or unable to reform their criminal ways.

2. *Maybe it will all add up and balance and vanish—corn, rug, fire; the terror and grief, the being pulled two ways like between two teams of horses—gone, done with for ever and ever.*

This quotation occurs after Major de Spain has informed Snopes that he owes twenty additional bushels of corn for destroying the rug. It is notable for the way Faulkner's narrative voice is able to vary throughout the story, approximating and mimicking the thoughts of Sartoris, his ten-year-old protagonist. The "for ever and ever" adds a childish lilt to the end of the phrase and underscores the impossibility of Sartoris's hopes ever being realized. Sartoris wants all the shame and burdens his father has heaped onto the family to merely disappear, to be erased. However, Snopes's transgressions are too vast to simply "vanish" as Sartoris hopes. Snopes's anger and sense of inferiority are not expressed merely through fire; rather, as is evident in this brief list—"corn, rug, fire"—he does not discriminate when it comes to destroying the property of others.

The quotation also reinforces the idea of a lack of peace in Sartoris's life; he is always aware of the reality in which he lives. The joy and peace of the de Spain property are fleeting, quickly giving way to the dark-coated, limping figure of the father arriving to unsettle the home. Faulkner fully captures young Sartoris's indulgent fantasies as well as the truly painful struggle he undergoes. Divided between family loyalty and loyalty to the law, he feels as though he is being torn apart by teams of horses pulling in opposite directions. Sartoris yearns for all of this—his father's transgressions, his own tumultuous emotions—to simply disappear. In a way, these things do disappear in the end, but only after Sartoris takes action by warning de Spain about the imminent fire. Sartoris himself eliminates them rather than waiting passively for them to vanish on their own.

Bartleby the Scrivener

Herman Melville
(1819–1891)

CONTEXT

Herman Melville was born in 1819 in New York City, the third of eight children. He came from an all-American family: one of his grandfathers had fought at Fort Stanwix, and another had taken part in the Boston Tea Party. Melville's family moved to Albany, New York, in 1830 after his family's import business went bankrupt. Two years later, Melville's father died, and the fifteen-year-old Melville and his brother, Gansevoort, found jobs to support the family.

Melville held a number of interesting and adventurous jobs in his lifetime. He worked as a surveyor, teacher, and cabin boy on a ship that traveled from New York to Liverpool, England. He also worked for a year and a half on the whaling ship *Acushnet*, which sailed to the South Pacific. Melville deserted the *Acushnet* to spend a few weeks with the inhabitants of Marquesas Island, some of whom were cannibals. Melville lived for four months in Honolulu, Hawaii, where he worked as a clerk, and found work in 1844 on the ship *United States*, which stopped in a Peruvian port on its way to Boston.

In 1847, Melville married Elizabeth Shaw. After three years in New York, the couple moved to the Berkshires in Massachusetts, where they stayed for the next thirteen years. It was in Massachusetts that Melville became friends with writer Nathaniel Hawthorne, author of *The Scarlet Letter* and *The House of the Seven Gables*. Hawthorne and his work would have a crucial influence on Melville's writing.

Much of Melville's work draws on his experiences as a sailor. *Typee* (1846) and *Omoo* (1847), for example, were inspired by his time spent with the natives of Marquesas Island, whereas the novels *Mardi* (1849), *Redburn* (1849), and *White-Jacket* (1850) drew heavily from his experiences at sea. *Moby-Dick* (1851), now an American classic, was a critical and commercial failure when it was first published, earning Melville less than $600. *Pierre* (1852), the novel that followed *Moby-Dick*, bombed so badly that Melville's publishers turned down his next book, *The Isle of the Cross*, a manuscript that has never been found.

"Bartleby the Scrivener" marked Melville's first foray into short fiction following the humiliating debacle of *Pierre*'s failure. During the next three years, Melville published fifteen stories and sketches, along with another novel, *The Confidence Man* (1857). Despite these efforts, his reputation remained tarnished, and he stopped trying to earn a living writing fiction. He lectured on his adventures at sea and worked as a customs inspector for the next twenty years. He eventually moved back to New York and lived in a house that his father-in-law had purchased for him. His book of Civil War poems, *Battle-Pieces* (1866) sold well, but his epic poem *Clarel* (1876) had an initial print run of only 350 copies. Melville died at age seventy-two in New York City in 1891. The *New York Times* got his name wrong in his obituary, identifying him as Henry Melville.

Interest in Melville's work didn't pick up until 1924, when his novella *Billy Budd* was published posthumously after it had been hidden in a tin can for thirty years. Several biographies of Melville followed—including Newton Arvin's biography, which won the National Book Award in 1950—as his works garnered more critical acclaim. Melville is now widely considered one of the finest writers in American history, and scholars praise his complex investigations of gender, race, and sexuality. Some see in his work the seeds of existentialist literature, a genre that wouldn't fully develop until the early twentieth century. Albert Camus, author of the existentialist novel *The Stranger* (1942), cited Melville as a crucial influence. Some scholars also identify Melville as the first modernist American poet.

"Bartleby the Scrivener" was published anonymously in *Putnam's Monthly Magazine* under the title "Bartleby, the Scrivener: A Story of Wall Street." It was published in two parts, the first of which appeared in November of 1853 and the second of which appeared the next month. It was later republished in Melville's short story collection called *The Piazza Tales* (1856).

PLOT OVERVIEW

The narrator begins the story by talking about scriveners, or law-copyists. In particular, his story will be about a man named Bartleby, a particularly strange and fascinating scrivener about whom little is known. The narrator describes his office. He is a master of chancery, a lawyer who works for rich men on property cases and once worked for the wealthy businessman John Jacob Astor. The narrator's office on Wall Street faces a tall brick wall. He employs men nicknamed Turkey and Nippers as copyists and a boy named Ginger Nut as an office boy. Turkey is well behaved in the morning but drinks during lunch and becomes sloppy in the afternoons. Nippers, meanwhile, dislikes his job and spends a great deal of time complaining about the poor quality of his desk. Unlike Turkey, Nippers is cranky in the morning and better behaved in the afternoon.

One morning, Bartleby comes to the narrator's office responding to an advertisement. He is "pallidly neat, respectable, incurably forlorn!" The narrator hires him and sets him up near a window with a view of the wall. Bartleby works tirelessly. One day, the narrator instructs Bartleby to compare two documents line by line, but Bartleby answers, "I would prefer not to." Shocked, the narrator repeats his request, but Bartleby only repeats his refusal, remaining perfectly calm. A few days later, the same thing happens. The narrator unsuccessfully tries to reason with him, and all the other employees confirm that the narrator is in the right.

The narrator worries at length about what to do with Bartleby. He asks Bartleby to compare the copies again, and as usual, Bartleby says he would prefer not to, prompting Turkey to threaten Bartleby with bodily harm. The narrator asks Bartleby to run to the post office and fetch Nippers, but Bartleby says he prefers not to both times. The narrator still can't decide what to do with him.

One Sunday morning, the narrator stops by the office on the way to Trinity Church and finds the front entrance locked. He knocks, and a disheveled Bartleby answers, saying he's busy. The narrator leaves, thinks about the situation, and returns, but he can't find Bartleby. Nevertheless, it's clear from the state of the office that Bartleby's been living there. The narrator feels terribly sad for Bartleby and discovers that Bartleby has been squirreling his wages away in a handkerchief. He realizes that Bartleby buys nothing and seems to have no family. As the narrator thinks, however, he starts to feel that there's nothing he can do to help Bartleby. He skips church, and as he walks home, he decides that he will try one more time to reason with Bartleby and will fire him if he still refuses to work.

The next morning, the narrator asks Bartleby where he was born, but Bartleby refuses to tell him. As the other employees converse, the narrator notices that they're using the word *prefer* much more often than before, and the observation unsettles him.

The next day, Bartleby announces that he won't write anymore, and the narrator assumes it's because Bartleby's eyes are hurting after working so hard. Days pass, and Bartleby says he has given up copying for good but also refuses to leave the office. At last the narrator tells Bartleby that he must leave in six days. When the time is up, Bartleby says he would prefer not to leave. The narrator gives him some money and goes home, thinking hard about the situation. The next morning, he arrives to find the door locked. Bartleby calls out that he's busy.

After walking around the block to think about the situation some more, the narrator returns and demands to know what right Bartleby has to stay in the office. He gets worked up and remembers the case of the businessmen Adams and Colt, one of whom killed the other in their office. The narrator remembers Jesus' words, "love one another," and resolves to behave charitably toward Bartleby. Days pass. The narrator reads Jonathan Edwards and Joseph Priestly and comes to the conclusion that Bartleby was predestined to be in his life.

Despite these resolutions, the narrator is swayed by his friends' opinion, who cannot understand why Bartleby is still in the office while refusing to do any work. The narrator decides that he can't throw Bartleby onto the street, bribe him, or even call the police. He believes the only thing to do is change offices. He relocates, leaving Bartleby alone in the now-empty offices. A lawyer named Mr. B sets up shop in the narrator's former office. Mr. B visits the narrator a few days after moving to discuss Bartleby, who still hasn't left the old office despite the fact that Mr. B now occupies it. The narrator denies any connection to or responsibility for Bartleby. A week later, a group of people visit the narrator and demand that he get rid of Bartleby. They say he is haunting the building. The narrator finally agrees that he'll try to get rid of Bartleby.

The narrator returns to his old office and finds Bartleby sitting on the landing. He offers him his choice of several jobs, but Bartleby says he would prefer not to take any of the jobs the narrator is offering. The narrator grows angry but then calms down and asks Bartleby whether he would like to come home with him. Bartleby says no, and the narrator leaves, feeling he has done everything he can possibly do.

He later learns that the police eventually removed Bartleby from the building and locked him up for vagrancy in a prison called the Tombs. The narrator visits Bartleby at the Tombs and finds him sitting in front of a wall. He doesn't want to talk to the narrator. On his way out, the narrator pays the grub-man to give Bartleby nicer food, even though Bartleby says he doesn't want to eat. A few days later, the narrator visits Bartleby again and finds him lying by the wall, dead, presumably from starvation.

The narrator says he later learned that Bartleby used to work in the dead-letter office in Washington. This fact strikes the narrator as extremely sad.

CHARACTER LIST

The Narrator   An unnamed lawyer. The narrator, who is probably in his sixties, is a master in chancery, a position that entails dealing with property rights. He treats his employees fairly, fosters a pleasant office atmosphere, and enjoys his work. Bartleby's appearance prompts a great deal of self-searching in the narrator, and he spends an immense amount of time and energy thinking about Bartleby's peculiar behavior and wondering what could possibly motivate it.

Bartleby   A copyist. Very little is known about Bartleby, other than the fact that he once worked in a dead-letter office in Washington, D.C. Bartleby is a plain, quiet, melancholy man who gently but firmly refuses to do tasks that do not appeal to him. His attitude is not insubordinate, but his decisions are absolute. He says little beyond what the narrator demands of him.

Turkey   A copyist. Turkey is a grubby, badly dressed, red-faced man who's about sixty. He is an excellent worker in the morning and speaks almost reverently to the narrator, but he gets sloppy and disrespectful in the afternoon after drinking alcohol at lunch. He believes that he's essential to the narrator's success.

Nippers   A copyist. A grouchy, dissatisfied man of about twenty-five, Nippers considers his job to be beneath him. He expresses his unhappiness by incessantly complaining about the table he uses for a desk. Unlike Turkey, Nippers is more bearable in the afternoons than he is in the mornings. Nippers writes well and behaves elegantly when it suits him.

Ginger Nut   The office boy. A twelve-year-old boy, Ginger Nut often fetches cake and apples for Turkey and Nippers. His nickname comes from the kind of cake he purchases most often.

Mr. Cutlets   The "grub-man" at the prison. Mr. Cutlets supplements the prison slop with better food for those inmates whose friends give him bribes.

Mr. B   A lawyer who occupies the narrator's offices after the narrator moves out. Mr. B asks the narrator how he knows Bartleby, but the narrator denies any responsibility for Bartleby.

ANALYSIS OF MAJOR CHARACTERS

THE NARRATOR   The narrator, who is never named, is a charming, intelligent, even lovable man. He sympathizes with the boring nature of his employees' jobs and overlooks their eccentricities. His humor, whether inadvertent or intentional, is winning and remarkably appealing even to modern readers. He is infinitely interested in himself and his own thoughts and reactions, analyzing every twist and turn of his own reactions to Bartleby. The narrator is also somewhat of a philosopher, offering interesting insights into human nature as he examines himself and those around him. Because he is so frank about himself and his failings, we come to trust him and consequently believe him when he says that he couldn't do anything to help save Bartleby from himself.

At the same time, however, the narrator may be read as a deluded hypocrite. He takes pains to portray himself as a religious man, peppering his speech with biblical imagery, and says that he turned into a pillar of salt—a reference to the fate of Lot's wife—when Bartleby first refused to obey him. Referring to Jesus' assertion that those who harm children should be drowned with millstones around their necks, the narrator also says that Bartleby is like a millstone around his neck, "not only useless as a necklace, but afflictive to bear." Taking on a pious tone, the narrator says he feels that both he and Bartleby are sons of Adam, united by their shared humanity, if by nothing else. Yet, when faced with a crisis, the narrator decides to skip church. He's also far less charitable than he believes himself to be and abandons Bartleby in an empty office rather than try to help him. In fact, if Bartleby is interpreted as a Christ figure, then the narrator becomes the Judas who betrays him, even saying that Bartleby is "nothing to him."

BARTLEBY   The title character's most crucial quality is his mysteriousness, his uninterpretability. Bartleby is calm, patient, and obstinate. A hard worker, he literally lives in the office. He is a trustworthy man who doesn't even pocket the spare change he finds on the floor. He is a tidy, sad, hushed man about whose life we and the characters know almost nothing. Yet he provokes passionate feelings in those he comes into contact with. Mystified by Bartleby, characters in the story foist their own interpretations on him. Many decide he's dangerous— so dangerous, in fact, that some people threaten to form a mob to forcibly remove him from the office. The narrator, however, characterizes him differently, as a ghost, a cadaver, a being that is not quite human. Our response to Bartleby is equally mixed: we may decide that he is a quiet but fervent anticapitalist who refuses to be another cog in the wheel, or we may think he's a good man who has suffered a trauma and can no longer function in society. Melville provides no answers, which is, in fact, the point of the story. Bartleby is fascinating not because of who he is, but because of the spectrum of how others react to him.

THEMES, MOTIFS, AND SYMBOLS

THEMES

THE RESPONSIBILITY OF SOCIETY   Melville's story asks us to consider the relationship between society and the individual. We may all agree that Bartleby should not be paid for work he refuses to do and may even agree that he should not be allowed to stay in a building in which he is not employed. But the level of hysteria with which people react to Bartleby suggests that society is not equipped to deal with people who don't conform to accepted standards of normalcy. Perhaps society is responding to Bartleby's quiet rebelliousness: he does not want to do any sort of work, and he would rather die than do something he finds unpleasant, an attitude that might enrage some people. Or perhaps society is responding to Bartleby's sheer strangeness: he has no family, personality, or need to eat anything other than ginger nuts. Melville asks us to consider, however, whether these qualities justify the threat of mob violence or imprisonment that Bartleby receives. People like Bartleby, he seems to suggest, should be expected to participate in civilization but also be treated with compassion even if they refuse.

THE PARADOXICAL NATURE OF OFFICE LIFE   The law office depicted in "Bartleby the Scrivener" is, in part, a gloomy, prisonlike place. A wall sits in front of the window, and the narrator suggests that light trickles down into the office as if the workers are at the bottom of a well. Melville makes the connection between the office and jail more explicit during the narrator's visit to the Tombs. There, the narrator finds Bartleby sitting in front of a wall, just as he had sat in the office. While the office is a kind of prison, however, it is at the same time a home. Bartleby literally lives in the office, and in many ways, his coworkers become his family. The narrator notes the quirks and personalities of Turkey, Nippers, and Ginger Nut and describes them as lovingly as he might those of his sons.

MOTIFS

THE WORD PREFER   The recurring word *prefer* illustrates the extent to which Bartleby influences those around him. Countless times, the narrator and his employees listen to Bartleby's calm pronouncement, "I would prefer not to." Depending on their moods and the passage of time, they are alternately mystified and enraged, but always resistant. Gradually, however, Bartleby's words and behavior begin to seep into their own thoughts, and the narrator is keen enough to notice the change. He realizes that he too has started to say *prefer* and worries that Bartleby is affecting his mind. Turkey and Nippers aren't so wise and merely use the word without realizing it. Bartleby may be a pale, mild man, but he is apparently also a powerful presence in the office. The recurrence of the word *prefer* is also indicative of Melville's immense skill. The first time Bartleby says, "I would prefer not to," it is puzzling to us. As he speaks the same phrase again and again, however, its meaning continually shifts, alternately annoying, mysterious, comical, infuriating, and ultimately sad.

SYMBOLS

DEAD LETTERS   Dead letters, which Bartleby used to sort and burn at his job at the dead-letter office, symbolize Bartleby himself. Dead letters are missives that for some reason cannot be delivered. They have become useless, just as Bartleby is considered useless by the world. Another meaning of the word *delivered* is "saved" (as in *deliver us from evil*), which applies equally well to Bartleby, because he's a person who can't be delivered from his suffering. He seems unsuited for life in normal society and doesn't encounter anyone who loves him enough to rescue him. The narrator reflects that letters may become dead because the intended recipient passed away before the letter could reach him. If Bartleby had an intended recipient—someone who could have saved him—that person does not materialize. The only candidate, the narrator, abandons Bartleby, and by the end of the story, Bartleby has died, just like the dead letters themselves.

SHORT STORY ANALYSIS

GENRE   Although it slips back and forth between several genres, "Bartleby the Scrivener" can be best categorized as a mystery or suspense story that revolves around Bartleby's unknown identity and behavior. Melville is anything but a hack, however, and instead of writing a story solely concerned with the shadowy history of one character, he writes a mystery that contains multiple spiritual mysteries. As the story progresses, for example, the narrator becomes preoccupied with the mystery of himself. He wonders why he responds to Bartleby as he does and how certain people manage to elicit inexplicable behavior from other people. The fact that Melville never solves the conundrum of Bartleby creates another mystery as to how others are to interpret such strangeness. Like the white whale in Melville's *Moby-Dick*, Bartleby is an almost infinitely interpretable figure. By putting such a character at the heart of a suspense story and then leaving the central puzzle unsolved, Melville challenges our expectations of the genre.

When Melville wrote "Bartleby," the short-story genre itself was relatively new, and perhaps partly because of that, Melville's story doesn't follow what would eventually become the standard conventions of the form. Instead of starting at the heart of the story, Melville's narrator sets the scene at length. Moreover, instead of introducing his central character, Bartleby, right away, Melville leaves him out of the narrative for some time. Instead of making sure that all of the characters remain involved in the plot for the duration of the story, he lets Turkey and Nippers slip out of the action. And instead of allowing us to get to know Bartleby, Melville keeps his past hidden until the end of the story. While some readers might accuse Melville of bad structuring, others might argue that each unconventional move is made on purpose. By delaying Bartleby's entrance and spending time setting the scene, Melville heightens the air of mystery that surrounds Bartleby.

B

HUMOR Melville reveals the narrator's character through the use of humor, and "Bartleby the Scrivener" is about its narrator just as much as it is about Bartleby himself. The narrator occasionally attempts to be funny for our amusement, making slightly stiff, long-winded jokes. In sarcastic praise, for example, he remarks that the brick wall is so close to his office window that you can see its beauty without the aid of a magnifying glass. More comical are the narrator's formal explanations and pronouncements, which he means to be utterly serious. After explaining that his employees are named Turkey, Nippers, and Ginger Nut, for example, he says, "in truth these were nicknames, mutually conferred upon each other by my three clerks." These sorts of remarks are humorous both because of their formality and because they explain what is already obvious. Funniest of all are the narrator's earnest, astonished accounts of his employees' oddities: Turkey's shabby, greasy clothes and drunken desire to fight; Nippers' furious struggles with his desk; and Ginger Nut's nut-strewn desk. These comments blend intentional humor with accidental humor—the narrator wants to amuse us but is most interested in painting an accurate picture of his office.

Melville balances tragedy and comedy, using humor to lessen the sadness of Bartleby's life. Nearly every description, line of dialogue, and observation about Bartleby blends humor, mystery, menace, and melancholy. Bartleby's refusal to work amuses us just as much as it surprises and annoys us. The phrase he uses repeatedly, "I would prefer not to," is always funny, even when it is also spooky or irritating. Bartleby often provokes other people to violent or cruel behavior, but even this behavior manages to be funny. Turkey longs to punch Bartleby, but because Turkey is drunk and repeatedly asks the narrator's permission to "black [Bartleby's] eyes," his threats are amusing. The new tenants violently object to Bartleby, but because their response is so over the top and includes threats of mob uprisings, they seem funny. Through the use of humor, Melville turns his story from the sad tale of a mysterious man into something far more complex and entertaining.

METAFICTION "Bartleby the Scrivener" is preoccupied with its own existence as a text. In a technique predictive of one that would become common in twentieth-century postmodern literature, Melville draws attention to the artifice of fiction. Much of this self-awareness is embodied by the narrator, who often comments on his own storytelling techniques. He begins by saying that ideally, he would write a biography of Bartleby but knows he can't because so little is known about Bartleby's life. The admission that his story is compromised and something less than it should be is disarming because it lowers our expectations for the story while simultaneously making us interested in learning why Bartleby is so remarkable. Throughout the story, the narrator also calls attention to the literary techniques he uses. For example, he announces that he is about to set the scene by describing his office and employees, and he sometimes interjects to explain how we should interpret certain scenes. At no time does he allow us to forget that we are being told a story.

Melville makes fiction and writing one of the key subjects of the story. The narrator's employees are parodies of writers. Drunken, quarrelsome, and obsessive, they embody most of the stereotypical qualities of novelists. Their job is to copy text, a task that is portrayed as tiresome and mindless. If Melville associates Turkey and Nippers with hack writers churning out reams of material, he associates Bartleby with the idealistic writer who would sooner fail to put a single word on paper than fall short of his own standards. The story's coda may be Melville's lament for the possible fate of fiction, his own and other writers'. Some novels and short stories are destined to become, quite literally, dead letters. Written with great passion, they may go forgotten and unread, just as the letters Bartleby handled were destined for the fire. Melville's interrogation of fiction is melancholic, but it is leavened with humor. He pulls off the literary equivalent of winking at us as he shows us what it means to be a writer.

IMPORTANT QUOTATIONS EXPLAINED

1. *So true it is, and so terrible too, that up to a certain point the thought or sight of misery enlists our best affections; but, in certain special cases, beyond that point it does not . . . To a sensitive being, pity is not seldom pain. And when at last it is perceived that such pity cannot lead to effectual succor, common sense bids the soul rid of it.*

This passage is representative of the narrator's facility with words, his astute insights, and his interest in his own reactions to Bartleby. He notes that in the beginning we feel sympathetic when we see a miserable person, but at some point the sympathy goes away. It pains sensitive people such as the narrator to observe someone else's pain, and if it becomes clear that feeling bad for a particular person will not help him, it makes sense to stop feeling bad and stop causing yourself pain. The narrator's conclusions seem logical, and we enjoy following his thought process. He is a lively writer and clear thinker. In fact, he is so logical, lively, and clear that he manages to pull the wool over our eyes and his own. In passages like these, he is doing little more than justifying his failure to help Bartleby. He truly believes in what he is saying, as do we, but his eloquence and conviction do not completely mask the heartlessness of his words.

2. *Somehow, of late I had got into the way of involuntarily using this word 'prefer' upon all sorts of not exactly suitable occasions. And I trembled to think that my contact with the scrivener had already and seriously affected me in a mental way. And what further and deeper aberration might it not yet produce?*

Bartleby scares people partly because they see themselves in him. On the surface, he seems perfectly normal, albeit a bit sad, and his behavior is fairly ordinary. He doesn't act wildly and quietly works hard at his white-collar office job. Yet something about Bartleby is off, and the perception that he isn't quite normal makes people worry that they too could turn into Bartleby one day. The narrator's increased use of the word *prefer* is most likely the natural consequence of spending time with a new person and picking up some of his verbal habits. But because the narrator is worried that Bartleby's strangeness might rub off on him, he imagines that Bartleby is having some kind of effect on his mental health. Like a pack of healthy animals leaving behind a sick member of their group, society shies away from Bartleby for fear that he will infect everyone.

B

The Birthmark

Nathaniel Hawthorne
(1804–1864)

CONTEXT

Nathaniel Hawthorne was born in 1804 in Salem, Massachusetts, to a family descended from Puritans. He was born Nathaniel Hathorne but changed the spelling of his name out of shame after learning that his paternal grandfather, John Hathorne, had been a judge at the Salem witch trials. When Hawthorne was four, his father, a sea captain, died in Dutch Guinea. Hawthorne spent much of his childhood in Maine with his mother, alone and sheltered. He attended Bowdoin College, earning his degree in 1825. Among his fellow classmates were several men who would go on to achieve great things, including poet Henry Wadsworth Longfellow and President Franklin Pierce. Hawthorne returned home after graduation and tried his hand at writing fiction, calling his efforts "articles" and "tales" rather than stories. Genre fiction was popular at the time, but Hawthorne was interested in going beyond the Indian stories and ghost stories that many magazines were publishing. In 1828, Hawthorne self-published a novel called *Fanshawe*, which failed to sell many copies and prompted Hawthorne to try to destroy every copy he could find. He succeeded in publishing some of his stories in the *United States Democratic Review* and the *Token*, among other publications.

In 1837, Hawthorne published a collection of stories entitled *Twice-Told Tales*. Two years later, U.S. senator and fellow Bowdoin alumnus Jonathon Ciley appointed Hawthorne to a post at the Boston Custom House. While at this post, Hawthorne became interested in transcendentalism, a philosophical movement led by Ralph Waldo Emerson that emphasized the individual over organized religion. For a time Hawthorne lived at Brook Farm, a utopian community near Boston that attempted to support itself via agriculture. In 1842, Hawthorne married his fiancée, Sophia Peabody, and moved to Concord, Massachusetts, which was also the home of Emerson, Henry David Thoreau, and Louisa May Alcott. The Hawthornes had three children: Una, who was mentally ill and died young; Julian, who was eventually convicted and jailed for defrauding the public; and Rose, who founded a Roman Catholic group called the Dominican Sisters of Hawthorne.

Hawthorne published his second collection of stories, *Mosses from an Old Manse*, in 1846, which was also the year he quit writing for a time and began working as a surveyor for the Salem Custom House to better provide for his family. His experiences as a surveyor inform his romance *The Scarlet Letter* (1850), which opens with a description of customs house business. Perhaps his most famous novel, *The Scarlet Letter* tells the story of a young woman who bears the illegitimate child of a preacher, keeps the father's identity secret, and is ostracized by her community. During the next several years, Hawthorne published what would become some of his best-known works, including *The House of the Seven Gables* (1851), *The Blithedale Romance* (1852), and *The Marble Faun* (1860). His other works include the children's books *A Wonder-Book* (1852), *Tanglewood Tales* (1853), *Grandfather's Chair: A History for Youth* (1841), and *Our Old Home* (1863). "The Birthmark," like much of Hawthorne's work, is set in New England and has a Puritan sensibility. Along with "Young Goodman Brown" (a favorite of Stephen King's), it is one of Hawthorne's best-known and most frequently anthologized stories.

In 1850, Hawthorne met the author Herman Melville. The two men were close friends for a time, so close that Melville dedicated his masterpiece, *Moby-Dick*, to Hawthorne. When his old college friend Franklin Pierce ran for president of the United States, Hawthorne wrote his campaign biography. Pierce rewarded Hawthorne in 1853 after winning the election by naming him the American consul in Liverpool, England. Hawthorne died in his sleep in 1864 at age sixty while taking a trip to the White Mountains with Franklin Pierce.

PLOT OVERVIEW

The narrator introduces Aylmer as a brilliant scientist and natural philosopher who has abandoned his experiments for a while to marry the beautiful Georgiana. One day, Aylmer asks his wife whether she has ever thought about removing the birthmark on her cheek. She cheerfully says no but grows serious when she sees that he asked the question seriously. Many people, she says, have told her the mark is a charm, and she has always thought maybe they were right. Aylmer says that because her face is almost perfect, any mark is shocking. Georgiana is angry at first, and then she weeps, asking how he can love her if she is shocking to him.

The narrator explains that the birthmark in question is a red mark in the shape of a tiny hand on Georgiana's left cheek. The mark disappears when she blushes. Georgiana's male admirers love the birthmark, and many would risk their lives just to kiss it. Some women think the mark ruins her beauty, but the narrator says this is nonsense.

Aylmer obsesses about the birthmark. For him, it symbolizes mortality and sin and comes to tower over Georgiana's beauty in his mind. He can think of nothing else. One night she reminds him of a dream he had. He spoke in his sleep, saying they must take out her heart. Aylmer remembers dreaming that he had removed the birthmark with a knife, plunging down until he had reached his wife's heart, which he decided to cut out. Georgiana says that she will risk her life to have the birthmark erased. Thrilled, Aylmer agrees to try. He professes complete confidence in his own abilities, likening himself to Pygmalion. He kisses his wife's unmarked cheek.

They decide to move to the apartments where Aylmer has his laboratory. He has already made stunning discoveries about volcanoes, fountains, mines, and other natural wonders. Now he will resume his studies of the creation of life. As the couple enters the laboratory, Aylmer shudders at the sight of Georgiana, and she faints. Aminadab, Aylmer's grotesque assistant, comes out to help. He says he would not remove the birthmark if Georgiana were his wife.

Georgiana wakes up in sweet-smelling rooms that have been made beautiful for her. Aylmer comforts her with some of his more magical creations: "airy figures, absolute bodiless ideas, and forms of unsubstantial beauty." He shows her moving scenes that mimic real life. Then he gives her a fast-growing flower that dies as soon as she touches it. Next he tries to create a portrait of her with a metal plate, but when the plate shows a hand, he throws it into acid.

Between experiments, Aylmer tells Georgiana about alchemy. He believes that he could turn base metal into gold and create a potion that would grant eternal life if he wanted to, even though he says he knows that doing so would be wrong. He disappears for hours and then shows her his cabinet of wonders. One such wonder is a vial that holds a powerful perfume. Another is a poison that, depending on the dose, would allow Aylmer to kill someone instantly or after a long period of time. Georgiana is appalled, but Aylmer says the poison is more good than bad. He shows her another potion that can wipe away freckles, but he says her birthmark needs a much deeper cure.

Georgiana realizes that Aylmer has been doctoring her food or making her inhale something in the air. Her body feels strange. She reads the books in his scientific library, as well as his accounts of his own experiments. She realizes that his achievements always fall short of the goals he originally sets. Still, the accounts of his studies make her worship him. Aylmer catches her crying over his journals, and although his words are kind, he is angry. She sings to him, restoring his spirits.

A few hours later, Georgiana goes to the laboratory to find Aylmer. When he sees her, he grows angry, accuses her of prying, and tells her to go away. She stands her ground and refuses, saying he should trust her and not try to hide his fears. She promises to drink whatever he tells her to drink. Moved, Aylmer says the mark goes deep into her body, and its removal will be dangerous. In her room, Georgiana thinks about how noble it is that Aylmer refuses to love her as she is, insisting instead to create his ideal version of her.

He brings her a potion that he says cannot fail. He shows her how it cures a geranium of blots. She drinks the liquid and sleeps. Aylmer watches her with tenderness but also as if he is watching a scientific experiment unfold. Gradually the birthmark fades. Aminadab laughs. Georgiana wakes, sees herself in the mirror, and tells Aylmer not to feel bad about rejecting "the best the earth could offer." Then she dies.

CHARACTER LIST

Aylmer   A brilliant yet misguided scientist and the protagonist of the story. Aylmer's experiments and creations have made him famous in the scientific community. He has investigated volcanoes, mines, and clouds; bottled the world's most delicious scents; created a powerful poison; and made a potion capable of erasing physical flaws such as freckles. Although his intentions are good, Aylmer is a selfish and cruel man whose delusions ultimately kill his wife.

Georgiana   Aylmer's wife. A beautiful, intelligent, and caring woman, Georgiana is physically and spiritually lovely. Her only flaw is a small red birthmark shaped like a tiny hand on her left cheek. Georgiana worships her husband and submits to his unreasonable demands, despite her suspicions that they will kill her.

Aminadab   Aylmer's assistant. A hulking, strong, grubby man, Aminadab is an able helper but simultaneously disgusted by Aylmer's desire to erase Georgiana's birthmark. Because Aminadab represents the physical side of existence, his disgust is a strong indictment of Aylmer. Ironically, Aminadab feels more compassion for Georgiana than her own husband does.

ANALYSIS OF MAJOR CHARACTERS

AYLMER   Aylmer is an intellectual run amok, a man whose mind has overpowered his sense of decency. An incredibly skilled scientist, he has made many exciting discoveries about the physical world. His inquiries into the spiritual world, however, tend to be more disturbing. Although he protests that he would never actually carry out his more outlandish ambitions — such as turning base metal into gold, making a potion that would give its drinker eternal life, or creating humans from nothing — he believes that he is at least capable of performing such miracles. And his actions belie his claim to respect life: he has invented a poison capable of killing a person instantly or during the course of years, depending on the administrator's whim. Such an invention proves that Aylmer longs to control nature itself. Aylmer's journals reveal that he considers his greatest achievements worthless in comparison to his ambition, which is nothing less than to exercise a godlike control over life.

Aylmer is a character, of course, but he also functions as a symbol of intellect and science. Unlike modern writers, Hawthorne is less interested in plumbing the psychological depths of his characters than he is in using them to prove a point. He also provides almost none of the details about Aylmer that we expect. We never learn his age, birthplace, childhood, or habits of speech. But it is not Hawthorne's aim to convince us that Aylmer is a real person. Indeed, he goes out of his way to make Aylmer a fantastical, nonrealistic being. By making Aylmer a symbol for the mind and then showing how dangerous it is when the mind operates independent of morality, Hawthorne warns us that unchecked ambition without regard for morality will result only in disaster and death.

GEORGIANA   A beautiful and passionate woman, Georgiana is undone by her allegiance to her husband. The ideal wife — at least according to the ideals of a bygone era — Georgiana considers Aylmer to be her master. Although every other man she has encountered has swooned over her beauty and many would risk death for the privilege of touching her birthmark, Georgiana cares only about Aylmer's opinion of her. Because he is horrified by her appearance, she discards years of praise and becomes disgusted with herself. Because she believes she should do anything to make Aylmer happy, she willingly risks death. Living in rooms decorated like elegant boudoirs; breathing in mysterious, character-altering fumes; and looking at fake vistas, Georgiana acts as if she is a robot under the control of her creator. If Aylmer is the villain of the story, Georgiana is the heroine. She acts as society says she should, trusting her husband absolutely, and her only reward for her obedience and deference is death. Perhaps Hawthorne is suggesting that although devotion is a laudable trait, women should not be expected to obey their husbands at all costs.

Even though Hawthorne's characters can often be two-dimensional people, Georgiana is far more complex and believable a character than is Aylmer. Even though she submits to her husband's demands, she is not simply the familiar and stereotypical downtrodden wife. A highly intelligent woman, she passes the time by reading the works of philosophy she finds in her husband's scientific library. She examines Aylmer's accounts of his experiments and understands everything she finds there. She is also far nobler than her husband, willing to risk her life to make someone else happy. When the occasion calls for it, she can also be feisty. She refuses to apologize for entering Aylmer's laboratory, for example, and chides him for keeping her in the dark about the danger of the experiment. And she does not die a silent martyr's death. Before passing away, she demonstrates a final burst of self-confidence by urging Aylmer not to feel bad about rejecting "the best the earth could offer."

THEMES, MOTIFS, AND SYMBOLS

THEMES

THE FOOLISHNESS OF STRIVING FOR PERFECTION   Aylmer's desire to make his wife perfect is doomed to failure because perfection, Hawthorne suggests, is the exclusive province of heaven and can't be found on earth. In fact, the very success of Aylmer's perfection-inducing potion may doom Georgiana to death. Because she becomes an ideal being, completely unmarred, she is no longer able to exist in this world. The desire for perfection not only kills Georgiana, it also ruins her husband because his desire to create the ideal woman becomes a fixation that prevents him from seeing the good in his wife. Eventually, her tiny imperfection is all he can see. It grows in his mind until the very sight of the beautiful Georgiana repulses him, a ludicrous turn of events. The wisest men in the story are those who understand that perfection is not a goal worth pursuing. These men, Georgiana's admirers, never appear in the story, but Hawthorne stresses that their appreciation of her is far more sensible than Aylmer's fixation on her single imperfection. For these men, Georgiana's slight flaw only enhances her loveliness. In the same way that life seems more precious because we know we'll die, Georgiana's beauty seems more amazing because it isn't seamless.

SCIENCE VERSUS NATURE   In a story full of wildly successful, almost magical, scientific experiments, it is untouched nature itself that is shown to be more powerful than any man-made creation. Aylmer has the ability to make lovely sights and amazing aromas from nothing, but he doesn't have the ability to control his wife's spirit or prolong her life. On the other hand, Georgiana does have some measure of power over her husband's spirit, a power that comes not from science but nature. For example, when Aylmer's spirits flag, he asks Georgiana to sing to him, and the beauty of her voice restores his good mood. Unlike her husband's potions, her voice is entirely natural but has a much greater effect. In addition, Georgiana's birthmark also demonstrates the power of nature because it captivates and intoxicates almost everyone who sees it. In the end, Aylmer's attempt to control nature with science ends only in death and unhappiness.

MOTIFS

RED AND WHITE   The colors red and white recur throughout "The Birthmark" to highlight both Georgiana's purity and imperfections. Hawthorne uses lyrical language to describe Georgiana's skin. Her birthmark is described as crimson and ruby-colored, while the skin around it is likened to snow and marble. These words reveal that the narrator thinks Georgiana's birthmark and the red and white shades of her face make her more beautiful, not less. The loveliness of the language he uses to describe her puts the narrator in opposition to Aylmer. So too does his description of the blending of the two colors. In general, the birthmark is red and Georgiana's skin is white, but these categories sometimes overlap: when she blushes, her skin turns the same color as the birthmark. This overlapping suggests that no clear boundary exists between Georgiana's beauty and one flaw.

SYMBOLS

THE BIRTHMARK   Georgiana's birthmark symbolizes mortality. According to the narrator, every living thing is flawed in some way, nature's way of reminding us that every living thing eventually dies. The hand-shaped mark on Georgiana's cheek is the one blemish on an otherwise perfect being, a blemish that marks her as mortal. Aylmer's revulsion for his wife's birthmark suggests the horror he feels at the prospect of death. He is a smart man, but his misinterpretation of the symbol on Georgiana's face leads him astray. He mistakenly comes to believe that if he can root out this symbol of transience, it will mean that he has the power to prolong life indefinitely. Aylmer also mistakenly believes that the birthmark represents Georgiana's moral decrepitude and spiritual flaws even though she isn't a woman prone to sin at all. If anything, the symbol of death on her cheek clashes with her natural generosity and sunny spirit.

SHORT STORY ANALYSIS

FORESHADOWING   "The Birthmark" is rife with the kind of foreshadowing that may strike modern readers as heavy-handed. Aylmer dreams of cutting off Georgiana's birthmark and finding that the roots plunge down into her heart, which he decides to cut out; Georgiana faints the first time she sees the laboratory; the beautiful, fast-blooming flower Aylmer creates withers and turns black as soon as Georgiana touches it; a reflection of Georgiana in a metal plate reveals the shape of a hand, so Aylmer throws the plate into acid, destroying it. Over and over, we see that Aylmer's experiments usually go awry and have destructive, unintended consequences. Georgiana's death, therefore, comes as no surprise to the attentive reader. In fact, some modern readers may feel disappointed that the final scene of the story adheres so closely to what has been foreshadowed and contains so little that is surprising.

If we are not shocked, however, neither is Georgiana, who serves as a stand-in for us, a reader of the events around her. Georgiana overhears Aylmer muttering in his sleep, realizes what he's dreaming about, and presses him to recall the dream the next morning. She interprets it correctly, firmly believing that the birthmark's removal may lead to her death. She analyzes the incidents of the past such as the broken flower and disfigured plate, and reads Aylmer's journals as catalogues of his failures. In this light, the lack of surprise at the end of the story emphasizes Georgiana's bravery: like us, she knew exactly what would probably happen, but she submitted to her husband's experiment to make him happy.

NARRATION   "The Birthmark" is told in a strong, subjective voice that draws attention to the narrator and makes him a key player in the story. At nearly every moment, we know what the narrator is thinking and how he views the characters' behavior. It is clear from the beginning that the narrator dislikes Aylmer and his quest to eliminate the birthmark and that he sympathizes with Georgiana. The narrator might be characterized as a chatty, intelligent friend sharing a particularly juicy piece of gossip. At several points in the story, he all but addresses us directly, imploring us, for example, to notice how bad Aylmer looks in comparison even to an animal like Aminadab. The narrator can also be characterized as a moralist who condescends to his readers. Rather than trusting us to figure out the symbolism of the birthmark, for example, or allowing us to draw our own conclusions about the soundness of Aylmer's experiment, the narrator rushes to explain every metaphor and symbol as if we might miss his point.

The strong narrative voice of "The Birthmark" epitomizes a key difference between modern American short stories and nineteenth-century American short stories. Modern stories are often told in an objective, distant, even ironic voice, whereas nineteenth-century stories were usually told by passionate narrators who infused their own strong opinions. Because we are not used to encountering this brand of subjective third-person narration, it is tempting to conclude that Hawthorne and the narrator of "The Birthmark" are the same person. In recent years, however, critics have suggested that Hawthorne never put himself into his stories but consciously created narrators who had distinct voices of their own. These critics argue that although Hawthorne's narrators are often pious and preachy, we shouldn't automatically conclude that he shared these characteristics. It would be a mistake, therefore, to decide that Hawthorne abhors Aylmer and likes Georgiana, simply because his narrator does.

B

THE STORY OF PYGMALION   Aylmer thinks of himself as a godlike creator, a self-perception that's revealed when he says that he will be happier than Pygmalion when he erases Georgiana's birthmark. The story of Pygmalion—originally from Ovid's *Metamorphoses* and recreated in countless poems, novels, and films—is about a sculptor who falls in love with an ivory statue of a woman he has made. Venus, the goddess of love, brings the statue to life, and Pygmalion marries it. Aylmer's reference to the story reveals much about his own character. By comparing himself to the smitten sculptor, Aylmer believes that he is clever enough to create the perfect woman. More important, he reveals a fundamental misunderstanding of his own project. Unlike Pygmalion, Aylmer isn't creating a woman where none previously existed. Rather, he is tampering with a perfectly beautiful woman whom, the narrator suggests, God created. The reference to Pygmalion reveals that Aylmer's self-regard has blinded him to the true nature of his experiment.

An earlier, subtler reference to sculpture reveals the narrator's distaste for Aylmer's image of himself as a magical creator of life. Before Aylmer refers to Pygmalion, the narrator condemns those jealous women who claim that the birthmark spoils Georgiana's beauty, saying that making such a claim is as silly as pretending that a tiny blue mark in marble would turn a statue of Eve into a monstrosity. It is a small moment, but a revealing one. The narrator suggests that God created Georgiana in the image of the mother of all humans and that just as Eve was tainted by sin and forgiven by God, so Georgiana is tainted and forgiven. In the narrator's estimation, Aylmer's classical reference could not be more misguided.

IMPORTANT QUOTATIONS EXPLAINED

---

1. "[H]ere is a powerful cosmetic. With a few drops of this in a vase of water, freckles may be washed away. . . . A stronger infusion would take the blood out of the cheek, and leave the rosiest beauty a pale ghost. . . . Your case demands a remedy that shall go deeper."

Even though Aylmer isn't evil, he is nevertheless despicable and sinister because he considers himself an apt judge of his wife's moral fiber. In this passage, we see that Aylmer doesn't merely want to wipe away the physical birthmark on his wife's cheek. If that were his aim, he would use the "powerful cosmetic" that he claims can wipe away freckles as if they were specks of dirt. Because he has become convinced that the mark is merely the external evidence of some deep moral and spiritual rot, he believes the so-called remedy must be applied internally. As we read the passage, we realize with mounting horror that Aylmer has become a madman. He no longer sees Georgiana's birthmark as a minor physical defect but as a terrifying symbol of death and sin.

---

2. *[W]ith her whole spirit she prayed that, for a single moment, she might satisfy his highest and deepest conception. Longer than one moment she well knew it could not be; for his spirit was ever on the march, ever ascending . . . [requiring] something that was beyond the scope of the instant before.*

This quotation investigates the myriad problems inherent in Aylmer's quest for perfection. Although Aylmer has managed to con Georgiana into believing that she isn't worthy of his affection, the narrator reveals here that Aylmer's insistence on perfection is insane. In fact, this passage makes it clear that even total perfection wouldn't satisfy him. Georgiana realizes that if she managed to satisfy his demands, her triumph would last only "for a single moment." After that, he would want still more from her. The removal of the birthmark is something of an artificial goal, and the narrator suggests that Aylmer wouldn't be happy even if she'd never had the birthmark in the first place. His lust for flawlessness will never be sated—he has become deranged.

Brokeback Mountain

Annie Proulx
(1935–)

CONTEXT

Edna Annie Proulx (pronounced *PROO*) was born in 1935 in Norwich, Connecticut, which was her mother's ancestral ground. For young Annie, Norwich was only a temporary home: the Proulx family, headed by a driven textile-executive father, moved frequently. Eventually they settled in Vermont, where Proulx attended the University of Vermont and studied history.

Proulx's studies continued in Canada, at Montreal's Sir George Williams University (now Concordia University), where Proulx became immersed in the philosophies of the French Annales school. According to this school of thought, history is best understood from the perspective of social science, incorporating qualitative and quantitative methodologies. The probing style of Proulx's prize-winning fiction, which invites readers to participate in thorough, intimate examinations of characters set against their particular time and place, owes much to the Annales approach. Proulx has also credited her fiction to the deft storytelling of her maternal grandmother and the observant qualities of her mother, a painter.

After graduate school, Proulx earned a modest income as a freelance journalist, writing mostly rural-interest pieces for various magazines. Her career as a reporter deepened her observational abilities, and between writing freelance articles, she wrote short stories. Careful research is integral to Proulx's fiction, which is invariably based on factual details of geography, landscape, culture, economy, history, and populace.

Until recently, Proulx was perhaps best known as the Pulitzer Prize–winning author of *The Shipping News* (1993), a novel (and later a film) that centers on a man named Quoyle, who, having lost his parents and wife, moves back home to a small Newfoundland harbor town. Following the release of Ang Lee's film adaptation of the short story "Brokeback Mountain" in 2005, Proulx has enjoyed even broader recognition. The critical and box office success of the film, which took home several Academy Awards in March 2006 as well as a slew of other industry honors, has catapulted the story on which it is based into the highest level of public consciousness. It has also made the story's protagonist, Ennis Del Mar (artfully portrayed onscreen by Heath Ledger), into an iconic film figure.

"Brokeback Mountain" was first published in 1997 in the pages of the *New Yorker*. The spare and deeply emotional tale was awarded both the National Magazine Award and the O. Henry Prize in 1998. One year later, Proulx's publisher, Scribner, collected "Brokeback Mountain" and other stories in a volume entitled *Close Range, Wyoming Stories*, which in circular but fitting fashion took home the *New Yorker*'s Book Award for Best Fiction in 2000.

Like most of Proulx's work, "Brokeback Mountain" concerns the struggle of individuals to carve out an existence in a world that is constantly in flux. Proulx pins her characters to concrete locations, painting vivid backdrops and evoking landscapes that speak volumes about their inhabitants. To her, time and place are of utmost importance to a piece of fiction; a story or a novel derives its impact from this ring of truthfulness. A human being cannot be understood out of context—this is Proulx's insistent refrain. Human behavior and relationships are outgrowths of economic, cultural, and geographical circumstances, which are never static. Proulx's fiction is, in her own words, an exploration of these "shifting circumstances overlaid upon natural surroundings." The characters of "Brokeback Mountain" may reel us in with their tragic stories, but it is the unflinching portrayal of the "grieving plains" of Wyoming—where Proulx planted roots in 1994—that affirm and explain their conditions in a profoundly moving way.

PLOT OVERVIEW

"Brokeback Mountain" begins with two italicized paragraphs in present tense that feature the story's protagonist, Ennis Del Mar, well after the story's main events have taken place. Ennis, a middle-aged ranch hand, wakes before five in his trailer. The ranch's owner has sold the place, and Ennis must move out this morning. He is unsure of what he will do, where he will go, or what his next job will be, but for now the uncertainty is assuaged by the pleasure of a dream he has just had about a man named Jack Twist.

The story leaps backward in time, to the spring of 1963, when Ennis and Jack first meet at the trailer office of Wyoming's Farm and Ranch Employment. The narration shifts into past tense, signaling the beginning of the narrative of which we have just glimpsed the ending. Jack and Ennis are teenagers, born and bred in opposite corners of Wyoming on poor ranches. Both are well acquainted with a life of hard work and rough living, and both are high school dropouts. Ennis lost both parents when he was young and grew up in the care of two older siblings. At age fourteen he received a hardship grant for a truck to drive to school, but the truck soon broke down and he went to work on a ranch. Now he is engaged to Alma Beers.

Jack and Ennis sign on to become sheep herder and camp tender, respectively, for a foreman, Joe Aguirre, whose livestock spend the summer on Brokeback Mountain. Jack has done this once before, but Ennis is new to the job. Aguirre instructs the herder to sleep with the sheep in a pup tent, armed but without a fire, to prevent coyotes from killing the animals. Jack and Ennis drink and talk in a bar, then head up the mountain and get to work. After Jack complains about the four-hour commute to get to the herd, the men switch roles: Ennis heads up the mountain while Jack prepares meals in the camp. When they are together, they talk, drink whiskey, and become friends.

The men move the sheep to graze in a farther field, increasing the distance between pasture and base camp. One cold night, after much talking and drinking, Ennis decides to remain in base camp rather than trek back to the herd. It's freezing and Jack tells him to join him in his sleeping roll inside the warm tent. In the tent, Jack reaches for Ennis's hand and pulls it to his groin, only to be roughly turned and entered from behind by Ennis—the first time Ennis has been with a man. The sex happens many times after that, but they deny their homosexuality.

During a surprise visit to the campsite, Joe Aguirre sees the men together through his binoculars. In August, the sheep get mixed up with a Chilean herd, and Ennis and the Chilean herder struggle to separate them. In late August, Aguirre calls the men and sheep down from the mountain and frowns as he pays Jack and Ennis, knowing that some of the sheep aren't his. The two men say goodbye, each evasive about his plans for the next summer. Jack has a bruised jaw—Ennis had punched him the day before. They part ways as though they don't care. Once Jack is out of sight, Ennis has to pull over because he is sick with grief.

Ennis marries Alma and has two girls, getting work as a wrangler and on a highway crew to support his family. Alma wants to live in town, but Ennis likes the impermanence of their remote apartment.

Four years pass. Jack sends Ennis a postcard saying he is coming to town, and Ennis replies with his address. When Jack arrives, Ennis runs to greet him. Alma steps outside and sees them kissing in front of their apartment, then quickly goes back inside. She comes out again when the men have separated, and Ennis introduces Jack to her. The men tell each other about the children they have. Jack has married a Texan girl, Lureen. The men go to a motel, where they have sex all night. The next day, they reminisce about their time on Brokeback and talk about their feelings. Ennis says he hasn't slept with other men, and Jack lies and said he hasn't either. Jack tells Ennis he thinks Aguirre knew what happened on the mountain. He tells Ennis he was surprised by the punch on the last day. Ennis says his brother used to punch him and that he finally punched his brother one day, taking him by surprise. Jack suggests they set up a ranch together. But Ennis tells Jack about the time his father took him, as a child, to see the mutilated body of a gay rancher. He says they just have to endure this separation.

A rift grows between Alma and Ennis, and she divorces him when their daughters are nine and seven. She remarries. At a Thanksgiving dinner, she confronts Ennis about his affair with Jack, and he storms out.

The two men continue to see each other occasionally, but they never return to Brokeback. They tell each other about their affairs with women. During one trip, Ennis tells Jack he won't be able to see him until November, although they'd planned to meet in August. While Jack has his wife's money and her inherited business to fall back on, Ennis lives paycheck to paycheck and can't miss work. Jack admits he travels to Mexico for sex because Ennis can't give him enough of a life. They argue, but nothing is resolved. Jack remembers a time on Brokeback when Ennis simply embraced him and stood with him by the fire.

Months later, a postcard Ennis has mailed to Jack is returned to him, stamped "DECEASED." Ennis calls Lureen, and she says that Jack had an accident: he was changing a tire when it blew up, sending the rim into his face. Ennis thinks it was no accident and that men killed him with the tire iron. Lureen says Jack wanted to have his ashes interred in a place called Brokeback Mountain, but she didn't know where it was, so she buried half the ashes and gave the rest to his parents. Ennis decides to visit Jack's family in Lightning Flat, Wyoming.

Ennis is met by Jack's mother and his disapproving father in their tiny, depressing ranch house. Mr. Twist says Jack had long spoken of coming home to Lightning Flat with Ennis to help run the ranch, but had recently begun talking of bringing home another man, a Texan, instead. His mother invites Ennis to see Jack's room. In the closet Ennis discovers an old shirt of Jack's, stained with Ennis's blood, layered over a shirt of Ennis's, from their Brokeback days. Jack's father says he's putting his son's ashes in the family plot.

Ennis buys a postcard of Brokeback and tacks it to his trailer wall; he hangs the two shirts beneath it on a nail. Around this time, Jack begins to appear in Ennis's dreams.

CHARACTER LIST

Ennis Del Mar   A rough-mannered, paycheck-to-paycheck ranch worker. Ennis's parents died in an auto accident when he was young, and he was raised by his older brother and sister. Although he falls in love with Jack Twist during their summer on Brokeback Mountain, he marries Alma Beers and has two daughters. Ennis is a stoic who, mired in the life he has made for himself, allows himself only stolen glimpses of the happy life he and Jack could have had with each other if circumstances had been different.

Jack Twist   A passionate, emotional ranch worker. Jack was raised on a humble ranch and has little money, although he is obsessed with the glitzy rodeo lifestyle. Though he is in love with Ennis, he marries Lureen and has a son. On the side, however, Jack has affairs and travels to Mexico to have sex with male prostitutes. He tries to coax Ennis into building a life together, but Ennis resists. Ultimately, Jack dies in a freak roadside accident that is more likely a violent murder.

B

Alma Beers   Ennis's long-suffering wife. For nine years, Alma tolerates Ennis's lack of affection, frequent trips with Jack, and poorly paying jobs. Although she sees Jack and Ennis kissing, she never says a word about it until well after they are divorced. She finally confronts Ennis about Jack during a Thanksgiving dinner, after which Ennis storms out and does not see her again.

Lureen   Jack Twist's wife. Lureen has money from her father's farm machinery business. She has a head for numbers, and she and Jack enjoy a financially comfortable life together. When Ennis calls her after Jack's death, her tone is icy, implying that she knows all about Ennis as well as Jack's other male lovers.

Joe Aguirre   The foreman who hires Jack and Ennis to work as herder and camp tender, respectively, on Brokeback Mountain in the summer of 1963. Aguirre spies on Jack and Ennis through his binoculars and later suggests to Jack that he knew what was going on between them up on Brokeback.

ANALYSIS OF MAJOR CHARACTERS

ENNIS DEL MAR   Ennis is a man of few words, whose actions often speak for him. When Ennis meets Jack, he is saddled with responsibility, engaged to Alma, and at the mercy of a conservative Wyoming culture that has no place for a gay ranch hand. Yet Ennis has nowhere else to go and no other profession at which to try his hand. An orphaned high school dropout dependent on hardship funds and raised to be pragmatic, he is trapped in a life over which he has little control. Rather than run off with Jack and try to build a happy life, as Jack repeatedly suggests, Ennis considers the reality of it all: the violent opposition that would greet two gay ranchers living together, his marriage to Alma, his love for his daughters. The life he builds, which involves financial hardship and eventually child support, effectively prohibits him from escaping.

Ennis is a prisoner of the life he has been born into. Without the financial wherewithal to escape, without any sort of community support for his sexual proclivities, and imbued with the belief that one must bear whatever one can't fix, Ennis is fated to live out the rest of his life as a man who tasted happiness once but has never again reached that peak. Though it is Jack Twist who, we infer, is murdered by those who oppose his sexual orientation, it is Ennis Del Mar—living in his trailer, confined to a sad life on the broad, flat plains of Wyoming—who is the story's tragic soul.

JACK TWIST   Jack Twist is the more verbally aggressive and outgoing of the story's two main characters. His name is onomatopoetic in its quick, light-footed sound, the clarity of its consonants strikingly dissimilar to the marbles-in-mouth quality of "Ennis Del Mar." Jack Twist is flashy and brazen, a would-be rodeo star, and later a glitzy Texan transplant who sports a brass belt buckle and large capped teeth. He is far less able and willing than Ennis to subjugate his sexual impulses to the demands of conservative married life. The initial tryst on Brokeback is Ennis's first sexual encounter with a man; but of Jack we may suspect that he is somewhat more experienced. And whereas Ennis muffles his sexual desire, Jack projects his desire for Ennis onto other men and women.

Ennis and Jack are complementary: Ennis the taciturn loner, Jack the performer who needs an audience; Ennis the hand-to-mouth earner, Jack the man who has married into money; Ennis the stoic who grits his teeth and bears his life, Jack the proponent of change. Yet for all his bravado and planning, Jack never seems to get what he wants. His father shrugs that most of his son's ideas "never come to pass," and Jack himself says, "Nothin never come to my hand the right way." When he tells Ennis his plan for them to run a ranch together, it doesn't occur to him how detached from reality his fantasy truly is, how impossible or ill-advised it would be to implement it. This divide between fantasy and reality drives the two men apart over the years, and Jack ultimately pays a steep price for his dreams.

THEMES, MOTIFS, AND SYMBOLS

THEMES

THE OVERWHELMING NATURAL FORCES OF DESIRE AND LOVE   Just as nature governs the ranch and mountain lifestyle, the natural force of desire directs every significant action taken by Ennis and Jack in "Brokeback Mountain," even when those actions are against their better judgment and against acceptable social dictums. The passion between the two men is so strong that they cannot explain it rationally or logically, and the way it ebbs and flows is not predictable or reasonable. Instead, it is irresistible and overwhelming—a point that Ennis makes emphatically when he tells Jack that "There's no reins on this one. It scares the piss out a me." "Brokeback Mountain" is a love story, and like many love stories, its end is tragic, not least because the natural force of the men's desire prevents them from ever fully fitting into the lives they were forced to pursue apart from each other.

The idea of two male ranch hands falling in love in conservative 1960s Wyoming epitomizes the suggestion that love, a natural force, persists against all odds. Indeed, Jack and Ennis have everything to lose because of their relationship. Society's powerful indictment of male love is woven deeply into Ennis's psyche; he tells Jack the story of how a gay rancher in his hometown was murdered, voicing his own apprehensions that the same thing could happen to them. The figure of Joe Aguirre, peering through his binoculars at the two men making love, is a stand-in for all those passing judgment on them. Even Alma has only disgust for Ennis's furtive sexual behavior: she calls his lover "Jack Nasty" and makes it plain that she finds the notion of two men in love reprehensible. But despite these opposing forces and the lives they build with their respective wives and families, Jack and Ennis are helpless in the clutch of their feelings for each other.

THE ENDLESS SHIFTING OF THE WORLD   "Brokeback Mountain" begins with movement and motion in Ennis's home, and the idea of the world being constantly in flux permeates the entire story. In the first few lines, Proulx describes the "wind rocking the trailer" and the hanging shirts that "shudder slightly in the draft." Despite the seeming permanence of Ennis's situation, despite the feeling of endlessness conveyed by the Wyoming plains, the winds of change are always blowing. Proulx has said she sees the world "in terms of shifting circumstances," and wind, for Proulx, suggests the meeting of opposing forces, of past, present, and future. Movement occurs when a kinetic force meets a static object, pushing it or acting on it in some way. In this sense, the shuddering shirts of the story's first line suggest a tension between the conservative, homophobic line that Jack has dared to cross (and been punished for crossing) and a time and place in which greater tolerance exists.

The notion of the world as constantly in flux is borne out more obviously in the span of years covered in the story. Along the way, the narrator comments on changes in the main characters' physical appearance—a thickening paunch, a patch of graying hair, the development of a benign growth over one of Ennis's eyes. The result is a sort of time-lapse view of the relationship between Jack and Ennis, one in which a single constant—their devotion to one another—is set against a backdrop of inevitable change.

MOTIFS

HOME AND LEAVING HOME   Both Ennis and Jack make frequent references to their parents and childhoods, and the opening description of the men's respective birthplaces suggests the significance of home and leaving home to the story. To "know where you are from" is to be of like mind with your family, kin, and community. Jack, a wandering soul who moves away from home and then out of state, is condemned by his father for wanting to be buried on Brokeback rather than in ancestral ground. Jack's desire to get away from home—in the sense of escaping its conventional values—is ultimately what gets him killed. Ennis, on the other hand, is mindful of his father's homophobia and being taken by him to see the dead body of a murdered gay rancher. He frequently professes his inability to break away from his home and upbringing. Home evokes safety, conservatism, status quo, and acceptance, whereas distance from home in this story becomes associated with progressiveness and risk.

Despite Ennis's declaration that "All the travelin I ever done is goin around the coffeepot lookin for the handle," traveling away from home proves influential to both Ennis and Jack, even if their travel covers little actual distance. If staying home is synonymous with stasis, permanence, and conventional thinking, then traveling away from home is an escape from all of that. Jack makes many trips to Mexico, a place that represents the gratification of his sexual desires, a place freer and more accepting than the rural plains of the American West that Jack calls home. When Ennis asks Jack what other people in their situation do, Jack cites travel as a solution: "It don't happen in Wyomin and if it does I don't know what they do, maybe go to Denver," he says. Just as the notion of home as tradition and continuity is a constant refrain in the story, the idea of leaving home and traveling marks the distance between an old-fashioned way of thinking and a forward-thinking mindset.

SYMBOLS

BROKEBACK MOUNTAIN   Brokeback Mountain looms large in a physical sense, casting its shadow on the plains below, and it rises up in the shared memories of Jack and Ennis and represents an idyllic, although temporary, life. The name "Brokeback" stands in for all that happens between the two men in the summer of 1963 and all they have lost since then. They refer simply to "Brokeback" rather than to specific events or feelings. When Jack says years later that "what we got now is Brokeback Mountain," he uses the phrase as shorthand for acts, emotions, and thoughts that, because he shares them with Ennis, he needs not articulate more explicitly. Brokeback Mountain also stands in stark contrast to the flatlands of Wyoming in an echo of the duality between Jack and Ennis, man and woman, resistance and acceptance, past and present, and, ultimately, life and death. In the postcard memorial that Ennis constructs to his dead lover, the mountain serves as a tombstone under which the men's relationship must finally be buried.

THE PLAINS OF WYOMING   If the high peak of Brokeback Mountain, thrusting into the sky, evokes the yearning to rise above and escape one's life, then the flatland of Wyoming represents all that is dull and desperate. Ennis and Jack are both raised on the plain, but while Jack takes off for Texas to live with his wealthy bride, Ennis is trapped by economic circumstance and responsibility. Proulx uses the noun *plain* just four times. First, the narrator describes how, from the extraordinary position of being atop the mountain, the plain is where "ordinary affairs" occur. The last three "plains" are used in conjunction with Jack's death, an event that renders Ennis "ordinary" once more. When Lureen confirms Jack's death, Ennis feels the "huge sadness of the northern plains" rolling over him. Later, driving to the Twist home, he notes the abandoned ranches scattered over the plain. Finally, leaving Lightning Flat, he notes the cemetery where Jack will be buried, calling it "the grieving plain."

By the end of the story, Ennis's pared down existence seems inseparable from the desolate Wyoming flatland, a locus of grief or of the status quo, which in this story is equated with grief. In the last line, another symbolic association becomes clear. The narrator describes the "open space" between what Ennis knows and believes about Jack's death, a reference to both the expansive, endless plains and the open-ended pain that will stay with Ennis forever.

SHORT STORY ANALYSIS

THE INDIVIDUAL IN CONTEXT   In "Brokeback Mountain," time and place are not incidental; rather, they are the foundations on which character is built and defined. In introducing the two main characters, Proulx does not separate them from their geographic and socioeconomic origins: "They were raised on small, poor ranches in opposite corners of the state, Jack Twist in Lightning Flat up on the Montana border, Ennis del Mar from around Sage, near the Utah line . . . ." Temporal setting, too, is critical. In the next paragraph, we learn that it is 1963 when Jack and Ennis first meet. No character, Proulx seems to say, can be understood out of his or her unique context—a notion affirmed by a glance at the author's autobiography, posted on her official website, which begins with a lengthy history of her maternal and paternal ancestors and the family's ancestral land. Indeed, the main tension of "Brokeback Mountain" derives from the pull of external, contextual forces on the two main characters, who are trapped in their circumstances like flies in a spider web. In another time, in another place, perhaps, Jack and Ennis could be happy together—but not in 1963 Wyoming.

LOCATION AND MEMORY   Significant memories tend to stand out in our minds, the way a mountain towers over a level plain. "Brokeback Mountain" is an allegory for the way a particular moment or moments in time can haunt us, turn our life in a particular direction, and forge a future we may never have anticipated. Jack and Ennis's first sexual encounter in the summer of 1963 is the pinnacle of their relationship: a single, untarnished, unpremeditated act with no painful history and no difficult future to chart or navigate. Many years afterward, Jack thinks back to embracing Ennis at that time and place and calls it, in his mind, "the single moment of artless, charmed happiness in their separate and difficult lives . . . they'd never got much farther than that." Proulx plants this flashback in the last third of the story, demonstrating structurally how a memory can crop up so long after the fact, disrupting the normal experience of time. In addition to being a temporal disruption, the memory of Brokeback is also a physical locus of pleasure and pain. In a fit of frustration, Jack yells at Ennis that all they have now, two middle-aged men with children, is Brokeback Mountain. Memory is a place from which it is difficult, if not impossible, to escape.

STOICISM   Ennis Del Mar is a stoic figure, and stoicism is central to "Brokeback Mountain." The ancient Greek school of stoic philosophy was founded on the principles of objectivity and detachment from emotional appeals, but that's not necessarily characteristic of Ennis. Rather than ignoring or suppressing his emotions, Ennis feels them intensely. He acts on them too, leaving his family for days at a time to go on fishing trips with Jack or lashing out at Jack in anger and frustration. However, Ennis is stoic in his belief that "if you can't fix it you've got to stand it," a depressing bit of folk wisdom that is, nevertheless, often true. Ennis is engaged to Alma when he meets Jack, and his obligation to her weighs heavy on his mind. Later, after they are married, Jack visits Ennis and says they need to figure out what to do. Ennis responds: "I doubt there's nothin now we can do." Jack seems to believe the opposite and is punished for pushing for change, leaving Ennis the stoic to bear an even greater burden.

IMPORTANT QUOTATIONS EXPLAINED

1. *They never talked about the sex, let it happen, at first only in the tent at night, then in the full daylight with the hot sun striking down, and at evening in the fire glow, quick, rough, laughing and snorting, no lack of noises, but saying not a goddamn word except once Ennis said, "I'm not no queer," and Jack jumped in with "Me neither. A one-shot thing. Nobody's business but ours."*

After their first sexual encounter on Brokeback Mountain, Ennis and Jack quickly fall into a passionate relationship—one in which, as this passage attests, actions speak much louder than words. The verbal silence that accompanies their sex hints at a relationship so fragile that to rationalize, explain, or defend it would put an end to its pleasure. Indeed, whenever Jack and Ennis give voice to their doubts, hopes, and fears, it results in an argument, not a resolution. There is, literally, no way for the men to talk their way into a good ending to their story. A similar wordlessness accompanies Ennis's lovemaking with Alma, and it too suggests the desire not to express the harsh reality of the situation at hand. The choice few words that *are* spoken between Jack and Ennis in this passage are desperate denials of the truth. Jack and Ennis have much more than a one-shot deal; their relationship is decades long. And although they try to tell each other that it isn't anyone else's business, the prevailing homophobic viewpoint is very much a third party in their love affair. At this early point in their relationship, alone on the mountain, it is easy and uncomplicated for the men to lie to themselves and each other. Over time, however, this denial becomes harder and harder to pull off—until, finally, it becomes impossible.

---

2. *"Tell you what, we could a had a good life together, a fuckin real good life. You wouldn't do it, Ennis, so what we got now is Brokeback Mountain. Everthing built on that. It's all we got, boy, fuckin all, so I hope you know that if you don't never know the rest."*

B

In this passage, Jack, looking back on what could have been, lashes out at Ennis for not allowing them to build a life together. In his frustration, Brokeback Mountain—the scene of their first tryst and the one-time emblem of their unblemished love—becomes a darker, more ominous symbol: it stands for all the tantalizing memories and pleasure they can never recapture. Jack's accusation highlights the differences between him and Ennis. Jack has pressured Ennis to settle down with him and give their relationship a more solid ground, regardless of wife and family, but Ennis has been steadfast in his refusals, citing his obligation to family as well as his desire to avoid scrutiny and punishment. By this point in the story, there is a sense of inevitability about their lack of a future together, and Jack knows it. They have only two options: move forward or keep gazing backward at their summer together on the mountain. Jack's declaration that "what we got now is Brokeback Mountain" underscores the sad fact that the latter option is their fate.

---

3. *There was some open space between what he knew and what he tried to believe, but nothing could be done about it, and if you can't fix it you've got to stand it.*

In this last line of the story, Ennis's stoicism is made explicit—and so is his self-doubt. Ennis has always been steadfast in his refusal to live with Jack, precisely to avoid the fate that has befallen Jack. But suppressing his nature and acting on his impulses only clandestinely has not made him any happier. By the end of the story, it seems that Ennis has begun to question his decisions. The "open space" between what Ennis knows and what he tells himself is a hazy area of what-ifs: what if he and Jack had made different choices? What if he had not married Alma and had two daughters? What if he had given into Jack's suggestions and thus prevented him from getting involved with the man in Texas? Would the outcome have been any different? Ever practical, Ennis knows that there is no way to know for sure. And because there is nothing he can do, he can only now live with the outcome of the choices they made.

Cathedral

Raymond Carver
(1938–1988)

CONTEXT

Raymond Carver was born in 1938 in the small town of Clatskanie, Oregon, to an alcoholic father who worked at a sawmill and a mother who worked as a waitress. He grew up in Washington state and married Maryann Burke, his high school girlfriend, when he was just eighteen. He and Maryann had two children by the time Carver was twenty-one. After high school, Carver and his family moved to California, where he worked a variety of odd jobs. He didn't resume his schooling until 1958, when he began taking classes at Chico State College. While there, he took writing classes with the writer John Gardner, who introduced him to the world of writing.

Carver began writing poetry and short stories while continuing to work odd jobs to support his family. In 1968 he published his first poetry collection, *Near Klamath*, followed not long after by *Winter Insomnia* (1970) and several other works in the early 1970s. He began teaching at various colleges, and in 1976 he published his first short-story collection, *Will You Please Be Quiet, Please?*, which has become one of his best-known works.

Although Carver earned critical acclaim for his writing, he simultaneously struggled with alcoholism. His alcoholism was so severe that he was hospitalized several times. He finally stopped drinking in 1977, after many failed attempts to quit. After a hiatus from writing, during which time he focused on staying sober, Carver published several more short-story collections: *What We Talk About When We Talk About Love* (1981), *Cathedral* (1983), and *Elephant* (published posthumously in 1988). Two compilations of Carver's stories have also been published: *Where I'm Calling From* (1988) and *Short Cuts: Selected Stories* (1993). A film version of *Short Cuts*, directed by Robert Altman, came out in 1993.

Carver has a distinct writing style, a strong, minimalist approach that critics often compare to the writing of Ernest Hemingway and Anton Chekhov. Carver liked to focus on down-and-out, blue-collar, middle-class people facing bleak truths, disappointments, and small revelations in their ordinary lives, all subject matter that places him firmly in the "dirty realism" school of writing. Other dirty realism writers include Bobbie Ann Mason, Ann Beattie, and Richard Ford. Besides the style and subject matter, Carver's short stories are known for their dialogue, which mimics realistic speech patterns, and their abrupt endings—also called zero endings—that fail to tie up the story neatly, if at all.

"Cathedral" features all of the well-known Carver characteristics and is often regarded as his best short story. Carver himself considered it one of his favorites and recognized it as an important step forward in his writing. "Cathedral" ends on a slightly more optimistic note than many of his earlier stories, and Carver believed that this story, as well as the other stories in the collection *Cathedral*, were "more hopeful" and more fully developed than his previous work.

As Carver wrote his later short-story collections, he divorced his wife, Maryann, and married a writer named Tess Gallagher. They were married for only a few months before Carver died from lung cancer in 1988. He was fifty.

PLOT OVERVIEW

The narrator says that his wife's blind friend, whose wife has just died, is going to spend the night at their house. He says that he isn't happy about this visitor and the man's blindness unsettles him. He explains that his wife met the blind man ten years ago when she worked for him as a reader to the blind in Seattle. He says that on the last day of her job there, the blind man touched her face and she wrote a poem about the experience. The narrator then describes his wife's past. She married her childhood sweetheart and became an officer's wife. Unhappy with her life, she tried to commit suicide one night by swallowing pills, but she survived. She and the blind man kept in touch by sending audiotapes back and forth to each other throughout her marriage, and she told everything to the blind man on tapes.

The narrator says that his wife once asked him to listen to one of the blind man's tapes. They started to listen but were interrupted before the narrator could hear anything about himself. The narrator suggests taking the blind man bowling. His wife reminds him that the blind man's wife, Beulah, just died and says that if he loves her, he'll welcome the blind man into their home. The narrator asks whether Beulah was "Negro," and his wife asks him whether he's drunk. She then tells him more about Beulah. Beulah became the blind man's reader after the narrator's wife stopped working for him, and they eventually got married. After eight years, however, Beulah died from cancer. The narrator thinks how awful it must have been for Beulah to know that her husband could never look at her. He speculates that she could have worn whatever she wanted.

The narrator's wife goes to pick up the blind man at the train station as the narrator waits at the house. When they arrive, he watches his wife laughing and talking with the blind man as she leads him by the arm to the house. The narrator is shocked to see that the blind man has a full beard. The wife introduces the narrator to the blind man, whose name is Robert. They all sit in the living room. The narrator asks what side of the train he sat on, and Robert says he sat on the right and that he hadn't been on a train for years. The narrator says his wife looks at him but doesn't seem to like what she sees.

The narrator says he's never known a blind person. He describes what Robert looks like and what he's wearing. Robert doesn't wear dark glasses, which the narrator finds strange. He wishes Robert would wear them because his eyes look weird and turn in strange directions. He pours scotch for all three of them, and they talk about Robert's trip.

Robert smokes several cigarettes. The narrator says he didn't think blind people could smoke. They sit down for dinner and eat ravenously, not speaking, eating so much that they are dazed. After dinner, they go back to the living room to drink more. The wife and Robert talk about things that have happened to them in the past ten years, while the narrator occasionally tries to join in. He learns that Robert and Beulah had run an Amway distributorship and that Robert is a ham radio operator. When Robert asks the narrator questions, he makes only short responses. The narrator then turns on the television, irritating his wife.

The wife goes upstairs to change clothes and is gone a long time. The narrator offers Robert some pot, and they smoke a joint. The wife joins them when she comes back. She says she's going to just sit with them on the couch with her eyes closed, but she immediately falls asleep. The narrator changes the channel and asks Robert if he wants to go to bed. Robert says he'll stay up with the narrator so that they can talk some more. The narrator says he likes the company and that he and his wife never go to bed at the same time.

There is a program about the Middle Ages on television. Nothing else is on, but Robert says he likes learning things. When the TV narrator doesn't describe what's happening, the narrator tries to explain to Robert what's going on. The TV narrator begins talking about cathedrals, showing different ones in different countries. The narrator asks Robert whether he has any idea what a cathedral looks like. Robert says he doesn't and asks the narrator to describe one. The narrator tries, but he knows he doesn't do a very good job. Robert asks him if he's religious, and the narrator says he doesn't believe in anything. He says he can't describe a cathedral because cathedrals are meaningless for him.

Robert asks the narrator to find a piece of paper and pen. Then he and the narrator sit around the coffee table, and Robert tells the narrator to draw a cathedral. He puts his hand over the narrator's hand, following the movement of the pen. The narrator draws and draws, getting wrapped up in what he's doing. His wife wakes up and asks what's going on, and Robert answers that they're drawing a cathedral. The wife doesn't understand.

Robert tells the narrator to close his eyes and keep drawing, and the narrator does so. Soon Robert tells him to open his eyes and see what he's drawn, but the narrator doesn't open them. He knows he's in his own home, but he feels like he's nowhere. With his eyes still closed, he says the drawing is "really something."

CHARACTER LIST

The Narrator   An unnamed man who describes his experience with Robert. The narrator is jealous of the men from his wife's past and doesn't want Robert to visit, but he eventually connects with him when they draw a cathedral together. While his eyes are closed, the narrator has an epiphany after finishing the drawing in which he feels like he isn't anywhere.

Robert   The blind man. Robert visits the narrator and his wife after his own wife, Beulah, dies. He is a caring, easygoing man who sets even the narrator at ease. He encourages the narrator to draw a cathedral when the narrator is unable to describe one in words.

The Narrator's Wife   A nameless woman who invites Robert to their home. The wife has kept in touch with Robert since they met ten years ago, exchanging audiotapes with him and telling him everything about her life. Before she married the narrator, she'd been married to a military officer and was so unhappy that she tried to kill herself.

ANALYSIS OF MAJOR CHARACTERS

THE NARRATOR   Even though the narrator of "Cathedral" is not literally blind, he displays a lack of insight and self-awareness that, in many ways, makes even him blinder than Robert. Unlike Robert, the narrator can see with his eyes perfectly well, but he has difficulty understanding people's thoughts and feelings that lie beneath the surface. He pities the deceased Beulah because Robert could never look at her and doesn't realize that Robert was able to see Beulah in a nonphysical way—that is, he could understand her intimately. Consequently, the narrator makes no effort to really get to know his own wife. Instead of welcoming her old friend to his home, he merely categorizes Robert as part of his wife's past, which makes him jealous, petty, and bitter. He doesn't care whether this visit is important to his wife or what role Robert may have played in helping her through her suicide attempt and divorce. The narrator is jealous of his wife's ex-husband but also cockily sure of his revered place in her life, expecting at one point to hear her tell Robert about her "dear husband." However, every comment he makes to his wife as well as everything he does seems designed to annoy and anger her. Far from being a "dear husband," the narrator is insensitive and arguably has no idea who his wife really is. The fact that he can recognize her on sight doesn't necessarily mean that he knows her intimately.

When the narrator draws a cathedral with Robert and closes his eyes, he has an epiphany during which he can see more than he ever could with his eyes open. Although he has been curt with and dismissive of Robert throughout the evening, he is forced to converse with Robert when his wife falls asleep. After some initial awkwardness, the narrator eventually taps into a core of compassion, clumsily describing what's on television. The narrator's good intentions are thwarted when he realizes he is unable to describe a cathedral. Even though he can see the cathedral, he is unable to describe the cathedral to Robert because he can't "see" its deeper significance. The act of drawing a cathedral with Robert with his eyes closed, however, lets the narrator look inside himself and understand the greater meaning. As a result, his description of the cathedral takes on a more human element, which liberates the narrator and allows him to truly see for the first time.

ROBERT   Robert is an insightful, compassionate man who takes the time to truly listen to others, which helps him to "see" them better than he could with his eyes. Robert and the narrator's wife have been listening to each other for the past ten years through the audiotapes they send back and forth. All the difficult details of the narrator's wife's past, including her marriage, suicide attempt, and divorce, have been recorded and sent to Robert, who has recorded responses in return. He is the person the narrator's wife turned to when she needed to talk. The fact that we never learn exactly what Robert says on the tapes is significant because it suggests that the mere act of listening to the tapes was more important than responding to them.

Robert's wife has recently died, but we learn little about his relationship with her and only slightly more about Robert himself. Though he is there in person, discussing his travels, Amway distribution business, and hobbies, he seems disembodied somehow and not really present. The narrator's wife is glad to see him, but since he cannot see her, their interaction is only slightly different from the back-and-forth conversation they've been carrying on through the tapes. Robert becomes wholly real, however, when he invites the narrator to draw a cathedral. With their hands touching, the two men work together and temporarily inhabit a space that excludes the narrator's wife. Robert is not a magical being in any way, but the effect this interaction has on the narrator is almost mystical.

THEMES, MOTIFS, AND SYMBOLS

THEMES

THE DIFFERENCE BETWEEN LOOKING AND SEEING   In "Cathedral," the act of look-ing is related to physical vision, but the act of seeing requires a deeper level of engagement. The narrator shows that he is fully capable of looking. He looks at his house and wife, and he looks at Robert when he arrives. The narrator is not blind and immediately assumes that he's therefore superior to Robert. Robert's blindness, the narrator reasons, makes him unable to make a woman happy, let alone have any kind of normal life. The narrator is certain that the ability to see is everything and puts no effort into seeing anything beyond the surface, which is undoubtedly why he doesn't really know his wife very well. Robert, however, has the ability to "see" on a much deeper level than the narrator. Even though Robert can't physically see the narrator's wife, he understands her more deeply than the narrator does because he truly listens. The wife obviously has a lot to say and has spent the past ten years confiding in Rob-ert on the audiotapes she sends him. The only interaction we see between the narrator and his wife, however, are snippy exchanges in which the narrator does little more than annoy her. True "seeing," as Robert demonstrates, involves a lot more than just looking.

ART AS INSIGHT   The narrator, his wife, and Robert find insight and meaning in their experiences through poetry, drawing, and storytelling. According to the narrator, his wife writes a couple of poems every year to mark events that were important in her life, includ-ing the time Robert touched her face. The narrator doesn't like the poems but admits that he might not understand them. The narrator gains insight into his own life when he draws a picture of a cathedral with Robert, realizing for the first time that looking inward is a way to gain greater knowledge and a deeper understanding of himself. Robert, too, gleans insight from the drawing. Although it's unlikely that he was able to visualize what the narrator drew, he shares the experience of the narrator's awakening. The narrator's mere act of retelling the story of his epiphany helps him make sense of his newfound understanding. Even though his narrative is choppy and rough and he frequently interrupts himself to make a defensive comment or snide remark, he gets the story out, passing along some of his insight to us. The narrator doesn't fully understand what happened when he closed his eyes and drew the ca-thedral, but he knows that it was an important experience.

MOTIFS

DRINKING   The physical act of preparing and consuming drinks gives the story rhythm and weaves the narrative together. Before every action in the story, someone prepares a drink or sips from a drink that's already been made. When the wife tries to kill herself, for example, she drinks a bottle of gin. Before the narrator begins listening to one of Robert's tapes, he makes drinks. When his wife tells him about Beulah, he drinks. When he waits for her and Robert to come home from the train station, he drinks. During the evening, the three of them drink constantly. Also, as the drinking continues into the night, compounded by ciga-rettes and marijuana, the story takes on a dreamy tone, with meaning lurking behind every corner but never quite clearly in focus.

SYMBOLS

THE CATHEDRAL The cathedral that the narrator draws with Robert represents true sight, the ability to see beyond the surface to the true meaning that lies within. Before the narrator draws the cathedral, his world is simple: he can see, and Robert cannot. But when he attempts to describe the cathedral that's shown on television, he realizes he doesn't have the words to do so. More important, he decides that the reason he can't find those words is that the cathedral has no meaning for him and tells Robert that he doesn't believe in anything. However, when he takes the time to draw the cathedral—to really think about it and see it in his mind's eye—he finds himself pulled in, adding details and people to make the picture complete and even drawing some of it with his eyes closed. When the drawing is finished, the narrator keeps his eyes shut, yet what he sees is greater than anything he's ever seen with his eyes open. Carver isn't specific about exactly what the narrator realizes, but the narrator says he "didn't feel like he was inside anything"—he has a weightless, placeless feeling that suggests he's reached an epiphany. Just as a cathedral offers a place for the religious to worship and find solace, the narrator's drawing of a cathedral has opened a door for him into a deeper place in his own world, where he can see beyond what is immediately visible.

AUDIOTAPES The audiotapes that Robert and the narrator's wife send back and forth to each other represent the kind of understanding and empathy that has nothing to do with sight. The narrator believes that Robert's wife, Beulah, must have suffered because Robert could never see her, but in his own way, the narrator has never truly seen his own wife. Robert's relationship with the narrator's wife is much deeper than anything the narrator can understand. When he hears a bit of Robert's tape, he says it sounds only like "harmless chit-chat," not realizing that this sort of intimate communication is exactly what his own marriage lacks. Only when the narrator closes his eyes to finish drawing the cathedral does he approach the level of understanding that his wife and Robert have achieved through their taped correspondence.

SHORT STORY ANALYSIS

POINT OF VIEW Carver uses a first-person narrator to tell the story of "Cathedral" to emphasize the bewildering aspects of the transcendent moment that he relates in the story. The unnamed narrator is self-absorbed, concerned only with how the visit from Robert will affect him and dismissive of what role Robert may have played in his wife's past. At the same time, the narrator lacks self-awareness. He pities Robert's wife, Beulah, because her husband could never look at her, never realizing that he doesn't really know his own wife despite the fact that he can see her. The narrator is not a very skillful storyteller either, putting his narrative together crudely, with rough transitions and defensive interruptions. For example, when he refers to his wife's childhood sweetheart, he breaks in, "Why should he have a name? He was the childhood sweetheart, what more does he want?" Interruptions such as these reveal the narrator's jealous insecurity and suggest that his relationship with his wife is not as stable as he makes it out to be.

When Robert arrives, the narrator does his best to make sense of him. He describes Robert's appearance, including his eyes, and observes Robert's actions with a kind of awe: the way Robert smokes his cigarettes, the way he cuts his meat during dinner. Carver's use of a first-person narrator is especially effective in these scenes because it makes Robert seem abnormal, even alien, because the narrator has no concept of what a blind man can and cannot do. Likewise, once Robert becomes more human for the narrator, he takes shape for us as well. At the end of the story, when Robert guides the narrator in drawing the cathedral with his eyes closed, the narrator revels in the strangeness of the experience, and his bewilderment makes this transcendent moment more poignant. It is a remarkable moment, but the narrator's unsophisticated description of it makes it a human moment as well.

OPTIMISM AND THE "ZERO ENDING" Carver finishes "Cathedral" with a "zero ending," leaving the narrator with his eyes closed, imagining the cathedral he has just drawn with Robert. A zero ending is an ending that doesn't neatly tie up the strands of a story. It may not even seem like an ending—in some cases, the writer may seem to have left off in the middle of a thought or idea. Instead of tacking on a florid conclusion that leaves everyone satisfied, Carver often stops his stories abruptly, at the moment when his characters are faced with a stark realization, glimmer of hope, or wall of confusion. Ernest Hemingway used the zero ending in many of his short stories as well. Also like Hemingway, Carver wrote in a sparse, masculine style, and this, along with his favored method of ending a story, has prompted many readers to compare the two writers.

The abrupt ending to the story leaves many questions unanswered, such as how exactly the narrator has changed, if his relationship with his wife will change, or how his opinion of Robert has changed. But the answers to these questions are not the point of the story. "Cathedral" concerns the change in one man's understanding of himself and the world, and Carver ends the story at exactly the moment when this change flickers in the narrator's mind. The narrator has not become a new person or achieved any kind of soul-changing enlightenment. In fact, the narrator's final words, "It's really something," reveal him to be the same curt, inarticulate man he's always been. The zero ending, however, adds an unexpected note of optimism to the story. Until this moment, the narrator has been mostly bitter and sarcastic, but he has now gained a deeper understanding of himself and his life. Far from leaving us unsatisfied, Carver's zero ending leaves us with our breath held as the narrator sees a new world start to crack open.

DIRTY REALISM The "dirty realism" school of writing became popular in the 1980s thanks to a group of writers who began writing about middle-class characters and the disappointments, heartbreaks, and harsh realities of their ordinary lives. *Granta*, a highly regarded literary journal, coined the label dirty realism in 1983 when it published its eighth issue, which featured writers from this school. *Granta 8*, as the issue became known, included stories by Angela Carter, Bobbie Ann Mason, Richard Ford, Tobias Wolff, Raymond Carver, and many others. Although each of these dirty-realism writers has a distinctive style, they are connected by their sparse prose, simple language, and direct descriptions of ordinary people and events. Much of the fiction published in the *New Yorker*, where many of these writers were and are still published, is of the dirty-realism school, but today the term—as well as the practice—has somewhat fallen out of fashion. Many of Carver's short stories, including "Cathedral," are prime examples of the dirty-realist style.

IMPORTANT QUOTATIONS EXPLAINED

---

1. *And then I found myself thinking what a pitiful life this woman must have led. Imagine a woman who could never see herself as she was seen in the eyes of her loved one. A woman who could go on day after day and never receive the smallest compliment from her beloved.*

This quotation appears near the beginning of the story when the narrator ruminates on what life must have been like for Robert's wife, Beulah, before she died. This passage reveals the extent of the narrator's self-delusion about what kind of husband he is and what really matters in a relationship. Though he calls Beulah's life "pitiful," everything his wife has told him about Beulah and Robert's relationship suggests the opposite. They were devoted to each other—"inseparable," the wife says. They'd worked together, and Robert had stayed by her bedside until her death. The narrator's sole criterion for deeming Beulah's life "pitiful" is the fact that Robert never knew what she physically looked like. For the narrator, the ability to see the other's appearance seems to be the defining element in a relationship.

The narrator tries to reflect on Beulah's life from her own perspective: she could never see herself as Robert saw her, and she could never receive a compliment on her appearance. What's ironic about the narrator's observation is that he himself can see, yet he fails to make his own wife happy. The narrator assumes that he is more capable of making his own wife happy than Robert simply because he can see. This assumption reveals that the narrator isn't aware of the difference between seeing and understanding.

---

2. *I stared hard at the shot of the cathedral on the TV. How could I even begin to describe it? But say my life depended on it. Say my life was being threatened by an insane guy who said I had to do it or else.*

This quotation appears near the end of the story when Robert asks the narrator to describe the cathedral that appears on television. Before this, the narrator has successfully described a parade in Spain in which people were dressed as devils and skeletons, but he doesn't have any idea how to describe a cathedral. The task seems impossible for the narrator, who doesn't have the words to describe what he sees. In a way, this is a crisis moment for the narrator, who realizes that he couldn't describe a cathedral even if his "life depended on it." The scenario he imagines—a crazy man forcing him to describe a cathedral—is absurd and comical but reflects his sense of panic. Even though he can see the cathedral, he can't describe what he sees because he really doesn't understand it. Only by drawing the cathedral with his eyes closed can the narrator bridge the gap between seeing and understanding.

The Chrysanthemums

John Steinbeck
(1902–1968)

CONTEXT

John Steinbeck was born in 1902 in Salinas, California, the third of four siblings. His father, John Ernst Steinbeck II, worked as a local government official, and his mother, Olive Steinbeck, was a teacher. Steinbeck read great literature when he was a young boy, including novels by Dostoevsky, Hardy, and Flaubert. He studied English at Stanford University off and on between 1919 and 1925 but never earned his degree. While beginning to write fiction, he worked to make ends meet as a lab assistant and fruit picker. During World War II, he worked as a war correspondent for the *New York Herald Tribune* and later took a trip to Vietnam for the *New York Daily News*. In 1930, he married Carol Henning, but their marriage dissolved in 1942. He quickly remarried and had two sons with his second wife, Gwyndolyn Congor, before they got divorced in 1949. His third marriage to Elaine Scott in 1950 lasted until his death in 1968.

Steinbeck published his first novel, *Cup of Gold*, in 1929. The fictionalized story of a seventeenth-century pirate, *Cup of Gold* was not a critical or commercial hit. His next novel, *Tortilla Flat* (1935), was much more successful, and it was turned into a film starring Spencer Tracy and Hedy Lamarr in 1942. Steinbeck is famous for his novels of California, so much so that Salinas, California, is sometimes referred to as Steinbeck Country. One of the best known of these California novels is *Of Mice and Men* (1937), the story of two struggling migrant workers. Director George S. Kaufman worked with Steinbeck to turn the novel into a stage play, which was a thundering success. Steinbeck never saw the play in person, saying that he didn't want to compromise the perfection of the production he imagined in his mind. The novel was made into a film in 1939, the same year that he published his most famous work, *The Grapes of Wrath*. Using an innovative narrative structure, *The Grapes of Wrath* tells the story of an impoverished family of farmers struggling to survive the Dust Bowl during the Great Depression. Widely hailed then and today as Steinbeck's best novel, *The Grapes of Wrath* won the 1940 Pulitzer Prize and was made into a film of the same name later that year.

Much of Steinbeck's work is overtly political because he spent time with labor-union leaders, radicals, leftists, and communists. Still, he was leery of far-left political persuasions, particularly socialism. The views expressed in Steinbeck's writing have offended some people, including members of his own family. He has been attacked for being both too left-leaning and not being left-leaning enough. He's also been criticized for perpetuating stereotypes. *The Grapes of Wrath*, for example, has been accused of sentimentalizing the poor, misrepresenting Oklahoma farmers, and shoving a liberal agenda down readers' throats. Nevertheless,

Steinbeck was elected to the American Academy of Arts and Letters in 1948 and won the Nobel Prize for Literature in 1962. In 1964, President Lyndon Johnson awarded Steinbeck the Presidential Medal of Freedom.

Even Steinbeck's detractors concede that his work is suffused with passion, social consciousness, and sometimes anger. Steinbeck felt a great deal for the downtrodden, working class, and dregs of society. His short story "The Chrysanthemums" (1938) also proves that he had an understanding of the struggles faced by women in his day. Like his novels, Steinbeck's short stories feature realistic dialogue, nerve-racking dramas, and sympathetic examinations of characters trying to find happiness in the face of poverty and oppression.

PLOT OVERVIEW

It is winter in Salinas Valley, California. The sun is not shining, and fog covers the valley. On Henry Allen's foothill ranch, the hay cutting and storing has been finished, and the orchards are waiting for rain. Elisa Allen, Henry's wife, is working in her flower garden and sees her husband speaking with two cigarette-smoking strangers. Elisa is thirty-five years old, attractive and clear-eyed, although at the moment she is clad in a masculine gardening outfit with men's shoes and a man's hat. Her apron covers her dress, and gloves cover her hands. As she works away at her chrysanthemums, she steals occasional glances at the strange men. Her house, which stands nearby, is very clean.

The strangers get into their Ford coupe and leave. Elisa looks down at the stems of her flowers, which she has kept entirely free of pests. Henry appears and praises her work. Elisa seems pleased and proud. Henry says he wishes she would turn her talents to the orchard. She responds eagerly to this suggestion, but it seems he was only joking. When she asks, he tells her that the men were from the Western Meat Company and bought thirty of his steers for a good price. He suggests they go to the town of Salinas for dinner and a movie to celebrate. He teases her, asking whether she'd like to see the fights, and she says she wouldn't.

Henry leaves, and Elisa turns her attention back to her chrysanthemums. A wagon with a canvas top driven by a large bearded man appears on the road in the distance. A misspelled sign advertises the man's services as a tinker who repairs pots and pans. The wagon turns into Elisa's yard. Her dogs and the man's dog sniff each other, and the tinker makes a joke about the ferocity of his animal. When he gets out of the wagon, Elisa sees that he is big and not very old. He wears a ragged, dirty suit, and his hands are rough. They continue to make small talk, and Elisa is charmed when the tinker says he simply follows good weather. He asks whether she has any work for him, and when she repeatedly says no, he whines, saying he hasn't had any business and is hungry. Then he asks about Elisa's chrysanthemums, and her annoyance vanishes. They discuss the flowers, and the tinker says that he has a customer who wants to raise chrysanthemums. Excited, Elisa says he can take her some shoots in a pot filled with damp sand. She takes off her hat and gloves and fills a red pot with soil and the shoots.

Elisa gives the tinker instructions to pass along to the woman. She explains that the most care is needed when the budding begins. She claims to have planting hands and can feel the flowers as if she's one with them. She speaks from a kneeling position, growing impassioned. The tinker says he might know what she means, and Elisa interrupts him to talk about the stars, which at night are "driven into your body" and are "hot and sharp and—lovely." She reaches out to touch his pant leg, but stops before she does. He says such things are not as nice if you haven't eaten. Sobered, Elisa finds two pans for him to fix.

As the tinker works, she asks him if he sleeps in the wagon. She says she wishes women could live the kind of life he does. He says it wouldn't be suitable, and she asks how he knows. After paying him fifty cents, she says that she can do the same work he does. He says his life would be lonesome and frightening for a woman. Before he leaves, she reminds him to keep the sand around the chrysanthemums damp. For a moment, he seems to forget that she gave him the flowers. Elisa watches the wagon trundle away, whispering to herself.

She goes into the house and bathes, scrubbing her skin with pumice until it hurts. Then she examines her naked body in the mirror, pulling in her stomach and pushing out her chest, then observing her back. She dresses in new underwear and a dress and does her hair and makeup. Henry comes home and takes a bath. Elisa sets out his clothes and then goes to sit on the porch. When Henry emerges, he says that she looks nice, sounding surprised. She asks him what he means, and he says she looks "different, strong and happy." She asks what he means by strong. Confused, he says that she's playing a game and then explains that she looks like she could break a calf and eat it. Elisa loses her composure for a moment and then agrees with him.

As they drive along the road toward Salinas, Elisa sees a dark spot up ahead and can't stop herself from looking at it, sure that it's a pile of discarded chrysanthemum shoots that the tinker has thrown away. Elisa thinks that he could have at least disposed of them off the road, and then realizes he had to keep the pot. They pass the tinker's wagon, and Elisa doesn't look. She says she is looking forward to dinner. Henry says she is different again, but then says kindly that he should take her out more often. She asks whether they can have wine at dinner, and he says yes. Elisa says she has read that at the fights the men beat each other until their boxing gloves are soaked with blood. She asks whether women go to the fights, and Henry says that some do and that he'll take her to one if she'd like to go. She declines and pulls her coat collar over her face so that Henry can't see her crying.

CHARACTER LIST

Elisa Allen   The protagonist. A robust thirty-five-year-old woman, Elisa lives with her husband, Henry, on a ranch in the Salinas Valley. Even though Elisa is associated with fertility and sexuality, the couple has no children. She is a hard worker, her house sparkles, and her flowers grow tremendous blooms. Nevertheless, Elisa feels trapped, underappreciated, and frustrated with life.

The Tinker   A tall, bearded man who makes his living repairing pots, pans, and other kitchen utensils. The tinker is a smart person and charming salesman. He is also down on his luck and not above pleading for work after Elisa initially turns him down. He may share her wanderlust, or she may only imagine that he does.

Henry Allen   Elisa's husband. Henry is a kind man, if slightly dimwitted. He loves his wife but doesn't really understand and appreciate her. Still, he is an adequate businessman who runs his ranch successfully and provides a comfortable life for his wife. He seems to love Elisa and tries his best to please her despite the fact that she mystifies him.

ANALYSIS OF MAJOR CHARACTERS

ELISA ALLEN   Elisa Allen is an interesting, intelligent, and passionate woman who lives an unsatisfying, understimulated life. She's thwarted or ignored at every turn: having a professional career is not an option for her, she has no children, her interest in the business side of the ranch goes unnoticed, her offers of helping her husband to ranch are treated with well-meant condescension, and her wish to see the world is shrugged off as an unfit desire for a woman to have. As a result, Elisa devotes all of her energy to maintaining her house and garden. The pride she takes in her housekeeping is both exaggerated and melancholy. Although she rightly brags about her green thumb, Elisa's connection to nature seems forced and not something that comes as naturally as she claims. She knows a great deal about plants, most likely because as a woman, gardening is the only thing she has to think about.

Elisa is so frustrated with life that she readily looks to the tinker for stimulating conversation and even sex, two elements that seem to be lacking in her life. Her physical attraction to the tinker and her flirtatious, witty conversation with him bring out the best in Elisa, turning her into something of a poet. Her brief flashes of brilliance in the tinker's presence show us how much she is always thinking and feeling and how rarely she gets to express herself. When the prospect of physical and mental fulfillment disappears with the tinker, Elisa's devastation suggests how dissatisfied she is with her marriage. She's so desperate to transcend the trap of being a woman that she seeks any escape, trying to banter with her husband, asking for wine with her dinner, and even expressing interest in the bloody fights that only men usually attend. None of these will truly satisfy Elisa, though, and it is doubtful that she'll ever find fulfillment.

THE TINKER   Elisa idealizes the visiting Tinker as exciting and smart, although it's difficult to tell whether he is actually either of these things. Although his misspelled advertisement for kitchen implement repair indicates that he hasn't had much schooling, the tinker comes across as a witty man who flirts and banters with Elisa. He is also clever and canny enough to convince the skeptical Elisa to give him work, begging at first and finally resorting to flattery. His ability to manipulate her may appeal to Elisa, who is used to manipulating her own husband. In fact, she seems to relish the chance to spar with a worthy partner, and the tinker produces an intense reaction in her. If we can trust her interpretation of him, he shares her appreciation for travel and her interest in a physical connection. However, Steinbeck suggests that although the tinker may actually possess these qualities, it is also possible that Elisa merely imagines that he possesses them because she's so desperate to talk to someone who understands her. In fact, the tinker may be bewildered and embarrassed by her intensity and want only to sell his services to her. The fact that he tosses away her chrysanthemum shoots—a symbol of Elisa herself—supports the idea that the tinker does not share Elisa's passions at all.

HENRY ALLEN   Elisa's husband, Henry, is a good, solid man who's unable to please his wife. By the standards of his society, Henry is everything a woman should want in a husband: he provides for her, treats her with respect, and even takes her out every now and then. At the same time, however, Henry is also stolid and unimaginative. He praises his wife as he would a small child, without understanding the genuine interest she takes in business or realizing that she has the potential to do so much more with her life. A traditional man, Henry functions in the story as a stand-in for patriarchal society as a whole. He believes that a strict line separates the sexes, that women like dinner and movies, for example, and that men like fights and ranching. His benevolent, sometimes dismissive attitude toward his wife—who is undoubtedly smarter— highlights society's inability to treat women as equals.

THEMES, MOTIFS, AND SYMBOLS

THEMES

THE INEQUALITY OF GENDER   "The Chrysanthemums" is an understated but pointed critique of a society that has no place for intelligent women. Elisa is smart, energetic, attractive, and ambitious, but all these attributes go to waste. Although the two key men in the story are less interesting and talented than she, their lives are far more fulfilling and busy. Henry is not as intelligent as Elisa, but it is he who runs the ranch, supports himself and his wife, and makes business deals. All Elisa can do is watch him from afar as he performs his job. Whatever information she gets about the management of the ranch comes indirectly from Henry, who speaks only in vague, condescending terms instead of treating his wife as an equal partner. The tinker seems cleverer than Henry but doesn't have Elisa's spirit, passion, or thirst for adventure. According to Elisa, he may not even match her skill as a tinker. Nevertheless, it is he who gets to ride about the country, living an adventurous life that he believes is unfit for women. Steinbeck uses Henry and the tinker as stand-ins for the paternalism of patriarchal societies in general: just as they ignore women's potential, so too does society.

THE IMPORTANCE OF SEXUAL FULFILLMENT   Steinbeck argues that the need for sexual fulfillment is incredibly powerful and that the pursuit of it can cause people to act in irrational ways. Elisa and Henry have a functional but passionless marriage and seem to treat each other more as siblings or friends than spouses. Elisa is a robust woman associated with fertility and sexuality but has no children, hinting at the nonsexual nature of her relationship with Henry. Despite the fact that her marriage doesn't meet her needs, Elisa remains a sexual person, a quality that Steinbeck portrays as normal and desirable. As a result of her frustrated desires, Elisa's attraction to the tinker is frighteningly powerful and uncontrollable. When she speaks to him about looking at the stars at night, for example, her language is forward, nearly pornographic. She kneels before him in a posture of sexual submission, reaching out toward him and looking, as the narrator puts it, "like a fawning dog." In essence, she puts herself at the mercy of a complete stranger. The aftermath of Elisa's powerful attraction is perhaps even more damaging than the attraction itself. Her sexuality, forced to lie dormant for so long, overwhelms her and crushes her spirit after springing to life so suddenly.

MOTIFS

CLOTHING   Elisa's clothing changes as her muted, masculine persona becomes more feminine after the visit from the tinker. When the story begins, Elisa is wearing an androgynous gardening outfit, complete with heavy shoes, thick gloves, a man's hat, and an apron filled with sharp, phallic implements. The narrator even describes her body as "blocked and heavy." The masculinity of Elisa's clothing and shape reflects her asexual existence. After speaking with the tinker, however, Elisa begins to feel intellectually and physically stimulated, a change that is reflected in the removal of her gloves. She also removes her hat, showing her lovely hair. When the tinker leaves, Elisa undergoes an almost ritualistic transformation. She strips, bathes herself, examines her naked body in the mirror, and then dresses. She chooses to don fancy undergarments, a pretty dress, and makeup. These feminine items contrast sharply with her bulky gardening clothes and reflect the newly energized and sexualized Elisa. At the end of the story, after Elisa has seen the castoff shoots, she pulls up her coat collar to hide her tears, a gesture that suggests a move backward into the repressed state in which she has lived most, if not all, of her adult life.

SYMBOLS

CHRYSANTHEMUMS   The chrysanthemums symbolize both Elisa and the limited scope of her life. Like Elisa, the chrysanthemums are lovely, strong, and thriving. Their flowerbed, like Elisa's house, is tidy and scrupulously ordered. Elisa explicitly identifies herself with the flowers, even saying that she becomes one with the plants when she tends to them. When the tinker notices the chrysanthemums, Elisa visibly brightens, just as if he had noticed her instead. She offers the chrysanthemums to him at the same time she offers herself, both of which he ignores and tosses aside. His rejection of the flowers also mimics the way society has rejected women as nothing more than mothers and housekeepers. Just like her, the flowers are unobjectionable and also unimportant: both are merely decorative and add little value to the world.

THE SALINAS VALLEY   The Salinas Valley symbolizes Elisa's emotional life. The story opens with a lengthy description of the valley, which Steinbeck likens to a pot topped with a lid made of fog. The metaphor of the valley as a "closed pot" suggests that Elisa is trapped inside an airless world and that her existence has reached a boiling point. We also learn that although there is sunshine nearby, no light penetrates the valley. Sunshine is often associated with happiness, and the implication is that while people near her are happy, Elisa is not. It is December, and the prevailing atmosphere in the valley is chilly and watchful but not yet devoid of hope. This description of the weather and the general spirits of the inhabitants of the valley applies equally well to Elisa, who is like a fallow field: quiet but not beaten down or unable to grow. What first seems to be a lyrical description of a valley in California is revealed to be a rich symbol of Elisa's claustrophobic, unhappy, yet hopeful inner life.

SHORT STORY ANALYSIS

POINT OF VIEW   Steinbeck displays an extraordinary ability to delve into the complexities of a woman's consciousness. "The Chrysanthemums" is told in the third person, but the narration is presented almost entirely from Elisa's point of view. After the first few paragraphs that set the scene, Steinbeck shrugs off omniscience and refuses to stray from Elisa's head. This technique allows him to examine her psyche and show us the world through her eyes. We are put in her shoes and experience her frustrations and feelings. Because she doesn't know what Henry is discussing with the men in suits who come to the ranch, we don't know either. Because she sees the tinker as a handsome man, we do too. Because she watches his lips while he fixes her pots, we watch them with her. As a result, we understand more about her longings and character by the end of the story than her husband does.

We learn that he was once married, but he no longer has a wife. We also learn that he has unsuccessfully tried to commit suicide in a desperate attempt to quell the despair for good. The only way the old man can deal with his despair now is to sit for hours in a clean, well-lit café. Deaf, he can feel the quietness of the nighttime and the café, and although he is essentially in his own private world, sitting by himself in the café is not the same as being alone.

The older waiter, in his mocking prayers filled with the word *nada*, shows that religion is not a viable method of dealing with despair, and his solution is the same as the old man's: he waits out the nighttime in cafés. He is particular about the type of café he likes: the café must be well lit and clean. Bars and bodegas, although many are open all night, do not lessen despair because they are not clean, and patrons often must stand at the bar rather than sit at a table. The old man and the older waiter also glean solace from routine. The ritualistic café-sitting and drinking help them deal with despair because it makes life predictable. Routine is something they can control and manage, unlike the vast nothingness that surrounds them.

MOTIFS

LONELINESS   Loneliness pervades "A Clean, Well-Lighted Place" and suggests that even though there are many people struggling with despair, everyone must struggle alone. The deaf old man, with no wife and only a niece to care for him, is visibly lonely. The younger waiter, frustrated that the old man won't go home, defines himself and the old man in opposites: "He's lonely. I'm not lonely." Loneliness, for the younger waiter, is a key difference between them, but he gives no thought to why the old man might be lonely and doesn't consider the possibility that he may one day be lonely too. The older waiter, although he doesn't say explicitly that he is lonely, is so similar to the old man in his habit of sitting in cafés late at night that we can assume that he too suffers from loneliness. The older waiter goes home to his room and lies in bed alone, telling himself that he merely suffers from sleeplessness. Even in this claim, however, he instinctively reaches out for company, adding, "Many must have it." The thought that he is not alone in having insomnia or being lonely comforts him.

SYMBOLS

THE CAFÉ   The café represents the opposite of nothingness: its cleanliness and good lighting suggest order and clarity, whereas nothingness is chaotic, confusing, and dark. Because the café is so different from the nothingness the older waiter describes, it serves as a natural refuge from the despair felt by those who are acutely aware of the nothingness. In a clean, brightly lit café, despair can be controlled and even temporarily forgotten. When the older waiter describes the nothingness that is life, he says, "It was only that and light was all it needed and a certain cleanness and order." The *it* in the sentence is never defined, but we can speculate about the waiter's meaning: although life and man are nothing, light, clealiness, and order can serve as substance. They can help stave off the despair that comes from feeling completely unanchored to anyone or anything. As long as a clean, well-lighted café exists, despair can be kept in check.

SHORT STORY ANALYSIS

HEMINGWAY'S ECONOMY OF STYLE   "A Clean, Well-Lighted Place" is arguably not only one of Hemingway's best short stories but also a story that clearly demonstrates the techniques of Hemingway's signature writing style. Hemingway is known for his economic prose—his writing is minimalist and sparse, with few adverbs or adjectives. He includes only essential information, often omitting background information, transitions, and dialogue tags such as "he said" or "she said. He often uses pronouns without clear antecedents, such as using the word *it* without clarifying what *it* refers to. Hemingway applies the "iceberg principle" to his stories: only the tip of the story is visible on the page, while the rest is left underwater—unsaid. Hemingway also rarely specifies which waiter is speaking in the story because he has deemed such clarification unnecessary. The essential element is that two waiters are discussing a drunk old man—the rest can be omitted according to Hemingway's economy of style. When the older waiter contemplates the idea of nothingness, Hemingway loads the sentences with vague pronouns, never clarifying what they refer to: "It was all a nothing. . . . It was only that. . . . Some lived in it . . ." Although these lines are somewhat confusing, the confusion is the point. This nothingness *can't* be defined clearly, no matter how many words are used. Hemingway uses fewer words and lets the effect of his style speak for itself.

THE DECEPTIVE PACING OF THE STORY   Hemingway does not waste words on changing scenes or marking the passage of time, leaving it up to us to keep track of what's happening and the story's pacing. For example, only a brief conversation between the waiters takes place between the time when the younger waiter serves the old man a brandy and the time when the old man asks for another. Hemingway is not suggesting that the old man has slugged back the brandy quickly. In fact, the old man stays in the café for a long time. Time has lapsed here, but Hemingway leaves it up to us to follow the pace of the story. The pace of "A Clean, Well-Lighted Place" may seem swift, but the action of the story actually stretches out for much longer than it appears to. The sitting, drinking, and contemplating that take place are languid actions. We may read the story quickly, but the scenes themselves are not quick.

Just as Hemingway doesn't waste words by trying to slow down his scenes, he also refrains from including unnecessary transitions. For example, when the older waiter leaves the café and mulls over the idea of nothingness, he finishes his parody of prayer and, without any transition that suggests that he was walking, we suddenly find him standing at a bar. Hemingway lets the waiter's thoughts serve as the transition. When he writes, "He smiled and stood before a bar," we're meant to understand that the waiter had been walking and moving as he was thinking to himself. And when the waiter orders a drink at the bar, the bartender offers him another just two sentences later. Again, Hemingway is not suggesting that the waiter gulps his drink. Instead, he conveys only the most essential information in the scene.

EXISTENTIALISM AND THE "LOST GENERATION"   The term *Lost Generation* refers to the writers and artists living in Paris after World War I. The violence of World War I, also called the Great War, was unprecedented and invalidated previous ideas about faith, life, and death. Traditional values that focused on God, love, and manhood dissolved, leaving Lost Generation writers adrift. They struggled with moral and psychological aimlessness as they searched for the meaning of life in a changed world. This search for meaning and these feelings of emptiness and aimlessness reflect some of the principle ideas behind existentialism. Existentialism is a philosophical movement rooted in the work of the Danish philosopher Søren Kierkegaard, who lived in the mid-1800s. The movement gained popularity in the mid-1900s thanks to the work of the French intellectuals Jean-Paul Sartre, Simone de Beauvoir, and Albert Camus, including Sartre's *Being and Nothingness* (1943). According to existentialists, life has no purpose, the universe is indifferent to human beings, and humans must look to their own actions to create meaning, if it is possible to create meaning at all. Existentialists consider questions of personal freedom and responsibility. Although Hemingway was writing years before existentialism became a prominent cultural idea, his questioning of life and his experiences as a searching member of the Lost Generation gave his work existentialist overtones.

IMPORTANT QUOTATIONS EXPLAINED

1. *"Each night I am reluctant to close up because there may be some one who needs the café."*

The older waiter makes this comment near the end of the story when he and the younger waiter are about to leave the café, and it reveals his own loneliness and despair. Until this point, the old man seemed to be the only one who wanted to stay at the café, but now the older waiter seems to need the café as well. A few lines before this, he reveals that he is someone who likes to stay at cafés late into the night, so his reluctance has two meanings. First, he understands why the old man and others may want or need to stay late, and he keeps the café open as a gesture of kindness and generosity. Second, he himself needs the café, so he is reluctant to close it because he, like the old man and others, will then be without a place to sit and wait out the night. While the younger waiter is rushing to get home, the older waiter leaves the café sadly, once again displaced and alone.

2. *What did he fear? It was not fear or dread, It was a nothing that he knew too well. It was all a nothing and a man was nothing too. It was only that and light was all it needed and a certain cleanness and order.*

This quotation appears near the end of the story, just after the older waiter leaves the café, and it explains the nature of what afflicts the older waiter and the old man, as well as all those people who want to stay in cafés late at night. We learn that this affliction is not fear or dread, and from the way the older waiter phrases his thoughts, we know that the affliction is not something that is clear, concrete, or easily described. Hemingway fills this passage with the vague pronouns *it* and *that*, never clarifying exactly what *it* and *that* refer to. We learn only that the affliction is "a nothing." The older waiter repeats "nothing" over and over again, emphasizing the idea.

The lack of specificity in this passage is confusing, but Hemingway is being vague on purpose. By using vague pronouns and saying only that everything is "nothing," he conveys the idea that the problem keeping the older waiter and the old man awake at night is related to something huge, even infinite, something beyond what language can describe: the purpose and meaning of life. Existential questions such as the meaning of life and existence make the night a dangerous, empty place for the people who dare to consider them. Only a clean, well-lighted café provides a refuge from these thoughts.

Continuity of Parks

Julio Cortázar
(1914–1984)

CONTEXT

Julio Cortázar was born in 1914 in German-occupied Brussels, Belgium, to Argentine parents Julio Cortázar and María Herminia Descotte. When Cortázar was age two, his family moved to Switzerland, where they waited for the end of World War I. Soon after they returned to Buenos Aires, Argentina, in 1918, Cortázar's father abandoned the family, a desertion that Cortázar found unforgivable. Cortázar attended the University of Buenos Aires and then worked as a teacher in small-town high schools. In 1944, he began teaching French literature at the National University of Cuyo in Mendoza.

Cortázar opposed the rule of General Perón and therefore moved to France in 1951. He would remain there until his death. Beginning in 1952, Cortázar worked as a translator for UNESCO. In 1953, he married Aurora Bernárdez, an Argentinean translator. He would later divorce and remarry twice, first to Ugné Karvelis and then to Carol Dunlop. A 1961 trip to Cuba marked the beginning of Cortázar's political shift leftward. He said that the trip, his first to Cuba, opened his eyes to his own "political uselessness" and showed him the value of being informed. He supported the Cuban Revolution and Nicaragua's Sandinista government, and some of his writings were used as part of Nicaragua's literacy campaign.

Cortázar demonstrated a talent for writing from an early age. He composed poetry when he was a boy and wrote his first novel when he was only age nine, a novel that was so accomplished that many in his family wondered if it was plagiarized. He launched his professional writing career as a poet and playwright. In 1938, he published a collection of poems called *Presencia* under the pen name Julio Denis. He published *Los reyes*, a play inspired by the Greek myth of Theseus, in 1949. *Los reyes* was the first work Cortázar published under his own name. Cortázar's novels and short stories, however, won him greater critical acclaim and financial success. He has spoken dismissively of his poetry collection *Presencia*, saying, "Happily, the book has been forgotten."

In 1951, Cortázar published the short story collection *Bestiaro*, which he followed in 1956 with the collection *Final del juego*. His novels include *Los premios* (*The Winners*), published in 1960, and *Rayuela* (*Hopscotch*), published in 1966. His work was introduced to an English-language audience in 1965, when *The Winners* was published in the United States. In 1967, a volume of his short stories translated by Paul Blackburn was published under the title *End of the Game and Other Stories*. The same volume was later republished under the title *Blow-Up and Other Stories*. Michelangelo Antonioni made a film called *Blow-Up* inspired by Cortázar's story "*Las babas del Diablo*" ("Blow-Up"). Perhaps Cortázar's most famous short stories are those that, like "Continuidad de los parques" ("Continuity of Parks"), have a fantastical quality. "Continuity of Parks" (1956) is a representative example of Cortázar's humor, elegant style, structural daring, and economy.

Cortázar wrote *Los autonautas de la cosmopista* (*The Autonauts of the Cosmoroute*) in 1983 with his third wife, Carol Dunlop, and gave the copyright to the Nicaraguan government. Cortázar's many other works, which run the gamut from essays to poetry to long fiction, include *Las armas secretas* (1959), *Historias de cronopios y de famas* (1959), *Último round* (1969), *Deshoras* (1982), *Adiós Robinson* (1995), and *Cartas* (2000). Cortázar died in Paris in 1984 at age seventy. He was buried in a tomb with his wife, Carol, in the cemetery at Montparnasse.

PLOT OVERVIEW

After taking care of some business matters, a man picks up a novel he had started reading a few days earlier. He sits in a green armchair with his back to the door. He likes the feeling of giving himself over to the story while simultaneously enjoying the presence of his cigarettes, his armchair, and the view of the park from his window. He sinks into the novel, in which a man and woman meet in a cabin. The woman kisses the man's face where a tree branch has scratched it, making it bleed. The man and woman are lovers, but their attention is now focused on murder: the man is going to kill the woman's husband. They leave the cabin and split up. The woman goes north, and he goes to her house. Following her instructions, knife in hand, the man goes inside and sees his victim: a man who's sitting in an armchair reading a book.

CHARACTER LIST

The Reader   A businessman. The reader seems well-to-do. He has interrupted his reading to attend important conferences, and he completes the novel while sitting in a comfortable room with a view of a park.

The Man   The hero of the reader's novel. The man is passionate and full of nervous emotion. He plans to kill his lover's husband, who sits reading in an armchair.

The Woman   The heroine of the reader's novel. The woman and her lover have convinced themselves of the absolute necessity of killing the woman's husband, a crime they think of as fated to occur.

ANALYSIS OF MAJOR CHARACTERS

THE READER   The reader has a distinct, quirky personality. He is a wealthy man who loves literature and delays gratification by waiting to open a book until he's finished his work for the day. He smokes and enjoys the view of the park from his favorite green velvet chair, all of which contribute to his ability to become absorbed in a good story. On one hand, these personality traits make him unique, but at the same time they also make him like every other reader. In this way, Cortázar's reader is a stand-in for all readers and everyone who has the ability to get lost in books. Although the reader is highly individualistic, his personality quirks represent the quirks of all avid readers, many of whom favor certain locations, times of day, and types of books to read. Cortázar therefore uses the reader, who is simultaneously unique and generic, to convey the universality of the pleasure of reading.

THEMES, MOTIFS, AND SYMBOLS

THEMES

THE DANGER OF SUBSUMING YOURSELF IN LITERATURE "Continuity of Parks" argues that your success in reading or writing fiction depends on your willingness to lose yourself utterly in the task. A true reader, like the protagonist of Cortázar's story, will tumble into fiction consciously and deliberately. He will subsume himself so thoroughly that he will feel as if he has become part of the fictional world. If we, Cortázar's audience, respond to "Continuity of Parks" in the way the reader responds to his book, we will come to the end of the story as if coming to the end of a vivid dream, not sure of what is real and what is imagined. The responsibility of a true writer is to create a world powerful and colorful enough to enable readers to lose themselves in it. At the same time, however, subsuming one's self in reading and writing can be dangerous—it's no coincidence that the reader's book concerns murder and betrayal. The story ends with a suggestion that the immersed reader is, at least metaphorically, on the brink of death. Cortázar implies that becoming engrossed in fiction is both a goal worth striving for and a way of losing hold of your identity.

MOTIFS

THE COLOR GREEN The color green, which recurs throughout "Continuity of Parks," highlights the power that fiction gives us to slip into another world while simultaneously remaining in our own world. As the reader lets himself fall into the novel, his green velvet chair acts as an anchor tying him to reality. He enjoys the feeling of the upholstery under his hand and behind his head as he lets the characters and plot wash over him. At the end of the story, when the man sneaks up on his victim, the green velvet armchair he sees sits right on the boundary of real and imagined, making us wonder which is which. Though unnamed, the color green is implied with each mention of the trees and the outdoors, elements that again suggest a simultaneous existence in two worlds. Trees link the two men: the reader senses the presence of the oak trees in his garden while the man in the story is scratched by a tree branch. The title "Continuity of Parks" also references the color green. On one level, the title refers to Cortázar's story, which begins and ends in the reader's park. On another level, the title refers to no less than life and fiction, which Cortázar characterizes as a long, interwoven series of green parks.

SYMBOLS

THE KNIFE The knife, which the man plans to use to kill his lover's husband, stands for the man's jealousy of his rival but, more important, also stands for the potentially lethal intersection between fact and fiction. When the man in the book creeps into the room containing a green armchair, we realize that fiction and reality have blended together and that the reader has become a part of the fictional world in his book. In this way, the knife serves as an anchor that links the two worlds together. Moreover, the fact that the knife symbolizes one thing in the book and something else in the story is typical of "Continuity of Parks," which argues that colors, themes, symbols, and characters leap back and forth between our lives and our books, weaving the two together.

SHORT STORY ANALYSIS

REALITY AND FANTASY   On first reading, "Continuity of Parks" seems to present a puzzle that readers must solve, as reality and fantasy intersect. In fact, however, no solution is possible, and Cortázar is not interested in puzzles in the first place. On a basic level, the short story seems to cry out for a tidy analysis and explanation. If we mistake Cortázar's story for an O. Henry tale with a pat twist ending or a detective story in which all becomes clear in the final moments, "Continuity of Parks" may tempt us into looking for one correct interpretation. We wonder how it is possible that the man reading the novel turns up in the summary of the novel's plot, and we may fall into the trap of trying out different theories that would explain this conundrum and trying to pin down the correct one. Perhaps the man is a character in a book about a man reading a book. Perhaps he is the husband the adulterous couple is setting out to kill. Perhaps he is so absorbed in the novel that he is vividly imagining its events encroaching on his life. A number of explanations seem possible.

Rather than a mystery, the story is actually a metaphor for the experience of reading: Cortázar's reader gets so lost in a fictional world that he literally becomes a participant in it. It is also a metaphor for *our* reading experience: we get so swept up in literature—literature including his own story, Cortázar hopes—that, like the reader in "Continuity of Parks," we can no longer distinguish between fiction and reality. It is also a metaphor for the writing experience: to create convincing fictional worlds, the writer must lose himself in his creations, just as Cortázar's reader loses himself in his book. We cannot identify one correct explanation for the puzzling ending because no single explanation exists. Instead, the story is an investigation of what it means to write and to read stories.

IMPORTANT QUOTATIONS EXPLAINED

1. "[He sat] [s]prawled in his favorite armchair, its back toward the door—even the possibility of an intrusion would have irritated him, had he thought of it.

While "Continuity of Parks" is a story of deep philosophical import and bold structural experimentation, it is not solemn or humorless. Cortázar's fiction is often noted for its glints and gleams of wry humor, and this story is no exception. In this passage, in which Cortázar describes the reader getting ready to plunge back into his novel, he sets up the end of the story by mentioning that the reader's back is to the door. He also does a sly and funny bit of foreshadowing by saying that "even the possibility of an intrusion would have irritated" the reader. This foreshadowing becomes humorous at the end, when, on one level, an actual intrusion takes place. It is also dark, however, in that, on another level, the intrusion takes place only in the reader's mind. It is he who lets the intruder in by allowing the story to take hold of him. Put another way, it is he who becomes the intruder in his own home.

The Dead

James Joyce
(1882–1941)

CONTEXT

James Joyce was born into a middle-class Catholic family in Rathgar, a suburb of Dublin, Ireland, in 1882. The family's prosperity dwindled soon after Joyce's birth, forcing them to move from their comfortable home to the unfashionable and impoverished area of North Dublin. Nonetheless, Joyce attended a prestigious Jesuit school and went on to study philosophy and languages at University College, Dublin. He moved to Paris after graduating in 1902 to attend medical school, but he turned his attention to writing instead. He returned to Dublin in 1903, where he met his future wife, Nora Barnacle, the following year. From then on, Joyce made his home in other countries.

From 1905 to 1915, Joyce and Nora lived in Rome and Trieste, Italy, where they had a son, George, and a daughter, Lucia. During his time in Italy, Joyce managed to convince three of his siblings to join his family there. He occasionally returned to Dublin to deal with business matters but refused to set foot in the city again after an unpleasant visit in 1912 with a publisher who refused to print his short story collection, *Dubliners*. The Joyces lived in near-destitution, especially because Joyce pursued a variety of ill-advised and unsuccessful business ventures. Joyce drank heavily in Italy, and he also suffered from severe problems with his eyes.

In 1915, Joyce and Nora moved to Zurich, Switzerland, where they stayed for four years. While there, Joyce was introduced to a publisher named Harriet Shaw Weaver, who would become his patron for more than two decades—that is, she provided funding so that Joyce could write without worrying about earning money. In 1920, Joyce and Nora moved to Paris, where they stayed for twenty years. In Paris, Joyce was among one of many writers who gathered in Sylvia Beach's famous bookshop, Shakespeare and Company, along with Ernest Hemingway and F. Scott Fitzgerald. Joyce wrote and published his two masterpieces, *Ulysses* (1922) and *Finnegans Wake* (1939), while he was living in Paris. The Joyces returned to Zurich in 1940, and Joyce died there a year later, in 1941. He was fifty-nine.

Joyce began publishing books when he was just twenty-five. In 1907, he published *Chamber Music*, a collection of poetry, and eventually published *Dubliners* in 1914. Although Joyce had written the book years earlier, the stories contained characters and events that were alarmingly similar to real people and places, raising concerns about libel. Joyce indeed based many of the characters in *Dubliners* on real people, and such suggestive details, coupled with the book's historical and geographical precision and piercing examination of relationships, flustered anxious publishers. Joyce's autobiographical novel, *A Portrait of the Artist as a Young Man*, followed *Dubliners* in 1916, and a play, *Exiles*, followed in 1918. Joyce is most famous for his later experimental novels, *Ulysses*, which maps the Dublin wanderings of its protagonist in a single day, and *Finnegans Wake*. These two works emblematize his signature stream-of-consciousness prose style, which mirrors characters' thoughts without the limitations of traditional narrative.

"The Dead" is the final and longest story in *Dubliners*. Set against a backdrop of a tumultuous Ireland, the story explores the intersection of life and death and concludes with an epiphany, a technique that Joyce used throughout the stories in *Dubliners*. "The Dead" is considered to be not only one of Joyce's most famous works but also one of the best short stories ever written. It was adapted for film by John Huston in 1987 and for the stage in 1999.

PLOT OVERVIEW

The housemaid, Lily, frantically greets guests arriving at the annual dance and dinner party given by Kate and Julia Morkan and their young niece, Mary Jane Morkan. Set at or just before the feast of the Epiphany on January 6—which celebrates the manifestation of Christ's divinity to the Magi—the party is held for a variety of relatives and friends. Kate and Julia particularly await the arrival of their favorite nephew, Gabriel Conroy, and his wife, Gretta. When they arrive, Gabriel attempts to chat with Lily as she takes his coat, but she snaps in reply to his question about her love life. Gabriel ends the uncomfortable exchange by giving Lily a generous tip, but the experience makes him anxious. He relaxes when he joins his aunts and Gretta, although Gretta's good-natured teasing about his dedication to galoshes irritates him. They discuss their decision to stay at a hotel that evening rather than make the long trip home. The arrival of another guest, the always-drunk Freddy Malins, disrupts the conversation. Gabriel makes sure that Freddy is fit to join the party while the guests chat over drinks. An older gentleman, Mr. Browne, flirts with some young girls, who dodge his advances. Gabriel steers a drunken Freddy toward the drawing room to get help from Mr. Browne, who attempts to sober Freddy up.

The party continues with a piano performance by Mary Jane. More dancing follows, which finds Gabriel paired up with Miss Ivors, a fellow university instructor. A fervent supporter of Irish culture, Miss Ivors embarrasses Gabriel by labeling him a "West Briton" for writing literary reviews for a conservative newspaper. Gabriel dismisses the accusation, but Miss Ivors pushes the point by inviting Gabriel to visit the Aran Isles, where Irish is spoken, during the summer. When Gabriel declines, explaining that he has arranged a cycling trip on the continent, Miss Ivors corners him about his lack of interest in his own country. Gabriel exclaims that he is sick of Ireland. After the dance, he flees to a corner and engages in a few more conversations, but he can't forget his chat with Miss Ivors.

Just before dinner, Julia sings a song for the guests. Miss Ivors leaves the party to the surprise of Mary Jane and Gretta and to the relief of Gabriel. Finally, dinner is ready, and Gabriel assumes his place at the head of the table to carve the goose. After much fussing, everyone eats, and finally Gabriel delivers his speech, during which he praises Kate, Julia, and Mary Jane for their hospitality. Framing this quality as an Irish strength, Gabriel laments the present age in which such hospitality is undervalued. Nevertheless, he insists, people must not linger on the past and the dead, but live and rejoice in the present with the living. The table breaks into a loud applause for Gabriel's speech, and the entire party toasts their three hostesses.

Later, as guests begin to leave, Gabriel recounts a story about his grandfather and his horse, which forever walked in circles even when taken out of the mill where it worked. After finishing the anecdote, Gabriel realizes that Gretta stands transfixed by the song that Mr. Bartell D'Arcy sings in the drawing room. When the music stops and the rest of the party guests assemble before the door to leave, Gretta remains detached and thoughtful. Gabriel is enamored with and preoccupied by his wife's mysterious mood and recalls their courtship as they walk from the house and catch a cab into Dublin.

At the hotel, Gabriel grows irritated by Gretta's behavior. She does not seem to share his romantic inclinations and in fact bursts into tears. Gretta confesses that she has been thinking of the song from the party because a former lover had sung it to her during her youth in Galway. Gretta recounts the sad story of this boy, Michael Furey, who died after waiting outside of her window in the cold. Gretta later falls asleep, but Gabriel remains awake, disturbed by what Gretta has told him. He curls up on the bed, contemplating his own mortality. Seeing the snow at the window, he envisions it blanketing the graveyard where Michael Furey rests and covering all over Ireland as well.

CHARACTER LIST

Gabriel Conroy   A university-educated teacher and writer. Gabriel struggles with simple social situations and conversations, and straightforward questions catch him off guard. He feels out of place due to his highbrow literary endeavors. His aunts, Julia and Kate Morkan, turn to him to perform the traditionally masculine activities of carving the goose and delivering a speech during their annual celebration. Gabriel represents a force of control in the story, but his wife Gretta's fond and sad recollections of a former devoted lover make him realize that he has little grasp on his life and his marriage lacks true love.

Gretta Conroy   Gabriel's wife. Gretta plays a relatively minor role until the conclusion of the story, when she is the focus of Gabriel's thoughts. She appears mournful and distant when a certain song is sung at the party, and she later plunges into despair when she tells Gabriel the story of her childhood love, Michael Furey. Her pure intentions and loyalty to this boy unnerve Gabriel and generate his despairing thoughts about life and death.

Lily   The Morkan sisters' housemaid who rebukes Gabriel when he teases her about a boyfriend.

Molly Ivors   The nationalist woman who teases Gabriel during a dance. Miss Ivors invites Gabriel to visit the Aran Isles, but Gabriel awkwardly declines. She leaves the party early.

Julia Morkan   One of the aging sisters who throw the annual dance party. Julia has a gray and sullen appearance that combines with her remote, wandering behavior to make her a figure sapped of life.

Kate Morkan   One of the aging sisters who throw the annual dance party. Kate is vivacious but constantly worries about her sister, Julia, and the guests' happiness.

Mary Jane Morkan   Kate and Julia's niece. Mary Jane lives with the Morkan sisters and plays the piano at the party.

Bartell D'Arcy   An opera singer who attends the Morkans' party. Mr. D'Arcy sings the song "The Lass of Aughrim," which Gretta recognizes from her past.

Freddy Malins   A drunken guest at the party.

ANALYSIS OF MAJOR CHARACTERS

GABRIEL CONROY   Gabriel, with his short temper, acute class-consciousness, social awkwardness, and frustrated love, is a man of many faces. To his aging aunts, he is a loving family man, bringing his cheerful presence to the party and performing typically masculine duties such as carving the goose. With other female characters, such as Miss Ivors, Lily the housemaid, and his wife, Gretta, he is less able to forge a connection, and his attempts often become awkward, even offensive. With Miss Ivors, he stumbles defensively through a conversation about his plans to go on a cycling tour, and he offends Lily when he teases her about having a boyfriend. Gretta inspires fondness and tenderness in him, but he primarily feels mastery over her. Such qualities do not make Gabriel sympathetic, but instead make him an example of a man whose inner life struggles to keep pace with and adjust to the world around him. The Morkans' party exposes Gabriel as a social performer. He carefully reviews his thoughts and words, and he flounders in situations in which he cannot predict other people's feelings. Gabriel's unease with unbridled feeling is palpable, but he must face his discomfort throughout the story. He illustrates the tense intersection of social isolation and personal confrontation.

D

Gabriel has one moment of spontaneous, honest speech, which is rare in "The Dead." When he dances with Miss Ivors, she asks him why he won't stay in Ireland and learn more about his own country. Instead of replying with niceties, Gabriel responds, "I'm sick of my own country, sick of it!" Gabriel pronounces his sentiment clearly and without remorse. Gabriel delivers his own message not only to Miss Ivors but also to himself and the readers of "The Dead." He dwells on his own revelation without suppressing or rejecting it. In the final scene of the story, when he intensely contemplates the meaning of his life, Gabriel has a vision not only of his tedious life but also of his role as a human being.

THEMES, MOTIFS, AND SYMBOLS

THEMES

THE INTERSECTION OF LIFE AND DEATH   "The Dead" invokes the quiet calm of snow that covers both the dead and the living and suggests that the dead are always present, intersecting uncomfortably with the living. The dead cast a shadow on the present, drawing attention to the mistakes and failures of people who are still alive. Michael Furey, who died many years ago, proves to be a vivid presence in Gretta's life, which Gabriel discovers only after the Morkans' party. Although Gabriel always thought he had mastery over his wife and that their marriage was rich and fulfilling, his illusions are shattered when he understands how important the dead Michael is to Gretta. Michael may be dead, but Gabriel cannot compete with him: Michael loved Gretta in a way that Gabriel knows full well he is not capable of. Ghosts such as Michael Furey—past loves, old family members, former acquaintances who have died or disappeared—are everywhere.

"The Dead" squarely addresses the intersection of life and death in Ireland, where present and past vie for loyalty. In his speech, Gabriel claims to lament the present age in which hospitality, such as that of the Morkan family, is undervalued. At the same time, he insists that people must not dwell on the past but embrace the present. Gabriel's words betray him, and he ultimately encourages a tribute to the past, the past of hospitality, that lives on in the present party. His later thoughts reveal this attachment to the past when he envisions snow as "general all over Ireland." In every corner of the country, snow touches both the dead and living, uniting them. Gabriel's thoughts in the final lines of the story, however, suggest that the living might in fact be able to free themselves from deadening routines and the past and live unfettered. Even in January, snow is unusual in Ireland and cannot last forever.

THE IMPORTANCE OF PASSION   Although Gabriel has always believed his marriage to Gretta was rooted in love, the actions of Gretta's former love, Michael Furey, reveal how different that love is from genuine passion and show that what Gabriel mistook for love is actually a desire for control. When Gabriel sees Gretta transfixed by the music at the end of the party, he yearns intensely to have control of her strange feelings. Although he remembers their romantic courtship and is overcome with attraction to Gretta, this attraction is rooted not in love or passion but in his desire to control her. At the hotel, when Gretta confesses to Gabriel that she was thinking of her first love, he becomes furious at her and himself, realizing that he has no claim on her and will never be "master." After Gretta falls asleep, Gabriel softens. Now that he knows that another man preceded him in Gretta's life, he feels sad that Michael Furey once felt an aching love that he himself has never known. Reflecting on his own controlled, passionless life, he realizes that life is short and that those who leave the world like Michael Furey, with great passion, in fact live more fully than people like himself.

THE DIFFICULTY OF HONEST COMMUNICATION   Gabriel's restrained behavior and his reputation with his aunts as the nephew who takes care of everything mark him as a man of authority and caution, but he struggles to communicate honestly with those around him, particularly with women. First, Gabriel clumsily provokes a defensive statement from the overworked Lily when he asks her about her love life. Instead of apologizing or explaining what he meant, Gabriel quickly ends the conversation by giving Lily a holiday tip. He blames his prestigious education for his inability to relate to servants like Lily, but his willingness to let money speak for him suggests that he relies on the comforts of his class to maintain distance. The encounter with Lily shows that Gabriel, like his aunts, cannot tolerate a "back answer," but he is unable to avoid such challenges as the party continues. During his dance with Miss Ivors, he faces a barrage of questions about his nonexistent nationalist sympathies, which he doesn't know how to answer appropriately. Unable to compose a full response, Gabriel blurts out that he is sick of his own country, surprising Miss Ivors and himself with his unmeasured response and loss of control. When Gabriel makes his speech during the party, his intention to please his aunts is genuine, but his speech is filled with platitudes. He intentionally tones down the speech, eliminating some poetry that he wanted to include, because he fears that the audience will not understand him and find him ridiculous and snobby.

Gabriel finds honest communication difficult even with his own wife. He desires her and remembers moments from their past, but he is completely unable to communicate these thoughts to Gretta. In the hotel room, instead of saying something kind or loving, he blurts out a pointless observation about a guest at the party. He is so flummoxed at trying to convey to Gretta how he feels and what he wants that he hopes she makes the first move. When Gretta does indeed approach him, however, she reveals information about her past, and Gabriel is utterly unprepared to respond to it. Instead of drawing them together, Gretta's open communication makes her seem like a stranger to Gabriel, and he resigns himself to never fully knowing his wife.

MOTIFS

ROUTINES   The Morkans' party consists of the kind of deadening routines that make existence so lifeless in "The Dead." The events of the party repeat every year: Gabriel gives a speech, Freddy Malins arrives drunk, everyone dances the same memorized steps, everyone eats. Like the horse that circles around the mill in Gabriel's anecdote, these Dubliners settle into an expected routine at every party. Such tedium fixes the characters in a state of paralysis. They are unable to break from the activities that they know, so they live life without new experiences, numb to the world. Routines are so deadening to Gabriel that even a small change in them, such as when he and Gretta stay the night in a hotel rather than go home, seems to be an escape. When he and Gretta arrive at the hotel, Gabriel feels as though they are embarking on a "new adventure." Instead, their routines follow them right into the room. Far from the adventure Gabriel had hoped for, they fall back into their patterns of poor communication and thwarted desire. Only Gretta, with the memories of her lost love, seems to have a refuge from the demands and habits of the day-to-day.

MUSIC   The Morkans' party, with the dancing, singing, and piano performances, seems like one long musical recital, which evokes feelings of nostalgia and longing for Gabriel and Gretta. Julia and Kate Morkan are music teachers, as is their niece, Mary Jane. The piano is constantly played during the party, both as background and when Mary Jane gives a brief performance. Talk at the dinner table is of music, and during his speech Gabriel calls the Morkans the "Three Graces of the Dublin musical world." At the end of the party, the opera singer Bartell D'Arcy gives a brief performance, which Gretta hears and which reminds her of Michael Furey. Later, when Gabriel remembers past years with Gretta, he compares a letter he wrote her to "distant music" and observes that her body is "musical." Although the party with its music seems lively, Gabriel's and Gretta's thoughts at the end of the night are sad and melancholy. Gabriel thinks about the fact that it won't be long before Julia dies, Gretta thinks about her first love, and Gabriel considers the fact that he has never know true love or passion, even for Gretta. The sonorous backdrop to "The Dead" may be beautiful, but the lives it touches are tinged with sadness and disappointment.

SYMBOLS

FOOD   The food in "The Dead" represents death rather than life or sustenance. When Gabriel observes the food on the Morkans' dinner table, he first notes the "fat brown goose," the "great ham, stripped of its outer skin," and the "round of spiced beef." Though succulent, these three dishes suggest the death of the animals that yielded them. The food appears at "rival ends" of the table, which is lined with parallel rows of various dishes, divided in the middle by "sentries" of fruit and watched from afar by "three squads of bottles." The military language transforms a table set for a communal feast into a battlefield, reeking with danger and death. Furthermore, the copious food highlights the numbing routine that plagues Gabriel and the other characters. This dinner proceeds in carefully planned steps that are repeated year after year, and it will be punctuated by Gabriel's annual speech. Food may sustain life, but it can also symbolize life's restraints.

SHORT STORY ANALYSIS

JOYCE'S IRELAND Ireland permeates all of Joyce's writing, especially Ireland during the tumultuous early twentieth century. The political scene at that time was uncertain but hopeful, as Ireland sought independence from Great Britain. The nationalist Charles Stewart Parnell, who became active in the 1870s, had reinvigorated Irish politics with his proposed Home Rule Bill, which aimed to give Ireland more autonomy from Britain. Parnell, dubbed the "Uncrowned King of Ireland," was hugely popular in Ireland, both for his anti-English views and support of land ownership for farmers. In 1889, however, his political career collapsed when his adulterous affair with the married Kitty O'Shea was made public. Kitty's husband had known for years about the affair, but instead of making it public, he attempted to use it to his political and financial advantage. He waited until he filed for divorce to expose the affair. Both Ireland and England reeled from the scandal, Parnell refused to resign, and his career never recovered. Parnell died in 1891, when Joyce was nine years old.

In the last part of the nineteenth century, after Parnell's death, Ireland underwent a dramatic cultural revival. Irish citizens struggled to define what it meant to be Irish, and a nationalist movement began to promote the Irish language and culture. The movement celebrated Irish literature and encouraged people to learn the Irish language, which many people were forgoing in favor of the more modern English language. Ultimately, the cultural revival of the late nineteenth century gave the Irish a greater sense of pride in their identity. Despite this revival, however, the bitter publicity surrounding Parnell's affair dashed all hopes of Irish independence and unity. Ireland splintered into factions of Protestants and Catholics, Conservatives and Nationalists. Such social forces form a complex context for Joyce's writing, which repeatedly taps into political and religious matters. Because Joyce spent little of his later life in Ireland, he did not witness these debates firsthand. Nevertheless, he retained his artistic interest in Dublin and the country of his birth and was able to articulate the Irish experience in his writings.

EPIPHANY Gabriel experiences a revelation in his everyday life, a moment that Joyce referred to as an *epiphany*, a word with connotations of religious revelation. Epiphanies on both a large and small scale are characteristic of Joyce's short stories. These epiphanies do not bring new experiences and the possibility of reform, as one might expect. Rather, these epiphanies allow characters to better understand their particular circumstances, usually rife with sadness and routine, to which they then return with resignation and frustration. The epiphany at the conclusion of "The Dead" is tinged with frustration, sadness, and regret and clarifies the connection between the dead and living, a significant theme of the story.

The holiday setting of the Epiphany in "The Dead" emphasizes the profoundness of Gabriel's difficult awakening that concludes the story. Gabriel experiences an inward change that makes him examine both his life and human life in general. Gabriel sees himself as a shadow of a person, flickering in a world in which the living and the dead meet. Even though he emphasizes the division between the past of the dead and the present of the living in his dinner speech, Gabriel recognizes after hearing that Michael Furey's memory lives on that such division is false. As he looks out of his hotel window, he sees the falling snow and imagines it covering Michael Furey's grave just as it covers the people who are still alive. The story leaves open the possibility that Gabriel might change his attitude and embrace life, even though his somber dwelling on the darkness of Ireland seems to close the story with morose acceptance.

IMPORTANT QUOTATIONS EXPLAINED

1. *He stood still in the gloom of the hall, trying to catch the air that the voice was singing and gazing up at his wife. There was grace and mystery in her attitude as if she were a symbol of something. He asked himself what is a woman standing on the stairs in the shadow, listening to distant music, a symbol of. If he were a painter he would paint her in that attitude.*

This quotation, which appears about halfway through the story, shortly before Gabriel and Gretta leave the party, marks the initial spark of Gabriel's lust for his wife and also reveals the extent to which he does not know her. As Gabriel watches Gretta, she seems like a stranger to him, and he doesn't seem to recognize this "grace and mystery." Indeed, Gretta's thoughts are a mystery to Gabriel. He has no inkling of what she may be thinking or what the song might mean to her. Unaware that his wife has a passionate love story in her past, he can't comprehend the meaning of her posture—he doesn't know what Gretta is "a symbol of." Gabriel is on the outside of his wife's thoughts, and he is unable to control them or her. He feebly attempts to exert control by imagining himself painting her—in a sense, capturing her on canvas.

2. *Yes, the newspapers were right: snow was general all over Ireland. It was falling on every part of the dark central plain, on the treeless hills, falling softly upon the Bog of Allen and, farther westward, softly falling into the dark mutinous Shannon waves. It was falling, too, upon every part of the lonely churchyard on the hill where Michael Furey lay buried.*

In the last paragraph of "The Dead," Gabriel gazes out of his hotel window, watching the falling snow and reflecting on Gretta's recent confession about her childhood love, Michael Furey. Previously in the story, Gabriel had been intoxicated and energized by Gretta's preoccupied mood, which reminded him of their courtship, but her outburst of sobbing undermines his self-assurance. This quiet moment of contemplation portrays Gabriel's muted, hushed acceptance that he was not Gretta's first love, and that in fact he has never felt love at all. The blanket of snow suggests this sense of numbness in Gabriel's character—he is literally frigid to emotion—but also the commonality of this trait. The snow does not fall only outside of Gabriel's window, but, as he envisions it, across the country, from the Harbor of Dublin in the east, to the south in Shannon, and to the west. In other words, everyone, everywhere, is as numb as he is.

A Death in the Woods

Sherwood Anderson
(1876–1941)

CONTEXT

Sherwood Anderson was born in Camden, Ohio, in 1876. Anderson's father, a charismatic Union Army veteran, ran a harness-making business. When that venture failed, he began drinking heavily and was reduced to working a series of low-paying odd jobs for the rest of his life. Anderson ended up shouldering a fair share of the family responsibilities, working so many part-time jobs that he earned the nickname "Jobby." At about age sixteen, Anderson dropped out of high school and left the family farm for Chicago, where he worked for several years as a manual laborer. He briefly served in the Spanish-American War, and, upon his return to the United States in 1900, he completed his secondary school education.

During the next ten years, Anderson built a solidly middle-class life for himself, working in various business ventures and marrying Cornelia Lane, the daughter of a wealthy businessman, with whom he fathered three children. At night, however, Anderson pursued the literary work that would someday make him famous. The competing demands of his personal, business, and artistic lives took a heavy toll in 1912, when Anderson suffered a mental collapse. After his recovery in 1913, he moved his family to Chicago, where he enjoyed much success as an advertising copywriter and later as an author. In the early 1920s, he left the corporate world, as well as any pretensions he may have had toward a respectably bourgeois life, for good. He divorced Lane in 1916. Before his death in 1941, he would marry three more times, eventually finding love and stability with his fourth wife, Eleanor Copenhaver.

Although his work would play a key role in the development of American fiction in the twentieth century, Anderson did not publish his first book, *Windy McPherson's Son* (1916), until he was forty. In subsequent years he wrote across several genres, publishing novels, short fiction, memoirs, and collections of journalism. The 1925 novel *Dark Laughter* was Anderson's only bestseller, but the short-story collection *Winesburg, Ohio* (1919) is far and away his most famous work. A series of linked stories that form a loosely connected novel about the inhabitants of a small Midwestern town, *Winesburg, Ohio* exemplifies many of the most prominent recurring features of Anderson's work: characters struggling with the difficulties of small-town life, an emphasis on experiences of loneliness and frustration, and a lyrical writing style that attempted to capture the rhythms of human thought. In 1998, the Modern Library named *Winesburg, Ohio* one of the one hundred best English language novels of the twentieth century.

Anderson is generally classified as a realist writer—that is, a writer concerned with representing human life and experiences with as much verisimilitude as possible. He is often grouped with naturalist writers such as Theodore Dreiser and Stephen Crane, who examined the social and scientific forces that shaped and, as the naturalists believed, ultimately determined individual human lives. In the 1910s and 1920s, Anderson became a member of Dreiser's so-called Chicago Group, joining the ranks of such influential American writers as Edgar Lee Masters and the poet Carl Sandburg. The modernist writer Gertrude Stein also exerted a powerful influence over Anderson, particularly her experimental novel *Three Lives* (1909). Through Stein, whom he met in Europe in 1924, Anderson met several other towering figures of the modernist movement, including the poets T. S. Eliot and Ezra Pound and the novelist James Joyce. Anderson's work, in turn, has influenced such important and varied American writers as Ernest Hemingway, William Faulkner, and John Steinbeck.

"A Death in the Woods," the title story of his 1933 anthology of short fiction, is generally considered Anderson's finest and most characteristic short story. In it, an unnamed narrator is haunted by a memory from his childhood. In an attempt to understand the enigmatic incident, he returns to the story again and again, seeming to circle closer to the truth with each telling. In composing "A Death in the Woods," Anderson went through a similar process. Although the story was published in 1933, Anderson had begun working on it at least seventeen years earlier. A ten-page, typewritten fragment—on the reverse side of which Anderson had drafted a portion of *Winesburg, Ohio*—sketches out several key elements of "A Death in the Woods," including a narrator who witnesses an eerie scene one snowy, moonlit night involving a pack of dogs who circle around the corpse of a dead woman bearing a pack of food. He completed various other sketches and drafts in the years between the first fragment and final publication.

Anderson himself experienced many of the things that both the narrator and the old woman undergo in "A Death in the Woods." Anderson spent time working as a laborer on the farm of a German man, and he too once had a strange encounter with a pack of dogs on a winter night in a forest. The character of old Mrs. Grimes is based, in part, on Anderson's own silent, hardworking mother. Although the narrator of the short story is not Anderson himself, the story's main subject—the ways in which an artist processes disjointed but powerful personal experiences through his art—certainly applies to its author, as well.

PLOT OVERVIEW

The narrator describes a certain type of poor, elderly woman. All country people have seen a woman like this, he says, but she is usually ignored. The narrator recalls a particular old woman who would walk past his house on her way in and out of town, laden with a heavy pack and followed by two or three large, gaunt dogs. The old woman was "nothing special," but thoughts of her have stayed with him and he suddenly recalls what happened to her.

The woman's name was Grimes, and she lived with her husband, Jake, and their son in a small house several miles out of town. Both men were tough and violent. The narrator recalls a time when he encountered Jake Grimes at Tom Whitehead's livery barn. None of the men there would speak to Grimes, who left after shooting the men a menacing glance.

Jake met his future wife at the farm of a German couple, where he was briefly employed and she labored as an indentured servant. The girl quickly agreed to leave the German, who had sexually assaulted her on several occasions. The German discovered their plan, and the two men engaged in a violent fight before Jake and the girl were able to escape. The narrator wonders how he came to know these details, because the events occurred long before he was born.

The woman and Jake had a son and daughter. The narrator mentions that the daughter died but says nothing else about her. The Grimes men work little, and the burden of maintaining the livestock falls to the old woman, who is always scheming about how to get everything fed. The woman's husband and son often go off for weeks at a time, leaving her with no money or support.

One day during the winter, the old woman goes into town with a few eggs tucked into her old grain bag. A few large farm dogs follow at her heels. At the butcher shop, the butcher, furious that an old, obviously sick woman should be out on such a cold day, tells her that he'd rather see her husband and son starve than get any of the meat he is about to give her. The old woman doesn't speak, but she is mildly surprised at his reaction.

Exhausted and sore, the old woman makes her way through the woods with the pack strapped to her back. She follows a path to a small clearing, where she sits down to rest, eventually closing her eyes and falling asleep.

The four Grimes dogs have picked up a few other farm dogs, and after going off to chase rabbits for a while, they come back to the clearing, excited about something. On a cold, clear night, the narrator says, some old instinct might take hold of these kinds of dogs. The dogs run silently around the clearing in what the narrator calls "a kind of death ceremony." Each dog takes turns nosing up against the old woman as she dies. The narrator says that, even though he wasn't present, he knows what happened because years later, as an adult, he once found himself in the woods on a winter night and saw a pack of dogs act the same way.

The old woman dies quietly, and when she does, the dogs stop running. They gather around her and drag the large pack of meat and soup bones away.

The dogs do not touch the old woman's body. When a rabbit hunter finds her a day or two later, her frozen body is so slight and narrow that she looks like a young girl. The narrator is following along on his brother's newspaper-delivery route when the hunter comes to town with his news. The hunter and the town marshal lead a group of townsmen out to the woods to see the body. When the group arrives at the clearing, the narrator notes that the woman does not, in fact, look old. Neither he nor his brother has ever seen a woman's naked body before. In the snow, she looks white and lovely.

When the party arrives back in town, the men take the body to the undertaker's and shut the door. The boys go home and the brother tells the family what happened, but the narrator keeps silent and goes to bed early. Jake Grimes and his son are found and questioned, and though they could not be implicated in the old woman's death, the townspeople's disapproval drives them out of town.

The narrator only remembers the image of the woman's body in the clearing. He says that somehow that scene has become "the foundation for the real story I am now trying to tell." In a disconnected fashion, he describes how, as a young man, he worked for a German farmer whose hired girl feared him. Later, he had a strange encounter with a pack of dogs in a forest on a winter night. He recounts how, as a child one summer day, he and a friend went to the old Grimes house, which had been abandoned except for a pair of tall, gaunt dogs.

The narrator compares the woman's story to a piece of faint music, heard from far away, which needs to be listened to slowly before it is truly understood. He claims that he and his brother were too young at the time to fully understand the point of the story. "A thing so complete has its own beauty," he says. He ends by saying that he won't emphasize the point: he's only trying to explain why, so many years later, he is telling the story over again.

CHARACTER LIST

The Narrator   As a boy, he joined the group that went to the woods to see the old woman's body. Many years later, the narrator suddenly remembers the event and begins to narrate the story of the old woman's life and death. Though he finds it difficult to articulate why, he feels compelled to retell this childhood tale. In the intervening years, the narrator has had several experiences that echo certain incidents in the old woman's life.

The Old Woman (Mrs. Grimes)   An old, sickly woman who lived on a farm near the narrator's childhood town. The old woman had a history of poor treatment. As a young orphan, she was legally bound to a German couple who abused her, and as an adult she lived in poverty on a small, remote farm with a husband and son who treated her just as poorly. The old woman bore her trials with a silent stoicism before dying in the woods in the company of a pack of dogs.

Jake Grimes   The old woman's husband. A rough, brutal man, Jake Grimes was a mean drunk who was distrusted and disliked in town. He was rumored to be a horse thief, but had never been caught. Like his wife, Jake Grimes spoke very little in the story, although his silence suggested menace rather than forbearance.

The Grimes's Son   The old woman and Jake Grimes's twenty-one-year-old son. Unnamed in the story, the Grimes's son inherited his father's violent, brutish ways.

The Grimes's Daughter   The old woman and Jake Grimes's daughter, who died before the story's events took place.

The German and His Wife   A couple to whom the young Mrs. Grimes was bound as an indentured servant. On several occasions, the German attempted to sexually assault the young girl, but he was always foiled by the wife's return. The wife, in turn, suspected the girl of being involved with her husband and harassed her because of it.

The Butcher   A man who took pity on the old woman on the day she died. The butcher gave her a liver and some dog bones for free. Angry at the husband and son who mistreated her so blatantly, he instructed her to not give them any of the meat.

The Hunter   A country fellow who discovered the woman in the woods a day or two after she died. Too frightened to look closely at the corpse, the hunter hurried into town and brought a group of men—including the narrator and his brother—to see what he thought was the body of a beautiful young girl.

The Narrator's Brother   A newsboy who abandoned his paper route to go see the body in the woods.

The Town Marshal   A large man with a Civil War injury who took charge of the party of men.

Tom Whitehead   The owner of the livery barn where several townsmen (including the narrator) encountered Jake Grimes.

ANALYSIS OF MAJOR CHARACTERS

THE NARRATOR Although the unnamed narrator of "Death in the Woods" appears only briefly as a character, his consciousness shapes the entire work. Whereas Mrs. Grimes remains silent throughout the story, we are constantly aware of the narrator's voice, which is conversational, colloquial, and immediate. The narrator often refers to us directly, such as when he stops short of describing the cruel treatment that bound children receive by saying, "You know what I mean." He also makes constant reference to himself and the functions of his own memory. By the end of the story, although we have learned few factual details about his life, we know the storyteller much more intimately than we know the subject of his tale, Mrs. Grimes.

Although the narrator never meets Mrs. Grimes while she is alive, the sight of her corpse has an intense and lasting effect on him. Seeing the woman's body turned the boy into an artist. All the men in the search party were struck by her death, but the young boy was stunned even more deeply by the beauty and mystery of the scene. As the years pass, the image lingers in the back of his mind like faint, far-off music. Details accrue to that original vision, and the narrator begins linking fragments of memory and his own personal experience in an attempt to shape the strange experience into a comprehensible form. Hence, he emphasizes moments that resemble his own life, such as the time she spent with the German farmers and the incident with the dogs. These points of connection between the storyteller and subject make the woman's existence seem more recognizable and familiar. The narrator's dissatisfaction with his and his brother's limited, childish understanding of the event compels him to return to the story in adulthood and tell it until he gets it right. In Freudian terms (Anderson was an early reader of the psychoanalyst Sigmund Freud), the image in the woods functions as a kind of primal scene: a key event witnessed as a child that shapes and informs the adult psyche.

THE OLD WOMAN (MRS. GRIMES) Abused and ignored, Mrs. Grimes is a pathetic figure whose suffering is both cyclical and unrelenting. From her parents' death (which is implied yet not described in the story) to her servitude with the Germans, and continuing through her difficult, loveless marriage, the old woman continually experiences fresh traumas as she trades one set of harsh circumstances for another. Each incident in her life seems to be evidence of a greater truth—namely, that she was born to suffer. The narrator further implies that Mrs. Grimes is only one example of a larger category of people. Early on in the story, the narrator insists that the woman is "nothing special" and that most people living in rural areas in America have encountered such a woman. By then going on to describe this supposedly insignificant woman's harrowing life, the narrator implies that many more women like Mrs. Grimes exist on the fringes of society, unseen in their suffering.

As the narrator asserts, Mrs. Grimes is "destined to feed animal life." In each situation, it has been the woman's responsibility to feed the men and animals in her care. On the Germans' farm, she is expected to feed the farmer's sexual appetites. On her husband's farm, she spends all her energy scraping together enough food to keep her husband, son, and animals from starving. Even in death, the old woman continues to feed others. In the dogs' case, she literally feeds them, as they take advantage of her death to steal away the pack of meat she has been carrying on her back. Metaphorically, however, the old woman also feeds the narrator's imagination, as the beautiful, cryptic image of her white corpse continues to fuel the narrator's art long into his adulthood.

THEMES, MOTIFS, AND SYMBOLS

THEMES

THE DEVELOPMENT OF THE ARTIST Although "A Death in the Woods" is ostensibly about the life and death of Mrs. Grimes, it is probably more appropriate to say that the short story's true subject is the narrator's own growth and development as an artist. The old woman's death is a kind of artistic initiation, as the image of the corpse triggered an intense aesthetic reaction in the young boy. To him, the body was a beautiful object, more like a "white and lovely" marble statue than the shell of a formerly living human being. Years later, the image continues to fascinate and trouble him. Dissatisfied with the way his brother told the story when they were children, the mature narrator now tells the story again. He struggles to discern patterns and meaning in the factual details. What he doesn't know, he invents, using his personal memories and experiences—even those unconnected to Mrs. Grimes herself—to fill out his fictions.

In his attempt to understand how the sight of the old woman's corpse has managed to exert such a strong, mystical power over his imagination, the narrator blends fact, memory, and invention to create a work of art—namely, the short story "A Death in the Woods." Just as the narrator reveals more about himself than about Mrs. Grimes, the true subject of "A Death in the Woods" is the short story's own creation, not the titular event.

MOTIFS

FEEDING Throughout her life—beginning with the Germans and continuing through her married life and on through her death—the old woman's energies were entirely focused on procuring food for the men and animals under her care. In its mindless relentlessness, the woman's situation represents a cruel parody of motherhood. Mothers (and, by extension, women) are expected to be nurturing and nourishing figures, but this woman's role has been limited to the simple, biological task of feeding, without any of the positive emotional or spiritual elements generally attached to the maternal role. Near the end of the story, the narrator claims that the woman was the "one destined to feed animal life." The assertion that Mrs. Grimes was inherently "destined" to lead such an existence is debatable, but it is clear that the harsh events of her life have reduced her to this state. The story goes on to suggest that all women may, at some point, have to take up the role of feeder, as the narrator notes that if he and his brother arrive home late after viewing the dead woman's body, "either our mother or our older sister would have to warm up our supper."

CIRCLES Circles, which appear throughout the story, help develop the story's mystical, spiritual aspects. On her way back to the farm, the old woman happens upon a round clearing in the woods. Despite the approaching darkness, the woman lays down to rest, an action that seems even stranger given the fact that we have never seen her rest before: indeed, her life thus far has been one of painful, slow, perpetual motion. The feeling that the story has reached an uncanny, mysterious crux is heightened when the pack of dogs begins running in circles around the woman's sleeping form. The dogs revert to primitive, instinctual behavior, performing what the narrator calls "a kind of death ceremony." The round clearing in the woods and the ceremonial circular movements become part of a strange ritual, the precise meaning of which eludes the narrator, although it seems to imply both a purification and blessing of the dead woman. Years later, when attempting to make sense of the cryptic event, the story he tells is circular as well. Rather than recounting the events in a straightforward, linear fashion, "A Death in the Woods" continually doubles back on itself, moving back and forth in time and between perspectives as the narrator finds himself returning, repeatedly, to the mysterious event from his childhood.

SILENCE Each of the most noteworthy people and moments in "A Death in the Woods" are characterized by their pervasive silence. When the old woman dies in the clearing, for example, the eerie quiet that hangs over the scene—not to mention the townsmen's stunned, reverential silence—heightens both the mystery and the significance of the moment. Similarly, it is partially because of Mrs. Grimes's lifelong muteness that the narrator finds himself attracted to her in the first place. On one level, it emphasizes her dramatically harsh life and pathetic separation from the rest of human society, two elements that make the old woman a compelling and rich character. Yet her silence also creates an aura of mystery around her. The character of Mrs. Grimes doesn't speak in the story, just as her dead body will not metaphorically "speak" to the narrator when he wishes to discover its secret, essential meaning. It is the silence of both the character and the corpse that the narrator finds so provocative and that prompts him to ritually retell the tale of the "A Death in the Woods."

As the narrator constructs his version of the events, nearly all the characters become silent ones. There is little directly quoted dialogue in this story. When characters appear to speak, their dialogue is generally revealed to be an internal monologue that the narrator has conjectured and placed within quotation marks. Like an oral storyteller who acts out all the voices in a given tale, the narrator speaks for all the people in this story. The only character who has any true quoted dialogue is the rabbit hunter, who erroneously describes the woman's corpse to the search party. The narrator makes this single exception so that he can then go on to discredit the hunter's report, just as he will later reject his brother's version of the night's events, asserting his own tale as the truest, most accurate portrayal of the story.

SYMBOLS

THE BUGGY Jake Grimes's buggy, which makes two appearances in "A Death in the Woods," is a constant reminder of his wife's confinement. When, as a young woman, the future Mrs. Grimes is an indentured servant on the German couple's farm, Jake arrives on the buggy seeking harvest work. He quickly convinces the girl to "go riding with him in his buggy"—a phrase that suggests both illicit sexual activity and the potential of a liberating romance. Later, he uses the buggy to carry the girl away from her abusive masters. The buggy offers the young girl the promise of freedom and a new beginning, but it soon becomes clear that in marrying Jake, she has only managed to trade one violent man for another. The buggy, formerly an optimistic symbol of progress and movement, ultimately reinforces the idea that Mrs. Grimes is doomed to repeat established patterns of abuse. This idea is emphasized when, many years later, Jake and their son drive away from the Grimes's shabby farm in the buggy, leaving the old woman isolated and on the brink of starvation for days at a time.

THE OLD WOMAN'S CORPSE The old woman's corpse represents artistic inspiration. As a child, the narrator sees the body, and many years later, as an adult, he finds himself writing stories about the fleeting yet haunting image. The story demonstrates how a true artist finds insight in the most unlikely places, as the narrator transforms an isolated, seemingly random event into a richly dramatic and significant piece of art. In its undeniable beauty, the corpse also represents the essential dignity of all human beings. Even though Mrs. Grimes was destitute and nearly invisible in life, in death she is revealed as possessing power and grace. When the townsmen come upon her body, they are each stunned into silence. Faced with the corpse, the narrator finds himself trembling "with some strange mystical feeling." The image seems to be a hopeful one at first, as a cruel, traumatic life is redeemed by a final moment of beauty. But the fact that a living woman has become a lifeless object injects an ominous strain of darkness into the scene.

SHORT STORY ANALYSIS

REALISM AND NATURALISM   Although Anderson wrote "A Death in the Woods" decades after the high point of American realism (generally traced from the Civil War through the turn of the century), the story demonstrates several hallmarks of the movement, whose goal is to faithfully and accurately represent reality. Its characters are ordinary people engaged in plausible activities; the language is common and vernacular, rather than heightened or poetic; and character and psychology are emphasized over plot and action. However, certain elements of "A Death in the Woods" depart from the realist model. Though none of the events are fantastical or supernatural, a strong current of mysticism runs throughout the story, as the narrator attempts to understand how an ordinary event—the sight of an old woman's corpse—could become such an influential experience. This attempt leads him to imagine a surreal scene: a pack of dogs performing a mysterious death ritual. He even imagines dialogue between the dogs. Most realist fiction confines itself to objective observations as a way of capturing verisimilitude (the appearance of being true or real). However, by exploring the narrator's internal thoughts, Anderson achieves a form of psychological realism, which depicts not how life appears from the outside, but how it is experienced from the inside.

"A Death in the Woods" fits more squarely in the realm of naturalism. Inspired by the work of Charles Darwin, naturalism is both a philosophical position and a literary movement. Naturalist writers believe that human beings are not substantively different from animals: people are simply animals of a higher order. In this worldview, humans are governed by instinct, not morality, and their lives are determined by external forces such as heredity, environment, and circumstance. Naturalist literature stresses the loss of individuality and the difficulty of exercising free will in an indifferent world. The story of Mrs. Grimes is a classically naturalist tale: reduced to the basic, biological task of feeding her family and her animals, she is reduced to a wordless beast herself. The fact that she dies in the woods, rather than on her farmstead or in the town, emphasizes the sense that the entire natural world contributed to her death. However, Anderson's narrative style complicates the classification of this story as naturalist. Naturalist literature tends to involve a dispassionate, scientific study of humans. Although the narrator views Mrs. Grimes from a fairly detached perspective, he himself has a much greater freedom, which suggests that only the poor and wretched must suffer the cruelty of the natural world.

FORM VERSUS PLOT   Sherwood Anderson pushed American literature to new heights by emphasizing form over the more conventional plot as a method of structuring short fiction.

Plot-based stories follow a linear sequence of events that eventually build to a climax and often conclude with a moral. Anderson found such stories to be contrived and unnatural. As he states in his autobiography *A Story Teller's Story* (1924), "there were no plot short stories ever lived in any life I had known anything about." In his attempt to write fiction that reflected real Americans' lives and psyches, Anderson wrote in a naturalistic, colloquial prose style and experimented with story forms that emphasized theme, character, tone, and setting over actions and events.

"A Death in the Woods" is a plotless short story. It narrates a sequence of events—the life and death of Mrs. Grimes—but ultimately, that tale is only a pretext for the story's *true* narrative: the ways in which the narrator has become haunted by the image of the old woman's corpse in the snowy clearing. The psychological journey the narrator undertakes to unlock the meaning of that image provides the form of "A Death in the Woods." We follow the narrator's mental processes as he strings together a series of half-remembered, half-fictionalized images, skipping freely from the old woman's history to his own, from past to present. Rather than standing back from the material and presenting it objectively, the narrator continually calls attention to the role he is playing in shaping the work. Early on, for example, he announces his tale by saying, "I have just suddenly now, after all these years, remembered her and what happened. It is a story." This and other remarks make the narrator a vibrant, immediate presence. In the end, it is his psychological condition that we become invested in, not the silent Mrs. Grimes's.

THE GROTESQUE   In the character of the old woman, Anderson creates one of his most significant examples of the "grotesque," which features prominently in his fiction. The concept was first elucidated in "The Book of the Grotesque," the opening story in the collection *Winesburg, Ohio* (1916). Generally, the word *grotesque* describes something that is exaggerated or misshapen in a strange, disturbing fashion. Anderson used the term to describe a certain kind of character whom he felt had proliferated in the increasingly industrialized America of the late nineteenth and early twentieth centuries. Anderson's grotesque figures are isolated, misunderstood people who become fixated on a particular way of thinking or behaving, thereby diminishing their existences and ceasing to be fully human.

Living on the fringes of society, ignored and detested by her own family, the old woman has become isolated to the point where even basic verbal communication with other human beings has ceased. Her entire existence has been reduced to the notion that she is "destined to feed animal life." Beyond this single responsibility, the woman no longer has any discernible identity, an idea emphasized by the fact that she is "nothing special." Mrs. Grimes remains trapped in this concept up until the very moment of her death. Because of this spiritual and emotional confinement, she is never able to become a fully realized human being. Still, Anderson treats the old woman with a measure of love and respect. Although she is pitied for her wretchedness, she is also dignified by her commitment and steadfastness. In the end, however, the narrator is far more taken with the old woman as an image or object than he is with her as a person. In death, the woman becomes beautiful, but she never becomes fully human.

IMPORTANT QUOTATIONS EXPLAINED

---

1. *She had got the habit of silence anyway—that was fixed.*

This description of the old woman appears in Part II, as the narrator describes her life with Jake Grimes. He offers this "habit of silence" as a reason why the old woman doesn't interfere with her husband's and son's violent arguments. The woman's silence functions as a protective shield, keeping other people at bay—people who have proven to be nothing but abusive. The woman's silence also prevents her from establishing any close relationships with other people. In this woman's world, verbal communication—normally a source of comfort and intimacy—has become painful and harmful, and her choice to give it up is unfortunate but understandable. The quotation leaves the cause of the woman's silence ambiguous. On one hand, it seems as if the harsh realities of her life have ground the words out of her, transforming her into just another mute beast of burden. On the other hand, her silence may also be an active decision that she makes to disengage herself from a life that has damaged her. The woman's retreat into a purely internal state may represent an attempt to preserve an element of humanity in an otherwise animalistic existence.

---

2. *Starve, eh? Well, things had to be fed. Men had to be fed, and the horses that weren't any good but maybe could be traded off, and the poor thin cow that hadn't given any milk for three months.*
   Horses, cows, pigs, dogs, men.

In these lines, which appear at the end of Part II, the old woman reacts with "a look of mild surprise in her eyes" to the butcher's admonishment to keep the meat he has sold her from her husband and son. The passage represents the extent to which the woman has come to accept her position in life. She no longer questions or is surprised by her fate: she understands that, no matter how futile her attempts, she cannot stop feeding those who depend on her to do so. The final line of the passage emphasizes how, in the absence of any demonstrable love or affection from her husband and son, the two men have ceased to become fully human in her eyes: nothing separates them from the animals in her care.

The reference to the "horses that weren't any good" and "the poor thin cow" with no milk also reminds us that the woman, like the farm animals, is a creature defined by her ability to perform work. Like these animals, the woman cannot (or perhaps chooses not to) look beyond her given role, and her resolute dedication to her responsibilities is both pathetic and admirable. The harsh nature of Mr. and Mrs. Grimes's shared existence ends up dehumanizing each of them in turn.

---

3. *A thing so complete has its own beauty.*

This line appears near the end of the story, when the narrator claims that both he and his brother were too young to really get the point of the old woman's death. It is unclear what exactly the word *thing* refers to in this sentence. On one hand, it suggests the woman's life, which has now been "completed." Although the woman's existence was one of pain and suffering, death gives us perspective on her life. By taking a step back from the harshness of her day-to-day existence, we can better appreciate the woman's essential humanity. Previously, her life was characterized by intense lack. As a complete entity, however, it achieves a wholeness and integrity that makes it both perfect and beautiful.

The word *complete* implies something that is closed off and, therefore, fixed and unchangeable. Death becomes a protective barrier for the woman, who finds peace when she is no longer subject to the abuse of others. The image of the woman's corpse—the same image that has lodged in the narrator's memory and that he has spent years trying to make sense of—can also be understood as a "complete," sealed object that possesses "its own beauty." The story's central symbol remains mysterious and cryptic and therefore alluring to the narrator. The fact that the image seems to keep its own secrets lends it an air of beauty.

D

The Death of Ivan Ilych

Leo Tolstoy
(1828–1910)

CONTEXT

Count Lev (Leo) Nikolaevich Tolstoy is widely recognized as Russia's premier novelist and one of the world's greatest literary figures. He was born to a wealthy landowning family in Russia on September 9, 1828, but spent most of his formative years with relatives after his parents' untimely deaths. He later studied law and Oriental languages at Kazan University, but he dropped out and returned home before earning his degree. His excessive drinking, gambling, and sexual escapades as a young Russian nobleman left him with a sexually transmitted disease and sizeable debts by his mid-twenties. He eventually left home with his brother and joined an artillery regiment in the Russian army in the 1850s. He first began writing while fighting in the Crimean War.

All of Tolstoy's early work is considered realist fiction because it attempts to accurately portray society, politics, and personal struggle. After suffering from depression in the 1870s, however, his writing turned to philosophical and religious themes. Tolstoy emerged from the depression with new faith in a form of Christianity that renounced violence and praised pacifism. His beliefs consequently pitted him against the ruling czar's militarism, earned him a reputation as an anarchist, and ultimately led to his excommunication from the Orthodox Church. Nevertheless, he continued to believe that individuals should seek happiness within themselves rather than in the church or society, a theme clearly evident in his short story "The Death of Ivan Ilych," which concerns a man who lives as a passive spectator of his own life until the moment before his death.

As one concerned with social injustice, Tolstoy had a deep respect for the peasants of Russia and felt that the poor suffered from the luxurious lifestyles of the wealthy landowners. In fact, Tolstoy felt guilty that he lived as one of the wealthiest members of the land-owning elite and therefore chose to support the peasantry in the many class upheavals that erupted throughout the latter half of the nineteenth century. He eventually opened a school for the peasants who worked his land and grew to admire their courage, spirit, and faith. His radical beliefs and distaste for the class system made him a hero in the eyes of the millions of Russian serfs and working classes and thus made him virtually untouchable. Not even the ruling czar felt it safe to publicly rebuke him.

Despite his initial happiness after marrying Sofya Andreevna Behrs in 1862 and having thirteen children over the subsequent years, Tolstoy's love soon turned to angst as their marriage withered. He used this experience as the basis for "The Death of Ivan Ilych," also incorporating his disgust about Russian social norms and his respect for the lower classes. This was the first story he wrote after his religious and philosophical reawakening, and many literary scholars consider it one of his best. Like his protagonist, Ivan Ilych, Tolstoy was eventually so disgusted with society that he abandoned his family, titles, and worldly possession (in 1910, at age eighty-two). Tragically, he contracted pneumonia and died at a remote train station, just days after leaving home.

Tolstoy's body of work has had a profound impact on Russia and the world. His call to abandon the class system, for example, affected revolutionaries like Vladimir Lenin, who toppled the czar and the Russian aristocracy in 1917. Perhaps more important, his writings also influenced peaceful activists such as Mohandas Gandhi and Martin Luther King, Jr., who applied Tolstoy's belief in nonviolent protest to their own struggles for freedom and equality.

PLOT OVERVIEW

Tolstoy's story begins in a private room where friends and colleagues of Justice Ivan Ilych have gathered to discuss a legal case. While perusing the daily paper, one man, Piotr Ivanovich, discovers that Ivan Ilych has died. Each of the men in the room privately hopes for a promotion to fill the now-empty position and also thinks of the tiresome obligations of attending the funeral ceremony and paying respects to Ivan Ilych's family.

Piotr Ivanovich pays his respects at Ivan Ilych's home, but he feels awkward and unsure of how to act or what to say. Ivan Ilych's widow, Praskovya Fiodorovna, greets Piotr Ivanovich and beckons him to join her in the drawing room. Piotr Ivanovich secretly fears that he will now have to stay longer than initially expected and will miss his weekly card game as a result. Praskovya Fiodorovna feigns grief, trying to find out from him whether she can extract more pension money from the government. Piotr Ivanovich, recognizing her insincerity, tells her that she cannot receive any more money and sneaks out to make it to his card game.

Tolstoy then takes readers back in time to relate the key events of Ivan Ilych's life. After finishing law school and years of work, Ivan Ilych eventually becomes a public prosecutor. He schmoozes with the right people in the important political circles and always does everything deemed appropriate by the social norms of the day. He marries Praskovya Fiodorovna, a pretty girl from a well-connected family, primarily because it seems appropriate and agreeable to everyone else. The couples lives happily for a while until Praskovya Fiodorovna becomes pregnant and transforms into a jealous and demanding woman. The change affects Ivan Ilych's leisure life, especially when Praskovya Fiodorovna's outbursts disrupt his card games with colleagues. Instead of addressing and resolving his wife's emotional grief, though, Ivan Ilych chooses to ignore the problem and devote more time to work to avoid her.

Ivan Ilych eventually gets a new job with a higher salary thanks to the help of a powerful friend. The family relocates to Petersburg, and Ivan Ilych takes great joy in decorating his new home, believing it to be both special and *comme il faut* (proper according to society). In reality, his house looks the same as all the other houses owned by people trying to appear wealthy. While hanging new curtains, he falls off a ladder and bruises his side, but he passes off the pain as a minor inconvenience because his family appreciates the new décor. For a time, they all live happily together again.

Soon, however, Ivan Ilych begins to feel uncomfortable pressure in his side and develops a strange taste in his mouth. When the discomfort turns to pain, he visits a doctor, who suspects damage to the kidney or the appendix. Despite treatments, the pain worsens. Ivan Ilych visits several more doctors, but each of them reaches different conclusions.

When Praskovya Fiodorovna's brother visits the family, he is shocked by Ivan Ilych's deathly appearance. After yet another visit to a doctor, Ivan Ilych feels better, but he can't help remembering his brother-in-law's initial surprise. For the first time, he realizes that he might die. He first sinks into depression and then tries to ignore both the constant nagging pain and the possibility of death. Nevertheless, Ivan Ilych can't stop thinking about death. Instead of feeling sorrow, pity, or sympathy for Ivan Ilych, his family and household servants can't wait until he dies and relieves them of the burden of taking care of him.

Ivan Ilych begins to resent and even despise his wife, who patronizes him and seems to think he is exaggerating his illness. In contrast, a servant named Gerasim shows great sympathy for Ivan Ilych's situation and faithfully stays with him through the night. Gerasim explains that it is a pleasant duty to be able to comfort a dying man. Ivan Ilych's son, Vladimir, also displays pity for his father and is clearly upset by his suffering.

Ivan Ilych begins to struggle with feelings that he has wasted his life. Most of his memories after his childhood seem worthless because he ignored his own desires and thoughtlessly pursued what society deemed appropriate. He ponders the meaning of life and believes that discovering the answer would ease his suffering. These thoughts bring terrible mental anguish that grieves him more than the physical pain.

D

As death draws nearer, Ivan Ilych cracks from the intense agony and regret. The house fills with his screams, which continue for three days. He flails his arms and shrieks desperately until his son kisses his hand and bursts into tears. Ivan Ilych realizes that despite a life full of mistakes, he is still alive and should now try to live according to his own desires. He feels immense pity for both his son and wife, who has now joined him by his deathbed. He also realizes that his death will alleviate their own suffering and tries to ask for their forgiveness.

Believing that he is finally living as he should, Ivan Ilych's pain immediately dissipates along with his fear of death. "Death is finished," he says and then stretches out and dies.

CHARACTER LIST

Ivan Ilych   The protagonist of the story. Ivan Ilych serves as a respected judge until an internal injury weakens and eventually kills him. As he dies, he begins to reevaluate his life and realizes that he should have lived as he wanted rather than as how society wanted. Confronting death in his final hours transforms and ultimately saves him. For the first time, he feels compassion and sympathy for others, but he also concludes that dying is the best thing he can do for his family.

Praskovya Fiodorovna   Ivan Ilych's wife. Praskovya Fiodorovna is a sweet, pretty, well-connected girl from a good family, and Ivan Ilych marries her primarily because it seems the appropriate thing to do. They live happily together until Praskovya Fiodorovna becomes pregnant. She becomes disagreeable and jealous and thinks only of money and status, even after Ivan Ilych's death. Her character represents the selfishness and hypocrisy of the entire social elite.

Gerasim   A lowly servant in Ivan Ilych's household. Gerasim feel sympathy for his master and comforts him when no one else will. He stays with Ivan Ilych throughout the night to elevate his legs and keep him company because he knows that he too will one day require help in his old age. Tolstoy uses the character of Gerasim to laud Russia's peasantry and vilify the upper classes.

Piotr Ivanovich   Ivan Ilych's childhood friend, who attends Ivan Ilych's funeral primarily because he feels that social conventions demand he do so. Praskovya Fiodorovna corners Piotr Ivanovich at the funeral and asks if she can extract any more pension money from the government. Annoyed, he tells her that she cannot and then leaves the funeral early to play a game of cards with his colleagues. His callousness, selfishness, and emotional emptiness typify the entire social elite.

Vladimir (Vassya)   Ivan Ilych's son. Vladimir and the servant Gerasim are the only characters who show any compassion for Ivan Ilych. His kindness prompts Ivan Ilych to feel compassion for others for the first time in his life and rekindles his desire to live.

Schwartz   A colleague of Ivan Ilych and Piotr Ivanovich. Schwartz calls on the house after Ivan Ilych's death but feels no compulsion to stay long. He takes his leave before the funeral service to attend his weekly card game.

Fiodr Vassilyevich   A colleague of Ivan Ilych.

Liza   Ivan Ilych's daughter.

Fiodr Petrovich Petrishchev   The magistrate who courts Ivan Ilych's daughter Liza.

Piotr   The footman.

Zahar Ivanovich   A powerful acquaintance who offers Ivan Ilych a promotion in Petersburg.

ANALYSIS OF MAJOR CHARACTERS

IVAN ILYCH   Ivan Ilych spends his entire adult life trying to live up to unrealistic social expectations and nearly dies without experiencing a single meaningful moment. In Tolstoy's words, his life was "most simple, most ordinary, and therefore most terrible." He consistently denies his own interests, passions, and desires to achieve the niceties and trappings of high society, such as nice houses, the perfect marriage, money, and prestige. Sometimes this self-denial proves advantageous: he never abuses his position as a powerful magistrate, spends long hours working to achieve success, and has the admiration of his family. On the other hand, his blind adherence to social norms and customs compromises his soul. As a young man, for example, he did things he personally considered "horrid" that made him feel disgusted with himself. Yet he always chose to ignore his conscience because none of his peers seemed to mind. He later studies law in his father's footsteps and marries Praskovya Fiodorovna primarily to win the esteem of those around him. He has no convictions of his own and always does what others expect him to do.

Tolstoy uses pleasant but blasé adjectives such as *intelligent, polished, agreeable, lively, sociable, capable, cheerful,* and *good-natured* to highlight Ivan Ilych's shallowness. Although it would be admirable to be known for one or several of these traits, being known for all of them suggests weakness of character and lack of depth or texture. Tolstoy even writes that Ivan Ilych willingly adopts the ways and opinions of the powerful people around him. These adjectives therefore dehumanize Ivan Ilych by making him seem perfect—*too* perfect. He lacks the internal struggles, dialogue, conflict, and self-doubt that normal people experience. As a result, readers never truly get to know the real Ivan Ilych, who never even really gets to know himself.

PRASKOVYA FIODOROVNA Praskovya Fiodorovna's deceitfulness and hypocrisy make her the least likeable character in "The Death of Ivan Ilych," and Tolstoy intends her to represent the entire Russian gentry. Her marriage to Ivan Ilych initially makes them both happy, but their relationship turns sour when she becomes pregnant within the first year. They bicker constantly, and she often makes fun of her husband in front of his colleagues. Instead of addressing the causes of her anger, Ivan Ilych chooses to ignore the problems, hoping they'll disappear on their own. Praskovya Fiodorovna becomes fixated with money, spending more than Ivan Ilych earns and complaining about the difference. Her superficiality and refusal to face death disgust Ivan Ilych and rouse an urge within him to live a better life. He associates her with the entire upper class: inconsiderate, unfeeling drones who live only for the dictates of society.

While Ivan Ilych lives in agony during the final months of his life, Praskovya Fiodorovna appropriates his suffering in a continual effort to play the victim. She makes self-pitying remarks to others about the grief that his illness caused her, even remarking to Piotr Ivanovich how much she suffered from Ivan Ilych's final screams. Yet one suspects that Praskovya Fiodorovna isn't entirely devoid of humanity. Even after seventeen years of a poor marriage, for example, she and her husband still have "rare periods of amorousness." And in his final minutes, Ivan Ilych even notices genuine tears on her nose and anguish in her eyes, which suggest she has the potential to one day find salvation too.

THEMES, MOTIFS, AND SYMBOLS

THEMES

THE EMPTINESS OF THE LIVES OF THE SOCIAL ELITE All of Tolstoy's wealthier characters in "The Death of Ivan Ilych" live meaningless lives devoid of any humanity. Ivan Ilych, for example, lives in denial of his true desires, striving only to increase his wealth, power, and prestige within society. All the choices he makes as an adult, from the woman he marries to the furnishings in his house, are made to conform to social conventions. Never once does he follow a dream, act upon a conviction, or even form his own opinions. Instead, he strives only to fulfill the duties that others dictate to him. In this sense Ivan Ilych is no different from his wife, Praskovya Fiodorovna, or his friend Piotr Ivanovich, both of whom Tolstoy uses to represent the vacuous social elite of Russian society who lack any compassion for others.

The only character who does feel sympathy and compassion for others is Ivan Ilych's household servant, Gerasim. Despite his lower social standing, he alone understands the greater significance of life and has the requisite maturity to contemplate the meaning of death. He comforts and stays with Ivan Ilych when no one else will, knowing that he too will one day need care in his old age. Gerasim's humanity contrasts sharply with the barren lives of the social elite and highlights Tolstoy's affinity for the hardworking lower classes.

DEATH AS SALVATION   Despite the obvious fact that death is unavoidable, most characters in the story try to convince themselves otherwise and consequently miss the opportunity
to see death as a chance for salvation. In the opening scene, for example, Ivan Ilych's colleagues callously perceive his death as unfortunate but trivial, and they fail to use the experience to reflect on their own mortality or life's greater meaning. Meanwhile, Ivan Ilych's wife
and daughter simply ignore the fact that he is dying. In fact, for them his illness is more
of an inconvenience and annoyance than a tragedy. Their inability to confront reality only
intensifies Ivan Ilych's suffering. Contemplating the prospect of death, however, does spark
a reawakening and transformation in Ivan Ilych, who begins to appreciate life and feels compassion for others. In this respect, dying becomes a positive experience for Ivan Ilych and
ultimately brings salvation. Tolstoy uses Ivan Ilych to convince readers that the inevitability of
death should serve as an incentive to follow one's own heart while living. Moreover, like all
Christians, Tolstoy perceived death as more of a new beginning than a final ending.

MOTIFS

LONELINESS   Most of the characters in the social elite, including Praskovya Fiodorovna,
Piotr Ivanovich, and even Ivan Ilych himself, value power and position over more meaningful human relationships, which leads to widespread loneliness. Ivan Ilych never mentions
his loneliness or is even consciously aware of it, but his interactions with Gerasim illustrate
his sense of alienation. When Gerasim enters his chamber, for example, Ivan Ilych finds reasons to keep him there. He finds Gerasim's presence and sympathy comforting when none of
his own family members can stand being near him. Despite his intense loneliness, however,
Ivan Ilych is also guilty of alienating others. He too has acted cold and distant, especially toward his own wife when he decided to spend more time at work rather than address his marital problems. Praskovya Fiodorovna is therefore as much of a victim of loneliness as her husband, which is why she grows increasingly hostile to Ivan Ilych throughout their marriage.

REVERSAL   Inversion and reversal appear throughout "The Death of Ivan Ilych," challenging the typical notion of narrative direction and progress to examine time and life in an
unconventional way. The story opens after Ivan Ilych has died, thus establishing death as a
beginning rather than an end. Ivan Ilych's ironic realization that dying will bring meaning
to his lonely life further suggests that death is a kind of salvation—and a new beginning.
Ivan Ilych's values are completely overturned as well. He realizes on his deathbed that the
quality of his life steadily declined as he worked to achieve success. As a result, the money,
possession, and prestige he once valued ultimately brought him the destitution he'd worked
so hard to avoid. In his final hours, however, he experiences an even greater reversal: the
realization that dying will finally bring meaning to his otherwise wasted life.

SYMBOLS

LIGHT AND DARKNESS   The darkness that Ivan Ilych perceives in death represents his
despair, regret, and, most important, fear of death. During his final hours, he feels as if he is
being buried alive by a relentless, invisible force stuffing him into the black hole of an open
sack. Light replaces the darkness, however, when he finally decides to confront death to ease

the suffering of those around him. The light he seeks symbolizes life and happiness. Ironically, Ivan Ilych reaches the light after falling through his black hole of despair, realizing that he still has time to live as he should have without regard to what others may think or want. The long, spiraling funnel downward thus becomes an unexpected tunnel upward toward redemption and salvation, suggesting that only by confronting death can one achieve true peace of mind.

MATERIAL OBJECTS The material objects that Ivan Ilych loves symbolize his own polished existence as a prized member of high society devoid of humanity and real worth. Throughout the story, Ivan Ilych constantly surrounds himself with luxury goods, such as antiques, screens, Japanese plates, rugs, damasks, bronzes, expensive cakes, and wines. He uses these items in a subconscious attempt to bring meaning to his life and fill the emptiness in his soul. Praskovya Fiodorovna; his daughter, Liza; and presumably the rest of Russia's upper crust do this as well so that their "drawing-rooms resembled all other drawing-rooms [as did their] enjoyable little parties resemble all other such parties." The absence of material goods in the lives of the peasants such as Gerasim conversely symbolizes their emotional and spiritual superiority over the social elite. Tolstoy's identification of material possessions as the cause of moral emptiness plagued him in his later years, until he finally renounced his wealth, land, and titles shortly before his death.

SHORT STORY ANALYSIS

THE MANIPULATION OF SPACE AND TIME Tolstoy manipulates space and time as the story unfolds to dramatize Ivan Ilych's final hours. The constriction of space, for example, gives readers the distressing sensation of claustrophobia and anxiety. In the opening chapters, Ivan Ilych moves frequently from province to province, constantly working to advance his career and increase his social standing. In time, however, he settles down, makes a home, and travels only within his town. Eventually, his world consists only of his study and then just his couch, as his health deteriorates in the final weeks of his life. Narrowing the scope of the story makes readers feel trapped along with Ivan Ilych.

The compression of time, meanwhile, accelerates readers toward the climax of the story as each subsequent chapter becomes shorter and shorter. Tolstoy devotes the first few chapters to entire decades of Ivan Ilych's life, passing over years of marriage as well as the births and deaths of his children. At one point, seventeen years pass by in a single sentence. Tolstoy then slows time dramatically as Ivan Ilych grows weaker, devoting later chapters to weeks and then finally to mere hours. To make this point even clearer, Tolstoy reduces the length of each chapter as the story progresses, making them pages long in the beginning but only paragraphs long by the end. As time slows, he describes Ivan Ilych's condition in greater detail, drawing out his death and magnifying the sense of pain and despair. Readers ultimately experience the agony of Ivan Ilych's final hours confined to his deathbed.

TOLSTOY'S WRITING AND CHRISTIAN BELIEFS "The Death of Ivan Ilych" blends elements from Tolstoy's older style of realistic fiction with the moralistic Christian principles he developed later in life. After a midlife bout with depression in the late 1870s, Tolstoy converted to a radical new form of Christianity based on Jesus' famous Sermon on the Mount, in which Jesus preached pacifism, selflessness, and finding happiness within oneself. Readers can see elements of his newfound faith in "The Death of Ivan Ilych," even though it may not initially seem like a story about Christianity. Death as salvation is a major theme that runs throughout the story, and the ideas of forgiveness and selflessness appear frequently as well. After realizing that he's made mistakes in his life, Ivan Ilych feels pity for his wife instead of hatred and doesn't seek revenge for years of hypocrisy and jealousy. It is on his deathbed when he also finally places the needs of others above his own and chooses death to make his family's life better. In this sense, Ivan Ilych becomes a Christlike figure in the final chapters, making the ultimate sacrifice to improve the lives of others.

Tolstoy divides his story into twelve segments, which in many ways mimic some of the Roman Catholic Stations of the Cross to further draw the comparison between Ivan Ilych and Christ. Roman Catholic and Orthodox Christians use the Stations of the Cross to trace Jesus' final steps from trial to crucifixion. At the first station, for example, Jesus is sentenced to death—just as readers learn that Ivan Ilych has died in the first segment of Tolstoy's story. The second stage and second segment respectively detail Jesus' burden carrying the cross and Ivan Ilych's burden living a dull life. The third stage and segment represent their fall as Jesus stumbles under the weight of the cross and Ivan Ilych stumbles off the footstool. Although the successive segments of the story don't follow the Stations of the Cross exactly, including the fact that there are actually a total of fourteen Stations of the Cross, enough similarities exist to suggest that their parallel structures are not accidental. Moreover, both Ivan Ilych and Christ finally die at the twelfth stratum with the words "It is finished." Mimicking the segments of the story on the Stations of the Cross transforms the deeply flawed Ivan Ilych into a martyr and an example for humanity.

DEPICTING THE EXPERIENCE OF DEATH   "The Death of Ivan Ilych" is remarkable for the way in which it takes the reader through the experience of death. Ivan Ilych's pain, for example, becomes an all-consuming specter called *It* that torments him: *It* would "stand" before him and "look" at him, *It* would penetrate his thoughts, and *It* would nearly drive him insane. Ivan Ilych's struggle to give his life meaning and confrontation with death force the reader to do the same: to realize that death is inevitable and live fully in this knowledge. Tolstoy, however, avoids condescension and preaching and doesn't sacrifice the quality of the story to convey this message. He simply places the reader in the mind of a dying man racked with guilt about his wasted life. Tolstoy also uses Ivan Ilych's death to explore the final moments of life. By the end of the story, Ivan Ilych is in an almost dreamlike state, perceiving his family's presence but unable to communicate. His inner thoughts seem both confident and childlike, as when he realizes that he is dying and exclaims, "So that's where [death] is! What joy!" Tolstoy also manipulates the perception of time throughout the story, climaxing with Ivan Ilych's enlightenment in the few seconds before his death. Although his death drags on for two hours, the time passes almost instantaneously for Ivan Ilych, bringing the reader to the edge of the experience of death.

IMPORTANT QUOTATIONS EXPLAINED

1. *Besides the reflections upon the transfers and possible changes in the department likely to result from Ivan Ilych's decease, the mere fact of the death of an intimate associate aroused, as is usual, in all who heard of it a complacent feeling that "it is he who is dead, and not I."*

When Ivan Ilych's colleagues learn of his death, they first think about his empty position and what it will mean for their careers. To readers, these men appear selfish and uncaring. In fact, they are actually much like Ivan Ilych before his injury and illness. These men live according to social convention, desiring what others desire and striving to climb the social ladder without any regard for their own interests and passions. The death of Ivan Ilych does not elicit any deep contemplation from his colleagues. Not one of them ponders the stark reality of death or even mourns the permanent loss of their friend. In fact, they even refrain from reflecting on their own mortality. For them, death is merely an abstraction, something that happens to other people but not them. Ivan Ilych also thought this way until his illness forced him to confront the prospect of dying. When Ivan Ilych realizes the inevitability of his death, he begins to reflect on his life and examines the way in which he lived. Tolstoy's writes so that readers will examine their own lives as well.

2. *[E]verything [Gerasim did] showed that he alone understood the facts of the case, and did not consider it necessary to disguise them, and simply felt sorry for the sick, expiring master. On one occasion . . . he even said straight out: "We shall all of us die, so what's a little trouble?"*

Unlike the members of his own family, Ivan Ilych's servant Gerasim selflessly stays with him through the night, alleviating both his physical pain and mental anguish. Gerasim is the only character with sympathy for Ivan Ilych, who consequently invents reasons to keep him around. Gerasim's presence is comforting because he alone understands the seriousness of his master's illness and doesn't pretend otherwise. No other adult demonstrates such an honest awareness of the facts. Gerasim feels sorry for Ivan Ilych and keeps him company, helping him wash and sit more comfortably and providing emotional support. In addition, he does these things without regard to the rules of social decorum, unlike everyone else. Gerasim's actions and thoughts compared to Praskovya Fiodorovna's, for example, illustrate Tolstoy's opinion of the class system. He conveys his deep respect for the peasantry by showing Gerasim's noble, simple, and brave outlook on life. Unlike the characters in the social elite, Gerasim faces death, perceives its inevitability, and understands that everyone must confront his or her own mortality.

3. *"Let the pain be. And death? Where is it?"*

He searched for his former habitual fear of death and did not find it.

"Where is it? What death?" There was no fear because there was no death either. In place of death there was light.

While on his deathbed, Ivan Ilych agonizes over how he could have lived a more fulfilling life. He screams continuously during his final days from the mental anguish until his son Vladimir approaches. Vladimir's compassion rekindles Ivan Ilych's desire to live, but Ivan Ilych concludes that he should face death to end his suffering and the suffering of his family. Confronting death finally frees Ivan Ilych from the confines of social convention and allows him to live life according to his own desires. The pity and sympathy he feels for his wife and son also mark the first time Ivan Ilych feels emotion for others. For once he feels in control of his life and destiny, represented by the light that has replaced the darkness that surrounded him. A feeling of peace comes over Ivan Ilych as his fear of death subsides.

D

Everyday Use

Alice Walker
(1944–   )

CONTEXT

Born in rural Eatonton, Georgia, in 1944, Alice Walker was the youngest of eight children. When she was eight years old, she was blinded in one eye by a BB shot by one of her brothers. Although she eventually had surgery on her scar and became valedictorian of her high school, she endured teasing and low self-esteem throughout her childhood. She received a scholarship to Spelman College, a traditionally black college in Georgia, and left home with three things given to her by her mother, Minnie: a sewing machine to encourage self-sufficiency, a suitcase to nudge her curious spirit, and a typewriter to nurture her budding writing talents. Walker eventually left Spelman to attend Sarah Lawrence College in New York, from which she graduated in 1965.

Walker is a prolific writer, working in a variety of genres including children's literature, poetry, nonfiction, and screenwriting. She is best known for her novels and short stories, in which she gives voice to a doubly oppressed group: African American women. Her novel *The Color Purple* (1982) is perhaps her most well-known, winning the Pulitzer Prize in 1983 and inspiring a film adaptation.

A tireless crusader on behalf of women, much of Walker's fiction speaks out against domestic violence, sexual abuse, racism, and genital mutilation, a ritual practiced by several native African cultures. Her concerns differ from ordinary "feminist" concerns, and she calls herself a "womanist," committed to freeing women from all forms of oppression. Walker's fiction has been the subject of controversy, because some critics believe she depicts men too harshly (such as in *The Color Purple*) and criticizes practices that she does not fully understand (such as genital mutilation, the subject of her 1992 novel *Possessing the Secret of Joy*).

"Everyday Use," published as part of the short story collection *In Love and Trouble: Stories of Black Women* (1973), includes some of the preoccupations that recur in Walker's later work, such as a focus on women's lives and the interconnection of the past and present. The stories in this collection take place in settings ranging from Walker's home territory in the American South to the multicultural world of New York City to the east African nation of Uganda. Walker's protagonists are portrayed as victims, variously manipulated and used by husbands and lovers, white society, or their own depleted self-esteem. Most of the stories have unhappy endings or cautious resolutions based on quiet, hard-won truths. Critics have seen "Everyday Use" as standing out from the other stories in the collection, partly because of the protagonist's confidence in defending her family's legacy.

In the time the story is set, the late 1960s or early 1970s, black American life and identity were undergoing a radical transformation. After enduring slavery and the violence and discrimination that came with eventual freedom, African Americans gradually gained civil rights in the 1950s and 1960s. A new generation emerged, some eager to break with the horrors of the past and others unable to emerge from the specter of poverty and inequality.

"Everyday Use" hinges on the tension created when these two worlds come together. In the story, Walker examines the intense, serious, sometimes militant rhetoric that characterized some strains of the rising black consciousness movement. But she gives her most intense scrutiny to the often tenuous bonds between family members.

PLOT OVERVIEW

Mama decides that she will wait in the yard for her daughter Dee's arrival. Mama knows that her other daughter, Maggie, will be nervous throughout Dee's stay, self-conscious of her scars and burn marks and jealous of Dee's much easier life. Mama fantasizes about reunion scenes on television programs in which a successful daughter embraces the parents who have made her success possible. Sometimes Mama imagines reuniting with Dee in a similar scenario, in a television studio where an amiable host brings out a tearful Dee, who pins orchids on Mama's dress. Whereas Mama is sheepish about the thought of looking a white man in the eye, Dee is more assertive. Mama's musing is interrupted by Maggie's shuffling arrival in the yard. Mama remembers the house fire that happened more than a decade ago, when she carried Maggie, badly burned, out of the house. Dee watched the flames engulf the house she despised.

Back then, Mama believed that Dee hated Maggie, until Mama and the community raised enough money to send Dee to school in Augusta. Mama resented the intimidating world of ideas and education that Dee forced on her family on her trips home. Mama never went to school beyond second grade. Maggie can read only in a limited capacity. Mama looks forward to Maggie's marriage to John Thomas, after which Mama can peacefully relax and sing hymns at home.

When Dee arrives, Mama grips Maggie to prevent her from running back into the house. Dee emerges from the car with her boyfriend, Hakim-a-barber. Mama disapproves of the strange man's presence and is equally disapproving of Dee's dress and appearance. Hakim-a-barber greets and tries to hug Maggie, who recoils.

Dee gets a camera from the car and takes a few pictures of Mama and Maggie in front of their house. She then puts the camera on the backseat and kisses Mama on the forehead, as Hakim-a-barber awkwardly tries to shake Maggie's hand. Dee tells her mother that she has changed her name to Wangero Leewanika Kemanjo to protest being named after the people who have oppressed her. Mama tells Dee that she was in fact named after her Aunt Dicie, who was named after Grandma Dee, who bore the name of her mother as well. Mama struggles with the pronunciation of Dee's new African name. Dee says she doesn't have to use the new name, but Mama learns to say it, although she is unable to master Hakim's name. Mama says that he must be related to the Muslims who live down the road and tend beef cattle and also greet people by saying "Asalamalakim." Hakim-a-barber says he accepts some of their doctrines but is not into farming or herding.

Mama wonders whether Hakim-a-barber and Dee are married. Sitting down to eat, Hakim-a-barber states that he does not eat collard greens or pork. Dee, however, eats heartily, delighted by the fact that the family still uses the benches her father made. Hopping up, she approaches the butter churn in the corner and asks Mama if she can have its top, which had been carved by Uncle Buddy. Dee wants the dasher too, a device with blades used to make butter. Hakim-a-barber asks if Uncle Buddy whittled the "dash" as well, to which Maggie replies that it was Aunt Dee's first husband, Stash, who made it. Dee praises Maggie's memory and wraps the items. Mama grips the handle of the dasher, examining the ruts and worn areas made by her relative's hands.

Dee ransacks the trunk at the foot of Mama's bed, reappearing with two quilts made by her mother, aunt, and grandmother. The quilts contain small pieces of garments worn by relatives all the way back to the Civil War. Dee asks her mother for the quilts. Mama hears Maggie drop something in the kitchen and then slam the door. Mama suggests that Dee take other quilts, but Dee insists, wanting the ones hand-stitched by her grandmother. Mama gets up and tries to tell Dee more about the garments used to make the quilts, but Dee steps out of reach. Mama reveals that she had promised Maggie the quilts. Dee gasps, arguing that Maggie won't appreciate the quilts and isn't smart enough to preserve them. But Mama hopes that Maggie does, indeed, designate the quilts for everyday use.

Dee says that the priceless quilts will be destroyed. Mama says that Maggie knows how to quilt and can make more. Maggie shuffles in and, trying to make peace, offers Dee the quilts. When Mama looks at Maggie, she is struck by a strange feeling, similar to the spirit she feels sometimes in church. Impulsively, she hugs Maggie, pulls her into the room, snatches the quilts out of Dee's hands, and places them in Maggie's lap. She tells Dee to take one or two of the other quilts. As Dee and Hakim-a-barber leave, Dee informs Mama that Mama does not understand her own heritage. Kissing Maggie, Dee tells her to try and improve herself and that it's a new day for black Americans. Mama and Maggie watch the car drive off, then sit in the quiet of the yard until bedtime.

CHARACTER LIST

Mama   The narrator of the story. Mama describes herself as a big-boned woman with hands that are rough from years of physical labor. She wears overalls and has been both mother and father to her two daughters. Poor and uneducated, she was not given the opportunity to break out of her rural life. A loving mother, her frank, open nature prevents her from deluding herself when it comes to her daughters' weaknesses. Mama has a strong understanding of her heritage and won't allow Dee to take the family quilts.

Maggie   The shy, retiring daughter who lives with Mama. Burned in a house fire as a young girl, Maggie lacks confidence and shuffles when she walks, often fleeing or hanging in the background when there are other people around, unable to make eye contact. She is good-hearted, kind, and dutiful. Rather than anger her intimidating sister, she is willing to let Dee have the quilts that had originally been promised to her.

Dee   Mama's older daughter, who has renamed herself Wangero Leewanika Kemanjo. Dee wears a brightly colored, yellow-and-orange, ankle-length dress that is inappropriate for the warm weather. Her hair stands up straight on top and is bordered by two long pigtails that hang down in back. Dee is educated, worldly, and deeply determined, not generally allowing her desires to be thwarted. When Mama won't let her have the quilts to display, she becomes furious. She claims that Mama and Maggie don't understand their heritage, but she is the one overlooking the important aspects of her family history.

Hakim-a-barber   Dee's boyfriend or, possibly, husband. Hakim-a-barber is a Black Muslim whom Mama humorously refers to as Asalamalakim, the Arab greeting he offers them, meaning "peace be with you." An innocuous presence, he is a short and stocky, with waist-length hair and a long, bushy beard. His desire to make a good first impression makes him seem awkward. He makes Maggie uncomfortable by forcing his attention and greetings on her.

ANALYSIS OF MAJOR CHARACTERS

MAMA Mama, the narrator of the story, is a strong, loving mother who is sometimes threatened and burdened by her daughters, Dee and Maggie. Gentle and stern, her inner monologue offers us a glimpse of the limits of a mother's unconditional love. Mama is brutally honest and often critical in her assessment of both Dee and Maggie. She harshly describes shy, withering Maggie's limitations, and Dee provokes an even more pointed evaluation. Mama resents the education, sophistication, and air of superiority that Dee has acquired over the years. Mama fantasizes about reuniting with Dee on a television talk show and about Dee expressing gratitude to Mama for all Mama has done for her. This brief fantasy reveals the distance between the two—and how underappreciated Mama feels. Despite this brief daydream, Mama remains a practical woman with few illusions about how things are.

Just as Dee embraces an alternative persona when she renames herself "Wangero," Mama rejected a traditional gender role when she worked to raise and provide for her daughters and took on an alternative, masculine persona. She is proud of her hardy nature and ability to butcher hogs and milk cows. In the story, she literally turns her back on the house, the traditionally female space. She feels that it confines her too much. Despite her willingness to operate outside of conventions, Mama lacks a broad view of the world and is, to some extent, intimidated by Dee. She doesn't understand Dee's life, and this failure to understand leads her to distrust Dee. Dee sees her new persona as liberating, whereas Mama sees it as a rejection of her family and her origins. It is not surprising that she names familiar Maggie as the caretaker of the family's heritage.

MAGGIE Nervous and maladjusted, Maggie is a figure of purity, uncorrupted by selfishness or complex emotional needs. Severely burned in a house fire when she was a child, her scarred, ugly appearance hides her sympathetic, generous nature. She lives at home and is protected by Mama, remaining virtually untouched by the outside world. As much as her homebound isolation protects her, she is also a victim of this seclusion: she suffers from a crippling shyness and lack of education. Maggie moves with a meek, shuffling gait and hovers awkwardly in doorways rather than getting involved in life around her. Although Mama mentions that Maggie is going to marry John Thomas, it is doubtful that even a marriage will help Maggie become a strong and clearly defined individual. Mama, protective as she is of Maggie, is frank about her shortcomings and problems.

Maggie's relationship with Dee is rife with jealousy and awe. Mama recalls how Maggie had always thought Dee had been gifted with an easy life in which her hopes and desires were rarely, if ever, frustrated. Maggie seems to have taken both sisters' difficulties onto her own shoulders, and although she never says explicitly that she finds it unfair, she clearly thinks so. The only time Maggie reveals the extent of her innermost desires is when Dee attempts to take the quilts that Mama had promised to Maggie. Maggie drops plates in the kitchen and then slams the door, outraged. Later, although she tries to win Dee's favor by giving up the quilts, her reluctance to do so stirs pity and anger in Mama. Maggie does have a will, and although it is buried deep inside her, it comes through when what she desires most in the world is about to be taken away.

DEE Dee is the object of jealousy, awe, and agitation among her family members, while as an individual she searches for personal meaning and a stronger sense of self. Dee's judgmental nature has affected Mama and Maggie, and desire for Dee's approval runs deep in both of them—it even appears in Mama's daydreams about a televised reunion. However, Dee does not make much of an effort to win the approval of Mama and Maggie. Unflappable, not easily intimidated, and brimming with confidence, Dee comes across as arrogant and insensitive, and Mama sees even her admirable qualities as extreme and annoying. Mama sees Dee's thirst for knowledge as a provocation, a haughty act through which she asserts her superiority over her mother and sister. Dee is also portrayed as condescending, professing her commitment to visit Mama and Maggie no matter what ramshackle shelter they decide to inhabit. Far from signaling a brand-new Dee or truly being an act of resistance, the new persona, Wangero, comes across as an attention-seeking ploy in keeping with Dee's usual selfishness. Dee says she is reclaiming her heritage, but she has actually rejected it more violently than ever before.

Through Dee, Walker challenges individuals—including activists, separatists, or otherwise—who ignore or reject their heritage. These people prefer to connect themselves to an idealized Africa instead of to the lessons and harsh realities that characterized the black experience in America. Dee and Hakim-a-barber are aligned with the abstract realm of ideology, which contrasts starkly with the earthy, physical, labor-intensive lifestyle of Mama and Maggie. Dee is intrigued by their rustic realism, snapping photographs as though they are subjects of a documentary, and in doing so effectively cuts herself off from her family. Instead of honoring and embracing her roots, Dee looks down on her surroundings, believing herself to be above them.

THEMES, MOTIFS, AND SYMBOLS

THEMES

THE MEANING OF HERITAGE Angered by what she views as a history of oppression in her family, Dee has constructed a new heritage for herself and rejected her real heritage. She fails to see the family legacy of her given name and takes on a new name, Wangero, which she believes more accurately represents her African heritage. However, the new name, like the "African" clothes and jewelry she wears to make a statement, is meaningless. She has little true understanding of Africa, so what she considers her true heritage is actually empty and false. Furthermore, Dee views her real heritage as dead, something of the past, rather than as a living, ongoing creation. She desires the carved dasher and family quilts, but she sees them as artifacts of a lost time, suitable for display but not for actual, practical use. She has set herself outside her own history, rejecting her real heritage in favor of a constructed one.

Mama and Dee have very different ideas about what "heritage" is, and for Mama, the family objects are infused with the presence of the people who made and used them. The family heirlooms are the true tokens of Dee's identity and origins, but Dee knows little about the past. She misstates the essential facts about how the quilts were made and what fabrics were used to make them, even though she pretends to be deeply connected to this folk tradition.

Her desire to hang the quilts, in a museumlike exhibit, suggests that she feels reverence for them but that to her they are essentially foreign, impersonal objects. Mama understands that Maggie, not Dee, should have the quilts, because Maggie will respect them by using them in the way they were intended to be used. When Dee contends at the end of the story that Mama and Maggie do not understand their heritage, Walker intends the remark to be ironic: clearly, it is Dee herself who does not understand her heritage.

THE DIVISIVE POWER OF EDUCATION   Although Mama struggled to send Dee to a good school, education proves to be more divisive than beneficial to Dee's relationship with her family. Mama herself was denied an education. When she was a child, her school was closed, and no one attempted to try to reopen it. Racism, passive acceptance, and forces beyond her control set Mama on the road that led to her life of toil. Dee was fortunate that Mama gave her the opportunity for advantages and refinements, but they have served only to create a wedge between Dee and the rest of the family. Dee uses her intellect to intimidate others, greeting her mother with "Wa-su-zo Tean-o," a greeting in an obscure African language Mama most likely doesn't speak. Dee, with her knowledge and worldliness, is a threat to the simple world Mama and Maggie inhabit, and Dee seems determined to lord her knowledge over them. Even as a child, Dee read to her mother and sister "without pity," "forcing" strange ideas on them and unsettling their simple domestic contentment.

Education has separated Dee from her family, but it has also separated Dee from a true sense of self. With lofty ideals and educational opportunity came a loss of a sense of heritage, background, and identity, which only family can provide. Dee arrives at the family home as a strange, threatening ambassador of a new world, a world that has left Maggie and Mama behind. Civil rights, greater visibility, and zero tolerance for inequality are characteristics of Dee's world. These things are not, in and of themselves, problematic. What's problematic is that Dee has no respect for anything *but* her world, leading her to alienate herself from her roots. Maggie, on the other hand, knows no world but the one she came from. Uneducated, she can read only haltingly. By doing what she is told and accepting the conditions of her sheltered life without question, Maggie has hampered her own self-fulfillment. Walker sets up this contrast to reveal an ironic contradiction: Dee's voracious quest for knowledge has led to her alienation from her family, while the lack of education has harmed and stifled Maggie. Both education and the lack of it have proven to be dangerous for the sisters.

MOTIFS

EYE CONTACT AND EYESIGHT   Throughout the story, the presence or absence of eye contact and strong eyesight reveals the difficulty that Mama, Dee, and Maggie have in relating to one another and, in Maggie and Mama's case, to the outside world. Mama is unable to look a white person in the eye, suggesting that she has never managed to embrace the idea of equality, whereas Dee can do so easily. Maggie can't look anyone in the eye at all, hanging her head as she walks, portraying herself as a silent victim. In describing Maggie's ability to read, Mama says that Maggie does the best she can despite not being able to see well. This qualified vision is associated with a lack of intelligence or mental acuity. Walker describes Dee as wide-eyed, always taking in the world around her. During the house fire that happened when she was a child, she was transfixed by the flames consuming the home that, to her, represented ignorance and poverty. Mama claims Dee's attention was often so rapt that she would not blink for long stretches of time. Dee's easy eye contact and intense gazes reveal her critical, condescending nature. Soon after arriving at the family home, Dee and Hakim send "eye signals" to each other, silently registering their disdain for Mama and Maggie's simple, rustic world.

NAMING AND RENAMING The act of naming—or, in Dee's case, renaming—is a way of connecting to the past and an indication of the fluid nature of identity. Walker doesn't tell us the origins of Maggie's name, and Mama's name is never given, but we know that these two characters are unchanging and have strong ties to their heritage. It therefore makes sense that their names and identities are stable and unremarkable. Dee, on the other hand, attempts to transform herself and embrace what she considers her true heritage by adopting an African name. Her boyfriend, Hakim-a-barber, may have taken on his name for similar reasons, as he grew to embrace Muslim ideas. Renaming is a sign of these two characters' attempts to leave behind their true selves by taking on a new identity. Dee believes that the name *Wangero* holds more power and significance than *Dee*, the name passed down through four generations. Dee's belief that she was named after her oppressors shows a critical lack of understanding. Quick to judgment, she sees her given name as an emblem of a racist, abusive world, as opposed to a tribute to a long line of strong women. Dee's decision to take on a new name highlights the confused views she has of her own heritage.

SYMBOLS

QUILTS "Everyday Use" focuses on the bonds between women of different generations and their enduring legacy, as symbolized in the quilts they fashion together. This connection between generations is strong, yet Dee's arrival and lack of understanding of her history shows that those bonds are vulnerable as well. The relationship between Aunt Dicie and Mama, the experienced seamstresses who made the quilts, is very different from the relationship between Maggie and Dee, sisters who share barely a word and have almost nothing in common. Just as Dee cannot understand the legacy of her name, passed along through four generations, she does not understand the significance of the quilts, which contain swatches of clothes once worn or owned by at least a century's worth of ancestors.

The quilts are pieces of living history, documents in fabric that chronicle the lives of the various generations and the trials, such as war and poverty, that they faced. The quilts serve as a testament to a family's history of pride and struggle. With the limitations that poverty and lack of education placed on her life, Mama considers her personal history one of her few treasures. Her house contains the handicrafts of her extended family. Instead of receiving a financial inheritance from her ancestors, Mama has been given the quilts. For her, these objects have a value that Dee, despite professing her desire to care for and preserve the quilts, is unable to fathom.

THE YARD Mama's yard represents a private space free of the regrets and shortcomings that have infiltrated Mama's life. The yard appears in the first and last sentences of the story, connecting the events and bookending the action. The yard has been meticulously prepared for Dee's arrival. Mama is sensitive to every detail of the yard's appearance, referring to the wavy designs she and Maggie have made in the dirt as they tidied it. Mama extols the comforts of the yard, comparing it to an extended living room. In many ways, Mama prefers the yard to the confining house, where the muggy air fails to circulate freely. The outdoors is a place of freedom, whereas the interior of the house offers restraint and discomfort. The tense discussion about who gets the quilts takes place inside, where the various objects provoke Dee's desire to reconnect with her past. In contrast, the yard is a blissful escape, a place where Mama's regrets can be sidestepped. For her and Maggie, the yard evokes safety, a place where they can exert what little control they have over their environment.

SHORT STORY ANALYSIS

HISTORICAL CONTEXT   "Everyday Use" is set in the late 1960s or early 1970s, a tumultuous time when many African Americans were struggling to redefine and seize control of their social, cultural, and political identity in American society. There was also a greater attempt to recognize the contributions that African Americans had already made in America's long history. At the time, both scholars and laypeople became interested in unearthing and reexamining the African American past. They were particularly interested in the aspects of African heritage that had survived centuries of slavery and were still present in African American culture. During this time, many blacks sought to establish themselves as a visible and unified group and take control of how their group was named. *Black* (and later *Afro-American*) replaced the term *Negro*, which took on offensive associations. Many black Americans, uninspired by a bleak history of slavery in North America, looked to their African roots in an effort to reconnect with their past.

The time period in which "Everyday Use" takes place was also an era when groups of all ideologies—some peaceful, some militant—emerged. The Black Panthers and Black Muslims were groups created to resist what they saw as a white-dominated society. Dee is possibly emulating the Cultural Nationalists, artists and writers who wore flowing robes and sandals and emphasized the development of black culture as a means of promoting freedom and equality. Walker may have created Hakim-a-barber with this new, younger, more militant generation in mind. When Mama describes the Muslims who live down the road, who lead a labor-intensive life, Hakim dismisses their hard lifestyle. He is unwilling to commit to the hard work of the cause and faith he claims to embrace. Ultimately, Walker's story is a critique of individuals who misapplied or misunderstood some of the ideals that black consciousness groups promoted during that time.

VOICE, DICTION, AND HUMOR   Colorful language, specialized diction, and Mama's unique phrases and observations give "Everyday Use" a sense of realism. Giving voice to a member of a group that had typically been silenced, Walker gives Mama the power to narrate and control and use language to convey her story and thoughts in her own way. Walker has Mama use the specialized language of butter churning and cheese making (Dee wants to take her mother's "dasher" and the "churn top"), which adds realism to the story. These objects evoke the self-supporting life of a rural farm family and endless cycles of labor its members face.

The story focuses on the disappointment Mama feels in both her daughters and the tension that arises when Dee forces her to make a difficult choice about who gets the quilts, but the tragedy is undercut by Mama's lively cadences and distinctive narrative style. Mama makes the language her own. For example, she refers to her husband carving benches when the family couldn't "effort" (instead of "afford") to buy chairs, and she describes the milk in the churn as "crabber" (soured). Walker uses humor as a way of lightening the story's grim observations, such as in the subtle comedy provoked by Mama's reaction to Dee's and Hakim's difficult-to-pronounce names. Mama eventually gives up on Hakim-a-barber's name and secretly addresses him as what she thinks he sounds like: a barber.

IRONY   The significance of the title "Everyday Use" and the effect of the story's portrayal of a daughter's brief visit hinge on the irony that comes from the sisters' differing intended use for the quilts. The quilts are most valuable to Mama and Maggie, not as objects to be hung on the wall and respected as folk art, but as the practical household items they are. Mama risks Maggie's harming or destroying the quilts, valuable and irreplaceable documents of family history, in exchange for the peace of mind that comes from knowing that they have been passed on to the right daughter. Mama contends that Maggie, supposedly mentally inferior to her sister, has an ability that Dee does not: she can quilt. While Maggie may subject the quilts to the wear and tear of everyday use, she can replace them and contribute a scrap of family history to the next generation. Dee wants to preserve the quilts and protect them from the harm her sister might inflict, but she shows no true understanding of their inherent worth as a family totem. She relegates the objects to mere display items.

Although claiming that the preservation of the quilts is of paramount concern, Dee has no real understanding of or respect for her mother's ancestors, viewing them much as she views her mother: a country clod she is glad to have left behind. While Dee claims to have reverence for the past, at the end of the story, she criticizes Mama and Maggie for remaining mired in the old ways of living and thinking. Creating a life altogether different from the past is Dee's primary objective. This attitude is yet another way in which she expresses her disconnection to and lack of appreciation for her heritage. To Dee, life in the country is something to escape, deny, and condemn. Her sudden turn to embrace the objects of the past is thus all the more empty and unbelievable. While she believes she is earnest, it is Mama, despite her poor education and lack of worldliness, who sees the shallowness of Dee's motives. For Mama, the best way to protect the spirit of the quilts is to risk destroying them while in Maggie's permanent "care." The irony of this is not bitter but touching: preserving the objects and taking them out of everyday use is disrespectful because it disregards the objects' intended, original uses. Keeping them in circulation in daily life keeps the family history alive.

IMPORTANT QUOTATIONS EXPLAINED

1. *She used to read to us without pity; forcing words, lies, other folks' habits, whole lives upon us two, sitting trapped and ignorant underneath her voice. She washed us in a river of make-believe, burned us with a lot of knowledge we didn't necessarily need to know.*

Mama speaks these words in reference to Dee's formative years, when she would return home from boarding school in Augusta, full of newly acquired knowledge that she would lord over Mama and Maggie. Rather than her daughter's intelligence and accomplishments triggering pride in Mama, Dee's schooling prompts fear and intimidation in her instead. Like the fire that destroyed the family's first house, knowledge is portrayed as a volatile and unwelcome presence that threatens the home's safety, simplicity, and stability.

Education is the means through which Dee rejects and belittles her family, thus leading to division and alienation. At the same time, knowledge is a provocation, reminding Mama of the exposure and opportunities she was never given. Mama gives voice to her resentment at her own stalled schooling and finds comfort in her physical strength and endurance. Infused with negative connotations, education is suggested as a destructive force that harms individuals by exposing them to worlds to which they will never really belong. Some are harmed or excluded by the struggle to acquire learning and are destined to be like Maggie, hanging meekly in the doorway of a room that she will never be able to enter, shut out from the ability to change. For Mama, this threat is as real and unwanted as a fire racing through the rafters.

---

2. *Have you ever seen a lame animal, perhaps a dog run over by some careless person rich enough to own a car, sidle up to someone who is ignorant enough to be kind to him? This is the way my Maggie walks. . . . She knows she is not bright. Like good looks and money, quickness passes her by.*

E

Mama narrates these words as Maggie joins her in the yard to wait for Dee. In this brief quotation she bluntly characterizes Maggie as a pathetic figure who shows the effects of her sheltered life and disfigurement. Maggie's crushed spirit and withering, withdrawn nature disappoint Mama, but she ultimately chooses Maggie's simplicity and faithfulness over Dee's shallow selfishness. Mama feels she is the protector of one daughter and the victim of the other. She dreams of the impending marriage that will relieve her of the burden of Maggie and leave her to a quiet life. On one hand, Mama's brutal honesty and lack of illusions seem closely connected to her strength. At the same time, Mama's honesty is also harsh. It dramatizes the subtle yet deep gulf that exists between Mama and her daughters. Whereas Dee represents a world of extreme change, Maggie relentlessly stays the same, an all-too-present reminder of the inequities of the past and present.

Everything That Rises Must Converge

Flannery O'Connor
(1925–1964)

CONTEXT

Mary Flannery O'Connor was born on March 25, 1925, in Savannah, Georgia, to Edward Francis O'Connor and Regina Cline O'Connor. Her family moved to Atlanta for her father's work when O'Connor was a teenager but had to return to their home in Milledgeville, Georgia, after her father contracted lupus. He died three years later. O'Connor later studied at a private high school before entering George State College for Women, where she worked for the student newspaper and literary magazine. She had enjoyed writing since childhood, and the stories she composed in college merited admission to the master's program at the University of Iowa's writer's workshop. There, she honed her craft and began publishing fiction. Her first story, "The Geranium," appeared in *Accent* when she was only twenty-one and earned her both an award and a publishing contract for her first novel. She began working on the novel *Wise Blood* while working as a teaching assistant at the University of Iowa after receiving her master's degree in 1947.

O'Connor accepted an invitation to work on *Wise Blood* at Yaddo, a respected artist's colony in Saratoga Springs, New York. Her publisher, however, disliked the initial drafts, so she switched publishers and submitted portions of the novel for publication in prominent journals such as the *Paris Review*. While visiting her mother in Georgia for Christmas, O'Connor's health began to decline, and doctors ultimately diagnosed her with lupus, from which she would eventually die. Fearing that she would live only three more years as her father had, she left New York and decided to live with her mother on their Georgian dairy farm, Andalusia. O'Connor lived there quietly for several years until she completed and published *Wise Blood* in 1952. Critics condemned the novel as an affront to Christianity for its satire on American religious life but recognized O'Connor's phenomenal talent as a writer.

O'Connor published her first collection of short stories, *A Good Man Is Hard to Find*, in 1955 and then followed up with a second novel in 1960, *The Violent Bear It Away*. Although critics loved her short fiction, her second novel suffered as *Wise Blood* had. Nevertheless, O'Connor's reputation grew, and she continued to write, lecture, and teach until her death in 1964. *Everything That Rises Must Converge*, her second volume of short stories, was published posthumously in 1965, and she posthumously won the National Book Award in 1972 for her *Collected Stories*. O'Connor's popularity has increased since her death, and many now deem her one of the best short story writers of the twentieth century.

"Everything That Rises Must Converge" was written in 1961 in the midst of the American civil rights movement. The ideas of intergenerational conflict and transforming social mores play out against the backdrop of racial desegregation in the South. O'Connor's story focuses on tensions that emerged after integration. Uncomfortable depicting the interior life of black Americans, she avoided incorporating black characters into her stories except as chorus figures or fringe characters, as is evident in this story. Still, the black characters' silence in this story adds to the sense of tension between whites and African Americans in the mid-twentieth-century South.

PLOT OVERVIEW

Julian, a recent college graduate, prepares to escort his mother to her weekly weight-loss class at the YMCA, which she attends to reduce her high blood pressure. He escorts her there every week because she has refused to take the bus alone since integration. She adjusts her garish new hat and contemplates returning it to pay the monthly gas bill. While walking through their dilapidated neighborhood, Julian imagines moving to a house in the country. He declares that he will one day make money, even though he knows he never really will. His mother encourages him to dream, saying that it will take time to establish himself.

She continues to chatter, mentioning that her grandfather once owned a plantation with 200 slaves. Embarrassed, Julian comments that the days of slavery are over, to which she replies that blacks should be free to rise but should do so separately from whites. Both think about the grandfather's house again, and Julian grows envious, despite the fact that he only saw the house in ruins as a boy. As his mother talks about her black nurse, Caroline, Julian resolves to sit next to a black person on the bus in reparation for his mother's prejudices.

When they arrive at the bus stop, Julian baits his mother by removing his tie, prompting her to exclaim that he looks like a thug. Julian retorts that true culture is in the mind and not reflected by how one acts or looks, as his mother believes. As they bicker, the bus pulls up and they board. Julian's mother strikes up conversation with other passengers, eventually pointing out with relief that there are only white people on the bus. Another woman joins in, and the subject of the discussion turns to Julian. Julian's mother comments that he works as a typewriter salesman but wants to be a writer. Julian withdraws into a mental bubble. He judges his mother for her opinions, believing that she lives in a distorted fantasy world of false graciousness. Although he feels nothing but disdain for her, she has made sacrifices so that he could have a good education.

The bus stops and a well-dressed African American man boards, sits down, and opens a newspaper. Julian imagines striking up conversation with him just to make his mother uncomfortable. Instead, he asks for a light, in spite of the no-smoking signs and the fact that he doesn't have any cigarettes. He awkwardly returns the matches to the man, who glares at him. Julian dreams up new ways to teach his mother a lesson, imagining that he will ignore her as she gets off the bus, which would force her to worry that he may not pick her up after her exercise class.

Julian retreats deeper into his thoughts, daydreaming about bringing a black lawyer or professor home for dinner or about his mother becoming sick and requiring treatment from a black doctor. Though he would not want to give his mother a stroke, he fantasizes about bringing a black woman home and forcing his mother to accept her. Despite these fantasies, he remembers how he has failed to connect with the African Americans with whom he has struck up conversations in the past.

The bus stops again, and a stern-looking black woman boards with her young son in tow. Julian senses something familiar about her, but he doesn't know why. The little boy clambers onto the seat next to Julian's mother, while the black woman squeezes into the seat next to

Julian. Julian's mother likes all children regardless of race and smiles at the little boy. He then realizes with delight that the black woman seems so familiar because she wears the same ugly hat as his mother, and he hopes the coincidence will teach his mother a lesson. The black woman angrily calls out to her son, Carver, yanking him to her side. Julian's mother tries to play peek-a-boo with the little boy, but the black woman ignores her and chastises her son instead.

Julian and the black woman both pull the signal cord at the same time to get off the bus. Julian realizes with horror that his mother will try to give Carver a nickel as she does with all little children. While they disembark, his mother searches through her purse but can find only a penny. Despite Julian's warnings, his mother calls after Carver and tells him she has a shiny new penny for him. Carver's mother explodes with rage, shouting "He don't take nobody's pennies!" She swings her massive purse and knocks Julian's mother down to the ground, then drags Carver away.

Julian berates his mother as he collects her items and pulls her up. Disoriented, she sways for a moment before stumbling off. Julian follows and lectures her, saying that she should learn from her encounter with the woman on the bus, who represents all African Americans and their distaste for condescending handouts. Reaching out to grab her arm, he sees a strange expression on her face. She tells him to call for Grandpa or her nurse, Caroline, to fetch her. Wresting herself from his grasp, she crumples to the pavement. Julian rushes to her and finds her face distorted, one eye rolling around and the other fixed on his face before finally closing. Julian starts to run for help but quickly returns to his mother's side.

CHARACTER LIST

Julian   An embittered recent college graduate who lives with his mother. Julian sells typewriters to make money while he halfheartedly pursues his ambition to be a writer. He has nothing but contempt for his doting mother, whom he believes has foolish, outdated manners and is detached from the realities of the changing world. Julian espouses the progressive ideologies of racial equality that he learned in college but finds himself unable to act on them or engage in any meaningful conversation with African Americans. He secretly longs for the comfort and privacy of his grandfather's mansion on the old family plantation, despite his avowed repudiation of the family's status as former slaveholders.

Julian's Mother   A middle-aged woman from an old southern family who is enrolled in an exercise class at the YMCA. Julian's mother dotes on her son and has made tremendous sacrifices so that he could have personal and educational opportunities. Julian's mother lives modestly and looks back longingly on the family history, reminiscing about the family plantation and the political and social influence held by previous generations of the family. She believes that the races should remain segregated and has a condescending way of treating blacks.

Carver's Mother   A tired and impatient black woman on the bus, the mother of young Carver. Carver's mother boards the bus and angrily chastises Carver for playing with Julian's mother. When Julian's mother gives Carver a penny, his mother flies into a rage and knocks Julian's mother to the ground with her large purse. She wears the same foolish purple-and-green hat that Julian's mother wears.

Carver   A four-year-old boy on the bus, the son of the imposing black woman. Carver seems oblivious to his mother's harsh attitude and tries to play with Julian's mother on the bus.

The Well-Dressed Black Man   A black man dressed in a suit and carrying a briefcase. He sits next to Julian on the bus and reads a paper, growing irritated when Julian asks him for matches. Julian·wants to chat with the black man to make his mother uncomfortable but fails in his attempts to make small talk.

The Woman with the Red-and-White Canvas Shoes   A white passenger on the bus. She shares Julian's mother's narrow view of race and moves to the back row of seats when the black man in the suit boards the bus.

The Woman with the Protruding Teeth   A white passenger on the bus. She chats with Julian's mother about the heat and gets off the bus when the black man in the suit boards.

ANALYSIS OF MAJOR CHARACTERS

JULIAN   Although he professes to have liberated, intellectual views about race, Julian is in many ways just as petty and small-minded as he perceives his mother to be. Julian has grown up with a narrow set of experiences, influenced by his overbearing mother's limited world-view. Because of his college education, however, he has acquired a new set of enlightened perspectives regarding race and social equality. Julian attempts to distinguish himself from his mother's antiquated beliefs by publicly demonstrating his liberal views on integration and racial relations. Throughout the story, he makes failed attempts to connect to blacks and repeatedly discovers that the people with whom he converses do not live up to his idealized expectations of them. When he tries to strike up conversation with the black man in the suit on the bus, for example, he comes across as awkward and intrusive. Julian desperately wants to demonstrate that he can communicate and connect to blacks, but he finds himself unable to connect to other people on their own terms, particularly across racial lines.

Julian seems to have no more understanding of African Americans than his bigoted mother, despite the liberal views he espouses. It becomes increasingly clear as the story progresses that he speaks of racial equality only to annoy his mother, not out of any compassion for black Americans. In fact, his irritation with his mother's outdated views may even reflect irritation with himself for being unable to connect with blacks or even engage in small talk with them. For him, African Americans are a class of people he doesn't understand, foreign enough that he fantasizes about bringing one or two of them home not as individuals but as trophies of his education and liberalism to be paraded in front of his mother. Julian's unrealistic perception of blacks and racial equality, therefore, isolates him from reality.

JULIAN'S MOTHER   Julian's mother's patronizing attitude toward blacks derives from fear and her dated perceptions of society and racial equality. Because of her upbringing, she has strict ideas about racial division, and her belief in segregation allows her to speak affectionately about her nurse, Caroline, while simultaneously believing that blacks were better off as slaves. In her mind, blacks should only be allowed to rise on their "own side of the fence" because full integration poses a danger to the social order. At the same time, she adheres to the older social norms, which prompt her to give Carver a penny without understanding the racist and patronizing nature of the act. She functions as a model of old southern gentility, harboring racist attitudes while maintaining a strong sense of social decorum. Ironically, the climax of the story pushes Julian's mother even further back into the past. After her apparent stroke, she becomes confused and disoriented, calling out for her father and her nurse, Caroline, both of whom are long dead, because she associates them with security and comfort.

THEMES, MOTIFS, AND SYMBOLS

THEMES

SOCIAL CONFLICT AS A GENERATIONAL CONFLICT O'Connor places the broader societal conflict of race relations within the context of the volatile relationship Julian has with his mother to connect the two issues that transformed the South in the 1960s. In many ways, Julian's mother still lives in the South of her ancestors, with strict social codes of conduct that determined the behavior of both whites and blacks. Even though these norms no longer apply, she still adheres to the old customs to resist the startling changes that the new desegregation and antidiscrimination laws have brought. Julian, meanwhile, eagerly seeks to embrace the new, integrated South and the promises of greater prosperity and racial equality. He rejects the older social order and espouses the liberal ideas of a younger generation, condemning older whites' attitudes regarding race. Like most young, idealistic Southerners, however, he has trouble acting on his convictions and fully treating blacks as equals or even people. Julian's clashes with his mother over dress, race, and appearances in general mimic the greater conflict in society and ultimately result in violence.

APPEARANCE AS A FAULTY MEASURE OF REALITY Both Julian and his mother rely heavily on appearances to separate and elevate themselves from the rest of society. Julian's mother, for example, hopes that her public demeanor and clothing will hide the fact that she no longer has any of her family's former wealth. In turn, she judges others on their appearance, including blacks, whom she automatically considers inferior. She looks down on the African American man on the bus who wears a suit, even though he is better dressed than Julian, and still places herself above the large black woman on board, even though she realizes that they wear the same hideous hat. Ironically, Julian relies on appearances to quickly judge others around him too, even though he criticizes his mother for this same shortcoming. He despises his own neighborhood with its rundown houses and evident poverty and resents the fact that his family no longer has any of its former wealth. Julian uses his education to distinguish himself from those around him, repeatedly claiming that true culture comes from the mind in a weak attempt to justify his apparent failure as a writer. Julian's and his mother's delusions illustrate the unreliability of appearances.

LINEAGE AS SAFETY Julian's and his mother's longing for the grandeur of the past suggests that neither character has fully come to terms with their lives as poor whites in an integrated South. For both characters, the past serves as safety net—a place filled with prosperity and sunshine, untroubled by poverty and social upheaval, and recalling the past allows them to continue living in a changing world they don't understand. For Julian's mother, the family heritage gives her an immutable social standing despite the fact that she lacks the money or prestige that her family once had. As a result, she has a distorted perception of her place in the world. Julian feels tormented by his family history and agonizes over the family connection to slavery, yet he still dreams of the past to escape his dreary life as an educated typewriter salesman.

MOTIFS

SOCIAL CONDUCT   Julian's mother believes that social conduct reflects a person's true nature, whereas Julian believes that social conduct reveals an unwillingness to adapt to social change. Julian's mother pays slavish attention to her manners and behavior, believing that the way a person does things reflects who they truly are. She emphasizes dressing well and behaving graciously, especially when in public. Although her family is no longer wealthy, she still conducts herself as though she is a woman of importance. Julian has an altogether different view of social conduct, believing that the content of a person's mind reveals who they are. He believes that his intellectual views, not his dress or manners, dictate who he is. Julian's mother's strict adherence to social conduct infuriates Julian, who believes that her actions demonstrate her ignorance and unwillingness to accept her lower social standing in a rapidly changing society.

SYMBOLS

THE HAT   The same hat that Julian's mother and the large black woman wear symbolizes the transforming cultural landscape of the 1960s South, which has put the two women on equal social footing. Historically, racial differences would have automatically placed Julian's mother on a higher social plane than the black woman, regardless of similarities or differences in wealth, education, and appearance. Desegregation, however, elevated African Americans and simultaneously stripped pretenses of superiority from poorer whites. The hat visually demonstrates that both women are now essentially the same: they both ride the same public transportation, shop in the same stores, and even have the same taste in clothing. It also highlights the absurdity of segregation and racial inequality, suggesting that people are more alike than different.

THE PENNY   The penny that Julian's mother gives to Carver represents her patronizing attitude toward all African Americans. Even though she wants to give the penny out of kindness, Julian's mother fails to recognize the offer's condescending and patronizing overtones. White Americans had denied blacks opportunity and access to material goods and wealth for hundreds of years, providing them only the necessities for basic living and expecting them to work happily as slaves. Giving money to Carver, therefore, is a symbolic continuation of blacks' dependence on whites. Fueled by centuries of anger and the promises of the growing civil rights movement, Carver's mother lashes out to establish her status as an independent being and reject historical subservience to white patronage.

SHORT STORY ANALYSIS

O'CONNOR AND THE SOUTHERN GOTHIC TRADITION   Although "Everything That Rises Must Converge" cannot be strictly classified as Southern Gothic literature, the story

nevertheless draws upon many aspects of the genre, most notably its treatment of setting and tone. A subgenre of American literature, Southern Gothic writing utilizes strange events, eccentric characters, and local color to create a moody and unsettling depiction of life in the American South. Southern history figures prominently, and stories usually draw upon the tragic history of slavery, lingering feelings of defeated regional pride after the Civil War, and isolated, often neglected, locales. People, places, and events in Southern Gothic literature appear to be normal at first glance, but they eventually reveal themselves to be strange, disturbing, and sometimes horrific. Although she loathed the label, O'Connor was a master of the genre while simultaneously keeping a tone of realism in her novels and short stories. Her prose, for example, emphasizes the truths of her characters' actions rather than their quirky peculiarities. Despite the often apocalyptic, surreal tone of her writing, her works always contain believable actions and choices. O'Connor grounds the story in reality by deemphasizing the eerie, disquieting tone of the backdrop and focusing instead on the relationships and events that drive the narrative.

The dark, strange setting emphasizes the mood of faded grandeur and urban decay and puts the story's events into context. O'Connor, for example, describes the houses near Julian's as "bulbous liver-colored monstrosities of a uniform ugliness" against the "dying violet" of the sunset. Dirty children squat outside these houses in a neighborhood that has long passed its prime. Southern history unfolds once again as both Julian and his mother fantasize about lost plantations and prestige, forcing readers to confront the uncomfortable and vexing legacy of slavery. The strange supporting characters, such as the imposing black woman and white woman with protruding buckteeth, also add to the unsettling feeling that permeates the town. The final moment of the story is apocalyptic in tone, with the major characters pushed back into the past as their perspective on the world becomes strange, distorted, and unfamiliar.

HISTORICAL CONTEXT   "Everything That Rises Must Converge" takes place during the civil rights movement when federal, state, and local governments made sweeping reforms in the North and South to end poverty and racial discrimination. By the 1950s, the aristocratic plantation system in the South had been fully dismantled, and urban areas swelled with an influx of job seekers from rural areas. At the same time, college admissions swelled as higher education became more affordable for a greater number of whites and a minority of blacks. American blacks in the North and South achieved a major milestone in the 1954 decision in *Brown v. Board of Education*, when the Supreme Court repealed the "separate but equal" guideline that had separated blacks from whites in almost all public areas. Rosa Parks's refusal to give up her seat on a public bus to a white passenger a year later in 1955, as well as her subsequent arrest, launched the Montgomery Bus Boycott and the peaceful protest campaign to end segregation.

All the characters in O'Connor's story struggle to either maintain or redefine their sense of identity as the drama of the civil rights movement unfolds. The white women on the bus, for example, deride black passengers in order to reestablish their social dominance. Julian's mother does this as well by repeatedly arguing—as if trying to convince herself—that her heritage makes her superior to blacks and even other whites. Julian, whose college education actually makes him a benefactor of the changing social climate, oscillates between classes and visions of society, often harping on social inequalities while simultaneously daydreaming of a bygone era. All the African American characters, meanwhile, take advantage of the growing equality to assert their individuality and respectability as an equal class of citizens. It is not surprising, therefore, that the black man Julies tries to befriend is the best-dressed person on the bus or that the large black woman with the ugly hat strikes Julian's mother for having offered Carver a penny. Like all American blacks in the 1960s, these characters refuse to accept further subjugation and condescension.

MORAL AMBIGUITY   Despite Julian's and his mother's racist attitudes toward blacks, neither character is truly immoral, allowing O'Connor to comment on the underlying racism prevalent throughout American society. O'Connor avoids conventional stereotypes of racist white Southerners to subtly demonstrate that most white Americans—including otherwise kind and well-intentioned people—often harbor racist attitudes without even realizing it. Even though Julian's mother plays peek-a-boo with the little boy, Carver, for example, she nevertheless believes blacks lived better lives as slaves underneath white masters than they do in the 1960s. She deplores the state of contemporary America but tempers her condemnation with optimism, promising Julian that his fortunes will eventually turn. Her decision to give Carver a penny, meanwhile, further demonstrates her kindness and love of children and simultaneously highlights her patronizing attitude toward blacks.

The inherently racist attitudes that lurk in Julian's subconscious belie his professed liberal opinions of race and equality and make him a morally ambiguous character as well. His longing for the material wealth of his great-grandfather's plantation implies that he hasn't fully accepted integration or racial equality. His inability to relate to African Americans also suggests that he may not see them as people like himself or even as people at all, given the fact that he daydreams of bringing influential black "catches" home just to parade in front of his mother. Yet at the same time, his liberal education and annoyance with the racist women on the bus set him apart. Unlike most white Southerners, he at least recognizes that segregation, not integration, is the fundamental problem of 1960s America. Readers consequently get a mixed view of Julian and his mother: neither are stereotypically evil people, but neither are accepting individuals either.

IMPORTANT QUOTATIONS EXPLAINED

---

1. *"True culture is in the mind, the* mind," *he said, and tapped his head, "the mind."*
    "It's in the heart," she said, "and in how you do things, and how you do things is because of who you are."

Despite Julian's and his mother's seemingly conflicting opinions, both opinions made in the beginning of the story on the bus ride to the YMCA reflect Julian's and his mother's inability to confront their own poverty and the changing social landscape around them. Julian's mother, for example, claims to believe that manners and gentility come from good breeding. The fact that her family once had political influence and wealth—not to mention power over the lives of 200 slaves—deeply troubles her, prompting her to overcompensate for this loss by always dressing and looking her best in public. She seems to relish the fact that she's the only woman at the YMCA who dresses up for classes and has a college-educated son. Equating family lineage with identity also allows her to live more happily under the false conviction that she is actually better than everyone else and certainly better than the descendents of "uppity" former slaves.

Julian, on the other hand, uses his college education to elevate himself above those around him. Although he professes to have liberal views regarding race, equality, and social justice, he rarely acts on these convictions and uses them primarily to boost his own fragile ego. His fantasies of finding influential black friends and lovers are testaments to just how unrealistic his views are. If he truly believed in racial equality, he wouldn't care about his friends' skin color. As it is, he can't even engage in small talk with fellow black passengers. Convincing himself otherwise, however, allows him to deal with his frustration as a typewriter salesman and separate himself from his mother and the poverty that surrounds him.

---

2. *"Don't think that was just an uppity Negro woman," he said. "That was the whole colored race, which will no longer take your condescending pennies. That was your black double."*

The black woman acts for all African Americans when she strikes Julian's mother with her purse at the end of the story, refusing to succumb to any more subjugation and condescension from whites. Julian understands this and tries to explain to his mother why the black woman hit her. The black woman seems to bristle with rage from the moment of her introduction, poised to explode like a volcano. Though she says little, she seems ready to lash out at any person who might treat her with disrespect. Her barely concealed anger represents the anger suppressed by blacks through years of slavery, mistreatment, and oppression under white patronage. The fact that she wears the same hat and rides the same bus as Julian's mother highlights the similarities between the two seemingly very different women. Integration has effectively equalized them.

The Fall of the House of Usher

Edgar Allan Poe
(1809–1849)

CONTEXT

Edgar Allan Poe was born in Boston, Massachusetts, on January 19, 1809, and died a mere forty years later on October 7, 1849. The manner in which he lived his life is not clear. The accounts of his friends, enemies, fans, and biographers are eclectic and contradictory, suggesting variously that he was a drug addict, drunk, and sober but chronically cheerless curmudgeon. Over time, the potent romance of Poe's work has infiltrated the potential romance of his life, and one of American literature's premier writers of psychologically dark tales is painted as though he were a gloomy, unstable product of his own writing.

What is known about Poe's life is not entirely cheery. Born to actor parents who were both in their early twenties, Poe was the second of three children. Abandoned by their father, David Poe, in 1811, Poe and his siblings witnessed their mother, Eliza, die of tuberculosis shortly thereafter. Poe was taken in by John and Frances Allan, a pair of wealthy theatergoers who knew his parents from their acting days in Richmond, Virginia. Poe's siblings went elsewhere. John Allan, a prominent tobacco merchant, agreed to give Poe a home and an education, but he never offered much in terms of financial stability. Poe was never officially adopted by the Allan family and complained of being neglected by Allan. They became estranged after Frances's death.

With this unstable familial foundation and early experience with loss, it is not surprising that Poe's work often deals with dark themes. However, his interests are also rooted in the literary traditions of his day. In the Gothic genre that was popular among British Romantics of the Victorian age, Poe found an effective framework for his interest in the gloomier side of human psychology and mysticism. Among the stories published in his first collection, *Tales of the Grotesque and Arabesque* (1845), "The Fall of the House of Usher" is one of Poe's greatest achievements, presenting many typically Gothic themes: fear, neurosis, death, haunting, and decay.

Poe began by writing poetry in college. He studied at the University of Virginia for one year but was forced to drop out due to gambling debts. He published his first collection of poetry in 1827, the same year he joined the army. Although he was eventually discharged from the forces, his interest in writing stuck. In 1835, he began working as editor and critic at the *Southern Literary Messenger,* work that would become a lifelong occupation. At that time, print magazines and literary journals held a prominent place in American culture, and Poe was able to both earn a living (though never an abundant one) and gain a certain level of influence through his involvement with many such journals.

Due to the popularity of magazines like the *Messenger*, a market for nonserialized short stories arose. Poe was not the first to embrace this genre, but he was the first to align it with coherent theoretic principles. In his preface to Nathaniel Hawthorne's *Twice-Told Tales* (1837), Poe wrote that the short story should create a singular "preconceived effect." "The Fall of the House of Usher" is the most perfect expression of this theory, and the single preconceived effect is fear.

Though Poe is recognized today both as the "father of the short story" and one of America's greatest horror writers, his writing was not as well received when it was first published. His reputation reached a national scale only after the publication of his poem "The Raven" in 1845, late in his career. A year after his marriage to his cousin Virginia Clemm ended in her death, "The Raven" finally allowed him to reach a state of financial independence and literary renown. At that point, Poe was considered a literary equal of the day's most esteemed writers, including Ralph Waldo Emerson, Henry David Thoreau, Nathaniel Hawthorne, and Henry Wadsworth Longfellow.

When Poe died in Baltimore in 1849, he was at the peak of his fame and skill. However, the details of his death, much like those of his personal life, have become obscured by mythology—he may have died of alcoholism, of rabies, in a gutter, or in a hospital. Wherever and however it was, one thing is clear: Poe lived a life dedicated to the creation of writing unparalleled in its innovation and unequivocal in its impact on American and world literature. With his short fiction alone, Poe is credited with the creation of the detective story and science fiction, with bringing the Gothic horror story across the Atlantic from Britain, and with helping to establish a uniquely American voice in literary criticism. And it's because of this, not his potentially sordid personal life, that he is still influential in the works of contemporary authors as diverse as Anne Rice and Paul Auster and still read widely today.

PLOT OVERVIEW

It is a cloudy day in autumn when an unnamed narrator arrives at the house of his boyhood friend Roderick Usher. The narrator sees the house is in a state of disrepair and finds the fog and decay surrounding the building frightening. However, he has come for a reason: to try and cheer up his friend, who recently wrote him a letter describing a state of physical and emotional illness that is afflicting him and has asked for help getting healthy. The narrator admits that although he is Roderick's only personal friend, he knows little about him. What he does know is that the Usher family, although an ancient bloodline, is known for having a peculiar temperament and never producing more than one heir per generation. Roderick is the current surviving heir. In addition, the narrator points out that the crumbling house and fatigued Usher line somehow mirror each other. Wondering which has greater influence on the other, he mentions that the surrounding peasant communities use the term "House of Usher" interchangeably to refer to both the physical "home" and its inhabitants.

Entering the house, the narrator is led through a series of shadowy passages. He finds the interior of the house to match the gloominess of the exterior. It is not the décor, he points out, that is familiar to him, but there's something *else* that causes this gloominess. He is then let into a dark, lofty room where Roderick lies on a sofa. Rising, Roderick shocks the narrator with his changed appearance: he is wan and almost inhuman looking. Roderick explains that he suffers from bad nerves and is experiencing heightened sensitivity to stimuli. The narrator suspects that the house is in some way the cause of his friend's misery. But the state of

Roderick's sister, Madeline, nearing death due to a mystifying illness, obviously adds to his distress.

During the next several days, the narrator tries, but fails, to cheer Roderick up. He listens to Roderick improvise songs with lyrics on his guitar, reads to him, and talks with him. Roderick eventually explains that he feels, like the narrator suspected, that the house is the cause of his gloomy familial temperament. Soon after, Madeline dies and Roderick asks the narrator to help him store her in a vault inside the house. He fears doctors curious about her illness might dig her up if she is buried in the conventional manner. While transporting Madeline's corpse, the narrator notices that her cheeks are still rosy and she bears a striking resemblance to Roderick, which terrifies him. Roderick explains that they were twins, and the narrator rationalizes that bodies often stay colorful after death.

After Madeline's entombment, Roderick descends into an even gloomier state, one that terrifies the narrator more. Days later, when an abstract fear is keeping the narrator from sleeping, Roderick comes to his room in a mad frenzy. Roderick points out that a strange storm is raging outside, with luminous gas and bright lightning. In an attempt to calm him, the narrator reads to Roderick from a medieval romance novel. However, as he reads, noises corresponding to those in the story seem to be audible in the house. At first, he is convinced that they are figments of his imagination. But soon it becomes obvious that they are actually occurring and cannot be ignored. Roderick, hunched in his chair, begins mumbling indistinguishable words. The narrator moves close to hear him and learns that he has been hearing similar sounds for days. He suddenly screams that he thinks they have buried Madeline alive and that the sounds are of her trying to escape. He screams that she is standing at the door, and suddenly a gust of wind exposes that she is. When the doors swing open, Madeline is standing in the doorway covered in blood. With a moan, she falls to her death onto her brother, who dies of terror under her weight. The narrator bolts, escaping from the house just as it crumbles, once and for all, into a heap of ruins.

CHARACTER LIST

The Narrator   The teller of the tale. The unnamed narrator has come to the House of Usher at the request of his boyhood friend Roderick Usher. They have not seen each other since youth, and the narrator has never before been to the house. Skeptical but prone to fright, the narrator immediately registers the sinister mood of the house. Once inside, he is skeptical of the specter until the end.

Roderick Usher   The last descendant of the "House of Usher," the Usher family line. Roderick suffers from hypochondria, is hypersensitive to stimuli, and is unable to leave the house. He invites the narrator to visit him because he wants someone to help him deal with his illness and the looming death of his twin sister, Madeline. Ultimately, he is killed by the same terror that caused his illness.

Madeline Usher   Roderick Usher's twin sister. Madeline serves as Roderick's doppelganger, or double. She suffers from a mysterious physical illness—possibly catalepsy, a sudden uncontrollable stiffness—that is the opposite of Roderick's nervous ailment. Her presence in the house is ghostlike, and we see her only once before her apparent death.

ANALYSIS OF MAJOR CHARACTERS

THE NARRATOR   The unnamed narrator is rational, analytical, and skeptical even of his own superstitions. When he visits the house of Usher, however, his rationality and resolve weaken, and he experiences a range of fear and terror. As the teller of the tale, the narrator imbues his language with the house's dark mood, which draws readers into the gloom that he feels and observes. Because the narrator is a participant in the story, Poe is better able to make the emotions convincing. Because the narrator has portrayed himself as so skeptical and rational, the terror of the story becomes more pronounced as his fear escalates and his superstitious suspicions are affirmed. Although the narrator is indeed a character in the story, his thorough portrayal of both actions and mood make him a vehicle through which Poe creates suspense and horror. Through him, Poe draws readers into the tale, and the narrator is ultimately a vessel to transmit terror from page to reader.

RODERICK USHER   Roderick is a pathetic antihero. Once handsome, his nerves have brought him to a state of disarray. Once a gifted artist, he is now unable to leave his house and consequently unable to share his art with an audience. In addition, he is afflicted with an illness that leaves him extremely sensitive to sensory stimulation. In a way, he is an ideal artist: extremely aware of aesthetic beauty but tragically unable to enjoy it in a conventional manner. Although frightening, his weaknesses make him pitiable, a combination that makes him an effective character in a horror story. He is in an upsetting state and responds to this state in an alarming way; he is frightened and passes that fright on to the reader.

Roderick exists in a state of reversed manhood, and when Madeline returns at the end of the story as an aggressive force, Roderick becomes an effeminate version of himself. Madeline is insensitive, whereas Roderick is overly aware of his sensory surroundings. Madeline breaks out of the vault and charges toward Roderick, whereas Roderick feels a kindred connection to Madeline and is intuitively aware of her survival. In other words, Roderick is passive, whereas Madeline is aggressive. When she attacks Roderick at the end of the story, he completely loses his place as the male heir to the Usher line. He is destroyed by Madeline, as is the entire Usher family line.

MADELINE USHER   Madeline appears in the story only two times, and in both instances, she is more ghost than person. When Madeline first appears, weak and sick, she functions almost as a ghost, as she is close to death. When she appears the second time, it is *after* she is pronounced dead. She really is a "skeleton in the closet" of the Usher house. Madeline personifies the constant presence of death. During the opening of the story, she is given a death sentence; at the end of the tale, she, Roderick, and the entire Usher line die completely. While much of the action of the story is taken up by the description of Roderick and the narrator's struggle to live and salvage the House of Usher from complete destruction, Madeline is so consumed by the evil in the house that she has come to embody its very existence. Madeline is so much a part of this spectral presence that it is unclear whether the house is haunted and therefore Madeline is ill or that the house is just haunted by Madeline.

THEMES, MOTIFS, AND SYMBOLS

THEMES

THE UNNATURALNESS OF ISOLATION   The Usher house and its demise reveal the unnaturalness of social isolation and the necessity of human social interaction. Before the narrator's arrival at the Usher house, it is in a state of almost complete seclusion. The Usher line has withdrawn from society by neither expanding its bloodline nor merging with other families. Roderick and his sister, Madeline, not only share this insular blood but are also twins and physical doubles. Even the non-Usher servants exist only in their relationship to the Usher family. They have no names, voices, or role beyond their part of the workings of the house itself. The house, called the "House of Usher," just like the family line, is even said to look like the Ushers. Inside the house, even light from the outside has trouble making its way in through the high windows. The house and its inhabitances are secluded completely from the larger world.

Because of this extreme seclusion, Roderick has fallen ill and Madeline has entered a ghostlike existence. When Roderick asks the narrator to visit, he may be making a final attempt to counteract the unhealthy nature of this isolation. Because the narrator is entirely separate from all things Usher, he may be able to break the family's isolation and rescue Roderick and Madeline from their afflictions. However, the narrator appears too late. He cannot lift Roderick from his stupor, and when Madeline is buried, Roderick becomes even more alienated from society. The ultimate consequence of the Usher insularity is complete annihilation. When Madeline returns from her burial, it is only to take Roderick and the entire "House of Usher"—family and building—away. At the end of the story, it is as if the "House of Usher" never existed. Only the narrator's memory of it remains.

MOTIFS

DOUBLES AND DUALITY   In the "Fall of the House of Usher," doubles and pairs accentuate the unnaturalness of the Usher family and their insularity. At the beginning of the story, the narrator notices the house reflected, upside down, in the tarn (a lake)—the image is the house's double. The central duality is the pair of Roderick and his sister, Madeline. Not only are Roderick and Madeline twins who look alike, but they also have dual illnesses: Roderick's senses are heightened, and Madeline's are dulled. The fact that they live together, apart from the rest of society, eerily suggests that the two are linked in a way that is not entirely natural. When Madeline dies, Roderick is unable to function on his own, and when they unite at the end of the story, their unity triggers the collapse of all the Usher doubles: the house falls into the tarn, and the twins fall into death together.

USHERS AND USHERING   The prevalence of ushers and ushering in "The Fall of the House of Usher" situates the story as happening between a corrupt world and more pure one. "Usher" has two meanings: as a verb, it means leading someone somewhere; as a noun, it means a person who leads someone else. When the narrator arrives at the House of Usher, he is both greeted by an usher and, in a sense, ushered into the mysterious world of the Usher family. Throughout the story, the narrator is ushered throughout the corridors of the house and through the strange terrain of Roderick's psychology. The longer the narrator stays at the house, the more he is able to understand the mystery around him. Likewise, the longer he stays, the more he is in danger of crossing over into the illness that afflicts the Usher clan. The Usher house ultimately serves as an usher between two worlds: the depraved world below, into which Roderick and Madeline descend, and the mortal world above, to which the narrator escapes after he flees the collapsing Usher mansion.

MEDIEVAL LITERATURE   Poe's allusion to medieval literary texts throughout "The Fall of the House of User" adds to the Gothic effect of the story. Like Gothic structures, those castles and far-away mansions that present a foreboding setting in Gothic stories, the obscure, ancient literature that appears in "The Fall of the House of Usher" gives Roderick's world a feeling of eerie obscurity. The medieval era dealt heavily in the supernatural and mysterious, and many of the texts in Roderick's library deal with supernatural themes. For example, "Chiromancy" by Robert Fludd is a well-known fifteenth-century book about palm reading—a mystical art shunned by the medical communities of Poe's day. When the narrator reads from "Mad Trist" by Sir Launcelot Canynge, the events he narrates actually take place between Madeline and Roderick. This paranormal concordance brings to life the suspicions aroused by the medieval texts. Like so many of the Gothic elements in the story, the medieval literature proves to be a clue about the presence of evil in the Usher house.

F

SYMBOLS

EYES AND SIGHT   In "The Fall of the House of Usher," eyes represent a person's essential humanity or true self. At the beginning of the story, Roderick looks physically ill, with pale skin and messy hair, but his eyes are still luminous—a clear indication that his inner self is still alive, although his body is failing. Madeline, however, is still vibrant physically, but she has died on the inside. She moves about the house but is sightless, unable to see or perceive where her body is. After Madeline dies, Roderick's eyes lose their luster, which indicates that he has begun to deteriorate in a more significant way. His humanness is fading, and his death is imminent. In addition to human eyes, the windows of the Usher house are described as seeming eyelike. Through these eyes, readers are given access to the life inside the Usher mansion. This description also contributes to the feeling that that house is alive and conscious of what it is going on inside of it.

SHORT STORY ANALYSIS

POE'S DOCTRINE OF UNIFIED EFFECT   In "The Fall of the House of Usher," Poe created the best expression of his belief that a short story should achieve a single "preconceived effect." Poe once wrote that he desired to produce one overriding singular feeling with each story. He hoped to use a focused mood to break through the mundane and tear away the conventional. Contemporary critical consensus is that "The Fall of the House of Usher" is his most focused story, centering most completely on the "grim phantasm, FEAR," as Roderick calls it. In other words, Poe's intention in "Usher" is to be as frightening as possible by depicting an overriding fear in each character and situation in the story and provoking a palpable sense of fear in the reader.

A close reading of "The Fall of the House of Usher" shows that Poe uses every opportunity to make his story frightening. The story, for example, is set in an obscure time period and an ambiguous place. Likewise, the narrator is constantly referring to the peculiarity of the land-scape and matching incongruity of the Usher house. All these details and, specifically, the language Poe uses to describe the setting are meant to create a frightening mood. Through-out the story, Poe also plants certain details that foreshadow death and destruction, such as the invisible crack on the front of the Usher house and the corpselike pallor of Roderick. Near the end of the story, the mood of fear intensifies and then finally comes to a head. On top of the violent storm raging outside, the narrator and Roderick hear puzzling sounds in the distance. First these sounds are undefined, and then we learn that they are the sounds of Madeline clawing her way out of the vault. In a final climactic moment, she bursts through the door and lands on Roderick. All the details from the story contribute to the true fearful-ness of this climax.

THE GOTHIC HORROR STORY   "The Fall of the House of Usher" is considered one of the greatest early examples of Gothic literature in America, a genre that later became popular in the American South. Originally, the Gothic genre was an offshoot of British Romantic literature, a school of writing advanced by the poets William Wordsworth, William Blake, Percy Shelley, and Lord Byron, among others. For the British Romantics, reality existed only on a spiritual plane, and external truth was a direct product of internal consciousness. Some writers began to explore these principles as forces that interact with the dark side of human nature, such as Mary Shelley did in *Frankenstein* (1818). Writing that explored these dark themes became known as Gothic literature. Originally, the term came from the fact that many of the stories were set in run-down, Gothic-style buildings, a type of architecture that many Europeans at the time considered ominous. Later, Gothic literature came to mean writing that explores human frailty in any frightening, dark, or haunted setting.

By the time Poe started writing Gothic stories, Gothic literature was associated with the exploration of spiritual corruption. In "Usher," this association plays out in Poe's fascina-tion with death, interest in impurity, and presentation of supernatural events, all of which are characteristics of Gothic literature in general. Many of these characteristics would later become clichés, such as the seeming resurrection of Madeline; the stormy night as an indica-tion of ominous events to come; the run-down, remote setting; and the ghostly pallor of the leading character. But Poe was among the first American writers to incorporate these charac-teristics and is often considered the most skilled practitioner of Gothic literature, especially in the short-story form.

ALLEGORY OF THE DEATH EXPERIENCE   Poe was greatly affected by the death of his mother, foster mother, and young wife, and his fiction often deals not only with the subject of death but also with the effects death has on those who outlive their most beloved family members. In "The Fall of the House of Usher," Poe presents an allegorical exploration of the experience of death. Roderick, who has spent many years alone in the Usher house with no companion except his sister, Madeline, asks the narrator to visit for the specific reason of help-ing him deal with her impending death. However, when Madeline first appears in the story, she seems as though she is already dead, because she floats through the house unaware of her surroundings. Although her body is alive, her spirit and soul have already died. In a way, the effects of Roderick's illness—his extreme sensitivity, corpselike whiteness, and inability to eat and enjoy life—are also effects of grief. The narrator is unable to "cure" Roderick's grief be-cause grief is not "curable." But he is able, for a while, to help soothe the symptoms.

Madeline's "living death" relates to a religious belief that was prevalent during the nineteenth century: the hope for everlasting life. Poe, who first experienced the grim realities of death at age two when his mother died, presents a horrific version of "life after death" in the character of Madeline, thereby firmly rejecting this common desire. Madeline seems to be alive at all only because of Roderick's need for her existence, and the fact that he insists she be buried inside the house emphasizes his unhealthy attachment. Roderick's grief becomes increasingly severe after he buries her in the vault, which suggests the perversity of his desire for her perpetual life and the impossibility of this desire. For Poe, the only appropriate ending is for Roderick to die with his sister; his grief ends only when he joins her in death. Mitigating grief through the belief in a life beyond the grave is, Poe seems to suggest, not only ineffective but irrational and insane.

IMPORTANT QUOTATIONS EXPLAINED

1. *During the whole of a dull, dark, and soundless day in the autumn of the year, when the clouds hung oppressively low in the heavens, I had been passing alone, on horseback, through a singularly dreary tract of country; and at length found myself, as the shades of the evening drew on, within view of the melancholy House of Usher.*

F

"The Fall of the House of Usher" opens with the clear, intelligent voice of the unnamed narrator. He is perceptive and describes the gloomy darkness that characterizes the House of Usher and land around it. Immediately, Poe situates his story within the Gothic genre and lets us know that the story will be a scary one. The lone narrator, on this dark autumn day, does not know what experiences he is about to have. However, the subtext of this passage is that he is about to stumble into a disturbed place and glimpse a dark world that will affect him deeply. These eerie overtones, which are conveyed through Poe's vivid, specific description, are present from the beginning of the story and persist until the end, when dark language and events take over completely.

2. *In the greenest of our valleys, / By good angels tenanted, / Once a fair and stately palace— / Radiant Palace—reared its head. / In the monarch Thought's dominion— / It stood there! / Never a seraph spread a pinion / Over fabric half so fair.*

Roderick's poem, called "The Haunted Palace," appears halfway through the story and is both a comment on Roderick's situation and a self-conscious comment on art in general. The "two luminous windows" in the third stanza suggest the windows of the Usher house as well as Roderick's eyes, which have also been described as "luminous." Likewise, "evil things" haunt the once-flourishing palace, just as evil things haunt the Usher house, which had once been the home of an artistic and generous family. At the end of the poem, evil entombs the palace, much like the Usher mansion will be entombed in the ground. This poem mirrors the Usher tale and speaks to the power of art to reveal the truth. Poe uses this technique to imbue his story with meaning in a way that adds to its frightening tone. He also forces readers to ask how it is that Roderick can create a poem that foreshadows his own demise.

Girl

Jamaica Kincaid
(1949–)

CONTEXT

Jamaica Kincaid was born Elaine Potter Richardson in 1949 in Antigua, in the British West Indies, but changed her name when she started writing because her family disliked her career choice. She came to New York at age seventeen, taking a job as a nanny for a rich family and met *New Yorker* columnist George S. Trow, who eventually helped her publish in the magazine. She wrote for the *New Yorker* for years and moved to Vermont in 1985. She has written ten books, including *Annie John* (1986); *A Small Place* (1988); *Annie, Gwen, Lilly, Pam and Tulip* (1989); *Lucy* (1990); *At the Bottom of the River* (1992); *The Autobiography of My Mother* (1996); *My Brother* (1997); *Talk Stories* (2001); *My Garden* (2001); and *Mr. Potter* (2003).

The *New Yorker* published Kincaid's short story "Girl" in 1978, her first piece of fiction. The story has since appeared in Kincaid's short-story anthology *At the Bottom of the River* and numerous other anthologies. The story is so popular in part because it speaks to so many audiences, including young people, African Americans, and women.

Much of Kincaid's work deals with ramifications of Antigua's history as a colony of Great Britain. The British controlled Antigua from 1632 until 1967, shortly before Kincaid left for New York. By 1967, the island had become self-governing, but it did not achieve independence within the British Commonwealth until 1981. The British imported many Africans to Antigua during the early colonial years to labor as slaves in the sugarcane fields. Despite independence, many of the descendents of these slaves still live in poverty there. Kincaid appreciated the education she received in the Antiguan school system but learned to hate almost everything about the British occupiers. Many themes in her stories—especially those of oppression and powerlessness—stem from her experiences in Antigua.

Kincaid visited her homeland in 1985, four years after independence. The rampant poverty shocked her so much that she felt compelled to write about it, describing the conditions in a nonfiction book called *A Small Place* (1988). She disliked colonialism but felt that Antiguans had squandered the opportunities that independence offered by relying too heavily on tourism. In her work, she also seeks to combat the negative effects of discrimination, detrimental environmental policies, and spread of AIDS, which killed her brother in 1996.

The short story "Girl," like many of Kincaid's books, deals with the experience of being young and female in a poor country. Kincaid's complicated relationship with her mother comes out in the mother-daughter dynamic in the story. She describes her mother as a literate woman who struggled against her poor circumstances, eventually feeling bitterness toward her children because of all her problems. Kincaid also wrote the book *Autobiography of My Mother* (1996), which explores the life of a woman stuck in poverty and resentful of her children. She has also said that her mother's anger toward her seemed to get worse when Kincaid became a teenager. Just as the voice of the mother in "Girl" resents and worries about her daughter becoming a woman, Kincaid's mother seemed to become more oppressive and bitter toward Kincaid as she grew older.

PLOT OVERVIEW

"Girl" consists of a single sentence of advice a mother imparts to her daughter, only twice interrupted by the girl to ask a question or defend herself. She intends the advice to both help her daughter and scold her at the same time. Kincaid uses semicolons to separate the admonishments and words of wisdom but often repeats herself, especially to warn her daughter against becoming a "slut." Besides these repetitions, "Girl" doesn't move forward chronologically: there is no beginning, middle, or end to the stream.

The mother dispenses much practical and helpful advice that will help her daughter keep a house of her own some day. She tells her daughter how to do such household chores as laundry, sewing, ironing, cooking, setting the table, sweeping, and washing. The mother also tells the girl how to do other things she'll need to know about, including how to make herbal medicines and catch a fish. These words of wisdom suggest that the women live in a poor, rural setting, where passing on such advice is essential for daily living.

Alongside practical advice, the mother also instructs her daughter on how to live a fulfilling life. She offers sympathy, such as when she talks about the relationships her daughter will one day have with men, warning that men and women sometimes "bully" each other. She also says that there are many kinds of relationships and some never work out. The mother also tells the girl how to behave in different situations, including how to talk with people she doesn't like.

Often, however, the mother's advice seems caustic and castigating, out of fear that her daughter is already well on her way to becoming a "slut." She tells the girl, for example, not to squat while playing marbles, not to sing any Antiguan folk songs in Sunday school, and to always walk like a lady. The girl periodically interjects to protest her innocence.

CHARACTER LIST

The Mother   The mother of a preadolescent daughter, and the main speaker in the story. The mother dispenses a long string of advice to her daughter to teach her how to properly run a household and live respectably. The mother intermittently scolds the girl between her words of wisdom because she fears her daughter will adopt a life or promiscuity. At the same time, however, the mere fact that she takes the time to impart her knowledge suggests a deeper caring for the girl.

The Daughter   The preadolescent daughter who listens to her mother's speech. The daughter says little, speaking only to defend herself against her mother's accusations that she will one day become a "slut." The girl's protestations suggest resentment, but Kincaid does not provide her true thoughts or feelings.

ANALYSIS OF MAJOR CHARACTERS

THE MOTHER   The mother sees herself as the only person who can save her daughter from living a life of disrespect and promiscuity. She believes the girl has already started down this path because of the way she walks, sits, and sings *benna* (Antiguan folksongs) during Sunday school, and she imparts her domestic knowledge to keep the girl respectable. In some ways, the mother is wise: not only does she know how to cook, clean, and keep a household, but she also has a keen sense of social etiquette and decorum, knowing how to act around different types of people. For her, domestic knowledge and knowing how to interact with people bring happiness along with respect from family and the larger community. Her instructions suggest that community plays a large role in Antiguans' lives and that social standing within the community bears a great deal of weight.

Yet at the same time, there is bitterness in the mother's voice, and she takes her anger and frustration out on her daughter. She seems to think that none of her wisdom will make any difference and that the girl is already destined for a life of ill repute. She even repeatedly hints that the girl wants to live promiscuously and be a "slut." Her fears for the girl actually belie deeper fears of the precarious state of womanhood in traditional Antiguan society. Despite the mother's caustic remarks and accusations, the fact that she knows how to make abortion-inducing elixirs implies that she has had some illicit relations with men or at least understands that such encounters sometimes occur.

THE DAUGHTER   Even though the girl says very little in the story, the fact that readers perceive the mother's words through her ears makes her the silent narrator and protagonist. The daughter narrates "Girl" as if recalling the memory of her mother from a distant future place. "Girl" is not a word-for-word transcript of an actual conversation between the mother and daughter but a compilation of advice the daughter remembers her mother saying. She remembers, for example, how her mother constantly accused her of promiscuity and impropriety, an accusation that has apparently haunted her through the years. The inclusion of such remarks in the story illustrates how deeply they affected her while growing up and just how powerful a mother's influence and opinions can be on her children.

THEMES, MOTIFS, AND SYMBOLS

THEMES

THE DANGER OF FEMALE SEXUALITY   Even though the daughter doesn't seem to have yet reached adolescence, the mother worries that her current behavior, if continued, will lead to a life of promiscuity. The mother believes that a woman's reputation or respectability determines the quality of her life in the community. Sexuality, therefore, must be carefully guarded and even concealed to maintain a respectable front. Consequently, the mother links many tangential objects and tasks to the taboo topic of sexuality, such as squeezing bread before buying it, and much of her advice centers on how to uphold respectability. She scolds her daughter for the way she walks, the way she plays marbles, and how she relates to other people. The mother's constant emphasis on this theme shows how much she wants her daughter to realize that she is "not a boy" and that she needs to act in a way that will win her respect from the community.

THE TRANSFORMATIVE POWER OF DOMESTICITY   The mother believes that domestic knowledge will not only save her daughter from a life of promiscuity and ruin but will also empower her as the head of her household and a productive member of the community. She basically believes that there are only two types of women: the respectable kind and the "sluts." Undoubtedly for many Antiguan women, domestic knowledge leads to productivity, which in turn wins respect from family and society. Household work therefore brings power and even prestige to women in addition to keeping them busy and away from temptation. Readers recognize the reverence the mother has for the power of domesticity because of the numerous specific instructions she gives her daughter, such as how to cook pumpkin fritters, sweep, grow okra, buy bread, and wash clothes. For her, domesticity brings respectability; sewing up a dress hem thus becomes more than an act of maintenance because it saves a woman's sexual reputation within the community.

MOTIFS

FOOD   The mother repeatedly emphasizes food throughout her lecture to reinforce her be-lief that happiness comes from domesticity. The acts—and art—of making pumpkin fritters, tea, bread pudding, *doukona*, and pepper pot thus take on greater meaning as elements that link women to their families, their households, and the greater community. In many ways, food will also be the mother's greatest legacy as she passes old family recipes and culinary traditions down to her daughter and future generations of women. Interestingly, foods such as *doukona* and pepper pot also act as anchors that squarely place the story in Antigua and the Caribbean. Mentioning these specific regional foods allows Kincaid to recreate a world that's vivid and different from our own without ruining the story's structure with unnecessary descriptions.

CLOTH   Cloth and its relationship to appearances and proper housekeeping reappear throughout the story to highlight the importance of respectability. The mother knows that a person's clothing reveals much about character and personality and that shabbiness implies laziness and poverty. Washing, sewing, and ironing allow women not only to project their status but also their productivity and self-worth. Neatness in appearance also corresponds to the community's perception of a woman's sexual respectability and morality. Organized, productive, well-groomed women appear competent and in control and consequently have much less chance of falling under suspicion of having had illicit relationships with men. The mother therefore stresses the importance of dress and appearance to save the daughter from a life of disrespect.

SYMBOLS

BENNA   Antiguan folksongs, or *benna*, symbolize sexuality, a subject the mother fears her daughter already knows too much about. Historically, native Antiguans sang *benna* to secret-ly spread scandalous rumors and gossip under the uncomprehending British people's noses. Singing *benna* in Sunday school, therefore, represents not only disobedience but also sinful, forbidden knowledge that can't be discussed openly in public, let alone in church. Even though the daughter may not consciously equate *benna* with sexuality as her mother does, her protestations nevertheless suggest she knows full well *benna*'s seductive power, mystique, and forbidden qualities. In fact, the girl's adamant, almost desperate denials may even hint that she actually has sung *benna* in Sunday school with her friends, an indication of her blossoming interest in boys as well as a sign of an increasing exasperation with her mother's advice and intrusions into her personal life.

SHORT STORY ANALYSIS

STRUCTURE AND THE PROSE POEM   Kincaid's use of semicolons to separate the mother's advice and commands creates a prose poem that vividly captures the daughter's conflicting feelings for her mother. A prose poem is one that lacks rhyme, lines, and the traditional form of poetry as well as the narrative structure of conventional fiction. The layers of advice and commands spoken in one long, unending breath create a smothering sense of duty and even oppression that stifles real, two-way communication. The daughter uses the few opportunities she has to speak to protest her mother's belief that she'll grow older to become a "slut," suggesting that the daughter has already begun to resent her mother. At the same time, however, Kincaid uses the run-on sentence structure almost as a list to display the mother's domestic accomplishments to highlight her wisdom and power.

LANGUAGE AND POSTCOLONIALISM   Like much of Kincaid's early fiction, "Girl" recreates the world of a young girl, focusing on the nuances and rhythms of Caribbean English. This evocation of the speech of the islands is reminiscent of other Caribbean writers such as Derek Walcott of St. Lucia and Edward Kamau Brathwaite of Barbados, whose stories have also been compared to prose poems. Kincaid's treatment of the lingering effects of slavery and colonialism on the minds of those descended from slaves and from the once-colonized Caribbean "natives" also places her in the company of Trinidadian novelist V. S. Naipaul and Dominican novelist Jean Rhys. Kincaid's work has found its place within the English tradition of anticolonial travel writing, a tradition stretching back to Jonathan Swift's mercilessly satirical writings on Ireland in the eighteenth century. The genre also includes George Orwell's classic essay "Shooting an Elephant" and works by Graham Greene and the American Paul Theroux. Kincaid's stories, novels, and essays have also been important to postcolonial theory, a branch of literary studies that is concerned with understanding how colonized peoples both internalize and resist the colonizing culture.

IMPORTANT QUOTATIONS EXPLAINED

---

1. *[A]lways squeeze bread to make sure it's fresh; but what if the baker won't let me feel the bread?; you mean to say that after all you are really going to be the kind of woman who the baker won't let near the bread?*

In this final line of the story, the mother interprets the baker's potential refusal to allow the daughter to touch the bread as a sign that the daughter has become a social outcast, undoubtedly a slut. Kincaid uses the words "feel" and "squeeze" to turn the act of buying bread into a metaphor for sexuality, and the baker's refusal is therefore a sexual rebuke. In response to her daughter's innocent question, the mother seems to explode in anger at her, as if one impertinent question demonstrates the futility of advising a stubborn and undisciplined girl bent on becoming a slut. The daughter's question and lack of an answer from the mother also highlight the inability of the mother and daughter to communicate on any level, much less a meaningful one. The mother's final words also make her seem unfair, unsympathetic, and almost cruel. Readers suspect that it won't be long before the young daughter grows to resent her mother and her implications of her promiscuity, if she doesn't already.

A Good Man Is Hard to Find

Flannery O'Connor
(1925–1964)

CONTEXT

Mary Flannery O'Connor was born in 1925 in Savannah, Georgia. She moved to Atlanta with her family as a teenager but moved to Milledgeville, Georgia, when her father was diagnosed with lupus. He died three years later when she was just fifteen. When O'Connor was a young woman, she began studying at Georgia State College for Women. An avid writer since childhood, she worked for the student newspaper and literary magazine and also wrote stories. These stories won her a place in the master's program at the University of Iowa's writer's workshop, where she honed her craft and began publishing fiction. When she was twenty-one, she published her first story, "The Geranium," in *Accent*, a publication that earned her both an award and a contract for her first novel. O'Connor received her degree in 1947, then worked as a teaching assistant at the University of Iowa while beginning to write her novel, *Wise Blood*.

O'Connor continued writing *Wise Blood* at Yaddo, a respected artist's colony in Saratoga Springs, New York, but her publisher disliked the first drafts. Rather than start from scratch, O'Connor chose a new publisher and submitted portions of the novel for publication in prominent journals. After leaving Yaddo, O'Connor lived in New York City and briefly in Connecticut. When O'Connor was twenty-five, her health began to decline, and doctors diagnosed her with lupus. Fearing that she would live only three more years as her father had, she left New York and moved in with her mother on their Georgian dairy farm, Andalusia. There, she raised and tended a variety of birds and kept up a complicated regimen of treatments for her lupus. She also wrote diligently and often gave lectures about writing.

O'Connor published *Wise Blood* in 1952. The novel, which satirized American religious life, was criticized for being an affront to Christianity, but O'Connor's talent did not go unnoticed. She published her first collection of short stories, *A Good Man Is Hard to Find*, in 1955 and followed up with a second novel in 1960, *The Violent Bear It Away*. Although critics loved her short fiction, her second novel suffered as *Wise Blood* had. Nevertheless, O'Connor's reputation grew, and she continued to write, lecture, and teach until her death in 1964 at age thirty-nine. *Everything That Rises Must Converge*, her second volume of short stories, was published posthumously in 1965. She also posthumously won the National Book Award in 1972 for her *Collected Stories*. O'Connor's popularity has increased since her death, and many now deem her one of the best short-story writers of the twentieth century.

"A Good Man Is Hard to Find" is one of the most famous examples of Southern Gothic literature. Southern Gothic writing focuses on strange events, eccentric characters, and local color to create a moody and unsettling depiction of life in the American South.

Southern history figures prominently, and stories usually draw upon the tragic history of slavery; lingering feelings of defeated regional pride after the Civil War; and isolated, often neglected locales. People, places, and events in Southern Gothic literature appear to be normal at first glance, but they eventually reveal themselves to be strange, disturbing, and sometimes horrific. Although she loathed the label, O'Connor was a master of the genre while simultaneously keeping a tone of realism in her novels and short stories. Her prose, for example, emphasizes the truths of her characters' actions rather than their quirky peculiarities. Despite the often apocalyptic, surreal tone of her writing, her works always contain believable actions and choices. O'Connor grounds the story in reality by deemphasizing the eerie, disquieting tone of the backdrop and focusing instead on the relationships and events that drive the narrative.

PLOT OVERVIEW

The grandmother tries to convince her son, Bailey, and his wife to take the family to east Tennessee for vacation instead of Florida. She points out an article about the Misfit, an escaped convict heading toward Florida, and adds that the children have already been there. John Wesley, eight years old, suggests that the grandmother stay home, and his sister, June Star, says nastily that his grandmother would never do that.

On the day of the trip, the grandmother hides her cat, Pitty Sing, in a basket in the car. She wears a dress and hat with flowers on it so that people will know she is "a lady" if there's an accident. In the car, John Wesley says he doesn't like Georgia, and the grandmother chastises him for not respecting his home state. When they pass a cotton field, she says there are graves in the middle of it that belonged to the plantation and jokes that the plantation has "Gone with the Wind." Later, she tells a story about an old suitor, Edgar Atkins Teagarden. Edgar brought her a watermelon every week, into which he carved his initials, E. A. T. Once he left it on the porch and a black child ate it because he thought it said *eat*.

The family stops at a restaurant called the Tower, owned by Red Sammy Butts. Red Sammy complains that people are untrustworthy, explaining that he recently let two men buy gasoline on credit. The grandmother tells him he's a good man for doing it. Red Sam's wife says she doesn't trust anyone, including Red Sam. The grandmother asks her if she's heard about the Misfit, and the woman worries that he'll rob them. Red Sam says, "A good man is hard to find." He and the grandmother lament the state of the world.

Back in the car, the grandmother wakes from a nap and realizes that a plantation she once visited is nearby. She says that the house had six white columns and was at the end of an oak tree–lined driveway. She lies that the house had a secret panel to make the house seem more interesting. Excited, the children beg to go to the house until Bailey angrily gives in. The grandmother points him to a dirt road.

The family drives deep into the woods. The grandmother suddenly remembers that the house was in Tennessee, not in Georgia. Horrified at her mistake, she jerks her feet. Pitty Sing escapes from the basket and startles Bailey, who wrecks the car. The children's mother breaks her shoulder, but no one else is hurt. The grandmother decides not to tell Bailey about her mistake.

A passing car stops, and three men get out, carrying guns. The grandmother thinks she recognizes one of them. One of the men, wearing glasses and no shirt, descends into the ditch. He tells the children's mother to make the children sit down because they make him nervous. The grandmother suddenly screams because she realizes that he's the Misfit. The man says it's not good that she recognized him. Bailey curses violently, upsetting the grandmother. The grandmother asks the Misfit whether he'd shoot a lady, and the Misfit says he wouldn't like to. The grandmother claims that she can tell he's a good man and that he comes from "nice people." The Misfit agrees and praises his parents.

The grandmother continues telling him he's a good man. The Misfit tells the other two men, Hiram and Bobby Lee, to take Bailey and John Wesley into the woods. The grandmother adjusts her hat, but the brim breaks off. The Misfit says he knows he isn't good but that he isn't the worst man either. He apologizes to the grandmother and the children's mother for not wearing a shirt and says that he and the other men had to bury their clothes after they escaped. He says they borrowed the clothes they're wearing from some people they met.

The grandmother asks the Misfit whether he ever prays. Just as he says no, she hears two gunshots. The Misfit says he used to be a gospel singer, and the grandmother chants, "pray, pray." He says he wasn't a bad child but that at one point he went to prison for a crime he can't remember committing. He says a psychiatrist told him he'd killed his father. The grandmother tells the Misfit to pray so that Jesus will help him. The Misfit says he's fine on his own.

Bobby Lee and Hiram come back from the woods, and Bobby Lee gives the Misfit the shirt Bailey had been wearing, but the grandmother doesn't realize it's Bailey's. The Misfit tells the children's mother to take the baby and June Star and go with Bobby Lee and Hiram into the woods. Bobby Lee tries to hold June Star's hand, but she says he looks like a pig.

The grandmother starts chanting, "Jesus, Jesus." The Misfit says he's like Jesus, except Jesus hadn't committed a crime. He says he gave himself this name because his punishment doesn't seem to fit the crime people said he committed. A gunshot comes from the woods. The grandmother begs the Misfit not to shoot a lady. Two more gunshots come from the woods, and the grandmother cries out for Bailey.

The Misfit says that Jesus confused everything by raising the dead. He says that if what Jesus did is true, then everyone must follow him. But if he didn't actually raise the dead, then all anyone can do is enjoy their time on earth by indulging in "meanness." The grandmother agrees that perhaps Jesus didn't raise the dead. The Misfit says he wishes he had been there so he could know for sure. The grandmother calls the Misfit "one of my own children," and the Misfit shoots her in the chest three times.

Bobby Lee and Hiram return, and they all look at the grandmother. The Misfit observes that the grandmother could have been a good woman if someone had been around "to shoot her every minute of her life." The Misfit says life has no true pleasure.

CHARACTER LIST

The Grandmother   An irksome woman who lives with Bailey and his family. During the family's journey to Florida, the grandmother suggests that they visit an old house she remembers, an idea that leads to a car accident and the murder of everyone in the group. Before she is killed, the grandmother remembers that the house is actually in Tennessee, nowhere near where she said it was. She tries to reason with the Misfit but only enrages him. She experiences a moment of grace right before the Misfit shoots her.

The Misfit   A wanted criminal who stumbles upon the family when they crash their car in the woods. The Misfit lives by a moral code that involves murder and remorselessness, but he also spends time wondering about Jesus. Because he doesn't know for sure whether Jesus really raised the dead, he has opted for "meanness" as a way of giving his life meaning. He doesn't see himself as a terrible person. His two henchmen kill the entire family, and the Misfit shoots the grandmother himself.

Bailey   The frazzled head of the family. Bailey seems to love his mother, but her needling behavior sometimes gets the best of him. He gives in to the grandmother's request to visit the old plantation house that she remembers only because the children are driving him crazy. When the grandmother's cat jumps onto his shoulder, he wrecks the car. He tries to quiet the grandmother and stop her from provoking the three criminals, but he is ineffective. He and John Wesley are the first to be killed by the Misfit.

John Wesley   A loud, obnoxious, eight-year-old boy. John Wesley wants to visit the house the grandmother talks about because she says it has a secret panel.

June Star   An obnoxious young girl. June Star loudly speaks her mind and makes cutting observations about those around her.

The Mother   Bailey's wife and the mother of John Wesley, June Star, and a baby. The mother breaks her shoulder in the car crash and is eventually killed by the Misfit's henchmen.

Red Sammy Butts   The owner of the Tower restaurant. Red Sammy is a good man according to the grandmother, trusting and even gullible to a fault.

Bobby Lee   One of the escaped criminals. Bobby Lee is fat and, according to June Star, looks like a pig.

Hiram   One of the escaped criminals. Hiram wears a gray hat and inspects the family's car.

ANALYSIS OF MAJOR CHARACTERS

THE GRANDMOTHER   The unnamed grandmother in "A Good Man Is Hard to Find" considers herself morally superior to others by virtue of her being a "lady," and she freely and frequently passes judgment on others. She claims that her conscience is a guiding force in her life, such as when she tells Bailey that her conscience wouldn't allow her to take the children in the same direction as the Misfit. She criticizes the children's mother for not traveling to a place that would allow the children to "be broad," and she compares the mother's face to a cabbage. She chastises John Wesley for not having more respect for Georgia, his home state. She also takes any opportunity to judge the lack of goodness in people in the world today. During all this, she proudly wears her carefully selected dress and hat, certain that being a lady is the most important virtue of all, one that she alone harbors.

The grandmother never turns her critical eye on herself to inspect her own hypocrisy, dishonesty, and selfishness. For example, the conscience the grandmother invokes at the beginning of the story is conveniently silent when she sneaks Pitty Sing into the car, lies to the children about the secret panel, and opts not to reveal that she made a mistake about the location of the house. When the Misfit systematically murders the family, the grandmother never once begs him to spare her children or grandchildren. She does, however, plead for her own life because she can't imagine the Misfit wanting to kill a lady. She seems certain that he'll recognize and respect her moral code, as though it will mean something to him despite his criminal ways. She tries to draw him into her world by assuring him that he's a good man, but even though he agrees with her assessment of him, he doesn't see this as a reason to spare her. Only when the grandmother is facing death, in her final moments alone with the Misfit, does she understand where she has gone wrong in her life. Instead of being superior, she realizes, she is flawed like everyone else. When she tells the Misfit that he is "one of [her] own children," she is showing that she has found the ability to see others with compassion and understanding. This is a moment of realization, one that is immediately followed by her death.

THE MISFIT   With his violent, wanton killing, the Misfit seems an unlikely source to look to for spiritual or moral guidance, but he demonstrates a deep conviction that the other characters lack. Unlike the grandmother, who simply assumes that she is morally superior to everyone else, the Misfit seriously questions the meaning of life and his role in it. He has carefully considered his actions in life and examined his experiences to find lessons within them. He has even renamed himself because of one of these lessons, believing that his punishment didn't fit his crime. Because the Misfit has questioned himself and his life so closely, he reveals a self-awareness that the grandmother lacks. He knows he isn't a great man, but he also knows that there are others worse than him. He forms rudimentary philosophies, such as "no pleasure but meanness" and "the crime don't matter."

The Misfit's philosophies may be depraved, but they are consistent. Unlike the grandmother, whose moral code falls apart the moment it's challenged, the Misfit has a steady view of life and acts according to what he believes is right. His beliefs and actions are not moral in the conventional sense, but they are strong and consistent and therefore give him a strength of conviction that the grandmother lacks. Twisted as it might be, he can rely on his moral code to guide his actions. The grandmother cannot, and in the last moments of her life, she recognizes his strength and her weaknesses. O'Connor called the Misfit a "prophet gone wrong," and indeed, if he had applied his moral integrity to a less depraved lifestyle, he could have been considered a true preacher, pillar, or teacher.

THEMES, MOTIFS, AND SYMBOLS

THEMES

THE ELUSIVE DEFINITION OF A "GOOD MAN"   The grandmother applies the label "good" indiscriminately, blurring the definition of a "good man" until the label loses its meaning entirely. She first applies it to Red Sammy after he angrily complains of the general untrustworthiness of people. He asks her why he let two strangers charge their gasoline—he's obviously been swindled—and the grandmother says he did it because he's "a good man." In this case, her definition of "good" seems to include gullibility, poor judgment, and blind faith, none of which are inherently "good." She next applies the label "good" to the Misfit. After she recognizes him, she asks him whether he'd shoot a lady, although he never says that he wouldn't. Because being a lady is such a significant part of what the grandmother considers moral, the Misfit's answer proves that he doesn't adhere to the same moral code as she does. The grandmother desperately calls him a good man, as though appealing to some kind of underlying value that the Misfit wouldn't want to deny. Her definition of "good," however, is skewed, resting almost entirely on her claim that he doesn't have "common blood."

The grandmother's wanton application of the label "good man" reveals that "good" doesn't imply "moral" or "kind." For the grandmother, a man is a "good man" if his values are aligned with her own. Red Sammy is "good" because he trusts people blindly and waxes nostalgic about more innocent times—both of which the grandmother can relate to. The Misfit is "good" because, she reasons, he won't shoot a lady—a refusal that would be in keeping with her own moral code. Her assumption, of course, proves to be false. The only thing "good" about the Misfit is his consistency in living out his moral code of "no pleasure but meanness."

THE UNLIKELY RECIPIENTS OF GRACE   In "A Good Man Is Hard to Find," the grandmother and the Misfit are both recipients of grace, despite their many flaws, sins, and weaknesses. According to Christian theology, human beings are granted salvation through God's grace, or favor, which God freely bestows on even the least likely recipients. In other words, God has the power to allow even bad people to go to heaven, which he does by granting them grace. The grandmother is an unlikely candidate for receiving grace. She lies to her grandchildren, manipulates her son, and harps constantly about the inadequacy of the present and superiority of the past. She has no self-awareness and seems oblivious to the world around her. Certain of her own moral superiority, the grandmother believes that she is the right person to judge the goodness of others as well as the right person to instruct other people on how to live their lives. However, she herself has an inherent moral weakness. She instructs the Misfit to pray, for example, even though she herself is unable to formulate a coherent prayer. She changes her mind about Jesus' rising from the dead as she grows more afraid of what will happen to her. The Misfit, for his part, is an unrepentant murderer. Both "bad" people in their own way, they are each unlikely—even undeserving—recipients of grace.

Grace, however, settles on them both, suggesting that even people like the grandmother and Misfit have the potential to be saved by God. The grandmother, moved by the Misfit's wish to know for sure what Jesus did and didn't do, experiences a moment of grace when her head momentarily clears and she exclaims, "Why you're one of my babies. You're one of my own children!" The Misfit isn't literally the grandmother's child; rather, this points to the fact that she realizes they are both human beings. Her comment seems inappropriate—even insane—given the circumstances, but this is actually the grandmother's most lucid moment in the story. She has clarity and, more important, compassion. God has granted her grace just before she dies. The Misfit, too, is open to grace at this moment. Although he had claimed earlier that there was "no pleasure but meanness" in life, he now denies that there is any pleasure in life at all. Killing has ceased to bring him happiness, suggesting that he, too, may harbor the possibility to change.

MOTIFS

NOSTALGIA   The grandmother, Red Sammy, and the Misfit's nostalgia for the past suggests that they all believe that a "good man" was easier to come by long ago and that pursuing goodness in the present day is difficult and even pointless. During the car trip, the grandmother reminisces about an old suitor, Edgar Adkins Teagarden, who brought her a watermelon every weekend. She suspects she should have married him because he was a gentleman—and therefore a "good man" as well—and became wealthy. Red Sammy and the grandmother reminisce about the past, when people could be trusted. Red Sammy says outright that "a good man is hard to find," considering himself—gullible and foolish—to be one of this dying breed. Even the Misfit remembers things his father said and did as well as the unfairness of his punishment for crimes that he can't remember committing. According to these characters, the present is rife with ambiguity and unhappiness, and things were much different long ago. In a way, this belief allows them to stop short of deeply exploring their own potential for goodness because they've convinced themselves that the world is not conducive to it.

SYMBOLS

THE GRANDMOTHER'S HAT   The grandmother's hat, which she wears for the sole purpose of showing that she is a lady, represents her misguided moral code. When the grandmother prepares for the car trip with the family, she dresses up to be prepared for a car accident so that anyone seeing her dead body would know that she'd been a lady. The grandmother seems to be entirely unconcerned with the fact that she's dead in this scenario and oblivious to the fact that other people—including her three grandchildren—would have probably died as well. For the grandmother, the only thing that matters is her standing as a lady, a ridiculous concern that reveals her selfishness and flimsy moral conviction. When the grandmother does become involved in a car accident, the hat—like her moral convictions—falls apart. After she is thrown from the car and the family is facing the Misfit, the brim of the hat falls off. She drops the broken hat as her self-conception as a lady dissolves.

SHORT STORY ANALYSIS

MORAL CODES   In "A Good Man Is Hard to Find," the grandmother and Misfit live by moral codes that affect their decisions, actions, and perceptions. A moral code is a set of beliefs and behaviors that people abide by to live what they consider to be a reasonable, fulfilling lives. The term *moral* doesn't necessarily mean "good"; it's simply a code of conduct, while the righteousness of a person's morals is entirely subjective. Although at first glance the Misfit's code seems to be misguided, it is actually the grandmother's code that proves to be flimsy and inconsistent. The grandmother has built her moral code on the characteristics that she believes make people "good." She places great stock in being a lady, for example, which emphasizes appearance over substance. At the same time, she repeatedly deceives her family and lacks even a rudimentary awareness of the world around her. Despite her professed love for Christian piety, she herself is unable to pray when she finds herself in a crisis and even begins to question the power and divinity of Jesus.

The Misfit, however, adheres to a moral code that remains consistent and strong. From his experiences as a convicted criminal, he believes that the punishment is always disproportionate to the crime and that the crime, in the end, doesn't even really matter. He also harbors a genuine bafflement about religion. Whereas the grandmother accepts faith unquestioningly and weakly, the Misfit challenges religious beliefs and thinks deeply about how he should follow them or not follow them. He has chosen to live under the assumption that religion is pointless and adheres to his own kind of religion: "No pleasure but meanness." His moral code is violent and never wavers, and in the end, his is the one that triumphs.

O'CONNOR AND CATHOLICISM Flannery O'Connor's Catholic upbringing influenced almost all her fiction, often garnering criticism because of her stark, sometimes harsh portrayal of religion. O'Connor's great-grandparents had been some of the first Catholics to live in Milledgeville, Georgia, and her family stood out in the predominantly Protestant South. O'Connor attended parochial school and frequently went to Mass with her family. Although her stories and novels are often violent and macabre, they are rooted in her belief in the mysteries of belief and divinity. Moreover, her characters often face violent or jarring situations that force them into a moment of crisis that awakens or alters their faith. Moments of grace—a Christian idea—are pervasive, such as the grandmother's moment of grace in "A Good Man Is Hard to Find." For O'Connor, writing was inextricable from her Christian beliefs, and she believed she wouldn't be able to write were it not for this background. In a lecture about "A Good Man Is Hard to Find" in 1943, O'Connor said, "Belief, in my own case anyway, is the engine that makes perception operate." She also attributed her desire to write to her Catholicism, writing once in a letter, "I feel that if I were not a Catholic, I would have no reason to write, no reason to see, no reason ever to feel horrified or even to enjoy anything."

IMPORTANT QUOTATIONS EXPLAINED

G

1. *"I found out the crime don't matter. You can do one thing or you can do another, kill a man or take a tire off his car, because sooner or later you're going to forget what it was you done and just be punished for it."*

The Misfit speaks these words near the end of the story, just before sending the children's mother, the baby, and June Star into the woods to be shot. The Misfit has told the grandmother that he had been punished for a crime that he can't remember, and this is the lesson he has taken away from it. According to the Misfit's theory, no matter what the crime, large or small, the punishment will be the same—even if one never remembers what one did. This idea of being punished for an unremembered crime alludes to the Christian belief in original sin. According to Christian theology, all human beings are born sinners for which they will be eternally punished. Only through God's grace can these people be saved. In this sense, humans "forget" their crime, yet are punished nonetheless, just as the Misfit suggests. The grandmother has her moment of grace when she recognizes the Misfit as one of her "own children," recognizing how similar she is to the Misfit for the first time. She isn't morally superior, as she has always believed. Instead, both are struggling in their own ways to come to terms with the difficult, often ambiguous tenets of the Christian faith.

2. *"She would have been a good woman," The Misfit said, "if it had been somebody there to shoot her every minute of her life."*

This quotation, at the end of the story, reveals the Misfit's understanding of what has occurred in the grandmother's final moments, and he seems to recognize two things about her. First, he fully understands that despite her obvious belief in her moral superiority—which she conveys through her self-proclaimed identification as a "lady" and religious instruction—

the grandmother is not, in fact, a good woman. She is flawed and weak, and her age grants her no particular rights for respect or reverence. Second, the Misfit recognizes that when facing death, the grandmother has the *capacity* to be a good woman. In her final moments, she foregoes the moral high ground she'd staunchly held and instead embraces her and the Misfit's common humanity. The Misfit observes this shift and seems to realize what it means: if the grandmother could have lived her life at gunpoint, so to speak, she could have gained the self-awareness and compassion that she'd lacked.

G

Harrison Bergeron

Kurt Vonnegut
(1922–   )

CONTEXT

Kurt Vonnegut, Jr., was born in Indianapolis, Indiana, in 1922. He edited his high school newspaper and attended Cornell University, where he studied chemistry and wrote for the *Cornell Daily Sun* for about two years. Then Vonnegut joined the army, where he served with the U.S. 106th Infantry Division during World War II and earned a Purple Heart. He was taken captive and, as a prisoner of war, saw the bombing of Dresden in Germany. After the war ended, Vonnegut earned an advanced degree in anthropology from the University of Chicago and worked for the City News Bureau of Chicago, where he worked as a police reporter. He eventually left Chicago for Schenectady, New York, to work for General Electric in the public relations department. In 1951, he left his job to devote himself to writing.

Vonnegut published his first short story, "Report on the Barnhouse Effect," in 1950. Numerous works of fiction followed, most of which are equal parts satire and science fiction. Some of his best-known works include *The Sirens of Titan* (1959), *Cat's Cradle* (1963), and *Slaughterhouse-Five* (1969). *Slaughterhouse-Five* tells the story of Billy Pilgrim, who has lived through the bombing of Dresden and become a time traveler. *Breakfast of Champions* (1973), another well-known novel, features an experimental form and the introduction of the author as a character. Vonnegut has produced many other novels as well as short story collections and plays and written essays about many subjects, including suicide. His mother killed herself when he was a young man, and Vonnegut attempted suicide himself in 1985. After the publication of *Timequake* (1996), Vonnegut said that he was through writing fiction. Since then, he has written essays for the magazine *In These Times*. He has taught at Smith College, the City College of New York, Harvard University, and the Iowa Writers' Workshop.

A fervent liberal, Vonnegut is a lifetime member of the ACLU (American Civil Liberties Union). Although he rarely makes explicit mention of real-world politics in his fiction, many of his works have been interpreted as oblique jabs at various governments and systems of thought. Many of Vonnegut's columns for *In These Times* criticize President George W. Bush and his handling of the Iraq war. The bestselling essay collection *A Man Without a Country* (2005) takes on both President Bush and Senator John Kerry. Never one to shy away from controversy, Vonnegut has tackled the debate about assisted suicide in his essay collection *God Bless You, Dr. Kevorkian* (2001) and has made much-criticized comments to an Australian newspaper about the bravery of terrorists who die for their beliefs.

"Harrison Bergeron" is one of Vonnegut's most important short stories. It was first published in *The Magazine of Fantasy and Science Fiction* in 1961 and was later republished as part of the short-story collection *Welcome to the Monkey House* (1968). Set in a dystopian America in 2081, it is often interpreted as a blistering critique of authoritarian governments. In its blend of satire and science fiction, "Harrison Bergeron" typifies Vonnegut's work. The story expands on an idea first introduced, in abbreviated form, in Vonnegut's novel *The Sirens of Titans*. In 1995, the short story was made into a TV movie.

PLOT OVERVIEW

It is the year 2081. Because of Amendments 211, 212, and 213 to the Constitution, every American is fully equal, meaning that no one is stupider, uglier, weaker, or slower than anyone else. The Handicapper General and a team of agents ensure that the laws of equality are enforced.

One April, fourteen-year-old Harrison Bergeron is taken away from his parents, George and Hazel, by the government. George and Hazel aren't fully aware of the tragedy. Hazel's lack of awareness is due to average intelligence. In 2081, those who possess average intelligence are unable to think for extended stretches of time. George can't comprehend the tragedy because the law requires him to wear a radio twenty-four hours a day. The government broadcasts noise over these radios to interrupt the thoughts of intelligent people like George.

Hazel and George are watching ballerinas dance on TV. Hazel has been crying, but she can't remember why. She remarks on the prettiness of the dance. For a few moments, George reflects on the dancers, who are weighed down to counteract their gracefulness and masked to counteract their good looks. They have been handicapped so that TV viewers won't feel bad about their own appearance. Because of their handicaps, the dancers aren't very good. A noise interrupts George's thoughts. Two of the dancers onscreen hear the noise, too; apparently, they are smart and must wear radios as well.

Hazel says she would enjoy hearing the noises that the handicappers dream up. George seems skeptical. If she were Handicapper General, Hazel says, she would create a chime noise to use on Sundays, which she thinks would produce a religious effect. The narrator explains that Hazel strongly resembles Diana Moon Glampers, Handicapper General. Hazel says she would be a good Handicapper General, because she knows what normalcy is. Before being interrupted by another noise, George thinks of his son, Harrison.

Hazel thinks George looks exhausted and urges him to lie down and rest his "handicap bag," forty-seven pounds of weight placed in a bag and locked around George's neck. He says he hardly notices the weight anymore. Hazel suggests taking a few of the weights out of the bag, but he says if everyone broke the law, society would return to its old competitive ways. Hazel says she would hate that. A noise interrupts the conversation, and George can't remember what they were talking about.

On TV, an announcer with a speech impediment attempts to read a bulletin. He can't overcome his impediment, so he hands the bulletin to a ballerina to read. Hazel commends him for working with his God-given abilities and says he should get a raise simply for trying so hard. The ballerina begins reading in her natural, beautiful voice, then apologizes and switches to a growly voice that won't make anyone jealous. The bulletin says that Harrison has escaped from prison.

A photo of Harrison appears on the screen. He is wearing the handicaps meant to counteract his strength, intelligence, and good looks. The photo shows that he is seven feet tall and covered in 300 pounds of metal. He is wearing huge earphones, rather than a small radio, and big glasses meant to blind him and give him headaches. He is also wearing a red rubber nose and black caps over his teeth. His eyebrows are shaved off.

After a rumbling noise, the photo on the Bergerons' TV screen is replaced with an image of Harrison himself, who has stormed the studio. He says that he is the emperor, the greatest ruler in history, and that everyone must obey him. Then he rips off all of his handicaps. He looks like a god. He says that the first woman brave enough to stand up will be his empress. A ballerina rises to her feet. Harrison removes her handicaps and mask, revealing a beautiful woman.

He orders the musicians to play, saying he will make them royalty if they do their best. Unhappy with their initial attempt, Harrison conducts, waving a couple of musicians in the air like batons, and sings. They try again and do better. After listening to the music, Harrison and his empress dance. Defying gravity, they move through the air, flying thirty feet upward to the ceiling, which they kiss. Then, still in the air, they kiss each other.

Diana Moon Glampers comes into the studio and kills Harrison and the empress with a shotgun. Training the gun on the musicians, she orders them to put their handicaps on. The Bergerons' screen goes dark. George, who has left the room to get a beer, returns and asks Hazel why she has been crying. She says something sad happened on TV, but she can't remember exactly what. He urges her not to remember sad things. A noise sounds in George's head, and Hazel says it sounded like a doozy. He says she can say that again, and she repeats that it sounded like a doozy.

CHARACTER LIST

Harrison Bergeron   The son of George and Hazel Bergeron. Fourteen years old and seven feet tall, Harrison seems to be the most advanced model the human species can produce. He is a genius who is also absurdly strong, a dancer who can also break out of prison, and a self-proclaimed emperor. If Harrison can't succeed in overthrowing the government, Vonnegut suggests, no one can. Harrison's assassination on live television means that the last, best hope of Americans has failed and there is no longer any chance of escaping the laws of equality.

George Bergeron   Harrison's father and Hazel's husband. To counteract his physical strength, George must wear weights around his neck. George, an intelligent man, must also wear a radio that prohibits him from thinking deeply. The noises broadcast at twenty-second intervals by this radio interfere with George's natural tendency toward intense thought. Despite his pensive nature, George is not bold. He believes in obeying the law and avoiding risks. He is also emotionally barren, urging his wife to forget her sadness and reacting to his son's televised adventure by going to the kitchen for a beer.

Hazel Bergeron   Harrison's mother and George's wife. Scatterbrained, dumb, and helpless, Hazel is also sweet and well intentioned. For every nonsensical comment she makes about the wonderful work the Handicapper General is doing or the commendable effort made by the incompetents on television, she makes a kind remark to George or sheds a few tears for her son's plight. Hazel is characterized as an average American.

Diana Moon Glampers   The Handicapper General of the United States. Diana Moon Glampers is in charge of dumbing down and disabling those who are above average. It is her minions who enforce the handicap laws and create new hindrances for superior beings such as Harrison. A woman much like Hazel, Diana Moon Glampers kills Harrison and his empress and threatens to murder the musicians if they don't put on their handicaps.

The Ballerina-Turned-Announcer   A dancer. George and Hazel can see that she is the best ballerina because she wears an immense amount of weight. She also wears a terrible mask to cover up what must be extreme beauty. When the announcer gives her the news to read, she speaks briefly in a beautiful voice before apologizing and making her voice ugly.

The Empress   A dancer, possibly the same character as the ballerina-turned-announcer. This dancer becomes Harrison's empress after he says the first woman to stand will be his mate. After Harrison removes her mental handicap, weights, and mask, she performs a lovely dance with him before being killed by Diana Moon Glampers.

The Announcer   A newscaster. The announcer has a severe speech impediment, as do all announcers, and cannot manage to read the news about Harrison's jailbreak.

ANALYSIS OF MAJOR CHARACTERS

HARRISON BERGERON   Harrison represents the part of the American people that still longs to try hard, flaunt their attributes, and outpace their peers. At age fourteen, Harrison is a physical specimen: seven feet tall, immensely strong, and extremely handsome. The government does everything in its power to squelch Harrison, forcing him to wear huge earphones to distort his thinking, glasses to damage his sight and give him headaches, three hundred pounds of metal to weigh him down, a ridiculous nose, and black caps for his teeth. But none of the government's hindrances, including jail, can stop Harrison. His will to live as a full human being is too strong. The government calls Harrison a genius, but he is remarkable less for his brains than for his bravery and self-confidence. When he escapes from jail, he is utterly convinced that he will succeed in overthrowing the government.

In addition to his remarkable strength of body and will, Harrison has an artistic, romantic soul. He removes his empress's handicaps with the careful touch of a sculptor. He instructs the musicians in their craft, showing them exactly how he wants them to play by singing to them. He dances so beautifully that he manages to defy gravity, springing thirty feet to the ceiling with his empress, where he kisses her. Vonnegut hints that Harrison is something of a sexual superman, and it is clear that if he succeeds in his plan to overthrow the government, he will father a line of superior children. But the murder of Harrison and his empress shows that in the America of 2081, those who are brave enough to show off their gifts will not be allowed to live, much less procreate.

GEORGE BERGERON   George is an everyman, a character most readers will understand and relate to. Smart and sensitive, George has been crippled by the government's handicapping program. He makes intelligent remarks and thinks analytically about society, but his mind is stunted. Every twenty seconds, noises broadcast by the government interrupt his thoughts, preventing sustained concentration. In addition to being smart, George is also stronger than the average man and must wear forty-seven pounds around his neck to weigh himself down. Although George is mentally and physically gifted, he is spiritually unremarkable. When Hazel suggests that he remove a few of the lead balls from the bag that weighs him down, George refuses to entertain the idea, unwilling to risk jail. A law-abiding man, he believes that America in 2081 is a much better place than it was in the old days, when competition existed. George, a slightly above-average person with a healthy respect for the rules, stands in for the reader, who may be all too willing to go along with government regulations that thwart individual freedoms and uniqueness. By showing us the unhappiness of George's existence, Vonnegut asks us to question our own passivity and perhaps even our support for the laws of the land.

HAZEL BERGERON   Hazel is a one-woman cautionary tale, an average American in an age when "average" has come to mean "stupid." She does not need a radio permanently affixed to her ear, as George does, because she was never capable of sustained thought. Hazel applauds those who are as incapable as she is, cheering on the unimpressive ballerinas and praising the pathetic performance of the announcer who cannot overcome his speech impediment. Hazel is a dim bulb, but she is also kind. She worries about George and suggests that he remove a few of his weights while he is at home, and she weeps over her son, although she cannot keep him in mind for more than a few seconds at a time. But Hazel is a cautionary tale precisely because her kindness makes no difference. Her stupidity overwhelms her good nature, preventing her from recognizing the absurdity of her society, let alone doing anything to change it.

THEMES, MOTIFS, AND SYMBOLS

THEMES

THE DANGER OF TOTAL EQUALITY   In "Harrison Bergeron," Vonnegut suggests that total equality is not an ideal worth striving for, as many people believe, but a mistaken goal that is dangerous in both execution and outcome. To achieve physical and mental equality among all Americans, the government in Vonnegut's story tortures its citizens. The beautiful must wear hideous masks or disfigure themselves, the intelligent must listen to earsplitting noises that impede their ability to think, and the graceful and strong must wear weights around their necks at all hours of the day. The insistence on total equality seeps into the citizens, who begin to dumb themselves down or hide their special attributes. Some behave this way because they have internalized the government's goals, and others because they fear that the government will punish them severely if they display any remarkable abilities. The outcome of this quest for equality is disastrous. America becomes a land of cowed, stupid, slow people. Government officials murder the extremely gifted with no fear of reprisal. Equality is more or less achieved, but at the cost of freedom and individual achievement.

THE POWER OF TELEVISION   Television is an immensely powerful force that sedates, rules, and terrorizes the characters in "Harrison Bergeron." To emphasize television's overwhelming importance in society, Vonnegut makes it a constant presence in his story: the entire narrative takes place as George and Hazel sit in front of the TV. Television functions primarily as a sedative for the masses. Hazel's cheeks are wet with tears, but because she is distracted by the ballerinas on the screen, she doesn't remember why she is crying. The government also uses television as a way of enforcing its laws. When dangerously talented people like Harrison are on the loose, for example, the government broadcasts warnings about them. They show a photograph of Harrison with his good looks mutilated and his strength dissipated. The photo is a way of identifying the supposedly dangerous escapee, but it is also a way of intimidating television viewers. It gives them a visual example of the handicaps imposed on those who do not suppress their own abilities. Television further turns into a means of terrorizing the citizens when Diana Moon Glampers shoots Harrison. The live execution is an effective way of showing viewers what will happen to those who dare to disobey the law.

MOTIFS

NOISE   The noises broadcast by the government increase in intensity and violence during the course of the story, paralleling the escalating tragedy of George's and Hazel's lives. When the story begins, a buzzer sounds in George's head as he watches the ballerinas on TV. As he tries to think about the dancers, who are weighed down and masked to counteract their lightness and beauty, the sound of a bottle being smashed with a hammer rings in his ears. When he thinks about his son, he is interrupted by the sound of twenty-one guns firing, an excessively violent noise that foreshadows Harrison's murder. Thoughts about the laws of equality and the competition that existed in the old days are shattered by the sound of a siren, a noise that suggests the extent to which the government has literally become the thought police. As Harrison barges into the television studio, George hears a car crash, a noise that connotes the injury of multiple people. The noise that interrupts George roughly at the same time that his son is being executed on live TV is described only as "a handicap signal," an ominously vague phrase. Vonnegut suggests that the noise is so awful that it can't be mentioned, just as the murder of Harrison is so awful that George and Hazel can't fully comprehend it. The final noise George hears is that of a riveting gun, an appropriate echo of the way Diana Moon Glampers killed Harrison.

SYMBOLS

HARRISON BERGERON   Harrison represents the spark of defiance and individuality that still exists in some Americans. He has none of the cowardice and passivity that characterize nearly everyone else in the story. Rather, he is an exaggerated alpha male, a towering, brave, breathtakingly strong man who hungers for power. When he storms into the TV studio and announces that he is the emperor, the greatest ruler who has ever lived, he sounds power-mad and perhaps insane. At the same time, however, his boastfulness is exhilarating. It is an exaggerated expression of the defiant urge to excel that some Americans still feel. When Harrison rips off his steel restraints and handicaps, the physical strength and beauty he reveals reminds some viewers that underneath their own restraints and handicaps, they too are still talented or lovely. But in the end, Harrison, symbol of defiance, is killed in cold blood by Diana Moon Glampers, the administrator of government power. The quick, efficient murder suggests that if a defiant spirit still exists in America in 2081, its days are numbered.

SHORT STORY ANALYSIS

VONNEGUT'S POLITICAL AND SOCIAL CRITIQUE   "Harrison Bergeron" offers vigorous political and social criticisms of both America in general and the America of the 1960s. The political system depicted in Vonnegut's story is distinctly American and founded on the principles of egalitarianism, which holds that people should be equal in every way. Equality is a beloved principle enshrined in America's constitution in the phrase "All men are created equal," but Vonnegut suggests that the ideals of egalitarianism can be dangerous if they are interpreted too literally. If the goal of equality is taken to its logical conclusion, we may decide that people must be forced to be equal to one another in their appearance, behavior, and achievements. "Harrison Bergeron" can also be interpreted as a direct critique of communism. In the 1960s, America was engaged with Russia in the Cold War and had recently struggled through the McCarthy era, when suspected communists were accused and blacklisted from artistic, literary, and political communities. The futuristic American society of "Harrison Bergeron" operates on communist principles, supporting the idea that wealth and power should be distributed equally and class hierarchies should not exist. Like the accused communists of the McCarthy era, anyone not conforming to society's accepted standards—in a reversal of sorts, anyone not adhering to the communist structure—is sought out and punished. In his story, Vonnegut argues that such principles are foolish. It is unnatural to distribute wealth and power equally, he suggests, and it is only by literally handicapping the best and brightest citizens that the misguided goal of equal distribution can be attained. Similarly, it is unnatural to seek out and punish those who reject social norms.

Some modern readers have interpreted the dystopia depicted in "Harrison Bergeron" as a preview of what might happen to America if such trends as psychiatric drugs and political correctness are allowed to proliferate. The characters in Vonnegut's story are passive, un-thinking, and calm. Although the means of achieving this mental state are externally applied to the body, rather than internally applied to the mind, some readers draw a parallel between the noises that destroy George's ability to think and the drugs that make modern Americans tranquil and detached. These critics argue that the characters in "Harrison Bergeron," who lack all passion, intelligence, and creative ability, should be interpreted as a warning about what happens to the members of a society that prizes calm happiness above artistry or intelligence. Other readers see "Harrison Bergeron" as a socially conservative argument against political correctness. Vonnegut himself has connected the story to recent attempts to make people equal using the language of political correctness. According to this argument, the respectful treatment of all marginalized groups may be a slippery slope, as "Harrison Bergeron" suggests. If we begin with the equal treatment of male athletes and their weaker female counterparts, for example, we may end with the insistence that ugly people should be treated as if they are beautiful, and so forth.

HUMOR "Harrison Bergeron," while full of dark themes, is also full of humor, which makes Vonnegut's serious message both easier to digest and more bitter. Almost every grim event in "Harrison Bergeron" is accompanied by a sly joke or moment of melancholy comedy. For example, the narrator explains that ballerinas are weighed down and masked to hide their light-ness and beauty. This deeply sinister image is leavened when we learn that such measures are meant to save viewers from the pain of feeling that they themselves look like "something the cat drug in" in comparison to the dancing beauties on their television screens. Later, the fearful announcement about Harrison's escape is accompanied by a mournful joke: the announcer has a speech impediment so bad that he must hand over the important news to a nearby ballerina so that she can read it. In a second joke, Hazel says she thinks the incompetent announcer should get a raise simply for trying hard. The pain of the ballerina-turned-announcer, who must hide the loveliness of her own voice, is mitigated by Vonnegut's description of her disguised voice as a "grackle squawk."

Even the most horrifying moments in the story are characterized by Vonnegut's dark brand of humor. We learn that Hazel, a sweet but deeply stupid woman, is very similar to

Diana Moon Glampers, the Handicapper General of the United States. Although it's upsetting to discover that the country is being run by imbeciles like Hazel, it is hard not to laugh at Hazel's idea for using religiously themed noises on Sundays to interrupt the thoughts of smart people like George. When Hazel and George attempt to discuss the difference between the competitive society of yesteryear and the America they live in, George's respect for the laws that have crippled him is heartbreaking. But the total breakdown of the conversation, brought about by George's and Hazel's inability to remember what they were talking about mere seconds earlier, produces a comical effect. Humor comes to the fore even after the Harrison's murder. In a disturbing exchange, George urges Hazel to "forget sad things" such as whatever made her cry (neither of them seem to know that their son's murder caused her tears). She answers that she always does forget sad things. Just after this conversation, George is interrupted by a noise that Hazel says sounded like a doozy. In a final bit of broad comedy, George, agreeing, says she can say that again, and Hazel repeats her remark verbatim. The effect is funny and a bit creepy, as the extent of the Bergerons' lack of self-awareness becomes fully clear.

IMPORTANT QUOTATIONS EXPLAINED

---

1. *"I think I'd make a good Handicapper General."*
   "Good as anybody else," said George.
   "Who knows better'n I do what normal is?" said Hazel.

This passage appears near the beginning of the story. Vonnegut seems to suggest that Hazel's similarity to Diana Moon Glampers is disturbing because it means that the country is being run by people just as clueless as Hazel. When George says that Hazel is as "[g]ood as anybody else," we get the idea that she is just as confused and incapable of serious thought as every other average American living in the year 2081. Hazel's confidence in her understanding of "normal" is both funny and sinister. Her self-confidence in understanding "normal" is amusing, especially because it comes on the heels of her ludicrous suggestion that the government should interrupt thoughts on Sundays with religious-sounding chimes. But it is also a disturbing and subtle reminder that in this futuristic America, the people who run the country are in power not because of their brains or savvy, but because of their normalcy.

---

2. *"The minute people start cheating on laws, what do you think happens to society?"*
   . . . . A siren was going off in [George's] head.
   "Reckon it'd fall all apart," said Hazel.
   "What would?" said George blankly.
   "Society," said Hazel uncertainly. "Wasn't that what you just said?"
   "Who knows?" said George.

This quotation, which appears near the beginning of the story, exemplifies the meandering, nonsensical human interactions that have become standard in Vonnegut's fictional America. Because he is smart, George is able to formulate an idea that society would disintegrate if people disregarded the laws and to pose that idea as a hypothetical question. But because his thinking is interrupted by one of the innumerable noises the government broadcasts over his radio, he loses track of the conversation completely. Even though Hazel is able to follow his reasoning, he can't remember what he was talking about moments before, and she isn't bright enough to get him back on track. The disturbing implication is that America's laws of equality go unchallenged not because citizens believe in them deeply but because they are too bewildered to figure out what they think of the laws in the first place. If George were able to think in peace for a few hours, he might come to believe that the laws he defends are absurd. However, these laws, against which he would likely protest if he could, are the ones that prevent him from thinking for more than a few seconds at a stretch.

---

3. *[T]hey remained suspended in air . . . and they kissed each other for a long, long time.*
   . . . . Diana Moon Glampers . . . came into the studio with a double-barreled ten-gauge shotgun. She fired twice, and the Emperor and the Empress were dead before they hit the floor.

Harrison's midair dance with his empress near the end of the story is the only moment of unadulterated beauty in "Harrison Bergeron," and its brutal conclusion suggests the beginning of still darker days for America. Harrison is as amazing as the rest of the world is dull. In a narrative full of stupidity, mediocrity, and terror, Harrison brings strength and beauty into the story by removing his and the empress's weights and disguises. Whereas his parents are so compromised that they can hardly put two logical sentences together and merely sit in front of the TV like automatons, Harrison is a whirlwind of activity. He bursts into the studio, takes control, and forces the musicians to play lovely music instead of hackneyed tripe. His physical vigor is superhuman: defying the laws of gravity, he manages to suspend himself and his empress thirty feet above the ground. The long kiss he exchanges with her also provides the only moment of sensual pleasure in the story. But Diana Moon Glampers interrupts Harrison's dance almost as soon as it has begun. The spare, unflinching language with which Vonnegut narrates her murder of the emperor and empress mirrors the cold, inhuman nature of the deed. It is clear that for all his braggadocio, Harrison never had a chance at unseating the government for good.

Hills Like White Elephants

Ernest Hemingway
(1899–1961)

CONTEXT

Ernest Miller Hemingway was born on July 21, 1899, the second of six children, and spent his early years in Oak Park, a suburb of Chicago. Both his mother and father were active members of the First Congregational Church and ran a strict household. All their children were required to abstain from any enjoyment on Sundays, for example, and were strictly punished for any disobedience. Hemingway later condemned them for their distinctly middle-class values and oppressive sense of morality.

Intelligent and an avid nature lover, Hemingway demonstrated a clear talent for writing from a young age. In fact, he published his first literary work at age seventeen. His father encouraged him to attend college after finishing high school, but Hemingway wanted to enter the army or become a writer. When his father refused to allow him to enlist, Hemingway left home and began reporting for the *Kansas City Star*.

Hemingway began to hone his now-famous literary style during his years as a reporter. His editors instructed him to write short, factual sentences without too many negatives to deliver the facts in his articles. He later incorporated this writing style into his own fiction writing. Hemingway soon grew restless and left the *Star* to serve in the Red Cross, where he worked as an ambulance driver in Europe during World War I. While recovering from a knee injury in a hospital in Milan, he fell in love with a nurse named Agnes von Kurosky. Although their relationship didn't last, he based his novel *A Farewell To Arms* (1929) on their romance.

After returning to America and finding new work as a journalist, Hemingway met and married Elizabeth Hadley Richardson. Soon after giving birth to their first child, however, the couple divorced because of Hemingway's affair with Pauline Pfeiffer. He subsequently married Pfeiffer and had two more children, but he left her after twelve years to marry another mistress, Martha Gellhorn. This third marriage lasted roughly ten years, but it dissolved like the others when he fell in love with yet another mistress.

Hemingway published "Hills Like White Elephants" in 1927 in his critically acclaimed second collection of short stories, *Men Without Women*. He wove many autobiographical elements into the story, particularly his lifelong difficulty building meaningful relationships. The story's numerous allusions and sparse style are also typical of Hemingway's writing.

Despite his success, Hemingway struggled with depression and alcoholism for most of his adult life. Many critics claim that his writing deteriorated after World War II, when his mental and physical health took a turn for the worse. He died in the summer of 1961 from a self-inflicted gunshot wound at age sixty-one.

PLOT OVERVIEW

"Hills Like White Elephants" opens with a long description of the story's setting in a train station surrounded by hills, fields, and trees in a valley in Spain. A man known simply as the American and his girlfriend sit at a table outside the station, waiting for a train to Madrid.

It is hot, and the man orders two beers. The girl remarks that the nearby hills look like white elephants, to which the American responds that he's never seen one. They order more drinks and begin to bicker about the taste of the alcohol. The American chastises her and says that they should try to enjoy themselves. The girl replies that she's merely having fun and then retracts her earlier comment by saying the hills don't actually look like white elephants to her anymore.

They order more drinks, and the American mentions that he wants the girl, whom he calls "Jig," to have an operation, although he never actually specifies what kind of operation. He seems agitated and tries to downplay the operation's seriousness. He argues that the operation would be simple, for example, but then says the procedure really isn't even an operation at all.

The girl says nothing for a while, but then she asks what will happen after she's had the operation. The man answers that things will be fine afterward, just like they were before, and that it will fix their problems. He says he has known a lot of people who have had the operation and found happiness afterward. The girl dispassionately agrees with him. The American then claims that he won't force her to have the operation but thinks it's the best course of action to take. She tells him that she will have the operation as long as he'll still love her and they'll be able to live happily together afterward.

The man then emphasizes how much he cares for the girl, but she claims not to care about what happens to herself. The American weakly says that she shouldn't have the operation if that's really the way she feels. The girl then walks over to the end of the station, looks at the scenery, and wonders aloud whether they really could be happy if she has the operation. They argue for a while until the girl gets tired and makes the American promise to stop talking.

The Spanish bartender brings two more beers and tells them that the train is coming in five minutes. The girl smiles at the bartender but has to ask the American what she said because the girl doesn't speak Spanish. After finishing their drinks, the American carries their bags to the platform and then walks back to the bar, noticing all the other people who are also waiting for the train. He asks the girl whether she feels better. She says she feels fine and that there is nothing wrong with her.

CHARACTER LIST

The American The male protagonist of the story. The American never reveals his name, nor does the girl ever directly address him by name. He is determined to convince the girl to have the operation but tries to appear as though he doesn't care what she does. He remains disconnected from his surroundings, not really understanding or even listening to what the girl has to say.

The Girl The female protagonist of the story. The American calls the girl "Jig" at one point in the story but never mentions her real name. Unlike the American, the girl is less sure of what she wants and appears reluctant to have the operation in question. She alternates between wanting to talk about the operation and wanting to avoid the topic altogether.

The Bartender   The woman serving drinks to the American man and the girl. The bartender speaks only Spanish.

ANALYSIS OF MAJOR CHARACTERS

THE AMERICAN   Throughout the story, the American behaves according to Hemingway's rigid conception of masculinity. Hemingway portrays the American as a rugged man's man—knowledgeable, worldly, and always in control of himself and the situation at hand. Even when vexed or confused, he maintains his cool and feigns indifference, such as when he tells the girl he doesn't care whether she has the operation. He initially avoids discussion of their problems, but when pressured, he tackles them head on by oversimplifying the operation and relentlessly pushing her to have it. Thinking himself to be the more reasonable of the two, he patronizes the girl and fails to provide the sympathy and understanding she needs during the crisis. Uncompromising, he seems to identify more with the other passengers "waiting reasonably" at the station than with his own girlfriend at the end of the story, which suggests that the two will go their separate ways.

THE GIRL   Compared to the American, Hemingway's overly masculine character, the girl is less assertive and persuasive. Throughout the story, the girl appears helpless, confused, and indecisive. She changes her mind about the attractiveness of the surrounding hills, for example; claims to selflessly care only for the American; and seems uncertain about whether she wants to have the operation. In fact, the girl can't even order drinks from the bartender on her own without having to rely on the man's ability to speak Spanish. Ironically, the girl seems to understand that her relationship with the American has effectively ended, despite her professed desire to make him happy. She knows that even if she has the operation, their relationship won't return to how it used to be. In many ways, the girl's realization of this fact gives her power over the American, who never really understands why they still can't have "the whole world" like they once did.

THEMES, MOTIFS, AND SYMBOLS

THEMES

TALKING VERSUS COMMUNICATING   Although "Hills Like White Elephants" is primarily a conversation between the American man and his girlfriend, neither of the speakers truly communicates with the other, highlighting the rift between the two. Both talk, but neither listens or understands the other's point of view. Frustrated and placating, the American man will say almost anything to convince his girlfriend to have the operation, which, although never mentioned by name, is understood to be an abortion. He tells her he loves her, for example, and that everything between them will go back to the way it used to be. The girl, meanwhile, waffles indecisively, at one point conceding that she'll have the abortion just to shut him up. When the man still persists, she finally begs him to "please, please, please, please, please, please" stop talking, realizing the futility of their conversation. In fact, the girl's nickname, "Jig," subtly indicates that the two characters merely dance around each other and the issue at hand without ever saying anything meaningful. The girl's inability to speak Spanish with the bartender, moreover, not only illustrates her dependence on the American but also the difficulty she has expressing herself to others.

MOTIFS

DRINKING   Both the American man and the girl drink alcohol throughout their conversation to avoid each other and the problems with their relationship. They start drinking large beers the moment they arrive at the station as if hoping to fill their free time with anything but discussion. Then, as soon as they begin talking about the hills that look like white elephants, the girl asks to order more drinks to put off the inevitable conversation about the baby. Although they drink primarily to avoid thinking about the pregnancy, readers sense that deeper problems exist in their relationship, of which the baby is merely one. In fact, the girl herself implies this when she remarks that she and the American man never do anything together except try new drinks, as if constantly looking for new ways to avoid each other. By the end of their conversation, both drink alone—the girl at the table and the man at the bar—suggesting that the two will end their relationship and go their separate ways.

SYMBOLS

WHITE ELEPHANTS   A white elephant symbolizes something no one wants—in this story, the girl's unborn child. The girl's comment in the beginning of the story that the surrounding hills look like white elephants initially seems to be a casual, offhand remark, but it actually serves as a segue for her and the American to discuss their baby and the possibility of having an abortion. The girl later retracts this comment with the observation that the hills don't really look like white elephants, a subtle hint that perhaps she wants to keep the baby after all—a hint the American misses. In fact, she even says that the hills only seemed to look like white elephants at first glance, and that they're actually quite lovely. Comparing the hills—and, metaphorically, the baby—to elephants also recalls the expression "the elephant in the room," a euphemism for something painfully obvious that no one wants to discuss.

SHORT STORY ANALYSIS

SETTING   Hemingway sets "Hills Like White Elephants" at a train station to highlight the fact that the relationship between the American man and the girl is at a crossroads. Planted in the middle of a desolate valley, the station isn't a final destination but merely a stopping point between Barcelona and Madrid. Travelers, including the main characters, must therefore decide where to go and, in this case, whether to go with each other and continue their relationship. Moreover, the contrast between the white hills and barren valley possibly highlights the dichotomy between life and death, fertility and sterility, and mirrors the choice the girl faces between having the baby or having the abortion. The girl seems torn between the two landscapes, not only commenting on the beauty of the hills but also physically walking to the end of the platform and gazing out at the brown emptiness around the station.

THE ICEBERG THEORY AND HEMINGWAY'S STYLE   Many first-time readers read "Hills Like White Elephants" as nothing more than a casual conversation between two people waiting for a train and therefore miss the unstated dramatic tension lurking between each line. As a result, many people don't realize that the two are actually talking about having an abortion and going their separate ways, let alone why the story was so revolutionary for its time. In accordance with his so-called Iceberg Theory, Hemingway stripped everything but the bare essentials from his stories and novels, leaving readers to sift through the remaining dialogue and bits of narrative on their own. Just as the visible tip of an iceberg hides a far greater mass of ice underneath the ocean surface, so does Hemingway's dialogue belie the unstated tension between his characters. In fact, Hemingway firmly believed that perfect stories conveyed far more through subtext than through the actual words written on the page. The more a writer strips away, the more powerful the "iceberg," or story, becomes.

Hemingway stripped so much from his stories that many of his contemporary critics complained that his fiction was little more than snippets of dialogue strung together. Others have called his writing overly masculine—there are no beautiful phrases or breathtaking passages, just the sheer basics. In "Hills Like White Elephants," for example, both the American man and the girl speak in short sentences and rarely utter more than a few words at a time. Hemingway also avoids using dialogue tags, such as "he said" or "she said," and skips any internal monologues. These elements leave the characters' thoughts and feelings completely up to the reader's own interpretations. Hemingway's fans, however, have lauded his style for its simplicity, believing that fewer misleading words paint a truer picture of what lies beneath.

IMPORTANT QUOTATIONS EXPLAINED

H

---

1. *"Yes," said the girl. "Everything tastes like licorice. Especially all the things you've waited so long for, like absinthe."*

Even though the girl had asked the American man to order the absinthe because she had never tried it before, she immediately puts her glass back on the table after the first taste, surprised by the drink's sharp bite. She remarks that her drink tastes like licorice and then tries to subtly broach the subject of her pregnancy again, because the American had ignored her earlier comment that the nearby hills look like white elephants. Basically rehashing the adage "be careful what you wish for because it may come true," the girl recognizes the irony in not liking the taste of the drink she'd asked the man to order for her, just as she presumably dislikes being pregnant when she'd always wished for a baby. The man, however, perhaps senses the underlying message of the girl's seemingly casual remark and tells her to be quiet, prompting her to once more bring up the subject of white elephants.

---

2. *"But if I do it, then it will be nice again if I say things are like white elephants, and you'll like it?"*

By this point, midway through the story, the girl has already retracted her previous comment that the surrounding hills look like white elephants, hinting that she wants to keep the baby instead of having an abortion. The man had been upset at this, feigning indifference but pushing for the abortion because he doesn't want the child. Still hoping to save their broken relationship, the girl asks her boyfriend whether things between them will return to the way they used to be if she goes through with the abortion. Her indecision and desire to placate the man demonstrate her dependence on him. At the same time, however, the mere fact that she asks the question may imply that she believes that nothing can save their relationship.

A Hunger Artist

Franz Kafka
(1883–1924)

CONTEXT

Born in Prague in 1883 to a Jewish father who excelled in business, Franz Kafka, along with his three sisters, had a comfortable childhood. He earned a doctorate of law degree by the time he was twenty-three and began working for a government agency, where he distinguished himself by publishing reports about worker safety that appeared in professional journals. He retired as Senior Secretary and was awarded a medal of honor for his contribution to the establishment and management of hospitals and rest homes. To his friends, Kafka was warm and charming. He had several girlfriends and two serious relationships, but he never married. Instead, Kafka devoted his life to writing, publishing his first story in 1909. He was well known among the small literary circles of Prague, and he often read his stories out loud to groups of friends. Kafka continued writing until his death at forty-one from tuberculosis in 1924, correcting the final proofs of the story "A Hunger Artist" while on his deathbed.

In the world of literature, Kafka holds a coveted distinction. Like William Shakespeare and George Orwell, he is one of the few authors whose name has become an integral part of the vocabulary used to characterize not only other literature but also the workings of the world around him. The term "Kafkaesque" has come to describe a nightmarish atmosphere resulting from pervasive, sinister, impersonal forces; feelings of guilt, fear, and loss of identity; and the sense of evil that permeates the logic of ruling powers. Much of Kafka's writing brims with this menacing, uneasy quality, and his protagonists are nearly always confined by alienation and anxiety. When reading Kafka's writing, we enter a world in which nothing is certain and in which every bad turn feels like the product of a conspiracy.

Although Kafka's body of work was the product of a unique, dynamic mind, it can also be traced to the personal unease Kafka felt during his seemingly peaceful life. In spite of his eccentricities, Kafka was a man of his times, and his experiences as a Jew in Prague at the turn of the twentieth century led him to distrust authority, a feeling that surfaced in his writing. Kafka's Prague was a civilized, cosmopolitan European city, but like most other cities of the Austro-Hungarian Empire, it was often hostile to Jews. Kafka lived in a ghetto all his life, segregated from mainstream society, and he felt disenfranchised by the faceless Austro-Hungarian bureaucracy. In his fiction, Kafka conveyed the horror he felt for a society that was highly organized but that also randomly assigned guilt and suffering. Kafka was in some ways a prophet, and his writing predated Stalin's Soviet Union and Hitler's Germany, where he lost his sisters and final girlfriend, by several years.

At the center of Kafka's literary vision is his relationship with his father. A brusque, domineering man, Hermann Kafka came to Prague and established a successful merchant business, sacrificing much of his identification with Judaism to do so. In his diaries, Kafka wrote that his father was too proud of his assimilation, and Kafka devoted himself to Jewish studies as if to rebel against his father. Aside from religious and cultural differences, Kafka's relationship with his father also suffered from the fact that they lived together in close quarters for much of Kafka's life. Hermann was surely insensitive to Kafka's feelings and indifferent to his literary ambitions. The effect on Kafka was drastic. Issues of tyrannical patriarchy abound in Kafka's works, and many of Kafka's protagonists, like Kafka himself, remain irredeemably in the wrong when confronted with such authority. In many ways, Kafka's relationship with his father was the defining influence on the harried, claustrophobic characters that make up the world of his fiction.

Like all of Kafka's fiction, "A Hunger Artist" joins ordinary life with eerie situations that seem to exist only in the realm of fantasy. Critics have pointed out that "A Hunger Artist" has many different interpretations—there is no simple, concrete message for readers to take away. Kafka must have realized the story's importance: it was one of the few pieces of fiction he thought worthy of saving when he directed his friend and editor Max Brod to destroy all his life's work when he died. Fortunately, Brod did not follow Kafka's instructions.

PLOT OVERVIEW

A man who is known only as "the hunger artist" and fasts for a living travels from town to European town with the impresario (his manager). In each town, the hunger artist chooses a public location and puts himself on display in a locked, straw-lined cage, where he fasts for periods of up to forty days. In the hunger artist's heyday, people from all over the surrounding area come to witness his performances. Children especially are drawn to him, and when the hunger artist is not hypnotically withdrawn in the cage, he talks to them and answers their questions with a smile. The adults also avidly monitor the hunger artist's progress, but they generally do so out of suspicion that the hunger artist is sneaking food. To the hunger artist's frustration, the townspeople assign men, usually butchers, to ensure that the hunger artist does not eat during the night. Even more annoying to the hunger artist, however, is that these men deliberately turn a blind eye to the hunger artist as if to allow him to steal a bite of food. The hunger artist sings to prove that he is not eating, but the people think he has simply mastered the art of eating and singing simultaneously.

Although the hunger artist is famous, he is perpetually unhappy. Because of the townspeople's incredulity, the hunger artist realizes that only he can be truly satisfied with his feats of self-denial. The hunger artist also feels constrained by the fasting limits imposed on him. Although the hunger artist finds fasting easy and can go much longer than forty days, the impresario always cuts the performance short because the spectators tend to lose interest. Furthermore, the ritual in which the impresario forces the hunger artist to break the fast is humiliating and unpleasant. First, doctors enter the cage to report the hunger artist's condition, which is announced with a megaphone. Next, two ladies chosen from the crowd try to help the hunger artist out of his cage. Unfailingly, the hunger artist objects, and the impresario intrudes to make a show of how frail the hunger artist has become. By the time the ritual is over, the hunger artist has been force-fed and the crowd moved by the hunger artist's seemingly desperate condition. In truth, however, the hunger artist is miserable only because he knows he could have fasted longer and that his supposed fans actually hate him.

The hunger artist goes on living in fame and quiet dissatisfaction, becoming hostile only when the occasional person theorizes that the root of his melancholy might be the fasting itself. At this suggestion, the hunger artist rattles his cage like a beast and can be calmed only by the impresario, who plays up the hunger artist's misery to the people by showing photographs of him withering away. Though these photos in reality capture the hunger artist looking wretched because he is being forced from the cage against his will, the impresario advertises it all as the effect of the fasting itself. The impresario's gesture never fails to cow the hunger artist, who sinks in submission, back into his straw, forever misunderstood.

Professional fasting eventually goes into decline, as audiences develop a taste for newer, more exciting forms of entertainment. The hunger artist and impresario dissolve their partnership, but because the hunger artist is too old to take up a new profession, he attempts to ride out the trend against fasting in the hope that it reverses itself. He joins a circus and becomes a sideshow, placed at the entrance of the menagerie of animals and other curiosities. As a result of his placement, the hunger artist is ignored by the throngs of people who have come for the livelier attractions inside. The hunger artist is nonexistent, save for a few stragglers who look at him as an anachronism. Left alone, the hunger artist finally exceeds his fasting record, although there is no way to tell exactly how long he has fasted because the circus attendants forget to change the sign on which his daily total appears. The hunger artist wastes away in his cage, unnoticed and unappreciated.

Many days pass before a circus overseer notices what seems to be an unused cage. Upon closer inspection, the overseer discovers the hunger artist buried in the straw, near death. Thinking the hunger artist insane, the overseer humors the hunger artist in his last words. The hunger artist asks to be forgiven, explaining that he has wanted only to be admired by everyone. When the overseer assures him that everyone does admire him, the hunger artist tells the overseer that they shouldn't, confessing that he has fasted only because in life he could not find food that he liked. With these words, the hunger artist dies. The circus attendants bury him with his straw and restock the cage with a young panther, which is unlike the hunger artist in nearly every way. Stalking about in its cage, the panther brims with life, feeding hungrily and expressing freedom and vitality. In no time, it becomes a major draw for the circus, and crowds of people edge close to the cage in breathless excitement.

CHARACTER LIST

The Hunger Artist   The miserable protagonist of the story. Dressed in black tights, the hunger artist is emaciated. Everything about his demeanor cries of desperation and tragedy. He sequesters himself in a cage, preferring to sit on the straw-lined floor rather than on a chair. Although he craves public attention and is delighted to display himself to wide-eyed spectators, he is often frustrated with the interactions he has with others. While in his cage, the hunger artist withdraws into himself, seemingly in a trance. He thinks of little more than the art of fasting and his desire to be the greatest faster of all time.

The Impresario   The hunger artist's manager. Until his partnership with the hunger artist ends, the impresario is wholly dedicated to the hunger artist's career and devotes all his resources to his advancement. As a result of spending so much time with the hunger artist, the impresario likely knows him better than anyone else. All the same, they do not seem to be friends, given the pleasure that the impresario takes in taunting the hunger artist during his performances to increase the drama and excitement.

The Overseer   A circus manager who discovers the hunger artist dying in his cage. The overseer hears the hunger artist's final words, but he clearly does not care whether he lives or dies. As soon as the hunger artist expires, the overseer callously orders that his body be taken away and replaces him with a panther.

ANALYSIS OF MAJOR CHARACTERS

THE HUNGER ARTIST   The key to the hunger artist's character lies in his identity as a professional faster, and at the center of his dedication to the perfection of his art is his ambition to achieve something that no one has ever achieved before. The hunger that the hunger artist willfully endures has a double meaning: it refers to his vocation of fasting as well as his insatiable yearning to defy human imagination by fasting indefinitely. Driven to renounce the nourishment that the rest of humanity embraces, the hunger artist literally lives in self-denial, forsaking comfort, companionship, and, most important, food, all of which are necessary to survival. Thus, the hunger artist's devotion to his art constitutes a thinly masked death wish. Unwilling to respond to the needs he has as a human being, let alone as a living thing, the hunger artist makes death the culmination of his life's work.

The hunger artist is doomed to be unhappy because he depends on others' understanding to validate his performance, which is, by his own description, "beyond human imagination." He feels deep disdain for his spectators, but because the nature of performance art requires spectators, the hunger artist is tied to the people he seeks to evade. He is, in a sense, a misfit in a showman's position, and he comes to depend on the praise and wide-eyed amazement of his spectators as if they themselves were the food of life. When he experiences their suspicion, cynicism, and indifference, he becomes frustrated, unable to understand that being an artist often means being alienated from others. Only at the end of his life does the hunger artist seem to approach an understanding of the paradox that defines his existence. At this point, he no longer thinks that "the world [is] cheating him of his reward," but rather that his aspirations could never be rewarded in the world in which he lives.

THE IMPRESARIO   The impresario is part of a class of people who exploit art and artists for their own personal gain. Though the impresario is the hunger artist's "partner in an unparalleled career," a description that would suggest camaraderie between the two men, he behaves for the most part as a parasite would, fattening himself on the proceeds presumably given to the hunger artist for his performances. The impresario finds sustenance by capitalizing on another man's starvation. In essence, the impresario commodifies the hunger artist's suffering, when all the hunger artist aspires to do is be recognized for his efforts and achievements. The impresario's career trajectory and business practices, when taken together, further indicate his parasitic nature. Just as the parasite is most effective when it does not drain its host completely, the impresario is most successful for shepherding the hunger artist back from the brink of death at the end of each performance. Finally, the impresario abandons his host when nourishment is no longer available.

While the impresario's motivations for associating with the hunger artist are primarily self-centered, the impresario plays an important role in enabling the hunger artist to come close to reaching his goal. The impresario may behave as the hunger artist's parasitic publicist, but he also functions as the hunger artist's only connection to the people on whom he depends to recognize his artistic achievement. By taking responsibility for the hunger artist's physical needs, even to the extent of force-feeding him, the impresario frees the hunger artist to focus solely on his aspiration to fast. Of the two, it is the impresario who most clearly perceives the disconnect between the hunger artist's apparent death wish and need to be recognized by the masses. By remaining with the hunger artist until he no longer possibly can, the impresario is in some ways the hunger artist's partner and devoted caretaker.

THEMES, MOTIFS, AND SYMBOLS

THEMES

THE SEPARATION OF ARTIST FROM SOCIETY   In "A Hunger Artist," the hunger artist's troubled relationship with his spectators suggests that the artist exists apart from society and must therefore be misunderstood. In the hunger artist's case, being an artist means cutting oneself off from the world, a conclusion reflected in the hunger artist's conscious choice to sequester himself in a cage. This physical separation of hunger artist and spectator mirrors the spiritual separation of the individual artistic ego and public will. This gap in mindset leads to a critical gap in understanding. Set apart from others, only the hunger artist realizes the importance of his ambitions and accomplishments, and only he knows that he is not cheating. The further the hunger artist goes in pursuit of perfection, as he does in the circus, the further away he moves from the understanding of the people for whom he performs. The artist will always be separated from society because the qualities that distinguish him as an "artist" and are worth preserving are the ones that ensure he will never be understood.

THE HARMFUL EFFECT OF PRIDE   Although the hunger artist's fierce pride in his art enables him to improve his fasting, it ultimately stops him from reaching his goals because it hurts his public appeal and connection to others. He looks on his emaciated frame and pro-truding ribcage with vanity, deeming them badges of honor, but his pitiful, grotesque body repulses the women who initially want to carry him from his cage at the end of his fast. In this case, his starved body—which is the manifestation of his pride—is the thing that ensures he will never be loved and admired by the public. Pride turns the hunger artist away from others and into himself, and he reinforces his isolation by imprisoning himself in a cage and meditating intensely. In the end, pride guarantees the hunger artist not fame and transcendence, but obscurity.

THE FRUITLESSNESS OF HUNGER   The hunger artist relishes in his hunger throughout the story, hoping that it will lead to spiritual satisfaction, but in the end, his fasting leaves him empty both physically and spiritually. The hunger artist refuses food, but his self-denial reveals his need for a different kind of nourishment: public recognition and artistic perfection. Hunger, for both physical and spiritual nourishment, is the subject of his performance. Beyond the performance, however, the hunger artist yearns only for what the physical world, including his audience, cannot give him. Fasting becomes the "easiest thing in the world" for the hunger artist, but what he struggles to do without is the spiritual nourishment that remains out of his reach.

While he performs with the impresario, the hunger artist never succeeds in fasting indefi-nitely, and this failure results in constant dissatisfaction. But the hunger artist fails to under-stand that the spiritual satisfaction he yearns for relies on the physical life he believes that he must give up. In renouncing his claims on life, the hunger artist makes himself incapable of achieving spiritual satisfaction. The panther that replaces him in the cage has a lust for life, satisfied "to the bursting point with everything that it needed." Even though it is trapped in a cage, the panther seems to need nothing because, in essence, it lacks nothing. The hunger artist dies empty, having given up everything and still attaining none of his goals.

MOTIFS

SPECTACLE AND SPECTATORS   The Europe of the hunger artist's time enjoys spectacle as a form of entertainment, which suggests that the society is one of mass culture and that individuals like the hunger artist are ruled by the crowd. The hunger artist turns the intensely private act of fasting into a spectacle and constantly seeks the public's approval. He is not content with knowing that he has achieved feats of fasting; he needs to know that others believe that he has not cheated. Knowledge of his own greatness is worthless because only the crowd's recognition can validate the hunger artist's effort. Only by becoming a spectacle does the hunger artist become real. Ironically, the hunger artist's reliance on spectators is why he never breaks his fasting records while he is famous: the public always forcibly ends the spectacle after forty days. By attempting to join the circus, the hunger artist is trying to ally himself with an even greater spectacle, but he falls out of the limelight. He fasts longer than ever, but there is no sense of victory because his final triumph is out of the public eye.

SYMBOLS

THE CAGE   The cage in which the hunger artist performs represents his alienation from society. In this sense, it suggests the division between spectators and spectacle and the barrier that prevents understanding. Unable to understand the artistic perfection for which the hunger artist strives inside his cage, the spectators see a pathetic madman who may be cheating on his fast. As the hunger artist suggests, the spectators' position outside the cage prevents them from truly appreciating the hunger artist's feat. The cage also represents security, protecting the hunger artist from those who do not understand him. On his side of the cage, the hunger artist may lament his separation from others, but he made the choice to isolate himself.

The cage has symbolic meaning not only for the hunger artist's relationship to others but also for the hunger artist himself. The cage represents the hunger artist's body, in which he feels he is imprisoned. After all, his body and its physical needs are the ultimate constraint on his ambition to fast indefinitely. His body is a prison to him, and his effort to break out of the prison is actually a death wish. By fasting, the hunger artist attempts to step outside his skin, an act associated both with death and divinity. Because of the limitations of his body, the hunger artist can achieve the out-of-body experience he covets only by giving up his life. This achievement constitutes the hunger artist's idea of artistic perfection.

THE PANTHER   The panther at the end of the story, with its power and liveliness, serves as the opposite of the hunger artist, who was powerless and, ultimately, lifeless. The hunger artist, who spent his life trying to achieve spiritual satisfaction, is replaced in the cage by the panther, which exhibits the uninhibited vitality of the physical world. The hunger artist lives in a state of constant want, for both food and recognition. The panther, on the other hand, wants for nothing. Though the panther is caged, it is so comfortable in its own skin that it projects an aura of freedom. The narrator claims that the panther's freedom lurks somewhere in its jaws, which suggests that hunting and consumption are what allow it to be so unconflicted. Ultimately, the panther embodies the power and grace that comes from engaging with the material world, which explains why the people crowd around its cage. Its vitality has attracted the recognition that the hunger artist failed to win.

THE CLOCK   The clock in the cage represents the artist's own biological clock and draws attention to his body's limitations. Convinced that perfection in his art is a noble and lasting human achievement, the hunger artist labors under the misperception that his powers of starvation will exist for all eternity. The clock's presence, however, exposes the hunger artist's delusions by constantly reminding him of the reality of the present. Like all other animate beings, the hunger artist is subject to physical and earthly demands, including the passage of time. Just as he cannot exist without food, he cannot exist outside of time. The clock is a mockery of the hunger artist's efforts to become immortal.

SHORT STORY ANALYSIS

RELIGIOUS IMAGERY   The religious imagery and references in "A Hunger Artist" make the story an allegory for the modern world's rejection of faith. An allegory is a story with a literal, surface meaning that corresponds to a secondary, symbolic meaning. In "A Hunger Artist," the hunger artist's life is parallel to Jesus Christ's, and the hunger artist's tragic end suggests that Kafka had a pessimistic outlook on the world's spiritual crisis. The hunger artist's simple black attire is priestly, marking him as a holy man, as Christ was. Like Christ, he travels from town to town and performs miracles in front of spectators. Both the hunger artist and Christ live ascetically, renouncing the material and physical worlds that they believe stand in the way of spiritual enlightenment. The hunger artist and Christ are most similar in that after expending themselves in so-called service to others, they undergo a public display of death.

The twist in Kafka's religious allegory is that the hunger artist's spectators are indifferent to his suffering. This indifference suggests that faith and spirituality have no place in the modern world. Kafka seems to suggest that the hunger artist's popularity, and, by extension, Christ's, is just a trend. Indeed, the hunger artist's popularity disappears in his own lifetime. Even when the hunger artist is famous and revered, the townspeople suspect trickery—no one has faith. His forty-day fasts, which mirror Christ's forty-day period in the desert during which he subjects himself to Satan's temptations, are greeted with cynicism and apathy. The spectators' apathy culminates in the hunger artist's final performance in the circus—no one pays him any attention. The fact that no one bothers to keep track of the days during the hunger artist's last and greatest effort underlines Kafka's message that the hunger artist, and thus Christ, do not truly die for others' sins. Ultimately, their martyrdom is false because the principles to which they devote themselves are quickly forgotten by the people left behind.

PROFESSIONAL FASTING IN KAFKA'S TIME   Kafka gleaned details for "A Hunger Artist" from the obscure real-life phenomenon of professional fasting, which was a popular form of entertainment in his time. The first well-known instance of fasting was by an American, Dr. Henry Tanner, who allegedly fasted under medical supervision for approximately forty days, much like the hunger artist in Kafka's tale. Imitators soon followed, the most famous of which was Giovanni Succi, an Italian who staged fasts as public performances across Europe. Whereas Tanner seems to have fasted as an experiment, Succi turned fasting into a profession, performing for the public upward of thirty times. Succi's performances were so similar to Kafka's fictional account of the hunger artist's performances, especially the fast's elaborate conclusion and the practice of selling photographic memorabilia, that some critics believe Kafka may have witnessed Succi or another professional faster firsthand. The professional faster's rise and fall in popularity, during a period of approximately forty years (from 1880 to 1922), coincided neatly with Kafka's life, which also ran approximately forty years (from 1883 to 1924).

KAFKA'S PARABLE   "A Hunger Artist" works as a parable—a story with a moral or principle. The morals that this parable illustrates are the dangers of pride and the artist's ineffectiveness as an agent of social or cultural change. The hunger artist's pride leads to his endless dissatisfaction and, ultimately, his death. Not content with the private knowledge that he has not cheated and has reached his goals, he wants mostly for others to recognize his successes. Pride keeps him from being fulfilled, even when he fasts for a longer period than ever before, because he succeeds out of the public eye. Because he can find no personal satisfaction without the validation of others, he dies having had no satisfaction at all. Not only has he been ineffective in changing his own fulfillment, he is also ineffective at changing others through his art. The hunger artist, in some ways, is not an artist at all, and his performance, although a form of entertainment, does or produces nothing of importance. His performance may seem to be a triumphant act, but this impression is provided mostly through the impresario's spin. The hunger artist is an individual fighting against and triumphing over powerful physical forces and urges, but he has set up those obstacles himself—which cheapens the accomplishment.

None of the characters in "A Hunger Artist" have names, which adds to the parable-like quality. They are referred to by their job titles, and all their experiences are filtered through their roles. For example, the hunger artist experiences all of his sensations—frustration, dissatisfaction, desire—through the prism of his role as "the hunger artist," rather than through the prism of a man, bachelor, or mystic. Without a name, and without more than this one dimension, the hunger artist could ultimately be anyone, and his trials provide universal lessons. The hunger artist is less an individual than an archetype (a universal figure), and his story of struggle, unfulfilled goals, and death is a warning for all mankind to let go of pride or face a life always lacking in satisfaction and contentment.

IMPORTANT QUOTATIONS EXPLAINED

1. *When . . . some leisurely passer-by stopped . . . and spoke of cheating, that was in its way the stupidest lie ever invented by indifference and inborn malice, since it was not the hunger artist who was cheating, he was working honestly, but the world was cheating him of his reward.*

This quotation, occurring toward the end of the story when the hunger artist joins the circus, epitomizes the misunderstanding that plagues the hunger artist throughout his career. The casual spectator's "inborn malice" refers to the spectators' heartless dismissal of the hunger artist's suffering as well as to their inability to identify with anything outside their familiar view of the world. To these people, the hunger artist's integrity is either false or a farce, and they quickly lose interest. This development suggests that crowds are fickle in their attention and demonstrates how alienated the hunger artist is from society. This passage is especially significant because the tone reveals the hunger artist's viewpoint more than at any other place in the story. The hunger artist's indignation indicates that he honestly remains convinced of his ambition's worth. This delusional belief comes into serious question only a page later, as the hunger artist finally starves himself to death.

---

2. *"If I had found [the food I liked], believe me, I should have made no fuss and stuffed myself like you or anyone else." These were his last words, but in his dimming eyes there remained the firm though no longer proud persuasion that he was still continuing to fast.*

This quotation, from the end of the story, exposes the contradiction implicit in the hunger artist's work: he has given up food only to gorge himself on the appreciation he longs for from others. The only thing that the hunger artist claims to want is the public's admiration. When this admiration, which has never been enough, is completely removed, the hunger artist has nothing on which to sustain himself and eventually dies. The hunger artist's life is ultimately a sham. The transcendence he always yearned for was unavailable because he worked for it under a misperception: that fasting could bring nourishment. No matter how long he fasted, and no matter how much recognition he received, the end result could only be death. The spiritual nourishment he longed for, even if he had received it, could not sustain his physical body.

H

I Stand Here Ironing

Tillie Olsen
(c. 1913–   )

CONTEXT

Tillie Olsen was born in either 1912 or 1913 in Omaha, Nebraska, the second of six children. Her parents were Russian Jews who fled to the United States after participating in the unsuccessful revolution of 1905, during which Russian peasants revolted against the government for a chaotic assortment of reasons, including their desire to have more land and higher wages. Olsen's parents settled in Nebraska, where Olsen's father became the secretary of the state's Socialist Party. The family struggled to make ends meet. When Olsen was age ten, she was forced to get a job shelling peanuts after school. Raised by political activists and often surrounded by orators and social commentators, many of whom stayed at the family home when in town for speaking engagements, Olsen developed an early awareness of the power of words. She was especially inspired by her mother, who was illiterate until her twenties and taught Olsen about the sacrifices women often make when they become mothers and wives.

Olsen was one of a few students in her neighborhood to go to the district's academically challenging high school, where teachers fed her love of learning and acquainted her with literature. In her mid-teens, Olsen began producing skits and musical sketches for the Young Socialist League. At eighteen, she joined the Young Communist League and was jailed for a month in Kansas City for distributing leaflets encouraging packinghouse workers to unionize. In 1932, Olsen moved to Faribault, Minnesota. She developed tuberculosis, and, during her recovery, had the luxury of bed rest and unlimited time to write. She produced the first few chapters of what would eventually become the novel *Yonnondio*, but pregnancy and the birth of her first child, Karla, interrupted her progress. Grinding poverty and an itinerant life, a period during which Karla's father left and returned numerous times, thwarted Olsen's initial literary efforts.

The 1934 publication of a short story called "The Iron Throat" garnered Olsen a sudden notoriety among critics and publishers. She soon found herself under contract with Random House and alone in Los Angeles, having sent her young daughter to be cared for by relatives. The separation proved too painful. Olsen forfeited her contract and moved to San Francisco to be reunited with Karla. In 1944, Olsen married fellow communist sympathizer Jack Olsen, with whom she had three daughters. From the mid-1930s to the late 1950s, Olsen worked a number of grueling jobs, attempting to write whenever she could.

At age forty-one, Olsen enrolled in a creative writing class at San Francisco State. A two-year fellowship at Stanford's prestigious writing program followed. An early draft of "I Stand Here Ironing," then entitled "Help Her to Believe," was the submission that won the admission committee's praise. At the end of the program, the return to a traditional workday almost thwarted the progress Olsen had made in those years. However, a grant from the Ford Foundation allowed her to finish one of her best-known stories, "Tell Me a Riddle," for which she won the esteemed O. Henry Award for Best Story of the Year in 1961. That story became the title piece in a collection of four short prose works, *Tell Me a Riddle* (1961), which also featured "I Stand Here Ironing." In 1974, Olsen finally published *Yonnondio*, the novel she had begun in 1932.

"I Stand Here Ironing" contains many autobiographical elements, including the narrator's recollection of being a teenage mother with limited opportunities who is abandoned by the baby's father. Olsen faced the same challenges, as her life was marked by the struggle to balance her family's demands and political activism. Those involved with the reenergized women's movement in the 1960s embraced the story's sensitive portrayal of the difficulties and self-doubts that infiltrated motherhood. They also praised the story's exploration of the effect that child rearing had on female identity during the Great Depression and World War II. The narrator attempts to accept responsibility for her failings as a mother, but she also recognizes the extenuating circumstances, such as inadequate pay for women and lack of social services, that frustrated her best efforts.

PLOT OVERVIEW

The unnamed narrator, a mother, is ironing while speaking on the phone with an unnamed individual who is most likely a social worker, teacher, or counselor. The mother likens the back-and-forth motion of the iron to her own mental process as she considers the cautionary statement made by this outside party. The person has asked the narrator to help him or her understand the narrator's daughter, Emily, a young woman whom the person claims is in need of assistance. The narrator balks, wondering what she can possibly do to change the situation. She believes that she has no special insight into Emily's behavior simply because she is her mother. The narrator feels she would become mired in the abstractions of the situation, all the things she should have done or those things that cannot be altered. The narrator remembers how beautiful Emily was as a baby, then her awkward phase, followed by the blossoming of her beauty in her late teens.

The narrator states that she breast-fed Emily, then questions why she cites that fact first in pleading her case to the unnamed "you." When Emily was eight months old, the narrator was forced to leave her in the care of a neighbor. Emily's father had left unexpectedly, unable to bear the family's poverty. The narrator recalls running home from work to retrieve Emily, who always cried when she spotted her. Eventually, the narrator sent Emily to live with her father's family. Emily returned to her mother's care when she was two, but the narrator worked long hours and placed Emily in day care. The narrator is still angry that she had no other choice. Emily would find any excuse to stay home from nursery school with her mother. The narrator recalls an old neighbor gently telling her that she should smile more at Emily. The narrator was more joyful in her treatment of her other four children and fears she is responsible for Emily's somber nature.

Despite her restrained temperament, Emily displays a talent for comedy and acting. The mother recalls sending Emily away to another's care a second time and Emily's subsequent return, this time adjusting to a new stepfather. The narrator and her second husband often left Emily alone for hours. Emily was sick with the measles when the narrator went to the hospital to have another daughter, Susan. The illness left her thin, weak, and prone to nightmares. The narrator tries to comfort Emily now, in the present, but it is too late. Suffering from tuberculosis at another point in her life, Emily was sent to a convalescent home, where she could be better cared for. During twice-monthly visits, the narrator had to shout to Emily, who stood on a balcony some distance away, because all the parents were forbidden from getting too close to their children. Emily returned home frail, distant, and rigid, with little appetite. She disliked the way she looked and had few friends and little luck attracting boys' attention. The family moved frequently, and Emily's feigned illnesses meant she was often absent from school, where she was labeled a "slow learner."

In rare peaceful moments, Emily and Susan played together. Otherwise, the girls were at odds. Susan would retell one of Emily's jokes in front of company to the praise and admiration of all. Emily's physical development as a teenager was slow, and her self-esteem issues deepened. The crying of the narrator's infant son, Ronnie, interrupts her reverie, and she cradles the child. She resumes her examination of Emily's life, serving as mother to her four younger siblings during and after World War II and helping to get the chaotic brood off to school, where Emily was lost in her classes. Good at imitations and comic performances, Emily, with the narrator's encouragement, entered and won the school talent show. She tearfully phoned the narrator at work to tell her the news. Emily began performing widely, blossoming into a talented performer. But without the money and encouragement to develop her talent, her potential remained unfulfilled.

In the story's present moment, Emily returns home and fixes herself something to eat. The narrator assures the person she is addressing that Emily will be fine just as she is. She then lists the multiple reasons Emily had a rocky childhood and hopes that Emily will come to view herself as a valuable creation.

CHARACTER LIST

The Narrator   An unnamed, approximately forty-year-old woman who struggles to explain the aspects of her daughter Emily's childhood that have made Emily who she is. The narrator was a young single mother during the lean years of the Great Depression. After her first husband left her, she struggled to work and raise Emily alone. She eventually remarried and had four more children. As she settles into a more stable life, she looks back on the intervening years and challenges she faced as a mother. Her guilt about the lack of attention she gave Emily as she grew up is especially pronounced.

Emily   The narrator's nineteen-year-old daughter, who, according to an unnamed person, needs help. Emily is the oldest child in the family, a beautiful baby who grew gaunt and sickly as a child. She is just entering womanhood and displaying the beauty and grace that will mark her adult years. Despite having a great talent for acting and comedy, she is a somber loner who has always been self-conscious of her dark hair and complexion.

Susan   The narrator's approximately fourteen-year-old daughter. Chubby, blond, and curly-haired, Susan is an articulate and self-assured child. Because of her social exuberance, she easily outshines Emily. Susan is clumsy, selfish, and less thoughtful than Emily, who has grown to despise Susan during the years for being everything that she herself is not.

Ronnie   The narrator's infant son and one of her five children. Ronnie cries and interrupts the narrator's meditation on Emily's life. He represents a fresh start and the hope of the future, the opportunity for the narrator to right the wrongs of the past.

Bill   The narrator's second husband. Bill is mentioned only in passing, as a limited presence in the family.

ANALYSIS OF MAJOR CHARACTERS

THE NARRATOR   The narrator, oppressed by personal and environmental circumstances, laments the choices she has made as a mother. She frankly reveals the dark side of being a parent and discusses the heartbreak, lack of control, and hopelessness that often infiltrate low-income and lower-middle-class households. Through her personal, interior monologue, she gives an honest view of motherhood that is typically absent from the image of the self-denying, long-suffering "ideal mother" that society expects women to embrace. At the same time, there is a resigned, distant tone to her ruminations, a sad acceptance that she feels about events that are beyond her control or too far in the past to change. As she indicates at the beginning of the story, the ability to pause, analyze a situation, and determine the best course of action was a luxury she never had when she was a young mother. The narrator is weighed down with domestic duties, and the constant demands of a large family run counter to a life of thoughtful consideration. Her extended meditation on the state of her daughter is framed by labor, the domestic duty of ironing the family's clothes.

As the narrator presses Emily's dress and privately considers her response to a concerned teacher or counselor who has called about an undefined problem, she knows full well that she will not respond to the person's request for a face-to-face meeting. The ironing serves as the backdrop for her reckoning of her life as a mother, but it does not indicate any kind of impending action. This lack of initiative and her passive belief that Emily will somehow find the right path subtly expose the narrator's failings as a guardian and inability to fulfill the ideal of what a sacrificing, loving parent should be. Although the narrator accepts responsibility for her role in Emily's unhappy development, at the same time she absolves herself of full responsibility, placing blame on environmental and social conditions that are unsympathetic to the needs of a single mother. She is unable to fully acknowledge the somber, tentative young adult Emily has become, because doing so would force the narrator to accept the ways her adult life has fallen short of expectation.

EMILY   Emily is the central character of "I Stand Here Ironing," the subject of a fractured portrait that emerges from the narrator's memories of the past. Emily seems to be a forgotten child, a muted presence in the family. However, through the narrator's obsessive focus on Emily's development and current, unspecified predicament, a complex portrayal of a vibrant presence comes into focus. Even though the narrator dwells on the details of Emily's gloomy and sickly nature, lack of popularity, and low self-esteem, she ultimately describes a sensitive, thoughtful, and selfless individual who has survived simply because she must. Emily has a grim, cheerless demeanor as well as an incongruous gift for comedy and performance. In a way, her acting ability serves as a dour comment on her conditions growing up. Her penchant for mimicry and bringing characters vividly to life reflects Emily's desire to become someone else, transcend her present reality, and escape the squalor, lack of attention, and compromised conditions that have marked her life so far.

THEMES, MOTIFS, AND SYMBOLS

THEMES

THE UNSPOKEN BURDENS OF MOTHERHOOD In "I Stand Here Ironing," Olsen suggests that the role of selfless mother that society expects women to embrace is actually an obstacle to any kind of successful self-discovery. Rather than help women achieve self-actualization, motherhood actually strands women in lives laden with toil and excessive responsibility. Olsen offers a representation of motherhood laid bare, shorn of any romantic embellishment. Instead of presenting an ideal example of a nurturing role model guiding her charges to success, Olsen gives us a protagonist who obsessively meditates on the harsher, more bitter realities of family life. The narrator deflates certain overblown notions regarding motherhood, in particular the primacy of the child-parent bond. The narrator no more understands Emily than the teacher or counselor who requests the mother's presence at a face-to-face meeting. The narrator is not evil, abusive, or intentionally neglectful, but she is a conflicted victim of circumstance whose personal resources can go only so far. The fact that the narrator did not or could not participate more fully in Emily's life may have led to the undefined issue that currently besets the young woman. The narrator is able to meet the basic physical needs of her children but is incapable of forming a deeper, more emotional bond with them.

Although the narrator remarks that with young children around, her ears are not her own because she is always listening for crying, it is a lack of listening that has likely sparked the problem with Emily that spurs the narrator's reflection. Although the narrator laments the past, she still seems to lack enthusiasm for Emily and her pursuits and will probably only perpetuate Emily's poor social adjustment and low self-esteem. The narrator can ignore Emily's difficulties and hope that they work themselves out, but this is an attitude of defeat. The narrator has endured a life marked by problems and assumes that Emily will endure the same. One reward of motherhood is providing a different or better life for one's child, and the narrator seems to have given up hope of winning even this fundamental pleasure.

THE NATURE OF GUILT AND REGRET As the narrator acknowledges her inability to improve Emily's fortunes in life, she faces a spiritual defeat, and "I Stand Here Ironing" is the narrator's meditation on the nature of guilt and regret in her life as a mother. The narrator recognizes the powerful influence of poverty and oppressive conditions that women were forced to accept in the early to mid-twentieth century, but she does not deny her own contributions to the maladjusted young woman Emily has become. The narrator's attempt to "total it all"—that is, to take stock of her actions and decisions as a mother—reads like a list of crimes, a succinct, painful summary of her shortcomings. She offers herself some degree of understanding for the difficulties she faced as a poor and sometimes single mother, but she offers herself no forgiveness.

Emily stirs up guilt and regret in the narrator in a way that the narrator's other children do not. Emily was the narrator's first child, the one born into a state of crisis—hard work, little money, and no father around to help. The narrator was too frazzled and desperate to make ends meet to fully meet the child's needs. With the other children, however, the narrator smiled more and became more emotionally engaged. In many ways, the narrator's guilt is rooted in the possibility that Emily absorbed the anxiety and distress that once characterized the narrator's life, as though Emily's grim demeanor is a relic of this early pattern. The narrator also held Emily to different standards than the other children. She chides herself for demanding "goodness" out of Emily—not just an even, agreeable temperament but a stoic endurance of hardship and lack of resistance to it. Emily did not have the luxury of misbehaving or registering her disapproval in appropriately childish outbursts; instead, she absorbed the narrator's expectation that she should simply endure unpleasantness. The narrator's guilt and regret stem from her worries about what the long-term effects of Emily's forced self-control will ultimately be.

MOTIFS

ABSENCE Absence figures heavily in "I Stand Here Ironing," as the narrator feels guilty about her emotional distance and decision to send Emily away for periods of care or recovery. Emily and the narrator have been absent from each other's lives during significant portions of Emily's development. In fact, Emily has known almost nothing but distance and displacement. The narrator sent her to an unaffectionate neighbor for day care when she was eight months old, then to the home of her father's relatives, then to another caretaker, and finally to a convalescence facility. Each time Emily returned, she was forced to reintegrate into the changing fabric of the household, and the narrator notes how Emily grew slowly more distant and emotionally unresponsive.

After so much absence, the narrator intensifies her attempts to show Emily affection, but these attempts are rebuffed, coming too late to prevent Emily's withdrawal from her family and the world. Although Emily is now at home with the narrator, the sense of absence continues even in the present moment of the story. Emily, the narrator's central preoccupation, appears only as a fleeting presence. She enters the story only long enough to interrupt the narrator's musings on the past. Mother and daughter exist on the edges of each other's lives, and the narrator sees Emily as a mystery, even a stranger. The narrator tells her audience that she is not a key to Emily and is as unsure as anyone else about what kind of help Emily needs. All the narrator can do is benignly hope that Emily's life will improve, although she must also confront the fear that what has been a virtually lifelong absence has created an unbridgeable gulf between them.

DOUBLES Emily is a double for the narrator, reflecting the narrator's fears that she has transferred her hard, hopeless life to Emily, continuing the legacy of poverty and lack of opportunity that plague some women of limited means. A "double" in fiction is a character that serves as a twin for another, usually more central, character, embodying either similar or opposite characteristics. In a flashback, the narrator recalls having Emily when she was only nineteen, the exact age Emily is in the present moment of the story. This similarity links the two characters, fusing their experiences and potential futures. The narrator remembers being nineteen and a single mother during the Great Depression, while Emily is now nineteen and in a similarly dire, though unspecified, situation. Both women began or are beginning their young adulthood facing a personal challenge of some kind.

Just as the narrator was left to deal with problems on her own two decades ago, Emily is left on her own to face whatever problem is plaguing her now. The narrator does not make an effort to help Emily or intervene in her life, despite an unnamed person's attempt to draw the narrator in. The narrator's own life could have been altered had she been helped, but she fails to see that the same could be true for Emily. In this way, Emily's life starts to clearly mirror the narrator's. Actual mirrors appear briefly in the story when the narrator brings Emily and Susan "two old dresser mirrors," subtly suggesting the ways in which a generation mirrors the one that came before it. The doubling of mother and daughter in this story is not positive. Instead, the narrator dreads the idea of Emily being a reflection of her, because she understands that Emily's grim nature is likely a result of the narrator's pervasive worries and inattention, and that Emily's future may turn out as burdened and unfulfilled as her own.

SYMBOLS

THE IRON The iron represents the chores and responsibilities that prevented the narrator from engaging with Emily's life more profoundly. As the story's title suggests, the narrator is constantly embroiled in the duties she must perform to effectively care for her family. This is ironic because it is these duties that drew her away from Emily and lessened the quality of her care. The repetitive motion of the iron moving back and forth across the surface of the ironing board mimics the narrator's thought processes as she moves back and forth over her life as a mother, attempting to identify the source of Emily's current difficulties. The distance the narrator feels from Emily is embodied in this simple act of ironing. Although Emily's welfare is the central concern of the story, the narrator is more actively engaged in unwrinkling her daughter's dress than in the life of the young woman who will wear it. The narrator's final wish is that Emily will have a strong sense of self-worth and believe that she is more than the dress that is "helpless before the iron." This comment suggests that the narrator hopes Emily will be able to transcend the narrator's mistakes, rather than succumb to the circumstances of her birth.

THE CONVALESCENT HOME AND EMILY'S BALCONY The convalescent home where Emily recovers from tuberculosis represents the narrator's inability to effectively care for her children. A social welfare agency has stepped in to provide Emily with the care and attention she does not receive at home—Emily can recover only if she is looked after by strangers in an unfamiliar place. The facility is supported by society women who have placed the children's convalescence center on their list of causes, and they help support the facility through fundraisers. These women couldn't be more different from the narrator, who has struggled for her entire life to make ends meet. The wide green lawns and "fluted flower beds" contrast starkly with the narrator's drab world of ironing in her cramped walkup apartment.

Emily's balcony in particular represents the emotional distance between the narrator and her daughter. While Emily is at the recovery center, she is cut off from almost all communication. Even the letters the narrator writes to her are read to her once and then thrown away. Parents are allowed to visit only every other Sunday, when the children line up on the balconies of their cottages and conduct shouted conversations with the parents who stand below. The narrator seems unable to establish direct contact with Emily, either in the recovery center or their home life. The narrator refers to the "invisible wall" that divides them, both then and now. A sign instructing visitors not to "contaminate" their children through "physical contact" suggests that the narrator herself is a source of contamination, allowing her daughter to sicken while she devoted her attention to other responsibilities. The mother's emotional neglect of Emily has permanently "contaminated" her as well, infusing her with a bleakness that the narrator fears will never disappear.

SHORT STORY ANALYSIS

STRUCTURE AND POINT OF VIEW   The narrator's stream-of-consciousness narration reflects the free-flowing, unstructured form of her thoughts and reveals her struggle to make sense of her situation and find logic among the fragments of her past. The narrator tries to excavate the past to gain a clear idea of how her history has shaped Emily, but clarity ultimately eludes her. The narrator's nonlinear, often jumbled thoughts and conclusions reflect Olsen's belief that a tangled web of familial and environmental causes is what shapes character and that no single explanation can illuminate the complexities of an individual's behavior. The narrator's associative leaps and often rambling narrative style also infuse the story with realism and immediacy. The mother often repeats herself, such as "She was a beautiful baby," and repeatedly mentions her struggle to "total"—draw conclusions from—her ruminations. These repetitions underscore the realism that infuses the story and offer insight into the issues that weigh most heavily on the narrator's mind.

The stream-of-consciousness structure allows the narrator to reveal herself on her own terms, a strategy that gives the narrator a fuller, unfiltered presence in the story. At the same time, this strategy forces us to consider that the narrator may be unreliable. An unreliable narrator may lie or alter or withhold information to make him- or herself look good or serve a personal agenda of some kind. In this story, the narrator may be holding some memories back or shaping the memories she reports to lessen her feelings of guilt. The narrator makes some startling confessions, such as revealing that she and her second husband often left Emily home alone for hours, which suggests that the narrator is being honest and open about her parenting. But the narrator also quietly asserts that she alone is not at fault. She gestures to "what cannot be helped," or broader social forces, such as the grinding poverty of the Depression years, that were beyond her control. The narrator has a personal reason for identifying a broad range of forces at play in shaping Emily: she wants to lessen her unbearable feelings of guilt. She is trying to convince herself that other factors are to blame as much as she is trying to convince us.

INTERIOR MONOLOGUE   Olsen has the narrator tell her story through an interior monologue, which is an aspect of stream-of-consciousness narration that focuses solely on one character's thoughts, feelings, and associations. An interior monologue is a device that writers use to reveal essential problems faced by a narrator. It may be addressed to an imagined audience or to oneself. In this story, the narrator addresses her monologue to the unidentified party who has expressed concern about Emily, and the monologue is emblematic of her passive response to a situation that actually requires action. Rather than engage with Emily's teacher or counselor and work toward finding a way to help, the narrator describes problems, causes, and thoughts—but only to herself. The interior monologue is private and unspoken, and she means it as a response, but in reality it is no response at all. Just as an imagined response is inadequate, the narrator's passive hope that Emily will be okay is inadequate as well. And because the interior monologue admits no voices but the narrator's, we get the sense that, because the narrator has chosen to stay uninvolved, Emily will be left entirely on her own.

HISTORICAL CONTEXT   "I Stand Here Ironing" is best understood in the context of two social forces that gripped the United States in the twentieth century: the lean years of the Great Depression and the burgeoning feminist movement of the 1950s and beyond. "I Stand Here Ironing" is highly autobiographical, and the narrator, a single, teenage mother raising a daughter in the depths of the Great Depression, is a double for Olsen. "It was the pre-relief, pre-WPA world of the depression," the narrator notes when she describes the reality into which Emily was born. The Works Progress Administration (WPA) was a relief agency that provided work rather than welfare to the nation's struggling families. Without employment assistance or financial relief, the narrator was left to her own devices, forced to face the grim specter of poverty and the need to work while raising her infant daughter alone. Those trying years have left an indelible mark on the narrator, who openly cites the permanent effect that this inescapable crisis had not only on her family but also on her psyche. Olsen also raised a child alone in the early 1930s and, like the narrator, faced economic hardship that led to great emotional strain.

During the Depression years, many single, working mothers struggled with a lack of so-cial services and financial support. Olsen's story provides a glimpse of a woman's experi-ence of economic deprivation, and her writing at the time added to the growing momentum of the feminist literary movement in the 1960s. Readers, particularly female readers, were drawn to Olsen's fictional portraits of working-class women who struggled to balance the demands of their professional and private lives, often at great expense to themselves and their self-identity. Olsen's work helped to shatter stereotypes of the ideal mother who effortlessly and selflessly nurtures her family while easily putting aside her own hopes. "I Stand Here Ironing" desanctified motherhood, giving voice to the self-doubt and ambivalence that some mothers felt when faced with the challenges of child-rearing.

IMPORTANT QUOTATIONS EXPLAINED

---

1. *I stand here ironing, and what you asked me moves tormented back and forth with the iron.*

The opening line of "I Stand Here Ironing" establishes the oppressive world of domestic tasks that punctuate the narrator's life and form the background for any consideration of more abstract concerns. The quotation also provides one of the story's central metaphors. Just as the narrator is pressing her daughter's dress, so too is she "ironing out" the path of Emily's development and the problem she is facing. The act of ironing imparts smoothness and order to a garment, and the narrator wishes that Emily's life could run more smoothly as well—although she stops short of taking steps to help Emily achieve this goal. The word *tormented* reveals the extent of the narrator's guilt at the lack of attention and limited op-portunities Emily has suffered. However, the act of ironing, part of the never-ending cycle of domestic duties, is what the narrator falls back on when she subtly pleads her defense. With so many chores to perform, the narrator argues, there was little time to devote too much at-tention to Emily's personal development. The narrator feels guilty about her shortcomings as a mother, but her guilt is not enough to make her put the ironing aside. The ironing is an inescapable fact of life, and the narrator, although "tormented," can do nothing about it.

2. *She is a child of her age, of depression, of war, of fear.*

This quotation appears at the end of the second-to-last paragraph, immediately preceding the narrator's exhortation regarding Emily to "Let her be." This attitude is representative of the narrator's feelings toward her performance as a mother. Although the narrator has guiltily listed the personal shortcomings that prevented her from adequately caring for Emily, she also indicts larger, uncontrollable forces—depression, war, and fear—that thwart even the best of intentions. The poverty that arose during the Great Depression clearly influenced what went on in the household. It kept the narrator away from home because she needed to work. Armed conflict and the ensuing climate of fear that accompanied the Cold War were other powerful and looming presences, diminishing the hope and faith that had prevailed after World War II.

This quotation encapsulates the narrator's belief that individual lives can be waylaid by uncontrollable, overpowering forces. This belief applies not only to Emily's life but to her own life as well. The narrator herself struggled with bleak prospects and despair, which she attributes to inescapable social factors. The narrator does bear some responsibility for Emily's problems, but as a single mother, she had no choice but to prioritize work and wage earning. Ultimately, the narrator admits her own guilt in creating Emily's unspecified problem, but she freely blames depression, war, and fear as well.

Interpreter of Maladies

Jhumpa Lahiri
(1967–)

CONTEXT

Jhumpa Lahiri was born in 1967 in London, England, and raised in Rhode Island. Her father and mother, a librarian and teacher, respectively, had emigrated from Calcutta, India, and Lahiri spoke Bengali with them at home. As Lahiri grew up, she never felt fully American because of her parents' deep ties to India, her own frequent visits there, and the fact that she was born in another country altogether. As a child, Lahiri wrote stories and short novels and for her school newspaper, but she never seriously considered writing as a true path. For most of her young adulthood, Lahiri didn't write at all, starting again only when she graduated from Barnard College, where she studied literature, and began figuring out what she should do next. Although she continued to write fiction and publish stories in small literary journals, Lahiri pursued three master's degrees, in English, creative writing, and comparative studies, as well as a Ph.D. in Renaissance studies, at Boston University.

In 1998, Lahiri was accepted to the Fine Arts Work Center in Provincetown, Massachusetts, an esteemed arts center that supports emerging and established writers and artists by providing them with short residencies that allow them time to work exclusively on their art. In the same year, she published "A Temporary Matter" in the *New Yorker* and began to garner immense critical praise. She went on to publish two more stories in the magazine within a one-year period, "Sexy" and "The Third and Final Continent." These stories eventually became part of the nine-story collection *Interpreter of Maladies*, which Lahiri published in 1999.

Interpreter of Maladies was Lahiri's first book and an immediate success. It won the Pulitzer Prize in 2000, making Lahiri the first person of South Asian descent to win an individual Pulitzer Prize. Her collection triumphed over the work of two established writers—*Close Range: Wyoming Stories*, by Annie Proulx, and *Waiting*, by Ha Jin. The title story, "Interpreter of Maladies," won an O. Henry Award for Best American Short Stories and was included in the anthology *Best American Short Stories* in 1999.

Although Lahiri never lived in India, her frequent visits to Calcutta familiarized her with the city, and she chose to marry there in 2001. Most of Lahiri's work focuses on the lives of Indian Americans, and the stories in *Interpreter of Maladies* are set in India or parts of the United States, including Cambridge, Massachusetts, and an unnamed university town very much like Cambridge. In her stories, characters come together for reasons that are not intimate and wind up finding themselves in intimate situations. For example, in "Interpreter of Maladies," the two main characters find themselves together in a car because one of them hires the other as a tour guide. Other stories in the collection involve a landlady and her tenants, an after-school caretaker and her ward, and a married couple in crisis. Lahiri tells many of the stories through the unexpected narrative perspective of someone who is not closely related to the person under observation. Few of the stories involve dramatic plot lines, although most involve the aftershocks of some major life-changing event, such as an affair, a miscarriage, or immigration.

India looms large in each story, although its influence varies in each story as it does in each character's life. India is a country of linguistic diversity. The central government uses both Hindi and English, as is required by the Indian constitution, and an additional twenty-two languages are recognized as official languages of India. By some counts, there are more than 400 languages spoken in India, while others prefer to say that there are more than 2,000 dialects. Indians have immigrated to the United States in astonishing numbers since the 1960s. Largely well educated and highly skilled, Indian immigrants come for a variety of reasons, but often to seek work in technological fields. Indian Americans now constitute the third-largest Asian American community in the United States.

In 2003, Lahiri published her second book, *The Namesake*, and continues to publish individual short stories. She lives in Brooklyn, New York, with her husband and two children.

PLOT OVERVIEW

The Das family is in India on vacation, and Mr. Das has hired Mr. Kapasi to drive them to visit the Sun Temple. The family sits in the car, which is stopped near a tea stall. Mr. and Mrs. Das are arguing about who should take their daughter, Tina, to the bathroom, and Mrs. Das ultimately takes her. Ronny, their son, darts out of the car to look at a goat. Mr. Das, who closely resembles Ronny, reprimands him but does nothing to stop him, even when he says he wants to give the goat a piece of gum. Mr. Das tells Bobby, the younger of their two sons, to go look after Ronny. When Bobby refuses, Mr. Das does nothing to enforce his order.

Mr. Das tells Mr. Kapasi that both he and his wife were born and raised in the United States. Mr. Das also reveals that their parents now live in India and that the Das family visits them every few years. Tina comes back to the car, clutching a doll with shorn hair. Mr. Das asks Tina where her mother is, using Mrs. Das's first name, Mina. Mr. Kapasi notices that Mr. Das uses his wife's first name, and he thinks it is an unusual way to speak to a child. While Mrs. Das buys some puffed rice from a nearby vendor, Mr. Das tells Mr. Kapasi that he is a middle-school teacher in New Brunswick, New Jersey. Mr. Kapasi reveals that he has been a tour guide for five years.

The group sets off. Tina plays with the locks in the back of the car, and Mrs. Das does not stop her. Mrs. Das sits in the car silently and eats her snack without offering any to anyone else. Along the road, they see monkeys, which Mr. Kapasi says are common in the area. Mr. Das has him stop the car so he can take a picture of a starving peasant. Mr. and Mrs. Das quarrel because Mr. Das has not gotten them a tour guide whose car has air-conditioning. Mr. Kapasi observes that Mr. and Mrs. Das are more like siblings to their children than parents.

Mr. Kapasi tells the Dases about his other job as an interpreter in a doctor's office. Mrs. Das remarks that his job is romantic and asks him to tell her about some of his patients. However, Mr. Kapasi views his job as a failure. At one time, he had been a scholar of many languages, and now he remains fluent only in English. He took the interpreting job as a way to pay the medical bills when his eldest son contracted typhoid and died at age seven. He kept the job because the pay was better than his previous teaching job, but it reminds his wife of their son's death. Mr. Kapasi's marriage was arranged by his parents, and he and his wife have nothing in common. Mr. Kapasi, seduced by Mrs. Das's description of his job as "romantic," begins fantasizing about Mrs. Das.

When they stop for lunch, Mrs. Das insists that Mr. Kapasi sit with them. He does, and Mr. Das takes their picture together. Mrs. Das gets Mr. Kapasi's address so that she can send him a copy of the picture, and Mr. Kapasi begins to daydream about how they will have a great correspondence that will, in a way, finally fulfill his dreams of being a diplomat between countries. He imagines the witty things he will write to her and how she will reveal the unhappiness of her marriage.

At the temple, Mrs. Das talks with Mr. Kapasi as they stare at friezes of women in erotic poses. Mr. Kapasi admires her legs and continues to dream about their letters. Dreading taking the Dases back to their hotel, he suggests that they go see a nearby monastery, and they agree. When they arrive, the place is swarming with monkeys. Mr. Kapasi tells the children and Mr. Das that the monkeys are not dangerous as long as they are not fed.

Mrs. Das stays in the car because her legs are tired. She sits in the front seat next to Mr. Kapasi and confesses to him that her younger son, Bobby, is the product of an affair she had eight years ago. She slept with a friend of Mr. Das's who came to visit while she was a lonely housewife, and she has never told anyone about it. She tells Mr. Kapasi because he is an interpreter of maladies and she believes he can help her. Mr. Kapasi's crush on her begins to evaporate. Mrs. Das reveals that she no longer loves her husband, whom she has known since she was a young child, and that she has destructive impulses toward her children and life. She asks Mr. Kapasi to suggest some remedy for her pain. Mr. Kapasi, insulted, asks her whether it isn't really just guilt she feels. Mrs. Das gets out of the car and joins her family. As she walks, she drops a trail of puffed rice.

Meanwhile, the children and Mr. Das have been playing with the monkeys. When Mrs. Das rejoins them, Bobby is missing. They find him surrounded by monkeys that have become crazed from Mrs. Das's puffed rice and are hitting Bobby on the legs with a stick he had given them. Mr. Das accidentally takes a picture in his nervousness, and Mrs. Das screams for Mr. Kapasi to do something. Mr. Kapasi chases off the monkeys and carries Bobby back to his family. Mrs. Das puts a bandage on Bobby's knee. Then she reaches into her handbag to get a hairbrush to straighten his hair, and the paper with Mr. Kapasi's address on it flutters away.

CHARACTER LIST

Mr. Kapasi   The Indian tour guide who accompanies the Das family on their trip. Mr. Kapasi was once fluent in many languages but now speaks only English. He once dreamed of being a diplomat but now works as a translator in a doctor's office, a job he acquired when his young son died from typhoid. Mr. Kapasi lives in a loveless, arranged marriage and no longer sees himself as a potential object of interest for women. He entertains fantasies about Mrs. Das but is ultimately horrified by her confession of infidelity and self-absorption.

Mrs. Mina Das   The self-absorbed wife of Mr. Das whose infidelity has isolated her from her husband and children. Mrs. Das cares only about herself and her needs and has little true connection to the people around her. After having an affair eight years ago and conceiving Bobby, she never told Mr. Das or Bobby the truth. Her need to confess her past transgressions horrifies Mr. Kapasi.

Mr. Das   The middle-school science teacher who hires Mr. Kapasi to accompany the family on their trip. Mr. Das takes a voyeuristic interest in India and its people, not really connecting with his surroundings except through his camera and guide book. Mr. Das is a passive, ineffective parent, incapable or unwilling to reprimand his children for misbehaving. In a moment of crisis, when Bobby is surrounded by monkeys, he fails to do anything but accidentally take a picture of the scene.

Bobby Das   The younger Das son, who is not actually Mr. Das's child. Bobby does not resemble Mr. Das physically or temperamentally. He is surly and treats Mr. Das disrespectfully.

Tina Das   The young Das daughter. Tina whines and misbehaves, seeking her mother's attention and failing to get it.

Ronny Das   The eldest Das child. Ronny does not listen to his parents, preferring to do what he wants to do.

ANALYSIS OF MAJOR CHARACTERS

MR. KAPASI   Mr. Kapasi believes that his life is a failure and longs for something more. In his efforts to lift his existence out of the daily, monotonous grind it has become, Mr. Kapasi develops a far-fetched fantasy about the possibility of a deep friendship between himself and Mrs. Das. This fantasy reveals just how lonely Mr. Kapasi's life and marriage have become. His arranged marriage is struggling because his wife cannot recover from her grief over the loss of their young son or forgive him for working for the doctor who failed to save their son's life. His career is far less than what he dreamed it might be. He uses his knowledge of English in only the most peripheral way, in high contrast to the dreams of scholarly and diplomatic greatness he once had. In his isolation, he sees Mrs. Das as a potential kindred spirit because she also languishes in a loveless marriage. He imagines similarities between them that do not exist, yearning to find a friend in this American woman. Not surprisingly, the encounter ends in disappointment. When Mrs. Das does confide in him, he feels only disgust. The intimacy he thought he wanted revolts him when he learns more about Mrs. Das's nature.

In both of Mr. Kapasi's jobs, as a tour guide and an interpreter for a doctor, he acts as a cultural broker. As a tour guide, he shows mostly English-speaking Europeans and Americans the sights of India, and in his work as an interpreter, he helps the ailing from another region to communicate with their physician. Although neither occupation attains the aspirations of diplomacy he once had, Mrs. Das helps him view both as important vocations. However, Mr. Kapasi is ultimately unable to bridge the cultural gap between himself and Mrs. Das, whether it stems from strictly national differences or more personal ones. Mr. Kapasi's brief transformation from ordinary tour guide to "romantic" interpreter ends poorly, with his return to the ordinary drudgery of his days.

MRS. MINA DAS Mrs. Das's fundamental failing is that she is profoundly selfish and self-absorbed. She does not see anyone else as they are but rather as a means to fulfilling her own needs and wishes. Her romanticized view of Mr. Kapasi's day job leads her to confide in him, and she is oblivious to the fact that he would rather she did not. She persists in confiding even when it is clear that Mr. Kapasi has no advice to offer her. Mrs. Das is selfish, declining to share her food with her children, reluctantly taking her daughter to the bathroom, and refusing to paint her daughter's fingernails. She openly derides her husband and mocks his enthusiasm for tourism, using the fact that they are no longer in love as an excuse for her bad behavior. Although Mrs. Das has been unfaithful, she feels the strain in her marriage only as her own pain. She fails to recognize the toll her affair takes on her husband and children. Rather than face the misery she has caused, Mrs. Das hides behind her sunglasses and disengages from her family. Likewise, when her attempt at confiding in Mr. Kapasi fails, she leaves the car rather than confront the guilt that Mr. Kapasi has suggested is the source of her pain.

Mrs. Das embodies stereotypically American flaws, including disrespect for other countries and cultures, poorly behaved children, and a self-involvement so extensive that she blames others for her feelings of guilt about her infidelity. She is messy, lazy, and a bad parent. She has no concern for the environment or her effect on it and drops her rice snacks all over the ground, riling the local wildlife. She represents what is often called the "ugly American," a traveler who stands out in every situation because of her expansive sense of self-importance and entitlement.

THEMES, MOTIFS, AND SYMBOLS

THEMES

THE DIFFICULTY OF COMMUNICATION Communication breaks down repeatedly in "Interpreter of Maladies," often with hurtful consequences. Mr. Kapasi, who is the interpreter of maladies, as Mrs. Das names him, has lost his ability to communicate with his wife, forcing him to drink his tea in silence at night and leading to a loveless marriage. He has also lost his ability to communicate in some of the languages he learned as a younger man, leaving him with only English, which he fears he does not speak as well as his children. Mr. and Mrs. Das do not communicate, not because of a language barrier but because Mrs. Das hides behind her sunglasses most of the time and Mr. Das has his nose buried in a guidebook. The children do not listen to their parents, nor do they listen to Mr. Kapasi about the monkeys. All these frustrated attempts at communicating with one another lead to hurt feelings. The Kapasis are trapped in a failing marriage. The Dases are openly hostile to each other. The Das children run rampant over their parents and everyone else. And Mr. Kapasi and Mrs. Das are unable to reach a level of friendship that they both may have sought, if only they could speak with one another openly. When Mrs. Das loses Mr. Kapasi's address at the end of the story, it marks the termination of the possibility that they could reach out to each other and the definite end to all communication between them.

THE DANGER OF ROMANTICISM Every time a character in "Interpreter of Maladies" fails to see the truth about another person, the results are in some way harmful. The main conflict of the story centers on two people who romanticize each other, although in different ways. Mr. Kapasi sees Mrs. Das as a lonely housewife who could be a perfect companion to him in his own loneliness. He misses or ignores cues that she may not be interested in him for his own sake because, at some level, he wants her to be this companion. He sees many details about her, such as her bare legs and Americanized shirt and bag, but he passes over others, such as the way she dismisses her children's desires and her selfishness with her snack. Such unflattering details do not fit with his conception of her. Likewise, Mrs. Das wants Mr. Kapasi to become a confidante to her and solve her personal and marital difficulties. She views him as a father figure and helper and misses or ignores indications that he may not fit those roles. For example, she doesn't notice that he is uncomfortable with her personal revelations and presses him for help even when he explicitly tells her that he cannot give it to her.

Besides romanticizing one another, the characters also romanticize their surroundings, resulting in insensitivity and danger. Mr. Das, for example, photographs the Indian peasant whose suffering he finds appropriate for a tourist's shot. He sees only what he wants to see—an interesting picture from a foreign land—not the actual man who is starving by the roadside. Even when Bobby is surrounded by monkeys, in genuine distress, Mr. Das can do nothing but snap a picture, as though this scene is also somehow separate from reality. Throughout their trip, Mr. Das fails to engage with India in any substantial way, preferring to hide behind the efficient descriptions in his guidebook. His romanticized tourist's view of India keeps him from connecting to the country that his parents call home.

MOTIFS

SEEING Each character in the story has a distorted way of seeing the others, as each views others through some artificial means. Mr. Das views the world through his camera. His camera is always around his neck, and he sees even harsh realities through its lens. For example, he takes pictures of the starving peasant, even though doing so blatantly ignores the peasant's essential reality. Mrs. Das hides behind her sunglasses, seeing the others through their tint and blocking others' view of her eyes. Additionally, her window does not roll down, so she cannot directly see the world outside the taxi cab. Mr. Kapasi watches Mrs. Das through the rearview mirror, which distorts his view of her and prevents him from looking at her directly. Each child is wearing a visor, which suggests that their vision will one day be as distorted as their parents' is. Finally, Mr. Das and Ronny closely resemble each other, whereas Mr. Das and Bobby have little in common. Mr. Kapasi simply observes this fact but draws no inference from it, even though this simple fact hints at the deeper truth: that Mr. Das is not Bobby's father. Because Mr. Kapasi sees the Das family as a unit, he never suspects this truth. His idea of family distorts the reality of the situation.

SYMBOLS

THE CAMERA Mr. Das's camera represents his inability to see the world clearly or engage with it. Because he views the world through his camera, Mr. Das misses the reality of the world around him, both in his marriage and in the scenes outside the cab. Mr. Das chooses to have Mr. Kapasi stop the cab so that he can take a photograph of a starving peasant, wanting the picture only as a souvenir of India and ignoring the man's obvious need for help. His view of the man's reality is distorted because he sees the man only through the camera lens. Mr. Das snaps pictures of monkeys and scenery, taking the camera from his eye only when he turns back to his guidebook. Rather than engage actively with the India that surrounds him, he instead turns to the safety of frozen images and bland descriptions of ancient sites. He has come to visit India, but what he will take away with him—pictures and snatches of guidebook phrases—he could have gotten from any shop at home in New Brunswick, New Jersey.

Mr. Das also uses the camera to construct a family life that does not actually exist. His children are insolent and his wife is distant, yet Mr. Das tries to pose them in pictures that suggest harmony and intimacy. When Mrs. Das refuses to leave the car when they visit the monastic dwellings, Mr. Das tries to change her mind because he wants to get a complete family portrait—something, he says, they can use for their Christmas card. This "happy family" that Mr. Das aspires to catch on film is pure fabrication, but Mr. Das does not seem to care. He would rather exist in an imaginary state of willful ignorance and arm's-length engagement than face the disappointments and difficulties of his real life.

MRS. DAS'S PUFFED RICE   Puffed rice, insubstantial and bland, represents Mrs. Das's mistakes and careless actions. Physically, Mrs. Das is young and attractive, but she is spiritually empty. She does not love her children or husband and is caught in the boredom of her life as a housewife. Her depression and apathy distance her from her family, but she harbors a secret that could tear the entire family apart. She carelessly scatters the puffed rice along the trail at the monastic dwellings, never thinking about the danger her actions pose to others. Even when she realizes the danger to Bobby, as monkeys surround and terrify him, Mrs. Das does not take any responsibility for the situation, just as she refuses to acknowledge any guilt about her affair with Mr. Das's friend. If Mrs. Das's secret is ever revealed, Bobby will be the true victim of that carelessness as well. Conceived out of anger, boredom, and spite and then lied to about his real father, Bobby is surrounded by deceit. Mr. Kapasi feels the urge to tell Bobby the truth as he carries him away from the monkeys. He knows that the safety he is providing for the boy—scattering the monkeys and lifting Bobby away from danger—is insubstantial. He delivers Bobby back to Mrs. Das, whose distance and carelessness fail to provide true safety.

SHORT STORY ANALYSIS

POINT OF VIEW   "Interpreter of Maladies" is told from third-person limited point of view—that is, the story is told by an objective narrator who reveals the perceptions of Mr. Kapasi's perceptions but not those of the other characters. Events unfold primarily as Mr. Kapasi, not Mrs. Das, sees them. For example, when the characters leave the taxi at the temple, the narrator follows Mr. Kapasi, who walks ahead so as not to disturb Mrs. Das, and does not show us what Mrs. Das is doing until she again enters Mr. Kapasi's view. Likewise, when Mrs. Das leaves the taxi to take Tina to the bathroom, the narrator stays in the car with Mr. Kapasi, who waits alone while the boys and Mr. Das get out of the car. Even the characters' names reflect the focus on Mr. Kapasi. Instead of calling Mrs. Das by her first name, Mina, as both her husband and her children do, the narrator refers to her exclusively as Mrs. Das, which is how Mr. Kapasi sees her. Likewise, the narrator does not disclose information that

Mr. Kapasi would not know. We do not, for example, ever learn the exact ages of Ronny and Tina. We do, however, hear about how Mr. Kapasi has only two suits, the better of the two is the one he wears in the story.

By using this point of view, Lahiri limits the scope of our knowledge about the Das family and emphasizes the disconnection between Mrs. Das and Mr. Kapasi. Although Mr. Kapasi interprets Mrs. Das's comments as flattering and even flirtatious, Mrs. Das likely did not intend her comments to be construed this way. Mr. Kapasi wishes for an intimate connection with Mrs. Das, but when she finally does spill her secrets—her affair, her true feelings about her husband, the heated beginning of their relationship—Mr. Kapasi is overwhelmed and disgusted. She was unaware of how crass and inappropriate her revelations would seem to Mr. Kapasi, just as she is oblivious to how insulting it is for her to expect him to have a "cure" for her pain. Mr. Kapasi thinks he and Mrs. Das have a connection because he recognizes in her situation the distant spouse and troubled marriage from his own life. However, any connection between them is only in his mind.

CHARACTER DEVELOPMENT   To develop characters in "Interpreter of Maladies," Lahiri layers small, specific details in her descriptions of each character, giving them depth and richness. From the first paragraph of the story, details such as the bickering about who will accompany Tina to the bathroom and the fact that Mrs. Das does not hold Tina's hand tell us that Mr. and Mrs. Das are at odds, at least in some small way, and that Mrs. Das is a somewhat careless mother. These details are important because the narrator tells us few explicit facts about the Das family. Rather, we must infer information about them from the way they act. We learn about Mr. Das's distance and willful ignorance from his picture taking and absorption in his guidebook, and we learn about the children's insolence through small behaviors, such as Tina's playing with the car locks and Ronny's approaching the goat with gum. Mr. Kapasi infers what he knows about the Das family from the same set of details.

The small pieces of information that we have about Mrs. Das almost overwhelm her big confession toward the end of the story. What we know of her character is based less on the substantial knowledge that she has committed adultery with her husband's friend and borne a child of the affair and more on the less significant fact that she does not share her puffed rice with her children or husband, does not care to be in the photographs they take at the monastery, and wears insensible shoes while she goes sightseeing. Mrs. Das is, with Mr. Kapasi, the most important character in the story, but what we know of her comes from the fact that she wears sunglasses, wears a shirt with a strawberry on it, shaves her legs, and carries a large, overstuffed purse. By providing so many small, specific details, Lahiri vividly portrays Mrs. Das but also allows for some ambiguity. Mr. Kapasi perceives the same details but misconstrues what they mean about Mrs. Das, mistakenly believing that she shares with him some problem or connection.

CULTURE CLASH   Central themes of all of Lahiri's work, "Interpreter of Maladies" included, are the difficulties that Indians have in relating to Americans and the ways in which Indian Americans are caught in the middle of two very different cultures. We learn quite a few details about where the Das family fits into this cultural divide. Mr. and Mrs. Das were both born and raised in America, although their retired parents have now moved to India to live. The Dases visit every few years, bringing the children with them. They are Indian but not of India, and their dress and manner are wholly American. Although Mr. Kapasi recognizes some common cultural heritage, the Dases are no more familiar with India than any other tourist. Mr. Das relies on a tourist guidebook to tell him about the country through which they are traveling, and Mrs. Das could not be more uninterested in her surroundings if she tried. Although India is their parents' home, Mr. and Mrs. Das are foreigners. Mr. Das even seems to take pride in his status as a stranger, telling Mr. Kapasi about his American roots with an "air of sudden confidence."

Though Mr. Kapasi and the Dases do share an Indian heritage, their marriages reveal the extent of how different their cultures really are. Mr. Kapasi believes that he can relate to Mrs. Das's unhappy marriage because he himself is in an unhappy marriage. He seeks this common ground as a way to find friendship and connection. However, the connection fails because the marriages are so vastly different. Mr. Kapasi's parents arranged his marriage, and he and Mrs. Kapasi have nothing in common. By contrast, Mrs. Das fell in love with Mr. Das at a young age, and although their union was encouraged by their parents, her marriage was not arranged. Mrs. Das's comments about her and Mr. Das's sexual behaviors during their courtship shock Mr. Kapasi, who has never seen his wife naked. Furthermore, Mr. Kapasi is offended by the concept of infidelity in Mrs. Das's marriage. This lack of understanding reflects a differing understanding of duty and family between the two cultures. The two marriages may both be unhappy, but the causes, remedies, mistakes, and results of that unhappiness have no overlap whatsoever. Mr. Kapasi's fantasy of forging a friendship with Mrs. Das is shattered even before he sees his address slip away in the wind. The cultural divide between him and Mrs. Das is, from his view, simply too vast.

IMPORTANT QUOTATIONS EXPLAINED

1. *The family looked Indian but dressed as foreigners did, the children in stiff, brightly colored clothing and caps with translucent visors.*

This quotation appears in the second paragraph of the story and highlights one of the story's central themes: the difficulty of communication, particularly between Indians and Indian Americans. Here, the narrator describes the Das family, emphasizing the ways in which they are and aren't Indian. The fact that the family seems both Indian and American forms part of what fools Mr. Kapasi into thinking he can communicate intimately with Mrs. Das. With his other tourists, who are foreign but non-Indian, Mr. Kapasi readily maintains an appropriate distance. He does not seek any sort of connection, nor does he expect to find one. However, the similarities between Mrs. Das and Mr. Kapasi lead him to mistakenly think they will find something significant in common. Their fraught interaction gestures to the idea that the cultural gap between Indian immigrants and those they leave behind in India can be enormous, a gap that widens further between the immigrants and second-generation Americans born in the United States. That gap leads to miscommunication and misunderstanding, which, in turn, leads to pain for everyone involved.

2. *She would write to him, asking about his days interpreting at the doctor's office, and he would respond eloquently, choosing only the most entertaining anecdotes, ones that would make her laugh out loud as she read them in her house in New Jersey.*

After Mrs. Das calls Mr. Kapasi's job "romantic," Mr. Kapasi begins to daydream about how they will become great friends. The international nature of their friendship appeals to him because it makes him feel like a diplomat or cultural broker. The daydream, however, will never come to pass. Mr. Kapasi fails to see the true Mrs. Das, and vice versa, and there is no way to bridge the gap between them and reach any sort of genuine connection. These fantasies illustrate how lonely Mr. Kapasi's life has become and how much he wants and needs a friend. They underscore his frustration with his daily existence, especially his feelings of failure about how he uses the languages that he spent his youth working hard to acquire. Mrs. Das makes Mr. Kapasi feel important, which makes him happy. This exaltation intensifies the disappointment Mr. Kapasi feels when Mrs. Das confesses her secret. Mr. Kapasi had misinterpreted Mrs. Das's comment, mistakenly believing it gestured to a deeper understanding between them. The truth is that there is no hope for a correspondence, much less a friendship. When his address flutters out of her handbag, ending all possibility of their ever communicating, Mr. Kapasi has already realized the impossibility of his fantasies.

3. *He decided to begin with the most obvious question, to get to the heart of the matter, and so he asked, "Is it really pain you feel, Mrs. Das, or is it guilt?"*

This quotation appears near the end of the story, after Mrs. Das has confessed to her affair and to the fact that Bobby is another man's son. Mr. Kapasi responds to Mrs. Das's confession in the worst possible way, from her perspective. He believes that he is beginning a conversation, but for her, his comment is the end of all possible discussion. She believes that she has privileged him by confiding her secret in him, but he is insulted that she would tell him such sordid personal matters and disgusted by her behavior in general. Mr. Kapasi here performs the ultimate act of interpretation: he reveals to Mrs. Das the true nature of her problem. He tells her the precise word for what she feels. For Mrs. Das, however, the diagnosis is too accurate. She cannot forgive such a judgmental proclamation of her situation. The heart of the matter is that Mrs. Das wants absolution, not questioning; she wants relief, not reflection. And Mr. Kapasi wants a friend whose actions and motives he can understand, even relate to. This breakdown in communication is heart wrenching because they are both lonely and believed they were reaching out to the other. Their differences, however, keep them apart.

The Jilting of Granny Weatherall

Katherine Ann Porter
(1890–1980)

CONTEXT

Katherine Anne Porter was born in Texas in 1890 as Callie Russell Porter. When she was two, her mother died during childbirth, so she went to live with her grandmother, Catherine Ann, along with her three siblings and her father. When Porter was eleven, Catherine Ann died, prompting the family to move frequently, often shifting between Texas and Louisiana. As a result, Porter received little formal education beyond elementary school. When she was sixteen, Porter ran away and converted to Catholicism to marry John Henry Koontz. Koontz was an alcoholic who subjected Porter to extreme physical abuse, and after eight years of marriage, Porter left him to start a career as an actress in Chicago and Texas. She formally divorced Koontz in 1915 and changed her named to Katherine Anne, a respelled version of her grandmother's name.

The same year she divorced Koontz, Porter contracted tuberculosis. For the next two years, she lived in sanatoriums. Porter's writing career began in 1917, when she worked as a drama critic and gossip columnist for the Fort Worth *Critic*, struggling to make ends meet. While working for a newspaper in Denver, Colorado, she fell victim to the great influenza epidemic that swept the nation in 1918 and 1919. After recovering, she moved to New York City, where she wrote fiction for children and did some ghostwriting. In 1920, Porter went to Mexico, a country that felt familiar to her because of the Mexicans she had known in Texas. She quickly became involved with the revolutionary movement seeking to overthrow the government, befriending infamous revolutionaries such as Diego Rivera. She also taught and worked as a journalist in Mexico and soon abandoned Catholicism.

In 1922, Porter published a book called *Outline of Popular Mexican Arts and Crafts*. That year also marked the publication of her first short story, "María Concepción." She wrote book reviews for various journals, along with articles for the *New Republic* and the *Nation*. In 1930, she published her first collection of short stories, *Flowering Judas and Other Stories*, which drew on Porter's firsthand experiences of the revolution in Mexico.

Porter's personal life, meanwhile, continued to be colorful and difficult: she had several miscarriages and endured a yearlong marriage to a man named Ernest Stock, who gave her gonorrhea. In the late 1920s, Porter traveled to Europe and eventually moved to Paris in the early 1930s, where she became friends with English writer Ford Madox Ford. In 1938, Porter returned to the states and married a man twenty years her junior, but she divorced him in 1942. She never remarried.

Porter blossomed as a writer during the 1930s. In 1937, she published *Noon Wine* and *Pale Horse, Pale Rider: Three Short Novels*. The latter features a southern family, the youngest daughter of which is often identified as a stand-in for Porter herself. When writing fiction, Porter often drew on her own life, creating rich blends of reality and imagination. As she wrote in one of her essays, "I shall try to tell the truth, but the result will be fiction." The title character in the story "The Jilting of Granny Weatherall" (1930) is largely based on Porter's grandmother, Catherine Ann Porter. The story also addresses religious belief and grave illness, subjects of which Porter had personal knowledge.

Porter worked on her novel *Ship of Fools* for more than twenty years, teaching at universities and giving lectures to earn money while she wrote. She finally published the novel in 1962, when she was seventy-two. Although Porter had already achieved critical success, *Ship of Fools* was the work that turned her into a widely known and read author. The novel spent twenty-six weeks at the top of the *New York Times* bestseller list and was made into a film starring Vivien Leigh in 1966. Porter won more acclaim in 1965, when her *Collected Stories* won the Pulitzer Prize and National Book Award. She was nominated for the Nobel Prize in Literature three times. Toward the end of her life, Porter returned to the Roman Catholic faith she had adopted as a young woman. She died in 1980, and her ashes were buried next to her mother's grave in Texas.

PLOT OVERVIEW

Sick in bed, Granny Weatherall is being visited by Doctor Harry, a man whom she considers little more than a child. Saying there is nothing wrong with her, Granny orders the doctor to leave. He speaks in a condescending tone to her, even after she snaps at him. Granny reminds him that she's survived more serious sicknesses before he was even born. Closing her eyes, Granny feels as if she is in a hammock. She hears the doctor and one of her daughters, Cornelia, talking about Granny's illness. It annoys her that they are talking about her when she is within earshot. Cornelia's goodness also irritates Granny, who says aloud that she would enjoy spanking Cornelia.

Granny thinks about what she has to do tomorrow. She believes it's important to keep the house clean and orderly. She decides that she must hide her letters that George and John had written her. Granny thinks about death, which she prepared herself for twenty years ago, when she felt that the end of her life was near. Her father, who lived until he was 102, attributed his longevity to his daily hot toddy, a liquor made from tree sap. Granny asks for a hot toddy and then snaps at Cornelia. It irritates Granny terribly to think that Cornelia is humoring her. She hates the small gestures people make when under the mistaken impression that she won't notice them.

Granny considers herself a better housekeeper and harder worker than Cornelia. She's still young enough for her children to come to her for advice. She longs for the old days, when her children were small. She imagines showing John how well the children turned out. They are older now than John was when he died. After his death, Granny changed. She had to fence in acres of land and act as a midwife and nurse. She thinks John would appreciate the way she kept nearly all her patients alive. She remembers lighting the lamps when her children were young. She recalls how they stood close to her, moving away once the frightening dark had been dissipated. Granny thanks God for his help and begins to say the Hail Mary. She then thinks about the necessity of picking all the fruit and not letting any go to waste.

Granny feels as if her pillow is suffocating her. She remembers the day she was supposed to get married for the first time. Her groom, George, never came to the church. She can't separate the idea of hell from the memory of George. She admonishes herself not to let her "wounded vanity" overpower her. Cornelia comes in and presses a cold cloth to Granny's forehead and comments that everyone will arrive at the house soon. Confused, Granny asks whether they are going to have a party for someone's birthday. Doctor Harry arrives. Granny protests that she just saw him five minutes ago, but Cornelia says that it's now night. Granny makes a witty retort, but when no one answers, she realizes she must not have spoken aloud. The doctor gives her an injection.

Granny thinks about Hapsy, the daughter she wants to see the most, and imagines seeing Hapsy holding a baby and greeting her. Cornelia asks if there is anything she wants to say or anything Cornelia can do. Granny wants to see George and tell him that she's forgotten him and has had a rich life. She wants him to know that she has everything he took from her. As she thinks these thoughts, however, it occurs to her that there's something she's still missing. A terrible pain cuts through her. She imagines that she's in labor and must send John for the doctor. She believes that after she gives birth to this last baby, she will regain her strength.

Cornelia says that Father Connolly has arrived. Granny thinks about the priest, who cares as much about tea and chatting as he does about the state of her soul and who often tells humorous stories about an Irishman confessing his sins. Granny is not concerned about her soul. She believes that her favorite saints will surely usher her into heaven. She thinks again of her first wedding day when her whole world crumbled and the priest caught her before she fell. He promised to kill George, but she told him not to. Granny thinks about herself and John comforting the children when they had nightmares and about Hapsy getting ready to deliver her baby. She looks at the room and sees a picture of John in which his eyes, which were blue, have been made to look black. She remembers that the man who made the picture called it a perfect copy, but she said it wasn't a picture of her husband. On the bedside table, Granny sees a candle, crucifix, and light with a blue lampshade. The lampshade looks ridiculous to Granny. Seeing a glow around Doctor Harry, Granny jokes that he looks like a saint, which is the closest he'll ever come to being one. No one understands what she said.

Granny imagines getting into a cart beside a man she knows. Up ahead, she sees trees and hears birds "singing a Mass." She holds her rosary while Father Connolly speaks Latin in a tone that strikes Granny as melodramatic. She imagines that he's tickling her feet. She thinks again of George. She hears thunder and sees lightning. She thinks Hapsy has arrived, but it is Lydia. Jimmy is there too. Granny realizes that she's dying. She feels surprised and unready. She thinks of small, last-minute advice and instructions she wants to give. Aloud, Granny tells Cornelia that she can't go yet. Granny worries about what will happen if she can't find Hapsy. She looks for a sign from God, but none comes. This absence is the worst sorrow of all, and she feels she has been jilted again. She dies.

CHARACTER LIST

Granny Weatherall   A woman who's about eighty. After she was jilted at the altar by George, Granny Weatherall married John, who died young, leaving her with several children to care for. Granny, whose given name is Ellen, used to be a midwife and nurse. Meticulous by nature, she is annoyed by Cornelia's and the doctor's attempts to make her more comfortable.

Cornelia   One of Granny's children. Cornelia is the primary caregiver during Granny's illness. Cornelia loves her mother and is devastated by the prospect of her death.

John   Granny's husband. John died when he was a young man, and Granny's memories suggest that he was a kind husband and father. She wishes he could see the children grown up and believes that he would admire her skill in caring for others.

George   The man who jilted Granny Weatherall, leaving her alone at the altar when she was a young woman. Granny still loves George, even though she has spent much of her adult life trying not to think about him.

Hapsy   Granny's favorite child. Granny longs to see Hapsy, who doesn't come to the house. There is some suggestion, never confirmed, that Hapsy died in childbirth. Granny has a vision of Hapsy holding a baby and welcoming her. And in her last moments of life, Granny thinks of Hapsy preparing to give birth.

Doctor Harry   A kind but condescending man who attends to Granny on her deathbed. Granny thinks of him as ludicrously young.

Father Connolly   The priest who delivers the last rites to Granny. Father Connolly affects a pious air while speaking Latin over Granny, but she remembers him as a jokester who was less interested in discussing religion than in gossiping over tea.

Lydia   One of Granny's children. Lydia often comes to Granny for advice when she is having trouble with her children. Granny thinks that because Lydia has an irresponsible husband, she will need the land.

Jimmy   One of Granny's children. Jimmy asks Granny for business advice.

ANALYSIS OF MAJOR CHARACTERS

GRANNY WEATHERALL   Granny Weatherall thinks of herself first and foremost as a gritty survivor. She prides herself on her strength, mothering skills, and ability to run a household single-handedly. After the death of her husband, John, Granny turned herself into both mother and father to her children. When she speaks of her life, she mentions traditionally feminine tasks such as cooking; making clothes; gardening; and tending to sick people, animals, and women in labor. She also speaks of masculine jobs such as paying bills and digging post holes across one hundred acres of land. Granny's last name, "Weatherall," is significant: she has weathered all kinds of difficulties and can't conceive of ever giving up the fight. Even when gravely ill, she tells herself that she's not tired or dying and will be up and about and back to her old self in just a few days. Because she identifies herself as a strong, capable matriarch, it enrages Granny when her own children treat her like a child, humoring her and shooting meaningful glances at each other as if she can't see them.

There are many attributes of Granny Weatherall's personality that she's not aware of—some endearing, some frustrating, and some tragic. She is a funny, wry woman, for example, who finds excessively good behavior annoying in everyone, including her children. She is also a smart woman, perceptive about people other than herself and capable of cracking jokes minutes before death. Her quips and observant remarks are largely unspoken because of her illness, but it is clear from her thoughts that she had a sharp, merciless tongue when she was in her prime. This sharpness often borders on unkindness, perhaps even cruelty. Granny is shamefully short-tempered with her daughter Cornelia, who clearly adores her mother and waits on her hand and foot. Granny's life has been a hard one, and she has coped with it by repressing many of her most painful feelings and maintaining strict, almost obsessive control over everything from the harvesting of fruit to the placement of hairbrushes. She thinks of life as an unmade bed and herself as the only person who can make it properly.

THEMES, MOTIFS, AND SYMBOLS

THEMES

THE USEFULNESS OF DENIAL Granny Weatherall is a woman in deep denial about the basic truths of her life and character. She refuses to believe that she is dying and that she never got over the man who jilted her at the altar. The story opens with her insistence that Doctor Harry should run along and stop wasting his time on someone who is not actually sick. As the narrative progresses, Granny tells herself repeatedly that she had a wonderful life with John and has forgotten George completely. Of course, her fixation on George makes it plain that she hasn't forgotten him at all, but she can't admit this essential fact to herself. Granny also doesn't see that she treats Cornelia harshly and won't admit that she regrets certain aspects of her life. She won't concede that her confusion is the result of her illness and not the fault of everyone around her.

Granny's state of denial is both a handicap and a necessity. If self-knowledge is a goal worth pursuing, it is one that Granny fails to achieve before her death. She seems to know little about herself and how she has lived her life. In addition, Granny's state of denial imposes hardships on those around her. It seems clear that her children have suffered at her hands. Because Granny won't admit even to herself that she has been hard on them, they never get the satisfaction of an apology or at least an acknowledgment of her failings from her. At the same time, however, Granny's deep-seated denial is what has enabled her to continue living, thrive, raise healthy children, and even save the lives of sick people and animals. She is not an inward-looking woman by nature, and it's possible that any slip into self-analysis would plunge Granny into despair. By simply refusing to acknowledge the persistence of her pain and ignoring the fact that she is permanently broken-hearted, Granny has managed to put her head down and soldier through her life.

MOTIFS

WASTE The fear of wasting food, which recurs in "The Jilting of Granny Weatherall," suggests Granny's fear of wasting life. As if rehearsing a speech that she wants to deliver to her children or turning to address the readers, Granny lies in bed silently exhorting an unnamed "you" to make sure that all the fruit gets picked and none of it goes to waste. She goes on to warn against losing things. These commands are partly practical in that Granny has had to support a family on not much money and has done that by using everything she can. The commands also show Granny's nervousness about squandering life itself. She seems to worry that she has wasted her own life and doesn't want her children to waste theirs by frittering away what is most important. Later, Granny thinks of her wedding cake, which went to waste after George stood her up at the altar. Her anxiety about this uneaten food suggests her sadness over wasting—losing—the man whom she loved best. On some level, Granny fears that because she lost her true love, the life she went on to live was a waste.

SYMBOLS

THE COLOR BLUE   Blue symbolizes the various stages of Granny Weatherall's life. The color is first introduced when Granny recalls her glory days of running a tidy, organized household. She visualizes the neatness of the white jars labeled in blue letters that identify their contents, such as coffee, tea, and sugar. This blue symbolizes the time at which Granny's youthful energy enabled her to act as head of the household. The blue letters on the white jars suggest order, just as at this stage of her life Granny was able to impose order. Blue recurs when Granny remembers the way her children watched her light the lamps at night, leaving her once the flame "settle[d] in a blue curve." This blue symbolizes the transitional moment in Granny's life during which her children, after drawing comfort from her strength, stopped needing her and were able to go off into the world on their own.

As Granny looks back on the way she was jilted and exhorts herself to be strong, "streamers of blue-gray light" fall on her eyes, frustrating her and making her worry that she will have nightmares. These bands of light stand for the stage in Granny's life when trouble poured down on her against her will. A hidden blue exists underneath a picture of John: a photographer made Granny's husband's eyes black, instead of the blue they were in real life. Granny agrees that the picture is attractive but says it doesn't depict her husband. This blue-turned-black symbolizes a stage in Granny's life that seemed to last for the duration of her marriage, during which she felt, despite her contentment, that she was married to the wrong man, instead of the one who was originally meant to be her husband. As Granny lies in bed, she thinks about the foolishness of Cornelia's lampshades, which turn the light blue. This time, blue suggests the point in Granny's life at which the world has passed her by. At last, blue becomes the color of the light in Granny's own mind, the light she snuffs out herself. It comes to symbolize the final stage of Granny's life, when she is easing into death.

SHORT STORY ANALYSIS

DIALOGUE   Porter uses dialogue to show that a gulf separates what we wish to say from what we're actually able to say. Granny is full of rage at the way her doctor patronizes her, for example, but she can't find the right words to express her anger. Her dialogue merely sounds querulous and complaining, and no one takes her seriously. Granny's inadequate words can't capture the passion and complexity of her thoughts, so they are dismissed or shrugged off. Porter's use of dialogue serves an instructive purpose. We are forced to realize that when we hear people use clichés—such as Granny's "respect your elders, young man"—we shouldn't ignore the speaker entirely. Well-worn expressions, meandering remarks, and general inarticulateness may mask intense feelings and complex thoughts.

As Granny's condition worsens, she can no longer understand those around her or make them understand her. Granny knows that Cornelia is speaking to her but can't hear the words coming from Cornelia's mouth. Here, Porter uses the absence of dialogue to show Granny's isolation. Not only does Granny fail to grasp what Cornelia says, but she also fails to express herself. Granny's mind teems with thoughts and last requests, but she can't articulate any of them. She makes caustic, funny jokes about Doctor Harry, and those at her bedside understand only that she is trying to say something, without understanding what it is. In another moment of failed communication, she insists that everyone leave her alone so that she can rest but realizes that she didn't actually speak her request aloud as she thought she had. In the final moments of life, the inadequacy of language leaves Granny deeply and tragically alone with her thoughts.

STRUCTURE   "The Jilting of Granny Weatherall," an essentially plotless story, takes its form from Granny's meandering thoughts, which leap back and forth in time. Porter uses this rather loose structure first and foremost to entertain us. Porter challenges herself by writing a story set entirely in bed but creating a structure that follows the twists and turns of the protagonist's thoughts, Porter transcends the physical limits of the story's setting. Although the actual events of the story never stray beyond Granny Weatherall's bed, Granny's mind wanders everywhere, taking her and us to all of the most important and dramatic events in her life. We come to understand Granny's rich, complicated life, which was full of both success and frustration.

Porter's timeless structure also creates a compelling portrait of the disintegration of a dying woman's mind. When the story begins, the structure is fairly conventional. People have logical conversations and the narration unfolds chronologically. This straightforward structure reflects the sanity of Granny's mind. As Granny begins to deteriorate, however, the structure of the story deteriorates with her. The narrator's remarks no longer correlate to what the characters are saying, for example. Instead of proceeding chronologically, the narration darts back and forth from the present moment to years long past. Finally, we're no longer sure of who is speaking, whether we're reading thoughts or spoken dialogue, which characters are in the room with Granny, or how her thoughts connect and lead to one another. By the end of the story, the structure has shifted from conventional to something approaching surrealistic, a change that reflects Granny's progressive descent into death.

IMPORTANT QUOTATIONS EXPLAINED

1. *There was the day . . . but a whirl of dark smoke rose and covered it, crept up and over into the bright field where everything was planted so carefully in orderly rows. That was hell. . . . For sixty years she had prayed against remembering him and against losing her soul in the deep pit of hell. . . .*

For a woman who prizes order above all things, disorder and confusion can be tormenting. Granny conceives of her planned life as a field "planted so carefully in orderly rows" and of George as a demon of chaos, a creeping, whirling cloud of smoke that covers her tidy field. His failure to show up at the church is disastrous for Granny not only because it humiliates her and robs her of the man she loves, but also because it throws her carefully planned future into disarray. This passage also illustrates the effects of Granny's state of constant denial. Granny has tried to forget George entirely for the past sixty years. The narrator suggests that Granny feared thinking about George because it would throw her into "the deep pit of hell," a state of rage, envy, or depression. These lines make it clear, however, that she has failed to eradicate him from her thoughts.

2. *For the second time there was no sign. Again no bridegroom and the priest in the house.*
   She could not remember any other sorrow because this grief wiped them all away. Oh, no,
   there's nothing more cruel than this—I'll never forgive it. She stretched herself with a deep
   breath and blew out the light.

In this passage, which ends the short story, Granny is jilted for a second time. Just as George never came to the church to marry her, God does not come to meet her in death. Wry and strong to the end, Granny notes the similarity between the situations: then, as now, there was "no bridegroom," and she was left with a priest. Granny's state of denial persists until the final moment of her life, and she feels that she'll never forgive this betrayal. This refusal is predicated on the assumption, which she now knows to be false, that there is an afterlife that will allow her to be conscious and capable of holding a grudge. It's possible to interpret this passage as an admonitory lesson on the oblivion that awaits people who, like Granny, treat religion lightly. However, many people read this passage to mean that everyone will die like Granny because there is no afterlife and that we'll all be jilted at the altar of death.

J

The Lady with the Pet Dog

Anton Chekhov
(1860–1904)

CONTEXT

Anton Chekhov was born in 1860 in Taganrog, Russia. Unlike most other great Russian writers, Chekhov came from an impoverished family. His grandfather was a serf who bought his own freedom, and his father, Pavel Yegorovich, was a grocer. A harsh, religious man, Pavel couldn't pay his debts and had to flee with his family to Moscow in 1875. He took five of his six children with him, leaving Anton behind to make his own way in Taganrog.

As a boy, Chekhov developed an interest in literature and theater. He inherited a gift for storytelling from his mother, Yevgeniya, and began to write short stories as a teenager. At age thirteen, he attended his first opera, a revelatory experience that turned him into an avid theatergoer. When his teachers refused to allow him to attend performances, he would often disobey them and go in disguise.

Chekhov worked as a tutor and in a warehouse to support himself during school. He moved to a Moscow slum after finishing school at age nineteen to join his family. Chekhov began publishing stories almost immediately and soon became the family's primary breadwinner. Nicknamed "Papa Antosha," he would bear the burden of supporting his family until his death. Besides the psychological impact, the family's poverty complicated Chekhov's writing in other ways. He had to write while living with his parents, siblings, and a rotating cast of boarders and relatives. In a letter to a magazine publisher, Nicholas Leikin, Chekhov wrote about the frustrations of writing in the midst of his noisy family with their phonographs, conversations, and squalling babies.

Chekhov was an extremely prolific writer who followed his own advice: "Write as much as you can! Write, write, write till your fingers break!" By age twenty-six he had published two story collections, more than 400 short stories and vignettes, and seven plays. This prodigious output is even more impressive given the fact that Chekhov achieved it while simultaneously earning his medical degree and becoming a licensed doctor by his twenty-fifth birthday. He said, "Medicine is my lawful wife and literature is my mistress. When I get fed up with one, I spend the night with the other." In addition to writing fiction, he found time to work for the eradication of cholera, famine relief, and the education of peasants.

Chekhov's stories were usually funny and observant, not to mention highly unique. Bucking long-established tradition, Chekhov didn't use his stories to push an agenda or tackle weighty issues. His stories were also different in that many didn't even feature eventful, action-packed plots. Instead, Chekhov liked to explore his characters' interior thoughts and emotions. As a result, his plots often hinged on shifting emotions rather than twists, coincidences, or dramatic incidents. Chekhov is also known for his brevity, a quality that some critics attribute to his experience as a magazine contributor. Chekhov wrote 162 magazine articles during his life, none of which were more than one hundred lines each. Although Chekhov detested this restriction, he may have eventually come to appreciate it because it taught him to compress complex ideas into the fewest number of words possible.

Chekhov also wrote his first play as an adolescent. His first major play, *Ivanov* (1887), was produced when he was twenty-seven. *The Seagull*, which has become one of Chekhov's best-known and most-loved plays, was produced in 1896 when Chekhov was thirty-six. A troupe of ill-prepared actors performed the drama in front of an audience that expected a comedy, which prompted catcalls and boos. Discouraged and embarrassed, Chekhov vowed never to write a play again. He did, though, and produced three of the most admired of all modern plays: *Uncle Vanya* (1899), *The Three Sisters* (1901), and *The Cherry Orchard* (1904). Chekhov always strived to capture the way people actually talk, and as a result, his characters speak simultaneously, interrupt each other, and sometimes just sit in silence.

Chekhov was exceedingly modest about his own achievements, yet he has become one of the most admired writers in history. Both his plays and short stories transformed their respective forms. "The Lady with the Pet Dog," for example, is considered one of the best short stories ever written because of its brevity, focus on psychology, and emphasis on detail.

In 1901, at age forty-one, Chekhov married an actress named Olga Leonardovna Knipper. Because of ill health, he spent a great deal of time in Nice, France, and Yalta, where "The Lady with the Pet Dog" opens. At age forty-four, Chekhov died of complications resulting from tuberculosis.

PLOT OVERVIEW

While staying in the holiday town of Yalta, Dmitry Dmitrich Gurov spots a young woman with a white Pomeranian dog. Gurov, who is younger than forty, is married to a rather dull woman and has three children. He doesn't enjoy being in his own home and has consequently had many affairs. He feels bitterness toward women but needs their company at the same time. He realizes that most of his affairs begin happily but grow complicated. Nevertheless, he embarks on every new affair with optimism.

Observing the woman with the pet dog walk into a restaurant one evening, Gurov surmises that she is an upper-class, married woman but alone and bored. Yalta is famous for inspiring wonton behavior, and although Gurov knows this reputation is exaggerated, it puts him in the mood for a fling. He initiates a conversation with her in hopes of pursuing her.

After eating, the couple takes a walk. Gurov tells the woman that at school he studied literature and languages and trained to be an opera singer but now works in a bank and owns two houses in Moscow. The woman, whose name is Anna Sergeyevna, lives in a town identified only as S—. She has been married for two years to a man who works for the local government, although she's not exactly sure what he does. The two end their stroll at Gurov's hotel, where they spend the night together.

Gurov and Anna continue to see each other every day during the course of the following week. One evening, as they watch a steamer pull into port, Anna seems excited and nervous until they go to her hotel room. Gurov thinks of all the women he has slept with before. Some appreciated the pleasure of sex; others, like his wife, faked passion and talked too much; and others looked stubborn and greedy. Anna is shy and awkward and always looks dejected afterward.

During a particularly impassioned fit of Anna's sobbing, Gurov watches her and calmly eats a slice of watermelon. After a half hour of silence, Anna delivers a passionate speech about the lowliness of her husband and the guilt she feels for betraying him, saying that the Evil One has set her on the wrong path. Although annoyed, Gurov speaks gently to her and tries to calm her. Anna feels jealous and worries that Gurov does not respect her even though Gurov repeatedly tells her how beautiful and attractive she is.

One day Anna learns that her husband is ill and tells Gurov that she must return to S—. At the train station, Anna says they will never see each other again. The silence after the train's departure shakes Gurov awake, and he regrets the way he treated her.

Gurov returns to a wintry Moscow, where the frost makes him want to put Yalta out of his mind. He plunges back into city life, reading the papers and attending fancy dinners and parties. Eventually, however, he begins thinking about Anna and wishes he could tell someone about the affair. One night, while leaving a club, he tells a friend that he met a woman in Yalta, but his friend merely responds that the fish they ate for dinner smelled bad. This remark disgusts Gurov and makes him hate his life in Moscow.

Gurov sleeps badly for several nights. Finally, that December, he goes to S— in the hopes of finding Anna and rents a room in a shabby hotel. He finds Anna's house, which is surrounded by a gray fence. She doesn't come out. The Pomeranian comes out with an old woman. As the minutes tick by, Gurov begins to worry that Anna is having an affair with another man.

After a nap at the hotel, Gurov wakes up feeling annoyed and rueful. He goes to see a play, *The Geisha*. Just as he'd hoped, Gurov sees Anna sitting in the front row next to her husband and realizes at that moment that he loves her more than anyone else on earth. He approaches her during intermission. She is horrified and scared but leads him down the corridors of the building to a secluded area. She tells him that she loves him dearly and is suffering because she can't be with him. Gurov kisses her, and she pulls away, appalled. She says she will visit him in Moscow, and Gurov leaves the theater.

After the incident at the theater, Anna frequently visits Gurov in Moscow, where she stays in a hotel. Gurov privately marvels that he hides his real life and shows his false life to the world. Anna cries after he visits her one night, and he assumes it's because she's sad that they have to hide their love. He goes to comfort her, and, in doing so, sees his own graying hair in the mirror. He realizes that this is the first time he has ever been in love, even though Anna is so much younger than him. He tries to soothe her by telling her that it will all work out in the end. They both know that their affair will last a long time.

CHARACTER LIST

Dmitry Dmitrich Gurov   The protagonist of the story. Gurov is in his late thirties and has a wife and three children. A prosperous banker, he owns two houses in Moscow. He lives the life of an upper-class Muscovite, entertaining important officials and frequenting clubs, restaurants, and formal events. He does not love his wife and has many extramarital affairs. Until he meets Anna, however, he has never really loved any of the women he's pursued.

Anna Sergeyevna   The woman with the pet dog whom Gurov meets in Yalta. Anna lives in a small, provincial town known only as S—. She is young and unhappily married to a wealthy but low-ranking government official. An emotional, high-strung woman, she loves Gurov but is tormented by guilt for having cheated on her husband.

ANALYSIS OF MAJOR CHARACTERS

DMITRY DMITRICH GUROV   Before he falls in love with Anna, Gurov is a worldly, slightly callous person. He is a ladies' man and frequently cheats on his wife, whom he doesn't even like. He also enjoys the company of women far more than the company of men. A flirtatious, confident man, he enters into new entanglements willingly, even though he knows from experience that most affairs sour with time. Gurov values calm, pleasant interactions, and even when he feels annoyed with women, he is able to mask his annoyance with kind, patient words. Sex is important to Gurov, and he categorizes women based on the way they behave in bed. For Gurov, sex is about pleasure rather than emotion, and he doesn't understand Anna's postcoital agony and guilt.

Gurov's liaison with Anna changes him from a diffident, self-controlled man into a vulnerable, emotional one. Even before he falls in love with her, something about Anna's company seems to transform him. In Moscow, Gurov's fixation on Anna causes him gradually to lose his suavity and worldliness. By the time he goes to S— to reunite with her, he has become endearingly anxious and vulnerable. When he wakes up in his shabby hotel room after trying and failing to catch a glimpse of her outside her house, he thinks sadly and humorously about the mess he has gotten himself into. It is a winning moment in which we see that Gurov has allowed himself to lose control. Instead of keeping his emotions firmly in check and controlling the terms of the relationship as he has always done, Gurov has become vulnerable. For the first time in his life, he has put himself at the mercy of another person and is suffering from the paranoia and self-doubt that come with being in love.

ANNA SERGEYEVNA   Although outwardly quiet and demur, Anna is actually highly sensitive and emotional. In public, she is shy and reserved. She blushes, stammers, and looks at the floor when nervous. In private, however, she reveals a storm of feelings: guilt about betraying her husband, scorn because he is nothing more than a low-ranking official, desperation to experience life, and self-loathing for sleeping with Gurov. Anna's strong emotions may be motivated by religion. Chekhov compares her to the Magdalene, the repentant prostitute and follower of Jesus in the Bible. Anna may even associate herself with the Magdalene because she believes that she has been led astray by the devil. She feels not only guilt but also that she is a sinner. Gurov notes that she's perpetually melancholy, even when they reunite after a long absence. Yet, she seems to love Gurov against her will. When he ambushes her at the theater in S—, for example, she appears overjoyed, despite being fearful that they will be caught. In many ways, Anna is just as sad and guilt-ridden at the end of the story, even though she knows that she'll continue to see Gurov for years to come.

THEMES, MOTIFS, AND SYMBOLS

THEMES

THE IMPOSSIBILITY OF KNOWING OTHER PEOPLE   In "The Lady with the Pet Dog," Chekhov suggests that you can never truly know other people. When Gurov first sees Anna at the restaurant in Yalta, he quickly concludes that she's a bored, married, upper-class woman traveling on her own and doesn't give any thought to her personality. In fact, the only time he thinks about her as a person rather than an object is when he considers her timid laugh, a quality that suggests her shyness. Because Chekhov writes the story from Gurov's point of view, we too are ignorant of Anna's true character for a time. It's therefore somewhat of a shock when she becomes hysterical after she sleeps with Gurov for the first time. This outburst clues Gurov and readers in to the fact that there is more to Anna than first meets the eye. Whatever ideas Gurov had about her, he has hardly scratched the surface of her personality.

Chekhov also argues that complete knowledge of another person's character is not a pre-requisite for love. Mere flashes of understanding or a collection of positive impressions can form the basis of deep affection. Gurov admits that women usually fall in love with their preconceived notions of him and not with his true self. And there is little doubt that Gurov himself loves Anna by the end of the story, even though he still really hasn't gotten to know her. Chekhov suggests that people are private creatures who can adore each other without fully understanding each other.

THE POWER OF ONE'S SURROUNDINGS   Environment has a strong effect on Gurov, whose mood is often shaped by his surroundings. He is open to meeting Anna and starting yet another affair only because he is in Yalta, which puts him in a philandering frame of mind. After he and Anna first make love, they sit in Oreanda, where they gaze at the mountains and listen to the birds and ocean. The lovely surroundings make Gurov think of the cycle of life and death, the beauty of the woman next to him, and the general goodness of the world. It is this mindset, brought on by Oreanda, that makes him feel his first twinge of real affection for Anna. On the other hand, whereas Anna pleases him when surrounded by natural beauty, she often irritates him in the cramped confines of his hotel room. When he sees her off, the sudden silence after the departure of the train seems to shake him awake, making him decide that the affair is over and he must return home. The snow and chill of Moscow invigorate Gurov and make him want to put Yalta, with its hills and sea, out of his mind.

At the same time, Chekhov argues that one's surroundings do not always determine one's behavior. Environment is a strong influence, but it is no match for passionate emotion. Gurov's strong feelings can color his surroundings, rather than the other way around. Even though Moscow is charming and sophisticated, Gurov can't stop thinking about Anna, and the city loses its luster. The theater in S— is a provincial place, and were Gurov not in love with Anna, such surroundings would likely make him see her as a rube among other com-moners. Because he's in love with her, however, he realizes that she is dearer to him than anyone in the world. In one of the most intense exchanges in the story, Gurov and Anna meet during intermission, and the strength of their emotions makes them literally forget their surroundings. Overwhelmed with emotion, Gurov wonders why the crowd and orchestra are there at all. He and Anna walk down halls and stairs without paying any attention to where they are going and kiss in full view of onlookers. The strength of their emotions allows them to transcend their surroundings altogether. They forget that they are in an opera house where decorum is required and are aware only that they are together.

MOTIFS

COLORS   Colors often reflect Gurov's mood. When he and Anna take a walk together after their first meeting in a restaurant, they remark on the "lilac color" of the sea and the "golden band of moonlight" that runs across it. The prettiness of the colors suggests the lightness of

Gurov's mood, and their unusual quality foreshadows the odd, powerful relationship that will evolve between him and Anna. White characterizes Moscow, which is frosty and brisk when Gurov returns from Yalta. The chilly white suggests a fresh start, and for a time at least, Gurov feels that he has escaped the languor of Yalta and started anew. When Gurov goes to S—, gray haunts him. The rug, dust, cover on his bed, and fence around Anna's house are all gray, which reflects Gurov's grumpiness and uncertainty. For the first time in his life, he is in love and unsure whether his feelings are returned.

SYMBOLS

THE WATERMELON   The watermelon that Gurov eats after sleeping with Anna represents his wonton sexuality. After she accuses him of losing respect for her, he sits and eats a slice of watermelon, taking his time with the task. He enjoys sex and classifies women according to their sexual behavior instead of thinking about them as individuals. The way he eats his slice of watermelon indicates the benign lack of interest he feels for Anna and his inability to relate to and truly know her as a fellow human being, let alone as a lover. It is crucial to point out, however, that Chekhov never relies on symbols to convey any messages. A strong argument can be made that "The Lady with the Pet Dog" is remarkable for its total absence of symbols. Chekhov consciously strived to depict life as realistically as possible and avoided using standard literary devices.

SHORT STORY ANALYSIS

STRUCTURE   Chekhov's short stories, particularly "The Lady with the Pet Dog," were revolutionary in that they didn't flow tidily from beginning to middle to end. Rather than subordinating character to a predetermined plot or relying on surprises or twist endings, the stories derive all of their drama from the shifting psychological states of the characters. By the literary standards of Chekhov's day, "The Lady with the Pet Dog" has no real plot. It ends in precisely the same place it begins, with a man and a woman having an extramarital affair, and hardly anything of note happens in between. Yet, despite its lack of conventional structure, great power and urgency come from Gurov and Anna's frustrations, emotions, and epiphanies.

Gurov and Anna's inner states of being shape the structure of "The Lady with the Pet Dog." When Gurov first meets Anna, he feels lighthearted, adventurous, and slightly careless, as he always does when beginning a new romance. The tension begins to increase after he and Anna consummate their affair. Gurov feels almost immediately bored with Anna and her histrionic guilt. As the affair continues in Yalta, Anna's anxiety persists, and Gurov is affectionate but removed. Chekhov raises the emotional stakes as Anna feels more and more guilty after each time she sees Gurov. If the story has anything approaching a conventional plot twist, it comes when Gurov realizes how much he actually loves Anna, causing him to feel suddenly disgusted with his life. When Gurov visits Anna's hometown, Chekhov ratchets up the suspense by making us wonder how she will receive him and whether the emotion she felt for him in Yalta has faded. The ending is a surprise not because it features an unforeseen event, but because it features unforeseen feelings of loyalty and love. As a result, the plot of "The Lady with the Pet Dog" hinges not on anything outside the characters but on their own shifting emotional states.

TONE   Even though "The Lady with the Pet Dog" is about two scandalous adulterers, Chekhov maintains a neutral, nonjudgmental tone throughout the entire story. Chekhov shies from extremes, neither criticizing his main characters for their illicit affair nor condemning the accepted, conservative norms of society. Rather, his tone is one of calm, observant interest. Modern readers, who are familiar with stories of adultery, may not immediately grasp the importance of Chekhov's neutrality. Contemporary readers, however, were not as blasé about the breaking of marriage vows. To them, it was surprising to read a story about adultery that ended without tragedy or repentance but with the promise of more adultery to follow. Chekhov's unwillingness to condemn his protagonists for betraying their spouses probably shocked audiences as well. The simple generosity he shows toward his characters and their situation represents a strong moral stance, one that prizes kindness over conventionality.

Instead of taking a moral stance either for or against adultery, Chekhov explores the personalities and quirks of the individuals involved. Gurov never feels the slightest twinge of guilt about his numerous extramarital affairs. When he thinks about the affairs at all, it is with affection and nostalgia. This attitude would shock traditionalists, but Chekhov merely reports it, without portraying Gurov as a cad, lothario, or sinner. In contrast to Gurov, Anna feels intense pangs of guilt about cheating on her husband. She is devastated after sleeping with Gurov for the first time. Even after their relationship is well established, guilt continues to plague her. Chekhov doesn't portray Anna's attitude, so different from Gurov's, as superior or inferior. On the other hand, he doesn't portray her as a harlot or a child who's been tempted by an older man. Instead, he merely captures their thoughts and emotions without passing judgment.

CHARACTERIZATION   In "The Lady with the Pet Dog," Chekhov demonstrates how his characters are feeling rather than simply telling us. Restraint was important to him. He once wrote in a letter to his brother, "God save us from vague generalizations! Be sure *not* to discuss your hero's state of mind. Make it clear from his actions." Chekhov demonstrates this belief in "The Lady with the Pet Dog." Although Gurov's emotional state is sometimes discussed in exposition, it is often arrestingly depicted through his actions. From the way he teases Anna for saying that Yalta is dull, we realize that he is in a flirtatious mood. After he sleeps with her for the first time, the way he eats a piece of watermelon while she grieves tells us that he does not share her feelings of guilt. When Anna gives an impassioned speech about her pent-up feelings and self-loathing, his laconic, unemotional responses show us that he is holding himself apart from her. Because of his intense irritation with his life in Moscow, we realize that he is actually longing for Anna. When he sleeps well in her hometown, it shows us what comfort he derives from the promise of seeing her.

Chekhov uses the same technique to convey Anna's moods. Because she blushes and looks at the ground in the café, we see that she is a shy woman. When she babbles and loses her train of thought, we realize that she is nervous. As she walks fast to the hotel, we see that she wants to sleep with Gurov just as much as he wants to sleep with her. When she grips her lorgnette and fan in her hands, we understand that the unexpected sight of Gurov terrifies her. Because she complains, cries, and calls out, we know that she is high-strung and emotional. In all of these instances, Chekhov allows us the pleasure of analysis. Instead of telling us how to interpret his characters, he invites us to interpret them for ourselves. This technique of showing rather than telling is one of Chekhov's many lasting legacies. Indeed, "show, don't tell" has become a maxim for most modern writers.

IMPORTANT QUOTATIONS EXPLAINED

---

1. *"You were right this evening: the sturgeon was a bit high."*
   These words, so commonplace, for some reason moved Gurov to indignation, and struck him as degrading and unclean. What savage manners, what mugs! What stupid nights, what dull, humdrum days! Frenzied gambling, gluttony, drunkenness, continual talk always about the same thing!

This moment outside the club in Moscow marks the climax of "The Lady with the Pet Dog." Gurov's friend tells Gurov that the fish they ate for dinner smelled bad, just after Gurov confides that he'd fallen in love with a woman in Yalta. The remark is a cheerful, careless one, but it makes something snap inside Gurov. Suddenly, the Moscow world to which he returned with such enthusiasm strikes him as both a boring wasteland and an orgy of self-indulgence. In his typically restrained fashion, Chekhov doesn't explain why this particular remark prompts such a drastic response or what exactly Gurov is thinking. In fact, Gurov himself may not consciously realize what has made him so disgusted with his world of drinking, gambling, and talking. To us, however, it is obvious that his fixation on Anna has soured him against Moscow. When Gurov goes to S— to find Anna a few days later, the reason behind his violent reaction to the sturgeon remark becomes even more clear: he detests Moscow because his life there contains none of the beauty, emotion, and intensity that characterizes his time with Anna.

---

2. *At the hotel [Gurov] took the best room, in which the floor was covered with gray army cloth, and on the table there was an inkstand, gray with dust and topped by a figure on horseback, its hat in its raised hand and its head broken off.*

This quotation exemplifies Chekhov's masterly use of details. The rug, inkstand, and statuette are decidedly unsymbolic. Rather, they are meant to conjure up the scene vividly in the reader's mind. The shabby carpet, dust, and beheaded figure convey the depressing gloom of this hotel. Also, and perhaps more important, these details are meant to reveal Gurov's frame of mind. He has been sleeping badly, is nervous about seeing Anna, and is likely uneasy about his surprising inability to stop thinking about a woman. There may be sunlight streaming in the window of the room, but because Gurov is feeling out of sorts, he can only notice the ragged, ill-kept nature of his surroundings. Russian novelist Vladimir Nabokov has written that this description of the hotel room is precisely the kind of thing that infuriated Chekhov's critics, who thought he should be conveying an ethical or moral lesson instead of wasting time on details. But it is exactly these details, Nabokov says, that make a fictional world spring to life and Chekhov great.

The Lottery

Shirley Jackson
(1916–1965)

CONTEXT

Shirley Jackson was born in 1916 in San Francisco, California, even though she claimed for the rest of her life that she was born in 1919. Jackson's socialite mother verbally abused her daughter, who consequently grew up with low self-esteem and a fragile sense of identity. Jackson began writing when she was a teenager and focused seriously on her work in high school and college. In 1940, she graduated from Syracuse University, where she had studied English, published stories in the school literary journal, and begun her own literary journal, the *Spectre*, with a classmate Stanley Edgar Hyman. After graduating, she and Hyman married. Hyman became a literary critic, and they eventually had four children.

Jackson published her first short story, "My Life with R. H. Macy," in the *New Republic* in 1941. From then on, she published stories frequently in well-regarded magazines and literary journals, dividing her time between writing and raising her children. In 1945, Jackson and Hyman moved from their home in New Hampshire to the small town of North Bennington, Vermont, where Hyman assumed a teaching position at Bennington College.

Jackson was unhappy in North Bennington. Independent and eccentric and with her own successful work as a writer, Jackson failed to fit into the role of "faculty wife" that she was expected to fill. She drank, smoked, was interested in magic and witchcraft, and often angered her children's schools by being too demanding. She was a devoted mother, but she was also devoted to her writing, and her parenting style was more haphazard than was commonly accepted at the time. Jackson did not fit in easily in North Bennington, and the town likely served as the basis for the New England town depicted in "The Lottery." After she published "The Lottery," a rumor began that she herself had actually been stoned by children in the town. She was also frequently rumored to be a witch and psychic because of her interest in black magic and witchcraft. According to some biographers, she once claimed that she had caused an acquaintance's accident by creating a wax sculpture of him with his leg broken.

The macabre subject matter of "The Lottery" caused outrage and controversy when it appeared in the *New Yorker* in 1948, but many critics now consider it to be Jackson's most famous work. The story also appeared in the collection *The Lottery and Other Stories* (1948). Jackson's six novels include *The Road Through the Wall* (1948), *The Hangsaman* (1950), *The Bird's Nest* (1954), *The Sundial* (1958), *The Haunting of Hill House* (1959), and *We Have Always Lived in the Castle* (1962). She also wrote two memoirs, *Life Among the Savages* (1953) and *Raising Demons* (1957). *The Haunting of Hill House* has been adapted to film twice, first in 1963 and again in 1999. Jackson also published a variety of plays, essays, articles, and children's books. One of her most famous works for children is *The Witchcraft of Salem Village* (1956), a history of the Salem witch trials. The story collection *Just an Ordinary Day* was published posthumously in 1995, when new stories were discovered among Jackson's belongings and papers. Almost all of Jackson's work is rooted in horror, hauntings, witchcraft, or psychological unease.

Jackson struggled with both mental and physical illnesses as an adult. She suffered from anxiety attacks and agoraphobia, eventually finding some relief from psychotherapy. She found solace in writing and always claimed that, unlike other writers, she found the writing process pleasurable. She wrote *We Have Always Lived in the Castle* at the height of her psychological turmoil, and many critics have drawn parallels between the novel and Jackson's personal life. Jackson died of a heart attack in 1965 while taking a nap. She was only forty-eight.

PLOT OVERVIEW

The villagers of a small town gather together in the square on June 27, a beautiful day, for the town lottery. In other towns, the lottery takes longer, but there are only 300 people in this village, so the lottery takes only two hours. Village children, who have just finished school for the summer, run around collecting stones. They put the stones in their pockets and make a pile in the square. Men gather next, followed by the women. Parents call their children over, and families stand together.

Mr. Summers runs the lottery because he has a lot of time to do things for the village. He arrives in the square with the black box, followed by Mr. Graves, the postmaster. This black box isn't the original box used for the lottery because the original was lost many years ago, even before the town elder, Old Man Warner, was born. Mr. Summers always suggests that they make a new box because the current one is shabby, but no one wants to fool around with tradition. Mr. Summers did, however, convince the villagers to replace the traditional wood chips with slips of paper.

Mr. Summers mixes up the slips of paper in the box. He and Mr. Graves made the papers the night before and then locked up the box at Mr. Summers's coal company. Before the lottery can begin, they make a list of all the families and households in the village. Mr. Summers is sworn in. Some people remember that in the past there used to be a song and salute, but these have been lost.

Tessie Hutchinson joins the crowd, flustered because she had forgotten that today was the day of the lottery. She joins her husband and children at the front of the crowd, and people joke about her late arrival. Mr. Summers asks whether anyone is absent, and the crowd responds that Dunbar isn't there. Mr. Summers asks who will draw for Dunbar, and Mrs. Dunbar says she will because she doesn't have a son who's old enough to do it for her. Mr. Summers asks whether the Watson boy will draw, and he answers that he will. Mr. Summers then asks to make sure that Old Man Warner is there too.

Mr. Summers reminds everyone about the lottery's rules: he'll read names, and the family heads come up and draw a slip of paper. No one should look at the paper until everyone has drawn. He calls all the names, greeting each person as they come up to draw a paper. Mr. Adams tells Old Man Warner that people in the north village might stop the lottery, and Old Man Warner ridicules young people. He says that giving up the lottery could lead to a return to living in caves. Mrs. Adams says the lottery has already been given up in other villages, and Old Man Warner says that's "nothing but trouble."

Mr. Summers finishes calling names, and everyone opens his or her papers. Word quickly gets around that Bill Hutchinson has "got it." Tessie argues that it wasn't fair because Bill didn't have enough time to select a paper. Mr. Summers asks whether there are any other households in the Hutchinson family, and Bill says no, because his married daughter draws with her husband's family. Mr. Summers asks how many kids Bill has, and he answers that he has three. Tessie protests again that the lottery wasn't fair.

Mr. Graves dumps the papers out of the box onto the ground and then puts five papers in for the Hutchinsons. As Mr. Summers calls their names, each member of the family comes up and draws a paper. When they open their slips, they find that Tessie has drawn the paper with the black dot on it. Mr. Summers instructs everyone to hurry up.

The villagers grab stones and run toward Tessie, who stands in a clearing in the middle of the crowd. Tessie says it's not fair and is hit in the head with a stone. Everyone begins throwing stones at her.

CHARACTER LIST

Tessie Hutchinson   The unlucky loser of the lottery. Tessie draws the paper with the black mark on it and is stoned to death. She is excited about the lottery and fully willing to participate every year, but when her family's name is drawn, she protests that the lottery isn't fair. Tessie arrives at the village square late because she forgot what day it was.

Old Man Warner   The oldest man in the village. Old Man Warner has participated in seventy-seven lotteries. He condemns the young people in other villages who have stopped holding lotteries, believing that the lottery keeps people from returning to a barbaric state.

Mr. Summers   The man who conducts the lottery. Mr. Summers prepares the slips of paper that go into the black box and calls the names of the people who draw the papers. The childless owner of a coal company, he is one of the village leaders.

Bill Hutchinson   Tessie's husband. Bill first draws the marked paper, but he picks a blank paper during the second drawing. He is fully willing to show everyone that his wife, Tessie, has drawn the marked paper.

Mr. Harry Graves   The postmaster. Mr. Graves helps Mr. Summers prepare the papers for the lottery and assists him during the ritual.

ANALYSIS OF MAJOR CHARACTERS

TESSIE HUTCHINSON   When Tessie Hutchinson arrives late to the lottery, admitting that she forgot what day it was, she immediately stands out from the other villagers as someone different and perhaps even threatening. Whereas the other women arrive at the square calmly, chatting with one another and then standing placidly by their husbands, Tessie arrives flustered and out of breath. The crowd must part for her to reach her family, and she and her husband endure good-natured teasing as she makes her way to them. On a day when the villagers' single focus is the lottery, this breach of propriety seems inappropriate, even unforgivable; everyone comes to the lottery, and everyone comes on time. The only person absent is a man whose leg is broken. Although Tessie quickly settles into the crowd and joins the lottery like everyone else, Jackson has set her apart as a kind of free spirit who was able to forget about the lottery entirely as she performed her chores.

Perhaps because she is a free spirit, Tessie is the only villager to protest against the lottery. When the Hutchinson family draws the marked paper, she exclaims, "It wasn't fair!" This refrain continues as she is selected and subsequently stoned to death, but instead of listening to her, the villagers ignore her. Even Bill tells her to be quiet. We don't know whether Tessie would have protested the fairness of the lottery if her family had not been selected, but this is a moot point. Whatever her motivation is for speaking out, she is effectively silenced.

OLD MAN WARNER   Old Man Warner, the oldest man in town, has participated in seventy-seven lotteries and is a staunch advocate for keeping things exactly the way they are. He dismisses the towns and young people who have stopped having lotteries as "crazy fools," and he is threatened by the idea of change. He believes, illogically, that the people who want to stop holding lotteries will soon want to live in caves, as though only the lottery keeps society stable. He also holds fast to what seems to be an old wives' tale—"Lottery in June, corn be heavy soon"—and fears that if the lottery stops, the villagers will be forced to eat "chickweed and acorns." Again, this idea suggests that stopping the lottery will lead to a return to a much earlier era, when people hunted and gathered for their food. These illogical, irrational fears reveal that Old Man Warner harbors a strong belief in superstition. He easily accepts the way things are because this is how they've always been, and he believes any change to the status quo will lead to disaster. This way of thinking shows how dangerous it is to follow tradition blindly, never questioning beliefs that are passed down from one generation to the next.

MR. SUMMERS   Despite his breezy, light-hearted name, Mr. Summers wields a frightening amount of power in the village, power that seems to have been assigned to him arbitrarily. A married, childless business owner, Mr. Summers is "jovial" and pitied by the townspeople for having a nagging wife. No one seems to question his leadership of the lottery, and it seems to have never been challenged. Perhaps he took on the role himself, or perhaps someone offered it to him. Whatever the case, he now has complete control. Mr. Summers not only draws the names on the day of the lottery, but he also makes up the slips of paper that go into the black box. It's up to him to make the black circle that ultimately condemns someone to death. Jackson never explains why the villagers put such pure faith in Mr. Summers, and the assumption that he will continue to conduct the lottery is just one more inexplicable but universally accepted part of the ritual.

THEMES, MOTIFS, AND SYMBOLS

THEMES

THE DANGER OF BLINDLY FOLLOWING TRADITION   The village lottery culminates in a violent murder each year, a bizarre ritual that suggests how dangerous tradition can be when people follow it blindly. Before we know what kind of lottery they're conducting, the villagers and their preparations seem harmless, even quaint: they've appointed a rather pathetic man to lead the lottery, and children run about gathering stones in the town square. Everyone is seems preoccupied with a funny-looking black box, and the lottery consists of little more than handmade slips of paper. Tradition is endemic to small towns, a way to link families and generations. Jackson, however, pokes holes in the reverence that people have for tradition. She writes that the villagers don't really know much about the lottery's origin but try to preserve the tradition nevertheless.

The villagers' blind acceptance of the lottery has allowed ritual murder to become part of their town fabric. As they have demonstrated, they feel powerless to change—or even try to change—anything, although there is no one forcing them to keep things the same. Old Man Warner is so faithful to the tradition that he fears the villagers will return to primitive times if they stop holding the lottery. These ordinary people, who have just come from work or from their homes and will soon return home for lunch, easily kill someone when they are told to. And they don't have a reason for doing it other than the fact that they've always held a lottery to kill someone. If the villagers stopped to question it, they would be forced to ask themselves why they are committing a murder—but no one stops to question. For them, the fact that this is tradition is reason enough and gives them all the justification they need.

THE RANDOMNESS OF PERSECUTION Villagers persecute individuals at random, and the victim is guilty of no transgression other than having drawn the wrong slip of paper from a box. The elaborate ritual of the lottery is designed so that all villagers have the same chance of becoming the victim—even children are at risk. Each year, someone new is chosen and killed, and no family is safe. What makes "The Lottery" so chilling is the swiftness with which the villagers turn against the victim. The instant that Tessie Hutchinson chooses the marked slip of paper, she loses her identity as a popular housewife. Her friends and family participate in the killing with as much enthusiasm as everyone else. Tessie essentially becomes invisible to them in the fervor of persecution. Although she has done nothing "wrong," her innocence doesn't matter. She has drawn the marked paper—she has herself become marked—and according to the logic of the lottery, she therefore must die.

Tessie's death is an extreme example of how societies can persecute innocent people for absurd reasons. Present-day parallels are easy to draw, because all prejudices, whether they are based on race, sex, appearance, religion, economic class, geographical region, family background, or sexual orientation, are essentially random. Those who are persecuted become "marked" because of a trait or characteristic that is out of their control—for example, they are the "wrong" sex or from the "wrong" part of the country. Just as the villagers in "The Lottery" blindly follow tradition and kill Tessie because that is what they are expected to do, people in real life often persecute others without questioning why. As Jackson suggests, any such persecution is essentially random, which is why Tessie's bizarre death is so universal.

MOTIFS

FAMILY Family bonds are a significant part of the lottery, but the emphasis on family only heightens the killing's cruelty because family members so easily turn against one another. Family ties form the lottery's basic structure and execution. In the town square, families stand together in groups, and every family member must be present. Elaborate lists of heads of families, heads of households within those families, and household members are created, and these lists determine which member draws from the box. Family relationships are essential to how the actions of the lottery are carried out, but these relationships mean nothing the moment it's time to stone the unlucky victim. As soon as it's clear that Tessie has drawn the marked paper, for example, her husband and children turn on her just as the other villagers do. Although family relationships determine almost everything about the lottery, they do not guarantee loyalty or love once the lottery is over.

RULES The lottery is rife with rules that are arbitrarily followed or disregarded. The intricate rules the villagers follow suggest that the lottery is an efficient, logical ritual and that there is an important purpose behind it, whereas the rules that have lapsed, however, reveal the essential randomness of the lottery's dark conclusion. Mr. Summers follows an elaborate system of rules for creating the slips of paper and making up the lists of families. When the lottery begins, he lays out a series of specific rules for the villagers, including who should draw slips of paper from the black box and when to open those papers. When someone is unable to draw, the lottery rules determine who should be next in line. At the same time, there are ghosts of rules that have been long forgotten or willfully abandoned altogether, such as those for salutes and songs that accompany Mr. Summer's induction as the chairman of the lottery. The fact that some rules have remained while others have disappeared underscores the disturbing randomness of the murder at the end of the lottery.

SYMBOLS

THE BLACK BOX The shabby black box represents both the tradition of the lottery and the illogic of the villagers' loyalty to it. The black box is nearly falling apart, hardly even black anymore after years of use and storage, but the villagers are unwilling to replace it. They base their attachment on nothing more than a story that claims that this black box was made from pieces of another, older black box. The lottery is filled with similar relics from the past that have supposedly been passed down from earlier days, such as the creation of family lists and use of stones. These are part of the tradition, from which no one wants to deviate—the lottery must take place in just this way because this is how it's always been done. However, other lottery traditions have been changed or forgotten. The villagers use slips of paper instead of wood chips, for example. There is no reason why the villagers should be loyal to the black box yet disloyal to other relics and traditions, just as there is no logical reason why the villagers should continue holding the lottery at all.

THE LOTTERY The lottery represents any action, behavior, or idea that is passed down from one generation to the next that's accepted and followed unquestioningly, no matter how illogical, bizarre, or cruel. The lottery has been taking place in the village for as long as anyone can remember. It is a tradition, an annual ritual that no one has thought to question. It is so much a part of the town's culture, in fact, that it is even accompanied by an old adage: "Lottery in June, corn be heavy soon." The villagers are fully loyal to it, or, at least, they tell themselves that they are, despite the fact that many parts of the lottery have changed or faded away over the years. Nevertheless, the lottery continues, simply because there has always been a lottery. The result of this tradition is that everyone becomes party to murder on an annual basis. The lottery is an extreme example of what can happen when traditions are not questioned or addressed critically by new generations.

SHORT STORY ANALYSIS

SPECIFIC DETAILS The specific details Jackson describes in the beginning of "The Lottery" set us up for the shocking conclusion. In the first paragraph, Jackson provides specific details about the day on which the lottery takes place. She tells us the date (June 27), time (about 10 A.M.), and temperature (warm). She describes the scene exactly: there are flowers and green grass, and the town square, where everyone gathers, is between the bank and post office. She provides specifics about the town, including how many people live there and how long the lottery takes, as well as about neighboring towns, which have more people and must start the lottery earlier. In the paragraphs that follow this introduction, Jackson gives us characters' full names—Bobby Martin, Harry Jones, and Dickie Delacroix, among others—and even tells us how to pronounce "Delacroix."

Far from being superfluous or irrelevant, these initial specific details ground the story in reality. Because she sets the story firmly in a specific place and time, Jackson seems to suggest that the story will be a chronicle of sorts, describing the tradition of the lottery. The specifics continue throughout the story, from the numerous rules Mr. Summers follows to the names of the people who are called up to the box. In a way, there is safety in these details—the world Jackson creates seems much like the one we know. And then the stoning begins, turning reality on its head. Because Jackson is so meticulous in grounding us in realistic, specific details, they sharpen the violence and make the ending so incredibly surprising.

FORESHADOWING AND SUSPENSE   Many of the seemingly innocuous details throughout "The Lottery" foreshadow the violent conclusion. In the second paragraph, children put stones in their pockets and make piles of stones in the town square, which seems like innocent play until the stones' true purpose becomes clear at the end of the story. Tessie's late arrival at the lottery instantly sets her apart from the crowd, and the observation her husband makes—"Thought we were going to have to get on without you"—is eerily prescient about Tessie's fate. When Mr. Summers asks whether the Watson boy will draw for him and his mother, no reason is given for why Mr. Watson wouldn't draw as all the other husbands and fathers do, which suggests that Mr. Watson may have been last year's victim.

Jackson builds suspense in "The Lottery" by relentlessly withholding explanation and does not reveal the true nature of the lottery until the first stone hits Tessie's head. We learn a lot about the lottery, including the elements of the tradition that have survived or been lost. We learn how important the lottery is to the villagers, particularly Old Man Warner. We go through the entire ritual, hearing names and watching the men approach the box to select their papers. But Jackson never tells us what the lottery is about, or mentions any kind of prize or purpose. She begins to reveal that something is awry when the lottery begins and the crowd grows nervous, and she intensifies the feeling when Tessie hysterically protests Bill's "winning" selection. And she gives a slight clue when she says that the villagers "still remembered to use stones." But not until the moment when a rock actually hits Tessie does Jackson show her hand completely. By withholding information until the last possible second, she builds the story's suspense and creates a shocking, powerful conclusion.

IMPORTANT QUOTATIONS EXPLAINED

---

1. *Mr. Summers spoke frequently to the villagers about making a new box, but no one liked to upset even as much tradition as was represented by the black box.*

This quotation, from the fifth paragraph of the story, reveals how firmly entrenched the villagers are in the lottery's tradition and how threatening they find the idea of change. The villagers have no good reason for wanting to keep the black box aside from a vague story about the box's origins, and the box itself is falling apart. Beyond shabby, it barely resembles a box now, but the villagers, who seem to take such pride in the ritual of the lottery, do not seem to care about the box's appearance. They just want the box to stay the same. Their strident belief that the box must not change suggests that they fear change itself, as though one change might lead to other changes. Already, some towns have stopped holding lotteries, but these villagers do not seem to be headed in that direction. Instead, they hold firm to the parts of the tradition that remain, afraid to alter even this seemingly insignificant part of it for fear of starting down a slippery slope.

---

2. *Although Mr. Summers and everyone else in the village knew the answer perfectly well, it was the business of the official of the lottery to ask such questions formally.*

This quotation appears about halfway through the story, just before the drawing of names begins. Mr. Summers has asked Mrs. Dunbar whether her son, Horace, will be drawing for the family in Mr. Dunbar's absence, even though everyone knows Horace is still too young. There is no purpose to the question, other than that the question is part of the tradition, and so Mr. Summers adheres to the rule despite the fact that it seems absurd. Even though other parts of the ritual have changed or been discarded over the years, this rule holds firm for absolutely no logical reason. Large things, such as songs and salutes, have slipped away, and wood chips have been replaced with slips of paper. Yet this silly, pointless questioning continues. The villagers seem strident in their adherence to the tradition. Old Man Warner, in particular, is adamant that tradition must be upheld and the lottery must continue. But the reality is that there is no consistency among what rules are followed and which are discarded. This lack of logic makes the villagers' blind observance of the ritual even more problematic because the tradition they claim to be upholding is actually flimsy and haphazard.

---

3. *Although the villagers had forgotten the ritual and lost the original black box, they still remembered to use stones.*

This quotation, which appears near the end of the story, distills the lottery down to its essence: murder. The villagers may talk of tradition, ritual, and history, but the truth—as this quotation makes clear—is that the traditional parts of it have long been discarded. The original ritual and box may indeed have borne along a tradition, violent and bizarre as it may be, but now, without the original trappings, songs, and procedures, all that remains is the violence. The haphazard ritual, the bits and pieces that have been slapped together into some semblance of the original, have led to this essential moment of killing. The villagers are all too eager to embrace what remains, eagerly picking up the stones and carrying on the "tradition" for another year.

The Man Who Was Almost a Man
Richard Wright
(1908–1960)

CONTEXT

Richard Wright was born in 1908 on a farm in Natchez, Mississippi. His father, Nathan, was a sharecropper who moved his family to Memphis, Tennessee, before deserting them. As Wright's biography reveals, his childhood was difficult and unhappy, much of it spent attending to his frail and sickly mother while squeezing in school whenever he had the time. After high school, he returned to Memphis with a forged note to gain entry to the city's library, where he read the works of Stephen Crane, Theodore Dreiser, and Sinclair Lewis, all of whom profoundly influenced his developing writing style. He later moved to Chicago and began publishing his stories in left-wing periodicals that reflected his political beliefs as a new member of the Communist Party. Wright eventually moved to New York City in the late 1930s, where he published his most famous novel, *Native Son* (1940), and memoir *Black Boy* (1945) and won fame as a rising star in the African American community.

Despite his success, however, Wright grew increasingly frustrated with the racial divide and therefore left New York for Paris around the mid-century. He quickly became part of Paris's vibrant literary circle, which included notable French writers such as Jean-Paul Sartre and Simone de Beauvoir. Wright continued to produce novels and nonfiction travelogues, but none had the brilliance of his earlier works. He tried to move to London several years later but failed to obtain status as a permanent resident. He ultimately returned to Paris, where he died on November 28, 1960.

Although Wright's fame has declined somewhat since his death, his legacy endures. His bold portraits of black Americans' struggle for recognition and assertion in an indifferent world added a rich new voice to the canon of American literature. Wright's fiction and memoirs graphically portray the experiences of African Americans in the early twentieth century, the conditions in which they lived, and their tenuous relationship with white society. In dissecting contemporary notions and observing the state of racial relations in the broadest context possible, Wright gravitated more and more to naturalism. Naturalist writers believed that larger, all-encompassing environmental, economic, and psychological forces shaped and controlled the lives of both individuals and groups of people in general. As a result, many characters in naturalist literature, such as Dave Saunders in Wright's "The Man Who Was Almost a Man," find themselves caught up in events and circumstances they can't control and don't understand. Although Wright primarily wrote about African Americans and their experiences, his work sought to address universal truths and experiences affecting people of all races.

Wright was the first major African American novelist to make his mark in the twentieth century, achieving both commercial and critical success. His success paved the way for other black writers to flourish, including Ralph Ellison and James Baldwin. His realistic portrayal of black Americans' lives injected an otherwise overlooked and silenced viewpoint into the nation's social and literary consciousness.

PLOT OVERVIEW

After a hard day at work, seventeen-year-old Dave heads across the fields for home, still thinking about a conflict he'd had with some other field hands that day. He vows to someday own a gun and get the respect he deserves, and he wants to prove to the others that he is no longer a child. He decides to head to the local store to examine the guns offered in a mail-order catalog, hoping that his mother will let him buy a pistol with the money he earns working in Mr. Hawkins's fields.

Entering the store, Dave feels his confidence drain from him when he sees Joe, the shopkeeper, but he manages to convince Joe to lend him the catalog overnight. Joe is surprised that Dave is thinking of buying a gun, especially because he knows that Dave's mother saves all his summer earnings. He nevertheless offers to sell Dave an old pistol he has on hand for $2. His interest piqued, Dave says he will come back for it later.

At home, Mrs. Saunders chides Dave for being late, and Dave tells her he was visiting his friends. On his way out to wash his hands, Mrs. Saunders notices the catalog and seizes it, giving it back when Dave explains he has to return it the next day. During supper, Dave is too engrossed in the catalog to eat or notice the arrival of his father and younger brother. Admiring the revolvers, he chokes down his dinner, knowing that he should ask his mother for the money instead of his father.

Dave finally works up enough courage after dinner to broach the subject, first asking his mother whether Mr. Hawkins has paid her for his time working in the fields. Mrs. Saunders responds that the money is solely for his school clothes and immediately dismisses the idea of buying a gun. Dave pleads his case, arguing that the family needs a gun and that he'll give it to Mr. Saunders. Still not fully convinced, Mrs. Saunders finally gives Dave the $2 on the condition that he bring the gun directly to her after buying it.

After buying the pistol, Dave walks around the fields with it, admiring the gun but too scared and unsure of how to fire it. He waits until it's dark and he's sure everyone has already fallen asleep before going home, and he puts the gun underneath his pillow instead of giving it to his mother as he'd promised. Mrs. Saunders approaches him in the middle of the night and quietly asks for the gun, but Dave tells her that he stashed it outside and will give it to her in the morning.

When he wakes up, Dave removes the gun and holds it in his hands, realizing that he now has the power to kill someone. He quietly gets out of bed and ties the pistol to his leg with an old strip of flannel. He then heads out to the fields where he works, and he accidentally runs into his boss, Mr. Hawkins. Surprised but not wanting to give away his secret, Dave tells Mr. Hawkins that he just wanted to get a head start on the day's work. He hitches the plow to a mule named Jenny and heads to the field farthest away so that he can fire the pistol without anyone noticing.

After holding and admiring the gun, Dave finally works up the courage to actually pull the trigger. He doesn't take proper aim, however, and accidentally shoots Jenny. Dave panics and desperately tries to stop the bleeding by plugging the wound with dirt, but Jenny soon dies. Sickened and frightened, he buries the gun at the base of tree and heads across the field, trying to concoct a believable story to explain Jenny's death to Mr. Hawkins.

Someone eventually finds Jenny, and a small group gathers around her body. When pressed, Dave lies and says that Jenny had been startled and fell on the point of the plow. Unconvinced, Mrs. Saunders urges him to tell the truth and then quietly asks about the gun when no one else is listening. Meanwhile, someone comments that Jenny's wound looks like a bullet hole. Crying and realizing that he has to tell the truth, Dave confesses. Mr. Saunders is shocked to hear about the pistol and Mrs. Saunders's complicity.

Mr. Hawkins tells Dave that he'll have to pay $50 for the mule even though her death had been an accident. He then tells Mr. Saunders that he'll take $2 out of Dave's pay each month until the debt has been paid. When Mr. Saunders asks Dave where he put the gun, however, Dave lies again and says that he threw it into the creek. His father tells him to retrieve it, get his $2 back from Joe, and give them to Mr. Hawkins as his first payment.

Unable to sleep that night, Dave skulks out to retrieve the gun. Cleaning it off, he forces himself to shoot it without closing his eyes and turning his head away as he'd done before. He fires the gun four times until there are no more bullets left. Putting the gun in his pocket, he heads across the field until he comes to Mr. Hawkins's large white house. If he had one more bullet, he muses, he would fire at the house to let Mr. Hawkins know that he is really a man. Dave then hears the sound of a train in the distance. Gun in hand, he heads for the tracks and hops into a moving boxcar as the train continues on into the night.

CHARACTER LIST

Dave Saunders   The adolescent protagonist of the story. Dave works on a plantation plowing fields during his summer break from school. Not quite a child but not yet a man, seventeen-year-old Dave struggles to win respect from the other fieldworkers even though he lacks the requisite maturity. Experiencing the turmoil and restlessness of adolescence, he grows resentful of his powerlessness and thinks that owning a gun will instantly make him a man.

Mrs. Saunders   Dave's mother. Beneath Mrs. Saunders's steely exterior lies a practical, upstanding woman caught between making her son Dave happy and doing what she knows is right. She suspects that buying a gun will bring trouble but can't refuse Dave. She is the first to realize that Jenny died from a gunshot wound and forces Dave to tell the truth, even though she tries to downplay her own complicity.

Mr. Hawkins   Dave's boss and the owner of a local plantation. Even though Mr. Hawkins seems to be a reasonable and fair employer, Dave still resents his authority on the plantation and in the community.

Mr. Saunders   Dave's father. A strict disciplinarian, Mr. Saunders seems more interested in Dave's earning potential and keeping good relations with Mr. Hawkins than in his son's happiness. He doesn't mind using violence to maintain discipline at home.

Joe   The local store's owner and shopkeeper. Amiable and plump, Joe lends the mail-order catalog to Dave, even though he thinks Dave is too young to own a gun. Still, he brushes aside his doubts and offers to sell Dave an old pistol that he has in stock for only $2.

ANALYSIS OF MAJOR CHARACTERS

DAVE SAUNDERS Dave is both an average adolescent struggling with growing up and the embodiment of all frustrated and impoverished African Americans without opportunities. On one level, Dave's experiences are not unique: he's a stereotypical teenager seeking a level of maturity and independence that he's not yet ready for. He can imagine the benefits of adulthood but doesn't understand the obligations that come with more freedom of choice. Searching for a quick way to become a man, he focuses on the guns for sale in Joe's mail-order catalogue, falsely believing that raw power will automatically win him the respect he desires. His murderous fantasies highlight his fixation with physical strength and misperception that the power to kill brings the power to control. Impatient, Dave tries to initiate his own rite of passage into manhood without making any of the sacrifices that come with adulthood.

Dave is a figure of the times, a field hand's son who has no choice but to become a field hand himself. Chained to a life of barely making ends meet, he lacks the education and opportunities to make his life better because white society forbids it. He feels that his life is so harsh and overwhelming that escape is the only solution. He expresses this urge in several ways, initially in the lies he tells, with his willful bending of the truth to make the world around him more in line with his hopes and desires. Dave's quest for adulthood and ultimate escape thus marks a shifting tide in society, as more black Americans broke with their past and ties to the South in search of new opportunities elsewhere.

THEMES, MOTIFS, AND SYMBOLS

THEMES

THE SEARCH FOR POWER Dave Saunders is trapped in a world that strips him of his personal and economic power. Dave sees his life as a series of abuses and humiliations: he's forced to obey his parents, work as a field hand for pay he never receives, and endure ribbing from the other field workers. His growing sense of degradation derives from the social and economic forces that keep him from achieving his potential and pursuing his dreams. The idea of owning a gun thus becomes Dave's outlet, a way to quickly become powerful and manly. He believes that a pistol in his hand will give him more control over others; however, Jenny's death only limits his future by forcing him to repay Mr. Hawkins the price of the mule. Although accidental, Jenny's death could be interpreted as Dave's unconscious desire to strike out against Mr. Hawkins. By destroying a symbol of Hawkins's prosperity and power as a landowner, Dave may be lashing out at an economic system and social order that he will always be excluded from merely because of his skin color.

COMING-OF-AGE STRUGGLES On many levels, "The Man Who Was Almost a Man" is a coming-of-age story in which the adolescent Dave Saunders must overcome numerous hurdles to become a mature adult. Restless, impatient, and taunted by the older men he works with, Dave believes that acquiring a gun will end his adolescence and transform him into a real man. Not surprisingly, however, Dave discovers that owning a gun only brings more problems and a much greater burden of responsibility. Ironically, possessing a pistol actually would have ushered Dave into adulthood if only he'd been able to handle the extra responsibility like an adult. Because he has to work for two years to repay Mr. Hawkins for

Jenny's death, the gun brings Dave greater commitment and obligation—the true hallmarks of manhood. But Dave discovers at the end of the story that he's really seeking escape, not more commitment. When owning a gun becomes a heavier burden than he'd realized, he chooses to leave, demonstrating even further that he's really not yet ready to become an adult. Still convinced that the gun is a more of a boon than a burden, he takes it with him, possibly inviting more trouble in the future.

MOTIFS

LIES AND LYING   Dave's lies indicate his disconnectedness from the world around him and prove that he is unprepared for the responsibilities of adulthood. Lying emerges as a behavior at odds with the moral qualities associated with adulthood and stereotypes of male behavior. Throughout the story, Dave tries to twist the truth in his favor so that he can buy a gun and avoid punishment. He convinces his mother to give him the $2 to buy the gun, for example, only after telling her that he plans to give it to Mr. Saunders. He reneges on his promise to give her the gun after buying it and later claims that he threw the gun in the river after shooting Jenny. Like a child, he fails to realize that lying won't protect him and will only bring more problems in the future.

DARKNESS   The darkness that pervades the story highlights the constraints, humiliation, and wounded pride that Dave associates with his work and family life. In the story's opening line, Dave makes his way across the fields "through parting light," fresh from another humiliating run-in with the older workers on the plantation. Thinking of the gun comforts him as the sun sets, caught between day and night just as he's caught between childhood and adulthood. After purchasing the gun, he stays out late, taking aim in the dark fields at "imaginary foes." Daytime only brings trouble and humiliation to Dave, whereas all his fantasies and imagined adventures take place at night. Wright describes Dave's relationship with the gun as a clandestine affair involving lies, deceit, and secret locales. Only in the darkened fields can Dave find the independence and masculinity he seeks.

SYMBOLS

THE GUN   The gun represents power, masculinity, respect, and independence—in short, everything that Dave desperately wants. He sees the gun as the solution to all his problems and compensation for all his weaknesses. Dave resents the fact that the other field hands treat him like a child and therefore mistakenly believes that owning a gun would instantly make a man out of him, even though he doesn't know how to fire one. He mistakenly reasons that owning a gun would also somehow provide him with independence, as if knowing how to fire it would keep him out of the fields and provide him with greater opportunities. Dave fantasizes about shooting at Mr. Hawkins's house, which suggests that Jenny's death has taught him nothing and has only made him crave power, independence, and masculinity even more.

THE MULE   Jenny, Mr. Hawkins's mule, represents Dave himself, who fears working as a subservient field hand on another man's land for the rest of his life. Dave consciously recognizes the similarities between himself and Jenny, even saying to himself before running away that everyone "treat[s] me like a mule, n they beat me," alluding to the thrashing his father had promised him. Dave believes that all he does is toil like Jenny, yoked to a plow with little hope of reward, escape, or becoming something better. The mule also represents commitment and responsibility, hallmarks of adulthood that Dave is still unwilling to accept. He wants only the freedom that he imagines adults have without any of their obligations. Jenny's death is consequently the symbolic death of Dave's childhood, which he wishes to erase to escape the community and a life of drudgery. Ironically, the power that Dave associates with owning a gun brings change but forces him to embark on a journey to manhood for which he's not yet ready.

SHORT STORY ANALYSIS

NATURALISM   Although much a typical coming-of-age story, "The Man Who Was Almost a Man" also depicts Dave's greater struggles with racism and poverty, and it is an exemplary piece of naturalist writing. Naturalists such as Wright incorporated stinging social criticism into their stories and novels by pitting their characters against social, economic, or environmental forces that they can't control. In making Dave a victim of racial oppression, for example, Wright attacks whites' lingering power over the lives of blacks. Like his parents, Dave is stuck in a life of subservience to men such as Mr. Hawkins, Joe the shopkeeper, and other financially secure whites and will never have the education or money necessary to achieve his full potential. He consequently believes that only brute power—the ability to shoot a gun—will win him the respect he wants. Dave's desire to own a gun thus reflects a greater desperation and psychological need to establish himself in the community as an empowered human being rather than a mere field hand.

Dave's struggle to overcome the uncontrollable forces pressing down on him speaks for all young people whom society has overlooked and dismissed. He therefore becomes Wright's unlikely hero, a young man who refuses to cave under overwhelming social forces while simultaneously shirking his debts and commitments like an irresponsible child. Even though readers know that Dave will probably never find the success, independence, or power he craves, the mere fact that he's willing to risk striking out on his own redeems him and makes him more than "almost a man."

HISTORICAL CONTEXT   Dave's struggle with racial oppression reflects the broader African American struggle to win more rights, freedoms, and opportunities since the end of the Civil War. Although many black Americans had pushed for equality and economic leverage in the latter half of the nineteenth century, the quest for civil rights didn't become a coordinated movement until the early twentieth century. Tired of second-class citizenship, African American activists such as W. E. B. DuBois, Marcus Garvey, and Thurgood Marshall began promoting strategies that would chip away at white dominance, just as the frustrated adolescent Dave Saunders finally decides to empower himself when he can no longer stand be ridiculed. Rather than indiscriminately striking out at those in power as Dave fantasizes, however, early civil rights leaders worked to change the oppressive social and legal systems. Only in the 1950s and 1960s—when this story was published—did civil rights activists actually rebel by quietly refusing to comply with white Americans' humiliating expectations.

Many factors conspired to extend the oppressive exploitation of blacks that slavery had established. For African Americans stuck farming small parcels of land owned by white overseers, sharecropping proved only slightly better than forced labor. Gang violence, lynchings, and Jim Crow laws that segregated blacks from whites also worked to keep blacks "in their place." Slowly, however, prevailing social patterns changed, especially between World War I and World War II, when hundreds of thousands of blacks fled their destitute lives in the South for better opportunities in the North. Dave's sudden flight at the end of the story mimics this so-called Great Migration. Seen in this light, his nighttime escape thus becomes a symbolic renunciation, a turning from the agrarian servitude that marked the past and a staunch refusal to accept the unfair conditions that kept families mired in poverty and robbed individual lives of hope and promise.

LOCAL DIALECT   Wright's use of local dialect provides unique voices for the story's black characters. Dave and his parents speak with an almost slurring drawl, dropping letters and syllables from their words, in contrast to the white-skinned Joe and Mr. Hawkins, who use more standard English. Although Wright's use of dialect often makes reading the story difficult, dialect gives the characters vitality and dimension. Readers can actually visualize Mrs. Saunders chastising Dave, for example, when she exclaims, "Lawd, chil, whut's wrong wid yuh?" Incorporating different dialects into the story also lends a ring of authenticity to Wright's portrayal of a rural southern community in the early twentieth century, a community in which whites and blacks coexist on unequal terms. Dialect helps separate these two groups, not only reflecting varying degrees of education but also highlighting inequalities in lifestyle and standards of living. As a result, readers are better able to understand Dave's frustration working on a plantation that affords no opportunities. If he doesn't escape, he'll undoubtedly work in the fields for the rest of his life, trapped, just like his father.

IMPORTANT QUOTATIONS EXPLAINED

M

1. Could kill a man with a gun like this. Kill anybody, black or white. And if he were holding his gun in his hand, nobody could run over him; they would have to respect him.

Withdrawing the pistol from underneath his pillow, Dave marvels at the gun's potential power and capabilities. Even though he doesn't actually know how to use it, the pistol gives Dave the sense of power and masculinity he desperately wants yet can't seem to muster on his own. Dave's musings, however, also reveal a darker desire to strike back at those he feels have abused and ridiculed him. He presumably daydreams not only about killing the other black plantation workers who laughed at him in the story's opening line, but also the empowered whites who unfairly control his and the other black workers' lives. Wright uses Dave in this way to explore the destructive influence of racism and lack of economic opportunity on the lives of black Americans. Although Dave never actually kills anyone, the fact that he runs away with the gun at the end of the story suggests that he still harbors the desire for power and maybe even revenge. Dave's musings may reflect his potential just as much as his desire: he could kill if he had a gun in his hand. These thoughts are probably nothing more than the fantasies of a typical adolescent boy, but Wright leaves open the possibility for future violence and never resolves the issue.

2. *Ahead the long rails were glinting in the moonlight, stretching away, away to somewhere, somewhere where he could be a man.*

Dave's sudden decision to hop on a train comes as an unexpected ending to the typical coming-of-age story and reflects Dave's deeper struggle with the oppressive social and economic forces of the day. Although Dave's wrangling to purchase the pistol and then covering up Jenny's death highlight the struggles of growing up that all teenagers face, the fact that he runs away suggests that Dave also feels oppressed and strangled in his community. He needs more than mere recognition and acceptance—he needs opportunities that field work can't provide. Running away allows Dave to exert control over his own destiny for the first time in his life, despite the fact that he's irresponsibly abandoning his family, debts, and commitments like a child. Trying to take control of his life in this way without serious regard to the consequences or future, therefore, makes Dave only "almost a man."

The Metamorphosis
Franz Kafka
(1883–1924)

CONTEXT

Franz Kafka was born in 1883, near the edge of the Jewish ghetto in Prague, where he lived with his parents and three sisters. His parents were not strict practitioners of their Jewish faith, and Kafka was raised speaking German and influenced by Germanic culture. Kafka led a lonely childhood, raised by nannies, while his parents tended the family business, a dry-goods store. Oppression and isolation, common themes in his adult writings, were not unknown to young Kafka. Kafka had an especially complicated relationship with his father, a domineering, practical man who, Kafka felt, took too much pride in his cultural assimilation and had little patience for Kafka's literary ambitions. Their relationship had such a lasting effect on Kafka that tyrannical father figures appear throughout his work. Kafka attended the state-run Altstädter Gymnasium, a competitive high school, before enrolling at Karl-Ferdinand University in 1901 to study law. During these years, Kafka became part of a loosely constructed group of acquaintances called the "Prague Circle," who met regularly to discuss philosophy and literature. They also strove to engage in the literary life, attending readings and staging presentations of their own writings.

In 1908, Kafka took a job with the Assicurazioni Generali, an Italian insurance company in Prague. Twelve-hour days soon took their toll on his writing schedule, and within months Kafka had secured a new position, working for the Arbeiter-Unfall-Versicherungsanstalt, the Workers Accident Insurance Institute. He remained with the firm for fourteen years, always struggling to balance his need to work with his desire to write. He published a segment of an early story, "Description of a Struggle," in 1908 in the literary publication *Hyperion* and two additional sections in 1909. In 1911, however, he agreed to work in a cousin's asbestos factory during the afternoon. He ended every day exhausted and unable to write a word.

Kafka's romantic leanings took the form of hundreds of letters written during a five-year period to a woman named Felice Bauer, whom he had met at the home of his closest friend, the novelist Max Brod. Despite occasional visits, the letters were the couple's main means of communication. Engaged twice, Kafka never could embrace the idea of melding the artist's life with the role of husband. Kafka always put his writing first. In late September 1912, after working all night, he completed "The Judgment," a story portraying a young man's confrontation with his father. During the next five years, Kafka created some of his most accomplished prose, including "The Metamorphosis" (1915), "In the Penal Colony" (1917), and portions of two of his best-known novels, *The Trial* (1925) and *Amerika* (1927), although some of these were not published until after he died.

Kafka was somewhat frail, susceptible to various medical conditions such as migraines and insomnia. After suffering a hemorrhage in his lungs in 1917, he was diagnosed with tuberculosis. Despite his failing health, Kafka still struggled to write. He completed the short stories featured in *A Hunger Artist* (1922) and began drafting *The Castle* (1926). While recuperating at a resort along the Baltic Sea in 1923, Kafka met Dora Diamant, the daughter of a rabbi, and moved with her to Berlin. They prepared to move to Palestine, but his rapid decline prevented it. In 1924, Kafka died at age forty-two.

At the time of his death, only a small portion of Kafka's writing had been published, and he was unknown beyond a limited circle of artists, thinkers, and literary enthusiasts. Before his death, Kafka asked Max Brod to destroy the manuscripts and drafts that would remain after he died, including stories, literary sketches, diaries, letters, and three unfinished novels. Brod, however, did not honor Kafka's request.

Kafka's best-known work is arguably "The Metamorphosis," a story that demonstrates Kafka's use of an extreme scenario to explore themes of alienation and isolation. The story displays Kafka's ability to capture the anxieties implicit in modern life, as bureaucracy, institutional organizations, and capitalist forces become more intrusive in individuals' lives. "The Metamorphosis" is suffused with paranoia, as the protagonist, Gregor Samsa, becomes victimized even in the nurturing realm of the family. Guilt, fear, resentment, and conditional love distort Gregor's physical form and mental state.

PLOT OVERVIEW

Gregor Samsa wakes up to find himself transformed into an insect. He tries to roll onto his right side and cannot. He worries about what he will tell his boss, noting that the family debt will be paid off in five to six years. His father, mother, and sister, Grete, try to rouse him, but the door is locked. Attempting to conceal his altered voice, Gregor tells them he will catch the next train. Gregor sidles out of bed and falls on his back to the floor. A knock at the door indicates the arrival of the office manager, who demands an explanation for Gregor's strange behavior.

The manager tells Gregor that he may lose his job. Gregor says he is feeling ill and will report to the office by eight o'clock, but his words are incomprehensible. Gregor crawls to the door, pulls himself up using his thin legs, turns the key with his jaws, and opens the door. When his parents and the manager see him, they recoil. Gregor exhorts the office manager to defend him at the office, but the manager slinks from the room. Gregor rights himself and enters the main room, frightening his mother. Gregor intends to pursue the manager, but his father drives him back into his room with a cane.

At the start of section two, Gregor wakes at dusk from a long nap. The house is silent. Gregor sees that Grete has left him a bowl of bread and milk, but he has lost his taste for it and leaves it uneaten. Late in the evening, the family tiptoes to bed. Gregor crawls under the sofa, where he spends the night in a trancelike state. Early the next morning, Grete enters, but she immediately slams the door when she sees him. Embarrassed by her reaction, she timidly comes back in. Seeing that he has not touched the bread and milk, she lays out a variety of foods so that he'll find something he likes. Each day, Grete feeds Gregor in the morning and again in the afternoon, while his parents take a nap.

Gregor has no communication with his family and listens at the door to their conversations. On the first day after Gregor's transformation, he overhears his father reviewing financial records, particularly the books of his business failure several years earlier. Money left from that plus saved portions of Gregor's salary have formed a considerable sum, but it would support the family for only a couple of years. Gregor is hurt by the fact that he has failed his family.

Grete continues her visits but must open the window for ventilation, and she is still frightened easily. Gregor's parents do not visit him, despite his mother's sometimes hysterical need to see him. Gregor takes to crawling on the walls and ceiling. To help him move around more easily, Grete proposes removing the furniture, but his mother feels the room will lose its human character and that it should remain as it is until Gregor returns to normal. Grete insists, so Gregor hides beneath a sheet draped over the sofa while Grete and his mother remove a heavy dresser. Gregor emerges to prevent the removal of any more of his things. He clings to the picture hanging on his wall. Grete sees him from the next room and stops their mother from going back in, but their mother spots him. Grete and their mother leave the room, and Gregor follows, intending to help Grete find some medicine for their shocked mother. But the women run from him. Gregor scuttles about the walls and ceiling and then falls onto the table. Gregor's father returns home and chases Gregor around the room, pelting him with apples. Mr. Samsa is about to kill Gregor, but Mrs. Samsa bursts in and stops him.

In section three, Gregor experiences a slow and only partial recovery from an apple that is embedded in his back. The family allows him to listen to their daily conversations and watch them gathered around the table. Tired from their new jobs, the family members have no time for Gregor. Grete feeds him and cleans his room with increasing irritation. The family fights over Gregor's care. The latest maid doesn't mind peeking in on Gregor but does not clean the room. She threatens to hit him with a chair when he tries to drive her away. Gregor loses his appetite, and his room becomes an increasingly cluttered storage area. The family takes in three boarders, who usurp the Samsas' place at the family table.

One night, during an impromptu violin performance by Grete, Gregor inches into the living room. When one of the boarders notices him, he alerts Gregor's father, who tries to allay their concerns. Incited, the boarders give notice and threaten legal action. Grete proposes getting rid of the entity that has replaced what was once Gregor. Gregor slowly returns to his room, and Grete locks him in.

In a state of peaceful contentment, Gregor dies early the next morning. Hours later, the boarders emerge, demanding their breakfast. Gregor's father insists that they leave. The three Samsas write excuses for their absence from work and send them to their employers. They then take a trolley car to the outskirts of the city, discussing their jobs and relatively bright future. They plan to move into a smaller apartment, and the parents muse on the prospect that Grete will marry well.

CHARACTER LIST

Gregor Samsa   A man who turns into a bug. Gregor was an army lieutenant and attended business college, but he is obliged to work as a traveling salesman to pay off the debt accrued after the failure of his father's business. When he discovers that he has been transformed into a large insect, his sense of duty initially prevents him from comprehending the gravity of his situation. Instead of outrage, he feels only pain at the discomfort he is causing others. He eventually dies.

Grete Samsa   Gregor's seventeen-year-old sister. Grete is initially helpless in the face of Gregor's condition, but her kindness eventually leads her to feed him and clean up after him. However, she grows increasingly irritable, resentful of the burden of caring for Gregor. Changed by the experience that the family has faced, she eventually advocates that the creature that replaced her brother be disposed of. During the final stage of Gregor's life, she helps the family by working in a shop and studies French in the evenings to improve her economic prospects. By the time Gregor dies, she has blossomed into a capable young woman.

Mr. Samsa   Gregor's father. A failed businessman, Mr. Samsa lacks the wherewithal to survive the tough conditions governing the marketplace. In the wake of his debt, he has retreated from the world, suffering from bad health and often assuming a stern presence in the family. Unable to change Gregor's condition, Mr. Samsa expresses himself through violence, twice injuring Gregor's insect body. Gregor's metamorphosis occasions a transformation in Mr. Samsa, who becomes a bank official and resumes his place at the helm of the family.

Anna Samsa   Gregor's mother. Initially a lively woman, Gregor's mother is weakened by Gregor's change. She suffers from severe asthma, and the sometimes turbulent atmosphere of the apartment triggers virulent attacks. Gregor's mother feels an instinctive maternal love for Gregor, yet she is repulsed by his transformation and unable to accept it. She finds a new lease on life in working outside the home.

The Office Manager   A high-ranking representative of the firm that employs Gregor. The office manager places duty over more human concerns. A supposed lecherous lady's man, his thin veneer of concern quickly devolves into criticism of what he views as Gregor's declining job performance and dubious future with the company.

The Maid   The last in a series of cooks and charwomen who either quit, ask to be confined solely to the kitchen, or are dismissed. Constitutionally the strongest among the domestic staff, the maid is not repulsed by Gregor and leaves his door open so that she can observe him. When he approaches her in a threatening manner, she lifts a chair to show him she can defend herself, and Gregor backs down. When Gregor dies, she discovers his body.

The Three Boarders   Professional men who rent a room in the Samsa home. The boarders represent encroaching capitalism, as the household, normally a refuge from the marketplace, is transformed into a business as well. They put the Samsas at their beck and call. When Mr. Samsa orders them to leave the house, he demonstrates that he has once again assumed a superior position in the household.

ANALYSIS OF MAJOR CHARACTERS

GREGOR SAMSA   Beneath his hard shell and arch-shaped ribs, Gregor Samsa remains the same gloomy, guilt-addled person he was in human form. He is capable of great tenderness, feeling guilty that he can no longer support his dependent family and experiencing pleasure when he can simply watch or hear his parents and sister when the door to his room is cracked. Gregor is also relentlessly passive and self-effacing. Although he harbors some anger at his situation, particularly his powerlessness to escape it, he displays no real desire to change back to human form. Rather, he passively accepts the conditions his world presents to him, just as he did as a traveling salesman. He has built his life around his ability to fulfill his duty to his family and seems incapable of envisioning any kind of duty he has to himself—even now, when his survival is at stake. Kafka never explains the reason for Gregor's sudden transformation, but one possible explanation is that Gregor's repulsive appearance is the projection of his own self-loathing and low self-esteem.

Gregor's chronic selflessness shines through when he first discovers his transformation. In one of the story's many instances of absurdity and black comedy, Gregor, having only partially recognized the full extent of his metamorphosis, immediately begins brooding on the difficult nature of his work, which is taxing for a man who is mobile and articulate, but now utterly impossible for an insectlike creature skittering around on many small legs. His changed appearance seems to have little bearing on his mounting concern about his professional and financial future—he is concerned only with how he will now go about supporting his family. However, the way Gregor is perceived and treated by his family triggers his realization of his true state. Although his physical alteration happened during one night, his internal transformation—of his character and sense of his own humanity—happens more slowly. As the remnants of his human life fall away, including his taste for food and the furniture in his room, he realizes that he may soon lose sight of his former self entirely, just as his family has done. When his family ceases to recognize him as simply a new form of the person he was and begins seeing him as a burden, he dies.

GRETE SAMSA   Just as Gregor experiences a change in "The Metamorphosis," Grete also experiences a transformation as she changes from an emotional girl into a capable young woman. Although the story's title refers mainly to Gregor's change, in some ways it also refers to the change Grete undergoes as she responds to Gregor's situation and transforms the role she plays in the family. Initially portrayed as an immature and ineffectual little sister, she quickly assumes the part of Gregor's caretaker, adopting a presumptuous authority over Gregor's life. Whereas her parents cannot stand to look at Gregor, she enters his room during the day and makes valiant attempts to quell her fear. By the end of the story, Grete has emerged from the family's ordeal with strength and wisdom. Although Gregor's possibilities for the future have disappeared entirely, Grete now harbors immense hope and potential.

Far from being a pure-hearted caretaker, Grete eventually loses patience with the burden of caring for Gregor and becomes a cold voice of reason in the family. Although she is the one feeding and caring for Gregor, she becomes convinced that the Gregor they all knew and loved is no longer present and that the creature who has replaced him is expendable. She loses her ability to see the humanity within the insect form. She is the one who forces recognition on the family, avowing that they will never have Gregor back as they once knew him. Mr. Samsa throws apples at Gregor, and Mrs. Samsa runs from him in repulsion, but only Grete gives voice to what they all believe: that Gregor must go. It is a forbidden and powerful sentiment: once his family has given up on him and forged ahead with their new lives, Gregor dies.

MR. SAMSA   Mr. Samsa is emblematic of the cold and distant patriarchs who loom large in Kafka's fiction, an emotionally stunted father figure who welcomes his son's death as a relief. Just as "The Metamorphosis" traces Grete's transformation in the wake of Gregor's decline, the story also shows Mr. Samsa's transformation as he regains power and pride in the family. After his business failure, Mr. Samsa retreated from reality, where he felt his humiliation too strongly. Beset by physical limitations, the emasculated Mr. Samsa was eclipsed by the younger and more resourceful Gregor, who supported the family as a salesman. However, once Gregor is trapped within the confines of his strange metamorphosis, Mr. Samsa

M

emerges once again as the true head of the family. He takes control of the family assets, gets a job, and resumes authority in the household by kicking out the bullying boarders. However, his newly regained power comes at the expense of his son, whom he must topple to resume his superior position. Mr. Samsa hits Gregor with a cane and throws apples at him, refusing to see any glimmer of Gregor within the insectlike creature. Only when Gregor finally dies can the Samsa family, with Mr. Samsa at the helm, sail unburdened into the future.

THEMES, MOTIFS, AND SYMBOLS

THEMES

THE DESTRUCTIVENESS OF ALIENATION In "The Metamorphosis," Kafka shows the many destructive forms that alienation can take, including alienation from the self, other individuals, society, the marketplace and workplace, and even one's own body. Alienation has always plagued Gregor's life, and it's only made worse by his transformation into an insect. At the beginning of the story, Gregor awakens to find himself in a "regular human" bedroom, a phrase that suggests how alienated Gregor has become from other people. By identifying Gregor's surroundings as "human," Kafka suggests that Gregor has felt separated from that human realm for some time. When Gregor becomes an insect, he is literally alienated from the human realm, an extreme step forward in those feelings of alienation. As Gregor's condition grows more acute, his alienation intensifies. Although at first he can see a hospital from his window, as his senses weaken he must rely on memory when he thinks about the hospital. His alienation from this potential source of help suggests that some problems, such as the yearnings of the modern wage slave, cannot be cured with the traditional medicines or procedures offered by society. In one of the story's few hopeful notes, the Samsas evaluate their favorable career prospects, looking to the future with a sense of command, as opposed to the listless existence of Gregor in his former life as a traveling salesman. Rootless and alienated from himself and other people, Gregor embodies this alienation when he turns into an insect. His metamorphosis marks the end of his aimless, doomed trek through a grinding existence.

THE NECESSITY OF METAMORPHOSIS In "The Metamorphosis," Kafka portrays change as not only inevitable but also necessary for a fulfilling life. Change helps Mr. Samsa and Grete overcome binding, unsatisfying family roles and become stronger, more fulfilled human beings. For example, Mr. Samsa transforms from a weak, passive failure into a strong family head and primary provider. Grete changes throughout the story, from a foolish teenager to a maternal caretaker to a shrewd pragmatist and, finally, to a fully realized woman. The high personal cost of Gregor's metamorphosis, including his disfigurement and alienation, turns out to be beneficial for those most dependent on him. Without Gregor to rely on and ease their lives, the family finds a renewed sense of purpose and new wells of resourcefulness. Even Gregor's metamorphosis proves necessary to pushing him into a new realm of his life. Gregor's metamorphosis changes everything—his physical existence and perspective and way of life. These changes are hardly positive for Gregor, but they do shake up his life in positive ways. Because he transforms into an insect, Gregor is freed of a job he detests and released from the burden of supporting his entire family. Gregor's metamorphosis ultimately leads to his death, but his routine prior to his metamorphosis would have led to death as well—although perhaps a slower and more painful one.

MOTIFS

VIOLENCE AND INJURY   The violence and injury that appear throughout the story highlight the alienation that Gregor feels from himself, his family, and society. When Gregor attempts to escape his room and reach his family and the office manager who is demanding his presence in the office, he hurts himself as he tries to get out of bed and open the door. Trying to unlock and open the door with his ungainly, insectlike jaw, Gregor shows how alienated he has become from the human world. In this scene, appeasing the office manager's concerns proves more important to Gregor than his physical safety, and Gregor bleeds a "brown liquid" from his mouth as he struggles with the key. He bleeds more when his father drives him back into his room with a cane, a violent prodding from which Gregor cannot escape. He injures himself as he tries to cram his ungainly body through the small doorway, and one of his insect legs hangs broken and useless after this hasty retreat. Later in the story, Mr. Samsa again uses violence by throwing apples at Gregor, and one cracks his hard shell. The rotting apple leads to an infection and speeds Gregor's demise. Gregor has become fully alienated from everyone around him, and the violence perpetuated against him emphasizes his complete transformation into a nonhuman entity.

ROOMS AND WALLS   The Samsas' small apartment, with its many rooms and walls, suggests the difficulties people have in communicating with one another and the limitations individuals face as they attempt to forge a life in the modern world. The Samsa family attempts to communicate through closed doors, and Gregor eavesdrops on their conversations by listening through a crack in the door. Gregor himself is confined to one room, although he does secure a bit of freedom for himself: he discovers his ability to walk along the walls and ceiling. Although Gregor is effectively imprisoned, he demonstrates resourcefulness in taking advantage of the limited space he has. However, Gregor will never truly escape his imprisonment within the walls of his room. Trapped in his insect body, unable to speak or communicate with the outside world, Gregor will never find his voice again and never reenter society. At the end of the story, the Samsa family rejects not only Gregor but also the walls that held him prisoner. They decide to move to a new home, someplace smaller and less extravagant, as though they are renouncing all traces of Gregor—even the comfort he once provided them.

SYMBOLS

THE INSECT   The insect that Gregor turns into represents the expendability of an individual life as well as the society that allows individuals to be treated as expendable. When we meet Gregor, he has already been transformed into an insectlike creature, and Kafka never describes what Gregor looked like as a regular human being. For all we know, Gregor has always been just as he is now, described throughout the story as a cockroach, beetle, and centipede with a rotating head. In other words, Gregor may have always been expendable, devoting his life to an uncaring business that needs bodies rather than individuals to carry out the necessary work. Only now, as an insect, does Gregor reflect that notion physically because insects are stepped on and exterminated without a second thought. Prone to depression, dissatisfied with his human existence, and unable to change his personal or professional life, Gregor finds the perfect physical form for his self-loathing and disappointment: a repulsive bug, without any human characteristics to differentiate it from the innumerable other bugs that populate the world and keep the business of society operating.

APPLES   The apples that Mr. Samsa throws at Gregor represent the fall of man and the overall lack of compassion that rules in the Samsa household. When Mr. Samsa throws the apples, he brings about Gregor's demise: an apple lodges in Gregor's outer shell, ultimately contributing to his death. Gregor, whose self-sacrifice and deprivations have been taken for granted by the family, is finally cast out from the family because of his altered state of existence. Gregor turns into an insect because his life is earmarked for nothing but drudgery, and his altered state requires his family's selfless love and attention, which they are not prepared to offer. Grete tries to show her brother compassion, although her kindness soon flags, whereas Mr. and Mrs. Samsa are unable to react to Gregor with anything but violence and fear, respectively. The throwing of the apples proves to be a turning point in the family's interactions with Gregor, the moment when they abandon any hope of rehabilitating Gregor and decide instead to focus on their own futures. Just as Adam and Eve were cast out of Eden when they ate the forbidden fruit, Gregor meets his own expulsion from his family and, ultimately, his life when the fruit lodges in his shell.

SHORT STORY ANALYSIS

STRUCTURE   "The Metamorphosis" is divided into three parts, a structure that reflects the fractured nature of Gregor's new existence. In each section, Gregor tries and fails to regain his place in the family and society. In section one, Gregor tries to escape his room so that he can explain himself to his family and the office manager, but Mr. Samsa drives him back inside with a cane. In the second section, Gregor leaves his room to help Grete and his mother, who has been overcome with shock at the sight of him, but he is once again driven back inside by his father, who pelts him with apples. In section three, Gregor timidly emerges from his room to hear Grete play the violin, but one of the boarders spots him and, along with the other two boarders, declares angrily that they will no longer live in the house. At this moment, Grete, with her parents' agreement, declares that Gregor is dead to them, referring to him now as an "it." Gregor retreats back to his room and dies.

Each section also teases out a particular aspect of Gregor's life as a creature rather than a human. In section one, the transformation is examined in light of its personal ramifications. Gregor worries intensely about how his current state will affect his ability to earn a salary and continue supporting his family. In the second section, the metamorphosis is evaluated as it relates to the domestic sphere: how Gregor's appearance has deeply affected family life. As in the first section, the second section features an aggressive physical attack on Gregor by Mr. Samsa. In section three, Gregor faces his family's desire that he sacrifice himself, increasingly looking inward and confronting his perceptions of himself and his situation. He accepts what he is—a doomed castoff alone in a locked room, a burden preventing his family from moving forward—and accepts death.

THE TERM *KAFKAESQUE* Like William Shakespeare and George Orwell, Kafka has achieved the distinction of having his name appropriated for a literary term. The term *Kafkaesque* describes a nightmarish atmosphere resulting from pervasive, sinister, impersonal forces; feelings of guilt, fear, and loss of identity; and the sense of evil that permeates the logic of ruling powers. Much of Kafka's writing brims with this menacing, uneasy quality, and his protagonists are nearly always confined by alienation and anxiety. When reading Kafka's writing, we enter a world in which nothing is certain and every bad turn feels like the product of a conspiracy. In a Kafkaesque scenario, protagonists are taken out of their normal lives, with their normal frames of reference, and placed in previously unthinkable or unforeseen situations in which they must renegotiate the terms of their existence. In his work, Kafka often employs grim or absurdist humor to draw attention to the underlying conditions that ordinary comedy would attempt to mitigate or disguise. Kafka's signature style and uneasy humor expose the serious, brooding, and highly emotional nature of Kafka's grim vision of modern life, with its intrusive bureaucratic institutions and fraught interpersonal relations.

Together, these two modes—the comic and tragic—create an unresolved tension, much like the opposing impulses buffeting the lives of Kafka's characters and undermining any semblance of stability that they have managed to construct. For example, in "The Metamorphosis," Gregor is gripped in an existential upheaval, and this crisis of identity leads to Gregor walking on the ceiling and walls and having apples lodged in his back—a tragic predicament underscored by dark comedy. Similarly, whereas Gregor was once preoccupied with life on the road, his goals change so abruptly that he finds himself positioning a sheet so as to conceal his insect body beneath a sofa. Gregor descends into an inhuman, animalistic state, but at the same time he ironically discovers his appreciation of music and still manages to feel tenderness for his family. Gregor's opposing impulses will never be unified or resolved, and in a world of such radical dislocation, Kafka argues that tragedy will ultimately dominate.

POINT OF VIEW AND NARRATIVE VOICE In "The Metamorphosis," Kafka employs a point of view and narrative voice that allow him to observe and relate, with grim humor, the tribulations Gregor faces when he is transformed into an insect. The story is told in the third-person point of view and is for the most part limited to Gregor's perspective. Only his thoughts and feelings are presented, and most of the events are relayed as they are seen through his eyes. Through this point of view, we get a picture of Gregor and the world as he understands it. This does not necessarily mean that all of Gregor's judgments are to be accepted. Rather, Kafka uses irony and black humor to indicate that Gregor is at times misled, such as when he believes he can still catch the eight o'clock train and make it to the office, despite barely being able to hoist himself out of bed and manipulate his insectlike legs.

For most of the story, the narrator's voice is closely aligned with Gregor. The narrator attempts to access Gregor's thoughts and impressions, but there is some detachment between narrator and subject. The dark comedy that punctuates the story is generated from this distance, as the narrator is able to wryly comment on the absurdity of Gregor's state. In his own grim assessment of his situation, Gregor finds nothing laughable. At the same time, although the narrator freely relates the events leading to Gregor's death, Kafka does not give the narrator the power to reveal the outcome. The narrator is bound with Gregor in his locked room, restricted to Gregor's oblique glances outside when the door is cracked and his reveries about the anxieties that mark his condition. Only after Gregor dies is the narrator freed from telling Gregor's personal story, and Kafka follows the Samsas out into the fresh air and brighter future that awaits them.

IMPORTANT QUOTATIONS EXPLAINED

1. *When Gregor Samsa woke up one morning from unsettling dreams, he found himself changed in his bed into a monstrous vermin.*

This is the opening line of "The Metamorphosis" and one of the most well-known opening lines in all of literature. Kafka unexpectedly places his climax at the beginning, forcing us to negotiate an unfamiliar world where humans morph into insects and then still worry about catching the eight o'clock train to work. By setting up this world from the outset, Kafka forces us to immediately abandon our prevailing sense of logic and realism, as well as our expectation that fiction will somehow reflect recognizable human experience. Kafka uses his absurd story premise as a way of logically examining the very real effects that personal and professional tensions have on Gregor Samsa. The black comedy and bleak realities that appear throughout the story reveal the essential pointlessness that characterizes human existence. Gregor is a helpless creature, devoid of any control over his life. His grasp of reality and a stable, ordered life is so tenuous that during the course of a night's restless sleep, the horror he feels at his enslavement to a capitalist system that will eventually consume him overtakes his physical self, bringing about the hideous metamorphosis that will ultimately cost him his life.

M

2. *The rotten apple in his back and the inflamed area around it, which were completely covered in fluffy dust, already hardly bothered him. He thought back on his family with deep emotion and love.*

This quotation, which immediately precedes Gregor's death in the middle of the night, captures Kafka's unique way of blending shocking abuse with the detached comic viewpoint that develops as a defense to the grim, hopeless conditions of Gregor's life. Gregor is dying of the wounds that his father inflicted on him, but this state only provokes strong pangs of affection. The peaceful meditation serves as Gregor's forgiveness of his family, the people to whom he entrusted his care and future but who renounced him. Kafka's words also invoke Gregor's passive final acceptance of his situation. He remains in a state of "empty and peaceful reflection" until he dies. This blissful oblivion that settles onto Gregor is the only escape he can find from his imprisonment in both his body and family home. Death is the only option that Gregor has. He has already lost the self he knew, and he must now forego his self and life entirely. For the sake of his family, Gregor wills his death. His family thinks that his death will free them, but now that the burden of supporting the family rests with them, his family will likely fall victim to the same alienation that afflicted Gregor during his life.

The Monkey's Paw

W. W. Jacobs
(1863–1943)

CONTEXT

W. W. (William Wymark) Jacobs was born in 1863 in London, England, to an impoverished family. His mother, Sophia, died when Jacobs was a young boy. His father, William Jacobs, managed a wharf in South Devon. After receiving his degree from Birkbeck College, the satirical magazines the *Idler* and *Today* published some of his stories in the early 1890s. Jacobs's first short-story collection, *Many Cargoes* (1896), won popular acclaim, prompting him to quit working as a clerk and begin writing full-time. Jacobs wed Agnes Eleanor, a prominent suffragette, in 1900, and they had five children together.

The success of Jacobs's fiction enabled him to escape his scrappy, hard-luck childhood and dull life as a civil servant. His early experiences benefited him greatly, however. He had spent a lot of time hanging around the wharves in London, and many of his short stories and novels concern seamen's lives and adventures. Jacobs's works include *The Skipper's Wooing* (1897), *Sea Urchins* (1898), *Light Freights* (1901), *Captains' All* (1902), *Sailors' Knots* (1909), and *Night Watches* (1914). All told, Jacobs published thirteen collections of short stories, five novels, and a novella, many of which sold tens of thousands of copies. He also wrote a number of one-act plays. His financial security was further solidified by the popular *Strand* magazine, which began publishing Jacobs's short stories in 1898 and continued to do so throughout much of his life. Jacobs died in 1943.

While modern readers associate Jacobs primarily with his suspenseful and frequently anthologized short story "The Monkey's Paw" and, to a lesser degree, with his short story "The Toll House," his contemporaries primarily knew him as a comic writer. Like many comic writers of the day, Jacobs explored the lives of the lower and middle classes and published many of his stories in magazines directed at this audience. The novellas *At Sunwich Port* (1902) and *Dialstone Lane* (1904) exemplify his ability to create humorous scenarios with vivid characters. Jerome K. Jerome, a popular comic novelist of the day, was a great fan of Jacobs's and praised his strong work ethic and painstaking approach. He said that Jacobs would often rewrite just one sentence for hours at a stretch. Many luminaries of literature have praised Jacob's work, including G. K. Chesterton, Henry James, Evelyn Waugh, P. G. Wodehouse, and Mark Twain.

"The Monkey's Paw" was published in Jacobs's short-story collection *The Lady of the Barge* (1902), and the story's popularity has been extraordinarily long-lasting. The story has been included in approximately seventy collections, from horror and gothic anthologies to the *New York Review of Books'* collection of classic fiction. The story has also been turned into a play, parodied on *The Simpsons*, and made into eight separate movies. Stephen King wrote about "The Monkey's Paw" in *The Dead Zone* (1979) and *Apt Pupil* (1982) and based his novel *Pet Sematary* (1983) on its themes. The spare but colorful characterization of the

White family, fascination with wishing and wishing gone awry, and story's mix of humor and terror have made "The Monkey's Paw" popular with generations of readers.

PLOT OVERVIEW

Part I opens on a dark and stormy night as the three members of the White family relax inside their cozy house. Herbert White and his father are playing a game of chess while Mrs. White knits near the fire. After his son wins, Mr. White complains about the terrible weather and nearly deserted road they live near.

A family friend, Sergeant-Major Morris, arrives for a visit. Over whisky, he tells stories of his exploits abroad. Mr. White expresses interest in going to India, but the sergeant-major says he would be better off staying at home. At Mr. and Mrs. Whites' urging, Sergeant-Major Morris takes a small, mummified paw out of his pocket. He explains that a *fakir* (a mystic miracle worker) placed a spell on the paw to prove that people's lives are governed by fate and that it is dangerous to meddle with fate. According to the sergeant-major, three men can wish on the paw three times each. The sergeant-major himself has already had his three wishes, as has another man, who used his third wish to ask for death. The sergeant-major has considered selling the paw, but he doesn't want it to cause any more trouble than it already has. Moreover, no one will buy the paw without first seeing proof of its effect. The sergeant-major throws the paw into the fire, and Mr. White quickly rescues it. The sergeant-major warns him three times to leave the paw alone, but he eventually explains how to make a wish on the paw.

Mrs. White says the story reminds her of the *Arabian Nights* and jokingly suggests that her husband wish her a pair of extra hands to help her with all her work. The sergeant-major doesn't find this joke funny, however, and urges Mr. White to use common sense if he insists on wishing. After supper and more tales of India, the sergeant-major leaves. Herbert says he thinks the sergeant-major is full of nonsense and jokes that his father should make himself an emperor so that he doesn't have to listen to Mrs. White's nagging. In mock anger, Mrs. White playfully chases her son.

Mr. White says he has everything he wants and isn't sure what to wish for. Herbert says that two hundred pounds would enable them to pay off the money owed for the house. Mr. White wishes aloud for two hundred pounds as Herbert accompanies him with melodramatic chords played on the piano. Mr. White suddenly cries out and says that the paw moved like a snake in his hand. After Mr. and Mrs. White go to bed, Herbert sits by the fire and sees a vividly realistic monkey face in the flames. He puts out the fire, takes the monkey's paw, and goes to bed.

Part II begins on the next morning, a sunny winter day. The room seems cheerful and normal in contrast to the previous evening's gloomy atmosphere and the mummified paw now looks harmless. Mrs. White comments on how ridiculous the sergeant-major's story was but remarks that two hundred pounds couldn't do any harm. They could, Herbert jokes, if the money fell out of the sky onto his father's head. Mr. White answers that people often mistake coincidence for granted wishes. Herbert then leaves for work.

Later that day, Mrs. White notices a stranger outside dressed in nice clothes. The stranger hesitantly approaches their gate three times before opening it and coming up to the door. Mrs. White ushers him in. He nervously states that he is a representative of Maw and Meggins, Herbert's employer. Mrs. White asks whether Herbert is all right, and the representative says he is hurt, but in no pain. For a moment, Mrs. White feels relieved, until she realizes that

Herbert feels no pain because he's dead. The representative says that Herbert was "caught in the machinery." After a pause, Mr. White says that Herbert was the only child they had left. Embarrassed, the representative stresses that he is simply obeying Maw and Meggins's orders. He then explains that the company will not take any responsibility for the death but will give the Whites two hundred pounds. Mrs. White shrieks, and Mr. White faints.

In Part III, the Whites bury Herbert. Several days pass, and the couple feels exhausted and hopeless. A week after the burial, Mr. White wakes up and hears his wife crying by the window. He gently urges her to come back to bed, but she refuses. He dozes off again until Mrs. White suddenly cries out that she wants the monkey's paw. In hysterics, she tells him to go downstairs and wish Herbert back to life. Mr. White resists and tells her that Herbert's death and the two hundred pounds they had received had nothing to do with his wish the previous night. Mr. White says that he didn't want to tell her before, but Herbert was so mangled that he had to identify the body by looking at the clothes. Mrs. White doesn't listen, however, and continues to insist on wishing Herbert back to life with the monkey's paw.

Mr. White retrieves the paw from its place downstairs. Mrs. White orders him to make the wish two more times until he finally complies. He makes the wish, and as they wait, the candle goes out. They hear the clock, the creak of a stair, and the sound of a mouse. At last Mr. White goes downstairs. His match goes out, and before he can strike another, he hears a knock at the door. Another knock sounds, and Mr. White dashes upstairs. Mrs. White hears the third knock and says it's Herbert. She realizes he hadn't returned right after the wish had been made because he'd had to walk two miles from the graveyard to their house.

Mr. White begs her not to open the door, but she breaks free and runs downstairs. As she struggles to reach the bolt, the knocking becomes more insistent. Mr. White searches frantically for the paw, which had dropped to the floor. As Mrs. White pulls back the bolt, Mr. White finds the paw and makes a final wish. The knocking stops, and Mrs. White cries out. Mr. White dashes downstairs and sees that beyond the door, the street is empty.

LIST OF MAJOR CHARACTERS

Herbert White   The son of Mr. and Mrs. White. Herbert is an irreverent, affectionate, and loyal young man and the only surviving child of the Whites. He works in an unidentified capacity with heavy machinery at a company called Maws and Meggins. It is possible, although not certain, that Mr. White's second wish reanimates Herbert as a terrifying corpse.

Mrs. White   Herbert's mother and Mr. White's wife. Mrs. White is an intelligent and passionate woman. She shares her husband's and son's fascination with Sergeant-Major Morris's stories and questions him just as eagerly as they do. She is lovingly attentive to her husband and son, although she also enjoys teasing them. Herbert's death traumatizes Mrs. White, and she forces Mr. White to wish Herbert back to life.

Mr. White   Herbert's father and Mrs. White's husband. Mr. White is an old man who is both curious and malleable. A poor man, he thinks longingly about the exotic lands he has never visited. The monkey's paw fascinates him in part because of its connection to those lands. Although it is Mr. White who makes all three wishes, he makes the first two only at the suggestions of his wife and son.

Sergeant-Major Morris   A friend of the Whites. A mysterious and possibly sinister figure, Sergeant-Major Morris enjoys talking about his adventures abroad and shows the Whites his monkey's paw, in spite of his professed reservations. A jaded and world-weary man, he discourages Mr. White from dreaming of India, suggesting that life is better and simpler at home in England. He throws the monkey's paw into the fire and urges Mr. White not to make any wishes, but he ultimately tells him exactly how to make a wish.

The Representative   The man who informs Mr. and Mrs. White of Herbert's death. The nervous representative sympathizes with the Whites and tries to distance himself from Maw and Meggins's failure to take responsibility, stressing that he is following orders and not expressing his own feelings. He gives Mr. and Mrs. White two hundred pounds from the company.

ANALYSIS OF MAJOR CHARACTERS

HERBERT WHITE   The possible transformation of Herbert White from a gentle, happy, and devoted young man into a threatening monster is the central horror of "The Monkey's Paw." A thoughtful and loving son, Herbert plays chess with his father and gently teases his mother. He is the only member of the family who works, so readers can assume that he supports his parents in their old age. Herbert believes that Sergeant-Major Morris's stories are nothing but a pack of tall tales and treats the monkey's paw with irreverent humor. He encourages his father to wish for an emperorship and then jokingly suggests he wish for two hundred pounds to pay off the mortgage. Herbert does not believe for a moment that the paw is magical, but he unwittingly predicts the outcome of the wish when he tells his parents that he knows he'll never see the money. The sunny, skeptical quality of Herbert's nature makes his eventual transformation, induced by his father's wish, more horrifying. Mr. White fears that his son has become a horribly mangled, evil being, after wishing him back to life. The fact that Jacobs never actually describes who—or what—knocks repeatedly on the Whites' door, however, suggests that the caller may not really be Herbert's revived corpse.

MRS. WHITE   Mr. and Mrs. White also undergo an upsetting change, transforming from a happy couple into parents racked by grief. During the sergeant-major's visit, Mrs. White is as eager as Herbert and Mr. White are to hear the tales of his exploits abroad. She is more willing to consider the truth of the monkey-paw story than Herbert is, but she is far less credulous than her husband. Indeed, she often shows herself to be more quick-witted than Mr. White. For example, she understands the significance of the Maw and Meggins representative's visit before her husband does, and she is the one to suggest wishing on the monkey's paw a second time to bring Herbert back to life. The death of her son and the belief that it might have been prevented nearly drive Mrs. White insane. Her transformation is far less dramatic than her son's, but she still changes from an intelligent, self-possessed woman into a raving, shrieking, weeping mourner.

MR. WHITE   Mr. White's grief is twofold as he laments his son's death as well as his decision to wish on the monkey's paw in the first place. Unlike his wife, Mr. White realizes he should have never invited trouble by wishing for the two hundred pounds or to bring Herbert back to life. The fact that he believes an unholy creature stands knocking at his door instead of his son suggests that he feels guilty for having let selfishness overtake him when he made his wishes. Instead of passing off the knocking as an unrelated coincidence, he immediately jumps to the conclusion that evil stands on the other side, as if believing the paw has punished him for being greedy. His decision to wish the unwanted visitor away with his third wish may reflect his desire to not only save his and Mrs. White's lives, but also redeem himself for his sins.

THEMES, MOTIFS, AND SYMBOLS

THEMES

THE DANGER OF WISHING The Whites' downfall comes as the result of wishing for more than what they actually needed. Even though Mr. White feels content with his life—he has a happy family, a comfortable home, and plenty of love—he nevertheless uses the monkey's paw to wish for money that he doesn't really need. As Jacobs suggests, making one seemingly harmless wish only intensifies and magnifies desire as each subsequent wish becomes more outlandish. After receiving two hundred pounds for Herbert's death, for example, Mrs. White jumps to the conclusion that the paw has unlimited power. She forces Mr. White to wish to bring Herbert back to life, a wish far more serious than their first. Unchecked greed, therefore, only leads to unhappiness, no matter how much more one asks for. Intense desire also often leads to unfulfilled expectations or unintended consequences as with Herbert's unexpected death and rise from the grave as a living corpse. Put simply, Jacobs is reminding readers to be careful what they wish for because it may just come true.

THE CLASH BETWEEN DOMESTICITY AND THE OUTSIDE WORLD Jacobs depicts the Whites' home and domestic sphere in general as a safe, cozy place separate from the dangerous world outside. The Whites' house is full of symbols of happy domesticity: a piano, knitting, a copper kettle, a chessboard, a fireplace, and a breakfast table. But the Whites repeatedly invite trouble into this cozy world. Sergeant-Major Morris—a family friend, seasoned veteran, and world traveler—disrupts the tranquility in the Whites' home with his stories of India and magic and warnings of evil. He gives Mr. White the monkey's paw, the ultimate token of the dangerous outside world. Mr. and Mrs. White mar the healthy atmosphere of their home again when they invite the Maw and Meggins representative inside, a man who shatters their happiness with news of Herbert's death. The final would-be invader of the domestic world is Herbert himself. Mr. White's terrified reaction to his dead son's desire for entrance suggests not just his horror at the prospect of an animated corpse, but his understanding, won from experience, that any person coming from the outside should be treated as a dangerous threat to the sanctity of the home.

MOTIFS

GROUPS OF THREE Jacobs's story is structured around a pattern of threes. The central force of the story is the monkey's paw, which will grant three separate owners three wishes each. The White family is made up of three people. Mr. White is the third owner of the paw. (The first owner was Sergeant-Major Morris, and the second owner used his third wish for death.) Sergeant-Major Morris begins talking about his adventures in India after three glasses of whisky and urges Mr. White three times not to wish on the paw. The representative from Maw and Meggins approaches the Whites' gate three times before he musters up the courage to walk up the path to their door. Mrs. White orders her husband three times to wish Herbert alive again before he retrieves the paw. And the reanimated corpse of Herbert knocks three times before his mother hears him. In addition to permeating the plot, the number three gives "The Monkey's Paw" its structure. The story is broken up into three parts, which take place at three times of day, during three types of weather. Part I occurs in the evening during a rainstorm. Part II takes place during the morning of a bright winter day. Part III is set in the middle of a chilly, windy night.

By stressing threes, Jacobs taps into a number of associations that are common in Western culture. Most relevant to the story is the saying "bad luck comes in threes." One well-known trinity, or three, is from Christian theology, in which God is composed of the Father, Son, and Holy Spirit. Disregard for threes has been superstitiously equated with disregard for the trinity. In the case of Jacobs's characters, faith in a non-Christian totem (the paw) may be interpreted as disrespect for Christianity. Finally, because twos commonly occur in nature (we have two legs, two eyes, two hands, and so on), threes are often used in literature to produce a perverse or unnatural effect.

SYMBOLS

THE MONKEY'S PAW   The monkey's paw is a symbol of desire and greed—everything that its owner could possibly wish for and the unrestricted ability to make it happen. This power makes the paw alluring, even to unselfish people who desire nothing and have everything they need. Mr. White, for example, hastily retrieves the paw from the fire, even though he himself admits that he wouldn't know what to wish for if he owned the paw. Its potential also prompts Herbert to half-jokingly suggest wishing for money the Whites don't really need, ostensibly just to see what happens. The paw grants Mr. White's wishes by killing Herbert and raising his corpse from the grave in an unexpected and highly sinister twist. At the same time, however, the paw's omnipotent power may be misperceived, because Herbert's death may have been entirely coincidental and the knocks on the door may be from someone other than his living corpse.

CHESS   Chess symbolizes life in "The Monkey's Paw." Those who play a daring, risky game of chess, for example, will lose, just as those who take unnecessary risks in life will die. When the story opens, Mr. White and Herbert play chess by the fire, and the game's outcome mirrors the story's outcome. Mr. White, the narrator explains, has a theory of "radical changes" concerning chess. He takes terrible, unnecessary risks with his king, risks that make his wife nervous as she watches the game unfold. As he plays, he notices that he has made a mistake that will prove deadly. The risks and mistakes Mr. White makes playing chess parallel the risks and mistakes he makes wishing on the monkey's paw. These mistakes ultimately lead to Herbert's death, the most "radical change" of all.

SHORT STORY ANALYSIS

THE HORROR GENRE   "The Monkey's Paw" is a classic of the horror genre that has been copied and adapted numerous times in the century since it was first published. Jacobs wove many common and recognizable elements of the genre into the story: the story opens on a dark and stormy night, the Whites live on a deserted street, doors bang unexpectedly, stairs squeak, and silences are interrupted by the ticking of the clock. These elements heighten the tension and inform readers that something dreadful could occur at any moment. Another element of classic horror is Jacobs's transformation of the happy, loving White family into people who live amidst death and misery. Herbert's transformation is the most obvious, from a joking and playful son to a living corpse. Parts of Mr. and Mrs. White also die after Herbert's accident, and they become obsessed with death and the loss in their lives. Jacobs also draws from classic horror fiction when he plays off the White family's happiness with readers' sense of impending doom. As the Whites make lighthearted jokes about the monkey's paw, for example, readers cringe, sensing that disaster will soon strike.

More than a classic horror piece, "The Monkey's Paw" is also a modern parable, infused with moral messages and instructions on how to live a more fulfilling life. As with all fables, the story's morals are familiar: don't tempt fate, and be careful what you wish for. The White family isn't wealthy, but they still have everything that's important, including love, happiness, and a comfortable life. Mr. White even says that he is so content that he wouldn't even know what to wish for. When he does make his first wish—partly in jest, partly out of curiosity—it is not for untold riches or worldly power, but merely for enough money to finally purchase their house. His small and sensible wish, however, is enough to tempt fate into killing Herbert. Jacobs's story adheres to the traditional belief that we do not really want what we think we want and that wanting more than what's sufficient may bring ruin.

LITERARY ALLUSIONS Jacobs drew from a number of widely known literary sources in writing "The Monkey's Paw" to make the story both familiar and unsettling. His most recognizable influence was the tale of Aladdin and the magic lamp, one of the more famous tales in *The Book of One Thousand and One Nights*, or simply *Arabian Nights*, as Mrs. White calls it. There are numerous variations to the Aladdin story—including Walt Disney's popular cartoon of the 1990s—but nearly all of them suggest that successful wishing is impossible because magic never works the way people want it to work. Jacobs also uses the same structural pattern in "The Monkey's Paw" featured in most other "three wishes" stories: the first wish leads to unexpected and dissatisfying results, the hastily made second wish fails to reverse the first wish and only worsens the situation, and the third wish manages to undo the disastrous second wish.

Jacobs's less obvious sources of inspiration, however, include the Bible and stories of Faust, the German scholar who sells his soul in exchange for the devil's service. Mr. White recoils in horror after wishing on the monkey's paw for the first time, insisting that the paw moved like a snake in his hand. This snake alludes to the biblical story of Adam and Eve, in which Eve discovers that the seemingly delicious fruit brings only misery. Similarly, the Whites—whose surname suggests unsullied innocence—discover that the powerful monkey's paw grants wishes with a heavy price. And just as in the Faust stories, the fulfillment of Mr. and Mrs. White's wishes brings only pain and suffering to others and therefore fail to satisfy them.

IMPORTANT QUOTATIONS EXPLAINED

---

1. *"He was caught in the machinery," said the visitor at length in a low voice. "Caught in the machinery," repeated Mr. White, in a dazed fashion, "yes."*

Herbert White's death has a literal meaning and two metaphorical meanings. Literally, Herbert died because he became entangled in the machinery, his body so mangled that Mr. White was able to identify his son only by examining his clothes. Metaphorically, however, Herbert died because after being caught in the machinery of fate, which went awry after Mr. White tampered with fate by making his wish for more money. A subtler metaphorical meaning has to do with Herbert's employer. An undercurrent of class consciousness runs through "The Monkey's Paw," a story that concerns the fate of three lower-middle-class people. It is possible to read the Whites' dire fate not as something they brought upon themselves through greediness, but instead as the unfair effect of a modest wish made by a family struggling with debts and a small income. Jacobs suggests that anyone, even the most moral reader, would behave exactly as the Whites did, making a small, practical wish just to see what might happen.

Jacobs uses Herbert's death to suggest that society is unfair to the good, hardworking people in the lower classes. Evidence of this worldview comes in the form of the Maw and Meggins representative, who shamefacedly announces that his company will decline to take any responsibility for the accident, but will effectively offer Mr. and Mrs. White a bribe to keep quiet. The first word of the company name, *maw*, means voracious, gaping mouth. The suggestion is that Herbert has been swallowed whole by a cruel world, and all because of one understandable wish made by a man who simply wants to own his own house.

---

2. *[H]e found the monkey's paw, and frantically breathed his third and last wish. The knocking ceased suddenly . . . a long loud wail of disappointment and misery from his wife gave him courage to run down to her side, and then to the gate beyond. The street lamp flickering opposite shone on a quiet and deserted road.*

The ambiguity of these final lines makes it possible to read "The Monkey's Paw" as something other than a horror story or cautionary tale. We never see Herbert's walking corpse with our own eyes, and neither do Mr. White, who is cowering upstairs, or Mrs. White, who cannot manage to open the door in time. One could therefore argue that the monkey's paw holds no power at all and that Herbert would have died had Mr. White never even made the wish. The frantic knocking at the door is perhaps someone else entirely who goes away just as Mr. White makes his third wish. The plausibility of this interpretation adds a new dimension to "The Monkey's Paw," making it more than just another horror story.

The Most Dangerous Game

Richard Connell
(1893–1949)

CONTEXT

Richard Edward Connell was born in Poughkeepsie, New York, on October 17, 1893. His father served in the House of Representatives for approximately one year before his death in October 1912. Precocious and verbal, Connell had a knack for writing since childhood and had become an editor for his local newspaper, the *Poughkeepsie News-Press*, by age sixteen. He served as his father's secretary and congressional aide while attending Georgetown but left Washington, D.C., after only a year to fight in Europe during World War I. He enrolled at Harvard University upon returning to the United States, editing both the *Harvard Lampoon* and *Harvard Crimson*.

Connell turned to freelance writing in 1919 and began a prolific period that spanned more than three decades. From his home in Beverly Hills, California, he published four novels, four collections of short stories, numerous Hollywood screenplays, and many articles for local newspapers. Critics quickly recognized him as a new master of short fiction, and his stories frequently appeared in *Collier's Weekly* and the *Saturday Evening Post* as well as foreign publications. He published more than 300 short stories during the course of his lifetime, including the well known "A Friend of Napoleon," "Big Lord Fauntleroy," "Hero of the Devil's Kitchen," and "Sssssssshhh." His short story "The Most Dangerous Game," first published in 1924, proved to be his greatest success and won him the prestigious O. Henry Memorial Award. He continued to write short stories until his death from a heart attack in 1949.

Adventurous and suspenseful, "The Most Dangerous Game" struck a chord with readers far and wide. Integrating elements of both popular and literary fiction, Connell's story provides fast-paced escapism and a menacing, Gothic atmosphere of mystery, horror, and the grotesque. Hollywood produced a silver-screen adaptation of the story eight years after its initial publication, pitting Rainsford and a shipwrecked brother-and-sister duo against the evil General Zaroff. The early "talkie" B-film's crisp pace, strong performances, and breathless suspense made it an instant classic. The story was twice adapted into popular radio dramas in the early to mid-1940s, the first starring Orson Welles as General Zaroff and the second starring Joseph Cotten as Rainsford. The human-hunting-humans scenario in "The Most Dangerous Game" has since inspired countless other films, television episodes, and novels, all trying to recapture the heart-pounding terror of Connell's original story.

PLOT OVERVIEW

On a yacht bound for Rio de Janeiro, a passenger named Whitney points out Ship-Trap Island in the distance, a place that sailors dread and avoid. He and his friend Rainsford are big-game hunters bound for a hunting trip in the Amazon River basin. As the yacht sails through the darkness, the two men discuss whether their prey actually feels fear. Rainsford believes that the world consists only of predators and prey, although Whitney is not as certain. Noticing the jitteriness of the crew, Whitney wants to sail past the mysterious island as soon as possible. He theorizes that sailors can sense danger and that evil emanates in waves like light and sound.

Whitney then decides to turn in for the night, but Rainsford opts to smoke his pipe on the afterdeck for a while. Suddenly, he hears three gunshots in the distance and moves toward the railing of the deck to investigate. Hoisting himself onto the rail to try and get a better look, Rainsford drops his pipe, loses his balance in an attempt to catch it, and accidentally plunges into the water. His cries for help go unanswered, and the yacht quickly disappears into the night.

Rainsford decides to swim in the gunshots' direction. He hears the screeching sound of an animal in agony and heads straight for it, until the cries end abruptly with a pistol shot. Exhausted, Rainsford reaches the rocky shore and immediately falls into a deep sleep. He wakes the next afternoon and sets off in search of food, forced to skirt the thick growth of the jungle and walk along the shore. He soon comes to a bloody, torn-up patch of vegetation where a large animal had thrashed about. He finds an empty rifle cartridge nearby.

He follows the hunter's footprints in the growing darkness and eventually comes upon a palatial chateau at the edge of a precipice that drops steeply into the rocky ocean below. At first, Rainsford thinks the chateau is a mirage, until he opens the iron gate and knocks on the door. Ivan, a burly man with a gun, answers and refuses to help Rainsford until another man, General Zaroff, appears from inside the chateau and invites Rainsford inside.

Zaroff greets Rainsford warmly and has Ivan show him to a room where he can dress for dinner. The huge, lavish dining hall features numerous stuffed and mounted heads, trophies that Zaroff has brought back from his many hunting adventures around the world. As the two men eat borscht, a red Russian soup made of beets, Rainsford praises his host's specimens, remarking on how dangerous it can be to hunt Cape buffalo. Zaroff states that he now hunts far more dangerous game on his island. He recounts past hunts, from his childhood in the Crimea to hunting big game around the world, but goes on to describe how the sport eventually became too easy.

Zaroff hints, however, that he has found a new kind of animal to hunt, one with courage, cunning, and reason. Rainsford's initial confusion turns to horror as he slowly realizes that the general now hunts human beings. Zaroff doesn't understand Rainsford's indignation but promises that his outrage will subside once he's begun the hunt. Rainsford declines Zaroff's invitation to join in the hunt that night and goes to bed. After a fitful night of insomnia and light dozing, the sound of a distant pistol shot awakens him in the early morning.

General Zaroff reappears at the chateau at lunchtime, sad that hunting humans no longer satisfies him. He laments that the sailors he lures to the island present less and less of a challenge. Rainsford demands to leave the island at once, but the general refuses and forces Rainsford to be his new prey in the next hunt, hoping that Rainsford, as a renowned big-game hunter, will provide the challenge he seeks. Zaroff promises to set Rainsford free if he lives through the next three days. Rainsford sets off into the jungle after receiving food, clothes, and a knife from Ivan. He cuts a complicated, twisting path through the undergrowth to confuse Zaroff and then climbs a tree to wait as darkness approaches.

Zaroff finds Rainsford easily but lets him escape to prolong the pleasure of the hunt. Unsettled that Zaroff found him so quickly, Rainsford runs to another part of the jungle and makes a booby-trap called a Malayan mancatcher to kill Zaroff. The trap only wounds Zaroff, who returns to the chateau and promises to kill Rainsford the following night.

Rainsford runs for hours until he mistakenly steps into a bed of quicksand. He manages to wrest free, then digs a pit in the soft mud a few feet in front of the quicksand. He lines the bottom of the pit with sharp wooden stakes, covers it with foliage, and then hides in the brush nearby. One of Zaroff's hunting hounds springs the trap and plunges to his death, forcing Zaroff to return to the chateau again. At daybreak, Rainsford hears the baying of the hounds and spots Zaroff and Ivan with a small pack of hunting dogs in the distance. Rainsford fashions another trap by tying his knife to a sapling.

The trap kills Ivan, but the hounds push on, cornering Rainsford at the edge of a cliff. Instead of facing the dogs, Rainsford jumps into the rocky sea below. Stunned and disappointed, Zaroff returns to his chateau. As he turns on his bedroom light, he is shocked to find Rainsford concealed in the curtains of the bed. Before they fight, Zaroff states that the dogs will eat one of them that night while the other will sleep in the comfortable bed. Rainsford later concludes that he has never slept in a more comfortable bed.

CHARACTER LIST

Sanger Rainsford   A world-renowned big-game hunter and the story's protagonist. Intelligent, experienced, and level-headed, Rainsford uses his wits and physical prowess to outwit General Zaroff. His understanding of civilization and the relationship between hunter and prey is radically transformed during his harrowing days on the island. Hiding from Zaroff, he recalls his days fighting in the trenches of World War I, where he witnessed unimaginable violence. At the same time, the three-day chase reverses his life of privilege and ease, forcing him to sacrifice comfort and luxury to survive.

General Zaroff   A Russian Cossack and expatriate who lives on Ship-Trap Island and enjoys hunting men. General Zaroff's high cheekbones, sharply defined nose, and pointed military mustache accentuate his mysteriousness and savagery. With a cultivated voice and deliberate, slightly accented way of speaking, his regal bearing and rarefied aristocratic air belie his dementia and sadism. He hunts human beings to experience the most satisfying thrill.

Whitney   Rainsford's friend and traveling companion. On the yacht, Whitney suggests to Rainsford that hunted animals feel fear. Highly suggestible, Whitney feels anxious as they sail near the mysterious Ship-Trap Island. He argues that evil emanates in waves like light and sound.

Ivan   A Cossack and Zaroff's mute assistant. A man of formidable physical stature, Ivan has a waist-length black beard and wears a black uniform. All of Zaroff's captives prefer to flee from Zaroff as prey rather than suffer torture and certain death at Ivan's hands.

ANALYSIS OF MAJOR CHARACTERS

SANGER RAINSFORD   The protagonist, Sanger Rainsford, is an adventurous big-game hunter who confronts the nature of life and death for the first time in his life during his few frightening days on Ship-Trap Island. Calm and composed, Rainsford coolly handles any challenge, be it falling overboard in the middle of the night or having to swim several miles to reach the shore. He's survived numerous near-death experiences, from fighting on the frontlines during World War I to hunting dangerous animals in some of the world's most exotic locales. Rainsford's wartime experiences have reinforced his ultimate belief in the primacy of human life and the respect it deserves. Only during Zaroff's relentless final pursuit does Rainsford truly feel fear and his own primal instinct to survive.

The long-term ramifications of Rainsford's harrowing ordeal remain indeterminate and unresolved, however, because Connell purposefully chooses to leave any transformation in Rainsford's character uncharted. Although Connell suggests that Rainsford now empathizes with the creatures he has hunted in the past, it is uncertain whether he will discontinue hunting in the future. On one hand, Rainsford could possibly abandon hunting altogether or at least approach it with a new respect for his prey. Conversely, Rainsford's ability to sleep so soundly after killing Zaroff may suggest that he has become even more ruthless or hasn't undergone any significant transformation at all.

GENERAL ZAROFF   General Zaroff's refined mannerisms conceal a maniacal desire to inflict suffering and death for his own amusement. In many ways, Zaroff considers himself a god who can snuff out life as he pleases. Zaroffs's madness stems from a life of wealth, luxury, and militarism, which inflate his ego and sense of entitlement and impose few limits on his desires. Zaroff began hunting at an early age when he shot his father's prized turkeys and continually sought out bigger game in his family's tract of wilderness in the Crimea, a peninsula on the Black Sea. Commanding a division of Cossack cavalrymen in Russia, meanwhile, familiarized Zaroff with the horrors and atrocities of warfare. His bloodlust and passion for hunting eventually prompted him to hunt men, the most cunning and challenging prey he could find.

Accustomed to death, General Zaroff has lost the ability to distinguish men from beasts, suggesting that he has slipped into barbarism and lost his humanity. The sanctioned violence of his youth and early manhood drained the general of his empathy and capacity to make moral judgments. His passion for the hunt and love of the refined, meanwhile, led him to devalue human life. In fact, Zaroff even praises his thoroughbred hounds over the lives of the sailors he hunts. Connell describes Zaroff's sharp pointed teeth and smacking red lips to dehumanize him and highlight his predatory nature. Ironically, Rainsford discovers that General Zaroff is far more repulsive than the "scum" he disdainfully hunts, devoid of all emotion and humanity despite his seeming gentility.

THEMES, MOTIFS, AND SYMBOLS

THEMES

REASON VERSUS INSTINCT   Pitting Rainsford and General Zaroff against each other in the hunt allows Connell to blur the line between hunter and prey, human and animal, to suggest that instinct and reason are not as mutually exclusive as people have traditionally thought. Writers and philosophers have traditionally placed human intellect and the ability to reason above the bestial instincts of wild animals, which have no moral compulsions and act solely to satisfy their own needs. Reason, therefore, transforms mere animals into people and allows them to live together in functioning societies. Connell first blurs the dichotomy between reason and instinct through Rainsford's friend Whitney, who asserts that animals instinctively feel fear and then confesses that Captain Neilson's description of Ship-Trap Island has given him the chills. Without realizing it, Whitney admits that his perception of the island has sparked a sense of dread in him, just as perceived danger induces fear in an animal.

Connell further turns the table on the idea that reason exists apart from instinct by reducing the gentleman hunter Rainsford to the role of prey in General Zaroff's sadistic hunt. Rainsford comes to realize that all creatures, including people, rely on fear and their instinct to survive to avoid pain and death, just as Whitney had originally argued. Nevertheless, Rainsford remains calm in spite of his fear and works methodically to evade death and even defeat Zaroff. Despite his desire to kill his pursuers, however, Rainsford keeps his perspective and continues to value human life, therefore remaining more man than beast. In contrast, the genteel General Zaroff reveals himself to be more animal than human by rationally concluding that people are no different from other living creatures and by ruthlessly hunting men to satisfy his inner bloodlust. Zaroff's and Rainsford's cool rationality and calculating cunning throughout the entire hunt belies the fact that each man acts only according to instinct, one to survive and the other to kill.

THE EFFECTS OF WAR   Although Rainsford and Zaroff have similar backgrounds and are both wealthy hunters, they have radically different interpretations of their wartime experiences. Zaroff tells Rainsford about his days slumming in the Russian army, a brief dalliance commanding a Cossack cavalry division that ultimately distracted him from his love of the hunt. He nevertheless conveniently retains the title of general in a nod to his thirst for power over other individuals' lives. Connell also suggests that Zaroff's martial experiences altered him and allowed him to think of other people as worthy prey. The general's inflated ego, disdain for humanity, and sadistic thrill at inflicting suffering all stem from seeing life through the sights of a rifle. Zaroff finds Rainsford's outrage naïve, primly Victorian, and overly puritan. Rainsford, however, remembers the grueling, harrowing aspects of warfare. He recalls desperately digging trenches with insufficient tools while on the European frontlines in World War I. The sense of desperation and powerlessness that his war years instilled in him revisit him during his three-day trial on the island.

MOTIFS

THE COLOR RED   The color red permeates the story to highlight the blood, violence, and death on Ship-Trap Island. In the beginning of the story, for example, Rainsford falls off his yacht into the "blood-warm waters" of the sea, symbolically marking him as a target of future violence. Upon reaching the shore, he discovers a crushed patch of weeds "stained crimson." As Rainsford moves deeper into the interior of the island, the color red becomes more directly linked with the bloodlust of General Zaroff, from the crimson sash his body guard, Ivan, wears to the steaming bowls of red borscht he serves Rainsford. Connell refers to the general's "red-lipped" smile twice, at one point extending the description to include a flash of Zaroff's pointed, fanglike teeth. Connell focuses less on the color red as soon as the hunt begins to emphasize Rainsford's level-headedness and foreshadow his ultimate triumph over Zaroff.

DARKNESS   The darkness that shrouds Ship-Trap Island accentuates the shadowy recesses that lie beyond the reach of logic and reason. As Whitney and Rainsford converse on the deck of the yacht in the opening passages, the moonless sultry night surrounds them with its "moist black velvet." Disoriented and isolated after falling overboard, Rainsford swims in the direction of the gunshots, the first of many such times on the island when he must rely on other senses to navigate the pitch-blackness that surrounds him. The darkness that envelops the island not only instills foreboding terror, but it also hints at the dementia that has lead Zaroff to hunt people. Interestingly, Connell contrasts this darkness with false beacons of light that draw unsuspecting victims to the island like moths to a flame. Rainsford, for example, heads toward the "glaring golden light" of Zaroff's chateau soon after awaking on the island. Similarly, the electric lights lining the channel to Ship-Trap Island appear to warn passing ships of the treacherous shoals and rocks, but they actually shipwreck more sailors for Zaroff to hunt. As a result, these false beacons only make the prevailing darkness more penetrating and foreboding.

SYMBOLS

THE JUNGLE   Teeming, wild, and ungovernable, the jungle serves as a powerful symbol of Zaroff's tangled psyche and the chaos within the island. The "snarled and ragged" growth shrouds the island, concealing Zaroff's grotesque hunt from the rest of the world. The jungle is also an emblem of restriction and Rainsford's loss of control because it impedes his effort to return to civilization. The morning he awakens on the island's shore, for example, he can see no way through the tangled trees and undergrowth before him. During the hunt, claustrophobia overtakes him as Zaroff closes in for the kill. Ultimately, Rainsford must free himself from this thorny physical and mental space and does so by rejecting the jungle altogether in favor of the sea.

THE ISLAND   Ship-Trap Island symbolizes a similarly uncharted region where the laws governing normal human discourse don't exist. Here, General Zaroff's plays out his homicidal whims unchecked, unimpeded, and a world apart from Rainsford's comfortable life of privilege and ease. In many ways, the island is an antiutopian society under the rule of a tyrant seeking to exterminate other people instead of sustaining them. The autocratic Zaroff, without any compassion or regard for human life, exerts absolute control over everything. Isolated, the island is a realm of wild, uncontrollable, and unspeakable desires recklessly pursued without any sense of morality. Subject to legend and superstition, the island is an unconscious embodiment of fear, abstract and impalpable, just like the chill and shudder that Whitney feels as the yacht first sails by.

SHORT STORY ANALYSIS

HISTORICAL CONTEXT   General Zaroff's Cossack background adds historical realism to the nightmarish hunt on Ship-Trap Island. *Cossack* is the general name given to a number of peoples in the Ural Mountains region of Eastern Europe in present-day Russia and the Ukraine. Many Russian Cossacks, such as Zaroff and his assistant, Ivan, were military specialists who fought for centuries as mercenary soldiers in service to the czar until the collapse of the Russian empire in 1917. The Cossacks played a crucial role in expanding Russia's borders and maintaining order along the frontier. Deeply feared, Cossacks were infamous for their swift and violent attacks and use of guerilla warfare tactics. Although Connell had no intention of promoting stereotypes in his story, he nevertheless wanted to capitalize on the mythic violence of Cossack warfare to heighten dramatic tension and expose the calculated madness of a single monstrous persona. Connell's extreme portrayal of the Cossacks thus provides a credible explanation for Zaroff's otherwise unfathomable motivations for killing.

Zaroff's Cossack heritage not only highlights his brutality but also foreshadows his doom, as the hunter becomes the hunted. In 1917, the once heavily persecuted Communists seized power after anarchists overthrew the ruling czar and the entire feudal system in the Russian Revolution. The newly empowered Soviets turned against the feared Cossacks and tried to exterminate them in a ruthless ethnic cleansing campaign. Zaroff briefly mentions the genocidal campaign to Rainsford, which he uses to explain his departure from the Crimea and subsequent retreat to the remote Ship-Trap Island. Like his Cossack brethren, however, Zaroff too finds himself trapped when Rainsford turns the tables on him in the final climatic scene, reversing the roles of predator and prey.

THE SERIAL GOTHIC ADVENTURE Connell weaves elements of Gothic fiction with the adventure serial genre to create a fun and fast-paced yet darkly probing story. The Gothic elements in "The Most Dangerous Game" add to the story's mysterious and suspenseful mood to expose the dark underside of the human psyche. In keeping with the Gothic tradition, Connell weaves the bizarre, grotesque, frightening, and unexpected into his story. The ominous Ship-Trap Island, for example, looms menacingly from the beginning of the story as a place that all sailors fear and avoid. Forbidding sounds such as gunfire and high-pitched cries then pierce the night, sending eerie chills down Rainsford's spine. The darkness and the jungle add to this feeling, as do the blood-stained weeds, the hidden fortress, Ivan's brooding presence, and the coldly calculating General Zaroff. These elements, among many others, build tension and pave the way for the shocking revelation that Zaroff kills people for sport on his island.

Combining these Gothic elements with the serial adventure genre ratchets the suspense even higher and adds to the sense of animalistic panic that all prey feel as a predator draws nearer. The jungle, chase, fashioning of traps, near escapes, and great white hunter taken out of his element and with the odds against him all help to expand the scope of the story and contribute to its increasingly breathless pace. Elements of the traditional, "literary" short story, such as the preoccupation with self-actualization and personal struggle, are still present, particularly in Connell's central concern with the nature of humanity and the interplay of instinct and reason. These elements highlight the story's seriousness and exploration of fear and death, but Rainsford's journey remains primarily a physical one and less emotional or philosophical. In fact, readers remain uncertain at the end about whether Rainsford truly learns from his experience on the island after finally killing Zaroff.

IMPORTANT QUOTATIONS EXPLAINED

---

1. *"Instinct is no match for reason."*

General Zaroff's smug formulation in his initial conversation with Rainsford over dinner summarizes the common assumption that instinct and reason are mutually exclusive. Connell explores this misperception by contrasting culture and society with the bestial, savage, and survivalist impulses all animals have. Although General Zaroff believes that logic and cool thinking always allow him to triumph over terrified prey, his physical injuries sustained from springing Rainsford's traps highlight the flaws in his reasoning and suggest that he's much more vulnerable than he'd like to believe. In the end, Rainsford survives the hunt only after fear forces him to jump off the cliff into the ocean, a rasher decision than he would ordinarily make. The animal and human elements work in tandem to ensure his survival.

---

2. *"I have played the fox, now I must play the cat of the fable."*

After creating a misleading path through the jungle to lose Zaroff on the first night of the hunt, Rainsford switches modes and hides in a tree to save some of his strength. Comparing Rainsford with foxes and cats allows Connell to highlight Rainsford's descent into a more animalistic state in which he must mimic the instinctive behavior of animals to survive. This quotation also reminds readers of Rainsford's earlier conversation with his friend Whitney on board the yacht when Rainsford dismisses the notion that prey feel fear. Such thoughts, he had initially believed, only personify animals and ascribe a complexity of thought and emotion that animals don't really possess. Playing the fox, however, with hunting hounds close on his heels, Rainsford feels the powerlessness and terror that all prey feel. Even though he jumps to his seeming death out of fear of the pursuing dogs, he manages to keep his fear in check enough to ultimately outwit General Zaroff and end the hunt.

The Necklace
Guy de Maupassant
(1850–1893)

CONTEXT

Henri Rene Albert Guy de Maupassant was born on August 5, 1850, to an affluent family at the Chateau de Miromesnil, in France. As a child, Guy adored his mother and loathed his absent father. His mother was very literary and passed on her love of books to her son, Guy, and his brother, Herve. Much of Guy's childhood was spent in the countryside playing sports or simply spending time outdoors.

The Franco-Prussian War erupted shortly after Maupassant finished college. Maupassant enlisted as a volunteer and then, in 1871, left the army to work as a clerk in the navy for the next ten years. During this time he became close with Gustave Flaubert, a friend of his mother's and the author of *Madame Bovary* (1857). Flaubert introduced him to several other prominent writers and spurred Maupassant to focus on his writing. As a result, Maupassant began producing a fair amount of short fiction on his own and eventually found work as a contributing editor for several prominent French newspapers in 1878. Despite this early focus on writing, however, Maupassant didn't publish any of his work until he turned thirty.

"The Necklace," or "La Parure" in French, first appeared in the Parisian Newspaper *Le Gaulois* in 1884. The story was an immediate success, and Maupassant later included it in his short-story collection *Tales of Day and Night* (1885). Flaubert's influence on Maupassant is evident in "The Necklace," and the story is in many ways similar to *Madame Bovary*. Both works, for example, revolve around attractive yet dissatisfied young women who seek to escape their destinies. More important, both works are also among the finest examples of realist fiction, a style of writing first appearing in the mid nineteenth century that sought to expose the grittier realities of ordinary people's lives. Above all else, Maupassant sought to explore the deeper meanings of everyday events, and his writing style has influenced other literary greats such as Anton Chekhov and O. Henry.

Maupassant's literary career peaked in the 1880s, around the time when he published "The Necklace." In the years just before and after he published *Tales of Day and Night*, Maupassant wrote more than 300 short stories and several successful novels, including *Un Vie* (1883), *Bel Ami* (1885), and *Pierre et Jean* (1888). He traveled extensively during this time and often produced his best writing on the road, writing newspaper articles, essays, and travelogues in addition to fiction. A powerful literary figure in his day, Maupassant formed and maintained friendships with other literary giants such as Ivan Turgenev and Émile Zola.

Despite his wealth and popularity, Maupassant never married, partly out of fear of being abandoned by a loved one as he was abandoned by his father. As he grew older, Maupassant became more withdrawn and obsessed with death. His infection with syphilis contributed to his growing dementia, and he was institutionalized after he tried to kill himself in 1891. He died two years later, on July 6, 1893.

PLOT OVERVIEW

Mathilde Loisel is "pretty and charming" but feels she has been born into a family of unfavorable economic status. She was married off to a lowly clerk in the Ministry of Education, who can afford to provide her only with a modest though not uncomfortable lifestyle. Mathilde feels the burden of her poverty intensely. She regrets her lot in life and spends endless hours imagining a more extravagant existence. While her husband expresses his pleasure at the small, modest supper she has prepared for him, she dreams of an elaborate feast served on fancy china and eaten in the company of wealthy friends. She possesses no fancy jewels or clothing, yet these are the only things she lives for. Without them, she feels she is not desirable. She has one wealthy friend, Madame Forestier, but refuses to visit her because of the heartbreak it brings her.

One night, her husband returns home proudly bearing an invitation to a formal party hosted by the Ministry of Education. He hopes that Mathilde will be thrilled with the chance to attend an event of this sort, but she is instantly angry and begins to cry. Through her tears, she tells him that she has nothing to wear and he ought to give the invitation to one of his friends whose wife can afford better clothing. Her husband is upset by her reaction and asks how much a suitable dress would cost. She thinks about it carefully and tells him that 400 francs would be enough. Her husband quietly balks at the sum but agrees that she may have the money.

As the day of the party approaches, Mathilde starts to behave oddly. She confesses that the reason for her behavior is her lack of jewels. Monsieur Loisel suggests that she wear flowers, but she refuses. He implores her to visit Madame Forestier and borrow something from her. Madame Forestier agrees to lend Mathilde her jewels, and Mathilde selects a diamond necklace. She is overcome with gratitude at Madame Forestier's generosity.

At the party, Mathilde is the most beautiful woman in attendance, and everyone notices her. She is intoxicated by the attention and has an overwhelming sense of self-satisfaction. At 4 A.M., she finally looks for Monsieur Loisel, who has been dozing for hours in a deserted room. He cloaks her bare shoulders in a wrap and cautions her to wait inside, away from the cold night air, while he fetches a cab. But she is ashamed at the shabbiness of her wrap and follows Monsieur Loisel outside. They walk for a while before hailing a cab.

When they finally return home, Mathilde is saddened that the night has ended. As she removes her wrap, she discovers that her necklace is no longer around her neck. In a panic, Monsieur Loisel goes outside and retraces their steps. Terrified, she sits and waits for him. He returns home much later in an even greater panic—he has not found the necklace. He instructs her to write to Madame Forestier and say that she has broken the clasp of the necklace and is getting it mended.

They continue to look for the necklace. After a week, Monsieur Loisel says they have to see about replacing it. They visit many jewelers, searching for a similar necklace, and finally find one. It costs 40,000 francs, although the jeweler says he will give it to them for 36,000. The Loisels spend a week scraping up money from all kinds of sources, mortgaging the rest of their existence. After three days, Monsieur Loisel purchases the necklace. When Mathilde returns the necklace, in its case, to Madame Forestier, Madame Forestier is annoyed at how long it has taken to get it back but does not open the case to inspect it. Mathilde is relieved.

The Loisels began to live a life of crippling poverty. They dismiss their servant and move into an even smaller apartment. Monsieur Loisel works three jobs, and Mathilde spends all her time doing the heavy housework. This misery lasts ten years, but at the end they have repaid their financial debts. Mathilde's extraordinary beauty is now gone: she looks just likes the other women of poor households. They are both tired and irrevocably damaged from these years of hardship.

One Sunday, while she is out for a walk, Mathilde spots Madame Forestier. Feeling emotional, she approaches her and offers greetings. Madame Forestier does not recognize her, and when Mathilde identifies herself, Madame Forestier cannot help but exclaim that she looks different. Mathilde says that the change was on her account and explains to her the long saga of losing the necklace, replacing it, and working for ten years to repay the debts. At the end of her story, Madame Forestier clasps her hands and tells Mathilde the original necklace was just costume jewelry and not worth anything.

CHARACTER LIST

Mathilde Loisel   The protagonist of the story. Mathilde has been blessed with physical beauty but not with the affluent lifestyle she yearns for, and she feels deeply discontented with her lot in life. When she prepares to attend a fancy party, she borrows a diamond necklace from her friend Madame Forestier, then loses the necklace and must work for ten years to pay off a replacement. Her one night of radiance cost her and Monsieur Loisel any chance for future happiness.

Monsieur Loisel   Mathilde's husband. Monsieur Loisel is content with the small pleasures of his life but does his best to appease Mathilde's demands and assuage her complaints. He loves Mathilde immensely but does not truly understand her, and he seems to underestimate the depth of her unhappiness. When Mathilde loses the necklace, Monsieur Loisel sacrifices his own future to help her repay the debt. He pays dearly for something he had never wanted in the first place.

Madame Forestier   Mathilde's wealthy friend. Madame Forestier treats Mathilde kindly, but Mathilde is bitterly jealous of Madame Forestier's wealth, and the kindness pains her. Madame Forestier lends Mathilde the necklace for the party and does not inspect it when Mathilde returns it. She is horrified to realize that Mathilde has wasted her life trying to pay for a replacement necklace, when the original necklace had actually been worth nothing.

ANALYSIS OF MAJOR CHARACTERS

MATHILDE LOISEL   Beautiful Mathilde Loisel was born into a family of clerks, and her utter conviction that her station in life is a mistake of destiny leads her to live her life in a constant rebellion against her circumstances. Although she has a comfortable home and loving husband, she is so unsatisfied that she is virtually oblivious of everything but the wealth she does not have. Her desire for wealth is a constant pain and turmoil. She cannot visit her wealthy friend Madame Forestier without being overcome with jealousy, and the idea of going to a party without expensive clothes drives her to tears. Mathilde is a raging, jealous woman who will do anything in her power to reverse the "mistake of destiny" that has plunged her into what she perceives as a wholly inappropriate and inadequate life.

Mathilde is happy at only one point in "The Necklace": on the night of the party, when her new dress and borrowed jewels give her the appearance of belonging to the wealthy world she aspires to. Fully at ease among the wealthy people at the party, Mathilde feels that this is exactly where she was meant to be—if it hadn't been for the mistake of destiny. She forgets her old life completely (her husband dozes in an empty room for most of the night) and immerses herself in the illusion of a new one. Her moment of happiness, of course, is fleeting, and she must spend the next ten years paying for the pleasure of this night. However, her joy was so acute—and her satisfaction, for once, so complete—that even the ten arduous years and her compromised beauty do not dull the party's memory. Just as Mathilde was oblivious to the small pleasures that her life once afforded her, she is oblivious to the fact that her greed and deception are what finally sealed her fate.

MONSIEUR LOISEL Monsieur Loisel's acceptance and contentment differ considerably from Mathilde's emotional outbursts and constant dissatisfaction, and although he never fully understands his wife, he does his best to please her. When he comes home bearing the invitation to the party, he expects Mathilde to be excited and is shocked when she is devastated. He cannot understand why Mathilde will not wear flowers to the party in lieu of expensive jewelry—in his view, that they cannot afford expensive jewelry is simply a fact of their life, not something to be railed against. When Monsieur Loisel tries to appease Mathilde, he does so blindly, wanting only to make her happy. When she declares that she cannot attend the party because she has nothing to wear, he gives her money to purchase a dress. While she complains she has no proper jewelry, he urges her to visit Madame Forestier to borrow some. When she dances all night at the party, he dozes in a coat room and allows her to enjoy herself.

Monsieur Loisel's eagerness and willingness to please Mathilde becomes his downfall when she loses the necklace. He is the one to venture back into the cold night to search for the necklace in the streets, even though he is already undressed and has to be at work in a few short hours. He is the one who devises a plan for purchasing a replacement necklace and orchestrates the loans and mortgages that help them pay for it. Although this decision costs him ten years of hard work, he does not complain or imagine an alternate fate. It is as though his desires do not even exist—or, at the very least, his desires are meaningless if they stand in the way of Mathilde's. The money he gives her for a dress had been earmarked for a gun, but he sacrifices this desire without a word—just as he mutely sacrifices any hope of happiness after he buys the necklace. Rather than force Mathilde to be accountable for her actions, he protects her, ultimately giving up his life so that she can relish her one moment of well-dressed happiness.

THEMES, MOTIFS, AND SYMBOLS

THEMES

THE DECEPTIVENESS OF APPEARANCES The reality of Mathilde's situation is that she is neither wealthy nor part of the social class of which she feels she is a deserving member, but Mathilde does everything in her power to make her life appear different from how it is. She lives in an illusory world where her actual life does not match the ideal life she has in her head—she believes that her beauty and charm make her worthy of greater things. The party is a triumph because for the first time, her appearance matches the reality of her life. She is prettier than the other women, sought after by the men, and generally admired and flattered by all. Her life, in the few short hours of the party, is as she feels it should be. However, beneath this rightness and seeming match of appearances and reality is the truth that her appearance took a great deal of scheming and work. The bliss of her evening was not achieved without angst, and the reality of her appearance is much different than it seems. Her wealth and class are simply illusions, and other people are easily deceived.

The deceptiveness of appearances is highlighted by Madame Forestier's necklace, which appears to be made of diamonds but is actually nothing more than costume jewelry. The fact that it comes from Madame Forestier's jewelry box gives it the illusion of richness and value; had Monsieur Loisel suggested that Mathilde wear fake jewels, she surely would have scoffed at the idea, just as she scoffed at his suggestion to wear flowers. Furthermore, the fact that Madame Forestier—in Mathilde's view, the epitome of class and wealth—has a necklace made of fake jewels suggests that even the wealthiest members of society pretend to have more wealth than they actually have. Both women are ultimately deceived by appearances: Madame Forestier does not tell Mathilde that the diamonds are fake, and Mathilde does not tell Madame Forestier that she has replaced the necklace. The fact that the necklace changes—unnoticed—from worthless to precious suggests that true value is ultimately dependent on perception and that appearances can easily deceive.

THE DANGER OF MARTYRDOM Mathilde's perception of herself as a martyr leads her to take unwise, self-serving actions. The Loisels live, appropriately, on the Rue des Martyrs, and Mathilde feels she must suffer through a life that is well beneath what she deserves. Unable to appreciate any aspect of her life, including her devoted husband, she is pained by her feeling that her beauty and charm are being wasted. When Mathilde loses the necklace and sacrifices the next ten years of her life to pay back the debts she incurred from buying a replacement, her feeling of being a martyr intensifies. She undertakes the hard work with grim determination, behaving more like a martyr than ever before. Her beauty is once again being wasted; this work eventually erases it completely. Her lot in life has gotten worse, and Mathilde continues to believe she has gotten less than she deserves, never acknowledging the fact that she is responsible for her own fate. Her belief in her martyrdom is, in a way, the only thing she has left. When Madame Forestier reveals that the necklace was worthless, Mathilde's sacrifices also become worthless, and her status as a martyr—however dubious— is taken away entirely. At the end of the story, Mathilde is left with nothing.

Whereas Mathilde sees herself as a martyr but is actually very far from it, Monsieur Loisel himself is truly a martyr, constantly sacrificing his desires and, ultimately, his well-being for Mathilde's sake. He gives up his desire for a gun so that Mathilde can buy a dress, and he uncomplainingly mortgages his future to replace the necklace Mathilde loses. Forced to sacrifice his happiness and years of his life to accommodate Mathilde's selfish desires, he is the one who truly becomes a martyr.

THE PERCEIVED POWER OF OBJECTS Mathilde believes that objects have the power to change her life, but when she finally gets two of the objects she desires most, the dress and necklace, her happiness is fleeting at best. At the beginning of "The Necklace," we get a laundry list of all the objects she does not have but that she feels she deserves. The beautiful objects in other women's homes and absence of such objects in her own home make her feel like an outsider, fated to envy other women. The things she does have—a comfortable home, hot soup, a loving husband—she disdains. Mathilde effectively relinquishes control of her happiness to objects that she does not even possess, and her obsession with the trappings of the wealthy leads to her perpetual discontent. When she finally acquires the dress and necklace, those objects seem to have a transformative power. She is finally the woman she believes she was meant to be—happy, admired, and envied. She has gotten what she wanted, and her life has changed accordingly. However, when she loses the necklace, the dream dissolves instantly, and her life becomes even worse than before. In reality, the power does not lie with the objects but within herself.

In contrast to Mathilde, Madame Forestier infuses objects with little power. Her wealth enables her to purchase what she likes, but more important, it also affords her the vantage point to realize that these objects are not the most important things in the world. She seems casual about, and even careless with her possessions: when Mathilde brazenly requests to borrow her striking diamond necklace, she agrees. And later, when Mathilde informs her that the necklace in her possession is actually extremely valuable, she seems more rattled by the idea that Mathilde has sacrificed her life unnecessarily. The fact that Madame Forestier owned fake jewels in the first place suggests that she understands that objects are only as powerful as people perceive them to be. For her, fake jewels can be just as beautiful and striking as real diamonds if one sees them as such.

MOTIFS

COVETING   Throughout "The Necklace," Mathilde covets everything that other people have and she does not. Whereas Monsieur Loisel happily looks forward to having hot soup for dinner, Mathilde thinks only of the grandness of other homes and lavish table settings that she does not own. When Monsieur Loisel obtains an invitation for a party, she covets a new dress so that she can look as beautiful as the other wives as well as jewelry so that she does not look poor in comparison to them. She is so covetous of Madame Forestier's wealth that she cannot bear to visit her, but she overcomes her angst when she needs to borrow jewelry for the party; there, her coveting is briefly sated because she gets to take one of the ornaments home with her. After the party, she covets the fur coats the other women are wearing, which highlight the shabbiness of her own wraps. This endless coveting ultimately leads to Mathilde's downfall and, along the way, yields only fleeting happiness. It is so persistent, however, that it takes on a life of its own—Mathilde's coveting is as much a part of her life as breathing.

SYMBOLS

THE NECKLACE   The necklace, beautiful but worthless, represents the power of perception and the split between appearances and reality. Mathilde borrows the necklace because she wants to give the appearance of being wealthy; Madame Forestier does not tell her up front that the necklace is fake, perhaps because she, too, wants to give the illusion of being wealthier than she actually is. Because Mathilde is so envious of Madame Forestier and believes her to be wealthy, she never doubts the necklace's authenticity—she expects diamonds, so diamonds are what she perceives. She enters willingly and unknowingly into this deception, and her complete belief in her borrowed wealth allows her to convey an appearance of wealth to others. Because she believes herself rich for one night, she becomes rich in others' eyes. The fact that the necklace is at the center of the deception that leads to Mathilde's downfall suggests that only trouble can come from denying the reality of one's situation.

SHORT STORY ANALYSIS

REALISM Maupaussant, like his mentor, Flaubert, believed that fiction should convey reality with as much accuracy as possible. He strived for objectivity rather than psychological exploration or romantic descriptions, preferring to structure his stories and novels around clearly defined plot lines and specific, observable details. However, he argued that calling fiction "realistic" was not correct—every work of fiction, he believed, was an illusion, a world created by a writer to convey a particular effect to readers. He was faithful above all to the facts and believed that close, focused observation could reveal new depths and perspectives to even the most common, unremarkable aspects of life. "The Necklace" clearly demonstrates Maupassant's fixation with facts and observations. Rather than explore Mathilde's yearning for wealth or unhappiness with her life, Maupaussant simply tells us about her unhappiness and all the things she desires. At the end of the story, he provides no moral commentary or explanation about Mathilde's reaction to Madame Forestier's shocking revelation; he simply reports events as they happen. There is no pretense, idealizing, or artifice to Maupaussant's prose or treatment of his characters.

Realism began in France in the mid nineteenth century and rejected the tenets from the romantic movement that came before it, a literary movement that emphasized the idealization of characters rather than realistic portrayal of them. Realist literature often focused on middle-class life—such as the tragic lives of Mathilde and her husband—and was most concerned with portraying actions and their consequences with little or no subjectivity. Social factors and cultural environment are often powerful forces in realist literature, as are elements of rationalism and scientific reasoning. Flaubert was one of the earliest practitioners of realism, as typified by his novels *Madame Bovary* (1857) and *Sentimental Education* (1869). Realism was also an influential artistic school that included French painters such as Gustave Courbet, Edgar Degas, and Éduard Manet.

THE SURPRISE ENDING AND IRONY "The Necklace" is most famous for its "whip-crack" or "O. Henry" ending. O. Henry, who wrote during the late 1800s, was famous for his twist endings that turned stories on their heads. In "The Necklace," the surprise ending unhinges the previously implied premise of the story. Until this point, the reader has been able to interpret Mathilde's ten years of poverty as penance for her stolen night of pleasure at the party and for carelessly losing the borrowed necklace. The ending shatters that illusion, revealing that the ten years of misery were unnecessary and could have been avoided if only Mathilde had been honest with Madame Forestier. Losing the necklace had seemed to be Mathilde's fatal mistake, but it was actually Mathilde's failure to be truthful with Madame Forestier that sealed her fate. This shocking realization sheds new light on the previous events and suggests that Mathilde's future—even though her debts are now repaid—will be none too rosy.

The horrible irony of the fact that the Loisels spent years paying off a replacement for what was actually a worthless necklace is just one instance of irony evident in "The Necklace." Also ironic is the fact that Mathilde's beauty, which had been her only valued asset, disappears as a result of her labor for the necklace. She had borrowed the necklace to be seen as more beautiful and winds up losing her looks completely. Perhaps the most bitter irony of "The Necklace" is that the arduous life that Mathilde must assume after losing the necklace makes her old life—the one she resented so fully—seem luxurious. She borrows Madame Forestier's necklace to give the appearance of having more money than she really does, only to then lose what she does have. She pays doubly, with her money and looks, for something that had no value to begin with.

IMPORTANT QUOTATIONS EXPLAINED

1. *She danced madly, ecstatically, drunk with pleasure, with no thought for anything, in the triumph of her beauty, in the pride of her success, in a cloud of happiness made up of this universal homage and admiration, of the desires she had aroused, of the completeness of a victory so dear to her feminine heart.*

This quotation appears near the middle of the story, during the party, when Mathilde is happier than she had ever been or ever would be again. Mathilde has schemed and strived to get to this moment: she wheedled money from Monsieur Loisel so that she could buy a new dress and borrowed jewels from Madame Forestier so that she would not look poor among the other women. And her angling has been successful—she is greatly admired at the party, and all the men want to dance with her. This is the moment for which she has been born. In this passage, her happiness is absolute. There is no thought of the past, nor any thought of the party's end, when she will return to her ordinary life. In the days that follow, she and Monsieur Loisel will be plunged into deeper poverty than they have ever known; but for now, she has immersed herself completely in the illusion of wealth. In her expensive dress for which her husband had to sacrifice, and in the necklace that does not even belong to her, she is filling the role she believes she deserves. In this moment, nothing else matters.

2. *[F]rightened by the pains yet to come, by the black misery which was about to fall upon him, by the prospect of all the physical privation and of all the moral tortures which he was to suffer, he went to get the new necklace, putting down upon the merchant's counter thirty-six thousand francs.*

This quotation, which appears close to the end of the story, marks the beginning of the Loisels plunge into poverty. Doomed to work for years to pay off his many loans, Monsieur Loisel nonetheless buys the replacement necklace so that Mathilde does not have to admit to her wealthy friend that she lost the original. Without complaining and with only this sick feeling in his gut, Monsieur Loisel faces the bleak future and moves forward. Unlike Mathilde, who cannot see the consequences of her actions and is oblivious to the sacrifices that her husband has made on her behalf, Monsieur Loisel can see clearly what is in store. This passage reveals the extent of his love for Mathilde—he knows he is giving up everything for her, and it has all been for a goal he never understood. Where Mathilde is selfish, Monsieur Loisel is selfless, and this purchase is his ultimate sacrifice.

3. *What would have happened if she had never lost those jewels? Who knows? Who knows?*
    How strange life is, how fickle! How little is needed to ruin or to save!

This quotation appears near the end of the story, when Mathilde daydreams during her housecleaning. When Mathilde imagines the night of the party, she idealizes it, even though this event led to her downfall. She seems to regret nothing about the night except losing the necklace, and she fails to realize that it was her desire to appear to be someone other than herself that ultimately ruined her. Despite her hardships, Mathilde has failed to learn from her mistakes. Instead of asking herself what would have happened if she hadn't lost the jewels, she should be asking herself what would have happened if she hadn't borrowed them in the first place. Mathilde believes that life is fickle, but it is she herself who has acted capriciously and brought about her own dire fate. Shortly after her reverie, she meets Madame Forestier again and learns that the necklace had been worthless. Had she simply told Madame Forestier she lost the necklace, she would have learned right away that it was costume jewelry and would not have sacrificed everything to buy a replacement. Truly, little would have been needed to save Mathilde.

N

An Occurrence at Owl Creek Bridge

Ambrose Bierce
(1842–1914)

CONTEXT

Ambrose Gwinnett Bierce was born in Meigs County, Ohio, in 1842, the tenth of thirteen children, all of whom had names beginning with the letter A. In 1846, the family moved to a farm in northern Indiana, where Bierce was exposed to periodic schooling, became a printer's apprentice on an antislavery newspaper, briefly attended the Kentucky Military Institute, and worked in a store and restaurant. His experiences fighting at the front lines of the Civil War proved to have a powerful influence on his writing. He enlisted in 1861, eventually achieving the rank of lieutenant and fighting in several noted battles and campaigns, including Shiloh, Chickamauga (the inspiration for his lauded story of the same name), and Sherman's March to the Sea.

After the war, he served as a treasury aide and topographical officer and then turned to journalism, embarking on a distinguished career both in the United States and abroad. He wrote for a variety of San Francisco periodicals and became the editor of the *News-Letter and California Advertiser* in 1868. Living in London in the early 1870s, he published three books of sketches and epigrams and wrote articles for various magazines. Settling once again in San Francisco, Bierce served as an editor of the *Argonaut* and then the *Wasp* from 1881 to 1886, and then went on to become a featured columnist in the Hearst publication the *Examiner*. There, he established himself as a leading literary critic and vocal opponent of realism, which dominated American letters at the time. Realist writers attempted to portray life objectively, without filtering it through the lens of artifice. From the late 1890s to 1913, he lived in Washington, D.C., where he continued to write for several well-known East Coast newspapers and magazines.

Bierce's reputation as an aphorist and epigrammist grew steadily in the latter part of the nineteenth century, as he showed great skill at producing pithy, observational, and often humorous sayings. Known for his wit and biting satirical style, his collected epigrams and aphorisms were first published as *The Cynic's Word Book* (1906) and later reissued under the title *The Devil's Dictionary* (1911). Today, he is known mostly for his short stories, which often have grim subject matter; a cynical or brooding tone; crisp, precise language; and a spare, stripped-down style. Arguably his most famous and well-received work is "An Occurrence at Owl Creek Bridge." Written in 1886 and first published in the collection *Tales of Soldiers and Civilians* (1891), the story is a much-anthologized classic that secured Bierce's place on the American literary map.

Critics have had mixed reactions to "An Occurrence at Owl Creek Bridge." Some have balked at the story's gimmicky, contrived ending and manipulation of readers' expectations.

Others have praised its innovative use of plot, structure, and time. In any case, Bierce was able to explore complex ideas of cognition and perception in his story, and he is often credited with being one of the first American writers to introduce psychology into his characters and scenarios. In doing so, he stretched the boundaries of the form, taking the short story out of a realm of closely observed lives and realistic, hard-won epiphanies.

By his early seventies, disillusioned and gripped most likely by depression, Bierce retired from writing after completing work on his twelve-volume *Collected Works* (1912). In 1913, he headed for Mexico, during the height of the country's revolution. The events of the last year of his life and the circumstances surrounding his death are shrouded in mystery. After posting a letter in Chihuahua, he was never heard from again. Some scholars believe he was killed in the siege of Ojinega on January 11, 1914, while other sensational explanations contend that he committed suicide in the Grand Canyon or was kidnapped by Brazilian Indians. However he died, his legacy remains. He has influenced a diverse array of modern writers, including William Golding, Jorge Luis Borges, and Carlos Fuentes, as well as the creators of suspense- and horror-based films and television programs.

PLOT OVERVIEW

"An Occurrence at Owl Creek Bridge" is divided into three sections. In section I, Peyton Farquhar is standing on a railroad bridge, twenty feet above the water. His wrists are bound behind his back, and around his neck is a noose that is tied to a beam overhead. He is positioned on loose planks that have been laid over the crossties of the train tracks to create a makeshift platform. Two soldiers from the Northern army, a sergeant, and a captain immediately surround him, awaiting the execution. Beyond them, armed sentinels stand at attention. The bridge is bordered on one side by forest and, across the stream, open ground that gives way to a small hillock on which a small fort has been erected. A motionless company of infantrymen, led by their lieutenant, stands assembled before the fort. As the two soldiers finalize the preparations, they step back and remove the individual planks on which they had been standing. The sergeant salutes the captain then positions himself on the opposite end of the board supporting Farquhar, as the captain, like the soldiers, steps off and away from the crossties.

Awaiting the captain's signal, the sergeant is about to likewise step away, sending Farquhar to dangle from the bridge's edge. Farquhar stares into the swirling water below. He watches a piece of driftwood being carried downstream and notes how sluggish the stream seems to be. He shuts his eyes to push away the distractions of his present situation and focus more intently on thoughts of his wife and children. He suddenly hears a sharp, metallic ringing, which sounds both distant and close by. The sound turns out to be the ticking of his watch. Opening his eyes and peering again into the water, Farquhar imagines freeing his hands, removing the noose, and plunging into the stream, swimming to freedom and his home, safely located outside enemy lines. These thoughts have barely registered in Farquhar's mind when the captain nods to the sergeant and the sergeant steps away from the board.

In section II, we learn that Farquhar was a successful planter, ardently devoted to the Southern cause. Unable to join the Confederate army, he yearned to help the South's war effort in some significant way. One evening in the past, Farquhar and his wife were sitting on the edge of their property when a gray-clad soldier rode up, seeking a drink of water. The soldier appeared to be from the Confederate army. While his wife was fetching the water, Farquhar asked for news of the front and was informed that Northern forces had repaired the railroads in anticipation of launching another advance, having already reached the Owl Creek bridge. Any civilian caught interfering with the North's efforts in the area, the soldier went on to reveal, would be hanged. Farquhar asked how a civilian could attempt some form of sabotage. The soldier told him that one could easily set fire to the driftwood that had piled up near the bridge after the past winter's flood. The man, who was actually a Northern scout in disguise, finished his drink and rode off, only to pass by an hour later heading in the opposite direction.

Section III brings us back to the present, at the hanging. Farquhar loses consciousness as he plummets down from the side of the bridge. He is awakened by currents of pain running through his body. A loud splash wakes him up even more abruptly, and he realizes that the noose has broken—sending him falling into the stream below. Farquhar sees a light flicker and fade before it strengthens and brightens as he rises, with some trepidation, to the surface. He is afraid he will be shot by Northern soldiers as soon as he is spotted in the water. Freeing his bound hands, then lifting the noose from his neck, he fights extreme pain to break through the surface and take a large gasp of air, which he exhales with a shriek. Farquhar looks back to see his executioners standing on the bridge, in silhouette against the sky. One of the sentinels fires his rifle at him twice. Farquhar can see the gray eye of the marksman through the gun's sights.

Farquhar then hears the lieutenant instructing his men to fire, so he dives down to avoid the shots. He quickly removes a piece of metal that sticks in his neck. Farquhar comes back up for air as the soldiers reload, and the sentinels fire again from the bridge. Swimming with the current, Farquhar realizes that a barrage of gunfire is about to come his way. A cannonball lands two yards away, sending a sheet of spray crashing over him. The deflected shot goes smashing into the trees beyond. Farquhar believes they will next fire a spray of grapeshot from the cannon, instead of a single ball, and he will have to anticipate the firing. Suddenly he is spun into a disorienting whirl, then ejected from the river onto a gravelly bank out of sight and range of his would-be executioners and their gunfire.

He weeps with joy and marvels at the landscape, having no desire to put any more distance between him and his pursuers, when a volley of grapeshot overhead rouses him. He heads into the forest, setting his path by the sun and traveling the entire day. The thought of his family urges him on. Taking a remote road, he finds himself in the early morning standing at the gate of his home. As he walks toward the house, his wife steps down from the verandah to meet him. He moves to embrace her but feels a sharp blow on the back of his neck and sees a blinding white light all about him. Then silence and darkness engulf him. Farquhar is dead, his broken body actually swinging from the side of the Owl Creek bridge.

CHARACTER LIST

Peyton Farquhar   A thirty-five-year-old Southern planter. A prosperous land- and slave-owner from an esteemed Alabama family, Farquhar is a civilian and an ardent supporter of the Confederacy. He assumes a kind expression at his execution, despite the grimness of his situation. Well-dressed, with large gray eyes and a pointed beard, he cuts a striking figure on the side of the bridge, a gentleman about to face a less-than-noble end.

Farquhar's Wife   A dutiful woman who serves as an emblem of the comfort and domestic security Farquhar seeks. Yet Farquhar's wife also represents the domain that Farquhar rejects in setting off on his reckless mission to cripple the North's campaign. His affluence and bliss at home are not enough; he is desperate to justify his existence and make his name in other ways. Still, it is her image and thoughts of his children that he returns to at his moment of greatest desperation.

The Northern Scout   A man disguised as a Confederate soldier. The Northern scout plants the seeds for Farquhar's sabotage and sets the disastrous course of events into action. His dual identity, which has him allied with the North but pretending otherwise, mirrors the gap between fiction and reality that serves as one of the story's main preoccupations.

The Sergeant   A Confederate officer. The sergeant conducts himself with the bearing of someone who may have been a deputy sheriff in civilian life. An all-but-invisible presence in the story, he is overly indulgent of the importance of his post and ceremonious nature of the execution.

ANALYSIS OF MAJOR CHARACTERS

PEYTON FARQUHAR   Peyton Farquhar, the protagonist of "An Occurrence at Owl Creek Bridge," is a shadowy figure who eventually becomes a two-sided character in the story. Little is known about him beyond the class distinctions that make him a seemingly unlikely candidate for execution as a Confederate agitator. Farquhar is a son of privilege and Southern dandy, and his life of ease has done little to prepare him for the rigors faced among the front lines of the Civil War. In section II, we learn that vague circumstances had prevented Farquhar from enlisting in the Confederate army, leaving him desperate to contribute to the Southern cause and prove his devotion. Because he is so determined to achieve distinction, he is vulnerable to the trap set for him by the disguised Northern scout. Unprepared and foolish, Farquhar allows his desire for renown to lead him right into his captors' hands. He has placed his own motives ahead of his responsibility to his family. Farquhar exhibits a damning gap between his true character and inflated perception of his abilities and role in the world.

The fantasized escape that runs counter to the actual execution in the story mirrors the gap between who Farquhar actually is and who he would like to be. In his world of illusion, he is able to outwit his captors and make it back to the family fold—whereas the reality of his situation is much more grim. Farquhar's overindulgence of fantasy in both his image of himself and his reimagining of his fate ultimately undoes him. He cannot realize his desires in the real world, and at the end of his life, he is prey to the same delusions and misinterpretations that led him to the gallows to begin with.

FARQUHAR'S WIFE   Farquhar's wife emerges as an embodiment of innocence and domestic safety, although throughout the story, she is an almost entirely imagined presence. The only time she appears as an actual physical being, as opposed to the object of Farquhar's projections, is when the Northern scout asks her to fetch him a drink of water. Even then, when she returns with it, she is depersonalized in Bierce's referring to her simply as "the lady." She exists to reflect her husband's glory and buttress his need for position and praise. She is a repository for Farquhar's various fantasies, fulfilling her function as an attractive ornament. She stands as a stereotypical feminine ideal, subservient, beautiful, silent, and ultimately dispensable in the name of Farquhar's higher cause. In the final moments of Farquhar's life, she is a source of the comfort that Farquhar is ultimately denied.

THEMES, MOTIFS, AND SYMBOLS

THEMES

THE FLUID NATURE OF TIME "An Occurrence at Owl Creek Bridge" is an elaborately devised commentary on the fluid nature of time. The story's structure, which moves from the present to the past to what is revealed to be the imagined present, reflects this fluidity as well as the tension that exists among competing notions of time. The second section interrupts what at first appears to be the continuous flow of the execution taking place in the present moment. Poised on the edge of the bridge, Farquhar closes his eyes, a signal of his slipping into his own version of reality, one that is unburdened by any responsibility to laws of time. As the ticking of his watch slows and more time elapses between the strokes, Farquhar drifts into a timeless realm. When Farquhar imagines himself slipping into the water, Bierce compares him to a "vast pendulum," immaterial and spinning wildly out of control. Here Farquhar drifts into a transitional space that is neither life nor death but a disembodied consciousness in a world with its own rules.

In the brief window of time between the officer stepping off the plank and Farquhar's actual death, time slows and alters to accommodate a comforting vision of Farquhar's safe return to his family. Despite Farquhar's manipulation of time, however, he cannot escape reality. Whether he lives a few moments or days longer, death ultimately claims him. Attempting to bend time to his own will is for naught. One of the most remarkable aspects of "An Occurrence at Owl Creek Bridge" is Bierce's realistic rendering of Farquhar's alternate conception of time, which suggests that the nature of time is to some extent subjective.

THE BLURRED LINE BETWEEN REALITY AND ILLUSION Reality and illusion operate side by side in "An Occurrence at Owl Creek Bridge," and until the end of the story, we aren't aware of any division between them—Farquhar's illusion is, for us as readers, reality. Farquhar creates his fantasy world out of desperation: he is about to die, and imagining his escape is a way of regaining control over the facts of his current state. His mind supplies the flight and successful escape that his body cannot achieve on its own. In the second section, when we learn what brought Farquhar to this moment, this hybrid world of the real and fantastic is mirrored in the figure of the Northern scout. Disguised in the gray attire of a Confederate soldier, he projects one version of the truth while actually embodying another—reality and illusion are blurred. By the time the fantasy world of the third section is in full swing, we are fully immersed in Farquhar's illusion, which has, for both him and us, become reality. Trying to distinguish one from the other is beside the point. Just as Farquhar's belief that the Northern scout is indeed a Confederate soldier leads him to execution, his belief that he is escaping can have but one outcome: the reality of his death.

MOTIFS

DISTORTED SENSORY EXPERIENCE As Farquhar faces death, he slips not only outside time but also outside his physical body. He is reduced to a network of raw, inaccurate sensory impressions, which allow him to create his fantasy of escape. Farquhar's distorted sensory impressions reveal the widening gap between reality and illusion. For example, Farquhar notes a gap between the sound of the cannon firing and the arrival of the shot. Similarly, he believes he can see the gray eye of the marksman through the rifle sights. The unrealistic, imagined realm he enters in the third section of the story is indicated through these increasingly chaotic and unreliable impressions. Churning in the eddies, Farquhar's distorted vision, in which the landscape is transformed into a series of swirling colored horizontal bands, suggests not only the lack of sound judgment Farquhar displayed in ending up in this predicament in the first place but also the distortion of reality that Bierce skillfully portrays.

THE COLOR GRAY The color gray appears throughout the story, suggesting the vague color lines dividing friend from foe as well as the clouded sense of reality in the final section of the story. Gray indicates the Confederacy and thus the cause to which Farquhar foolishly sacrifices himself, and the "gray clad" rider approaches Farquhar and his wife in the second section. However, the color gray is a misleading indication of the rider's affiliation, as he is only pretending to be a Confederate soldier. In this sense, the color gray indicates a distortion of the truth—the soldier is actually a Northern scout disguised in the enemy's colors. When Farquhar begins his fantasized escape, he operates under a gloomy gray sky. Gray is the color of Farquhar's eyes as well as the eyes of the sentinel who takes aim at him from the bridge. Farquhar recalls reading that the most famous marksmen, and thus those with the keenest eyesight, had gray eyes, and he can see the sentinel glaring ominously at him through the rifle's sights. This seemingly paranoid detail, impossible to actually see from such a distance, establishes a link between Farquhar and the man who is apparently attempting to kill him. At that moment, the distinctions separating North from South, aggressor from victim, and ally from enemy are collapsed, as Farquhar slips deeper into his fantasy realm.

SYMBOLS

DRIFTWOOD Driftwood, as it makes its way downriver, represents both Farquhar's unattainable freedom and Farquhar himself as he begins imagining his own escape in the water. At first, the driftwood distracts Farquhar from thoughts of his wife and children. Later, it becomes an extension of Farquhar himself, as Farquhar imagines floating in the water as though he is driftwood. The driftwood also indicates Farquhar's distorted sense of time. As he looks down, he sees the water "racing madly" beneath him, then sees the "dancing" driftwood. He is struck by how slowly it seems to be moving in the suddenly "sluggish" stream. This abrupt change in his perception marks Farquhar's transition from reality to fantasy. From then on, he takes liberties with the details of his own story and supplies the ending he desires: a brave escape rather than an execution for being a war criminal. Ironically, although he envisions himself as driftwood of sorts, it is driftwood that led to his capture in the first place. When Farquhar initially encounters the undercover Northern scout, the scout advises Farquhar to set fire to the pieces of wood that the winter flood swept to the base of the bridge. The driftwood thus serves as his means of undoing just as it ultimately represents an unattainable freedom.

THE OWL CREEK BRIDGE The Owl Creek bridge suggests connection and transition. Confederate forces or sympathizers had presumably destroyed the bridge in an attempt to prevent the North from advancing deeper into enemy territory. With the important artery restored by Union forces, the North's war effort once again gained momentum in northern Alabama, ushering in the ultimate defeat of the Confederacy and bringing an end to the Civil War. Ironically, the target of Farquhar's sabotage attempt becomes the platform on which his execution is staged. By sabotaging the bridge, Farquhar was attempting to erode order and connection, just as he erodes order by fantasizing, in the final moments of his life, about disconnecting himself from his physical body. The bridge serves as an intermediary space, joining the creek's opposite banks—it is neither one side nor the other, but a connection between them. Similarly, the bridge joins life and death for Farquhar. As Farquhar "escapes" into the water, the bridge suggests a transitional psychological space between fantasy and reality.

SHORT STORY ANALYSIS

REALISM   The success of Bierce's surprise ending in "An Occurrence at Owl Creek Bridge" depends on the believability of the world he establishes at the beginning of the story. He carefully lays out all of the details: the setting is northern Alabama, and the time is the Civil War. Bierce precisely describes the complicated series of beams, planks, and ropes needed to hang Farquhar. Bierce's descriptions of the positioning of the soldiers, the way they hold their guns, the minutiae of military ritual and conduct, and the exact terminology and diction all establish a recognizable world. To give his story authenticity and authority, Bierce drew on his experience fighting for the North during the Civil War. Such specific details ground readers in the story, and only at the end does Bierce reveal his structural innovations. In the final section, a fantasy world replaces reality, but this fantasy world is deceptively similar to the real world. Without such elaborate, realistic detail at the beginning of the story, the final revelation would be far less jarring. If we expected that Farquhar was simply imagining his escape—that is, if Bierce had failed to provide enough realistic details to make the fantasy world believable—then the story would lose its shocking effect.

By invoking the gritty details of an enemy's execution, Bierce participates in a realist tradition that helped to transform popular conceptions of war. He takes his place among other writers, artists, and photographers of the era who did not romanticize or avoid the war's horrific nature. Instead, they presented shockingly detailed portrayals of violence and death. For example, in the novel *The Red Badge of Courage* (1895), Stephen Crane, Bierce's contemporary, brought a startling psychological realism to the story of protagonist Henry Fleming's wartime experience. Crane attempted to capture the barbaric ways in which an untrained soldier proved his mettle, and in doing so he exposed the unenviable side of military life: wanton killing. Similarly, photographer Matthew Brady's battlefield photographs brought a harrowing realness to the conflict. The images of fly-strewn, bloody corpses stripped the war of its glory and underscored the high cost of victory. The reality these artists brought to the public forced a new realization on many Americans. They saw that lives were often senselessly sacrificed in the name of an abstract cause.

FORESHADOWING AND TONE   Bierce uses subtle instances of foreshadowing in "An Occurrence at Owl Creek Bridge" to gesture to the gap between reality and illusion that widens throughout the story. Bierce's story hinges heavily on the unexpected final revelation—that Farquhar, far from escaping, has actually been hanged. Although Bierce intends the unexpected ending to startle the readers' assumptions, he peppers his story with various clues to signal in advance the unreliable and completely fantastical nature of the concluding section. For example, the description of the soldiers' weapons in the first section—with the company of infantrymen holding their guns at "parade rest" with the butts to the ground and the commanding officer standing with the point of his sword also to the ground—stands in stark contrast to the rounds fired and volley of shots lobbied at Farquhar during his imagined escape. The weapons are in truth merely ceremonial and harmless, and Farquhar is and remains in the company's custody throughout.

To separate his authorial voice from Farquhar's thoughts and signal the unreliable nature of Farquhar's sensory impressions, Bierce qualifies Farquhar's perceptions, describing how things "seem" to him as opposed to how, in reality, they truly are. In doing so, Bierce adds an unreliable slant to the otherwise realistic style and authoritative tone, and this slant foreshadows the revelation that things are not as they appear. The shifts in tone also call attention to Bierce's manipulation of the narrative. For example, when Farquhar frees his hands after plunging unexpectedly into the river, the narrator's voice contains a hint of sarcasm, as though Bierce is mocking storytelling conventions. Adventure fiction, in particular, often involves elaborate and seemingly impossible means of escape. By tipping his hand in this way, Bierce calls into question readers' assumptions about reality and foreshadows the eventual revelation that the "action" of the story was not actually action, but fantasy.

NARRATIVE STRUCTURE AND CONVENTIONS   The ending of "An Occurrence at Owl Creek Bridge" has drawn many reactions from critics. Some believe the ending is contrived and more appropriate for a thriller, suspense, or mystery tale than for a literary work. Others see the ending as Bierce's attempt to transform the traditional conventions of narration. The story of Farquhar's execution, like a traditional story, follows a logical order: from introduction to development to conclusion. Bierce's "trick" is that the conclusion is not what it seems. Although the story does not end after the first section, Farquhar's life does, extended for a few agonizing seconds as he swings from the end of the rope. By adding the third section, Bierce calls into question the essential nature of a story's resolution. Endings, his story reveals, can often be unresolved or manipulated. They do not always have to be tidy, as they often are in more traditional prose.

Bierce's innovations in the story's structure reveal his unique understanding of plot. For Bierce, competing versions of the truth can exist within the same story. The third section takes us into Farquhar's interior life, marking a departure from the more objective tone in the story's first section. In making this shift, Bierce shows that a short story can portray both internal and external points of view. Bierce also has a unique understanding of the way time can be used in a story. The first two sections occur in real time, whereas the final part plays out over just a few moments—in the time it takes for Farquhar to die from his violent plunge from the bridge—although it seems to Farquhar to take place during the course of the next day. Bierce's greatest innovation comes in the way the seemingly consistent, seamless surface of his story nearly hides the competing versions of reality.

IMPORTANT QUOTATIONS EXPLAINED

---

1. *As these thoughts, which have here to be set down in words, were flashed into the doomed man's brain rather than evolved from it the captain nodded to the sergeant. The sergeant stepped aside.*

This quotation appears at the end of the first section of the story, immediately before Farquhar plunges to his death, and marks an important turning point. The execution itself won't resume until the third section of the story, so for now, Bierce uses the break in the action to give us details about Farquhar's past. After this flashback in the second section, the action resumes not in reality but in fantasy. Although Farquhar will die in a matter of seconds after he plunges from the bridge, his final thoughts of escape and reunion with his family fuel the imaginative flight that makes up the third section of the story. By portraying Farquhar's final thoughts and impressions as reality, Bierce reveals his preoccupation with the conventions of prose. The passage serves as an early indication of the surprise ending to come.

---

2. *Death is a dignitary who when he comes announced is to be received with formal manifestations of respect, even by those most familiar with him.*

Although most of "An Occurrence at Owl Creek Bridge" maintains a consistent tone, there are several moments, such as in this quotation from the end of the second paragraph of the story, where a brief shift in tone appears. This quotation, which reflects Bierce's penchant for aphorisms and epigrams, breaks the silent and formal way the Union forces prepare for Farquhar's hanging. The troops take their duties seriously, and there is a ritualistic quality to the event. Bierce asserts that their hushed attention is a form of respect to the man they are under orders to execute. Though death is not unexpected for Farquhar—the disguised Northern scout had warned Farquhar of this potential punishment during their brief exchange at the plantation—he is ultimately unable to accept it. Rather than "respect" the magnitude of the moment, he resists death by unspooling an elaborate fantasy of an alternate fate.

Odour of Chrysanthemums

D. H. Lawrence
(1885–1930)

CONTEXT

Born in 1885 in Eastwood, Nottinghamshire, England, the fourth child of a failed school-teacher and an illiterate coal miner, David Herbert Lawrence was a frail and delicate child who deeply sympathized with the struggles his mother endured in her unhappy marriage. Many of the female characters in Lawrence's fiction mirror his mother: sensitive women who are shackled to coarse husbands and suffer from the difficulties of supporting a family in the harsh labor conditions of the day. Like Elizabeth Bates, the protagonist in "Odour of Chrysanthemums," Lawrence's mother, Lydia Beardsall Lawrence, spent many nights lamenting her choices in life, particularly her marriage to a man who made the village pub, not the family home, his primary after-work destination.

Through a combination of hard work, savings, and scholarship assistance, Lawrence completed high school and eventually college, while at the same time beginning to explore his interest in writing. Eventually, he became a poet, a dramatist, a critic, an essayist, a novel-ist, and a short-story writer, and his works provoked high praise and controversy during his lifetime and beyond. His first novel, *Sons and Lovers*, was published in 1913, followed by *The Rainbow* in 1915. Deemed obscene, copies of *The Rainbow* were seized by authorities, foreshadowing the controversy that many of Lawrence's literary creations would go on to pro-voke. His best-known novel, *Lady Chatterley's Lover* (1928), was initially published privately. In 1960, when it was released by a mainstream, commercial publisher, it was overwhelmed by scandal and an obscenity trial. Such controversy often overshadowed the less sensational-istic, less sexual aspects of Lawrence's work, selling short his deft portrayal of individuals gov-erned by circumstances beyond their control. His sensitive explorations of the natural world stood in sharp contract to the mechanized world of industry and its rules regarding human conduct and relationships.

Many critics view Lawrence's short stories, including "The Horse Dealer's Daughter" (1922) and "The Rocking-Horse Winner" (1926), as his greatest literary accomplishments. "Odour of Chrysanthemums," among Lawrence's most highly regarded, was completed in 1909. The writer Ford Madox Ford first published it in the June 1911 issue of the *English Review*, the influential literary magazine he edited. A longer version was published in *The Prussian Officer and Other Stories* (1914). This version, referred to in this note, features an expanded final section in which Elizabeth confronts the illusions and failures of her life after washing her husband Walter's dead body. This version emphasizes Elizabeth's harsh real-izations about her own responsibility in the shortcomings of her marriage. Much has been written about the connection between Elizabeth's difficult conclusions and the bittersweet liberation Lawrence felt after his mother's death in 1910.

In "Odour of Chrysanthemums," as in many of his other prose works, Lawrence writes about a world he knew intimately: the hardscrabble existence of the miners in Nottinghamshire, who performed dangerous work to support their families. As in other works of Lawrence's fiction, a life-altering event, in this case a miner's death, serves as a turning point and leads the protagonist to reassess all that has led to such a tragic moment. In writing the story, Lawrence drew from not only his own childhood experiences but also his evolving perceptions of his days growing up in Nottinghamshire. Although Lawrence's fiction is not wholly autobiographical, Lawrence used fiction to confront his own tenuous relationship with his father and move closer to understanding the sacrifices that Arthur Lawrence made on behalf of his family. Like Elizabeth in "Odour of Chrysanthemums," Lawrence was able to embrace a more nuanced understanding of human relationships and the ramifications of environment, choice, and consequence.

Lawrence, who was antimilitary, and his wife, Frieda, whose father was German, were viewed suspiciously in wartime England during the early 1900s, and they left in 1917 under orders from the government. For years, they traveled extensively, returning to England only rarely. Lawrence died in France in 1930.

PLOT OVERVIEW

A locomotive engine comes chugging along the tracks, pulling seven loaded cars behind it. It is late afternoon in the autumn, nearing dusk, in England's coal country. The locomotive pulls into the colliery's loading area, as various miners make their way home. Nearby is a low cottage with a tiled roof and a garden, a sparse apple orchard, and a brook beyond. Elizabeth Bates emerges from the chicken coop, watching the miners walk along the railroad. She turns and calls her son, John, who emerges from the raspberry patch. She tells him that it is time to come in. The locomotive her father is driving appears in the distance. As John makes his way to the house, she chides him for tearing off the petals of the chrysanthemums and scattering them on the path. She picks a few of the flowers and, after holding them against her cheek, sticks a sprig in her apron.

The train comes to a stop near the gate, and Elizabeth brings her father tea and bread and butter. He tells Elizabeth that it is time he remarried. He also informs her that her husband, Walter, had gone on another drinking binge and was heard bragging in the local pub about how much he was going to spend. Done with his tea, the old man drives off. Elizabeth enters the kitchen, where the table is set and awaiting Walter's return so that the family can have their tea. With no sign of Walter, Elizabeth continues preparing the meal. Her daughter, Annie, enters the room, and Elizabeth mildly scolds her for being late. She asks Annie whether she has seen Walter; she has not. Elizabeth fears that Walter is again at the pub, and at Annie's urging, they start to eat. Annie is transfixed by the slowly dying fire. Eating little, Elizabeth grows increasingly antsy and angry.

Elizabeth goes to get coal and drops a few pieces on the fire, which snuffs out almost all the light in the room. John repeatedly complains about the darkness, and Elizabeth lights the overhead lamp, revealing for the first time that she is pregnant. Annie exclaims at the sight of the chrysanthemums in Elizabeth's apron. She removes them and puts the flowers to her lips, enthralled by their scent. Looking at the clock, Elizabeth realizes that Walter will not get home until he is again carried in, intoxicated, by his friends. She vows not to clean him after his day of work and to leave him lying on the floor.

The children play quietly, afraid of angering Elizabeth, who sews in her rocking chair. After a while, she sends them to bed, although Annie protests, as Walter has not come home yet. Elizabeth states that when he does appear he will be all but unconscious from drinking. Putting the children to bed, she angrily and fearfully resumes her sewing. At eight o'clock, she leaves the house. She makes her way to a row of dwellings and enters a passage between two of the houses, asking Mrs. Rigley whether her husband is at home. Mrs. Rigley answers that he has had his dinner and then gone briefly to the pub and that she will go find him. Mrs. Rigley soon returns, with her husband in tow. He tells Elizabeth that he last saw Walter at the coal pit, finishing a job. Elizabeth suggests that Walter is simply at another pub, and Mr. Rigley offers to go and find out. He walks her home, as Mrs. Rigley runs immediately to her neighbor's house to spread the fresh gossip.

After Elizabeth has waited for another forty-five minutes, her mother-in-law enters the cottage, crying hysterically. Elizabeth asks whether Walter is dead, but all her mother-in-law tells her is that he has been in a serious accident. As the mother-in-law laments and defends her son's gradual slide into debauchery, a miner arrives to inform the women that Walter has been dead for hours, smothered after a cave-in. Elizabeth's mother-in-law dissolves into tears, and Elizabeth quickly silences her, afraid that her wailing will wake the children. She moves into the parlor to clear a space on the floor where the body can be laid. She spreads cloths on the floor to protect the carpet, takes out a clean shirt to air it, and then waits in the pantry.

Shortly, the pit manager and another man arrive with the body on a stretcher. As they bring Walter into the parlor and lay him on the floor, one of the men accidentally tips over a vase of chrysanthemums. Elizabeth quickly cleans up the water and broken glass. Annie, who has woken up, calls from upstairs, and Elizabeth rushes up to comfort her. The men try to silence Walter's mother, who is still sobbing loudly. With Annie finally calmed and the men gone, Elizabeth and her mother-in-law prepare to undress, clean, and lay out the body. Elizabeth embraces the body, trying to make a connection to her husband's still-warm corpse. She and Walter's mother wash the body. Elizabeth presses her cheek against the body but is repulsed by the dead flesh. She laments her marriage and the hand she had in its failure. Walter's mother rouses Elizabeth from her musing. Elizabeth, unable to weep, goes to fetch a shirt. With difficulty, she dresses Walter. Covering him in a sheet and locking the parlor door, she tidies the kitchen, afraid and ashamed of the harsh realizations she has come to as a result of Walter's death.

CHARACTER LIST

Elizabeth Bates   The protagonist of the story. Stern, cold, and pragmatic, Elizabeth is deeply resentful of finding herself married to an alcoholic and living in a coal community. A good mother, she feels she cannot afford to indulge emotional weakness or sentimentality but must be strong for the sake of her children. Elizabeth attains a deep understanding of her life, husband, and marriage only when Walter is dead and she is forced to confront her circumstances and her own role in her fate.

Walter Bates   Elizabeth's alcoholic husband who has just died in a cave-in. Walter was a handsome man, blond and fleshy, with strong limbs and a moustache. Although he never appears in the story alive, he casts a dark shadow over the story's proceedings. He emerges as a caricature, the monstrous drunken husband, who is gradually redeemed by Elizabeth's growing recognition of the ways she has denied or ignored his essential humanity.

Walter's Mother   An emotional woman of sixty who is with Elizabeth when Walter's body is brought home. Walter's mother laments Walter's louche tendencies and the gradual shirking of his responsibilities to his family, while at the same time justifying his irresponsible behavior. She is slightly competitive with Elizabeth when it comes to ministering to her son's body.

Annie Bates   Elizabeth's young daughter. Annie has large blue eyes and curly hair that is changing from blond to brunette. A sensitive girl, she is attached to her father but deferent to her mother's harsh opinions of him and his carousing. Annie is drawn to the scent of the chrysanthemums.

John Bates   Elizabeth's five-year-old son. A small and sturdy boy with black hair, John wears clothes made from a man's suit that has been cut down to fit him. Childishly self-absorbed, and often indifferent to what is going on around him, he reminds Elizabeth of Walter.

Elizabeth's Father   A short man with a gray beard and cheerful disposition. Pragmatic like Elizabeth, Elizabeth's father is resigned to remarrying in an effort to fill the domestic void in his life. He appears only briefly at the beginning of the story, when his train passes Elizabeth's house.

Mrs. Rigley   A miner's wife with twelve children. Mrs. Rigley offers Elizabeth a sympathetic ear while at the same time exploiting the gossip potential of the Bates's shaky marriage.

Mr. Rigley   A miner who helps Elizabeth look for Walter. Mr. Rigley is a large man with a bony head and blue scar on his temple, which he got from working in the coal pits. Kind and helpful, he is alert to the potential dangers of life as a miner.

ANALYSIS OF MAJOR CHARACTERS

ELIZABETH BATES   Though Elizabeth initially emerges as a long-suffering wife who deserves sympathy, her response to Walter's death reveals that she is not as blameless for her unhappiness as she first appears. At first, Walter seems to be the clear cause of Elizabeth's difficult life. He regularly comes home drunk after working in the mine, making the local pub more of a home than his actual home. Elizabeth is accustomed to the dull, dreary routine of waiting for him, but she still feels anger and annoyance when dinner must be delayed. Every comment she makes is said "bitterly," and she herself is described as "bitter." At times she seems so harsh that we may wonder whether she is capable of any other form of emotion. However, early in the story, Lawrence shows Elizabeth giving tea and bread to her father, which suggests that she is capable of nurturing. On the day on which the story takes place, her anger and annoyance change to anxiety as the night wears on with no sign of Walter. He seems to be a recognizable brand of "bad husband," and Elizabeth, the put-upon wife and mother, seems to be a clear victim. Her frustration and harsh words about Walter seem fully justifiable. Elizabeth clearly sees herself as having wasted her life with Walter, missing out on a better life she could have had with someone else.

Elizabeth's dismal view of her fate changes once Walter's corpse is brought home. As Elizabeth and her mother-in-law undress and wash Walter's body, Elizabeth confronts her role in the marriage's failure. When she looks at the corpse, she realizes that for years, she has not really seen Walter. He was her husband but chronically distant from her, and she feels "ashamed" because she had not allowed him to be himself. Instead of feeling anger and resentment, she recognizes that her own expectations and refusals helped tear them apart. The pity she feels for Walter sharply contrasts with her earlier harsh view of him, serving as an epiphany—she suddenly recognizes Walter as a human being, rather than simply a difficult burden. Elizabeth realizes she has been culpable in her own unhappiness. At the end of the story, she submits to both life and death as her "masters," humbled by her own mistakes and, we may assume, about to carry on with a new perspective.

WALTER BATES Although Walter never appears in the story alive, he plays an essential role in shaping the Bates family's life and bringing about Elizabeth's revelation. From the comments made by Elizabeth, her father, and Walter's mother, we get the sense that Walter is little more than an insensitive drunkard who opts to spend his evenings at a bar rather than with his wife and children. Even his mother says, "I don't know why he got to be such a trouble." His long absences mean that his children must wait for dinner and that Elizabeth must struggle with both anger and anxiety, facing gossip from the neighbors. The only kind words spoken about Walter come from his mother when she fondly remembers him as a child, calling him "a good lad." When Walter's body is brought home, however, a different side of Walter reveals itself. Dead, he is naked and vulnerable, and Elizabeth is stunned by this stark humanity of him. Because she can no longer blame him for her unhappiness, she turns inward and acknowledges her role in their marriage's demise. First absent and then inanimate, Walter nevertheless proves to be a catalyst for change in Elizabeth and her vision for the future.

WALTER'S MOTHER Although Walter's mother mourns Walter's death loudly and dramatically when she arrives in Elizabeth's home, the Walter she is mourning is not the Walter who lies dead on the parlor floor. Described variously as an "old woman," "grandmother," "elder woman," and "old lady," Walter's mother reveals herself to be connected to the past much more than the present. She lectures Elizabeth on what a wonderful child Walter had been, only reluctantly acknowledging how much trouble Walter had brought to his family as an adult. Even her criticisms are veiled with indulgence, however, and she explains that because he was her son, she has always been able to excuse his bad behavior. Elizabeth's stunned, stoic reactions stand out against Walter's mother's loud sobbing, but rather than make Elizabeth seem cold, the contrast serves to make the dead Walter more distant from both women. Walter's mother knew Walter deeply as a child, but we can assume that she knew all but nothing about him as a grown man. Elizabeth thought she knew her husband simply as an uncaring, difficult burden, but she realizes as she looks at the corpse that she might have overlooked some essential pieces of who he was. Dead, Walter can reveal nothing about himself to either woman, but Walter's mother's presence illuminates at least one dimension of Walter that Elizabeth will forever be unable to know.

THEMES, MOTIFS, AND SYMBOLS

THEMES

THE ISOLATION OF THE HUMAN SOUL As Elizabeth tends to Walter's body, Lawrence writes that she feels "the utter isolation of the human soul," and this sense of isolation permeates the entire story. Early on, Elizabeth is isolated in her home as she waits helplessly for Walter, and she is further isolated when she seeks help in finding him and thus becomes the subject of gossip among the other wives. Pregnant and left alone with her other two children, Elizabeth loses herself in anger and resentment. When Walter's mother arrives and the two women learn of Walter's death, both women are isolated in their own way. Walter's mother is lost in grief for a man she knew best as a child, whereas Elizabeth must face the fact that her husband was little more than a stranger to her.

With Walter's corpse unclothed and stretched out on the parlor floor, Elizabeth finally understands, when it is too late, the grave injustice they have done each other in respectively giving up on their marriage. For years, Elizabeth has perceived herself as a victim of her husband's habits, failing to see her own possible role in their strained relationship. She has willingly given up on their partnership, separating herself from Walter while also lamenting her solitude and isolation. Although we know nothing of Walter beyond what Elizabeth and her mother-in-law reveal, we can assume that Walter felt isolated in his marriage as well, unknown and unseen by Elizabeth. In death, he has achieved the ultimate isolation, and widowed, Elizabeth is now even further isolated than she was before.

THE NATURE OF LOVE The nature of love between mother and child and between husband and wife stand in sharp contrast to each other in "Odour of Chrysanthemums." Although she is often short with them, Elizabeth clearly loves her children, John and Annie. She protects them from Walter's indiscretions whenever she can and shields them from seeing his dead body. When she struggles to figure out how to carry on when she fears that Walter is dead, she understands that, first and foremost, she must worry about her children. Similarly, Walter's mother indulges Walter's weaknesses because he is her son, and her deep love for him overshadows his adult flaws. More complicated is Elizabeth's relationship with her unborn child. It was conceived not out of love but out of a cold coupling between isolated individuals, and the child is described as "a weight apart from her" and "ice." At this point, Elizabeth seems to connect the unborn child to her relationship with Walter rather than to her life as a mother. The baby seems less a part of her than a part of her distant relationship with Walter.

The nature of love between Elizabeth and Walter is much darker than the love between Elizabeth and her two existing children. Little is left of their love, having been replaced by resentment, disgust, and anger, and not even physical intimacy can overcome the fact that they are "two isolated beings, far apart." Neither spouse was willing to try to forgive or understand the other, and this inflexibility resulted in permanent estrangement. Until she ministers to Walter at the end of the story, Elizabeth seems unable to see Walter beyond her own disappointments. As she waits and waits for him, she berates herself for being a "fool" and says, "And this is what I came here for, to this dirty hole, rats and all, for him to slink past his very door"—neglecting entirely any love that may have once existed between them and that drew her into the marriage.

MOTIFS

SUFFOCATION Suffocation brings about Walter's death, when he is trapped in the coal pits after a cave-in, but the idea of suffocation also appears throughout the story in Elizabeth's domestic unhappiness. In a way, the coal pits have smothered Elizabeth, because she came to this remote community only because she married Walter. Rather than advancing her interests or opening up new possibilities, the role of wife has been a diminishment, a slow, agonizing humiliation and gradual suffocation. Elizabeth is trapped in the confined and parochial world of the cottage and community and sees no way out. Before she knows that Walter is dead, she speculates on what may happen if he is simply injured, and she feels a fleeting moment of hope as she envisions this as her chance to rid Walter of his drinking habits. But this moment quickly gives way to the news that Walter is dead, and Elizabeth, shocked, is almost suffocated by the erratic rushing of her heart once it "surged on again." Elizabeth must now carry on in an even weightier, more burdensome situation than before.

DARKNESS "Odour of Chrysanthemums" takes place almost entirely under the cover of darkness, and natural light appears only at the beginning, when Elizabeth's father rolls through town. Once he leaves, Elizabeth retreats to her home, lit only by candles and a waning fire. She scolds Annie for coming home after dark, although Annie claims it's "hardly a bit dark." John complains of the lack of light in the cottage as the children eat their dinner, and Elizabeth can barely see their faces. Darkness obscures various dangers: when Elizabeth ventures out into the darkness to find Walter, rats scuffle around her; she senses eavesdropping housewives who are prone to gossip; and as Mr. Rigley escorts Elizabeth home, he warns her of the ruts in the earth that she cannot see in the blackness of the night.

Darkness has a life-giving element as well as a dangerous or threatening one. When Elizabeth prepares to receive Walter's dead body in the parlor, the one paltry candle she brings does little to dispel the gloom. She can barely see Walter in a literal sense, but now, for the first time, she gets a glimpse of who he is as a person. In life, she knew almost nothing about Walter, and even their closest physical encounters took place in the dark. Now, with darkness surrounding her and with Walter in the permanent darkness of death, startling truths come to light for Elizabeth. In this sense, darkness serves as a kind of renewal. Morning will come for Elizabeth, but her life will be very different.

SYMBOLS

CHRYSANTHEMUMS Throughout the story, chrysanthemums primarily suggest unpleasantness and death, and Elizabeth cannot look at or smell them without being plagued by unhappy associations. We first see chrysanthemums as Elizabeth's son, John, strews them over the path toward the house, and Elizabeth chastises him because the petals look "nasty." At home, waiting for Walter to return, Elizabeth remembers bitterly the first time Walter came home drunk, sporting brown chrysanthemums in his buttonhole. When Elizabeth is told that Walter is dead, she notices two vases of chrysanthemums and their "cold, deathly smell" in the parlor, where she plans to lay out Walter's body. When the men eventually carry him in, one knocks over a vase of chrysanthemums, and Elizabeth tidies up the mess before she turns to face the body.

Chrysanthemums, although primarily a symbol of death, occasionally have life-affirming associations as well. Annie, Elizabeth's daughter, is enamored with the chrysanthemums that Elizabeth has placed in her apron and thinks they smell beautiful. When Elizabeth tells her daughter about the time Walter came home drunk, she prefaces the memory with other celebratory moments when chrysanthemums have punctuated her life: her marriage and the birth of Annie. The fact that Elizabeth keeps vases of chrysanthemums in her home suggests that Elizabeth continues to have mixed feelings about the flowers, both resenting and embracing the memories they evoke.

SHORT STORY ANALYSIS

IMAGERY Throughout the story, Lawrence's dark, ominous imagery forms a threatening backdrop to the characters' struggles. For example, when describing the Bates's house, Lawrence writes, "A large bony vine clutched at the house, as if to claw down the tiled roof." We first see young John near raspberry plants that are "like whips." Lawrence twice compares humans to shadows: miners who walk past the house are "like shadows," and Elizabeth returns to the house "like a shadow" after she puts a dustpan outside. We get the sense that these people are somehow disappearing, even as they go about their daily lives. Fire, in particular, appears repeatedly in the story, almost always as a threatening force. At the beginning of the story, Lawrence describes the flames rising from the coal pit as "red sores licking its ashy sides," as though the flames themselves are alive. Inside the house, when Annie cries out in pleasure at seeing the flowers in Elizabeth's apron, Elizabeth is startled, fearing that "the house was afire." Mrs. Rigley, whom Elizabeth approaches for help in finding Walter, asks Elizabeth to make sure the children don't "set theirselves afire." Fire brings warmth and light into the Bates's home, but the characters are always conscious of the threat that accompanies it.

The animal and natural imagery that Lawrence uses suggests that the characters are part of a larger, more unpredictable natural cycle of life and death. John is "like a frog" when he crawls out from underneath the sofa, and Elizabeth says angrily that when Walter comes home drunk he'll be "like a log." One of the miners who brings Walter home compares the cave-in to a "mouse-trap," which suggests that Walter himself was a mouse as he worked in the dark, narrow mines. Walter's mother's tears are like "drops from wet leaves," so impersonal that Lawrence says she was "not weeping." The unborn child feels "like ice" in Elizabeth's womb, an inhuman image that emphasizes how separate Elizabeth feels from both the child and its father. Finally, life and death themselves take on human qualities at the end of the story, when Elizabeth says they are her "immediate master" and her "ultimate master," respectively. These are forces beyond her—or anyone else's—control, and she realizes that she will always be subservient to this natural cycle.

LOCAL DIALECT Lawrence's dialogue is full of local dialect, which adds to the authenticity and vitality of the story's setting and supports the idea of isolation among the characters. Lawrence grew up among mining families in Nottinghamshire, and his father was a miner, so Lawrence was familiar with the intonations, elisions (omissions), and distinctive verbal patterns used in the community. These local details make the characters come alive. When Elizabeth goes to Mrs. Rigley to find out whether her husband had seen Walter that evening, Mrs. Rigley asks "'Asna 'e come whoam yit?" The men who eventually bring Walter's body home tell Elizabeth "E wor smothered!" when describing Walter's fate. Surrounding these interludes of coarse dialect is Lawrence's elegant, carefully calibrated prose, which helps emphasize the separateness of this particular community from the rest of the world.

Perhaps most significant, the dialect used by the locals stands in sharp contrast to Elizabeth's more standard speech patterns and emphasizes her isolation from the rest of the community. We get the sense that Elizabeth is truly an outsider, perhaps coming from a distant community or even a higher social station. Her father speaks in standard English as well, although his is a bit rougher than Elizabeth's, confirming that Elizabeth's family comes from somewhere else. She clearly resents having come to this place, and though Lawrence never tells us exactly what she gave up or what other options had been open to her, we know that she has been disillusioned by what life has offered her. The absence of dialect in Elizabeth's speech emphasizes that she is isolated not only from her husband but also from the community in which she lives.

FORESHADOWING   Numerous examples of foreshadowing crowd "Odour of Chrysanthemums," providing a sense of inevitable tragedy. Lawrence gives us clues to Walter's fate from the beginning of the story, when Elizabeth bitterly says to the children that he "can lie on the floor" when he comes home and that he'll be "like a log." After Elizabeth puts the children to bed, she attempts to distract herself with her sewing, her anger at the situation becoming "tinged with fear." Later, when she seeks the help of Mr. Rigley, he escorts her down the dark alleyway in front of his house, warning her to be careful of the deep ruts in the earth, afraid that someone could slip in the uneven surface of the ground. This idea of accidental physical harm is echoed in Walter's death, caused by a cave-in at his mine.

Developments beyond the scope of the story are foreshadowed as well, particularly in Lawrence's description of the children. Annie is divided in her affections, respectful of her mother's ire yet loyal in her love for her father. How her affections will eventually tilt is suggested in Annie's hair, which is changing from blond, the color of Walter's hair, to brunette, the color of Elizabeth's. This detail subtly suggests the fact that Annie will be forced to transfer her affections exclusively to Elizabeth when Walter dies. The clothes that John wears carry the weight of foreshadowing as well. When he first emerges from the raspberry patch, he is wearing pants and a waistcoat made out of a larger set of men's clothes that had been cut down to fit him. Essentially dressed up as a man, John unwittingly predicts the potentially grim future that awaits him because he will be expected to be the "man of the house" now that Walter is gone. In these small details of the children's physical appearance, we get hints of their bleak future.

IMPORTANT QUOTATIONS EXPLAINED

---

1. *She worked at her sewing with energy, listening to the children, and her anger wearied itself, lay down to rest, opening its eyes from time to time and steadily watching, its ears raised to listen. Sometimes even her anger quailed and shrank, and the mother suspended her sewing . . .*

In this passage, just before the end of section I, Elizabeth tries to distract herself from waiting for Walter, and her anger takes on a life of its own. While Elizabeth sews, her anger keeps vigil, resting or rousing itself whenever footsteps go by outside. This description makes

Elizabeth's anger almost catlike, and we can imagine the anger like a restless pet that seems to be watching and listening even as it sleeps. Attributing animate qualities to this anger suggests that Elizabeth has harbored it for so long that it has taken on a life of its own. It is outside of her control, persisting even when she herself would rather quiet her mind and wait in peace. At the end of the story, when Elizabeth understands that both she and Walter were responsible for the disintegration of their marriage, we can assume that this constant, rootless anger is partly to blame for their problems. Walter was far from innocent, and Elizabeth's anger often had a just cause. It is the animate quality of her anger, however, that makes it more than just an ordinary emotional response. It has become, for Elizabeth, a way of life and constant companion.

---

2. *She looked at his naked body and was ashamed, as if she had denied it. . . . She looked at his face, and she turned her own face to the wall. For his look was other than hers, his way was not her way. She had denied him what he was—she saw it now. She had refused him as himself. . . . She was grateful to death, which restored the truth. And she knew she was not dead.*

At the end of the story, as Elizabeth tends to Walter's body, she suddenly understands that she was culpable in creating the rift that had grown between her and Walter. In this moment, the anger that had been such a part of her life has dissolved, and she yearns to feel a connection to her husband. However, when she looks closely at his body and face, he seems like a stranger. Only now can she see her husband clearly, separate from the anger and resentment that colored her view of him throughout their marriage. Her shame at realizing that she had "denied him" his true self leads to her epiphany. No longer shielded by her martyrdom, she understands the truth: she has done harm to Walter by constantly trying to make him into someone he wasn't and never embracing the man he actually was. She had let her own disappointments and annoyances overshadow the crux of their partnership. Only now, with Walter dead before her, does she understand the truth, and her realization that she herself is not dead suggests that she will now change her outlook on her life.

The Open Boat

Stephen Crane
(1871–1900)

CONTEXT

Born in 1871 in Newark, New Jersey, Stephen Crane hailed from a line of strong-willed men who took active roles in the founding and building of America. On his father's side, one man sailed to America with Sir Francis Drake, and another served as a representative to the pre–Revolutionary War Continental Congresses. Crane was always proud of his family's part in American history, and it motivated him to carve out his own place in history, albeit in a style all his own. It is a marvel that in his short life, Stephen Crane produced so much memorable fiction; he died in 1900, at the young age of twenty-eight. Although his last years were dominated by poor health, Crane left a grand mark on American literature. His influences were few, but his disciples were many, among them Hemingway and Joseph Heller as well as many twentieth-century war novelists. Crane was probably unaware of the literary legacy he would leave, but he always had a good idea of the legacy he inherited.

Although he began writing at a very young age, Crane first made his presence felt in the literary world at age twenty-two with *Maggie: A Girl of the Streets* (1893), which he wrote while living in the slums of New York and for which he needed money from his brother to publish. *Maggie* was instantly notable not only for the conditions in which Crane wrote it but also for its unblinking look at its subject: the underbelly of New York. Crane attempted to depict what he saw as the enslavement of the poor by their own poverty. He was committed to naturalism and realism, as he would be throughout his life, no matter what subject he was writing about. A "naturalist" writer approaches subjects objectively, almost scientifically, staying detached as much as possible. "Realist" writers strive to portray their subjects as realistically as possible. Crane's best-known work, *The Red Badge of Courage* (1895), was a naturalistic novel set during the Civil War. Told from a private's point of view, *Red Badge* resonated with readers who were familiar with the life of the grunt: the constant threat of the unknown, the feeling of being a pawn in someone else's schemes, the suppression of personality, and self-doubt.

"The Open Boat" (1897) evolved from Crane's real-life experience of being stranded in a dinghy on the Atlantic Ocean. On December 31, 1896, Crane sailed out of Jacksonville, Florida, bound for Cuba, to cover the emerging war as a correspondent. His ship sank in the morning of January 2, and Crane and three crew members spent thirty hours in a dinghy before coming ashore near Daytona Beach. Crane immediately wrote "Stephen Crane's Own Story," a newspaper account of the sinking, but he shied away from further telling of his experience, writing only that "The history of life in an open boat for thirty hours would no doubt be instructive for the young, but none is to be told here now." Crane waited for years before he turned his experience into "The Open Boat."

"The Open Boat" confronts both Crane's time aboard the dinghy and the symbolic implications of fighting for one's life amidst forces that are uncaring about one's survival. The correspondent in the story is based on Crane himself, while the injured captain, the cook, and Billie the oiler all have their real-life counterparts in the men who shared the dinghy with Crane. The actual captain did indeed injure himself in the ship's foundering, and William Higgins, the actual oiler, did indeed die on the shore. Although all of Crane's characters are based in reality, Crane turns them into archetypes (ideal models) of humanity and submits them to the whims of nature. The critical reception of "The Open Boat" was enthusiastic, with both H. G. Wells and Joseph Conrad praising the story. Unfortunately for Crane, the experience that gave him this story also took away his health. Following his experience at sea, Crane became vulnerable to the diseases that would eventually kill him.

Despite his poor health, Crane never stopped moving in an attempt to be on the frontline of some of the grimmer scenes of his time. His travels took him to Greece to report on the Greco-Turkish War; to England, where he befriended contemporaries such as Henry James, H. G. Wells, and Joseph Conrad; back to Cuba to cover the Spanish-American War; and finally to England and Germany, where he succumbed to tuberculosis. During all this time, Crane persisted in writing fiction and poetry, much of it characterized by his naturalistic perception of man caught in the throes of the conflicting, alienating forces that define the human condition. Ultimately, Crane tried to follow his own maxim that "the nearer a writer gets to life the greater he becomes as an artist." For him, this meant a commitment to reality in life as well as in art. Crane lived this maxim so deeply that in the end, his desire to report from the thick of war was responsible for putting him in contact with the diseases that killed him while he was still in his twenties.

PLOT OVERVIEW

It is just before dawn, and not far off the coast of Florida, between the open sea and the surf, are four men in a dinghy. The ship on which they were sailing sank overnight, and they are the only survivors, left to bob up and down in the waves until their bathtub-sized boat capsizes and they too drown. They do not have a moment's peace. The ocean is so rough that one indelicate move will upset the dinghy and send them into the winter waters. Each man, despite not having slept for two days, works tirelessly to keep the boat afloat. The correspondent and the oiler share the work of rowing, while the cook huddles on the floor of the dinghy, bailing water. These men take their direction from the captain, who was injured during the shipwreck and sits grimly in the bow, the memory still fresh of his ship engulfed in the sea and the crew's dead faces in the water.

As day breaks and the cook and correspondent bicker about being rescued, the men begin to make progress toward the shore. Fighting hopelessness, they row silently. Gulls fly overhead and perch on the water. The gulls are at ease on the ocean, so much so that one lands on the captain's head. The men see this as a sinister, insulting gesture, but the captain cannot swat the bird off because the sudden movement would likely topple the boat.

Eventually, the captain shoos the bird away, and they go on rowing until the captain sees a lighthouse in the distance. Although the cook expresses reservation that the nearby life-saving station has been abandoned for more than a year, the crew heartens at approaching land, almost taking pleasure in the brotherhood that they have formed and in attending to the business of the sea. The correspondent even finds four dry cigars in a pocket, which he shares with the others.

The men's optimism evaporates when, approaching land yet unable to master the turbulent surf, they realize that help isn't coming. They again make for the open sea, exhausted and bitter. Another sign of hope comes when the captain sees a man on shore. Each crew member looks for signs of hope in the man's gestures. They think the man sees them. Then they think they see two men, then a crowd and perhaps a boat being rolled down to the shore. They stubbornly think that help is on the way as the shadows lengthen and the sea and sky turn black.

During the night, the men forget about being saved and attend to the business of the boat. The correspondent and oiler, exhausted from rowing, plan to alternate throughout the night. But they get tired in the early hours of the morning, and the cook helps out. For the most part, the correspondent rows alone, wondering how he can have come so far if he is only going to drown. Rowing through phosphorescence and alongside a monstrous shark, the correspondent thinks of a poem he learned in childhood about a soldier dying in a distant land, never to return home.

When morning comes, the captain suggests that they try to run the surf while they still have enough energy. They take the boat shoreward until it capsizes, and then they all make a break for it in the icy water. The oiler leads the group, while the cook and correspondent swim more slowly and the captain holds onto the keel of the overturned dinghy. With the help of a life preserver, the correspondent makes good progress, until he is caught in a current that forces him to back to the boat. Before he can reach the dinghy, a wave hurls him to shallower water, where he is saved by a man who has appeared on shore and plunged into the sea to save the crew. On land, the correspondent drifts in and out of consciousness, but as he regains his senses, he sees a large number of people on the shore with rescue gear. He learns that the captain and cook have been saved but the oiler has died.

CHARACTER LIST

The Correspondent   A reporter and the central character of the story. The correspondent is presumably young and able-bodied, given that he shares rowing duties with the oiler. The correspondent is also, by virtue of his profession, inclined to be cynical of men. He is pleasantly surprised to find his heart warmed by the brotherhood that he and the crew have formed in the boat. Several times, the correspondent curses nature and the gods who rule the sea and wonders whether he is really meant to drown.

The Captain   The captain of the ship, injured when the ship floods. The captain is calm and quiet, talking for the most part only to give directions and lead the crew to shore. The captain commands complete authority, and although he does not take part in keeping the dinghy afloat, he bears the full responsibility of getting everyone to safety. He is always alert and cool-headed, even when it looks as though he might be sleeping.

The Cook   The ship's cook, who maintains a positive, even naïve, outlook on the men's rescue. The cook is the first to suggest the presence of a lifesaving station and cannot help but turn his mind to the simple pleasures of living on land, such as his favorite pies and meats. Although he is not fit enough to help with the rowing, the cook makes himself useful by bailing water.

The Oiler (Billie)   The only refugee from the ship to die in the final attempt at reaching land. Before the ship sank, the oiler worked a double watch in the engine room, and he is most likely to be exhausted in the dinghy. The oiler is staunch, obedient to the captain, and generous and polite to the correspondent whenever he is asked to row. The oiler also seems to be the most realistic of the men, never losing sight of the task at hand or the slim chance they have of surviving.

ANALYSIS OF MAJOR CHARACTERS

THE CORRESPONDENT   For Crane, each crewmember is an archetype that, when joined with his fellow castaways, constitutes part of a microcosm of society. The captain represents the leaders; the cook the followers; the oiler the good, working men; and the correspondent the observers and thinkers. As his profession as a reporter suggests, the correspondent functions as the eyes and voice of the story. Crane underlines this point in his introduction of the characters in the first section. While the cook is cowering on the boat's floor and the oiler is silently working at his oar, the correspondent watches the waves and wonders why he is caught on the ocean, a question that reveals the correspondent's search for purpose in life. With this question alone, the correspondent begins to shape our perceptions of the ordeal the men are undergoing.

In the first five sections of "The Open Boat," the correspondent's challenges to the sea, which he associates with nature and fate, reveal his desire to make sense of surviving the ship only to drown in the dinghy. Although he understands that nature and fate do not act and think as men do, the correspondent nevertheless goads them because he believes that there is a purpose to nature, that it in some way validates his struggle for survival. The correspondent initially thinks he finds the answer when he considers the "subtle brotherhood of men" that develops among the crew in response to the overwhelming cruelty of nature. At this point, he takes pleasure in the pain caused by rowing in the rough sea because he believes that this pain is the healthy byproduct of his effort at community, which nature has forced them to create and is the only thing that really matters. As the men realize that no one is coming to save them, however, the correspondent comes to lose hope in the "subtle brotherhood" that had seemed to be the noble purpose of submitting to nature's punishment.

THE CAPTAIN   The captain is the consummate leader, a man who never shirks from the responsibility he takes for those who have entrusted their safety to him. When he loses his ship to the sea at the beginning of the story, the captain suffers infinitely more than the other survivors. Deprived of his ship, he becomes a broken man who has lost the very thing that grants him his authority. Yet the captain, through his dedication to guiding the men to safety, retains a degree of dignity to go with the ineffable sense of loss he feels at having failed in his charge. In this sense, the captain is at once a majestic and tragic figure, one who has not measured up to the standards he has set for himself but continues to fight for his fellow men. His quiet, steady efforts in the boat are not self-motivated and afford him no personal redemption. Instead, his actions are directed toward the others.

THE OILER (BILLIE)   Of the four characters in the boat, the oiler represents the everyman, the one whom Crane intends to resemble the average person most closely. The oiler functions as the lynchpin of the crew, holding everyone together through his staunch heroism. He has the fewest delusions about the men's physical plight, but he never gives in to the hopelessness that the others mask with idle talk about nonexistent opportunities for rescue or meditations about the cruelty of nature. Instead, the oiler maintains an image of strength, warmth, and integrity. He echoes the captain's orders, reinforcing the social structure of the crew and instilling confidence in the others, whose outlook rises and falls with the waves.

THEMES, MOTIFS, AND SYMBOLS

THEMES

NATURE'S INDIFFERENCE TO MAN Despite the narrator's profusion of animistic (animal-like), humanistic (manlike), and deistic (godlike) characterizations of nature, Crane makes clear that nature is ultimately indifferent to the plight of man, possessing no consciousness that we can understand. As the stranded men progress through the story, the reality of nature's lack of concern for them becomes increasingly clear. The narrator highlights this development by changing the way he describes the sea. Early in the story, the sea snarls, hisses, and bucks like a bronco; later, it merely "paces to and fro," no longer an actor in the men's drama. In reality, the sea does not change at all; only the men's perception of the sea changes. The unaltered activity of the gulls, clouds, and tides illustrates that nature does not behave any differently in light of the men's struggle to survive.

Crane strengthens the idea that nature is indifferent to man by showing that it is as randomly helpful as it is hurtful. For every malevolent whim that the men suffer, they experience an unexpected good turn in the form of a favorable wind or calm night. The fact that the men almost seem to get assistance from nature destroys the notion of nature as an entirely hostile force. Nothing highlights this point so much as the correspondent's final rescue. Plowed to shore and saved by a freak wave, the correspondent must embrace the fact that the very thing that has put him in harm's way has saved him. This freak wave, however, may also be responsible for killing the much hardier oiler, a turn of events that demonstrates two ideas: nature is as much a harsh punisher as it is a benefactor, and nature does not act out of any motivation that can be understood in human terms.

MAN'S INSIGNIFICANCE IN THE UNIVERSE "The Open Boat" conveys a feeling of loneliness that comes from man's understanding that he is alone in the universe and insignificant in its workings. Underneath the men's and narrator's collective rants at fate and the universe is the fear of nothingness. They have an egotistical belief that they should have a role in the universe, that their existence should mean something. When the correspondent realizes by section VI that fate will not answer his pleas, he settles into despair. His subsequent recollection of the poem about the soldier who lies dying in Algiers reflects his feelings of alienation at being displaced from his position in the universe. Like the soldier who dies in alien territory, the correspondent fears that he too will perish without a connection to whatever gives him his sense of self.

Throughout "The Open Boat," the correspondent understands pain to be the necessary byproduct of his efforts to overcome nature, the willful enemy. He comes to value his suffering because it is nobly derived; in the earlier sections, the correspondent, whom the narrator says is cynical, is often cheerful and talkative in his descriptions of the physical pain he experiences. By the end of the story, however, the correspondent's new awareness that the universe is unconcerned with the situation's outcome makes him physically and spiritually weary. He decides that there is no higher purpose to surviving other than prolonging a life that is meaningless. His comment in section VII that the coldness of the water is simply "sad" underscores this despair. At this point, all sensations of pain and pleasure are merely physical and have no spiritual meaning.

SOCIETY AS MEANING IN A HARSH WORLD   In assembling the men in the dinghy and creating a microcosm of mankind, Crane sets up man's greatest invention, society, against what first seems to be a cruel, unrelenting nature. When faced with the savage, stormy sea, the men in the dinghy immediately band together because they recognize that society is the best defense against the chaos of nature. The men derive meaning from their fellowship, created to oppose nature, which they view as the force that seeks to undo them. Even when they become disheartened by the fact that nature shows no regard for them, they can still turn to one another. In creating society, they have created an obligation to one another that they must honor to survive. The narrator observes that the men's cooperation is "personal and heartfelt," which suggests that the men derive some spiritual satisfaction from the arrangement. Although they are shut out of the realm of cosmic importance, these men nevertheless construct something that is meaningful to them.

MOTIFS

DROWNING   As the narrator attempts to capture the men's thoughts as they endure many demoralizing episodes, he inserts a refrain into the text three times that suggests that the men's general fear of death is exacerbated by the unconcern of nature. The refrain is a rant against fate, which the narrator personifies as an incompetent fool unable to govern men's lives. The narrator is not really trying to tell us that fate is cruel. Instead, he is suggesting that the men are furious because they believe that fate has toyed with their lives. The men consider their situation unfair, and in the refrain, they protest against it. The fact that the narrator intrudes on the story with this refrain at the moments when fate seems to have let the men down creates the impression that this is, in fact, the men's reaction. The refrain acts as the narrator's interpretation of how the men themselves interpret their situation

Hidden deeper in the refrain is the narrator's conviction that a higher power does not exist to weigh in on men's affairs. By making outright references to "the seven mad gods who rule the sea," the narrator clues us in to the mythical implications of the story, insinuating that these pagan gods, who are traditionally involved in men's lives, have abandoned the stranded men. More important, the narrator hints at the absence of an overseeing God through a subtle use of numerology. The thrice-repeated phrase "If I am going to be drowned" in the refrain alludes to the New Testament Gethsemane scene in which Peter denies Jesus three times. In the Bible, man denies God, but Crane inverts the scene so that it is God denying man.

WAVES   A ceaseless presence in the story and constant nuisance to the refugees, the ocean waves suggest both the forces of nature and uncontrollability of life. At the beginning of the story, the narrator presents the waves as the men's primary concern, the thing they must master if they are to survive the shipwreck. In this sense, the waves resemble the ever-changing demands of the present, the part of life that demands the most attention but allows for the least reflection. Crane seems to imply that because the men cannot control the waves' ebb and flow, man in general cannot affect the outcomes of his life and can hope only to respond constructively to what he encounters. Just as the waves are constantly changing, becoming sometimes violent and sometimes favorable, the pressures in man's life will continue to jostle his progress toward whatever he seeks. The narrator's final mention of the waves as "pacing to and fro" emphasizes this point by suggesting that the waves, in their motion, are impatiently waiting for the men, who must eventually venture out again onto the seas of fortune.

SYMBOLS

THE BOAT   The boat, to which the men must cling to survive the seas, symbolizes human life bobbing along among the universe's uncertainties. The boat, no larger than a bathtub, seems even smaller against the vastness of the ocean. The boat is inconsequential and always in danger of capsizing, much as we as humans are inconsequential and frail in the context of the world around us. The fact that the boat is characterized as "open" supports this interpretation: the boat is unprotected and thus open to suffering the unexpected turns of fortune that are unavoidable in life. For the men, being in the open boat becomes the reality of their lives, and they realize from their experience on the boat how little control they have over where they can go and what they can do. Through the boat, Crane implies that life is not something we can control, but rather life is what we must hang onto as we make our way in the world.

THE OILER'S DEATH   The oiler's death and lack of explanation surrounding it reinforce the randomness of nature's whims and symbolize the indifference of nature toward man. Because he is no more deserving of death than any other crew member, and in some cases is less deserving because he has worked the hardest under the most physical strain, his death highlights the fact that nature is arbitrary in how it chooses its victims. The events surrounding the oiler's death also uncover the fact that the "subtle brotherhood of men" sensed by the crew is nothing more than a delusion. The men make a break for land on their own, and the good-natured oiler leaves everyone behind to reach the shore. In this way, Crane illustrates that there is a limit to what working together can accomplish and that all men ultimately end up alone.

THE POEM   The poem that the correspondent recites about the soldier who pitifully lies dying in a foreign land represents the correspondent's understanding of his own plight. Just as in youth he never considered it a tragedy that the fictitious soldier dies away from home, the correspondent realizes that, as a grown man, his situation is like the soldier's and that it is nature that now regards his death as inconsequential. This understanding forces the correspondent to see the soldier's story as tragic because it is the only way to give his own life weight. The correspondent endows the fictitious soldier with humanity, a gesture that reveals both his maturity at understanding what his life really amounts to and his self-delusion for using fiction to give meaning to his own situation. In truth, the poem does not make the correspondent's plight any more real. Rather, it only reinforces the meaningless of his struggle, which the narrator later describes as "the plight of the ants."

THE CIGARS The four wet cigars and four dry cigars serve as a complex symbol of hope for spiritual salvation and as the ultimate loss of that salvation. When the correspondent finds these cigars in his pockets, Crane makes it clear that there are two interpretations of the men's plight. First, like the four sodden cigars, the four men are physically and spiritually soaked by the heavy, demoralizing forces of nature—they are broken and useless. Second, like the four dry cigars hidden deep inside the correspondent's pocket, there is something inside the men that remains untouched by the cold, drenching despair that the sea imparts. At the moment when the correspondent digs through his pocket, the men are likely to see themselves optimistically—as the four dry cigars—because their cooperation and hard work has seemingly put them on track to defeat nature. Yet by the end of the story, the men's optimism is not intact, and they feel misery, not triumph. The wet cigars more aptly illustrate the tragedy of the men's spirits.

SHORT STORY ANALYSIS

SHIFTING FRAMES OF REFERENCE AND IMPRESSIONISM Although Crane was foremost a realist and naturalist writer who valued firsthand, close-up experience as the key to understanding, Crane in "The Open Boat" relies on impressionism to communicate the gulf between objective reality and what his characters perceive as reality. Whereas the logic of realism and naturalism calls for experience and perception to be nearly identical, impressionism differs from the other two in that it allows for the fact that a character's grasp of reality is at best fleeting or even impossible. Crane's impressionistic technique in "The Open Boat" is ideal for placing his readers into the same frame of reference as his characters. The story's first sentence, "No one knew the color of the sky," thrusts the reader into the position of his characters, who have a limited perspective of the world. Each character lives alone in his own reality, as does the narrator, whose lack of omniscience (the ability to be all-knowing) underscores one of the story's central messages: no one truly knows anything.

Crane enriches his impressionistic technique by juxtaposing close-up, sensory descriptions of the men's experience in the dinghy with the narrator's detached perspective. The narrator says that the mountainous gray waters obstruct the men's view of everything outside the boat, but in the next sentence the narrator comments on how the whole scene would have been picturesque if viewed from afar. The point of shifting the frame of reference is to convey that the significance of intense moments, such as the men's experience in the dinghy, depends on the perspective from which they are seen. This idea becomes relevant to the characters themselves as they realize that, from a cosmic perspective, their lives are inconsequential.

EXISTENTIALISM AND IRONY In "The Open Boat," Crane conveys an existential view of humanity: that is, he depicts a human situation in which the individual is insignificant in the universe and yet, through free will and consciousness, must interpret a reality that is essentially unknowable. The men in the dinghy, particularly the correspondent, try desperately to justify their survival in the struggle against the sea, but the values by which they live and the appeals they make to the heavens are inadequate. The universe is indifferent to their courage, valor, and brotherhood, and there is no response to the men's furious appeals to fate and God to answer for the outrageous misfortune that has befallen them. Crane's use of the word *absurd* in the narrator's refrain challenging fate—"The whole affair is absurd"—resonates well with the existentialist creed that the universe itself is "absurd" and that there is no meaning in the natural order of things. At best, these men can construct their own meanings, such as the "subtle brotherhood of men" they form, but in Crane's vision, they are shut out from the cosmos.

The irony in Crane's vision of "The Open Boat" is that, in describing the situation of the correspondent, who has come to understand his insignificant position in the natural universe through the manmade tower, the narrator continues to give human qualities to inhuman things. For example, the narrator calls nature a "she." For both the narrator and correspondent, nature is an old, inscrutable mistress whose workings are always beyond their grasp. At the end of the story, the captain, correspondent, and cook are no more able to converse with nature than they were at the beginning. Indeed, they finally realize that there is no such thing as conversing with nature. This awareness drives home the irony of the final sentence in the story, in which the narrator says that the three surviving men feel that they can be interpreters of the ocean's voice. The men's capacity to interpret nature for other people refers simply to their understanding that the sea's voice is incoherent and the universe a cosmic void. There is nothing to interpret.

ALTERNATIVE INTERPRETATIONS Critics generally agree that "The Open Boat" is an examination of man's relationship to the universe as well as of man's relationship to other men. But there are different opinions about the precise nature of these relationships. On one hand, Crane's work seems to be anti-Romantic. Romanticism argues that human beings exist in harmony with nature. The sea in this story, with its constant snarls and hisses, is a hostile force to mankind and certainly not in harmony with the men who are fighting for their lives. American writers such as Ralph Waldo Emerson and Henry David Thoreau believed that nature is a mystic wonderland that in every corner holds tiny clues to how man fits seamlessly into the universe. "The Open Boat" suggests the opposite: man is alienated from the universe and doomed to lead a cold, unnatural existence.

On the other hand, "The Open Boat" could be seen as a Darwinian story that shows how man is intimately connected to nature. Whereas the anti-Romantics tried to separate man completely from nature, the Darwinians understand Crane to be embracing nature so tightly that his plot simply expands on Darwin's idea of "survival of the fittest." In this interpretation, nature has no will or purpose. Just as the men come to realize that nature has not actually taken up arms against them, they begin to devote themselves to "the business of the boat"—to survival. Although the oiler's death seems to undermine the Darwinian interpretation of the story, because he is clearly the strongest of the group and therefore should have survived, it actually reinforces the idea of "survival of the fittest." While the cook, captain, and correspondent all depend on a manmade or naturally occurring device to help them to the shore, the oiler goes it alone, relying only on his human strength and not on his more evolved capacity for thought and strategy. The "fittest" are the men who have relied on man's ability to intelligently adapt and create.

IMPORTANT QUOTATIONS EXPLAINED

1. *When it occurs to a man that nature does not regard him as important . . . he at first wishes to throw bricks at the temple, and he hates deeply the fact that there are no bricks and no temples . . . . Thereafter he knows the pathos of his situation.*

This passage, from the beginning of section VI, serves as a preface to the correspondent's epiphany that the sea is a formless, voiceless phenomenon that lacks the consciousness he requires to validate his own existence. Until this point, the correspondent has thought of the sea, nature, and the universe as part of a higher power that intelligently governs the cosmos, a higher power against which he can define himself and through which find meaning in his own life. Instead, the correspondent finds out that he is nothing to the universe or God, who remains as distant and cryptic as "a high cold star." In the absence of this power, the correspondent loses his identity. Crane creates a sense of irony by having the narrator personify nature. The narrator gives it human actions such as "regard" and "maim," whereas he's actually denying that nature has any humanlike consciousness. The irony inherent in Crane's language in this passage suggests that he believes that man will always go on believing in something that he knows isn't there.

2. *This tower . . . represented . . . the serenity of nature amid the struggles of the individual— nature in the wind, and nature in the vision of men. She did not seem cruel to him then, nor beneficent, nor treacherous, nor wise . . . she was indifferent, flatly indifferent.*

This passage, from the beginning of section VII, denies the distinction between reality and what man perceives as reality and supports the idea that nature is indifferent to man. Much as the narrator does in section I when describing the picturesque quality of the men in the dinghy when seen from afar, the correspondent uses a new, broad-picture perspective to remove himself from the hostility of his immediate surroundings and take in a larger picture of nature. His consideration of the giant, immovable wind tower in the distance opens him up to the reality that might exist outside himself or the "nature in the wind" that is separate from the "nature in the vision of men." The main difference between these two natures is that whereas the former works inexplicably within the confines of itself, the latter depends on an intelligent higher power that directs nature's affairs. The correspondent accepts the possibility of true objective reality, confessing that he is no longer certain that there is a benevolent, rational God at the center of the universe.

Paul's Case: A Study in Temperament
Willa Cather
(1873–1947)

CONTEXT

Willa Cather, the oldest of seven children, was born on December 7, 1873. She lived in Virginia until age nine, when her family moved to Nebraska. The shift from the mountains of Virginia to the plains of Nebraska affected Cather strongly, as did the immigrant population she encountered in Red Cloud, the second Nebraska town in which her family lived. Cather attended the University of Nebraska, where she was a star student. Although she initially wanted to be a doctor, she soon decided to concentrate on the classics. During college, Cather discovered her talent for writing and quickly entered the world of journalism. By the time she was twenty, she had a column in the *Nebraska State Journal*, and during her junior year, she became the paper's drama critic. After graduation, she took a job in Pittsburgh, Pennsylvania, as managing editor for *Home Monthly*, a women's magazine. About a year later, she became a drama critic for a Pittsburgh newspaper called the *Leader*.

Beginning in 1901, Cather did a five-year stint as a high school English teacher, a job she hoped would give her plenty of time for her own writing. In 1903, she published a book of poetry called *April Twilights*. After she met S. S. McClure, editor of *McClure's Magazine*, McClure offered her a job as an editor at the magazine, which was famous for its muckraking journalism. She accepted and moved to New York. Cather's biography of Christian Science founder Mary Baker Eddy was published serially in *McClure's*, and in 1909, it was published as a book. The biography infuriated Christian Scientists, who attempted to buy every copy in an effort to contain the damage.

In 1913, Cather followed the advice of her mentor, writer Sarah Orne Jewett, and left the magazine to focus on writing full-time. Cather considered her first novel, *Alexander's Bridge* (1912), derivative of Henry James's and Edith Wharton's fiction. She found her true voice in *O Pioneers!* (1913), a novel set on the prairie. In 1918, Cather published *My Ántonia*, the story of a boy named Jim who, like Cather, moves to Nebraska from Virginia. The novel received rave reviews, and its popularity persists today. Cather won the Pulitzer Prize for *One of Ours* (1922). In her novel *Death Comes for the Archbishop* (1927), Cather explored the life of a French Catholic missionary in the southwestern United States.

Cather's other works include the novels *The Song of the Lark* (1915), *The Professor's House* (1922), *A Lost Lady* (1923), *My Mortal Enemy* (1926), *Shadows on the Rock* (1931), *Lucy Gayheart* (1935), and *Sapphira and the Slave Girl* (1940) and the short-story collections *Youth and the Bright Medusa* (1920) and *Obscure Destinies* (1932). Cather died of a cerebral hemorrhage in 1947.

Although Cather is most often associated with the prairie, her adult life was cosmopolitan. She lived in a number of big cities, including New York. Most modern scholars agree that she was a lesbian. She wrote her books for her friend Isabelle McClung, with whom she lived and traveled in her twenties. For forty years, Cather lived with Edith Lewis, an advertising woman who also hailed from Nebraska. Many details of Cather's personal life are unknown, however, because both she and Lewis destroyed their letters.

In recent years, critical interest in Cather has increased dramatically. Once dismissed as a folksy Midwestern writer, Cather's reputation has undergone a transformation. Feminist scholars, among others, find much to interest them in such novels as O, Pioneers! and My Antonia, and Cather's work is increasingly taught in high schools and colleges.

"Paul's Case," one of Cather's most frequently anthologized short stories, was originally published in McClure's. It later appeared in Cather's first short-story collection, The Troll Garden (1905). It was written and is set in Pittsburgh, where men such as J. P. Morgan and Andrew Carnegie were making vast fortunes during the early 1900s. These "iron kings" and steel magnates are the giants who employ Paul's neighbors and who fire Paul's imagination. Carnegie Music Hall in Pittsburgh, where Paul works as an usher, is named for steel magnate and philanthropist Andrew Carnegie. Carnegie's name and influence loom large over the story, because it is at the Hall that Paul first finds a means of escaping his unhappy life.

Cather claimed that her teaching experiences inspired "Paul's Case." Her career as a young journalist also seems to inform the story, as Cather spoke of the intoxicating effect of seeing her name in print for the first time. Her instant addiction to the world of journalism and the arts is mirrored in Paul, who is hypnotized by theater and music.

PLOT OVERVIEW

Paul has been suspended from his high school in Pittsburgh. As the story opens, he arrives at a meeting with the school's faculty members and principal. He is dressed in clothes that are simultaneously shabby and debonair. The red carnation he wears in his buttonhole particularly offends the faculty members, who think the flower sums up Paul's flippant attitude. Paul is tall and narrow-shouldered, with enlarged pupils that remind one of a drug addict's eyes.

The faculty members have a difficult time articulating their true feelings about Paul. Deep down, they believe that Paul loathes, feels contempt for, and is repulsed by them. They lash out at Paul, but he betrays no emotion. Instead, he smiles throughout the barrage of criticism. After Paul leaves, the drawing master says aloud that Paul's mother died in Colorado just after Paul was born. Privately, the drawing master remembers seeing Paul asleep one day in class and being shocked at his aged appearance. As the teachers depart, they feel embarrassed about their viciousness toward Paul.

Paul goes straight to Carnegie Hall in Pittsburgh, where he works as an usher. Because he is early, he goes to the Hall's gallery and looks at paintings of Paris and Venice. He loses himself in one particular painting, a "blue Rico." After changing in the dressing room, where he roughhouses with the other ushers, Paul begins to work. He is excellent at his job, performing every aspect of it with great enthusiasm. He is annoyed when his English teacher arrives and he must seat her, but he comforts himself with the knowledge that her clothes are inappropriate for so fancy a venue.

The symphony begins, and Paul loses himself in the music. As he listens, he feels full of life. After the performance, he trails the star soprano to her hotel, the Schenley, and imagines vividly that he is following her inside the luxurious building. As if awaking from a dream,

Paul realizes that he is actually standing in the cold, rainy street. He dreads returning to his room, with its ugly knickknacks and pictures of John Calvin and George Washington.

As he reaches Cordelia Street, where he lives, Paul feels depressed and repulsed by the commonness and ordinariness of his middle-class neighborhood. Unable to face his father, Paul sneaks into the basement, where he stays awake all night imagining what would happen if his father mistook him for a burglar and shot him—or recognized Paul in time, but later in life wished that he had shot his son.

The next day, Paul sits on the porch with his sisters and father. Many people are outside, relaxing. It is a pleasant scene, but Paul is disgusted by it. His father chats with a young clerk whom he hopes Paul will emulate. This clerk took his boss's advice: he married the first woman he could and began having children immediately. The only tales of business that interest Paul are those of the iron magnates' expensive adventures in Cairo, Venice, and Monte Carlo. He understands that some "cash boys" (low-level employees) eventually find great success, but he does not enjoy thinking about the initial cash-boy work.

After managing to get carfare from his father by pretending that he needs to study with a friend, Paul goes to see Charley Edwards, a young actor who lets Paul hang around his dressing room and watch rehearsals. The narrator notes that Paul's mind has not been "perverted" by novels, as his teachers suspect. Rather, Paul gets pleasure solely from theater and music, which are the only things that make him feel alive.

At school, Paul tells outrageous lies about his close friendships with the members of the theater company and the stars who perform at Carnegie Hall. Paul's effort to prove that he is better than his classmates and teachers winds up alienating him from them. In the end, the principal speaks with Paul's father, and Paul is forbidden to return to school, Carnegie Hall, or the theater where Charley Edwards works. The theater company's members hear about Paul's lies and find them comical. Their lives are difficult, not the glamorous dream worlds that Paul imagines.

Paul takes an overnight train and arrives in New York City, where he buys expensive clothes, hats, and shoes. After purchasing silver at Tiffany's, he checks into the Waldorf, paying for his rooms in advance. The eighth-floor rooms are nearly perfect. All that's missing are flowers, which Paul sends a bellboy out to buy. The narrator explains what has happened to make all this possible: Paul got a job with Denny & Carson's, and when asked to take a deposit to the bank, he deposited only the checks and pocketed $1,000 in cash. He is using this stolen money to fund his spree in New York.

After a nap, Paul takes a carriage ride up Fifth Avenue. He notices banks of flowers, bright and vibrant, protected by glass from the snow. He dines at the hotel while listening to an orchestra play the *Blue Danube*. He feels utterly content. The next day, Paul meets a rich boy who attends Yale. The two of them enjoy a night on the town, staying out until 7 a.m. The narrator notes that although the boys begin the evening in a happy mood, they end it in a bad one.

A lovely week passes, and then Paul finds that his theft has been discovered and reported by the Pittsburgh newspapers. According to the stories, his father has paid back the $1,000 and is headed to New York to find his son. Paul enjoys one last dinner at the Waldorf. The next morning, he wakes up, hungover, and looks at the gun he purchased on his first day in New York. In the end, he takes cabs to a set of railroad tracks in Pennsylvania and leaps in front of an oncoming train. Before he dies, he recognizes "the folly of his haste" and thinks of the places that he will never see.

CHARACTER LIST

Paul   The protagonist and antihero of the story. An idealistic, lying, suicidal young man, Paul fits in nowhere and looks down on nearly everyone he knows. He is class-conscious and reserves his approval for rich people and those involved in the art world. Desperate for both acceptance and superiority over others, he lies about his friendships with actors to make himself seem important. He ends his life after stealing money and spending it all on a lavish spree in New York City.

Paul's Father   An unnamed widower. Paul's father, in Paul's view, is simply a potential disciplinarian. However, Cather portrays Paul's father as a deeply generous man who provides for his children and looks after their well-being. His concern about Paul's troubles in school, his willingness to pay back the $1,000 Paul stole, and his quest for his vanished son all demonstrate his deep kindness.

Charley Edwards   A young actor in a Pittsburgh theater troupe. Charley Edwards allows Paul to hang out backstage, help him with his costumes, and observe rehearsals. However, when Paul is forbidden to return to Carnegie Hall, Charley agrees not to see him anymore. Cather hints that Charley may recognize and share Paul's homosexual tendencies.

The Soprano   A German singer. To Paul, the soprano seems to be a highly romantic figure, when in fact she is a middle-aged mother. This gap between perception and reality is typical of Paul, who idealizes what he does not understand. The soprano also lives (at least in Paul's mind) a life of glamour and beauty that Paul craves. Her stay at the Schenley, a posh hotel, may inspire Paul's flight to the Waldorf in New York.

The Drawing Master   One of the faculty members. The drawing master defends Paul to the other teachers, positing that he is disturbed rather than simply rude. He makes the only mention of Paul's dead mother in the story and worries about Paul's physical weakness.

The English Teacher   One of the faculty members. The English teacher is keenly aware of the contempt Paul feels for her and the other teachers. She knows that he has a "physical aversion" to her that he cannot control, and this knowledge hurts her feelings. She spearheads the attack against Paul during the meeting. Later, when she attends the symphony at Carnegie Hall, she covers her confusion at encountering Paul by acting snobby.

The Young Clerk   A twenty-six-year-old man held up as an example by Paul's father. The clerk embodies everything Paul wants to avoid in his own life. He married an unattractive woman, fathered four children, lives on Cordelia Street, and brags about his boss, a steel magnate.

The Yale Student   A rich boy from San Francisco. Something unmentionable happens between Paul and the Yale student, who spend a night out on the town together in New York. The narrator says only that they part on bad terms, without explaining why. It is possible that a sexual encounter, or an attempt at one, soured their friendship.

ANALYSIS OF MAJOR CHARACTERS

PAUL   Paul moves through his world awkwardly, never truly fitting in anywhere or ever feeling comfortable in his own skin. He is obsessed with art, theater, and music, and his job as an usher at Carnegie Hall in Pittsburgh allows him to indulge these obsessions. Paul has an unrealistic idea that the art world is an ideal fantasyland, and he uses art as a sort of drug to escape his dreary existence. He has no desire to join the art world he admires; rather, he wants to sit back and observe other people. Paul feels contempt for his teachers, classmates, neighbors, and family members, all of whom he sees as hopelessly narrow-minded. Besides art, Paul is also obsessed with money. He longs to be rich and believes that great wealth is his destiny. Because of his selfishness and desperation to escape his own unspectacular life, Paul lies constantly, sometimes to get out of a sticky situation and sometimes to impress his classmates and teachers. Cather makes it clear that Paul has homosexual tendencies, although it is not clear whether he acknowledges or acts upon them. He feels alienated from society because of his homosexuality and general disdain for other people.

Paul's self-destructive impulses intensify throughout the story. At first, he wishes to escape life by submerging himself in art. When Paul stands outside the soprano's house and listens to the symphony, Cather's language suggests his longing for oblivion. He wants to let art take him away, "blue league after blue league, away from everything." Paul spends an entire night imagining what would happen if his father took him for a burglar and shot him. More disturbingly, he also imagines what would happen if his father one day regretted *not* killing him. The implication is that Paul assumes that he will fail and disgust his father so drastically that his father will wish him dead. Toward the end of the story, we learn that Paul bought a gun when he arrived in New York because even at the outset of his adventure, he foresaw that he might need "a way to snap the thread." Several times, the narrator mentions a darkness in Paul, a fear that he has felt since he was a child. Paul ultimately commits suicide not because of one event or character trait. Rather, all his reasons for unhappiness, loneliness, and alienation converge and lead him to his decision to leap in front of a train.

THEMES, MOTIFS, AND SYMBOLS

THEMES

THE DANGER OF MISUNDERSTANDING MONEY   Paul is obsessed with money, and his belief that money will solve all his problems leads to unrelenting disappointment in his life. He thinks almost constantly about the humiliation of those who have little money and the power wielded by those who possess lots of it. He keenly analyzes his own slightly impoverished existence and hates every detail: cramped houses, grubby bathrooms, simple clothes, women's inelegant conversations, and men's worshipful attitude toward their bosses. He believes that money is the one way out of the existence he loathes. But it becomes clear that Paul will never become one of the prosperous men he idealizes because he has no understanding of the relationship between work and money. The narrator points out that there are boys like Paul who started at the bottom of the ladder and worked their way up until they became kings. Paul's father and the young clerk discuss just such men as Paul listens on the front porch. But while Paul is fascinated by the exotic haunts and exploits of these rich men, he has no interest at all in the "cash-boy stage" of their lives, those first days when they were as poor as he is. He longs for the spoils of hard work but cannot conceive of doing the hard work that leads to the spoils.

Paul views the small economies of his neighbors disdainfully, believing that only he understands the best way of building wealth. The fathers around him pinch pennies and pass on their thrifty ways to their children, taking pleasure in their skill with arithmetic and ability to accumulate coins in piggybanks. Paul sneers at this petty fixation on money, not understanding that the careful accumulation of funds is the best chance that he or anyone in his neighborhood has of moving up in the world. He believes that some people are born rich and others are born poor and dismisses the idea that in America, the boundaries between the two groups are fluid. Paul further believes that he was meant to be rich and that only by some terrible mistake was he born poor. Because Paul is so certain that he was destined for wealth, it comes as no surprise when he steals $1,000 in cash from his company. In some sense, he feels that he deserves money without working for it. In the end, Paul's obsession with money and failure to understand it are key causes of his downfall.

THE ADDICTIVE NATURE OF ART   In "Paul's Case," art acts as a dangerous drug, and Paul's addiction to it causes him endless problems. Although Paul feels happiest and most alive when he is surrounded by art—at the theater, listening to music, or gazing at paintings—his happiness is an illusion because he does not truly understand what he sees. Instead, he consumes art voraciously and unthinkingly, as if it is an addictive drug. For example, the narrator writes that although the music at Carnegie Hall means nothing to Paul, he loves it because it lets loose "some hilarious and potent spirit within him." This phrase describes an involuntary but highly pleasurable reaction, similar to the reaction inspired by addiction.

Much as addicts use their drug of choice to escape their everyday lives, Paul uses art to escape his own consciousness. When he gazes at the painting in the Carnegie Hall gallery and again when he listens to the symphony, he is described as losing himself. The aftermath, however, is ugly, and Paul is shaken and irritable after his bouts with the arts. His high does not linger, and coming down from it is difficult. Cather emphasizes Paul's unintellectual response to art by pointing out that he does not read novels. He avoids books, the narrator says, because "he got what he wanted much more quickly from music." Just like an addict in search of a fix, Paul needs to consume art as easily and fast as he can. Anything that requires sustained concentration or intellectual appreciation, such as novels, is too time-consuming. Theater, music, and paintings provide Paul with instant, though shallow, gratification.

THE ALIENATION OF HOMOSEXUALS   Cather suggests strongly that Paul has homosexual leanings that make his life difficult and contribute to how alienated he feels from others. Modern readers might find her portrait of his homosexuality shallow and uncomfortably stereotypical: Paul is petrified by rats, splashes cologne on himself, and is fastidious about odors and dirt. The only woman who interests Paul is the soprano he sees at Carnegie Hall, a middle-aged woman described as "the mother of many children" and a clear substitute for Paul's own deceased mother. The prospect of heterosexual relations seems to repulse Paul. He is unsettled, for example, by the young clerk's marriage to a nearsighted schoolmistress and by the couple's four children. Paul is most interested in boys. He tussles with the other young ushers at the theater and latches on to Charley Edwards, who allows Paul to help him dress for performances. The narrator notes that Charley thinks Paul has a vocation. The kind of vocation is not specified, and we infer that Paul has an affinity both for the theater and for men, as does Charley.

Paul's homosexuality makes him feel deeply alienated from society. Although he seems to achieve a certain acceptance from a few groups and individuals, the details are so vague that we can assume the acceptance was hardly overt or fulfilling. He has no close friends, and the narrator suggests that his advances are often rebuffed. When Paul meets the rich student from Yale, he makes a brief connection, and the two share a wild night out on the town. But although their friendship begins with "confiding warmth," they part coldly. The narrator describes this change in the space of one sentence, which suggests how quickly the tone of the relationship goes from hot to cold. It is possible that the change occurs because Paul made a pass at the Yale student and was turned down. It is also possible that the two boys shared an encounter that left both of them embarrassed and upset. Whatever happened, Paul is again left alone, and the stage is set for his solitary descent into despair.

MOTIFS

COLORS Cather often uses colors to suggest personality and mood. Yellow is associated with the repulsion Paul feels for his home. After following the soprano to her hotel, he dreads returning to his room with its yellow wallpaper. Later, surrounded by luxury at the Waldorf, he thinks with horror of that yellow wallpaper. The young clerk is associated with red. His face and mouth are red, which reflects his formerly wild nature, now tamed by his conventional life. Riches are associated with the color purple. Paul scorns his teachers for failing to decorate their buttonholes with purple violets, as rich people might. He orders violets and jonquils for his rooms at the Waldorf. He is happy during dinner in the hotel, feeling that no one will question "the purple"—that is, that no on will question his masquerade as a rich boy.

Cather uses white and blue to portray Paul himself. His teeth, lips, and face are pale, which suggests his emotional strain. White is also a positive color for him: white snow often falls during his days in New York, where he is happiest. The drawing master notices the blue veins on Paul's face. Paul loses himself in the "blue Venetian scene or two" and the "blue Rico" in the gallery, and listens to the *Blue Danube* at the Waldorf. He longs to let art carry him away into a blue sea. The two colors combine in his imagination. The theater is described as Paul's "bit of blue-and-white Mediterranean shore," and he thinks of the sea just before he dies.

FOOD Mentions of food as well as the smell and preparation of it recur throughout "Paul's Case." Paul associates nauseating food with his house on Cordelia Street. After following the soprano to her hotel, he feels revulsion at the thought of ordinary food and scent of cooking spread throughout a house. The narrator describes Paul's ordinary life as a "flavorless, colorless mass," a phrase that would apply equally well to an unappetizing plate of food. Paul is also disgusted by the dishtowels and dishwater that must be used to clean plates dirtied by food. Before visiting Charley Edwards, he tries to rid his fingers of the smell of dishwater by putting cologne on them.

Although the food of his own people repulses Paul, the food of rich people tantalizes him. He pores over pictures of fancy dinner parties in magazines and imagines the delicious food and drink the soprano will enjoy in her hotel. Once he reaches the Waldorf, he is overwhelmed by the dining room's beauty and amazing sight of champagne frothing in his glass.

In fact, food is not mentioned in the description of Paul's first dinner at the Waldorf. It is as if the most genteel food hardly has any smell at all. During that first dinner, Paul can hardly believe that he comes from a place where the men's clothes smell like food.

SYMBOLS

RED CARNATIONS   The red carnations Paul often wears in his buttonhole represent Paul himself. At the beginning of the story, when Paul wears a red carnation to meet his teachers and principal, the adults correctly interpret its presence as evidence of Paul's continued defiance. They want him to show remorse, but the jaunty flower proves that he feels none. At the end of the story, Paul buys red carnations. As he walks to the train tracks, he notices that they have wilted in the cold. He buries one of the flowers in the snow before leaping in front of a train. The carnation's burial is a symbolic prelude to Paul's actual suicide.

SHORT STORY ANALYSIS

A CLINICAL VIEW OF A SUICIDAL YOUNG MAN   "Paul's Case" is notable for its complete absence of dramatized scenes. Typically, short-story writers strive for a balance of exposition (discourse in which the narrator simply provides information and description for the reader) and dramatization (fully drawn scenes in which characters speak to each other). "Paul's Case" is composed entirely of exposition. It contains only three pieces of dialogue: Paul's weak explanation of his bad behavior, the art teacher's mention of Paul's mother's death, and the young clerk's awed account of his boss's productivity. Even these words of dialogue come in the midst of exposition.

The story's subtitle, "A Study in Temperament," provides the explanation for this unusual structure. Cather is less interested in writing a traditional short story than she is in providing a case study of a suicidal young man. Each piece of exposition explains or elaborates on a motivation for Paul's eventual suicide. By the time Paul leaps in front of the train, we recognize a number of reasons for his action: the death of his mother, his longing to join the upper class, his idealized love for the arts, his homosexual tendencies, his alienation from society, and his impossible craving for money. By doing away with dramatized scenes, Cather produces the effect of a story extrapolated from a doctor's notes on the causes of a patient's suicide. Modern critics have diagnosed Paul as delusional and narcissistic. These terms were not in common usage when "Paul's Case" was first published; Cather wrote the story several years before Freud became popular in America. However, the story certainly anticipates America's fascination with analysis, and Cather's subtitle emphasizes her own interest in studying Paul's psyche.

THE SELF-ABSORPTION OF THE CLINICALLY DEPRESSED   "Paul's Case" is intentionally claustrophobic. Told in close third-person narration, it hardly ever strays outside the confines of Paul's mind. This extremely focused point of view conveys the intense self-involvement of deeply unhappy people. Paul is so wrapped up in his own depression that he cannot think about others. Not until midway through the story do we learn about the existence of Paul's sisters. Even then, they are mentioned only in passing and never named. After using one of them to justify a lie to his classmates, Paul never thinks or speaks about them again. He doesn't consider the feelings of his father, who lost his wife when his children were very young. Instead, he dismisses his father as an annoyance to be avoided and lied to. It doesn't occur to him that his father worries about his whereabouts only because he loves him. Paul also never thinks about what it means that his father paid back the money he stole and set out for New York to find him. Like the sisters, Paul's father is never named.

Cather's tight focus on Paul's point of view mirrors his self-absorption. His egoism blots out everyone, not just his family. The only people he observes with interest are those he idealizes—and he fails to see them as they really are. The soprano, Charley Edwards, and the Yale student are not real people for Paul but rather figures in a fantasyland of theater and money. He imagines that the soprano is a queen of romance, when in fact she is a middle-aged mother of several kids. He believes that Charley walks through a magic portal into the theater world, when Charley is actually a youngster in an unremarkable local troupe. He views the Yale student as the boy he himself was meant to be, when in reality the two can hardly get along for the space of one night. Whether Paul is ignoring the people who love him or fantasizing about those who hardly know him, he demonstrates his inability to think of anyone but himself. Even in the seconds before he dies, his last thought is for the places he won't get to see, rather than the family members who will mourn his death.

PAUL'S SCORN FOR THE MIDDLE CLASS Some of the most memorable passages in "Paul's Case" are the descriptions of Paul's neighborhood, which seethe with anger and resentment. Paul's beloved worlds of theater and money are often described in vague terms because Paul knows almost nothing real about them. In contrast, the world of Cordelia Street brims with concrete details, and it is these details that are so upsetting to Paul. The narrator describes Paul's wooden bed, the cushions on which the housewives sit, the bellies of the men, the conversations about the children's progress in school, and the portraits of George Washington and John Calvin that hang in Paul's room. The details that horrify Paul the most get repeated: the yellow wallpaper, smell of cooking, and love of arithmetic. The repetition of these details reveals the class hatred that plays continuously in Paul's mind. Every mention of the neighborhood and its trappings drips with loathing. Paul hates the piety and work ethic of the people he comes from. He despises the very place that is most real in his mind and longs for the abstract world of the upper class.

The angry tone of these passages brings up an issue that recurs throughout the story: the extent to which the narrator—and, by extension, Cather—sympathizes with Paul. On first reading, it is tempting to conclude that the narrator presents Paul as a hero or at least a traditional protagonist. We might assume that the narrator considers Paul's suicide the only way out of a world that does not understand him. A closer look, however, shows that the narrator is highly critical of Paul. In the passages about his middle-class neighborhood, the narrator is showing, rather than sharing, Paul's fury. Cather wants her readers to understand that despite what Paul believes, the residents of Cordelia Street are actually hardworking, decent people. And although Paul's depression is treated with sympathy, his scornfulness and other shortcomings are not. Cather asks us to recognize that Paul's anger at his family and his neighbors is the typical product of teenage sullenness, not a valid or romantic reason for suicide.

IMPORTANT QUOTATIONS EXPLAINED

---

1. *The members of the stock company were vastly amused when some of Paul's stories reached them—especially the women. They were hardworking women, most of them supporting indigent husbands or brothers, and they laughed rather bitterly at having stirred the boy to such fervid and florid inventions.*

This quotation appears midway through the story, after Paul has been removed from school, and reveals one of the subtler tragedies of "Paul's Case": the nonexistence of the art world that Paul dreams of. The art world exists, of course, but it is not the land of romance, happiness, and elegance that Paul imagines. He thinks of theater people as far more refined and elegant than his neighbors are. Ironically, the professionals in the art world must work *harder* than Paul's neighbors. The women on Cordelia Street have conscientious husbands and are free to relax on their porches on the weekends; the women of the theater must toil to support their "indigent husbands or brothers." When these theater women hear about Paul's "fervid and florid inventions" concerning their livelihood, they laugh "rather bitterly," a phrase that suggests their impatience with Paul's unrealistic dreams. It is distressing to reflect that Paul's hatred of his own life is founded on a misunderstanding. If he knew the truth about the art world, Cather suggests, he would see that it is not more desirable than the world of Cordelia Street.

---

2. *Until now he could not remember the time when he had not been dreading something. Even when he was a little boy it was always there—behind him, or before, or on either side. There had always been the shadowed corner, the dark place into which he dared not look, but from which something seemed always to be watching him—and Paul had done things that were not pretty to watch, he knew.*

This passage comes after the narrator's revelation of Paul's theft and flight to New York. Safe in his room at the Waldorf, Paul feels content, not fearful, for the first time in his life. "[T]he shadowed corner, the dark place" Paul cannot bear to think about may refer to his homosexuality. The ambiguous assertion that "Paul had done things that were not pretty to watch" may be an oblique reference to socially unacceptable sexual acts. The narrator's evasions and hints about Paul's homosexuality mirror Paul's inability to think about his orientation. However, "the dark place" may also be a catch-all phrase to describe Paul's sizable collection of neuroses and causes for depression. He never knew his mother, does not fit in anywhere, has no friends, is unable to think of anyone but himself, and dreams of losing consciousness. All of these difficulties may be crammed into "the shadowed corner" that Paul would rather ignore than confront.

The passage is also notable for its focus on watching and being watched. Throughout the story, Paul acts as if he is being observed, much as an actor on a stage might. Often, as in this passage, he seems tormented by his imaginary audience. He longs to know that any onlooker would find him well-dressed, debonair, confident, and normal, but he knows that he is none of these things. His discomfort with the idea of being watched may explain his disinclination to be an active member in the art world he idealizes. Paul would much rather be in the audience than onstage.

3. *It occurred to him that all the flowers he had seen in the glass cases that first night must have gone the same way, long before this. It was only one splendid breath they had, in spite of their brave mockery at the winter outside the glass; and it was a losing game in the end, it seemed, this revolt against the homilies by which the world is run.*

Before he leaps in front of a train to his death, Paul thinks about the flowers that he saw in New York. In this passage, Cather explicitly makes a connection between the glass-protected flowers, which make one brief stand against the winter, and Paul, who makes one brief stand against society. Like the flowers struggling to survive in the midst of winter, Paul is attempting to live in a world that he feels is hostile to him. The flowers' "one splendid breath" parallels Paul's eight-day stint impersonating a rich boy. Neither the flowers nor Paul have a chance at survival. They are fragile, out of place, and doomed.

Paul is egocentric, naïve, snobbish, and weak, but in passages like these, Cather shows sympathy for him. She asks us not to condemn him too harshly, despite his unjustifiable actions. She suggests that Paul cannot help his nature any more than the flowers can help their color or constitution. Although it is clear that his ways of thinking and acting are undesirable, it is also clear that, in his way, he is noble. He does try to "revolt against the homilies by which the world is run," even if his revolt ends up being a misguided failure.

P

A Perfect Day for Bananafish

J. D. Salinger
(1919–   )

CONTEXT

Jerome David (J. D.) Salinger is one of the most beloved and secretive American novelists of the twentieth century, as famous for being a recluse as he is for his fiction. Born in 1919 to a Jewish father and Irish-Catholic mother, Salinger spent his childhood in New York City, where he was part of the affluent social circles that he would later write about. Salinger attended the Valley Forge Military Academy and served in the army during World War II. After the war, he enrolled at Ursinus College in Pennsylvania and later took writing courses at Columbia University. Salinger began his literary career by writing short stories for magazines in the late 1940s. He admired and emulated the sparse prose style of Hemingway and Fitzgerald and, like Hemingway, wrote about darker aspects of human nature, death, and suicide.

"A Perfect Day for Bananafish" appeared in the *New Yorker* in 1948 and was later republished as the opening story in the collection *Nine Stories* (1953). In "A Perfect Day for Bananafish," Salinger introduces the Glass family, who would become recurring characters in his fiction. In the next ten years, Salinger published three other Glass family stories in the *New Yorker*: "Franny," "Zooey," and "Raise High the Roof-Beam, Carpenters." These stories appear in Salinger's other books, which include *Franny and Zooey* (1961) and *Raise the Roof Beam, Carpenters, and Seymour: An Introduction* (1963). Critics revered *Nine Stories*, but Salinger's other works were not so well received. The siblings of the Glass family were criticized for being unkind and obnoxious.

Salinger's first novel, *Catcher in the Rye* (1951), was the critical and popular success that launched Salinger into both literary fame and social scandal. *Catcher* quickly became an American classic, and its protagonist, Holden Caulfield, became the voice of a generation that was coming of age in the postwar era. After the popular success and controversy of *Catcher* and the criticism of his subsequent works, Salinger isolated himself from the world, publishing little and maintaining a private life.

Salinger wrote "Bananafish" in postwar America, when many veterans of World War II were struggling with the readjustment to civilian life. The story includes many of the elements that Salinger revisits throughout his career, including the idea of the outsider, male angst, critique of New York society, contempt for materialism, and the redemptive nature of children. Seymour Glass, like many of Salinger's other protagonists, is an unhappy outsider, critiquing the society of which he is part. Salinger's heroes are most like him in this regard — outsiders who are dissatisfied with society and therefore remove themselves from it by either self-seclusion (like Salinger himself) or suicide.

PLOT OVERVIEW

Muriel Glass waits in her Florida hotel room for the operator to put her call through to her mother. The hotel is full for a sales convention, so she must wait a long time. She fixes her clothing, paints her nails, and reads a magazine. When the call does go through, Muriel reassures her anxious mother about her safety. Her mother is concerned about the erratic, reckless behavior of Seymour, Muriel's husband. She hints at a car accident that Seymour and Muriel were involved in and suggests that Seymour deliberately crashed Muriel's father's car into a tree. She reminds Muriel of the strange and rude things Seymour has said to members of Muriel's family. Seymour has recently returned from the war, and Muriel's mother believes that he was discharged from the military hospital prematurely. Muriel is not as concerned as her mother. She is preoccupied by the fashion at the resort and the evening's events. In the evenings, there are formal dinners and cocktail parties, at which Seymour often sits apart, playing the piano. The resort is full of society people, although Muriel feels that the quality of these people has diminished since the war. She tells her mother that Seymour is on the beach by himself.

On the beach, three-year-old Sybil Carpenter lets her mother put sunscreen on her body. Mrs. Carpenter then sends Sybil away so that she can go have cocktails. Sybil wanders far from the part of the beach where the hotel guests are situated. Eventually, she finds Seymour, who knows her. He tells her he likes her blue bathing suit, but her suit is yellow. Sybil accuses him of letting another little girl, Sharon Lipschutz, sit on the bench with him while he played the piano. Seymour assures Sybil that she is his favorite. Sybil tells Seymour he should push Sharon off the piano bench next time. As they get ready to go into the ocean, Seymour tells Sybil they should look for bananafish. They then discuss the tigers in one of Sybil's children's books, *Black Sambo*, as well as Sybil's fondness for olives and wax. Sybil asks Seymour whether he likes Sharon Lipschutz, and Seymour tells her that he does, especially the fact that she is nice to small dogs and always kind.

In the water, Seymour puts Sybil onto the raft and says it's a perfect day for bananafish. He explains that these are normal-looking fish that swim into banana holes and greedily eat all the bananas inside. As a result, the bananafish become so fat that they cannot leave their holes and die. Doubtful of the fish at first, Sybil tells Seymour that she sees a bananafish with six bananas in his mouth. Seymour kisses the arch of Sybil's foot. Sybil protests, and when they get out of the water, Sybil runs back to the hotel.

Seymour, alone again, collects his things and returns to the resort. On his way to his room, he accuses a woman in the elevator of looking at his feet. When the woman denies it, Seymour becomes irate, calling her a "God-damned sneak." The woman leaves the elevator. Seymour proceeds to his room, where Muriel is napping. Sitting on the other bed, he watches her. Then he takes a gun from his luggage and shoots himself in the head.

CHARACTER LIST

Seymour Glass   A man who has recently returned from the war, where he suffered psychological trauma. A strange outsider, Seymour rejects the company of his wife, Muriel, and other adults at the Florida resort where he and Muriel are on vacation. He prefers to play with children at the resort and on the beach. He has an easy rapport with children and fully immerses himself in a childlike world of imagination when he is with them. When a child named Sybil claims she sees a bananafish, a creature that Seymour has invented, he kisses her foot. Seymour ultimately kills himself in the hotel.

Muriel Glass   Seymour's pretty, socialite wife. Muriel is unconcerned with Seymour's mental condition, although whether she is unconcerned because of indifference or deep love for him is never fully clear. Enamored with beauty and materialistic society, Muriel is firmly rooted in the materialistic world that Seymour rejects as well as in the adult world of woman-hood and sexuality. In rejecting Muriel, Seymour rejects both society and adulthood.

Sybil Carpenter   A young child vacationing with her mother. Sybil befriends Seymour on the beach and is able to understand him better than any other character, perhaps because her innocence has been untainted—unlike Seymour, she has not seen the ugliness of the world. However, Sybil is unnerved by Seymour when he kisses her foot in the ocean. Although Sybil is part of the childhood innocence Seymour would like to repossess, the kiss is an inappropriate gesture. Seymour has crossed a line, and Sybil runs away from him when they return to shore.

Muriel's Mother   A nosey socialite who is frantically concerned with Muriel's safety around the erratic Seymour. Muriel's mother reveals some of Seymour's past transgressions, including strange, dangerous behavior and rude comments to family members, all of which suggest the extent of Seymour's psychological distress.

Mrs. Carpenter   Sybil's mother. Preoccupied with drinking and gossiping, Mrs. Carpenter carelessly allows Sybil to play by herself on the beach, unaware that she is associating with a strange man.

ANALYSIS OF MAJOR CHARACTERS

SEYMOUR GLASS   Seymour is an unrepentant outsider among his wife, his wife's family, the guests at the Florida resort, and society in general. Intelligent but psychologically damaged from the war, he has lost his footing in accepted adult society and renounces this society in favor of poetry, music, and children. He is pale whereas the other guests are tan, and antisocial whereas the others enjoy mingling at cocktail parties and dinners. While Muriel socializes, Seymour plays the piano by himself or spends time with children at the beach. Always, he is apart from the crowd, moving through a world that is saturated more with yearned-for innocence than with adult realities. For much of the story, Seymour seems placid and quiet, a stark contrast to the unbalanced, erratic Seymour that Muriel and her mother discuss on the phone. His outsider status seems, if not "normal," then at least harmless. However, when Seymour angrily accuses the woman in the elevator of looking at his feet, another side of him becomes clear. Ultimately, Seymour is unable to reconcile his outsider status with society and kills himself.

Although Seymour's interactions with children, particularly Sybil, are rooted in his desire for a return to innocence, modern readers may find it difficult to ignore the uncomfortable sexual undertones. On the surface, Seymour's actions are harmless, even childlike. For example, he plays with Sybil and talks to her in a silly, childlike way, and he allows Sharon Lipschutz to sit with him on the piano bench, as though they are both children retreating from the adults in the room. However, Seymour also disrobes in front of Sybil, which he will not do in front of Muriel. He is a lone, adult man playing with a child not his own while her mother is not around, touching her physically as he lifts her onto a raft and kisses her foot. He also spins the tale of the bananafish, which seem blatantly phallic. Nothing comes of this talk, and Seymour's struggle to achieve a kind of new innocence ultimately renders his words harmless. But as the scene on the beach is followed by his violent outburst in the elevator and then his suicide, his actions and words take on a darker, more adult character, unfair and inaccurate as that characterization may be.

MURIEL GLASS   Muriel, a pretty and self-interested socialite, is firmly entrenched in the superficial, materialistic world in which Seymour is an outsider. She places great importance on her appearance, spends time reading vapid magazines, and is concerned with the horrendous fashion she sees at the Florida resort. When Sybil asks Seymour where Muriel is, Seymour says, "She may be in one of a thousand places. At the hairdresser's. Having her hair dyed mink." Muriel elicits nothing but scorn from Seymour presumably since he came home from the war, although she is not overly concerned with his behavior, even his calling her "Miss Spiritual Tramp 1948."

Muriel's unconcern suggests devotion to Seymour as well as indifference and naïveté. She willingly drove to Florida with him even after he crashed her father's car, and she defends him against her mother's wild, worried accusations. Though her mother criticizes Seymour's erratic behavior, Muriel dismisses it and seems to accept that Seymour's behavior is part of who he is. However, her unconcern also suggests that she is indifferent to Seymour's mental health and well-being. Clearly, he has been psychologically damaged in the war, yet Muriel only half-heartedly pursues answers and information from a psychiatrist at the resort. She all but ignores Seymour during their trip, never pressuring him to make more effort to be social or trying to make him fit into social norms. Ultimately, her lack of concern reveals her naïveté. Seymour is and has been truly disturbed, but even at his moment of greatest crisis—when he takes the gun from his luggage and shoots himself in the head—Muriel has no idea of the extent of Seymour's distress. Her lack of concern may well have been a strange form of devotion, but it ultimately enabled Seymour to carry out his violent suicide.

SYBIL CARPENTER   Young Sybil, like Seymour, is alone and misunderstood. Her mother misunderstands her chanting of Seymour Glass's name as the nonsense words "see more glass," which suggests that Sybil, too, lives in a world were no one understands her. With Seymour, however, she speaks freely and randomly, and Seymour listens intently and responds in kind. More important, she seems to understand Seymour in a way that adults cannot. She enters his imaginary world easily, willingly engaging in his silly talk and fantastical claims about bananafish. For a brief time, she and Seymour inhabit the same imaginary universe, creating life on their own terms, from their own minds. Sybil breaks the dream, protesting when Seymour kisses her foot. Although she is the child and Seymour is the adult, she is the one who is more willing to return to the real world, and when she runs from Seymour back to the hotel, she does so "without regret."

The name *Sybil* suggests an allusion to Greek mythology, in which sibyls are figures who can see the future. Sybil is a kind of seer because she is able to see the bananafish that Seymour describes. In some ways, she seems to be wise beyond her years, recognizing that Seymour needs for her to "see" what he sees. Her ability to "see" the bananafish ultimately suggests her ability to understand Seymour. Her connection with him, however, cannot save his life, even though it granted him a final moment of happiness.

THEMES, MOTIFS, AND SYMBOLS

THEMES

THE DIFFICULTY OF TRUE COMMUNICATION   Throughout "A Perfect Day for Bananafish," characters struggle to communicate with one another, and each attempt is fraught with difficulty. Muriel and her mother engage in a haphazard conversation in which Muriel never really hears her mother's worries and Muriel's mother never really hears Muriel's reassurances that she is fine. The two women talk *at* rather than *with* each other, and neither woman succeeds in truly communicating her thoughts to the other. When Muriel attempts to talk with the psychiatrist at the resort, their communication is hindered by the noise around them. Seymour is entirely unable to communicate with other people at the resort, preferring to sit alone playing the piano or spend time at the beach rather than try to enter into a society in which he feels like an outsider. Sybil's mother fails to communicate with Sybil clearly, believing that Sybil says "see more glass" when she is actually talking about Seymour Glass. Only Sybil and Seymour seem able to communicate effectively, although their discourse is on a child's, not an adult's, level.

Though Muriel and Seymour do not speak with each other in the story, their communication is so fraught as to be nonexistent. Muriel has no idea what is really going on in Seymour's mind, and Seymour seemingly has no desire to explain to her how he feels. The most tragic lack of communication is Muriel's mistaken certainty that Seymour's mental health is fine. Seymour's violent suicide is, perhaps, the one truly successful act of adult communication in the story, the one gesture that cannot be misread or ignored.

THE FUTILE SEARCH FOR INNOCENCE   Seymour hovers uncomfortably between the world of adult sexuality and world of childhood innocence. Scarred from his experiences in the war and suffering from psychological distress, Seymour finds refuge in children. Innocent and simple, they exist in a world that is free from adult suffering and greed. Unlike Muriel, who is fixated on appearances and class, Sybil can communicate with Seymour in a way that calms him. By speaking Sybil's language, Seymour may hope to reconnect to or return to a childlike, innocent state. Children and their world seem to hold the possibility of redemption.

A return to innocence proves to be impossible for Seymour. Though he is clearly distanced from Muriel emotionally, she is very much physically present. Their hotel room is suffused with the scents of her calfskin luggage and nail polish remover, and the physical space they share—in the car as they drove to Florida, in their hotel room, and at the resort—is small. Seymour's self-isolation is temporary at best, as he opts out of parties to play the piano or retreats to the beach. The world of childhood innocence has long been lost for Seymour, and he chooses suicide as an escape from the oppressive adult world in which he must otherwise live as an outsider.

MOTIFS

MATERIALISM   Salinger is critiquing the shallowness of materialism through Muriel and her world of wealth. Each time we see Muriel, she is luxuriating in wealth—she wears a white silk dressing gown, fixes her Saks blouse, meticulously paints her nails, and uses fine leather luggage. Seymour tells Sybil that Muriel may be getting her hair dyed "mink." These suggestions of a luxurious lifestyle demonstrate the divide between Muriel and Seymour. She reads women's magazines while Seymour reads poetry. She is more concerned with her clothes and the current fashion trends than with her husband's emotional and psychological problems. Even when she and her mother are discussing Seymour's erratic, dangerous behavior and unstable mental state, the talk keeps floating back to fashion and idle gossip. Muriel's obsession with material goods alienates Seymour from Muriel and her world, just as Mrs. Carpenter's indulgence in martinis and gossip shuts out Sybil.

SEEING   The idea of seeing permeates "A Perfect Day for Bananafish." Seymour's name sounds like "see more," a confusion that Sybil's mother falls prey to when Sybil talks to her about "see more glass." Sybil's name also references seeing; in Greek mythology, a sibyl was a seer. Seymour, or "see more," suggests that Seymour is literally able to see more than other people. Because of his traumatic experiences in the war, he has a greater understanding of life and can recognize the materialism and superficiality of the world around him. Like Seymour, Sybil can see what others cannot, though her openness is a function of her childishness rather than of trauma and regret. She easily sees the imaginary bananafish that Seymour tells her about and is therefore able to "see" Seymour in a way the adults in his life cannot.

SYMBOLS

BANANAFISH   Bananafish, the imaginary creatures that gorge themselves on bananas and then die of banana fever, represent Seymour and his struggles to reengage with society after returning from the war. Seymour, an outsider in a world that seems to be guided by materialism, greed, and pettiness, has no real outlet for the complicated emotions he carries around inside him. He has been psychologically damaged by the war and, having been released early from the Army hospital, is clearly not getting the care he needs. Muriel and her family exist in a world he does not understand, and his behavior in that world is inappropriate, disturbing, and dangerous. His devotion to Sybil and other children reveals his heartbreaking yearning for innocence and clarity, feelings that have no outlet in the adult world. Just as the bananafish become too fat to leave their holes, Seymour is "fat" from the overflow of painful emotions he cannot express. At the end of the story, he, like the bananafish, dies.

SHORT STORY ANALYSIS

HISTORICAL CONTEXT   Through his writing, Salinger critiques his cultural environment—the United States in the post–World War II era. In "A Perfect Day for Bananafish," Salinger critiques the materialistic consumer society of postwar America, which reveled in excess and gluttony. The country's economic boom prompted people to buy things that they or their parents had never before been able to acquire. This prosperous period marked a drastic departure from the scarcity necessitated by the war and the Depression that preceded it.

During this time, women were the target audience of marketing campaigns for products ranging from kitchen appliances to luxury clothes to magazines. For a returning solider like Salinger or Seymour who was coming home from a devastated Europe, this new American boom led to disorientation and unease.

The criticisms conveyed in "A Perfect Day for Bananafish" would not become a mainstream movement for another ten years, and Salinger's work fits into the larger artistic movement of postmodernism, which began in the 1960s. Postmodernist writers created works that were often minimalist in style, ambiguous in content, and heavily reliant on dialogue to convey meaning. The postmodern writing of Hemingway, Faulkner, and Salinger was the building block for the antiestablishment movement of the 1960s. The antiestablishment movement in literature, music, and society in general rejected the empty materialism of the postwar era and strived to regain a state of childlike innocence. Salinger's influence on this movement can been seen in writers such as Jack Kerouac and Tom Wolfe, both of whom use outsider antiheros of dubious moral worth.

IMPORTANT QUOTATIONS EXPLAINED

1. *"Did you see more glass?"*
   "Pussycat, stop saying that. It's driving Mommy absolutely crazy."

This exchange between Sybil and her mother, which appears about halfway through the story, is an example of how difficult clear communication is for the characters in the story. While Sybil is referring to Seymour Glass, Mrs. Carpenter hears "see more glass" and thinks Sybil is being silly. Mother and daughter are speaking different languages — Seymour Glass is a figure who exists solely in Sybil's world of childhood, whereas the phonetic interpretation, "see more glass," is Mrs. Carpenter's adult take on the phrase. This exchange also reveals Sybil as an outsider in her mother's adult world, just as Seymour is. This exchange is markedly different from the conversations between Sybil and Seymour. Seymour, unlike Mrs. Carpenter, understands Sybil and is kind and patient with her — in a way, he speaks the language of childhood.

2. *"If you want to look at my feet, say so," said the young man. "But don't be a God-damned sneak about it."*

As Seymour returns to his room at the end of the story, he accuses a woman in the elevator of looking at his feet. When she denies this claim, he becomes irate. This unfounded anger illustrates two parts of Seymour's character. First, such a violent and unprovoked outburst shows that he really is mentally unstable. While Muriel has spoken with her mother about Seymour's psychological condition, this is the only direct evidence in the story that Seymour is in fact not well. Second, Seymour is angry with the woman for being a "sneak" — that is, for being inauthentic. This is a criticism against the materialistic world of the hotel, where appearances rule. Shortly after this exchange, Seymour commits suicide, and in a way, this outburst is an attempt to have one final interaction or communication with the adult world. His effort is inappropriate and disturbing, but its violence reveals the extent of Seymour's psychological distress.

3. *Then he went over sat down on the unoccupied bed, looked at the girl, aimed the pistol, and fired a bullet through his right temple.*

The final sentences of the story demonstrate Salinger's control of language to create tone and tension. These short phrases portray Seymour's actions as calm and matter-of-fact—there is no room for doubt or hesitation in the abrupt phrases. Tension builds as the actions pile up, and until the last moment, there is some ambiguity about whom Seymour will shoot—this may be the crazy act that Muriel's mother worried Seymour would perpetrate. Instead, Seymour shoots himself, ending his life and the story at the same time. The suicide is so sudden, and at first Seymour's reasons for doing it seem wholly unclear—he seems unhappy and cut off from the world, yes, but his afternoon on the beach with Sybil did little to suggest that this was to come. However, the story can be read as a slow, simmering buildup of actions and problems, which makes Seymour's suicide shocking but not necessarily a surprise.

The Red-Headed League

Arthur Conan Doyle
(1859–1930)

CONTEXT

Born in Edinburgh, Scotland, on May 22, 1859, Doyle was the son of an Irish painter who specialized in fantasy scenes. Doyle was sent to England at age nine to attend boarding school, an experience he deeply loathed. He then enrolled in medical school, after which he briefly served as a naval doctor before entering into private practice. He moved around southern England until he finally settled in the town of Southsea. Doyle had written for his own pleasure up until this point in his life but succeeded in publishing A *Study in Scarlet* in 1887, a slim novel that introduced the world to Sherlock Holmes.

Doyle wrote another Sherlock Holmes novel, *The Sign of Four*, in 1890, and moved with his wife, Louise, to London in 1891. By this time, Doyle had decided to become an eye doctor, especially because his first two Sherlock Holmes novels had not been financial successes. Ironically, however, Doyle found that he had few patients and was consequently left with plenty of time to write. By switching formats and writing Holmes mysteries as short stories rather than novels, Doyle was able to capitalize on his talent for writing rapid, engrossing plots and minimize some of the tedium that had plagued his earlier work. Serialized in the popular magazine, the *Strand*, Sherlock Holmes and his adventures became an overnight phenomenon, electrifying readers throughout the English-speaking world. "The Red-Headed League" first appeared in the *Strand* in 1891 and was published a year later with eleven other stories as *The Adventures of Sherlock Holmes*.

In a matter of months, Doyle went from a struggling eye doctor to one of the most famous writers in the world. He quickly grew tired of being solely identified with Holmes, however. So in 1893, he killed off his fictional detective in a climactic battle with the evil Professor Moriarity. Readers in Britain and the United States mourned the loss of their hero, and grown men were seen to wear black armbands for weeks afterward.

Doyle continued to write both fiction and nonfiction throughout the 1890s, although none of his works were as popular as the Sherlock Holmes stories. Hoping to boost his popularity and sales, Doyle revived Sherlock Holmes again in 1901 with *The Hound of the Baskervilles*, a novel many critics regard as one of the greatest mysteries ever written. In 1903, he began writing Holmes stories again and continued to do so almost until his death in 1930. In addition to many other works, he published *The Lost World*, a popular science-fiction novel, in 1912.

The success of the Sherlock Holmes stories can hardly be overstated. Almost single-handedly, Doyle inaugurated two massive changes in literature. First, he transformed the short story from a mildly successful exercise into a major literary form capable of sustaining both an enormous readership and a longstanding critical interest. Second, Doyle perfected and popularized the detective story, which went on to become the most popular new genre of fiction in the twentieth century. Previous writers such as Edgar Allen Poe had published short stories and mysteries before, but all had failed to energize readers to the degree that Doyle's Holmes energized them. Readers also identified with Holmes's real-world London and liked the fact that they had the opportunity to solve the mysteries along with the hero. Sherlock Holmes had become so popular that by the end of the twentieth century he'd appeared in more than 100 films, more than 700 radio dramas, and more than 2,000 stories and novels. Perhaps only Mickey Mouse rivals Holmes as the most recognizable fictional character of the past century.

Much of Doyle's popularity today stems from his vivid description of late-Victorian London. From the defeat of Napoleon in 1815 to the start of World War I in 1914, Britain was the dominant military power in the world. As a result, London was both the world's largest city and the center of the most extensive and powerful empire in history by the end of the nineteenth century. Victorian London was also a city of mystery: a place of dark fogs, horse-drawn carriages, and Jack the Ripper. In other words, even though London at the end of the nineteenth century was the de facto capital of the world, Londoners were still deeply interested in their city's dark undercurrents. Readers today find this mix of power and mystery fascinating and share with Doyle's contemporaries a love for the way in which the intellect of Sherlock Holmes cuts through the shadows, illuminating the darkness with pure reason.

PLOT OVERVIEW

Doctor John Watson steps into the home of his friend, the famous private detective Sherlock Holmes. Watson, the story's narrator, finds Holmes deep in conversation with Jabez Wilson, a man who would be entirely unremarkable except for his blazing red hair. Holmes asks Watson to stay and lend his assistance, claiming that he has never heard a case as bizarre as Jabez Wilson's.

Wilson reveals that he is a pawnbroker and has an assistant named Vincent Spaulding, who is working for half the usual salary to learn the business. Wilson says that Spaulding is a fine worker, although he is interested in photography and often goes alone into the basement of the shop to develop photos. About two months ago, Spaulding drew Wilson's attention to an advertisement in the paper for an opening in the League of Red-Headed Men. According to Spaulding, the league is a foundation established by an eccentric and wealthy American to promote the interests of redheaded men by paying them to perform small tasks. Spaulding encouraged Wilson to apply, and the two went to the offices listed in the advertisement. After fighting through a crowd of redheaded men waiting outside, Spaulding and Wilson made their way to the manager, another redheaded man by the name of Duncan Ross, who promptly hired Wilson. The league paid Wilson to copy pages of the *Encyclopedia Britannica*, forbidding him from leaving the office for any reason during his four-hour shifts.

Wilson says that he worked for the league for eight weeks and was paid handsomely for his efforts. The morning on which the story begins, however, Wilson arrived at the offices to find that the Red-Headed League had been dissolved and that Duncan Ross was nowhere to be found. Wilson went immediately to Sherlock Holmes, hoping that Holmes could help him find out whether he had been the victim of a practical joke. Holmes asks Wilson a few questions about Vincent Spaulding and discovers that Spaulding came to work for Wilson only about a month before the whole mysterious affair began. Holmes tells Wilson that he will have an answer in a few days.

After smoking three pipes in a row, Holmes leaps up and asks Watson to accompany him to a concert. Along the way, they stop in front of Wilson's shop, where Holmes thumps his walking stick on the pavement and knocks on the door to ask Spaulding for directions. After Spaulding and Holmes finish talking, Holmes tells Watson that he believes that Spaulding is the fourth-smartest man in London. Holmes also tells Watson that he saw on the knees of Spaulding's trousers exactly what he wanted to see. Even though Watson is mystified by these remarks, Holmes refuses to explain them further and instead leads Watson around to a busy street behind Wilson's shop. Holmes notices aloud that there's a bank behind Wilson's shop, and, finished for the day, he and Watson go to the concert.

After the concert, Holmes asks Watson to meet him at his office at ten o'clock that night, saying that a serious crime is about to be committed. Watson agrees but is entirely bewildered by Holmes's actions. Watson notes that he and Holmes have seen and heard exactly the same information about the case but that Holmes seems to have arrived at some conclusions that he himself has failed to draw.

That night, Watson meets up with Holmes, along with two other men—a Scotland Yard detective named Peter Jones and a bank manager named Mr. Merryweather. Holmes says that the four men are about to have a run-in with John Clay, a notorious criminal. The men depart in carriages to Mr. Merryweather's City and Suburban Bank—the same bank Holmes and Watson had discovered behind Wilson's shop. The four men wait for an hour in the darkness of the cellar filled with French gold. Suddenly, they notice a light shining through a crack in the floor. The light gets brighter and brighter, until the crack finally widens and a man's hand breaks through. The man climbs out of the opening the floor and begins to help another man through when Holmes and Detective Jones leap on the two men. They capture the first man, John Clay, also known as Jabez Wilson's hardworking assistant, Vincent Spaulding. The other man escapes through the crack in the floor.

Later that night, Holmes tells Watson how he solved the case. Holmes realized from the beginning that the Red-Headed League was simply too preposterous to be real and that it must therefore have been a ploy to get Wilson out of his shop for a few hours every day. The fact that Spaulding was willing to work for so little money and spent a lot of time alone in the basement suggested to Holmes that Spaulding was doing something illicit in the cellar. When he noticed the bank nearby, Holmes had suspected that Spaulding was digging a tunnel to the bank. Holmes pounded on the sidewalk outside Wilson's shop to determine whether the ground was hollow underneath, and he knocked on the door for directions so that he could see whether the knees of Spaulding's pants were worn away. The fact that the league dissolved so suddenly suggested to Holmes that the robbery was imminent, and he was therefore able to make preparations and capture John Clay.

CHARACTER LIST

Sherlock Holmes   A private detective and the story's protagonist. Sherlock Holmes's keen observations and ability to reason allow him to solve puzzles that stymie everyone else. Sometimes quiet and contemplative, other times bursting with energy, Holmes uses methodology that can confuse and frustrate others. He is somewhat of a mystery, rarely divulging his thoughts until he's already solved the crime.

Dr. John Watson   Sherlock Holmes's partner and the story's narrator. Good-natured, brave, and down-to-earth, Watson is Sherlock Holmes's sidekick, even though he rarely helps Holmes actually solve any mysteries. His confusion with the mysteries and Holmes often mirrors readers' own confusion.

Jabez Wilson   A London pawnbroker. Jabez Wilson is an average man whose only remarkable feature is his shock of fiery red hair. His slow and trusting nature prevents him from seeing anything suspicious about either Vincent Spaulding or the preposterous Red-Headed League.

John Clay/Vincent Spaulding   A notorious criminal working at Jabez Wilson's pawnshop under the pseudonym Vincent Spaulding. Sinister and haughty, John Clay wins the respect of Sherlock Holmes because of his ingenious plot to rob the City and Suburban Bank.

Peter Jones   A Scotland Yard detective. Peter Jones is a tough police officer who both respects and distrusts Sherlock Holmes.

Mr. Merryweather   The manager of the City and Suburban Bank.

Archie/Duncan Ross/William Morris   John Clay's partner in crime. Archie's red hair prompts John Clay to devise the Red-Headed League to lure Wilson out of his pawnshop for four hours every day.

ANALYSIS OF MAJOR CHARACTERS

SHERLOCK HOLMES   Sherlock Holmes is one of the most recognizable figures in all of world literature, and it can often be difficult for readers to strip away their preconceptions about Holmes and see how the stories actually portray him. Most people think of Holmes as a force of pure reasoning, an almost superhuman mind capable of solving any puzzle. Although Doyle's stories do confirm this stereotype to some degree, they also complicate this image, as is clear in "The Red-Headed League." Here readers see multiple sides of Holmes: he moves from quiet contemplation to frantic activity, virtually asleep one moment and practically pushing Watson out the door in hot pursuit of clues the next. Watson comments that Holmes has a "dual nature," and readers see evidence of this throughout the story, as when Holmes transitions instantly from fervently investigating the clues at Wilson's house to lounging the day away in a concert hall. Holmes veers wildly from one extreme to the next, making him far more eccentric than first-time readers might expect.

Although these extremes of behavior might suggest that Holmes is not a realistic, well-rounded character, close readers of the story will notice that he is also capable of more complicated emotions. Holmes displays warm friendship for his "dear Watson" but usually rebuffs his friend's attempts to find out what he is thinking. Even more troubling is the question of Holmes's motives in solving cases. While Holmes does hand criminals over to the police, serving justice is not his primary concern. Instead, Holmes is primarily interested in the case as an intellectual challenge, a puzzle to be solved. At the end of the "The Red-Headed League," for example, Holmes suggests that his reward came from hearing an interesting case and settling a private score with John Clay, not from keeping the public safe by putting a known criminal behind bars. Even in the story's final moments, Doyle further complicates readers' image of Holmes, who responds indifferently to Watson's praise and says that he pursued the case solely to escape the boredom of everyday life. Holmes is therefore a character readers easily recognize as superhuman, but also one who is just as human as everyone else.

DR. JOHN WATSON   Even though he's the narrator of the story, Watson plays a surprisingly limited role. In fact, he does not help solve the case or even contribute to the action of the story in any way. That is not to say, however, that Watson is irrelevant. In fact, Watson is just as much the center of the story's form as Sherlock Holmes is the center of the story's plot. Watson shapes the story for readers, who see and understand only what Watson himself experiences. Watson's good nature, eagerness, and warm feelings for Holmes enliven the story and transform it from a mere recounting of a crime and its solution into a rich study of human behavior.

Doyle transforms the story from a straightforward mystery into a complex study by putting readers directly into Watson's shoes. Although far from dull, Watson is like most readers in that he simply isn't as observant as Holmes. The fact that he is so average and genial also makes him instantly accessible to readers. Readers don't always understand Holmes's reasoning, but they admire him all the more because of Watson's warm descriptions of him. Watson also tries to redeem Holmes for readers by suggesting that he is a benefactor of humanity, even though Holmes himself admits that he solves cases merely for his own recreation.

THEMES, MOTIFS, AND SYMBOLS

THEMES

THE PRESENCE OF THE BIZARRE IN EVERYDAY LIFE   "The Red-Headed League" depicts a world in which everyday life is filled with bizarre occurrences. Doyle's story is realistic in that it portrays recognizably human characters in recognizable settings, but it is unusual in its emphasis on the idea that the real world is a somewhat grotesque place, with the mundane and outlandish existing side by side. Watson notes, for example, that pawnbroker Jabez Wilson would be an entirely average man were it not for his absurdly bright red hair. The story of Wilson's misadventure further underscores this point by showing how an average man with a dull occupation can be suddenly and unexpectedly thrust into a strange and seemingly inexplicable situation. The story contains details and images that would almost be better suited to science fiction or a dream, such as Wilson's description of the streets of London being completely filled with redheaded men. The fact that Doyle portrays such images so realistically emphasizes his view that even everyday experiences can be utterly bizarre.

THE POWER OF REASON   Doyle emphasizes the power of logical reasoning throughout "The Red-Headed League" and in every other Sherlock Holmes story. Unlike other detectives, Holmes uses pure logic to cut right to the heart of any matter. Readers catch a glimpse of Holmes's powers of observation early, when he pieces together Jabez Wilson's past simply by paying attention to minor details that other people overlook, such as Wilson's worn coat jacket, his tattoo, and the firmness of his handshake. After Holmes explains how he reached his conclusions, Wilson remarks that Holmes's method is actually very simple, a point emphasized throughout the story. Although everyone has the ability to rationalize, few people take the opportunity to do so, even the intelligent Dr. Watson. Though Watson should be able to solve the case as easily as Holmes, he doesn't, and instead sits back to watch Holmes unravel the mystery. Like Watson, most people prefer to let others do the thinking for them.

MOTIFS

RED HAIR   Red hair highlights the presence of the bizarre in everyday life. Doyle repeatedly describes Jabez Wilson's and Archie's red hair to make this point, in addition to describing the unforgettable throng of redheaded men packing the streets of London. Doyle also emphasizes red hair to make a subtle pun on the term *red herring*, which is a false clue that writers often insert into their mysteries to thwart the hero's attempts to solve the puzzle. In this case, Wilson's and Archie's red hair really is a red herring, because the Red-Headed League is a false clue used to divert readers' attention from John Clay's intended bank robbery. Doyle is nudging readers to make the connection that red hair and the Red-Headed League are mere decoys, which should theoretically make the central mystery much easier to solve.

SYMBOLS

THE CELLAR   The pitch-black cellar where Watson, Holmes, Jones, and Merryweather wait for the bank robbers to appear represents the dark and seemingly impenetrable mystery of the Red-Headed League. Watson compares being in the cellar to being in a state of darkness he's never before experienced, the same way he feels about the entire bizarre pawnshop scenario, Wilson, and the confusing Red-Headed League. As with the story's central mystery, Watson and readers wait in the blackness of the cellar, comprehending nothing until a light penetrates the darkness and makes everything clear in accordance with Holmes's logical conclusions.

SHORT STORY ANALYSIS

THE FAIR-PLAY MYSTERY   "The Red-Headed League" is a quintessential "fair-play" mystery, in which readers know all the relevant clues at the same time that the detective does and therefore should theoretically be able to solve the crime on their own. This type of detective fiction is now common, thanks largely to the popular success of early fair play mysteries such as "The Red-Headed League" and other Sherlock Holmes stories. Because Doyle's story is such an early example of a fair-play mystery, readers can see Doyle experimenting with this new form of fiction, especially when he has Holmes tell Watson that he should be able to solve the mystery too. Because Watson is a stand-in for readers, Doyle is consequently instructing his audience that they too can piece together the puzzle if they just think things through.

Some readers have complained that Doyle withholds some evidence because Holmes rarely shares his thoughts with Watson. Watson is confused, for example, when Holmes taps the sidewalk outside Wilson's shop and asks Vincent Spaulding for directions. However, Doyle skirts this criticism by claiming that Holmes often behaves mysteriously because he's already solved important pieces of the riddle in his head. In this case, he's already figured out that Spaulding is digging an underground tunnel between the pawnshop and bank and merely wants to confirm his suspicions by listening for hollows under the ground and examining Spaulding's trousers. Although these actions aren't necessarily clues, they confirm what readers could have concluded themselves. The influence of fair-play mysteries such as "The Red-Headed League" on detective fiction has been enormous, because many readers enjoy feeling involved in the case, even if the ending still surprises them.

THE DYNAMISM OF VICTORIAN LONDON   One of the major elements of "The Red-Headed League" is the story's representation of the dynamic urban world of late-Victorian London. During the course of the nineteenth century, London more than quintupled in population, so it was easily the largest city in the world by 1900. Due to both its sheer size and crooked, irrational layout, many people saw London as fascinating but entirely mysterious and even somewhat dangerous. Although crime rates in London at the end of the nineteenth century were almost impossibly low by modern standards, London had an aura of darkness and risk that existed simultaneously with its atmosphere of imperial might and constant energy. "The Red-Headed League" captures both sides of London, describing it as both a city of light and a city of darkness.

Doyle's Sherlock Holmes stories illustrate the ways in which sinister mysteries unfold behind the seemingly nondescript storefronts of an average street in London. The proximity of Wilson's pawnshop in a quiet and dilapidated square to the City and Suburban Bank on the bustling avenue highlights London's diversity. Watson describes the difference between these two sides of the same block as being like the difference between the front of a picture and the back, one side all life and activity, the other a dark blankness. This contrast is reinforced by the different ways that Watson describes the city during the day and night. During the day, he and Holmes take the subway to Wilson's neighborhood, walk down some recognizable streets, and finally go off to enjoy some of the high culture that urban life provides. Upon returning at night, however, Watson describes the exact same location as "an endless labyrinth of gas-lit streets," suggesting that the dark and mysterious side of the city has come to the forefront.

THE RISE OF THE DETECTIVE GENRE   Nineteenth-century England witnessed the emergence of the modern police force, and "The Red-Headed League" is one of many Sherlock Holmes stories that familiarized the public with the new business of solving crimes. Modern police forces didn't exist in England until 1829, and even then the police were more concerned with preserving public order than investigating crimes committed by unknown perpetrators. Londoners had become more familiar with police and detectives by the time Doyle wrote "The Red-Headed League," but detectives weren't especially admired, especially in the wake of the brutal and unsolved Jack the Ripper slayings in the late 1880s. English novelists Charles Dickens and Wilkie Collins both wrote novels featuring detectives long before Doyle invented Sherlock Holmes, but their detectives acted more like hyperactive cops than rational professionals.

Doyle makes fun of such detectives in "The Red-Headed League" when Holmes refers to Detective Jones as a brave man but "an absolute imbecile." Subtly ribbing the contemporary police detectives was Doyle's way of calling for changes in the profession, particularly the way in which crime solvers worked. Even though Sherlock Holmes does Detective Jones's work for him, Jones can't quite bring himself to admit Holmes's superior crime-solving strategy, remarking instead that Holmes has the potential to be a good detective. Watson's skepticism of Holmes before readers discover that Holmes was right all along actually lends credence to this new, almost scientific method of solving crimes. Thus Doyle is both playing off the emergence of the detective in public consciousness and trying to stir that same public into demanding more from their police forces.

IMPORTANT QUOTATIONS EXPLAINED

1. *"As a rule," said Holmes, "the more bizarre a thing is the less mysterious it proves to be. It is your commonplace, featureless crimes which are really puzzling, just as a commonplace face is the most difficult to identify."*

Sherlock Holmes's remark after hearing Jabez Wilson's story highlights one of the central themes of the story: the connection between the bizarre and mundane. Holmes claims that what appears to be the strangest, most out-of-the-ordinary occurrence can actually be explained through simple means. The Red-Headed League and Jabez Wilson's story, for example, prompt Watson and readers to expect a complicated explanation for such a confusing scenario. The truth, however, is far simpler, as Holmes reveals that John Clay concocted the whole Red-Headed League scheme to assist a common bank robbery. What's more, Holmes declares that even though he can solve this seemingly bizarre case, the incomprehensible crimes are the ones that people see and hear about every day. In other words, Doyle suggests that although a great mind like Holmes's can penetrate the rare bizarre cases, nothing seems to be able to explain the fact that we live in a world in which crime itself is, as Holmes says, "commonplace."

2. *Here I had heard what he had heard, I had seen what he had seen, and yet from his words it was evident that he saw clearly not only what had happened, but what was about to happen, while to me the whole business was still confused and grotesque.*

In many of the Sherlock Holmes stories, Watson's reactions mirror readers' own thoughts. Watson, for example, comments at the story's end that he has seen the same evidence Holmes has, and yet can't quite solve the case as quickly or thoroughly as Holmes can. Although many contemporary readers have been just as confused as Watson, they take pleasure in watching Holmes unravel the case. Doyle therefore simultaneously pulls and pushes readers, compelling them to sharpen their intellect and help solve the mystery. On the other hand, Watson's perpetual bewilderment allows readers the pleasure of merely watching Holmes's astonishing powers of reasoning. This dual reaction, in which readers want to watch and actually be Holmes, is a large reason why Doyle's stories have remained so popular for so long.

Rita Hayworth and the Shawshank Redemption

Stephen King
(1947–)

CONTEXT

Stephen King was born on September 21, 1947, in Portland, Maine, his home state for the majority of his life. King's father, Donald, abandoned his family when King was only two, and King never saw or heard from him again. His mother, Nellie, was left with the burden of raising him and his adopted brother, David. In his early years, King occasionally went to live with relatives on both sides of his family. The family moved around, living in a succession of small towns before finally settling in the Maine community of Durham when King was eleven. When King was a teenager, he found a box of his father's old horror and science-fiction magazines, a discovery that would change his life. He began writing his own tales of horror while still a high school student at Lisbon High School in the mid-1960s and even attempted to write a few novels. After graduating, King accepted a scholarship to the University of Maine, Orono.

War protests and the politically charged atmosphere of the late 1960s transformed King from a conservative into a student radical who led marches to express dissent about the United States' involvement in the Vietnam War. Shortly after graduation in 1970, King married another aspiring novelist, Tabitha Spruce, and worked as a high school English teacher during the day and at an industrial laundry at night to make ends meet. The couple had a daughter, Naomi, in 1971 and two more children in the following years. Despite his demanding work and family life, King never abandoned his love for writing and eventually published his first novel, *Carrie*, in 1974. The novel and subsequent 1976 movie raked in enormous profits and catapulted King to instant fame and fortune.

King's second novel, *The Shining* (1977), made the bestseller lists, as has every novel he's written since, making him one of the most popular writers in the world. In the 1980s, he was the author of seven of the decade's top twenty-five bestsellers, and his works have been translated into nearly every major language. A prolific author, King has produced an average of a book per year for nearly three decades. In addition to his novels and short fiction, King has also written numerous essays, writing guides, and screenplays. Because of his association with horror and the occult, however, King is often overlooked as a serious novelist, even though he's won critical acclaim for a number of his more literary works. In 1996, for example, his short story "The Man in the Black Suit," which first appeared in the *New Yorker*, won the O. Henry Award for best short story of the year. He also received a National Book Award medal in 2003 for his distinguished contribution to American letters.

Although King's genre and artistic preoccupations have remained fairly consistent over the years, he's refined his writing style and modes of inquiry, allowing him to write tighter novels and more serious short fiction. Although works such as *The Stand* (1978) still reflect King's epic sweep with their apocalyptic themes and sprawling cast of characters, his more recent works focus on the interpersonal relationships and the often extreme behaviors that mark the relations between men and women. All of King's work, however, shares certain consistent qualities and hallmarks, such as strong evocation of setting, atmosphere, and character.

"Rita Hayworth and the Shawshank Redemption" is the opening story in the collection *Different Seasons* (1982) and embodies classic King themes of fear, confusion, and loss of control, albeit transformed and shifted to the fractured domesticity of a high-security prison. The chills and breathless horror commonplace in much of King's other writings have been replaced by the psychological torture of living in a confined space for an indeterminate amount of time. The story was eventually made into a popular film released in 1994 under the title *The Shawshank Redemption*.

PLOT OVERVIEW

Red, the narrator, recounts how he planned and carried out his wife's murder by disabling her brakes, which accidentally killed a neighbor and child as well and earned him a life sentence at Shawshank Prison. Red also remembers the arrival of an inmate named Andy Dufresne, whose tenure at Shawshank affected the lives of everyone at the prison. Andy was sent to Shawshank for life in 1947 for the cold-blooded murder of his wife, Linda, and her lover, tennis pro Glenn Quentin. Despite the damning evidence placing him at the scene of the crime on the night of the murders, Andy has always maintained his innocence, which Red eventually comes to believe in as well.

Andy has some initial difficulty adjusting to prison life, especially because many of the other prisoners think he's a snob. A gang of men known as the Sisters frequently attack and rape him in the laundry room while the guards look the other way. Andy fights the Sisters, even though it always lands him in the infirmary and sometimes solitary confinement. Despite these hardships, however, Andy never complains or loses his confidence.

Soon after arriving at Shawshank, Andy approaches Red and asks him to procure a rock hammer because he's interested in rock collecting and carving. After a while, he also pays Red to smuggle in some polishing cloths and then, rather nervously, a large poster of pinup Rita Hayworth. Red fulfills Andy's requests.

After a few years, Red and Andy both find themselves on a work crew, tarring the roof of the prison's license plate factory. Andy overhears Byron Hadley, a prison guard, complaining to the other guards about the taxes he'll have to pay on the $35,000 he just inherited from his long-lost brother. Andy offers Hadley some financial advice by telling him to give the money to his wife as a one-time tax-free gift. Andy even offers to fill out the paperwork for Hadley in exchange for giving three beers to each prisoner on the work crew. After some initial hesitation and suspicion, Hadley agrees. The deal wins Andy the respect of everyone involved and makes him a mythic hero in the eyes of the prisoners. Andy also becomes a valuable financial resource to those who run the prison. As a result, the guards and the warden protect Andy from the Sisters, make him the prison librarian, and don't assign other inmates to his cell. Andy relishes his new position and works hard during the next two decades to significantly expand the library.

Andy's financial responsibilities start with filing the guards' tax returns, but they soon expand to laundering money for the various prison wardens, including Bible-thumping Samuel Norton. Andy has no moral objection to hiding the money that Norton receives from construction companies, but he doesn't realize that doing so also hurts his chances of ever leaving Shawshank.

A new inmate named Tommy Williams arrives at Shawshank and tells Andy that he served time in another prison with Elwood Blatch, a man who privately admitted to killing tennis pro Glenn Quentin. When Andy asks Norton to request a retrial, Norton dismisses Andy's claims and puts him in solitary confinement for more than a month on the "grain and drain" diet of bread and water. Norton, meanwhile, transfers Tommy Williams to another prison out of fear that Andy would expose his money laundering operation if paroled. After another aborted attempt to reason with the warden and another stint in solitary, Andy drops the issue and becomes more brooding and introspective.

Eventually Andy emerges from his lengthy depression and tells Red one day that he had a friend set up a false identity for him. Under the false identity, the friend invested $14,000 of Andy's money, which has since become more than $370,000. Andy, however, can't touch the money, saved under his alternate identity, because he would risk exposing himself and losing everything. The documents and lucrative bonds are kept in a safe-deposit box at a local bank, the key to which has been stashed under a black volcanic rock wedged into a stone wall in the countryside near the prison. Andy dreams of escaping, assuming the new identity, and becoming the proprietor of a small hotel in Mexico. Andy also imagines Red going with him.

Red thinks nothing of this until years later when the prison guards find Andy's cell empty one morning. The guards search the prison but find nothing, until an extremely frustrated Norton rips the pinup poster from the wall to reveal a gaping hole in the thick concrete. The hole leads to the sewage drainpipe, which empties into the marshes surrounding Shawshank. Red figures that Andy slowly and systematically used the rock hammer and polishing cloths every night for nearly twenty years to carve through the wall. After completing his hole, Red also figures that it took Andy roughly eight years to muster the courage to actually try to escape.

A search of the marshes and nearby towns reveals nothing, however, and Norton has a nervous breakdown and resigns. Red never hears anything from Andy but receives a blank postcard from a border town in Texas some months later. The story of Andy's escape spreads throughout the prison and gives him an even greater mythic status. He becomes the symbol of hope for many prisoners, not only as someone who successfully escaped, but also as a man who never let prison crush his spirit.

Red adds a postscript to his story about a year later, writing from a hotel in Portland, Maine, after being released from Shawshank. The transition to life on the outside has been tough, and Red thinks of Andy when he feels the urge to commit a petty crime or violate the terms of his parole so that he'll be put back in prison. Now working as a bag boy at a supermarket, Red uses his days off to explore the countryside, partly because he likes the freedom and the space but also because he's looking for the volcanic rock where Andy hid the key to the safe-deposit box.

Red walks the rural hayfields in search of the stone wall Andy had described years earlier, and after several weeks of searching, he finally finds the rock. Underneath, Red discovers a letter addressed to him from Peter Stevens, Andy's pseudonym. The letter invites Red to join Andy in Mexico and includes a gift of $1,000. Red concludes the postscript with renewed hope for the future as he decides to abandon his job, violate his parole, and make his way to Mexico to find Andy.

CHARACTER LIST

Red   The narrator of the story. A convicted murderer serving a life sentence, Red writes the story to try to make sense of his friendship with Andy, his life in prison, and his hopes for the future. Red is a key figure inside prison, a lifeline to the outside world who can smuggle almost anything into the prison—for a price. Once paroled, he struggles with his newfound freedom, dissatisfied with his job and still without hope for a better future.

Andy Dufresne   The protagonist. The former vice president of a bank in Portland, Maine, Andy is thirty years old when he arrives at Shawshank and approximately fifty-eight when he escapes. A short, neat, meticulous man with sandy blond hair, he has small hands and wears gold-rimmed glasses. Most of the other inmates think that Andy is cold and snob-bish because he's always so calm and composed, rarely revealing his inner thoughts or true character. Andy eventually becomes the prison librarian and financial wizard, offering free tax advice to guards and wardens in exchange for protection and favors. He's one of the few innocent inmates at Shawshank.

Samuel Norton   One of the prison wardens. Norton institutes the new "Inside-Out" program that forces prisoners to work on chain gains to repair roads and public buildings. Even though he claims to be a devout Baptist, he accepts bribes from local construction companies so that the Inside-Out program won't put them out of business. He uses Andy's financial expertise to hide his illegal earnings and therefore refuses to help Andy win a retrial. Norton eventually resigns in disgrace after Andy's escape.

Byron Hadley   A prison guard. A tall man with thinning red hair, Hadley speaks loudly and uses the threat of violence to control the prisoners. Pessimistic, cynical, and paranoid, he feels the world is out to get him, even when he inherits $35,000 from a long-lost brother. Andy's offer to help Hadley avoid paying taxes on the money marks the beginning of Andy's career as the prison's financial wizard. Hadley eventually has a heart attack and retires.

The Sisters   The gang of inmates who prey on weaker prisoners. The Sisters, including in-mates Bogs Diamond and Rooster MacBride, maintain their dominance in the hierarchy of prisoners by beating and gang-raping new inmates, including Andy. Andy always fights back even though he usually loses. Andy eventually wins protection from the Sisters after helping the guards and wardens with their finances.

Tommy Williams   A young inmate. A career criminal, Tommy has served time in another prison with Elwood Blatch, the man who privately admits to killing Andy's wife and her lover. Tommy offers to help Andy prove his innocence, but Norton transfers Tommy to a minimum-security prison to keep Andy from leaving Shawshank.

ANALYSIS OF MAJOR CHARACTERS

RED   Red is the lifeline of the prison, the man who can smuggle almost anything into Shawshank from the outside world. By making himself indispensable to the other inmates, Red affords himself protection and an esteemed place in the pecking order of the prison yard. He forces the other men to do business on his terms and knows full well the need to defend his own interests in a world where violence and exploitation are the norm. Ultimately, however, Red's hardened stance conceals his fear and insecurity as he struggles to make sense of his life both in and out of prison. Even though Red's narrative focuses on Andy and his eventual escape, Red admits that the story is really all about himself. Andy's inner confidence and sense of self-worth represent the part of Red that Hadley, Norton, and the other prison authorities never managed to crush. Although Red has undoubtedly thought of escaping numerous times during his thirty-eight years in prison, it is Andy's resolute sense of hope that Red admires. Red knows that hope is what keeps him and every other inmate alive.

ANDY DUFRESNE   Andy is an enigma to Red and the other inmates, a man they admire but never really understand. An element of fantasy infuses the characterization of Andy: at one point King even refers to the mysterious "myth-magic" that his protagonist seemingly possesses. In truth, Andy is an anomalous figure who stands out from the rest of the inmates at Shawshank Prison, but not for any mythical or spiritual reason. Andy's calm, cool collectedness govern his interactions with the world around him, and he rarely succumbs to emotion or cheap sentiment. What many inmates take for snobbery is actually reserve and caution as Andy tries to stay one step ahead of his adversaries. Without this strength and inner resolve, Andy would never have survived his twenty-eight years in prison nor managed to escape. Andy emerges as an object of fascination for many of his fellow prisoners, a figure onto whom they project their various embellishments of the ideal man: Andy, the man who can talk down the guards; Andy, the man who can manipulate the warden; and Andy, the man who can escape out from under everyone's noses.

SAMUEL NORTON   Warden Norton embodies the hypocrisies and contradictions of the penitentiary system. The national exposure and adulation he gets for his "Inside-Out" program belies and conceals the corruption that prevails during his tenure and the campaign of threats, intimidation, abuse, and excessive cruelty he employs to maintain control of the inmates. At times aligned with images of death—his face is compared to a cold slate tombstone—Norton is a self-deluded despot who justifies his exploitation and the promotion of his self-interest at the expense of others in the name of his faith and the fire-and-brimstone Bible passages he often quotes.

THEMES, MOTIFS, AND SYMBOLS

THEMES

THE BURDEN OF ISOLATION AND IMPRISONMENT   Each of the inmates inside Shawshank Prison is locked up metaphorically as well as literally, hiding from himself or unable to function in the unregulated world that extends beyond the prison walls. There are many levels of isolation inside Shawshank, from the large, enclosed recreation yard to the smaller work crews down to the cellblock, cells, and, finally, solitary confinement. The prison is thus a multilayered world, a microcosm of the world outside that the prisoners have been forcibly removed from. The bars, strict schedules, sadistic keepers, and predatory Sisters only add a sense of entrapment and suffocation to these layers of isolation.

Shawshank's confines, however, also highlight the extent to which the prisoners have isolated themselves and compromised their sense of identity. Beneath the hardened criminals lie insecure, maladjusted outcasts, many of whom believe they can't function outside the prison system. Elwood Blatch, for example, is a braggart and an egomaniac whose exaggerated accounts of his exploits fool none of his listeners into believing that he is the master criminal whom he makes himself out to be. Red, meanwhile, identifies Andy as the part of himself who never let go of the idea of freedom. Freedom is a frightening concept for Red, who dreams of being paroled but eventually struggles to find his place in society after almost forty years in prison. Recounting Andy's escape, therefore, allows Red to face his fears and find the psychological freedom he seeks.

THE POWER OF HOPE   Hope, more than anything else, drives the inmates at Shawshank and gives them the will to live. Andy's sheer determination to maintain his own sense of self-worth and escape keeps him from dying of frustration and anger in solitary confinement. Hope is an abstract, passive emotion, akin to the passive, immobile, and inert lives of the prisoners. Andy sets about making hope a reality in the form of the agonizing progress he makes each year tunneling his way through his concrete cell wall. Even Andy's even-keeled and well-balanced temperament, however, eventually succumb to the bleakness of prison life. Red notes that Tommy Williams's revelation that he could prove Andy's innocence was like a key unlocking a cage in Andy's mind, a cage that released a tiger called Hope. This hope reinvigorates Andy and spreads to many of the other inmates in the prison. In his letter addressed to Red, Andy writes that "hope is a good thing," which in the end is all that Red has left. Red's decision to go to Mexico to find Andy is the ultimate proof of Red's own redemption, not from his life as a criminal but from his compromised state, bereft of hope and with no reason to embrace life or the future. Red's closing words, as he embarks tentatively onto a new path, show that hope is a difficult concept to sustain both inside the prison and out.

MOTIFS

CORRUPTION AND CRIME   Shawshank blurs the line between right and wrong and challenges the notion that isolating and reforming criminals will turn them into law-abiding citizens. Instead, the prison is a den of corruption, greed, bribery, and money laundering. Everyone exploits the system for their own gain, from Red, who can smuggle anything into the prison, all the way up to the wardens, who profit from forced prison labor. Andy's willingness to launder Warden Norton's slush money initially serves as a survival technique, a means of protecting himself by extending his good will to the administration. His complicity and knowledge of the warden's illegal enterprises, however, keep Norton from ever releasing him for fear that Andy would reveal the warden's secret. The fact that Shawshank is as corrupt and tainted as the outside world further justifies Andy's escape from a hypocritical, exploitative system that cares little for the prisoners' lives or rehabilitation.

TIME   Time serves as both a source of torment as well as the backdrop for the slow, eventual achievement of Andy's escape, his seemingly impossible goal for nearly twenty-eight years. Shawshank redefines the passage of time for the inmates, especially for the "lifers" like Andy and Red, who can only look forward to death. Hours can seem like a lifetime, and every day seems indistinguishable from the next, adding to the loneliness and burden of imprisonment. Ironically, however, time also proves to be the means of Andy's escape and salvation and gives him hope throughout his quarter-century in Shawshank. An amateur geologist, Andy realizes that dripping water can erode stone over the span of several million years and that with his small rock hammer and a lot of patience, he too can break through concrete. His devotion to chipping away at the concrete not only allows him to measure the passage of time but also gives him the sense of hope that the other inmates lack.

SYMBOLS

RITA HAYWORTH   The pinup posters of Rita Hayworth and the other women represent the outside world, hope, and every inmate's desire to escape to a normal life. Andy admits as much when he tells Red that sometimes he imagines stepping right through the photograph and into another life. More literally, Rita Hayworth really does remind Andy of his desire to actually break out of Shawshank because of the chiseled hole in the concrete that the posters conceal. As a result, Rita Hayworth embodies the sense of hope that keeps Andy alive and sane and distinguishes him from the other inmates. Even though it takes Andy more than twenty-five years to hammer his way through the wall, the mere fact that he has something to work for keeps him from lapsing into bouts of self-pity as the other inmates do. Having a mission and something to look forward to—even before he knew he would use the hole to break out—kept Andy alive and gave him his "inner light."

ROCKS   The rocks Andy sculpts serve as a cover to justify owning a rock hammer, but they also represent the spirit of hope that he exudes. As an amateur geologist, Andy is undoubtedly distracted from the doldrums of daily prison life by the rocks. Continuing to pursue his hobby gives him a sense of normality and control over his life that many other inmates lack. Displaying his collection of polished rocks on the windowsill of his cell also gives Andy a sense of accomplishment and means to measure the passage of time. More important, however, sculpting the pebbles give Andy hope and a means to fend off despair. Giving these sculptures away to Red and other inmates also represents Andy's ability to transfer his sense of hope—his "inner light" as Red calls it—to some of the other inmates.

SHORT STORY ANALYSIS

FIRST-PERSON NARRATIVE   "Rita Hayworth and the Shawshank Redemption" is presented in the form of a monologue, a written narrative that Red prepares to come to terms with his life in prison and the aftermath of his incarceration. Although Red spends much of his time recounting Andy's story, he admits that the narrative is as much about himself as it is about his friend. Red merely uses Andy's story as a parable to convey his own sense of frustration, despair, and, ultimately, hope. King's use of the first-person also gives the story credibility and authenticity. Red's frank, down-to-earth voice, grammatical mistakes, and use of prison slang, such as *screws* instead of *guards*, make the story much more real.

At the same time, first-person narration reveals the limits of individual perception and the human tendency to remember details selectively. Red describes how Andy became a Shawshank legend and says that dozens of men could recall seeing Andy confront Byron Hadley on the roof of the prison's license- plate factory, even though only a dozen or so men had actually been there. For this reason, readers must question Red's account of events as a biased observer who freely admits that so much of what he knows about Andy comes from rumor and hearsay. Furthermore, Red's admiration of Andy makes the story less credible as a factual account but insightful as a window into Red's own psyche. Andy's hopes and dreams of life outside reflect Red's own, just as Andy's eight-year struggle to overcome his fear of escaping Shawshank mirrors Red's own fears of the future and life on the outside. So while Red's warm, immediate, and engaging style of storytelling infuses the novel with directness and authenticity, Red is an unreliable narrator, attempting to overcome his limitations as an imprisoned observer to construct the story he wants to tell about both himself and the inmate who changed his life.

IMPORTANT QUOTATIONS EXPLAINED

---

1. *All I know for sure is that Andy Dufresne wasn't much like me or anyone else I ever knew. . . . It was a kind of inner light he carried around with him.*

Red writes these lines after recalling how Andy traded tax advice with Byron Hadley in exchange for three beers apiece for the crew of prisoners tarring the roof of the Shawshank license plate factory. Andy's reputation soars to legendary status after taking on Hadley and returning a sense of self-worth and dignity to the prisoners in the work crew. Red realizes that what some prisoners had originally written off as snobbishness or the swagger of self-satisfaction was merely Andy's unrelenting sense of self-worth. In a system designed to undermine personal identity and label individuals as unworthy of being normal members of society, Andy's composure and confidence stand out from the rest of the prisoners, whose aspirations and attitude become slowly blighted during the grinding years of incarceration. Andy's sense of self-worth exists as another form of freedom, the liberation of knowing he is in full possession of himself no matter how suffocating and claustrophobic the prison becomes. In that sense, Andy never actually loses his freedom because no one can take it away from him.

---

2. *I hope Andy is down there.*
   I hope I can make it across the border.
   I hope to see my friend and shake his hand.
   I hope the Pacific is as blue as it has been in my dreams.
   I hope.

Red's words at the end of his narrative reinforce the central role hope plays in "Rita Hayworth and the Shawshank Redemption." Finding Andy's letter could not have come at a better time, because Red has reached an impasse within his first few tentative months of freedom after being paroled. Red's difficult transition and struggle with finding his place in society place him at risk of violating the terms of his probation and intentionally returning to the familiar surroundings of Shawshank. Upon first entering prison, many inmates resent the loss of control of their lives, but they later miss that level of control once they've been released. The regulated, ordered lifestyle offers structure, routine, and discipline. Freedom and release, once so highly prized, become foreign and threatening. Women, for example, seem threatening to Red, and his job is unfulfilling. Andy's request to join him in Mexico, however, gives Red the direction and purpose that he had lacked. Even though Red fears that the waters of the Pacific will not be as blue as he has imagined them to be and realizes that he may not even be able to find Andy, their friendship has once again infused him with a strength that he would not otherwise possess.

R

A Rose for Emily
William Faulkner
(1897–1962)

CONTEXT

William Faulkner was born in New Albany, Mississippi, in 1897. One of the twentieth century's greatest writers, Faulkner earned his fame from a series of novels that explore the South's historical legacy, its fraught and often tensely violent present, and its uncertain future. This grouping of major works includes *The Sound and the Fury* (1929), *As I Lay Dying* (1930), *Light in August* (1931), and *Absalom, Absalom!* (1936), all of which are rooted in Faulkner's fictional Mississippi county, Yoknapatawpha. This imaginary setting is a microcosm of the South that Faulkner knew so well. It serves as a lens through which he could examine the practices, folkways, and attitudes that had divided and united the people of the South since the nation's inception.

In his writing, Faulkner was particularly interested in exploring the moral implications of history. As the South emerged from the Civil War and Reconstruction and attempted to shed the stigma of slavery, its residents were frequently torn between a new and an older, more established world order. Religion and politics frequently fail to provide order and guidance and instead complicate and divide. Society, with its gossip, judgment, and harsh pronouncements, conspires to thwart the ambitions of individuals struggling to embrace their identities. Across Faulkner's fictional landscapes, individual characters often stage epic struggles, prevented from realizing their potential or establishing their place in the world.

"A Rose for Emily" was the first short story that Faulkner published in a major magazine. It appeared in the April 30, 1930, issue of *Forum*. Despite the earlier publication of several novels, when Faulkner published this story he was still struggling to make a name for himself in the United States. Few critics recognized in his prose the hallmarks of a major new voice. Slightly revised versions of the story appeared in subsequent collections of Faulkner's short fiction—in *These 13* (1931) and then *Collected Stories* (1950)—which helped to increase its visibility.

Today, the much-anthologized story is among the most widely read and highly praised of Faulkner's work. Beyond its lurid appeal and somewhat Gothic atmosphere, Faulkner's "ghost story," as he once called it, gestures to broader ideas, including the tensions between North and South, complexities of a changing world order, disappearing realms of gentility and aristocracy, and rigid social constraints placed on women. Ultimately, it is the story's chilling portrait of aberrant psychology and necrophilia that draws readers into the dank, dusty world of Emily Grierson.

Faulkner won the Nobel Prize in Literature in 1949 and the Pulitzer Prize in both 1955 and 1962. He died in Byhalia, Mississippi on July 6, 1962, when he was sixty-four.

PLOT OVERVIEW

The story is divided into five sections. In section I, the narrator recalls the time of Emily Grierson's death and how the entire town attended her funeral in her home, which no stranger had entered for more than ten years. In a once-elegant, upscale neighborhood, Emily's house is the last vestige of the grandeur of a lost era. Colonel Sartoris, the town's previous mayor, had suspended Emily's tax responsibilities to the town after her father's death, justifying the action by claiming that Mr. Grierson had once lent the community a significant sum. As new town leaders take over, they make unsuccessful attempts to get Emily to resume payments. When members of the Board of Aldermen pay her a visit, in the dusty and antiquated parlor, Emily reasserts the fact that she is not required to pay taxes in Jefferson and that the officials should talk to Colonel Sartoris about the matter. However, at that point he has been dead for almost a decade. She asks her servant, Tobe, to show the men out.

In section II, the narrator describes a time thirty years earlier when Emily resists another official inquiry on behalf of the town leaders, when the townspeople detect a powerful odor emanating from her property. Her father has just died, and Emily has been abandoned by the man whom the townsfolk believed Emily was to marry. As complaints mount, Judge Stevens, the mayor at the time, decides to have lime sprinkled along the foundation of the Grierson home in the middle of the night. Within a couple of weeks, the odor subsides, but the townspeople begin to pity the increasingly reclusive Emily, remembering how her great aunt had succumbed to insanity. The townspeople have always believed that the Griersons thought too highly of themselves, with Emily's father driving off the many suitors deemed not good enough to marry his daughter. With no offer of marriage in sight, Emily is still single by the time she turns thirty.

The day after Mr. Grierson's death, the women of the town call on Emily to offer their condolences. Meeting them at the door, Emily states that her father is not dead, a charade that she keeps up for three days. She finally turns her father's body over for burial.

In section III, the narrator describes a long illness that Emily suffers after this incident. The summer after her father's death, the town contracts workers to pave the sidewalks, and a construction company, under the direction of northerner Homer Barron, is awarded the job. Homer soon becomes a popular figure in town and is seen taking Emily on buggy rides on Sunday afternoons, which scandalizes the town and increases the condescension and pity they have for Emily. They feel that she is forgetting her family pride and becoming involved with a man beneath her station.

As the affair continues and Emily's reputation is further compromised, she goes to the drug store to purchase arsenic, a powerful poison. She is required by law to reveal how she will use the arsenic. She offers no explanation, and the package arrives at her house labeled "For rats."

In section IV, the narrator describes the fear that some of the townspeople have that Emily will use the poison to kill herself. Her potential marriage to Homer seems increasingly unlikely, despite their continued Sunday ritual. The more outraged women of the town insist that the Baptist minister talk with Emily. After his visit, he never speaks of what happened and swears that he'll never go back. So the minister's wife writes to Emily's two cousins in Alabama, who arrive for an extended stay. Because Emily orders a silver toilet set monogrammed with Homer's initials, talk of the couple's marriage resumes. Homer, absent from town, is believed to be preparing for Emily's move to the North or avoiding Emily's intrusive relatives.

After the cousins' departure, Homer enters the Grierson home one evening and then is never seen again. Holed up in the house, Emily grows plump and gray. Despite the occasional lesson she gives in china painting, her door remains closed to outsiders. In what becomes an annual ritual, Emily refuses to acknowledge the tax bill. She eventually closes up the top floor of the house. Except for the occasional glimpse of her in the window, nothing is heard from her until her death at age seventy-four. Only the servant is seen going in and out of the house.

In section V, the narrator describes what happens after Emily dies. Emily's body is laid out in the parlor, and the women, town elders, and two cousins attend the service. After some time has passed, the door to a sealed upstairs room that had not been opened in forty years is broken down by the townspeople. The room is frozen in time, with the items for an upcoming wedding and a man's suit laid out. Homer Barron's body is stretched on the bed as well, in an advanced state of decay. The onlookers then notice the indentation of a head in the pillow beside Homer's body and a long strand of Emily's gray hair on the pillow.

CHARACTER LIST

Emily Grierson   The object of fascination in the story. A eccentric recluse, Emily is a mysterious figure who changes from a vibrant and hopeful young girl to a cloistered and secretive old woman. Devastated and alone after her father's death, she is an object of pity for the townspeople. After a life of having potential suitors rejected by her father, she spends time after his death with a newcomer, Homer Barron, although the chances of his marrying her decrease as the years pass. Bloated and pallid in her later years, her hair turns steel gray. She ultimately poisons Homer and seals his corpse into an upstairs room.

Homer Barron   A foreman from the North. Homer is a large man with a dark complexion, a booming voice, and light-colored eyes. A gruff and demanding boss, he wins many admirers in Jefferson because of his gregarious nature and good sense of humor. He develops an interest in Emily and takes her for Sunday drives in a yellow-wheeled buggy. Despite his attributes, the townspeople view him as a poor, if not scandalous, choice for a mate. He disappears in Emily's house and decomposes in an attic bedroom after she kills him.

Judge Stevens   A mayor of Jefferson. Eighty years old, Judge Stevens attempts to delicately handle the complaints about the smell emanating from the Grierson property. To be respectful of Emily's pride and former position in the community, he and the aldermen decide to sprinkle lime on the property in the middle of the night.

Mr. Grierson   Emily's father. Mr. Grierson is a controlling, looming presence even in death, and the community clearly sees his lasting influence over Emily. He deliberately thwarts Emily's attempts to find a husband in order to keep her under his control. We get glimpses of him in the story: in the crayon portrait kept on the gilt-edged easel in the parlor, and silhouetted in the doorway, horsewhip in hand, having chased off another of Emily's suitors.

Tobe   Emily's servant. Tobe, his voice supposedly rusty from lack of use, is the only lifeline that Emily has to the outside world. For years, he dutifully cares for her and tends to her needs. Eventually the townspeople stop grilling him for information about Emily. After Emily's death, he walks out the back door and never returns.

Colonel Sartoris   A former mayor of Jefferson. Colonel Sartoris absolves Emily of any tax burden after the death of her father. His elaborate and benevolent gesture is not heeded by the succeeding generation of town leaders.

ANALYSIS OF MAJOR CHARACTERS

EMILY GRIERSON   Emily is the classic outsider, controlling and limiting the town's access to her true identity by remaining hidden. The house that shields Emily from the world suggests the mind of the woman who inhabits it: shuttered, dusty, and dark. The object of the town's intense scrutiny, Emily is a muted and mysterious figure. On one level, she exhibits the qualities of the stereotypical southern "eccentric": unbalanced, excessively tragic, and subject to bizarre behavior. Emily enforces her own sense of law and conduct, such as when she refuses to pay her taxes or state her purpose for buying the poison. Emily also skirts the law when she refuses to have numbers attached to her house when federal mail service is instituted. Her dismissal of the law eventually takes on more sinister consequences, as she takes the life of the man whom she refuses to allow to abandon her.

The narrator portrays Emily as a monument, but at the same time she is pitied and often irritating, demanding to live life on her own terms. The subject of gossip and speculation, the townspeople cluck their tongues at the fact that she accepts Homer's attentions with no firm wedding plans. After she purchases the poison, the townspeople conclude that she will kill herself. Emily's instabilities, however, lead her in a different direction, and the final scene of the story suggests that she is a necrophiliac. *Necrophilia* typically means a sexual attraction to dead bodies. In a broader sense, the term also describes a powerful desire to control another, usually in the context of a romantic or deeply personal relationship. Necrophiliacs tend to be so controlling in their relationships that they ultimately resort to bonding with unresponsive entities with no resistance or will—in other words, with dead bodies. Mr. Grierson controlled Emily, and after his death, Emily temporarily controls him by refusing to give up his dead body. She ultimately transfers this control to Homer, the object of her affection. Unable to find a traditional way to express her desire to possess Homer, Emily takes his life to achieve total power over him.

HOMER BARRON   Homer, much like Emily, is an outsider, a stranger in town who becomes the subject of gossip. Unlike Emily, however, Homer swoops into town brimming with charm, and he initially becomes the center of attention and the object of affection. Some townspeople distrust him because he is both a Northerner and day laborer, and his Sunday outings with Emily are in many ways scandalous, because the townspeople regard Emily—despite her eccentricities—as being from a higher social class. Homer's failure to properly court and marry Emily prompts speculation and suspicion. He carouses with younger men at the Elks Club, and the narrator portrays him as either a homosexual or simply an eternal bachelor, dedicated to his single status and uninterested in marriage. Homer says only that he is "not a marrying man."

As the foreman of a company that has arrived in town to pave the sidewalks, Homer is an emblem of the North and the changes that grip the once insular and genteel world of the South. With his machinery, Homer represents modernity and industrialization, the force of progress that is upending traditional values and provoking resistance and alarm among traditionalists. Homer brings innovation to the rapidly changing world of this Southern town, whose new leaders are themselves pursuing more "modern" ideas. The change that Homer brings to Emily's life, as her first real lover, is equally as profound and seals his grim fate as the victim of her plan to keep him permanently by her side.

THEMES, MOTIFS, AND SYMBOLS

THEMES

TRADITION VERSUS CHANGE Through the mysterious figure of Emily Grierson, Faulkner conveys the struggle that comes from trying to maintain tradition in the face of widespread, radical change. Jefferson is at a crossroads, embracing a modern, more commercial future while still perched on the edge of the past, from the faded glory of the Grierson home to the town cemetery where anonymous Civil War soldiers have been laid to rest. Emily herself is a tradition, steadfastly staying the same over the years despite many changes in her community. She is in many ways a mixed blessing. As a living monument to the past, she represents the traditions that people wish to respect and honor; however, she is also a burden and entirely cut off from the outside world, nursing eccentricities that others cannot understand.

Emily lives in a timeless vacuum and world of her own making. Refusing to have metallic numbers affixed to the side of her house when the town receives modern mail service, she is out of touch with the reality that constantly threatens to break through her carefully sealed perimeters. Garages and cotton gins have replaced the grand antebellum homes. The aldermen try to break with the unofficial agreement about taxes once forged between Colonel Sartoris and Emily. This new and younger generation of leaders brings in Homer's company to pave the sidewalks. Although Jefferson still highly regards traditional notions of honor and reputation, the narrator is critical of the old men in their Confederate uniforms who gather for Emily's funeral. For them as for her, time is relative. The past is not a faint glimmer but an ever-present, idealized realm. Emily's macabre bridal chamber is an extreme attempt to stop time and prevent change, although doing so comes at the expense of human life.

THE POWER OF DEATH Death hangs over "A Rose for Emily," from the narrator's mention of Emily's death at the beginning of the story through the description of Emily's death-haunted life to the foundering of tradition in the face of modern changes. In every case, death prevails over every attempt to master it. Emily, a fixture in the community, gives in to death slowly. The narrator compares her to a drowned woman, a bloated and pale figure left too long in the water. In the same description, he refers to her small, spare skeleton—she is practically dead on her feet. Emily stands as an emblem of the Old South, a grand lady whose respectability and charm rapidly decline through the years, much like the outdated sensibilities the Griersons represent. The death of the old social order will prevail, despite many townspeople's attempts to stay true to the old ways.

Emily attempts to exert power over death by denying the fact of death itself. Her bizarre relationship to the dead bodies of the men she has loved—her necrophilia—is revealed first when her father dies. Unable to admit that he has died, Emily clings to the controlling paternal figure whose denial and control became the only—yet extreme—form of love she knew. She gives up his body only reluctantly. When Homer dies, Emily refuses to acknowledge it once again—although this time, she herself was responsible for bringing about the death. In killing Homer, she was able to keep him near her. However, Homer's lifelessness rendered him permanently distant. Emily and Homer's grotesque marriage reveals Emily's disturbing attempt to fuse life and death. However, death ultimately triumphs.

MOTIFS

WATCHING Emily is the subject of the intense, controlling gaze of the narrator and residents of Jefferson. In lieu of an actual connection to Emily, the townspeople create subjective and often distorted interpretations of the woman they know little about. They attend her funeral under the guise of respect and honor, but they really want to satisfy their lurid curiosity about the town's most notable eccentric. One of the ironic dimensions of the story is that for all the gossip and theorizing, no one guesses the perverse extent of Emily's true nature.

For most of the story, Emily is seen only from a distance, by people who watch her through the windows or who glimpse her in her doorway. The narrator refers to her as an object—an "idol." This pattern changes briefly during her courtship with Homer Barron, when she leaves her house and is frequently out in the world. However, others spy on her just as avidly, and she is still relegated to the role of object, a distant figure who takes on character according to the whims of those who watch her. In this sense, the act of watching is powerful because it replaces an actual human presence with a made-up narrative that changes depending on who is doing the watching. No one knows the Emily that exists beyond what they can see, and her true self is visible to them only after she dies and her secrets are revealed.

DUST A pall of dust hangs over the story, underscoring the decay and decline that figure so prominently. The dust throughout Emily's house is a fitting accompaniment to the faded lives within. When the aldermen arrive to try and secure Emily's annual tax payment, the house smells of "dust and disuse." As they seat themselves, the movement stirs dust all around them, and it slowly rises, roiling about their thighs and catching the slim beam of sunlight entering the room. The house is a place of stasis, where regrets and memories have remained undisturbed. In a way, the dust is a protective presence; the aldermen cannot penetrate Emily's murky relationship with reality. The layers of dust also suggest the cloud of obscurity that hides Emily's true nature and the secrets her house contains. In the final scene, the dust is an oppressive presence that seems to emanate from Homer's dead body. The dust, which is everywhere, seems even more horrible here.

SYMBOLS

EMILY'S HOUSE Emily's house, like Emily herself, is a monument, the only remaining emblem of a dying world of Southern aristocracy. The outside of the large, square frame house is lavishly decorated. The cupolas, spires, and scrolled balconies are the hallmarks of a decadent style of architecture that became popular in the 1870s. By the time the story takes place, much has changed. The street and neighborhood, at one time affluent, pristine, and privileged, have lost their standing as the realm of the elite. The house is in some ways an extension of Emily: it bares its "stubborn and coquettish decay" to the town's residents. It is a testament to the endurance and preservation of tradition but now seems out of place among the cotton wagons, gasoline pumps, and other industrial trappings that surround it—just as the South's old values are out of place in a changing society.

Emily's house also represents alienation, mental illness, and death. It is a shrine to the living past, and the sealed upstairs bedroom is her macabre trophy room where she preserves the man she would not allow to leave her. As when the group of men sprinkled lime along the foundation to counteract the stench of rotting flesh, the townspeople skulk along the edges of Emily's life and property. The house, like its owner, is an object of fascination for them. They project their own lurid fantasies and interpretations onto the crumbling edifice and mysterious figure inside. Emily's death is a chance for them to gain access to this forbidden realm and confirm their wildest notions and most sensationalistic suppositions about what had occurred on the inside.

THE STRAND OF HAIR   The strand of hair is a reminder of love lost and the often perverse things people do in their pursuit of happiness. The strand of hair also reveals the inner life of a woman who, despite her eccentricities, was committed to living life on her own terms and not submitting her behavior, no matter how shocking, to the approval of others. Emily subscribes to her own moral code and occupies a world of her own invention, where even murder is permissible. The narrator foreshadows the discovery of the long strand of hair on the pillow when he describes the physical transformation that Emily undergoes as she ages. Her hair grows more and more grizzled until it becomes a "vigorous iron-gray." The strand of hair ultimately stands as the last vestige of a life left to languish and decay, much like the body of Emily's former lover.

SHORT STORY ANALYSIS

FAULKNER AND THE SOUTHERN GOTHIC   Southern Gothic is a literary tradition that came into its own in the early twentieth century. It is rooted in the Gothic style, which had been popular in European literature for many centuries. Gothic writers concocted wild, frightening scenarios in which mysterious secrets, supernatural occurrences, and characters' extreme duress conspired to create a breathless reading experience. Gothic style focused on the morbid and grotesque, and the genre often featured certain set pieces and characters: drafty castles laced with cobwebs, secret passages, and frightened, wide-eyed heroines whose innocence does not go untouched. Although they borrow the essential ingredients of the Gothic, writers of Southern Gothic fiction were not interested in integrating elements of the sensational solely for the sake of creating suspense or titillation. Writers such as Flannery O'Connor, Tennessee Williams, Truman Capote, Harper Lee, Eudora Welty, Erskine Caldwell, and Carson McCullers were drawn to the elements of Gothicism for what they revealed about human psychology and the dark, underlying motives that were pushed to the fringes of society.

Southern Gothic writers were interested in exploring the extreme, antisocial behaviors that were often a reaction against a confining code of social conduct. Southern Gothic often hinged on the belief that daily life and the refined surface of the social order were fragile and illusory, disguising disturbing realities or twisted psyches. Faulkner, with his dense and multilayered prose, traditionally stands outside this group of practitioners. However, "A Rose for Emily" reveals the influence that Southern Gothic had on his writing: this particular story has a moody and forbidding atmosphere; a crumbling old mansion; and decay, putrefaction, and grotesquerie. Faulkner's work uses the sensational elements to highlight an individual's struggle against an oppressive society that is undergoing rapid change. Another aspect of the Southern Gothic style is appropriation and transformation. Faulkner has appropriated the image of the damsel in distress and transformed it into Emily, a psychologically damaged spinster. Her mental instability and necrophilia have made her an emblematic Southern Gothic heroine.

TIME AND TEMPORAL SHIFTS   In "A Rose for Emily," Faulkner does not rely on a conventional linear approach to present his characters' inner lives and motivations. Instead, he fractures, shifts, and manipulates time, stretching the story out over several decades. We learn about Emily's life through a series of flashbacks. The story begins with a description of Emily's funeral and then moves into the near-distant past. At the end of the story, we see that the funeral is a flashback as well, preceding the unsealing of the upstairs bedroom door. We see Emily as a young girl, attracting suitors whom her father chases off with a whip, and as an old woman, when she dies at seventy-four. As Emily's grip on reality grows more tenuous over the years, the South itself experiences a great deal of change. By moving forward and backward in time, Faulkner portrays the past and the present as coexisting and is able to examine how they influence each other. He creates a complex, layered, and multidimensional world.

Faulkner presents two visions of time in the story. One is based in the mathematical precision and objectivity of reality, in which time moves forward relentlessly, and what's done is done; only the present exists. The other vision is more subjective. Time moves forward, but events don't stay in distant memory; rather, memory can exist unhindered, alive and active no matter how much time passes or how much things change. Even if a person is physically bound to the present, the past can play a vibrant, dynamic role. Emily stays firmly planted in a subjective realm of time, where life moves on with her in it—but she stays committed, regardless, to the past.

THE NARRATOR   The unnamed narrator of "A Rose for Emily" serves as the town's collective voice. Critics have debated whether it is a man or woman; a former lover of Emily Grierson's; the boy who remembers the sight of Mr. Grierson in the doorway, holding the whip; or the town gossip, spearheading the effort to break down the door at the end. It is possible, too, that the narrator is Emily's former servant, Tobe—he would have known her intimately, perhaps including her secret. A few aspects of the story support this theory, such as the fact that the narrator often refers to Emily as "Miss Emily" and provides only one descriptive detail about the Colonel Sartoris, the mayor: the fact that he enforced a law requiring that black women wear aprons in public. In any case, the narrator hides behind the collective pronoun *we*. By using *we*, the narrator can attribute what might be his or her own thoughts and opinions to all of the townspeople, turning private ideas into commonly held beliefs.

The narrator deepens the mystery of who he is and how much he knows at the end of the story, when the townspeople discover Homer's body. The narrator confesses "Already we knew" that an upstairs bedroom had been sealed up. However, we never find out *how* the narrator knows about the room. More important, at this point, for the first time in the story, the narrator uses the pronoun "they" instead of "we" to refer to the townspeople. First, he says, "Already we knew that there was one room. . . ." Then he changes to, "They waited until Miss Emily was decently in the ground before they opened it." This is a significant shift. Until now, the narrator has willingly grouped himself with the rest of the townspeople, accepting the community's actions, thoughts, and speculations as his own. Here, however, the narrator distances himself from the action, as though the breaking down of the door is something he can't bring himself to endorse. The shift is quick and subtle, and he returns to "we" in the passages that follow, but it gives us an important clue about the narrator's identity. Whoever he was, the narrator cared for Emily, despite her eccentricities and horrible, desperate act. In a town that treated her as an oddity and, finally, a horror, a kind, sympathetic gesture—even one as slight as symbolically looking away when the private door is forced open—stands out.

IMPORTANT QUOTATIONS EXPLAINED

---

1. *Alive, Miss Emily had been a tradition, a duty, and a care; a sort of hereditary obligation upon the town . . .*

This quotation appears near the beginning of the story, in section I, when the narrator describes Emily's funeral and history in the town. The complex figure of Emily Grierson casts a long shadow in the town of Jefferson. The members of the community assume a proprietary relationship to her, extolling the image of a grand lady whose family history and reputation warranted great respect. At the same time, the townspeople criticize her unconventional life and relationship with Homer Barron. Emily is an object of fascination. Many people feel compelled to protect her, whereas others feel free to monitor her every move, hovering at the edges of her life. Emily is the last representative of a once great Jefferson family, and the townspeople feel that they have inherited this daughter of a faded empire of wealth and prestige, for better or worse.

The order of Faulkner's words in this quotation is significant. Although Emily once represented a great southern tradition centering on the landed gentry with their vast holdings and considerable resources, Emily's legacy has devolved, making her more a duty and an obligation than a romanticized vestige of a dying order. The town leaders conveniently overlook the fact that in her straightened circumstances and solitary life, Emily can no longer meet her tax obligations with the town. Emily emerges as not only a financial burden to the town but a figure of outrage because she unsettles the community's strict social codes.

---

2. *Then we noticed that in the second pillow was the indentation of a head. One of us lifted something from it, and leaning forward, that faint and invisible dust dry and acrid in the nostrils, we saw a long strand of iron-gray hair.*

These lines end the story. Emily's secret, finally revealed, solidifies her reputation in the town as an eccentric. Her precarious mental state has led her to perform a grotesque act that surpasses the townspeople's wildest imaginings. Emily, although she deliberately sets up a solitary existence for herself, is unable to give up the men who have shaped her life, even after they have died. She hides her dead father for three days, then permanently hides Homer's body in the upstairs bedroom. In entombing her lover, Emily keeps her fantasy of marital bliss permanently intact.

Emily's excessive need for privacy is challenged by the townspeople's extreme curiosity about the facts surrounding her life. Unsatisfied with glimpses caught through doorways and windows, the townspeople essentially break into the Grierson home after Emily's death. Convincing themselves that they are behaving respectfully by waiting until a normal period of mourning has expired, they satisfy their lurid curiosity by unsealing the second-floor bedroom. There is no real moral justification for their act, and in light of their blatant violation of Emily's home and privacy, Emily's eccentric, grotesque behavior takes on a layer of almost sympathetic pathos. She has done a horrible, nightmarish thing, yet the confirmation of the townspeople's worst beliefs seems sad, rather than satisfying or a cause for celebration.

Shiloh

Bobbie Ann Mason
(1942–   )

CONTEXT

Bobbie Ann Mason was born in Kentucky in 1942. As a girl, Mason was fascinated by the Bobbsey Twins and Nancy Drew, young characters who got to travel and have adventures. She loved growing up on a farm but saw that the women in her community did little besides give birth and work on the land or in schools, stores, or factories. She longed to explore the world and get an education. She attended the University of Kentucky, where she majored in journalism. After graduation, she moved to New York and worked at several magazines, writing articles about pop culture. She applied to the writing program at Stanford University but was rejected. Taking refuge in the study of literature, she earned an M.A. from the State University of New York at Binghamton and a Ph.D. in literature from the University of Connecticut. Her dissertation was eventually published under the title *Nabokov's Garden* (1974). In 1975, she published *The Girl Sleuth: A Feminist Guide to the Bobbsey Twins, Nancy Drew, and Their Sisters*.

As a southerner living in the Northeast, Mason often felt shy and awkward. She had absorbed the idea that northerners were authoritative sophisticates who believed that southerners were inferior. On the rare occasions when she talked about her Kentucky background, her listeners often fit the stories into their own stereotypes of the South as a charmingly picturesque and backward place. She attempted to get rid of her southern accent and for years looked outside of the South for inspiration. Eventually, she figured out that her home was her true subject. In her fiction, she strives to depict middle-class and lower-middle-class people, whose lives she says "are just as important as the lives of those who read the *New York Times* and go to the opera."

After composing short stories in college, Mason set the form aside for fifteen years. In the mid-seventies, she attended a writing workshop in the Adirondacks, where she studied with prominent writers, including Margaret Atwood. After submitting stories to the *New Yorker*, she heard back from Roger Angell, a celebrated writer and editor at the magazine. Angell mentored Mason, responding to each of her submissions with suggestions and encouragement. "Offerings," Mason's twentieth submission to the magazine, was accepted for publication.

Shiloh and Other Stories, Mason's first collection, was published in 1982. It won the PEN/Hemingway award and was nominated for the National Book Critics Circle Award, American Book Award, and PEN/Faulkner Award. Mason's 1985 novel *In Country* earned high praise from reviewers for its focus on generational concerns such as the Vietnam War. In 1989, the novel was made into a film starring Joan Allen and Bruce Willis. Mason's memoir *Clear Springs: A Family Story* (2000) was a finalist for the Pulitzer Prize. Mason's other works include the short-story collections *Love Life* (1989), *Midnight Magic* (1998), and *Zigzagging Down a Wild Trail* (2002); the novels *Feather Crowns* (1993), *Spence + Lila* (1998), and *An Atomic Romance* (2005); and the biography *Elvis Presley* (2002). She has also written nonfiction essays and articles.

"Shiloh," the title story from Mason's first collection, is one of her most frequently anthologized works. Like much of her fiction, it explores the ennui and restlessness of southerners living in a changing society and examines a world in which traditional values and communities are being replaced by divorce, chain stores, and television. It is peopled by sympathetic characters dissatisfied with their lots in life and leavened by frequent touches of melancholy humor. Its publication in book form prompted a reviewer at the *New York Times* to marvel at Mason's characters, whose lives, he said, seemed amazingly strange and foreign to northerners from big cities. It has been Mason's project, beginning with "Shiloh," to bring news of these supposedly mysterious southerners to the wider world.

PLOT OVERVIEW

As the story opens, Norma Jean Moffitt is exercising her pectoral muscles. Leroy Moffitt, Norma Jean's husband, was injured four months ago while driving his truck. He wouldn't want to return to truck driving even if he could. To pass the time, he constructs crafts and dreams of building a log cabin. Norma Jean supports herself and her husband by working at a Rexall drugstore in the cosmetics department.

Leroy is happy to be home and feels affectionate toward his wife, but he worries that she does not return these feelings. She doesn't seem overjoyed about his constant presence. He wonders whether having him around reminds her of Randy, their son, who died as an infant. Leroy realizes that the death of a child drives many couples apart, and he feels lucky that his marriage is intact.

One night, Leroy buys marijuana from Stevie Hamilton, the son of a former schoolmate of Leroy's. Stevie's father is a well-to-do doctor. Leroy tries to make conversation about his plans to build a log cabin, but Stevie isn't interested. We learn that Leroy and Norma Jean, who are now thirty-four, got married when they were eighteen and had Randy a few months afterward. While the family was at a drive-in watching *Dr. Strangelove*, Randy died of SIDS (Sudden Infant Death Syndrome). He was four months and three days old.

When Leroy returns home, his mother-in-law, Mabel Beasley, is at the house. She keeps tabs on the state of Norma Jean's laundry and plants. She gives Norma Jean and Leroy a dust ruffle that she made in the upholstery shop where she works. Leroy jokes that they can use it to hide things. Mabel still resents him for impregnating Norma Jean.

Mabel makes fun of Leroy's *Star Trek* needlepoint pillow cover, calling sewing a woman's hobby. Leroy claims that football players sew and then explains his plans to build a cabin. Norma Jean says the first thing he needs to do is get a job. Mabel urges them to take a trip to Shiloh, the Civil War battlefield where she and her late husband, who died when Norma Jean was a girl, went on their honeymoon.

When Mabel leaves, Norma Jean presents Leroy with a list of possible jobs, including guarding, carpentering, and working in a lumberyard. He says he can't be on his feet all day, and she reminds him that she does exactly that at Rexall's. As she speaks, she does leg exercises. Leroy reiterates his desire to build a cabin, but Norma Jean says she doesn't want to live in one. Norma Jean and Leroy used to have fun when he came home from work, eating food that Norma Jean made, playing cards, and watching television. Now Norma Jean eats healthy cereal. This is one of the many small details that Leroy has learned about his wife now that he's been home.

Leroy goes for pointless drives and looks around the new subdivisions. After one of these excursions, he arrives home and finds Norma Jean making a casserole and crying because Mabel found her smoking. Leroy comforts her. While he smokes a joint, she plays "Sunshine Superman" and "Who'll Be the Next in Line?" on the organ he got her for Christmas. He thinks about an old friend, Virgil, who organized a drug bust. Again he mentions the cabin, and again Norma Jean dismisses the idea. He longs to get to know his wife again but doesn't say anything.

On Saturday, Mabel comes over and tells a story about a dachshund that killed a baby, claiming that the mother was neglectful. Leroy warns Mabel to watch what she says. Afterward, Norma Jean says the story was meant to punish her for smoking. She and Leroy are thinking about Randy, but neither of them says his name.

Norma Jean enrolls in a composition class at night school. Leroy is defensive about his own English. She starts cooking more exotic foods. Instead of playing her organ, she writes a paper about music. Leroy knows she will leave him. He and Mabel commiserate about the change in Norma Jean, and Mabel again suggests a trip to Shiloh. When Norma Jean arrives home, she is rude to her mother. That night, she tells Leroy that his name means *the king*.

They go to Shiloh on Sunday. It looks like a park, not a golf course, as Leroy imagined. They see a log cabin. Close to the cemetery, they eat a picnic. Leroy feels nervous around his wife, as if she is an older woman and he a bumbling boy. After they eat, Leroy smokes a joint. Silence falls, and Norma Jean says she wants to leave Leroy. He suggests starting over, and she says they already did start over. He asks her if it's a "women's lib" issue. Norma says something changed when Mabel caught her smoking. She says she feels like she's eighteen, which she hates. She walks away.

Leroy continues smoking and thinks about the war and the way it relates to Mabel's marriage and to his and Norma Jean's marriage. He realizes that he has left a space in the middle of this history, just as there is a space in the middle of a log cabin, and a space in the middle of his marriage. He realizes that building a log cabin was a terrible idea. He begins to follow Norma Jean, whom he sees walking toward the Tennessee River. On the bluff, she faces Leroy and moves her arms in what could be a gesture to him or an exercise for her pectoral muscles. The sky reminds Leroy of the dust ruffle that Mabel gave them.

CHARACTER LIST

Leroy Moffitt   A thirty-four-year-old truck driver from Kentucky. Leroy married his wife, Norma Jean, when they were both eighteen. Leroy adores Norma Jean but feels he no longer knows her. Their only child, Randy, died of SIDS (Sudden Infant Death Syndrome). Because of an accident that injured his left hip and leg, Leroy is unable to drive his rig and sits at home with too much time on his hands. A pot-smoker and craft-maker, Leroy spends more time thinking and worrying than he does taking concrete steps to improve his life.

Norma Jean Moffitt   Leroy's wife. At thirty-four, Norma Jean is restless, unhappy, and annoyed by Leroy's constant presence. She preferred it when he was on the road much of the time and came home only for short visits full of food, television, and cards. Norma Jean keeps the family afloat with her job at a Rexall's drugstore, where she sells makeup. She works on strengthening her body and mind, taking weightlifting classes and enrolling in night school. Norma Jean is a smart, fiery woman, but she struggles to understand her own feelings and express herself.

Mabel Beasley   Norma Jean's mother. A dumpy, unattractive woman who works in an upholstery shop, Mabel keeps tabs on the cleanliness of her daughter's house. She was widowed when Norma Jean was ten, and holds a special place in her heart for Shiloh, the battleground where she and her late husband took their honeymoon. Mabel is a nag and constant critic. She makes nasty remarks about Leroy's leisure pursuits and tells a story meant to make Norma Jean feel responsible for Randy's death. Still, she loves her daughter and son-in-law and worries about the changes she sees in them. It upsets her to see Norma Jean smoking and studying. She fears that her daughter will addle her brains if she reads and thinks too much. Leroy's inactivity and aimlessness also bothers her. She would like it best if Norma Jean and Leroy stuck to their traditional, narrowly defined gender roles.

Randy   Leroy's and Norma Jean's son. At four months and three days old, Randy died of SIDS at the drive-in while his parents watched *Dr. Strangelove*. Leroy and Norma Jean think of him often, but they don't talk about him. He is a vague but painful memory that they can refer to only occasionally and obliquely. His death has left a void in their lives.

Stevie Hamilton   The local kid who sells marijuana to Leroy. The son of a thirty-six-year-old doctor who was two classes ahead of Leroy in school, Stevie is the same age that Randy would have been had he lived. Leroy is interested in this link between Stevie and Randy and tries to make conversation with the young drug dealer. Stevie sees Leroy only as a source of income and brushes off his attempts at friendliness.

ANALYSIS OF MAJOR CHARACTERS

LEROY MOFFITT   Leroy is a man adrift in his own life, casting about for an identity and a sense of purpose. Although he has almost recovered from his accident, he is shaken up and frightened of driving the rig again. No longer the primary breadwinner, he begins to lose his identity as a provider. He is less interested in pursuing the carpentry and guarding jobs that Norma Jean suggests than he is in sewing needlepoint, building models, and dreaming of constructing a log cabin for himself and Norma Jean to live in. Leroy has also lost his identity as a father. His son, Randy, is dead, and although Leroy often thinks of him, his memories of Randy have faded, and Leroy does not consider himself a paternal figure. At loose ends, Leroy latches on to Norma Jean. He is something of a romantic and imagines that his wife will appreciate his constant presence around the house and that their marriage will flourish as a result. When it turns out that Norma Jean is annoyed and oppressed by his homecoming, Leroy begins to lose his identity as a husband.

Mason portrays Leroy as lovable, perceptive, and kind, but a loser nonetheless. Leroy adores Norma Jean and watches her anxiously, trying to guess what she is feeling and thinking. He treats his abrasive mother-in-law with respect, showing sympathy and kindness toward her even when she insults him. When tensions simmer or Norma Jean and Mabel squabble, Leroy diffuses the situation by staying calm and refusing to be provoked. He misses his son and makes friendly overtures to Stevie Hamilton, who is the same age Randy would have been and cruelly rejects Leroy's attempts at conversation. If Leroy wins our hearts, however, he also earns Norma Jean's criticism. Instead of pulling himself together and finding a new job, he lies on the couch smoking pot or drives aimlessly around town. He allows himself to be intimidated by his wife's increased independence, rather than accepting it or even encouraging it. He anticipates Norma Jean's departure, but he passively watches it happen rather than try to prevent it. Although he remains hopeful, wondering whether his wife is beckoning to him in the distance, it is clear to us that his lovable nature will not outweigh his negative qualities in Norma Jean's eyes.

NORMA JEAN MOFFITT Norma Jean undergoes a transformation during the course of "Shiloh," changing from a stunted housewife into a woman taking steps toward complete independence. Before the story opens, Norma Jean played a traditional feminine role, keeping the home fires burning and plying her husband with food and entertainment when he returned from his long trips. When the story begins, she is chafing under the yoke of her wifely duties. Leroy's presence weighs on her. After so much time spent away, he seems like a stranger, someone who does not understand her. She has begun to improve her mind and her body, taking weightlifting classes and eating healthily. As the story progresses, she enrolls in night school and stays up late studying instead of going to bed early, as she used to do. She admits that she might not tell Leroy if she were having an affair. She clashes with her overbearing mother, who is baffled by the changes in her daughter.

Far from portraying this transformation as a smooth forward movement, Mason stresses Norma Jean's confusion and self-doubt. When Mabel catches her smoking, Norma Jean weeps. She lets Mabel rattle her with the story of the baby-killing dachshund. She tackles night school but writes essays about casseroles, a symbol of her former existence as a simple housewife. In the climactic scene during which Norma Jean says she wants to leave Leroy, she confusedly traces the change back to the day her mother caught her smoking, says she doesn't want to feel like a child anymore, and decides that she was unhappy even before the smoking incident. In the end, she says she doesn't know what she means. The scene presents a microcosm of Norma Jean's mentality: she is able to be braver and speak her mind more freely than she could as a young woman, but she is still insecure. She makes great gains during the course of the story, but the process of self-discovery is slow, painful, and unfinished.

THEMES, MOTIFS, AND SYMBOLS

THEMES

THE PERSISTENCE OF GRIEF Although Randy's death occurred years before the story takes place, it continues to permeate the consciousnesses of Leroy and Norma Jean. They never speak of the death, and Leroy's memories of the baby are fuzzy. Nevertheless, grief about the tragedy persists. Until it begins to seem self-pitying, Leroy tells every hitchhiker he picks up about Randy. Seeing grown-up kids the age Randy would be, had he lived, reminds Leroy of his son. Leroy thinks of Randy when he sees Mabel, who believes that Randy's death was a cruel trick of fate because she opposed Norma Jean's teenage pregnancy. When Mabel tells a nasty story about a dog killing a baby and claims that the mother was to blame for the disaster, both Leroy and Norma Jean immediately assume that she is taking a jab at them. Their sensitivity to Mabel's insinuations suggests that Randy is always at the forefront of their minds.

Randy's death contributes to the dissolution of Leroy and Norma Jean's relationship. The habit of avoiding any mention of the baby becomes an oppressive force in their marriage. Leroy considers saying something about Randy to dispel the discomfort he and his wife sometimes feel around each other, but he seems unable to bring up the topic. Even after Mabel tells the story about the baby killed by the dog, they refer to the death of their son only abstractly. When Norma Jean complains about her mother's spitefulness, Leroy pretends not to know what she is talking about. Norma Jean says he knows exactly what she means, but she will not actually say Randy's name out loud. Rather than continue the discussion, they both fall silent, and such persistent silence drives a wedge between them. At the beginning of the story, Randy thinks about how lucky he and his wife are to be together despite the tragedy; he has heard that the death of an infant can spoil a marriage. But by the end, it is clear that he has been overconfident: the death has affected him and Norma Jean exactly as it affects most couples.

THE INSTABILITY OF GENDER ROLES   Leroy and Norma Jean swap traditional gender roles, which emasculates Leroy and leads to the breakdown of the Moffitts' marriage. Scared and confused by the accident that left him unable to drive his rig, Leroy sits at home all day like a bored housewife, pursuing hobbies that are stereotypically feminine. He makes craft objects from kits and sews needlepoint pillows, which Mabel claims is a womanly pursuit. He thinks of his rig, which sits unused in the backyard, as an unwanted piece of furniture, an image that suggests a woman's dissatisfaction with her shabby possessions. Even his fixation on building a log cabin indicates a traditionally feminine eagerness to settle down in a house of one's own. Leroy feels unsettled by his inability to play the role of the powerful husband. He is shy around his wife, whom he begins to think of as strong and smart. As time goes on, the role-swap convinces Leroy that his wife will leave him.

Norma Jean is confused by her own masculine behavior but also emboldened by it. She is the sole breadwinner after Leroy's accident. When Leroy complains that he can't take a job that requires standing, she reminds him that she has the strength to stand behind a cosmetics counter all day long. She takes a bodybuilding class, and the story begins and ends with a description of her pectorals, muscles that are usually associated with a man's chest. She also enrolls in night courses and works hard at improving herself. These changes, although positive, don't always sit comfortably with Norma Jean. She wants Leroy to play the traditional role of husband and provider and gives him a list of jobs he should consider. With her mother, she behaves like a petulant girl, weeping when she is caught smoking and snapping at Mabel to shut up about Shiloh. But despite her occasional regressions, Norma Jean ultimately begins to embrace her newfound independence. The gender-role reversal continues to bewilder her—after she tells Leroy she wants to leave him, she talks confusedly about feeling eighteen and says she doesn't know what she means—but she is strong enough to say clearly that she wants to end her marriage.

MOTIFS

MUSIC   Norma Jean's changing relationship with music runs parallel to the changes in her marriage to Leroy. Initially, the organ represents an emotional bond between the couple. Leroy buys Norma Jean the organ as a Christmas present, and at first, the songs she plays on it are romantic. One of the tunes mentioned is "Can't Take My Eyes Off You," which mirrors Leroy's admiration for his pretty, youthful spouse. Another is "I'll Be Back," which makes Leroy think of his return to his wife after fifteen years of long absences on the road. But as the months progress, the new songs Norma Jean plays reflect the deterioration of the marriage. The song "Sunshine Superman" may be an ironic joke about Leroy, who lies on the couch smoking weed and looking like anything but a superman. "Who'll Be the Next in Line?" foreshadows Norma Jean's faltering loyalty to her husband. Eventually, Norma Jean stops playing the organ altogether and instead begins writing about the importance of music in her life. She moves away from the present that Leroy gave her and toward the academic world that intimidates him.

SYMBOLS

THE LOG CABIN   The log cabin that Leroy dreams of building for his wife symbolizes his marriage. The cabin is an impractical idea, and the project does not interest Norma Jean. Leroy clings to his dreams of building the cabin with the same touching and misplaced tenacity with which he clings to his wife. Nothing dissuades him, even the straightforward words of Mabel and Norma Jean, who repeatedly tell him that living in a cabin is unpleasant, that new developments wouldn't allow such a structure, that building is too expensive, and that, in any case, Norma Jean hates the idea. Just as Leroy won't let go of the idea of the cabin in the face of strong opposition, he won't give up on his marriage in the face of clear evidence that his wife already has. At Shiloh, Leroy at last realizes that his marriage is as hollow as the boxy interior of a log cabin. Too late, the symbolic link between his dreams of a cabin and his failed marriage becomes clear to him.

THE DUST RUFFLE   The dust ruffle that Mabel gives Leroy and Norma Jean symbolizes the couple's attempts to keep their troubles out of sight. When Mabel brings over the dust ruffle, a present she made by hand, Leroy jokes that it will enable him and Norma Jean to hide possessions underneath the bed. Like a ruffle that conceals objects, silence conceals Leroy's and Norma Jean's difficulties. They both sense the serious rifts that exist between them, but instead of examining them head-on, they ignore issues such as the death of their son, their deep unfamiliarity with each other after years of Leroy's traveling, and their mismatched ambitions. At the end of the story, Leroy looks at the sky, and its bleached shade reminds him of the dust ruffle. The comparison of the sky, a huge expanse, to the dust ruffle, a small scrap of fabric, suggests that Leroy has belatedly understood the enormous destructive power of silence.

SHORT STORY ANALYSIS

LEROY'S POINT OF VIEW   "Shiloh" is narrated in the third-person limited point of view, which means that we get only Leroy's perspective. We see the other characters through Leroy's eyes, rather than getting a wholly objective view of them. Because Norma Jean has become a mystery to Leroy, she is a mystery to us too, and we must initially guess at her motivations and thoughts. As the story opens, Leroy wonders whether she returns his feelings of affection and whether she has ever cheated on him. As the months go by, the time he spends at home allows him to learn new details about his wife: what she eats for breakfast, the way she cuts onions, where and when she puts on her slippers, what she feeds to the birds in their backyard. For the first time in years, Leroy gradually comes to understand his wife's character, an understanding that leads him to anticipate her desire to leave the marriage. As Leroy progresses from being puzzled to noticing details and understanding character, we undergo an identical progression.

Many writers tackle the challenge of writing from the viewpoint of someone of a different age, gender, religion, ethnicity, or sexuality, with varying results. In "Shiloh," Mason's male viewpoint is wholly convincing. Ironically, it is Leroy's stereotypically feminine qualities, such as his sensitivity and sentimentality, that make him a three-dimensional man rather than a stereotype of masculinity. With his affection for his wife, grief about his son, quirky interest in crafts, pot-smoking, and self-doubt, Leroy is a fully drawn human being. Mason's experiment with the male point of view succeeds because she treats it not as a chance to show off her writing chops but as an opportunity to fully enter the mind of a person who happens to be male.

SHOPPING-MALL REALISM   Mason writes in a straightforward, populist fashion that some critics have dubbed "shopping-mall realism," a style that both roots her story in reality and reflects and dignifies the lives of her Kentuckian characters. Mason's sentences are unadorned and rely on the vivid but plain words that her characters might use. The text is filled with references to icons of pop culture, including *Star Trek, Dr. Strangelove, Donohue,* and songs from the 1960s. Mason also makes mention of parking lots, shopping centers, Yodels, Coca-Cola, Diet Pepsi, casseroles, marijuana, orange sneakers, and Rexall drugstores. Many writers would avoid mentioning these sorts of pop culture items, brand names, and places in their fiction for fear of seeming too prosaic or unsophisticated. But Mason prizes accuracy over elevated prose style. She is interested primarily in creating a true portrait of the lives of middle- and lower-middle-class southerners. By faithfully reporting what her characters eat, watch, listen to, and think about, she makes their lives real to us. Her shopping-mall realism also grants dignity to people who have often been overlooked in fiction. Leroy and Norma Jean are not the sort of eloquent and highly educated people familiar from the fiction of, for example, John Updike, but Mason shows that they are as intelligent, sensitive, and complicated as their higher-class fictional counterparts.

Mason's style also allows occasional moments of transcendence to occur amid the detritus of everyday life. Leroy and Norma Jean may be products of a charmless town and relentless consumer culture, but they gravitate toward whatever beauty they can find. Leroy observes the goldfinches that come to the feeder and wonders whether they keep their eyes shut when they fall toward the ground before spreading their wings and flying upward again. Norma Jean aspires to make her body strong and beautiful, possibly from a desire to transcend the ugliness that surrounds her. At Shiloh, she leaves the trees by the parking lot and walks toward the Tennessee River, where she waves her arms in an ambiguous gesture. In a world comprising subdivisions, stores, and vast stretches of cement, these glimpses of melancholy beauty shine all the brighter for their rarity.

HISTORICAL CONTEXT   "Shiloh" is rooted in two wars: the battle for women's rights and the Civil War. Feminism was beginning to take hold in America around the same time that Norma Jean and Leroy were married. After more than fifteen years, its precepts have started to permeate Norma Jean's consciousness. Although she does not articulate her motivations or chalk them up to feminism, she begins a gradual process of reclaiming her independence.

She lifts weights, takes classes, supports the family, and stays up late working on her writing. Instead of cooking delicious, high-fat food for Leroy, as she used to do, she feeds herself with nutritious cereal before heading out to work. When Leroy asks her whether her desire to end the marriage is "'one of those women's lib things,'" she thinks—or pretends to think—that he is joking. But it's clear that women's lib is exactly what is motivating her to strike out on her own.

The Civil War, specifically the battleground at Shiloh, is a counterpart to the feminist struggle; Mason uses the war to underline the confusing, debased, violent, and sometimes romantic institution of marriage. Shiloh is the site of one of the bloodiest battles in American history, but Mabel associates it with marriage because she visited there on the day after her wedding. She thinks of it as a beautiful and romantic spot and repeatedly urges Leroy and Norma Jean to go there on a second honeymoon. When they finally visit the battleground, Leroy senses its many parallels to his own marriage. He is surprised by the direction his marriage has taken, just as he is surprised to find that Shiloh looks not like a golf course but an enormous park full of trees and ravines. He and Norma Jean have struggled to go on, just as the Union and Confederate troops fought to live. And the battleground is now polluted with tourists, parking lots, and cars, just as their lives are polluted by the ordinary and mundane. In the penultimate paragraph of the story, Leroy tries to comprehend the fact that 3,500 men died at Shiloh, but all he can think about is the way his life, and the lives of Mabel, her husband, and Norma Jean, are linked to the battleground. Mason suggests that it is impossible to wrap our minds around abstractions such as war and marriage and that all we can do is understand how they relate to our own lives.

IMPORTANT QUOTATIONS EXPLAINED

1. *"Your name means 'the king," Norma Jean says. . . . she is reading a book about another century. . . .*

    "Am I still the king around here?"

    Norma Jean flexes her biceps and feels them for hardness. "I'm not fooling around with anybody, if that's what you mean. . . ."

This quotation, which appears near the end of the story, reveals that Norma Jean's foray into education both empowers and drives her away from Leroy. When she learns, for example, that *le roy* means "the king" in French, she seems aware of the irony in the definition. Her husband, an out-of-work pothead, strikes her as anything but kinglike. When Leroy asks, "Am I still the king around here?" he reveals his uneasiness. He knows that Norma Jean's books, which he can identify only vaguely as "about another century," are taking her beyond his reach, and he senses that she may have ceased to consider him the head of the household. In answer to Leroy's question, Norma Jean "flexes her biceps," a gesture that should confirm Leroy's suspicions. Norma Jean is literally flexing her muscles and showing her husband that she is the one in charge of things now. She then provides a grudging and stereotypically male reassurance that she is not having an affair. Both mentally and physically, Norma Jean is toughening up.

2. *Leroy has the sudden impulse to tell Norma Jean about himself, as if he had just met her. They have known each other so long they have forgotten a lot about each other. . . . But . . . he forgets why he wants to do this.*

The quotation appears near the middle of the story, as Leroy smokes a joint on the couch. "Shiloh" is in part a story about the impossibility of knowing other people, even people with whom you have spent more than sixteen years. Leroy's long absences on the road have distanced him from Norma Jean, as has the couple's inability to talk about Randy's death. The institution of marriage itself has also separated the couple. In marriages, Mason suggests, chit-chat and comfortable silences can easily replace honest communication, leading to a paradoxical state in which people "have known each other so long they have forgotten a lot about each other." Although Leroy feels a connection to his wife, he no longer understands her motivations or is privy to her thoughts. In fact, her actions often bewilder him. Occasionally he imagines starting over from the beginning and talking to his wife as if they are strangers getting to know each other for the first time. But everything from shyness to marijuana to general stasis prevents him from acting on this impulse. The estrangement only increases as the story goes on, until Leroy is sitting in a car with his wife and feeling as awkward as a young guy on a date with a sophisticated older woman.

S

Sonny's Blues

James Baldwin
(1924–1987)

CONTEXT

James Arthur Baldwin was born on August 2, 1924, in New York's Harlem neighborhood. As the center of African American culture at that time, Harlem was at once a culturally vibrant community of artists and musicians and a neighborhood deeply affected by poverty and violence. Baldwin's mother, after being abandoned by Baldwin's legitimate father, worked as a domestic servant and eventually married David Baldwin, a preacher whose strong influence on his stepson was evident not only in James Baldwin's writing but also in his strong religious devotion. While still a teenager, Baldwin experienced a religious epiphany that led him to become a preacher, an experience that Baldwin used as the basis for his most famous novel, *Go Tell It on the Mountain* (1952), and incorporated into his play *The Amen Corner* (1968) and much of his other writing.

Baldwin's religious fervor had its complications. He had a difficult relationship with his stepfather, and while attending De Witt Clinton High School in the Bronx, he grew to accept his homosexuality, further complicating his role in the church. At De Witt Clinton, Baldwin stood out for his literary talent and ambition. He began spending his spare time in Greenwich Village, the heart of the post–World War II artistic community. There, he met Richard Wright, who had already established himself as an author. Wright helped Baldwin win a fellowship to work on his first novel, which went unpublished.

Baldwin turned toward literary criticism as he struggled to make a career for himself as a writer. Frustrated with life in America, Baldwin left New York for Paris, where he met some of the most noted writers and philosophers of the era, including Saul Bellows and the French philosopher Jean Paul Sartre. Baldwin also began to establish a name for himself through a series of essays, some of which were pointedly directed at Baldwin's first literary mentor, Richard Wright. Despite the success of his essays, Baldwin had yet to fulfill his dream of publishing a novel. In 1951, he retreated to a small village in the Swiss Alps to write what would become his first and most celebrated novel, *Go Tell It on the Mountain*. Highly autobiographical, the novel is set in the Harlem of Baldwin's youth and concerns the religious salvation of a young man, John Grimes, and his problematic relationship with his stepfather.

Go Tell It on the Mountain brought Baldwin wide recognition. The novel was nominated for a National Book Award and brought Baldwin into the forefront of American literature. A few years later, in 1956, Baldwin published *Notes of a Native Son*, a collection of essays that focused on race in America. The civil rights movement had just burgeoned into a national struggle, and Baldwin became one of its most outspoken and eloquent advocates. He appeared on the cover of *Time* magazine and published another highly regarded essay collection, *The Fire Next Time* (1963). Baldwin's third novel, *Another Country* (1962), received mixed reviews but went on nonetheless to sell millions of copies.

Baldwin reached the peak of his fame and popularity as the civil rights movement began its gradual decline, after a number of major victories and the death of Martin Luther King,

Jr., in 1968. Baldwin continued to turn out an almost relentless series of books, both fiction and nonfiction. Although none of his new books were as well received as his earlier writing, Baldwin's work continued to express the dominant themes and images from his life. Racial segregation, Harlem, and the nearly overwhelming obstacles faced by young African American men raised in poverty occur again and again throughout his work.

"Sonny's Blues" was one of Baldwin's earliest short stories. Originally published in the *Partisan Review* in 1957, "Sonny's Blues" follows the narrator as he comes to discover who his drug-addicted, piano-playing younger brother, Sonny, truly is. Set in Harlem, like many of Baldwin's other work, "Sonny's Blues" is a constant struggle between light and darkness, failure and redemption. The story was included in the short-story collection *Going to Meet the Man* (1965). The collection, which spans more than a decade's worth of Baldwin's stories, is notable for the insight it gives into Baldwin's development as a writer. Like much of Baldwin's later fiction, the collection was met with mixed reviews by critics, who noted that in many of these stories Baldwin was revisiting the same themes he had covered in his previous work. Nonetheless, the stories in the collection, "Sonny's Blues" in particular, demonstrate Baldwin's ability to transform his social and political concerns into art. In "Sonny's Blues," Baldwin takes on Harlem's deterioration, religion, drug addiction, and post–World War II America all at the same time. The story, like the characters in it, literally struggles under the weight of so much pressure.

In his later years, Baldwin spent less of his time in America. In December 1987, at age sixty-three, Baldwin died of stomach cancer at his home in the south of France.

PLOT OVERVIEW

The unnamed narrator of the story discovers from a newspaper that his younger brother, Sonny, has been arrested for selling and using heroin. As he prepares to teach his algebra class, the narrator remembers Sonny as a young boy. His students, he realizes, could someday end up like Sonny, given the obstacles and hardships they face growing up in Harlem. At the end of the school day, the narrator heads home, but he notices that one of Sonny's old friends, who is always high and dirty, is waiting for him by the school. The two men walk together, talking about Sonny. The narrator simultaneously hates and pities Sonny's friend, who, despite his problems, makes it painfully clear to the narrator just how difficult Sonny's drug-addicted life has been and how difficult it will continue to be.

Time passes, but the narrator never writes to Sonny in prison until the narrator's young daughter, Grace, dies. Sonny writes a long letter back to his brother in which he tries to explain how he ended up where he is. The two brothers then stay in constant communication. When Sonny gets out of jail, the narrator is there for him. He takes Sonny back to his own family's apartment.

In an extended flashback, the narrator recalls how Sonny and their father used to fight with each other because they were so similar in spirit. He remembers the last day he saw his mother while on leave from the army, when she told him to watch out for his brother. She told him that when his father was a young man, he watched his own brother get run down by a car full of white men who never bothered to stop. The experience traumatized and damaged the narrator's father for the rest of his life.

After that conversation with his mother, the narrator went back into the army and didn't think about his brother again until their mother died. After the funeral, the two brothers sat and talked about Sonny's future. Sonny told his brother about his dream of becoming a jazz pianist, which the narrator dismissed. The narrator arranged for Sonny to live with his wife's family until Sonny graduated from college. Sonny reluctantly agreed to do so. He didn't want to live in the house and spent all his spare time playing the piano. Although Sonny loved the music, the rest of family had a hard time bearing his constant practicing.

While living with his sister-in-law, Sonny got into trouble for skipping school. He tried to hide the truancy letters, but one eventually made it to the house. When his sister-in-law's mother confronted him, Sonny admitted to spending all his time in Greenwich Village, hanging out with musicians. The two fought, and Sonny realized what a burden he'd been on the family. After two days, Sonny joined the navy. The narrator didn't know whether Sonny was dead or alive until he received a postcard from Greece. After the war, the two brothers returned to New York, but they didn't see each other for quite some time. When they eventually met, they fought about Sonny's decisions in life. After one especially difficult fight, Sonny told his brother that he could consider him dead from that point on. The narrator walked away, telling himself that one day Sonny would need his help. The flashback ends there.

After having Sonny live with him for a few weeks, the narrator debates whether he should search Sonny's room. As he paces back and forth, he sees a street-corner revival occurring outside his window and thinks about its significance. Eventually Sonny comes home and invites his brother to watch him perform later that evening. The two brothers go to a small jazz club where everyone knows and respects Sonny. Sonny and the band get on stage and play, and as they play, the narrator watches Sonny struggle with the music. He watches all his brother's struggles come pouring out as he plays, and only then does he finally realize who Sonny is and what he's made of.

CHARACTER LIST

The Narrator   Sonny's older brother. Compared to Sonny and many of the young men in Harlem, the narrator is a success, working as a math teacher and raising a family. However, he also feels trapped in Harlem, where he has lived his entire life. He knows he has an obligation to Sonny, but it takes him a while to get over his skepticism and devote himself to helping Sonny as best he can.

Sonny   The narrator's wayward younger brother. Sonny is a troubled young man who becomes addicted to heroin at an early age. Unlike many of the young boys in the neighborhood, Sonny is not hard or brutal. He keeps all of his problems bottled up—except when he plays music. Music, for Sonny, is a freeing and ultimately redemptive outlet and perhaps the only means he has for keeping himself away from prison and drugs. He channels into his performance not only his own frustration and disappointment but also that of the entire community.

Isabel   The narrator's wife. Unlike the narrator, Isabel can make Sonny feel comfortably at home in their house after Sonny is released from prison. She draws him out of his shell and makes him laugh. She can, in her own way, accept Sonny with less hesitation than the narrator. She is a caring wife and mother who watches over the narrator much the same way his mother watched over his father.

Mother   The mother of Sonny and the narrator. She dies while Sonny is still a boy. Before she dies, she expresses her deep concerns about Sonny's future to the narrator. She is acutely aware of the dangers facing her youngest son, and her final request to the narrator is that he protect his brother, just as she protected their father. Kind and loving, she has spent much of her life trying to protect her family from the darkness of the world.

Sonny's Friend   A drug addict who meets the narrator early in the story to tell him what happened to Sonny. Despite his addiction, he is able to eloquently explain the hardship that comes with drug addiction. He is a troubled, nameless soul whose brief presence in the story speaks for the countless young men in Harlem who struggle with a drug addiction.

Father   The father of Sonny and the narrator. He has the same spirit as Sonny, and as a result he fights constantly with his son. When he was a young man, he lost his brother and was haunted by it his entire life. He constantly searched for a better reality but died without finding it.

Creole   The leader of Sonny's band. An imposing older black man, Creole guides Sonny through his performance at the end of the story. He controls the playing of every member in the band.

Grace   The narrator's daughter. Grace dies of polio while Sonny is prison. Her death prompts the narrator to write to Sonny. Her dying, although not discussed in great detail, becomes an act of grace, allowing the narrator to reach out to his brother for the first time.

ANALYSIS OF MAJOR CHARACTERS

THE NARRATOR   The narrator of "Sonny's Blues" provides insight not only into Sonny and their life together but also into their environment. Although the story invokes Sonny in its title, it is through the narrator's eyes that Sonny and Harlem are revealed. Compared to most of the men in his community, the narrator has succeeded: he has a wife, two children, and a good job as a teacher. However, he is constantly aware of Harlem's darker, more dangerous side. He notes the open drug dealing that happens in the playgrounds near the housing projects, the disappearance of old homes, and, of course, his brother's ongoing battle with the world. Far from worrying solely about his family's difficulties, he frames Sonny's struggles within a larger context, situating him within the poverty, crime, and drug abuse that plague the entire community.

Though the narrator is fully conscious of his community's dark side, he tries his best to keep those problems at arm's length, refusing to let any tragedy affect him too much emotionally. Unlike Sonny, the narrator has a difficult time expressing his ideas and emotions, and only when his young daughter dies does he open up and write to his brother. The narrator believes that he has been called upon to watch over Sonny, but this knowledge doesn't lessen the burden he feels. He is constantly torn by his emotions, which shift quickly from love to hate, concern to doubt. As much as he cares for Sonny, he seems to be unable to fully accept that his brother has the capacity for change.

SONNY   From a young age, Sonny is haunted by the burden of being poor, black, and trapped within the confines of his community. As a young African American male born in Harlem, he is aware of the limits and obstacles he faces. He struggles to defy the stereotypes by moving away from Harlem and beginning a career as a musician. Unlike his brother, Sonny wants and needs an escape from Harlem and the traditional social order. Instead of being free, however, Sonny winds up being confined in prison—far from feeling trapped in his community, he is now literally captive. Even after Sonny is released from prison, the narrator describes him as a caged animal that is trying to break free from the effects that prison has had on him and from the drug addiction that led to his incarceration.

Sonny's one saving grace is his music, through which he can express all of his deep-seated longing and frustration. Sonny's music offers him a chance at redemption, but at the same time it also threatens to destroy him. To create music, Sonny has to bear the suffering and tragedies of his life and all the lives around him. He translates that suffering into an artistic expression that ultimately, even if only temporarily, redeems his audience. There is something heroic, almost Christlike, to the way Sonny offers himself up to his music. He knows that playing music may destroy him by leading him back into a life of drugs, but he also knows that it's a burden that he has to bear.

MOTHER   The mother in "Sonny's Blues" is an almost saintlike figure who guards and protects her children and husband from the darkness of the world, and Baldwin's biblical imagery and undertones come through clearly in her character. She shepherds her husband through the overwhelming grief that follows his brother's death, thereby living up to the biblical challenge to be "your brother's keeper." She has done more than just live a decent life: she helped bear her husband's tragedy as her own. Just as Jesus is often depicted as a shepherd, so too is the narrator's mother, whose presence makes her husband's life manageable. Her life story is a direct challenge to the narrator, who, unlike his mother, initially fails to care for his brother as he should.

In addition to her compassion, the mother also has a prophetic role to play in the narrative. She can see her own impending death and the dangers her youngest son will face. As a mother, she has protected her family, but now that she knows she is going to die, she knows she will no longer be able to guide and protect her family as she once did. Her foreshadowing of her death signals a shift in the narrator's relationship with his brother. It makes him the new protector of Sonny against the greater darkness of the world that has always threatened to invade their lives.

S

THEMES, MOTIFS, AND SYMBOLS

THEMES

THE OBLIGATION TOWARD BROTHERLY LOVE   The narrator's mother, by charging him with watching over Sonny, is asking him to serve as his brother's keeper. The dynamic between the two brothers echoes, in part, the relationship between the brothers Cain and Abel in the Bible. In that narrative, Cain, after murdering Abel, asks whether he is supposed to be his brother's keeper. The narrator, following his mother's death, is presented with a similar dilemma. Since their mother's death, Sonny's life has been marred by prison and drug abuse. The tension between the two brothers is so great that after one particular fight, Sonny tells his brother to consider him dead from that point on, a statement that, again, deliberately echoes the biblical narrative of Cain and Abel. Like Cain, the narrator turns his back on his brother and fails, at first, to respond to Sonny when he is prison. He has failed to live up to his mother's commandment that he watch over his brother—but the failure is only temporary. By the end of the story, the narrator has taken Sonny back into his home. He finally takes on the role of his brother's keeper, constantly watching and worrying over Sonny as he emerges from the darkness of prison and drug abuse.

The idea of brotherly love extends beyond the relationship between the narrator and Sonny into the community as a whole. Harlem is plagued by drugs, poverty, and frustration, but members of the community come together to watch over and protect one another. The adults spend their Saturday afternoons sharing stories, providing a sense of warmth and protection to the children around them. The narrator, although initially angered by one of Sonny's old drug-addicted friends, in the end recognizes his connection to the man and offers him money. Even Sonny, for all his problems, helps the people around him endure and survive by channeling their frustrated desires into his music.

THE PREVALENCE OF RAGE AND FURY   Throughout the story, the narrator repeatedly remarks on the barely concealed rage in the people around him as a way of showing both the internal and external conflicts that haunt the characters. Fury and rage are products not only of the limited opportunities that came with being African American at that time but of life in Harlem as well. Early in the story, the narrator notes that his students are "filled with rage." They are aware of the limited opportunities available to them, and that knowledge breeds an internal, destructive rage that threatens to destroy their lives. With nowhere left to go, they inevitably turn their anger onto themselves, leading them into a life of darkness.

An equally strong rage is present in the streets of Harlem. While looking out the window, Sonny notes with amazement the simple fact that Harlem has not yet exploded. The narrator observes a "furious" man as he drops change into a church bucket. The fury that underlies daily life in Harlem is evident everywhere, even in the religious revivals held on the streets. It's a fury fueled by desperation and desire, and it finds its truest form of expression in the music Sonny plays at the end of the story. As painful and difficult as that fury is, it also makes the type of jazz Sonny plays possible. It gives life to the religious revival Sonny passes on the street, and although it inevitably exacts an enormous toll on all of the people who bear its weight, it also offers something in return.

MOTIFS

IMPRISONMENT   The characters in "Sonny's Blues" are trapped both physically and emotionally. Throughout the story, the narrator and Sonny are constantly struggling to break free from one barrier or another. Sonny is physically imprisoned in jail as well as by his addiction to drugs. The narrator is confined to Harlem and, more specifically, to the housing projects that he clearly detests. In addition, he is also trapped within himself, unable to express his emotions or live up to his obligations as a brother until his daughter's death gives him the motivation he needs to change.

The narrator and Sonny are imprisoned and also free in exactly opposite ways. Sonny, while in prison, is physically locked up, and yet as a young man, he was able to do what his brother never did: escape from Harlem and create a life of his own. On the other hand, the narrator is physically free. He is not in jail or, unlike Sonny and many of the young men in his community, addicted to drugs. Nonetheless, he is trapped inside Harlem and its housing projects. As a musician, Sonny is able to express the frustration and rage that derive in part from his imprisonment. While playing the piano, he is able to break loose and live as free as any man. The narrator, however, lives his life trapped inside of himself. He has a difficult time communicating with his brother and even fails to do so because he cannot bear the emotions that come with it. He is, in the end, temporarily freed by Sonny, whose music offers him a rare glimpse into himself.

SALVATION   The narrator and Sonny are both seeking a form of salvation, not only from the world but also from themselves. The world they live in is plagued by darkness, despair, drugs, and confinement, leading each brother to seek a form of redemption that can cleanse them of their sins. Salvation in "Sonny's Blues" comes in several forms. The narrator is haunted by his failure to respond to his brother, a failure that is a denial both of his brotherly obligation to Sonny and his mother's dying request. The death of Grace, the narrator's daughter, is ultimately an act of grace. It spurs the narrator into immediately writing to his brother, whom he knows he has failed and whose forgiveness he seeks. Sonny, at the same time, has been through a form of hell and, upon his release from prison, wants to be saved from the life of drugs that destroyed him. Just before Sonny invites his brother to watch him perform, he passes a revival on the street, where salvation is promised but never fully attained. During Sonny's performance, both the narrator and Sonny find the salvation they've been seeking, even if only temporarily.

SYMBOLS

THE CUP OF TREMBLING   At the end of the story, the narrator describes a glass sitting over Sonny's piano as shaking "like the very cup of trembling" to highlight what a difficult and complicated position Sonny is in. This image is borrowed from the Bible, where the cup of trembling is used as a symbol to describe the suffering and fear that have plagued the people. The biblical passage promises a relief from that suffering, but Baldwin's use of the cup of trembling as a symbol is less overt. Sonny's drinking from the cup of trembling serves as a reminder of all the suffering he has endured, while also offering the chance for redemption and peace. As a musician, Sonny takes all his suffering and that of those around him and transforms it into something beautiful.

Like the figures from the Bible, Sonny is moving toward salvation, but his fate remains uncertain. Perhaps he will continue to suffer, suffering being the cost he has to pay for being a musician. There is something Christlike about Sonny's pain, and suffering for Sonny is at once inevitable and redemptive. At the end of the story, it remains unclear whether he will continue to suffer in order to play his music or whether a greater peace and redemption awaits everyone involved. The fact that the glass is filled with scotch and milk only further highlights the tension and duality Sonny faces.

HOUSING PROJECTS   The housing projects in Harlem were for Baldwin clear symbols of Harlem's decline and fall. He describes the projects as "rocks in the middle of a boiling sea." It is an apocalyptic image, one meant to convey the awful conditions of life inside of the projects. The phrase also has a biblical undertone in that it invokes a type of hell on earth. As rocks in a boiling sea, the projects are massive, lifeless objects surrounded by misery. The word *rocks* highlights the buildings' cold, brutal nature.

The projects offer up a false image, a "parody of the good," in that they were initially built with the supposedly noble intention of providing affordable housing but in fact became almost immediately broken-down, drug-infested buildings. The projects symbolize a perversion of the real world, one in which good ideas are actually living nightmares. The projects have playgrounds that are populated by drug dealers; they have large windows that no one wants to look out of. The people who live in them are bitterly aware of what the projects are, making their existence cruel and bitterly ironic.

LIGHT AND DARKNESS   Light and darkness are in constant tension throughout "Sonny's Blues," and Baldwin uses them to highlight the warmth, hope, gloom, and despair that mark his characters' lives. Baldwin uses light to describe Sonny's face when he was young and the warmth that came from sitting in a room full of adults after church. Light represents all of the positive and hopeful elements that are a part of life. It also has a religious undertone. Not only does light represent the best elements of life, but it also symbolizes a form of salvation and grace. To live in the light is to live a proper, moral life.

In exact opposition to the light is the darkness that constantly threatens the characters in the story. The darkness, which represents a roster of social and personal problems, can be found everywhere. The darkness literally haunts the figures in the story, something they are acutely aware of once the sun goes down. Sonny's life in prison, his addiction to drugs, and the general state of life in Harlem are all embodied by the darkness. As pervasive as the darkness is, however, it is always balanced against a measure of light. Light, ultimately, comes to signify salvation, comfort, and love, whereas darkness represents the fear and desolation that always threatens to extinguish it.

SHORT STORY ANALYSIS

MUSIC   From the title of the story to the closing scene, music plays a central role in defining the characters and culture of Harlem in "Sonny's Blues." At a young age, Sonny decides he wants to grow up to become a musician, a decision that his brother has difficulty accepting. Sonny lists the great jazz musicians of his era, most notably Charlie Parker, who had broken out of the traditional conventions of jazz to create a new, freer form of musical expression. Unlike earlier forms of jazz, which relied heavily on well-developed and thoroughly planned arrangements, the music of men such as Charlie Parker and Dizzy Gillespie was created spontaneously as the men listened and responded to each other. The music relied on instinct rather than on rigid structures. Sonny contrasts his music idols with those of the previous generation, whose rigid, classical form of musical expression is no longer valid. For Sonny, the world is an entirely different place from the one his older brother grew up in and, as a result, needs new artistic forms to convey its reality.

The music that Sonny plays and loves is based less on a strict formal order than on a pure expression of the soul. Bebop, as it came to be known, was a radical new form of jazz. For musicians like Sonny, the freedom of expression that came with bebop was a chance to live freely, defy social conventions and norms, and create something utterly original. For many of the great musicians of that era, drugs were a constant temptation. Sonny's stated musical hero, Charlie Parker, was himself addicted to drugs and died a very early death partly as a result. At the end of the story, the narrator witnesses Sonny's playing firsthand. The experience is similar to the religious revival the narrator witnessed earlier, with one major exception: there is a real redemption available through the music.

HISTORICAL CONTEXT "Sonny's Blues" is set in post–World War II New York, in the midst of an important cultural and political revolution that permanently changed the country. Artists from all over the world had made New York a new cultural capital, establishing Greenwich Village, where Sonny briefly lives, as the bohemian center of the city. A diverse array of artists, including the painter Jackson Pollack, musician Charlie Parker, and writer Jack Kerouac, all converged in New York around this time. These artists learned and borrowed from one another, and although there were great differences in style and subject matter, many of the artists were responding to what they believed was America's unique cultural and political crisis following the end of the war. In "Sonny's Blues," Sonny wants to move past the traditional conventions of music, as did many postwar artists whose work expressed radical new notions of individual freedom and artistic liberty.

At the same time that the art scene in New York was exploding, thousands of African American soldiers were returning home from the war and heading north toward communities like Harlem, where, instead of finding new job opportunities and equal rights, they found newly constructed housing projects and vast urban slums. Sonny and his brother both serve in the war, and each returns to find a radically different life in America. It was an experience that thousands of other African Americans faced following the war's conclusion. The civil rights movement, which had begun in the South early in the decade, had quickly begun to spread across the country as millions of African Americans began to agitate for equal rights. Although America in the 1950s was generally more conservative, the groundwork for the radical political movements of the 1960s was being laid. Hundreds of homes in Harlem were leveled to build the housing projects, which would eventually become symbols of urban blight and poverty. Harlem was at a critical juncture in its history, seemingly ready, as Sonny notes, to explode. "Sonny's Blues" is a testimony to both the frustration of life in America's cities and the eventual transformation of that frustration into a political and artistic movement.

BALDWIN'S STYLE Baldwin's prose style is one of the most distinctive in American literature, known for both its eloquence and rhetorical force. The Bible was one of Baldwin's earliest literary influences. Throughout his novels and stories, he constantly relies on biblical imagery and phrases to make his moral and political points. In "Sonny's Blues," there is the "cup of trembling" and the description of housing projects as "rocks in the middle of a boiling sea," a phrase that could have been lifted directly from the Book of Revelations in the Bible. Baldwin's sentences also contain a biblical tone and rhythm. For example, near the conclusion of "Sonny's Blues," Baldwin describes the effect that Sonny's playing had on him: "I seemed to hear with what burning he had made it his, with what burning we had yet to make it ours, how we could cease lamenting." The message and particular words that Baldwin employs also have a biblical tone. At the heart of the sentence is a desire for peace and salvation, ideas that occur repeatedly throughout the Bible.

Baldwin was a preacher before he became a writer, and there is a hint of this former preacher in much of his writing. At times, this background helped Baldwin to reach new heights of poetry and eloquence. At other times, however, Baldwin's style was criticized for being too overbearing and direct in its use of moral statements. In "Sonny's Blues," Baldwin strikes a fine balance between employing the occasional rhetorical flourishes and creating morally complicated characters. The closing scene of the story highlights Baldwin's talent as a stylist. Sonny's performance is like a religious sermon, but instead of the words of a preacher, there is only the music. Baldwin describes the music's effect on the narrator with as much grace as a preacher.

IMPORTANT QUOTATIONS EXPLAINED

1. *Yet, when he smiled, when we shook hands, the baby brother I'd never known looked out from the depths of his private life, like an animal waiting to be coaxed into the light.*

The narrator makes this observation about Sonny when he sees him after he's released from prison. Prison, for Sonny, was a hellish experience, as was his addiction to heroin. Both experiences have altered Sonny, but he remains, at heart, the same person he's always been. The narrator notes, somewhat mournfully, that he never actually knew his baby brother, even though he can see traces of him buried beneath the darkness of prison life and drug addiction. It's a painful realization, one that he is forced to confront now that Sonny has become, to some degree, his responsibility. The question that remains for Sonny is whether he can be brought back into the light, whether he can ultimately be saved. While in prison, Sonny lived like a caged animal, trapped in the misery of his life. He is physically free now, but whether he is free of his addiction and sorrow is still unclear.

2. *"All that hatred down there," he said. "All that hatred and misery and love. It's a wonder it doesn't blow the avenue apart."*

Sonny, following his release from prison, makes this observation about the street outside the window. He has just passed a religious revival being held on the street, which promises salvation even though none will actually be granted. Baldwin's story is as much about Harlem as it is about Sonny's life. This observation captures perfectly the complicated nature of the community. It is neither wholly terrible nor wholly wonderful, but rather a mixture of love and hatred. This mixture is what makes Harlem such a vibrant place, but it also threatens to destroy Harlem and the people who live there. Baldwin's concern with the particular streets in Harlem is evident throughout this story. The avenue Sonny is referring to is most likely Lenox Avenue, one of the most important streets in Harlem, which Baldwin frequently wrote about.

3. *For, while the tale of how we suffer, and how we are delighted, and how we may triumph is never new, it always must be heard. There isn't any other tale to tell, it's the only light we've got in all this darkness.*

Near the middle of Sonny's performance at the end of the story, the narrator makes this claim about the music's function. The statement also holds true for Baldwin's writing. "Sonny's Blues" is a story about suffering and triumph, subjects that have been addressed countless times by other writers. Baldwin believed that these were the only things worth writing about, and throughout his prolific career he returned to the same themes again and again. Each exploration was a chance at redemption, an opportunity to make meaning out of the cruelty and hardships in life. Sonny is trying to do precisely that with his music, just as Baldwin tried to do that with his stories and essays. Art becomes the redeemer, the means by which we can save our souls.

The Story of an Hour

Kate Chopin
(1850–1904)

CONTEXT

Kate Chopin was born in St. Louis, Missouri, in 1850, one of five children but the only one to live through her twenties. Her father, Thomas O'Flaherty, died when she was five, and she spent her childhood among women: her mother, Eliza; grandmother; great-grandmother; and the nuns who ran her school. In 1870, Chopin married Oscar Chopin and moved with him to New Orleans, where they had six children.

Chopin was an independent spirit who smoked cigarettes, walked alone through the city, and argued passionately with others about politics and social problems, much to the dismay of the other New Orleans housewives in her social circle. Not long after the family moved to Cloutierville, Louisiana, Oscar died unexpectedly. Chopin mourned his death deeply but eventually embraced her independence, even going so far as to having an affair with a married man. Chopin soon returned to St. Louis, where she would spend the rest of her life.

Chopin began writing fiction in 1889. She wrote about life and people in Louisiana and focused her attention on love, sex, marriage, women, and independence. She published her first novel, *At Fault*, in 1890, when she was forty. The novel was well received, and she went on to publish short stories and essays addressing similar topics. She published two collections of short stories, *Bayou Folk* (1894) and *A Night in Arcadie* (1897), and became known as a writer with a keen eye for local culture. "The Story of an Hour" was published in 1894 and, along with "The Storm" (1898), is among Chopin's most famous stories. Although Chopin's female protagonists act in unconventional, even scandalous, ways, readers accepted this as simply part of the storytelling and didn't suspect Chopin of moralizing or trying to insert her personal opinions into her work.

In 1899, Chopin published her second novel, *The Awakening*. The novel, which chronicles a married woman's adulterous affair, shocked readers. Chopin had allowed her support of women's independence and sexual freedom to shine through, which proved to be unacceptable. The publication of this novel marked the beginning of the end of Chopin's writing career, and the novel soon fell out of print, remaining undiscovered until the 1950s.

Today, Chopin is known for addressing feminist issues many years before the feminist movement became a major social and political force in America. When Chopin was writing, the feminist movement had barely begun, and in Louisiana, women were still considered to be their husbands' lawful property. As a result, Chopin's brazen, sensual, independent protagonists were years ahead of their time. "The Story of an Hour" reflects Chopin's view of the repressive role that marriage played in women's lives as the protagonist, Louise Mallard, feels immense freedom only when her husband has died. While he is alive, she must live for him, and only when he dies does her life once again become her own.

Chopin died of a brain hemorrhage in 1904. She was fifty-two.

PLOT OVERVIEW

Louise Mallard has heart trouble, so she must be informed carefully about her husband's death. Her sister, Josephine, tells her the news. Louise's husband's friend, Richards, learned about a railroad disaster when he was in the newspaper office and saw Louise's husband, Brently, on the list of those killed. Louise begins sobbing when Josephine tells her of Brently's death and goes upstairs to be alone in her room.

Louise sits down and looks out an open window. She sees trees, smells approaching rain, and hears a peddler yelling out what he's selling. She hears someone singing as well as the sounds of sparrows, and there are fluffy white clouds in the sky. She is young, with lines around her eyes. Still crying, she gazes into the distance. She feels apprehensive and tries to suppress the building emotions within her, but can't. She begins repeating the word *Free!* to herself over and over again. Her heart beats quickly, and she feels very warm.

Louise knows she'll cry again when she sees Brently's corpse. His hands were tender, and he always looked at her lovingly. But then she imagines the years ahead, which belong only to her now, and spreads her arms out joyfully with anticipation. She will be free, on her own without anyone to oppress her. She thinks that all women and men oppress one another even if they do it out of kindness. Louise knows that she often felt love for Brently but tells herself that none of that matters anymore. She feels ecstatic with her newfound sense of independence.

Josephine comes to her door, begging Louise to come out, warning her that she'll get sick if she doesn't. Louise tells her to go away. She fantasizes about all the days and years ahead and hopes that she lives a long life. Then she opens the door, and she and Josephine start walking down the stairs, where Richards is waiting.

The front door unexpectedly opens, and Brently comes in. He hadn't been in the train accident or even aware that one had happened. Josephine screams, and Richards tries unsuccessfully to block Louise from seeing him. Doctors arrive and pronounce that Louise died of a heart attack brought on by happiness.

CHARACTER LIST

Louise Mallard   A woman whose husband is reportedly killed in a train accident. When Louise hears the news, she is secretly happy because she is now free. She is filled with a new lust for life, and although she usually loved her husband, she cherishes her newfound independence even more. She has a heart attack when her husband, alive after all, comes home.

Brently Mallard   Louise's husband, supposedly killed in a train accident. Although Louise remembers Brently as a kind and loving man, merely being married to him also made him an oppressive factor in her life. Brently arrives home unaware that there had been a train accident.

Josephine   Louise's sister. Josephine informs Louise about Brently's death.

Richards Brently's friend. Richards learns about the train accident and Brently's death at the newspaper office, and he is there when Josephine tells the news to Louise.

ANALYSIS OF MAJOR CHARACTERS

LOUISE MALLARD An intelligent, independent woman, Louise Mallard understands the "right" way for women to behave, but her internal thoughts and feelings are anything but correct. When her sister announces that Brently has died, Louise cries dramatically rather than feeling numb, as she knows many other women would. Her violent reaction immediately shows that she is an emotional, demonstrative woman. She knows that she should grieve for Brently and fear for her own future, but instead she feels elation at her newfound independence. Louise is not cruel and knows that she'll cry over Brently's dead body when the time comes. But when she is out of others' sight, her private thoughts are of her own life and the opportunities that await her, which she feels have just brightened considerably.

Louise suffers from a heart problem, which indicates the extent to which she feels that marriage has oppressed her. The vague label Chopin gives to Louise's problem—"heart trouble"—suggests that this trouble is both physical and emotional, a problem both within her body and with her relationship to Brently. In the hour during which Louise believes Brently is dead, her heart beats strongly—indeed, Louise feels her new independence physically. Alone in her room, her heart races, and her whole body feels warm. She spreads her arms open, symbolically welcoming her new life. "Body and soul free!" she repeats to herself, a statement that shows how total her new independence really is for her. Only when Brently walks in does her "heart trouble" reappear, and this trouble is so acute that it kills her. The irony of the ending is that Louise doesn't die of joy as the doctors claim but actually from the *loss* of joy. Brently's death gave her a glimpse of a new life, and when that new life is swiftly taken away, the shock and disappointment kill her.

THEMES, MOTIFS, AND SYMBOLS

THEMES

THE FORBIDDEN JOY OF INDEPENDENCE In "The Story of an Hour," independence is a forbidden pleasure that can be imagined only privately. When Louise hears from Josephine and Richards of Brently's death, she reacts with obvious grief, and although her reaction is perhaps more violent than other women's, it is an appropriate one. Alone, however, Louise begins to realize that she is now an independent woman, a realization that enlivens and excites her. Even though these are her private thoughts, she at first tries to squelch the joy she feels, to "beat it back with her will." Such resistance reveals how forbidden this pleasure really is. When she finally does acknowledge the joy, she feels possessed by it and must abandon herself to it as the word *free* escapes her lips. Louise's life offers no refuge for this kind of joy, and the rest of society will never accept it or understand it. Extreme circumstances have given Louise a taste of this forbidden fruit, and her thoughts are, in turn, extreme. She sees her life as being absolutely hers and her new independence as the core of her being. Overwhelmed, Louise even turns to prayer, hoping for a long life in which to enjoy this feeling. When Brently returns, he unwittingly yanks Louise's independence away from her, putting it once again out of her reach. The forbidden joy disappears as quickly as it came, but the taste of it is enough to kill her.

THE INHERENT OPPRESSIVENESS OF MARRIAGE Chopin suggests that all marriages, even the kindest ones, are inherently oppressive. Louise, who readily admits that her husband was kind and loving, nonetheless feels joy when she believes that he has died. Her reaction doesn't suggest any malice, and Louise knows that she'll cry at Brently's funeral. However, despite the love between husband and wife, Louise views Brently's death as a release from oppression. She never names a specific way in which Brently oppressed her, hinting instead that marriage in general stifles both women and men. She even seems to suggest that she oppressed Brently just as much as he oppressed her. Louise's epiphany in which these thoughts parade through her mind reveals the inherent oppressiveness of all marriages, which by their nature rob people of their independence.

MOTIFS

WEEPING Louise's weeping about Brently's death highlight the dichotomy between sorrow and happiness. Louise cries or thinks about crying for about three-quarters of "The Story of an Hour," stopping only when she thinks of her new freedom. Crying is part of her life with Brently, but it will presumably be absent from her life as an independent woman. At the beginning of the story, Louise sobs dramatically when she learns that Brently is dead, enduring a "storm of grief." She continues weeping when she is alone in her room, although the crying now is unconscious, more a physical reflex than anything spurred by emotion. She imagines herself crying over Brently's dead body. Once the funeral is over in her fantasies, however, there is no further mention of crying because she's consumed with happiness.

SYMBOLS

HEART TROUBLE The heart trouble that afflicts Louise is both a physical and symbolic malady that represents her ambivalence toward her marriage and unhappiness with her lack of freedom. The fact that Louise has heart trouble is the first thing we learn about her, and this heart trouble is what seems to make the announcement of Brently's death so threatening. A person with a weak heart, after all, would not deal well with such news. When Louise reflects on her new independence, her heart races, pumping blood through her veins. When she dies at the end of the story, the diagnosis of "heart disease" seems appropriate because the shock of seeing Brently was surely enough to kill her. But the doctors' conclusion that she'd died of overwhelming joy is ironic because it had been the loss of joy that had actually killed her. Indeed, Louise seems to have died of a broken heart, caused by the sudden loss of her much-loved independence.

THE OPEN WINDOW The open window from which Louise gazes for much of the story represents the freedom and opportunities that await her after her husband has died. From the window, Louise sees blue sky, fluffy clouds, and treetops. She hears people and birds singing and smells a coming rainstorm. Everything that she experiences through her senses suggests joy and spring — new life. And when she ponders the sky, she feels the first hints of elation. Once she fully indulges in this excitement, she feels that the open window is providing her with life itself. The open window provides a clear, bright view into the distance and Louise's own bright future, which is now unobstructed by the demands of another person. It's therefore no coincidence that when Louise turns from the window and the view, she quickly loses her freedom as well.

SHORT STORY ANALYSIS

STRUCTURE AND STYLE   In "The Story of an Hour," Chopin employs specific structural and stylistic techniques to heighten the drama of the hour. The structure Chopin has chosen for "The Story of an Hour" fits the subject matter perfectly. The story is short, made up of a series of short paragraphs, many of which consist of just two or three sentences. Likewise, the story covers only one hour in Louise Mallard's life—from the moment she learns of her husband's death to the moment he unexpectedly returns alive. The short, dense structure mirrors the intense hour Louise spends contemplating her new independence. Just as Louise is completely immersed in her wild thoughts of the moment, we are immersed along with her in this brief period of time. This story can be read quickly, but the impact it makes is powerful. Chopin surprises us first with Louise's elated reaction when she first murmurs "free" to herself. She shocks us again at the conclusion when she dies upon Brently's return. The "heart disease" mentioned at the end of the story echoes the "heart trouble" discussed at the beginning, intensifying the twist ending and bringing the story to a satisfying close.

Because such a short story leaves no room for background information, flashbacks, or excessive speculation, Chopin succeeds in making every sentence important by employing an almost poetic writing style. She uses repetition to highlight important points, such as when she repeats the word *open* throughout the story to emphasize the freedom of Louise's new life. She has Louise repeat the word *free* over and over again as well, which is one of the few words Louise actually speaks aloud in the story and indicates how much she cherishes her newfound freedom. Besides repeating words, Chopin also repeats phrases and sentence structures to highlight important points. For example, Chopin writes, "She breathed a quick prayer that life might be long. It was only yesterday that she had thought with a shudder that life might be long." The identical phrasing of the second half of each sentence reveals how drastically Louise's life has changed—she once shuddered at the thought of a long life, but now she prays for it. Finally, Chopin makes the prose of the story beautiful by using alliteration and internal rhymes. For example, Josephine "revealed in half concealing" when she tells Louise the news, and Brently reappears "composedly carrying" his belongings. All of Chopin's stylistic and structural techniques combine to make this very short story powerful.

IMPORTANT QUOTATIONS EXPLAINED

1. *But now there was a dull stare in her eyes, whose gaze was fixed away off yonder on one of those patches of blue sky. It was not a glance of reflection, but rather indicated a suspension of intelligent thought.*

This quotation appears after Louise has gone alone to her room to deal with the news of Brently's death. After an initial fit of tears, Louise looks out her window at the wide-open spaces below. This quotation is our first hint that Louise's reaction to Brently's death will be surprising and that Louise is very different from other women. Whereas most women would gaze reflectively at the sky and clouds, Louise's gaze suggests something different, something shrewder or more active. What she sees as she gazes out the window is different from what other women would likely see after their husbands have died. Not long after this passage, Louise acknowledges the joyous feeling of independence that Brently's death has given her. Here, at the window, the first breaths of these feelings are stirring, and her "intelligent thought" will quickly engage once again as she processes these feelings and allows herself to analyze what they mean.

---

2. *She breathed a quick prayer that life might be long. It was only yesterday she had thought with a shudder that life might be long.*

This quotation appears close to the end of the story, just before Louise leaves her bedroom to go back downstairs, and illuminates the extent of Louise's elation. Before Brently's death, Louise viewed her life with trepidation, envisioning years of dull, unchanging dependence and oppression. The "shudder" she felt was one of dread. Now, however, she is free and independent, and her life is suddenly worth living. Whereas she once hoped life would be short, she now prays for a long, happy life. This passage, besides showing us how fully Louise feels her independence, also highlights the unexpectedness of Louise's reaction. Rather than dread a life lived alone, this solitude is, for Louise, reason enough to anticipate the future eagerly. When Brently returns, she dies, unable to face the return of the life that she'd dreaded so much.

Super-Frog Saves Tokyo

Haruki Murakami
(1949–)

CONTEXT

Haruki Murakami was born in Kyoto, Japan, in 1949 and raised mostly in the cosmopolitan port city of Kobe, where his mother and father both taught Japanese literature. Murakami's childhood was spent in the traumatic wake of World War II. The Japanese had surrendered to the Allies in August 1945, after atomic bombs were detonated over the cities of Nagasaki and Hiroshima. Earlier that year, half of Tokyo had burned, and American firebombs had killed more than 100,000 Japanese. After the war, the United States occupied and ruled Japan from 1945 until 1952. Murakami was thus born during an intense period of self-examination by the Japanese as they attempted to redefine their national identity while living under an increasingly dominant American presence.

In 1968, Murakami went to Tokyo to attend Waseda University, where he studied dramatic literature. Murakami's love for popular music was well established by the time he graduated. He worked at a record store during college and eventually opened a jazz bar in Tokyo called Peter Cat, which he ran for seven years. Murakami didn't write his first novel until he was almost thirty. According to a now well-worn anecdote, Murakami was watching a baseball game when an American player named Dave Hilton hit a double. At the moment Hilton's bat made contact with the ball, Murakami claims, he knew he could write a novel. Murakami wrote his first book, *Hear the Wind Sing* (1979), at nights after closing the bar and submitted it for the Gunzou Literature prize for emerging authors. He won first prize. *Hear the Wind Sing* became the first part of a series known as "The Rat Trilogy," which also includes *Pinball, 1973* (1980) and *A Wild Sheep Chase* (1982). His novel *Norwegian Wood* (1987), a bittersweet story about sexual revolution in 1960s Tokyo (with a title that alludes to a Beatles' song), became a runaway bestseller in Japan, particularly among younger readers, and catapulted Murakami to a new level of fame.

Murakami and his wife, Yoko, settled for a time in Rome in 1986 and later moved to the United States, where he spent two years as a visiting scholar at Princeton and another two years as a writer in residence at Tufts University, in Boston. In January 1995, a massive earthquake devastated Murakami's hometown of Kobe, killing more than 6,000 people and striking a heavy blow to the Japanese economy. Two months later, in March 1995, Japan received another shock when the Aum Shinrikyo cult released deadly sarin gas into the Tokyo subway system, killing twelve and injuring thousands more. Still in Boston, Murakami followed the events on television. The overwhelming emotions he felt watching his homeland suffer convinced him that it was time to return.

Back in Japan, Murakami set to work on his first nonfiction project. *Underground* (1997) is a collection of sixty interviews with survivors of the subway attack, interspersed with essays written by Murakami. His next work of fiction, the short-story collection *after the quake*, also drew from the tragedies of 1995. (Murakami specifically instructed his English translator, Jay Rubin, to print the titles of the collection and its six stories in lowercase letters.) The characters in *after the quake* experience serious repercussions from the Kobe disaster, although only indirectly. None of the stories are set in Kobe, and although "Super-Frog Saves Tokyo" is built around the threat of an earthquake in Tokyo, none of the stories depict scenes from the actual Kobe quake. The protagonists in each story, however, are profoundly shaken by some kind of upheaval, whether social or personal. A lingering sense of dread and anxiety filters through the stories, as if the shaking ground in Kobe had forced every Japanese person to question their deepest-held beliefs.

Murakami enjoys a level of popularity in America unmatched by most international writers. His short stories are frequently published in major American magazines such as the *New Yorker*, *GQ*, and *Harper's*, and his novels regularly receive high-profile reviews before landing comfortably on bestseller lists. For Western readers, Murakami's work can be a bracing blend of the familiar and exotic. Although his stories generally take place in Japan and almost always feature Japanese characters, those characters often display a thorough grounding in American popular culture. References to rock music and Western philosophers abound, as do nods to American consumer culture—KFC mascot Colonel Sanders even has a small but pivotal role in Murakami's novel, *Kafka on the Shore* (2002; translated into English in 2005).

Murakami's narratives continuously balance the mundane and strange. His writing style is plain and unadorned, and his protagonists are usually ordinary middle-class men who remain passive and unobtrusive until pushed into action by external forces. This flatness, however, is often paired with a strong sense of the surreal. In Murakami's stories, animals speak, ghosts return from the grave, and parallel universes exist calmly in the shadows of our own.

PLOT OVERVIEW

On February 15, 1995, Katagiri, a longtime collections officer for the Tokyo Security Trust Bank, is surprised to find a giant frog waiting for him politely outside his apartment. Frog introduces himself and apologizes for barging into Katagiri's home, claiming to have an urgent matter to discuss. He has come because Tokyo is about to be destroyed. Katagiri thinks that it must be a prank, but Frog assures him that they are the only ones present. Frog tells him that he isn't crazy and that Katagiri isn't dreaming. Confused and overwhelmed, Katagiri asks whether Frog is "a real frog." Frog replies in the affirmative and demonstrates his realness by tilting back his head and letting out a wall-rattling series of *ribits*. Frog tells Katagiri that there will be an earthquake three days from now, much bigger than the one that struck Kobe a month earlier. More than 150,000 people will die, and the city's infrastructure will be destroyed. The epicenter will be right under Katagiri's bank office. Frog tells Katagiri that to stop the earthquake from happening, the two of them must go underground and do mortal combat with Worm.

Frog explains that Worm is a giant worm that has slept deep beneath Tokyo for decades, his eyes and brain slowly atrophying. Worm absorbs reverberations as he sleeps and replaces those impulses with rage through a mysterious chemical process. When the rage builds to a certain level, he releases it in the form of an earthquake. Frog says that he feels no personal animosity toward Worm but that Worm has nevertheless become too dangerous to ignore. Katagiri accepts this explanation, but he still doesn't understand why Frog has chosen him for the mission.

Frog says that he's been watching Katagiri for a long time. He's seen Katagiri do the dirty, difficult work of collecting money from thugs without ever receiving the recognition he deserves. He's also seen the sacrifices Katagiri made for his siblings. Frog says there is no one in Tokyo he would rather have by his side in this battle. Katagiri suggests that Frog will be better off with someone who's stronger, maybe a martial arts expert. Frog waves him off, saying that he'll do the fighting but needs Katagiri for moral support. Frog is also frightened and reluctant to fight Worm, but he quotes Nietzsche's maxim that "the highest wisdom is to have no fear."

As a final reassurance, Frog offers to solve a sticky loan situation for Katagiri involving a company called Big Bear Trading. Then Frog flattens himself up and slips out through the door crack. The next morning, a lawyer calls Katagiri to say that that Big Bear will pay off all debts as long as Frog stays away. Frog comes to Katagiri's office at lunch. He tells Katagiri not to worry because no one else can see him. Now that he's proven his existence, Frog wants confirmation that Katagiri will help him fight Worm. There will be no glory in their battle, he warns, because no one besides the two of them will ever know it has taken place. Katagiri tries to convince Frog once again that he's not worthy, but Frog says that people like Katagiri are the reason why Tokyo is worth saving and that only someone like Katagiri could help him win the battle. Katagiri reluctantly agrees.

Frog describes how the two of them will head underground through a hidden shaft in the bank's boiler room on February 17. He assures Katagiri that he has battle plans but refuses to divulge them when Katagiri asks for details. Katagiri pushes again, asking what Frog will do if Katagiri gets scared and runs away. Frog thinks and then answers that he would just have to fight alone, even though he would have about as much hope of defeating Worm alone as Anna Karenina would have had of beating the speeding locomotive that killed her. Frog seems disappointed that Katagiri has not read Tolstoy's novel.

On the evening of the battle, however, Katagiri is shot while returning from his collection rounds. A young man in a leather jacket jumps in front of him and puts a slug in his right shoulder. Other shots follow. Katagiri wakes up in a hospital, where the attending nurse explains that it's 9:15 a.m., February 18. Katagiri asks about the previous night's earthquake and is relieved to discover that nothing happened. He's perplexed, however, to learn that he wasn't shot. He was found lying unconscious on the street and had apparently been yelling Frog's name in the hospital all night long.

Frog appears in Katagiri's hospital room that night, exhausted and wounded. Katagiri begins to apologize for not meeting him in the boiler room, but Frog explains that Katagiri did help him—in his dreams. The battle took place in the area of imagination, Frog explains. He describes how Katagiri brought in a foot-powered generator to light Frog's way in the battle to fight off the encroaching darkness. In the end, Frog was unable to defeat Worm, able only to call a draw and prevent the earthquake from taking place.

Frog then slips into a coma. He begins to twitch, and boils break out all over his body. The boils pop, and creatures that look like worms, maggots, and centipedes start crawling out. Frog's eyeballs fall to the floor, where they're eaten by bugs. The entire room is covered with insects, blotting out the light, overwhelming Katagiri in his bed. He screams. The nurse turns on the light, and the bugs are suddenly gone. She gives Katagiri an injection and tells him that he had another nightmare. Delirious, Katagiri tells the nurse that Frog sacrificed himself to save Tokyo from an earthquake. The nurse says that Katagiri must have been very fond of Frog. "Locomotive," he says. "More than anybody." She wipes the sweat from his brow as he drifts into a deep sleep.

CHARACTER LIST

Katagiri   A collections officer for the Tokyo Security Trust Bank and protagonist of the story. Katagiri is short, balding, and seemingly unremarkable. Nevertheless, Katagiri is a tough, reliable man, and Frog chooses him for the battle with Worm because he sees a courage and staunchness in the man whom everyone else seems to overlook.

Frog   A giant talking frog. Frog enlists Katagiri to help him battle Worm to save Tokyo from a giant earthquake. Frog has a deeply philosophical temperament, both in the sense that he enjoys knotty philosophical puzzles and that he is thoughtful, careful, and articulate. Even though Frog takes pains to prove that he is an actual frog, it remains unclear whether he truly exists.

Worm   A giant worm that slumbers deep beneath Tokyo city, directly under the offices of Katagiri's bank. Worm absorbs vibrations from the city, which slowly build up in his body until they are transformed into pure rage. When the rage reaches a critical point, Worm releases that energy in the form of devastating earthquakes.

The Nurse   A woman who tends Katagiri in the hospital after he is found passed out in the street. She is patient and motherly and treats Katagiri with great sympathy.

Young Man   The man who shoots Katagiri shortly before he's supposed to battle Worm. Because Katagiri shows no signs of having been wounded, it seems likely that the young man is a figment of Katagiri's imagination.

Shiraoka   An attorney for Big Bear Trading, a company that had been defaulting on loan payments to Katagiri's bank. After Frog pays a mysterious visit to the company leaders, Shiraoka is dispatched to tell Katagiri that Big Bear will pay its debt as long as Frog is kept away.

ANALYSIS OF MAJOR CHARACTERS

KATAGIRI   On the surface, there doesn't seem to be much to Katagiri. Forty and socially awkward, with flat feet and a receding hairline, Katagiri has little family and fewer friends. Underneath his unremarkable exterior, however, Katagiri harbors some truly remarkable qualities. Frog respects Katagiri for his wisdom and courage as well as for the quiet, steady way he faces challenges without ever seeking any reward. Katagiri's isolation might be seen as a manifestation of his modesty, evidence of a desire to avoid imposing himself on the world or asking too much of it. Companionship is one of the many rewards that Katagiri deserves but never receives.

In Frog and his mission, Katagiri finds recognition and validation for an entire life of silent struggles. Although Katagiri appears to be right back where he started at the end of the story—with no friends, reward, or recognition for having helped save Tokyo—the deep, tranquil sleep that Katagiri falls into is one of satisfaction and relief. Not only did he save 150,000 lives, but for once, after a life of slipping through the shadows and hovering in the background, Katagiri knows he has truly been perceived and witnessed by another person—even if that person happened to be a giant, talking—and possibly imaginary—frog.

FROG   Frog is a blend of contradictions. He is a lighthearted pacifist who loves art and nature, yet when Worm's growing instability threatens the city of Tokyo, Frog shoulders his mission bravely and resolutely. He speaks courteously and respectfully to Katagiri yet proves capable of stirring fear and terror in his enemies such as Big Bear Trading and Worm. Frog is also surprisingly bookish, and his speech is littered with highbrow references to Western thinkers, including the philosopher Friedrich Nietzsche and the writers Joseph Conrad, Leo Tolstoy, and Fyodor Dostoevsky.

Perhaps the greatest contradiction in Frog's character concerns the nature of his existence. Frog claims to be "a real frog" that looks and sounds like an ordinary frog (that is, when he isn't speaking Japanese with Katagiri). He's also real in the sense that he can have an effect on the world around him, as he proves with Big Bear. However, real frogs—that is, the animals we commonly see in lakes and in pet stores—cannot walk on their hind legs, speak, or change their bodily form at will. Frog is clearly a supernatural, fantastic creature, and in that sense, he cannot be real. The question of Frog's reality is never truly resolved in "Super-Frog Saves Tokyo," and throughout the story, Frog points out several philosophical paradoxes that may shed light on his existence, such as Conrad's assertion that people can be terrified most by their own imaginations.

WORM   Worm is the enemy in "Super-Frog Saves Tokyo," but he's not a true villain. Frog knows that Worm must be stopped to save the citizens of Tokyo, but he doesn't necessarily believe that Worm is evil or that Worm doesn't have a right to exist. Even though he has a frightful appearance and is prone to violence, Worm is as morally neutral as an actual earthquake. In fact, Frog's description of Worm's awakening seems to place some of the blame on human beings, because it is the clamor and tumult of the city itself that produces Worm's rage. The figure of Worm evokes the two tragedies Japan suffered in 1995, both of which took place deep underground. Frog claims that the Kobe earthquake in January 1995 pushed Worm's patience over the limit, while the pointed comparison of Worm and a commuter train evokes the Aum Shirinkyo subway tragedy of March 1995.

THEMES, MOTIFS, AND SYMBOLS

THEMES

VIRTUE AS ITS OWN REWARD   One of the major themes of "Super-Frog Saves Tokyo" is that there are some obligations a person must assume in life, even if recognition or reward is unlikely. Katagiri has spent his whole life taking on these kinds of duties. When his parents died, Katagiri dedicated himself to raising his brother and sister, putting them through college and arranging their marriages. At work, Katagiri takes on the hardest jobs, dealing with violent clients in a dangerous part of the city without ever receiving the praise he deserves. Frog changes Katagiri's life because he helps him to understand that virtue is its own reward. He knows that Katagiri is already strongly motivated by a sense of duty and obligation. When

Katagiri expresses reluctance to fight Worm, Frog appeals to this sensibility by telling him that this battle is "a matter of responsibility and honor," not glory. If they succeed, no one will know, and if they are killed, no one will feel bad about the way they died. Yet Frog manages to make this sacrifice seem worthwhile, even desirable. He references Hemingway and Tolstoy, great authors who lend a heroic gloss to their characters' decisions to go to battle without the promise of acknowledgment or gratitude.

At the same time, however, Frog does reward Katagiri for his service. At the end of the story, Katagiri has the satisfaction of having participated in a truly glorious, monumental battle, after having spent his life occupied with more mundane labors. But perhaps more importantly, Frog offers Katagiri recognition, honoring the daily struggles of his previous life and providing him with an emotional release he had never experienced. At the end of the story, it seems clear that Super-Frog saved not only Tokyo but Katagiri as well.

THE INSTABILITY OF LIFE   The first line of "Super-Frog Saves Tokyo"—"Katagiri found a giant frog waiting for him in his apartment"—recalls the famous opening to Franz Kafka's story "The Metamorphosis," which begins with the main character discovering that he'd transformed into an insect overnight. Like Kafka, Murakami tells the story of an ordinary man confronted with a shocking, unprecedented event that upends his life completely. In "Super-Frog," the arrival of the amphibian stranger turns the normal order of things topsy-turvy so that frogs can be six feet tall, speak, and make tea. Earthquakes, previously assumed to be the product of plate tectonics, are revealed to be the work of a giant, angry worm. Katagiri experiences a sudden and shocking upheaval as well when, after years of working in the criminal districts of Tokyo, he is shot on the street near his office. The ground beneath the characters feet is literally unstable, as evidenced by both the Kobe earthquake and potential Tokyo quake.

The instability depicted in "Super-Frog" parallels the situation found in mid-1990s Japan. The Kobe earthquake, gas attack on the Tokyo subway, and collapse of the Japanese economy all weighed heavily on Murakami as he wrote the stories collected in *after the quake*. "Super-Frog" offers consolation to a traumatized Japan by showing how radical upheaval can sometimes lead to higher wisdom or satisfaction. Frog claims that an earthquake in Tokyo would make people appreciate the fragility of their city and, by his unspoken extension, the fragility of their existence. Katagiri gains an understanding of his own vulnerability, but he also emerges from the experience rejuvenated and with a deep sense of satisfaction.

MOTIFS

THE UNDERGROUND   The space beneath the earth's surface is fraught with peril and anxiety as the home of the enemy and source of the potentially devastating earthquake. To reach Worm's lair, Frog and Katagiri must pass through a series of places that are hidden from public view, just like the figurative "underground" in which Katagiri spent so much of his earlier life. Katagiri deals primarily with the shady criminal underworld in the red-light district of Kabuki-cho, which is filled with gangsters and "money flowing beneath the surface from one murky den to another." This image of dirty, subterranean rivers makes the figurative concept of an underground economy a literal one. The thugs and gangsters of Kabuki-cho and fraudulent executives of Big Bear Trading all traffic in concealed corruption. Murakami thus uses the underground motif to draw parallels between the sleeping, monstrous Worm and criminal underworld, both of which are portrayed as lurking threats to Japanese society. The notion of the underground also connects "Super-Frog Saves Tokyo" to the Aum Shinrikyo subway attack and real-life Kobe earthquake. Both of these incidents, which had shaken the collective Japanese identity, were subterranean terrors.

SYMBOLS

WORM Murakami has described Worm as a symbol of inner evil, which is a broad and flexible definition. Worm may represent the wickedness hidden inside the city of Tokyo (the criminal corruption that Katagiri battles every day) or the malice hidden inside the hearts of individual people. He may also represent the internal terrors of the imagination, a notion that Frog discusses often throughout the story. Because Worm apparently cannot be killed and his violent outbursts occur cyclically, Murakami seems to be arguing that human beings' inner evil is similarly persistent and difficult to defeat. Frog complicates this reading when he says that he doesn't consider Worm to be "the embodiment of evil." Worm is not evil himself; rather, he is like a vessel that collects hatred from other sources.

SHORT STORY ANALYSIS

MAGICAL REALISM Magical realism is a genre of literature that places fantastical or surreal elements in a recognizably ordinary setting. Sometimes these disparate elements sit comfortably alongside one another, and characters accept fanciful or supernatural occurrences as a part of everyday life. However, in some magical realist stories, the ordinary world is shocked by the introduction of the extraordinary, and in these cases it is usually the tension between the two elements that drives the story forward. In "Super-Frog Saves Tokyo," for example, the pitiable bank officer Katagiri spends most of the story wondering whether he can believe his eyes and his senses, which seem to tell him that a giant frog is talking to him and seeking his help in a battle against a giant worm. Katagiri's ordinariness and the relative poorness of his social and emotional life make the distinction between his previous life and the magical experience he shares with Frog even more pronounced.

In "Super-Frog Saves Tokyo," the magic serves a healing purpose. If we choose to accept Frog's claims at face value—that Tokyo is indeed being threatened with imminent destruction—then magic, as embodied by Frog, has come as a savior to heal the city's psychic damage by destroying Worm. But even if we don't believe this surreal premise and assume that Katagiri has imagined or hallucinated Frog, then we can still say that magic has healed him—even if the magic only lives in Katagiri's mind. Katagiri is a solitary, friendless man with no real connection to the world he lives in. When Frog comes to him, telling him that he has secretly been selected for a gloriously dangerous task, Katagiri's life gains a sense of meaning. Everything he has done thus far in his life has prepared him for this moment— none of his efforts were wasted or unappreciated. Perhaps more important, Katagiri has gained a true friend in the surreal, monstrous Frog, someone he is drawn to, cares for, and respects. The deep satisfaction Katagiri feels at the end of the story suggests that something inside him has indeed been healed by his extraordinary encounter.

THE QUESTION OF REALITY Frog recruits Katagiri to battle Worm with him, but the true quest Katagiri embarks on in "Super-Frog Saves Tokyo" is primarily philosophical in nature.

Throughout the story, Katagiri struggles to determine whether his experiences are real, wondering whether he can trust his senses and trying to figure out what's going on around him. Philosophers call this branch of inquiry, which seeks to understand the nature of human knowledge, *epistemology*. Epistemologists examine the ways in which human beings draw conclusions about the world around them. Katagiri's attempts to figure out whether Frog, Worm, and the imminent earthquake are actually "real" place his quest firmly within an epistemological framework.

According to the dictionary, *real* means having a physical presence or existing as fact and not imagination. Katagiri's experiences with Frog confound these definitions, however. Frog seems to be a solid, corporeal being at times, but only in front of Katagiri. Even after he self-destructs in a putrid mess at the end of the story, his remains vanish instantly when the nurse flips on the lights. Just prior to his death, Frog explicitly admits to moving within the realms of dreams and imaginations, which would make him unreal. He claims to have fought Worm in the "area of the imagination," for example, and claims that Katagiri traveled to his side on the battlefield in his dreams. Finally, just before he dies and his body erupts in boils, Frog warns Katigiri, "What you see with your eyes is not necessarily real." The fact that no other witness can confirm what Katagiri has seen with his eyes—except, perhaps, for the unseen and unnamed Big Bear executive—adds to the sensation that nothing in "Super-Frog" was actually real.

However, the story's emotional impact makes it hard to dismiss the unreal events so easily. Like the reader, Katagiri is teased with a series of riddles that do not lead him to true intellectual understanding. And yet, when he closes his eyes and sighs at the end of the story, we can see that he has drawn great satisfaction from his experiences with Frog, whether they were real, imagined, or otherwise. There may never have been a "real" threat to the citizens of Tokyo, but the effect that Frog has on Katagiri is real and tangible. Although Murakami engages with questions of epistemological philosophy, in the end, he seems to suggest that faith and imagination can sometimes trump the intellect.

IMPORTANT QUOTATIONS EXPLAINED

1. *I just gave them a little scare. A touch of psychological terror. As Joseph Conrad once wrote, true terror is the kind that men feel toward their imagination.*

This is Frog's response to Katagiri when he asks about the visit to Big Bear Trading. Frog tells him that he didn't use any actual, physical violence to achieve his ends. He simply played on the executive's fear. In his explanation, Frog paraphrases an excerpt from Joseph Conrad's novel *Lord Jim* (1900), in which one of Conrad's characters remarks that "the reality could not be half as bad, not half as anguishing, appalling, and vengeful as the created terror of his imagination."

The notion that the imagination can be the source of terrible, horrifying experiences recurs throughout "Super-Frog Saves Tokyo." When Frog recounts the battle with Worm that Katagiri cannot remember participating in, Frog tells him that the battle had actually been fought in Katagiri's imagination. Earlier in the story, when Katagiri is shot, he remembers Frog's Conrad quotation and turns off his own imagination, immediately falling into unconsciousness. When the nurse tells him the next day that he hasn't actually been shot, his memory of the incident becomes hazy. Perhaps Katagiri imagined the shooting, but if he did, then that would mean that an imaginary creature managed to have an effect on him. This refutes Frog's earlier attempt to prove his own existence, in which Frog claims that, by making the Big Bear executive change his mind about the payment he owes to the bank, he has proven that he exists as a real creature capable of producing results in the real world. These inconsistencies and ambiguities make it impossible to say definitively whether Frog, Worm, and the battle actually "existed," and if so, what kind of existence they may have had.

---

2. *Smiling, the nurse toweled the sweat from his forehead. "You were very fond of Frog, weren't you, Mr. Katagiri?"*

"Locomotive," Katagiri mumbled. "More than anybody." Then he closed his eyes and sank into a restful, dreamless sleep.

Murakami ends "Super-Frog Saves Tokyo" on a cryptic note. Just before he dies, Frog says, "The locomotive is coming." This is a reference to the novel *Anna Karenina*, by Russian author Leo Tolstoy, in which the title character commits suicide by throwing herself in front of a train. Tolstoy strongly believed in personal integrity and that the meaning of life comes from unselfishly following the path of righteousness. Anna Karenina, however, is selfish, fixated on the opinions of society. Unable to be true to herself, she sees no way out besides death. When Frog alludes to the locomotive in the final seconds of his life, he signals his own awareness of his imminent death.

Frog references *Anna Karenina* earlier in the story as well, when he says that if Katagiri abandoned him on the battlefield, he would go on fighting alone, even though he'd have about as much chance of defeating Worm that way as Anna Karenina had of defeating the oncoming train. This first reference to Tolstoy's novel is not arbitrary. Frog staunchly believes that his mission is a righteous one. He warns Katagiri that the two of them may die underground and that even if they are successful, they will never be recognized for their sacrifice. Katagiri seems to accept this at the end of the story when he falls into a "restful, dreamless sleep." He realizes that society doesn't need to know about the sacrifices he's made—either in the battle with Worm or in his previous life—because he made them to satisfy his own internal sense of virtue. Katagiri comes to accept Tolstoy's philosophy, as Frog has before him, that self-gratification doesn't lead to happiness. One finds harmony by following the dictates of one's inner integrity.

The Swimmer

John Cheever
(1912–1982)

CONTEXT

Born in 1912 in Quincy, Massachusetts, John Cheever grew up with only his mother and older brother, Fred, after his bankrupted father abandoned the family. At seventeen, he was expelled from high school for smoking. He wrote a short story called "Expelled" about the experience, which he sold to the *New Republic*, then moved to Boston, where he lived with his brother and wrote. Eventually he moved to New York City, where he lived on next to nothing while he worked on his stories. He published a short story in the *New Yorker* when he was twenty-three, the first of his 121 appearances in the magazine. In 1938, Cheever joined the army and fought in World War II, but he continued writing and publishing stories. He published his first collection, *The Way Some People Live*, in 1943.

In 1941, Cheever married Mary Winternitz, with whom he had three children, Susan, Benjamin, and Frederico. Both Susan and Ben Cheever eventually became writers themselves. After Benjamin was born, Cheever and his family moved from the Upper East Side of New York City to the suburb of Westchester County, New York, where Cheever was immersed in a landscape that he would incorporate into much of his writing. It was here that Cheever began struggling with excessive drinking, a problem that would plague him for many years to come and all but destroy his life. Not surprisingly, alcohol figures prominently in almost all of his fiction.

Cheever wrote and published stories and novels steadily throughout his life, and his deep, razor-sharp focus on life in suburban America led critic John Leonard to dub him "the Chekhov of the suburbs." Cheever published his second story collection, *The Enormous Radio and Other Stories*, in 1953, followed by *The Housebreaker of Shady Hill and Other Stories* (1959); *Some People, Places and Things That Will Not Appear in My Next Novel* (1961); and *The Brigadier and the Golf Widow* (1964). His novels and novellas include *The Wapshot Chronicle* (1957), which won the National Book Award, *The Wapshot Scandal* (1964), *Bullet Park* (1969), *Falconer* (1977), and *Oh What a Paradise It Seems* (1982). In 1978, *The Stories of John Cheever*, a monumental collection of Cheever's work, won the Pulitzer Prize.

"The Swimmer" appeared in the collection *The Brigadier and the Golf Widow* and is considered to be one of Cheever's best short stories. In 1968, director Frank Perry adapted the story for a film starring Burt Lancaster, which brought the already-famous Cheever even greater renown. Cheever wrote and published the story when alcohol had begun to take over his life. In the years that followed, he destroyed many personal and professional relationships and stopped writing almost completely. Although he taught at both Boston University and the University of Iowa during this time, he was barely functioning. He was suicidal, made drunken scenes in public, and became intolerable to live with. In 1975, he checked himself into a rehab clinic and later stayed sober with the help of Alcoholics Anonymous.

In 1982, Cheever died from cancer in Ossining, New York. He was seventy.

PLOT OVERVIEW

On a Sunday afternoon in midsummer, Neddy and Lucinda Merrill and Helen and Donald Westerhazy sit around the Westerhazys' pool, complaining about their hangovers. They are all drinking. Neddy feels young, energetic, and happy. He decides to get home by swimming across all the pools in his county. He feels like an explorer. He dives into the Westerhazys' pool, swims across, and gets out on the other side. He thinks about all the pools that lie ahead and the friends that await him.

He walks to the Grahams' pool, swims across, then has a drink. He next swims across the Hammers' pool, then several others. At the Bunkers' pool, a party is going on. Enid Bunker greets him, telling him that she's happy he could come to the party after all. He has a drink, then moves on. The Levys aren't home, but Neddy swims across their pool anyway and helps himself to a drink, feeling very contented. A storm begins, and Neddy waits it out in the Levys' gazebo. After the storm, he notices that red and yellow leaves are scattered all over the lawn.

Neddy heads toward the Welchers' pool. On his way, he finds that the Lindleys' horse-riding area is overgrown, and he can't remember whether he heard that the Lindleys were going away for the summer. At the Welchers' house, he finds that the pool is empty, which Neddy thinks is strange. There is a for-sale sign in front of their house. Neddy tries to remember when he last heard from the Welchers. He wonders whether his memory is failing him or he has just repressed unpleasant information.

Neddy waits for a long time to cross a highway, and people in the cars going by yell and throw things at him. He knows that he should head back to the Westerhazys', but he can't bring himself to do so. He finally manages to cross to the median and then to the other side. He walks to a public pool, showers, and swims across, disgusted by the crowds and the overly chlorinated water. Then he walks to the Hallorans'. He takes off his swim trunks because he knows the Hallorans enjoy being naked and swims across the pool. The Hallorans greet him and say that they're sorry for all his "misfortunes," hinting that he's sold his house and something has happened to his family. Neddy denies that anything has happened, puts his swim trunks back on, and leaves. He feels cold and weak and smells burning wood. He wishes he could have a drink of whiskey so that he could warm up and get some energy.

Neddy asks for a drink when he gets to Helen and Eric Sachses' pool, but Helen says they haven't been drinking since Eric had an operation three years ago. Neddy has no recollection that Eric had been sick. He swims across their pool, then tells them he hopes to see them again soon.

He goes to the Biswangers' house. The Biswangers regularly invite him and Lucinda to dinner, but they always refuse because the Biswangers are of a lower social standing. A party is going on, and Neddy goes to the bar. Grace Biswanger greets him coldly, and the bartender is rude to him. Neddy knows that their odd behavior means something has happened to his own social standing because caterers and bartenders always know what's happening in his social circle. In the background, Grace says something about someone losing all their money and asking her for a loan. Neddy swims across the pool, then leaves.

He expects to get a warm welcome at Shirley Adams's pool because Shirley had been his mistress, although he can't remember how long ago the affair had ended. Shirley tells him she won't give him any more money and that she won't give him a drink because someone is in the house. Neddy swims across the pool, but he has trouble getting out and must use the ladder. As he walks away, he smells fall flowers and sees fall constellations in the sky.

Neddy starts crying for the first time since childhood, feeling cold and confused. He thinks that he has just been swimming too long and needs a drink and dry clothes. He swims weakly across a few more pools. Finally, he reaches his own house. The lights are all off, and Neddy doesn't know where everyone could be. Every door is locked, and no one answers when he knocks. He looks in the windows and sees that his house is empty.

CHARACTER LIST

Neddy Merrill   The protagonist, who decides to go home from his friends' house by swimming through all the pools in his neighborhood. Neddy and his wife, Lucinda, enjoy a high social standing in their affluent neighborhood. As he swims home, he loses his strength, and his friends begin saying things that suggest that a great deal of time has gone by. When he arrives home, he finds his house empty.

ANALYSIS OF MAJOR CHARACTERS

NEDDY MERRILL   Neddy Merrill, with his perfect family, high social standing, and pricey suburban home, has few problems in his life and seems to see himself and all his friends as blessed. Neddy has mastered all the rules of the world he inhabits. He accepts and rejects invitations according to a rigid social hierarchy and engages in all the expected trappings and activities: tennis, drinking gin, and sailing. He has many friends, and his position in this privileged world allows him to hop from pool to pool uninvited, confident that he will be welcomed wherever he goes. If there is any unpleasantness in Neddy's world, Neddy opts not to see it. Although he is no longer young, he prides himself on his youthful strength and vigor and seems to see himself as invincible. He exists in a state of bliss that leaves no room for anything but health and happiness.

As Neddy undertakes his watery journey home, he begins to understand that the discontent he's always stubbornly ignored is more present in his life than he realized. Neddy has made a habit of rejecting invitations, and as friend after friend remarks on how long it's been since they've seen him, it becomes clear that he has distanced himself from those around him: he hadn't been aware of his friend's illness, friends have moved away, and he himself has suffered from some unknown misfortune that has cost him his wealth and family. The robust health and strength that Neddy enjoys leaves him, and he gets weaker as his journey progresses. Rather than being eternally youthful, Neddy is actually aging and moving toward death. Everything he once considered his right—his family, mistress's affection, youth, and social standing—have disappeared, and at the end of the story he is left entirely alone. Neddy is not an evil man in any way, but his willful ignorance of the unpleasant side of life eventually leads to his downfall.

THEMES, MOTIFS, AND SYMBOLS

THEMES

THE INEVITABLE PASSAGE OF TIME   Neddy's journey home through the pools of his neighborhood turns into a journey through many years of his life, showing that the passage of time is inevitable, no matter how much one might ignore it. Neddy has mastered the art of denial. At the beginning of the story, the narrator tells us that Neddy is "far from young," but he does his best to act young by sliding down a banister and diving headlong into a pool. The long afternoon at the Westerhazys' pool seems timeless, no different, we can assume, from many other afternoons spent exactly the same way. Neddy's idea to swim home seems like just one more idea in a series of ideas that have popped up on many similar occasions.

As Neddy's journey progresses, we see that time is actually passing much more quickly than Neddy realizes. Leaves and hedges turn yellow and red, the constellations in the sky change, and the air gets colder. Friends are not at home when he expects them to be, he faces scorn from the people he'd once scorned, his mistress wants nothing to do with him, and he learns that a friend has been very ill. All of these changes have happened without Neddy's knowledge. Neddy questions his memory, but he also wonders whether he has simply denied reality to a dangerous degree. His peers have acted their age and faced adult problems, whereas he has resisted. His former mistress even asks him, "Will you ever grow up?" Only at the end of the story when Neddy faces his dark, empty house does he realize that time has passed. He has tried to ignore it, but its passage has proven to be inevitable.

THE EMPTINESS OF SUBURBIA   As Neddy makes his journey across the county, we see that emptiness and despair lie beneath the sunny façade of suburbia. Although Neddy seems to have a full, happy life, he nevertheless remains isolated from others. He makes a habit of rejecting invitations and has been out of touch with many people whom he considers friends. Neddy can't even seem to remember personal details about many of them, such as when Mrs. Levy bought her Japanese lanterns. He knows the rules of the social world he occupies, but this is a world built primarily on appearances. Along his path, he encounters the comfortable trappings of high society, but no genuine friends. And everywhere he goes, people are drinking heavily, which suggests that there is something from which they are trying to escape or hide.

The emptiness of suburbia also applies to Neddy's love life. Even though Neddy names his pool path after his wife, Lucinda, he is cut off from her as well by virtue of his affair with Shirley Adams. The affair, however, also lacks genuine love. When Neddy thinks about Shirley, he defines "love" as "sexual roughhouse," which is what he looks to for comfort and warmth. At the end of the story, when Neddy is actually alone and facing his empty house, the true state of his life is, for the first time, clear. The foundations were flimsy and his relationships weak.

MOTIFS

ALCOHOL   The pervasive consumption of alcohol throughout the story sharpens the distortion of time and Neddy's sense of unhappiness. The drinking, serving, and desire for alcohol become significant motivators for Neddy as well as a way to measure his social standing. At the beginning of the story, everyone is complaining of having drunk too much the night before, but they have gathered companionably at the Westerhazys' pool to drink again. Neddy drinks gin before he decides to swim from pool to pool, and his swim home is marked as much by fresh drinks as by new swimming pools. At the Bunkers' party, Neddy feels comforted and happy when he is given a drink, whereas at the Biswangers' party, he feels slighted by the way his drink is served. As his journey grows more difficult, Neddy wishes deeply for a drink but is often turned down, once at the Sachses' and once at Shirley Adams's. His desire for a drink grows stronger as he grows weaker, and the amount of alcohol he has consumed during his journey could explain the harsh, bewildering emotional place in which Neddy finds himself at the end of the story.

MAPS AND EXPLORATION Images of maps and exploration regularly punctuate "The Swimmer," highlighting the gap between Neddy's perceived understanding of his happiness and direction in life and the messy confusion that eventually takes over. When Neddy gets the idea to swim home through the pools in his county, he sees himself as a brave explorer, setting off for the unknown from a home base that is stable and secure. Neddy likens himself to a "legendary figure" who is making an important discovery, and as he begins his journey, he calls himself a "pilgrim" and an "explorer." When Neddy envisions his friends' pools, he sees them through a mapmaker's eyes, even though the narrator tells us that Neddy's maps are imaginary at best—the first hint that Neddy's sense of direction and place is flimsy. The lighthearted fantasies about exploring eventually disappear as Neddy's journey grows harder and stranger. By the end of the story, Neddy has literally lost his way. He thought he was moving through familiar territory, but the home where he finds himself, dark and empty, is someplace he's never been before.

SYMBOLS

SWIMMING POOLS The pools that Neddy swims through as he makes his way home represent periods of time that Neddy passes through. At the beginning of the story, Neddy is strong and active, feels deep contentment with his life, and is admired by his friends. Warm in the sun, he feels like a "legendary figure," as though there is nothing he can't accomplish. As he progresses from pool to pool, however, Neddy changes. Physically, he grows weaker, unable to pull himself out of pools without a ladder and unwilling to dive in as he once did. Instead of being warm, he eventually feels chilled to the bone. Around him, the sunny summer day grows increasingly cooler, and a storm passes. The trees, meanwhile, lose their leaves, and the constellations change to those of autumn. His standing in his social circle has changed as well. Once respected and given to snubbing those who aren't part of his group, he is now snubbed by Grace Biswanger and the bartender at her party. Other acquaintances pity him for his "misfortunes," which Neddy isn't aware that he has suffered. A lot has happened as he's been moving from pool to pool, and Neddy has undergone these changes unwittingly.

Neddy has named the chain of pools the "Lucinda River," invoking the security and longevity of his marriage and family, but his choice of name becomes sad and ironic when he winds up at his dark, deserted home. Neddy has taken Lucinda, just as he took his comfortable life, for granted. We don't know much about their marriage, but we know of Neddy's affair with Shirley, an affair he treated lightly and to which he attached no meaning. Treating adultery so casually implies that Neddy assumed that Lucinda would always be there, supportive and secure. When the Lucinda River deposits him at a lonely, unfamiliar place, he faces the consequences of his actions and harsh reality of the passing years for the first time.

CHANGES IN WEATHER AND SEASON   The changes in weather and season that occur throughout "The Swimmer" mirror Neddy's changing life circumstances, particularly the deterioration of his comfort and security. At the beginning of the story, Neddy is warm in the sunshine, conscious of nothing but his own happiness and the pleasures of the day. As he begins his swim, the water and air are of comfortable temperature, and he can walk easily from pool to pool in his swim trunks. Shortly into his journey, a storm passes, marking a turning point in Neddy's plans. He is alone for the first time, waiting out the storm in a deserted gazebo; and when the storm ends, the warmth is gone. He is chilly, and the red and yellow leaves on the ground suggest fall—Neddy feels a "peculiar sadness," the first time he feels anything other than happiness. Weather and season are not kind to Neddy from this moment on. He gets colder, sees more signs of fall, and changes from a robust traveler into a pathetic figure by the highway. Autumn arrives in full as Neddy finishes his journey, and the final pool he swims in has freezing-cold water. Just as Neddy's happy life has come to a close, the cycle of seasons has been completed as well, and it is clear by the end of the story that Neddy is entering the winter of his life.

SHORT STORY ANALYSIS

CHEEVER'S FICTIONAL WORLD   John Cheever is famous for the fictional world within his novels and short stories, a world where wealth and privilege do not protect his characters from despair, heartbreak, and disaster. Cheever generally sets his fiction in the Northeastern United States, usually the affluent suburbs of New Jersey, New York, and Connecticut. His characters are preppy, wealthy, and white and not above snobbery and elitism. Extramarital affairs, family drama, and family feuds—particular between brothers—are commonplace. Happiness, although seemingly promised by wealth and all its comfortable trappings, always seems just out of reach. And alcohol—primarily gin—plays a prominent role in almost every social interaction.

The world of "The Swimmer" is typical Cheever, full of all the trappings of the upper middle class as well as the persistent malaise that accompanies them. Cheever bombards us with details from Neddy's world: in the first paragraph of the story, he mentions the church, golf course, tennis court, Audubon group, and adults who have been drinking excessively. Immediately, we understand that this is a wealthy, privileged world, where adults can spend entire afternoons drinking gin by the poolside, secure with their position in society. Beneath this security and bloated comfort, however, lie a strict, punitive social hierarchy; fragile relationships; and unhappiness. Neddy experiences some undefined misfortune that pushes him down in the social ranks, and in his world, the snubbing by a bartender is a significant offense. He loses track of friends and doesn't even know about their moves or illnesses. He cheats on his wife, abandons his mistress, and consequently ends up alone. Although not all of Cheever's stories take the surreal, twisting path of "The Swimmer," many revolve around this theme of fragile happiness and existential meaninglessness.

IMPORTANT QUOTATIONS EXPLAINED

1. *He was not a practical joker nor was he a fool but he was determinedly original and had a vague and modest idea of himself as a legendary figure.*

This quotation, which appears in the third paragraph of the story, reveals the rosy, self-satisfied view Neddy has of himself and his world. Neddy has achieved all the trappings of success and is surrounded by friends and family. He takes comfort in the privileges that his social standing affords, content to know that he is a respected member of society. In this quotation, he reveals his self-perception: he is "original" and sees himself as a "legendary figure." This idea is delusional at best, especially because Cheever writes that Neddy has a "modest" view of himself—envisioning oneself to be legendary certainly does not suggest modesty. As "The Swimmer" progresses, we see that Neddy's worldview is indeed faulty. His friends have become distant acquaintances, his family has disappeared, and he has grown weak. At the end of the story, Neddy is no longer original or legendary. He is simply cold, alone, and confused.

2. *Why, believing as he did, that all human obduracy was susceptible to common sense, was he unable to turn back? Why was he determined to complete his journey even if it meant putting his life in danger? At what point had this prank, this joke, this piece of horseplay become serious?*

This passage, which appears about halfway through the story, suggests that Neddy's journey, which had begun as simply a fun exploit, is actually more meaningful than Neddy had anticipated. Neddy began his pool-to-pool journey with a view of himself as an explorer, doing something unexpected on an ordinary afternoon. Neddy just wanted to take a new way home and didn't conceive of it as a life-changing decision. At this point, however, Neddy is standing in his swim trunks beside a busy highway, and the journey suddenly becomes something more than just a lark. He doesn't understand why he is persevering or why the journey has become something serious, but he recognizes that the fun is gone.

This quotation points to a larger idea of "The Swimmer" as well. Neddy claims to be satisfied and happy with his life, but he doesn't seem to realize that this life is all he has and his actions have consequences. All his rejected invitations have gained him enemies and a host of friends kept at arm's length. He has also ruined his marriage and apparently lost his fortune. His life, as the quotation suggests, is indeed serious, not a prank or joke. Just as he feels unable to stop his strange journey home, he is unable to turn back the clock and make up for past mistakes. There is nowhere to go but forward, across the highway and on into the future.

The Tell-Tale Heart

Edgar Allan Poe
(1809–1849)

CONTEXT

Edgar Allan Poe didn't live long enough to fully enjoy his reputation as one of America's most original and influential writers, as he died at forty, after years of alcohol, poverty, and poor health had taken their toll. Poe's life had always been difficult. Poe was born in 1809 to actor parents. Within two years, his father had abandoned the family, and his mother had died of tuberculosis. Poe was taken in by foster parents in Virginia. He attended boarding school for a time in England before returning to America and matriculating at the University of Virginia, where he ran up gambling debts and left after a year. Poe drifted from a two-year stint in the army to a short-lived position at West Point to the house of his aunt in Baltimore, where he tutored his cousin, Virginia Clemm. He married Virginia in 1836, when she was thirteen and he was twenty-seven.

During this time, Poe was committed to writing. He published his first book of poetry in 1827 and a second two years later. He took editing jobs at small literary journals. His reviews, criticism, articles, and stories began to bring small-scale notoriety. Despite these successes, poverty dogged Poe and Virginia. They moved often, seeking out cheap housing in New York and Philadelphia. In 1842, Virginia was singing to Edgar when blood began flowing from her mouth—it was the first sign of tuberculosis. Within five years, she was dead.

Virginia's declining health and untimely death hit Poe hard, and his writing in those years was often preoccupied with the macabre. Poe returned again and again to death, disease, and other dark themes. "The Tell-Tale Heart" was first published in 1843 and reflects an author not unfamiliar with anxiety and morbidity. Nervousness and impending doom fuel the story's action.

These interests, although rooted in Poe's personal tragedies, were not unique to Poe. His dark short stories are virtuoso examples of gothic literature, a genre that had begun in Europe almost a century before. The killing, dismembering, and insanity of "The Tell-Tale Heart" are characteristic of other gothic works. Gothic style itself was an offshoot of the larger movement of romanticism. Romanticism highlighted intense emotional responses, in contrast to the intellectual coolness that marked the opposing field of classicism. Also prevalent in romanticism was a great respect for the artist's individual power. Poe's original worlds and atmospheres, such as the nightmarish one of "The Tell-Tale Heart," are typical of the romantic imagination.

Despite working in an established genre, Poe was a major innovator. The fantastical feel of "The Tell-Tale Heart" and other Poe stories inspired the later emergence of science fiction. Poe's brooding atmospheres and use of deranged narrators helped form the horror genre. Even the detective story owes some of its provenance to Poe. Although he wasn't the first author to put a detective in a story, Poe pioneered the form. The modern mystery story also owes a great debt to Poe, especially stories such as "The Tell-Tale Heart."

Poe's reputation took years to be fully established, and when he died, events that could have come right from one of his own stories contributed to the delay. Rufus Griswold, a rival in the literary scene of the day, managed to convince Poe's mother-in-law that he was the appointed executor of Poe's estate. Griswold took Poe's letters and manuscripts with the promise that they would produce income for the destitute Mrs. Clemm. Not only did Griswold stiff Mrs. Clemm on her share of royalties, but he proceeded to tarnish Poe's name in a subsequent biography. Portraying Poe as an abusive madman, Griswold blurred the line between Poe's narrators and Poe himself. It was twenty-five years before a revised biography was released, time enough for Poe's fictionalized life history to gain traction in the public mind.

Today, Griswold is all but forgotten, whereas Poe's work is as vital as ever. Franz Kafka and Jorge Luis Borges are two examples of writers whose imaginations were freed by Poe's pioneering example. Talents as diverse as the poet Charles Baudelaire, writer Ray Bradbury, and filmmaker Alfred Hitchcock have cited Poe as a major inspiration.

PLOT OVERVIEW

An unnamed narrator admits that he's nervous but denies that he's insane, even though he admits to having extra-sharp senses, especially hearing. He says that he will tell his story calmly to prove he isn't mad. He goes on to describe the events that led up to the murder.

The narrator says he committed the crime because of the old man's eye, which looks like a vulture's eye, with a film covering its blue iris. To escape the eye, the narrator resolves to kill the old man. The narrator begins an elaborate planning process. Every night at midnight, he opens the door of the old man's room, so the old man becomes accustomed to sleeping through the sound of his door being opened. The narrator sticks a darkened lantern through the crack, then follows it with his head. On some nights, the narrator takes an hour to complete this process. Once inside, the narrator opens the lantern so that a ray of light shines on the old man's face. The eye doesn't open, however, so the narrator never makes a move against the old man. Every morning at dawn, the narrator visits the old man and asks him how he slept, just to make sure he doesn't suspect anything.

On the eighth night, the narrator follows his routine, cracking the door and sliding his head in. This time, however, his thumb slips on the clasp when he goes to open the lantern. The noise wakes the old man, who sits up and demands to know who is in his room. The narrator freezes. He stays motionless for an hour, waiting for the old man to lie back down. Finally a terrified groan comes from the bed. The narrator pities the old man as he imagines the train of his thoughts, the way he must be trying to explain the sound away as the wind, a mouse, or a cricket. At the same time, the narrator knows the old man's terror cannot be soothed because the old man has recognized Death.

Eventually the narrator opens a crack in the lantern. A single ray of light shoots out and falls directly onto the old man's eye, which is open. The sight of it brings out the violence in the narrator, violence that is intensified by a beating sound. It sounds like a ticking watch wrapped in cotton. The narrator believes that his superhuman hearing is picking up the sound of the old man's heart. The beat gets faster and louder, becoming so overwhelming that the narrator fears a neighbor will hear it. He screams and opens the lantern fully, and the old man screams. The narrator pulls him out of bed and throws him to the floor, where he smothers him with the bed. The heartbeat sound grows soft and eventually subsides as the old man dies.

To hide the body, the narrator cuts off the old man's head, arms, and legs. He uses a tub to catch the blood. The narrator pulls up the floorboards and stashes the corpse there. He rearranges the floorboards so that they look undisturbed.

Someone knocks at the front door. The narrator has hidden everything perfectly, so he opens the door without fear. Three policemen come in, investigating a scream reported by a neighbor. The narrator smiles and says he must have screamed in a dream. To prove his innocence, he walks the men through the house, including the old man's room. He tells them that the old man is away in the country and points out that his possessions haven't been disturbed.

The narrator, confident that he has hidden his crime perfectly, brings chairs into the old man's room so that they can sit there. He puts his own chair on top of the floorboards that conceal the corpse. As the men talk, the narrator's ears begin to ring. To cover his anxiety he starts to talk more, but the ringing gets worse. The narrator becomes convinced that the sound is not coming from his ears. It is a sound like a ticking watch wrapped in cotton. Trying cover up the sound, the narrator talks even more, gestures wildly, walks up and down the room, and even rubs the chair over the floorboards. The sound just gets louder. Meanwhile, the cops act as if nothing is wrong, continuing their light conversation. The narrator thinks the cops are mocking him by acting so casual. The thumping sound gets louder.

The narrator reaches his breaking point. He admits his guilt and tells the cops to pull up the floorboards. The awful sound, he shouts, is the beating of the old man's heart.

CHARACTER LIST

The Narrator   The protagonist of the story. The narrator murders the old man because his eye disturbs him, then he hides the body in the floorboards. Although the narrator claims to be sane and cunning, his words and actions reveal that he is actually insane.

The Old Man   The man who shares a house with the narrator. The old man has a blue, filmy eye that infuriates the narrator. The old man is murdered, dismembered, and hidden in the floorboards of his bedroom.

ANALYSIS OF MAJOR CHARACTERS

THE NARRATOR   From the first words of "The Tell-Tale Heart," the narrator reveals himself to be delusional and insane. Although he is well aware of his nervousness and the necessity of proving his innocence, he is fully unaware of how he is portraying himself and of his own madness. The things he blurts out, such as that his senses have been sharpened by disease, are rendered insane by the hyperbolic details he conveys, such as the fact that he hears "all things in the heaven and in the earth." To prove his sanity, the narrator brags about how "wisely" and with what "caution," "foresight," and "dissimulation" he has committed his crime. The narrator has indeed acted in a steady, obsessive manner, but he hasn't plotted the "perfect triumph" that he claims. The narrator's arrogance makes him overconfident and ultimately leads to his undoing.

Poe creates in the narrator a compelling and believable portrait of both mental instability and the power of a guilty conscience. Poe never diagnoses the narrator, but the narrator is likely suffering from paranoid schizophrenia or a similar disorder. He hears things, has acute anxiety, and is deeply self-delusional. Poe also lets us see how powerful a guilty conscience can be. His crime is so big and hideous that he believes everyone can see he did it—the beating that batters the narrator is too powerful for him to ignore. The narrator claims to have no guilt about what he's done, but he is ultimately overcome by his awareness of the crime and his overwhelming compulsion to confess.

THEMES, MOTIFS, AND SYMBOLS

THEMES

THE DANGER OF ARROGANCE   The narrator brags about his cunning and skill in killing the old man and boasts about the clever way he concealed the body, but he has overestimated his abilities and ultimately brings about his own downfall. The narrator perceives that he has pulled off a truly difficult crime, but in reality he has simply smothered an elderly man whom he has taken by surprise in the middle of the night. Because he has miscalculated his abilities and feels far too much pride in them, the narrator is overconfident when three policemen arrive at his house. Rather than just explain away the shriek that's been reported and bid them goodnight, he invites them in and deliberately takes them through every room, encouraging them to search thoroughly. He sets up chairs for them in the old man's room and puts his own chair right over the floorboards that hide the dismembered body, a gesture that suggests both the height of arrogance and the narrator's unconscious desire to confess to his crime.

The narrator believes he has the ability to stay calm and deflect any and all suspicion, but his already nervous temperament intensifies in the face of such stress, and he becomes overwhelmed by anxiety. Pushed to the limit by the maddeningly oblivious cops, who do not hear the beating, and the violent distress of his own conscience, the narrator cracks and confesses. Although his conscience is likely what ultimately leads him to confess, his arrogance is what puts him in the precarious situation in the first place. By underestimating the power of his guilty feelings and ability to suppress them, he brings about his downfall.

THE POWER OF THE CONSCIENCE   In "The Tell-Tale Heart," the narrator's conscience proves to be the single most powerful force in his life, even more powerful than his madness. The narrator conveys endless rationalizations for why he is plotting to kill his housemate. He makes the case for his own principles, pointing out that he isn't motivated by base impulses such as pride, greed, or spite but by something more sinister—the eye. Separating the eye from the old man it belongs to, as if they were two unrelated entities, further allows the narrator to evade guilty feelings. He argues that eliminating the eye is an act of self-preservation or self-defense, ignoring the reality that he is committing murder. Despite these efforts, however, his attempts to dehumanize the old man ultimately fail, and his conscience wins out. It takes the form of a persistent sound, what the narrator decides is the beating of the old man's heart. The sound grows too great for the narrator to bear and he cracks, revealing his crime and finally gaining relief from the torture of his conscience.

MOTIFS

PROJECTION   The narrator of "The Tell-Tale Heart" has an inaccurate self-image, unable to see his own madness, and projects onto others the twisted qualities within himself. For example, the narrator describes the old man as having a "vulture eye," but the narrator himself is like a vulture, a predatory bird that feeds on dead flesh. The narrator hovers like a bird of prey as he plots to kill the old man. The narrator describes the eye as having a "hideous" film over it, and he likewise describes the old man's heart hidden under the floorboards as "hideous." What is truly hideous is the vicious nature of the narrator. The narrator similarly projects his traits onto the policemen. When they converse in the old man's room, the narrator takes their friendliness as a mockery and refers to their "hypocritical smiles." However, the officers aren't being hypocritical; they sincerely don't suspect anything, and it is really the narrator who is wallowing in hypocrisy. At the end of the story, when the narrator breaks down, he shrieks, "Villains . . . dissemble no more!" The narrator is again projecting his own villainous and dishonest nature onto the others.

PULSE   Throughout "The Tell-Tale Heart," the narrator is aware of a throbbing sound, an awareness he attributes to an "over-acuteness of the senses." Although he often believes the sound to be coming from external sources, in reality it is internal, the sensation of his own pulse. The sound first appears just before he kills the old man. To the narrator, the beat sounds like a watch "enveloped in cotton," which he inaccurately believes is the sound of the old man's beating heart. The narrator smothers the old man and hears the pulsation long after the old man has died. The beating sound returns when the narrator starts to panic in front of the police. Again, the narrator is convinced it is coming from outside his head, and again it sounds like a watch in cotton. As his panic grows, so does the sound, which becomes "louder — louder — *louder!*" In the final line of the story, the narrator is overcome by what he believes is the "beating of his hideous heart!" and confesses his crime to the police.

SYMBOLS

THE EYE   Although the old man's eye has a practical function in "The Tell-Tale Heart," it also works on a deeper symbolic level. The eye is filmed-over, probably by disease. The narrator likens it to a vulture, a creature that is associated with death. Early in the story, the narrator further refers to the old man's eye as his "Evil Eye." Capitalizing these words indicates the narrator probably believes in the notion of the Evil Eye, a superstition wherein a person can do harm to another simply through the power of their gaze. For the narrator, the eye represents the dark forces of the world. It also symbolically corresponds with an awareness of his own mortality and fears of death and disease.

LIGHT AND DARKNESS   Most of the action in "The Tell-Tale Heart" takes place at night in the old man's chambers. The shutters are tightly closed, so the only light that can come into the room is from the narrator's lantern. The narrator nightly releases a "single thin ray" onto the old man's eye. This ray interrupts the normal order of things, one that includes a darkened room and the old man's closed eye. On the eighth night, however, the eye is open. The light shining onto the "vulture eye" infuriates the narrator so much that he is driven to kill. Darkness generally has negative associations, whereas light usually suggests illumination or the revelation of truth. In "The Tell-Tale Heart," however, the associations of light and darkness are reversed. The narrator's light reveals his misperception of the world. Light helps to project "hideous" qualities onto the old man. And in darkness, the old man is safe; only when the narrator shines the light on him is he in danger.

SHORT STORY ANALYSIS

POE'S USE OF IRONY Irony is apparent from the first lines of "The Tell-Tale Heart," where the narrator begins to build a case for his own sanity. The narrator cites his over-acute senses as proof of his sanity and later claims to be able to hear the beating of the old man's heart. Because hearing another's heartbeat in a room is impossible, the narrator's efforts to burnish his sanity ironically affirm a portrait of insanity. This insanity leads the narrator to attempt to protect himself from the old man's "Evil Eye." In this attempt, the narrator ironically harms himself. If instead of plotting against the old man the narrator had simply left the house, he would have come to no harm from the eye. Likewise, if he had just ignored the eye, it surely would not have damaged him. By actively setting out to destroy the eye, the narrator begins the chain of events that lead to his downfall. By admitting the murder to the police, the narrator condemns himself to the gallows. His efforts to protect himself have led to his death.

The narrator preemptively attacks sight, but ironically his downfall can be attributed to sound. At first, sight seems to be the most hazardous sense for the narrator. His seeing the eye and the eye seeing him intensify his paranoia. Sound, however, is the sense that makes the "perfect triumph" of the narrator's crime something less than perfect. After sneaking into the old man's room, he makes a noise with the lantern that awakens the old man. This is further ironic because on the previous seven nights the narrator has successfully used light—a visual element—to spy on the old man. With the old man awake, the narrator loses much of the element of surprise. When he finally goes to smother his housemate, the old man emits a shriek. This sound is heard by a neighbor, who files a report with the police. Sound ultimately dooms the narrator. He has paid much attention to putting all the evidence out of sight, but he is unable to stand the sound of what he believes is the old man's beating heart. The narrator has protected himself from a visual menace, but he has ironically let himself be destroyed by an auditory cue.

SENSATIONALIST INFLUENCES In "The Tell-Tale Heart," Poe uses a sensationalistic murder as a vehicle for expressing complex universal themes. Poe's story could pass for a contemporary horror film or gruesome urban murder. The innocence of the victim; the elaborate plot; the gory details, such as the blood-draining and the dismemberment; and the stashing of the body under the floor form a scenario that could fill the pages of a modern tabloid for weeks. Poe does more than simply recount a murder, however. He delves deeply into the mind of a murderer and creates a portrait of feelings such as panic and terror, the nightmare of insanity, and the torture of a haunted soul.

Like his contemporaries Nathaniel Hawthorne and Herman Melville, Poe was an avid journal- and newspaper-reader and kept abreast of the scandals of the day. Critics point out that Poe probably read an article in 1841 that discussed some comments made by an attorney named Daniel Webster regarding a murder trial. Webster mentioned the calmness of the murderer and the fact that he had killed an elderly man while he slept. He also discussed the weight that such a crime puts on the murderer, who must live with what he has done, mentioning specifically the idea of a beating heart, which Webster claimed feels like "a vulture is devouring it." The details Poe read may have planted the seeds for "The Tell-Tale Heart." The image of the vulture and the impression of an incessant beating heart both appear in the story. Poe's final scene, where the narrator is flooded by the demands of his conscience and believes that the police are onto him, also bears a strong resemblance to Webster's descriptions. Poe did not intend the story to simply recount a real-life event, but its roots in reality help magnify the horrific effect of the tale.

ATTEMPTS AT EMPOWERMENT   The old man in "The Tell-Tale Heart" is the instigator of the narrator's fear, and the narrator tries repeatedly to empower himself to overcome this fear. The narrator is terrorized by the old man's eye, which he likens to a vulture's. A vulture is a predator, feeding off of dead meat, and is often associated with death itself. The narrator is particularly unnerved by the film that covers the eye, which suggests disease and, by extension, death. By destroying the eye, the narrator is attempting to gain power over death, and in a way he becomes like a vulture as he stalks the old man. When the old man groans, the narrator attributes it to the terror of death, who has "stalked with his black shadow" into the room. By conflating death with the old man, the narrator deludes himself into thinking that by destroying the old man, he will be conquering death.

The narrator's attempts at empowerment succeed at first, such as when he successfully spies on the sleeping old man. The narrator momentarily gains power over life and death as he waits for seven nights in the doorway. When he acts on the eighth day, the narrator indulges this power. He inwardly laughs at the old man's terror, because it is under his control. He takes the old man's life, exercises complete authority in concealing the crime, and relishes his "perfect triumph." This power is fleeting, however, and he eventually succumbs helplessly to panic. Fear wins out in the end.

IMPORTANT QUOTATIONS EXPLAINED

1. TRUE!—nervous—very, very dreadfully nervous I had been and am; but why will you say that I am mad? The disease had sharpened my senses—not destroyed—not dulled them. Above all was the sense of hearing acute. I heard all things in the heaven and in the earth. I heard many things in hell. How, then, am I mad?

From the first lines of the story, Poe creates an insightful portrait of insanity. One key aspect of the narrator's insanity is his lack of awareness of it. His diction alone reveals that his mind is troubled. For example, the italics on the word "will" seem to be misplaced, emphasizing the wrong word in the sentence. The narrator's attempts to reaffirm his sanity are also undermined by the symptoms he describes, such as his overly acute hearing, which he attributes to a "disease." Poe never specifies what the disease is, but it may well be schizophrenia, of which auditory hallucinations are a common symptom. This passage reveals that the narrator is also afflicted by a deep anxiety. Poe sets up an immediate tension between the narrator's denial of his instability and clear lack of solid grounding. Finally, this passage demonstrates the narrator's attempts to justify his actions. He is defensive and seems to be recoiling from an accusation that he is insane.

2. *For a whole hour I did not move a muscle, and in the meantime I did not hear him lie down. He was still sitting up in the bed listening; — just as I have done, night after night, hearkening to the death watches in the wall.*

In this quote, Poe references "death watches," which in the context of the story take on multiple meanings. A *death watch*, or *deathwatch* in the modern spelling, is a type of beetle. It makes a clicking sound as it burrows through wood, a sound reminiscent of a watch's ticking. The beetle got its name from a superstitious belief that the sound of one indicated an impending death. The narrator, with his hypersensitivity to sound, may have driven himself crazy staying up at night listening to the beetles crawling through the walls. He may be hearing them again later when he convinces himself that he hears the beating of the old man's heart.

This quote also contains existential overtones. We see the narrator's suffering in his admission that he has stayed up "night after night" listening in bed. The sound surely intensified his anxiety. The narrator's fear of the "Evil Eye" indicates a superstitious temperament. He may have been tortured by the notion that someone in the house was soon to die and wondered whether it was he whose time had come. A deathwatch has a second meaning as well: a vigil kept over a dying person. This immediacy of death, which soon overtakes the old man, may also have terrorized Poe's paranoid narrator.

---

3. *I saw it with perfect distinctness — all a dull blue, with a hideous veil over it that chilled the very marrow in my bones; but I could see nothing else of the old man's face or person; for I had directed the ray as if by instinct, precisely upon the damned spot.*

The narrator makes a dramatic separation between the vexing eye of the old man and the old man himself. In this description, he is unable to see the old man as a whole. The narrator can see only his obsession, the eye. In objectifying the old man, removing aspects of a shared humanity, the narrator makes the act of killing easier for himself. The somewhat awkward phrase "damned spot" to describe the location of the eye is an allusion to Shakespeare's play *Macbeth*. In the play, Lady Macbeth is driven insane by her guilty feelings over the murder of the King of Scotland. While sleepwalking one night, she imagines that the dead king's blood has stained her hand. "Out, damned spot! Out, I say!" she shouts, before going on to contemplate, "who would have thought the old man to have had so much blood in him?" In using this phrase, Poe is making a clear parallel with Shakespeare's classic portrayal of a guilty conscience. Although objectification will allow the narrator to complete the murder, Poe has foreshadowed that there will be a price to pay.

The Things They Carried

Tim O'Brien
(1946–)

CONTEXT

Tim O'Brien was born on October 1, 1946, in Austin, Minnesota, and was raised in Worthington, a small town in southern Minnesota. As a child, the overweight and introspective O'Brien spent his time practicing magic tricks and making pilgrimages to the public library. His father's accounts of fighting in Iwo Jima and Okinawa during World War II that appeared in the *New York Times* inspired O'Brien to consider a career in writing. When O'Brien arrived at Macalester College in St. Paul, Minnesota, he decided to focus his studies on political science. He spent many of his college years, however, trying to ignore the Vietnam War or protesting against it—he attended peace vigils and war protests and aspired to join the State Department to make a difference. When he graduated, he intended to accept his offer of admission to a Ph.D. program at Harvard's Kennedy School of Government but was drafted before he could begin.

Faced with the prospect of fighting in the war that he so actively opposed, the twenty-two-year-old O'Brien felt pulled between his personal convictions and the expectations of the people in his hometown. Although torn, he entered the military for basic training at Fort Lewis, Washington, on August 14, 1968. When he arrived in Vietnam in February 1969, he served in the Fifth Battalion of the 46th Infantry, 198th Infantry Brigade, American Division until March 1970. O'Brien served in Vietnam's Quang Ngai Province, which eventually served as the setting for his short-story collection *The Things They Carried*.

O'Brien's service brought him to the South Vietnamese village of My Lai a year after the infamous massacre of 1968. He was wounded and returned home with a Purple Heart, Bronze Star, and Combat Infantry Badge. He also had a storehouse of guilt and an endless supply of observations and anecdotes that would later constitute his memoir *If I Die in a Combat Zone, Box Me Up and Ship Me Home* (1973). This work was published as O'Brien was abandoning his graduate studies for a career as a national affairs reporter for the *Washington Post*, a job he held for a year. In 1975, he published *Northern Lights*, an account of two brothers in rural Minnesota. His novel *Going After Cacciato*, about a platoon forced to chase one its own AWOL soldiers, won the National Book Award in 1979 and solidified O'Brien's reputation as a masterful writer concerned with the ambiguities of love and war. Following this success came *The Nuclear Age* (1985), a novel about a draft dodger obsessed with the idea of nuclear holocaust.

O'Brien then returned his attention to the battlefields. He wrote a short story, "Speaking of Courage," that was originally meant for inclusion in *Going After Cacciato*. In 1990, "Speaking of Courage" was one of twenty-two stories he included in *The Things They Carried*, a sequence of lyrical, interconnected short stories that has been heralded as one of the finest volumes of fiction about the Vietnam War. The work received acclaim not only for its subject matter but also for its honesty and specificity, discussion of fact and fiction, and commentary on the act of storytelling itself. O'Brien drew much of the material in the work from his own experiences and blurred the line between fact and fiction by naming the narrator and protagonist (who does not appear by name in the title story) Tim O'Brien.

The Things They Carried was a finalist for both the Pulitzer Prize and National Book Critics Circle Award. Since then, he has published several more novels: *In the Lake of the Woods* (1994), *Tomcat in Love* (1998), and *July, July* (2002).

PLOT OVERVIEW

Lieutenant Jimmy Cross carries various mementos that remind him of his love for Martha, a girl from his college in New Jersey. Even though Martha doesn't love him in return, Cross carries her letters in his backpack and her good-luck pebble in his mouth. After a long day's march, he unwraps her letters and imagines the prospect of her loving him someday. Martha is an English major who writes letters that quote lines of poetry, and she never mentions the war. Even though the letters are signed "Love, Martha," Cross understands that she uses the word colloquially and doesn't really love him. He wonders whether Martha is a virgin. He carries photographs of her, including one of her playing volleyball, and remembers the time they spent together. They went on a single date, to see the movie *Bonnie and Clyde*. When Cross touched Martha's knee during the final scene, Martha looked at him and made him pull his hand back. Now, in Vietnam, Cross wishes that he had carried her up the stairs, tied her to the bed, and touched her knee all night long. He is haunted by the knowledge that his affection will most likely never be returned.

The narrator describes the things all the men of the company carry. Each man carries a load of munitions and gear—weapons and ammunition, mosquito repellent and marijuana, pocketknives and chewing gum. The things they carry depend on several factors, including the men's priorities and physical strength. Because the machine gunner, Henry Dobbins, is exceptionally large, for example, he carries extra rations. And because he is superstitious, he carries his girlfriend's pantyhose around his neck. Nervous Ted Lavender carries marijuana and tranquilizers to calm himself, and the religious Kiowa carries an illustrated New Testament that his father gave him.

Some things the men carry are universal, such as a compress to stop excessive bleeding and a two-pound poncho that can be used as a raincoat, groundsheet, or tent. Most of the men are common, low-ranking soldiers and carry a standard M-16 assault rifle and several magazines of ammunition. Several men carry grenade launchers. They sometimes carry each other when one is sick or wounded, and they even carry Vietnam itself, in the heavy weather and dusty soil. The things they carry are also determined by their rank or specialty. As leader, for example, Lieutenant Jimmy Cross carries the maps, compasses, and responsibility for his men's lives. The medic, Rat Kiley, carries morphine, malaria tablets, and supplies for serious wounds. All the men, however, also bear the burden of psychological turmoil caused by the war.

One day, when the platoon is in the Than Khe area on a mission to destroy enemy tunnels, Cross imagines Martha and himself becoming trapped in a collapsed tunnel. Daydreaming about whether she is a virgin distracts him from the mission, and on the way back from going to the bathroom, Lavender is shot, falling particularly hard under the burden of his loaded backpack. Still, Cross can think of nothing but Martha. He thinks about her love of poetry and her smooth skin.

While the soldiers wait for the helicopter to carry Lavender's body away, they smoke his marijuana. They make jokes about Lavender's tranquilizer abuse and rationalize that he probably was too numb to feel the pain when he was shot. The platoon burns the village of Than Khe in retaliation for Lavender's death and then begins a long march in the late afternoon heat. When they stop for the evening, Cross digs a foxhole in the ground and sits at the bottom of it, crying. Meanwhile, Kiowa and Norman Bowker sit in the darkness discussing the short span between life and death in an attempt to make sense of their situation. In the ensuing silence, Kiowa marvels at how Lavender fell so quickly and how he was zipping up his pants one second and falling dead the next. Kiowa finds something un-Christian about the lack of drama surrounding Lavender's death and wonders why he cannot openly lament it.

The morning after Lavender's death, Cross crouches in his foxhole and burns Martha's letters and photographs. He plans the day's march and concludes that he will never again have such fantasies. He plans to call the men together and assume the blame for Lavender's death. He reminds himself that despite the men's inevitable grumbling, his job is to lead, not be loved by his men.

CHARACTER LIST

Jimmy Cross   The lieutenant in charge of the platoon. Cross is well intentioned but unsure of how to lead his men. He is racked with guilt because he believes that his preoccupation with Martha caused the death of one of his soldiers, Ted Lavender.

Ted Lavender   A young, scared soldier. Lavender carries tranquilizers and marijuana with him to help him deal with the stress of war. He is shot in the head when he momentarily steps away from the group.

Kiowa   A Native American soldier who carries a copy of the New Testament. Kiowa sleeps with the book as a pillow. After he sees Ted Lavender get killed, he can't stop describing how hard he fell after he was shot.

Henry Dobbins   The platoon's machine gunner, who wears his girlfriend's pantyhose around his neck.

Dave Jensen   A member of the platoon who carries dental-hygiene items.

Mitchell Sanders   The radiotelephone operator. Sanders carries condoms.

Norman Bowker   A member of the platoon who carries a diary.

Rat Kiley   The platoon's medic. Kiley carries comic books and M&M's in addition to his medical supplies.

Lee Strunk   A soldier in the platoon who carries a slingshot.

ANALYSIS OF MAJOR CHARACTERS

JIMMY CROSS   Jimmy Cross shows the profound effect that responsibility has on those who are too immature to handle it. Cross's immaturity radiates from everything he does and thinks. He carries a picture of Martha from a high school yearbook, and when he fantasizes about her, he thinks primarily about touching her knee. Although terrified of the war, Cross understands his huge responsibility and feels overwhelming guilt when one of his men dies. Right before Ted Lavender is killed, Cross allows thoughts of Martha and mementos of her to distract him. His innocent reverie is interrupted by Lavender's death, and Cross's only conclusion is that he cares for this faraway girl more than he cares for his men.

Jimmy Cross can be viewed as a Christ figure because he assumes the position of the group's savior. Cross is linked to Christ not only on a superficial level—they share the same initials and are associated with the cross—but also in the nature of his role. Just as Christ suffered for all of mankind, Cross suffers for the sake of the entire platoon. He bears the grief of Lavender's death for the soldiers in his platoon who, like Kiowa, are too dumbfounded to mourn. Cross also makes a personal sacrifice, burning the photographs and letters from Martha so that the thought of her will no longer distract him. In both cases, Cross makes a Christlike sacrifice so that his fellow men can carry on without being crippled by grief and guilt.

THEMES, MOTIFS, AND SYMBOLS

THEMES

THE BURDENS OF WAR   The things that O'Brien's characters carry are both literal and figurative and demonstrate the enormous burdens of war that the young soldiers must bear. They all carry heavy physical loads, including weapons, ammunition, communication devices, medical supplies, and provisions. These are the trappings of war, the things these soldiers will literally die without. The soldiers also carry heavy emotional loads, composed of grief, terror, guilt, love, and longing. Ted Lavender, for example, is weighed down by intense fear, and Jimmy Cross is weighed down by guilt after Lavender is shot. Often, a man's physical burden underscores his emotional burden. Henry Dobbins, for example, carries his girlfriend's pantyhose and, with them, the longing for love and comfort. Jimmy Cross carries compasses and maps and, with them, the responsibility for the men in his charge. Ted Lavender carries tranquilizers and marijuana to cope with his terror.

The emotional burdens that the soldiers bear are intensified by their young age and inexperience. Most of the men who fought in Vietnam were in their late teens and early twenties—they were children, students, sons, and boyfriends who had no perspective on how to rationalize killing or come to terms with their friends' untimely deaths. From the beginning, O'Brien uses explicit details to illustrate what the experience was like for the scared men. The dense and detailed lists of objects that the men carry may seem tedious or irrelevant at times, but the specific details emphasize the soldiers' humanity. They may carry weapons and other items that point to the violence of war, but they also carry candy and letters from girls. They are soldiers but also just scared, young boys.

THE POWER OF STORYTELLING   In the chaos and violence of war, the soldiers try to make sense of events and feelings by telling stories. For example, when Ted Lavender dies, Kiowa describes over and over again how Lavender looked when he fell and how he fell hard and instantly, just like cement. His descriptions are not ornate, and he doesn't vary them. The repetition of the story is Kiowa's way of trying to make sense of Lavender's sudden death and figure out how he feels about it. Similarly, the men often repeat the phrase "there it is," which is a catchall explanation for the inexplicable things that happen that they have no control over. The narrator explains that such repetition is "a balance between crazy and almost crazy," a way of protecting themselves for thinking too much about the things they see and experience. Along with "there it is," the men often look for morals in the horrific things that happen, trying—sometimes ironically—to find meaning or purpose in death and violence that is actually senseless. Turning difficult events into stories allows the men to cope with the horrors around them.

Even though the men feel death very deeply, they are aware that grief and fear could easily overwhelm them, so they try to minimize death by discussing it in irreverent, made-up words and phrases. Instead of saying "killed," for example, they use "greased," "offed," "lit up," and "zapped" because the words strip away the horror of death. Language and stories help the soldiers face the reality of war by allowing them to stand outside of it. By talking about war and death through repeated stories and invented language, they remove themselves from the experience and find the strength to carry on.

MOTIFS

AMBIGUOUS MORALITY   "The Things They Carried" suggests that the war blurs boundaries between right and wrong, and the story contains several instances of ambiguous morality. The brutal killing of innocents on both sides can't be explained, and during moments of shock, the men deal with the pain of their feelings by pointing out the irony. Many of the soldiers look for a moral to take away from the senseless death and destruction, which only emphasizes the immorality of it. After Ted Lavender is fatally shot by the enemy, for example, Sanders jokes that the moral of Ted Lavender's accidental and tragic death is to stay away from drugs. When exposed to these horrors, the men's notions of right and wrong shift. After Lavender's death, for example, Cross deals with his guilt by burning the entire village of Than Khe. Other men, instead of grieving for Lavender, simply feel relieved that they are still alive. In another instance, the soldiers come upon an enemy's corpse and feel no qualms about slicing off the dead boy's thumb. In war, mutilating a dead body is a gesture done without blinking, and the morality of the action is irrelevant. War is ambiguous and arbitrary because it forces humans into extreme situations that have no obviously right or wrong solutions.

DAYDREAMS   To cope with the stress and horror of war, many soldiers in "The Things They Carried" escape to a dream world, rooted in the lives they've left behind. Jimmy Cross loses himself in daydreams about Martha whenever he has time to rest, such as when he's in his foxhole at night. When he's marching, his daydreams help him bear the weight of all the things he carries, because thinking about Martha makes him feel like he's in another world. But daydreams about Martha overtake him even at difficult moments, such as when he's waiting for the helicopter to take Ted Lavender's dead body away. For Cross, daydreams are both a way to pass the time and a way to escape from his surroundings.

Not all the daydreams of the men are so romantic, though. Even though they'd never admit it to one another, many of them fantasize about shooting off their own fingers or toes so that they can go home. They fantasize about simply giving up, succumbing to their fear and fatigue, and having a nervous breakdown so that they can leave Vietnam. They also daydream about "freedom birds," helicopters or planes that could sweep them safely away from the jungle. Their daydreams are detailed: the men imagine what they would yell, how it would feel to fly away, and what they would see from the sky. These daydreams about freedom give them "lightness," allowing them to escape the tremendous burdens of their reality.

SYMBOLS

MARTHA   Martha, through her letters, photographs, and presence in Jimmy Cross's mind, represents the world that the men have left behind. Cross relies on his memory of his only date with Martha to provide comfort and escape and harbors the hope that she might one day return his love. Martha is a real person, but Cross doesn't know her intimately: he doesn't know her thoughts, fears, or needs. Instead of being a real woman whom Cross misses and yearns for, she's merely a fantasy that motivates him to survive the war. At the same time, Martha also represents the danger of becoming too immersed in memories and thoughts of home. When Ted Lavender dies, Cross blames himself, believing that he had prioritized thinking about Martha over protecting his men. When he burns Martha's letters and pictures, he is symbolically accepting his duty as a soldier and a leader. He lets go of his ties to home and fully commits himself to his role as the leader of his platoon.

SHORT STORY ANALYSIS

NONLINEAR NARRATION   O'Brien uses nonlinear narration (narration that doesn't follow a traditional beginning-middle-end sequence) in "The Things They Carried" to demonstrate that conventional ideas of time and order don't apply during war. The story begins by describing Jimmy Cross and his letters from Martha as well as the things the other soldiers carry with them. The story drifts from one moment to another, with no mention of specific days, dates, hours, or even periods of time. Instead, O'Brien constantly draws us back to Lavender's death: things happen either before the death or after it, and his death becomes the standard for measuring time. This alternative way of measuring time is appropriate for the chaos of war and emphasizes how different the soldiers' world is from ours. Events and memories are a jumble, and days of marching, hiding, and carrying blur together into an indistinguishable mass. Conventional time measurements—such as beginning, middle, and end—are too neat for the messy warfare the story describes. Instead, O'Brien weaves Lavender's death throughout the narrative, suggesting that it is part of the soldiers' lives even before it actually happens. Death is as real in their imaginations as it is in reality.

THE VIETNAM WAR   The Vietnam War was rife with paradoxes: in the name of protecting democracy, the United States propped up a dictatorial regime in South Vietnam. Later in the war, the U.S. military destroyed villages to "save" them. Not surprisingly, a profound sense of confusion pervaded the entire war. The U.S. involvement in Vietnam is inseparable from the larger context of the Cold War. Ever since the end of World War II, the United States and Soviet Union had been in the midst of a worldwide struggle for spheres of influence, each superpower wanting to exert cultural, political, and ideological control over various regions of the globe. At the same time, the United States and USSR both wanted to stop the other country from gaining any ground. Southeast Asia, and Vietnam in particular, were important spheres of influence in the minds of both U.S. and Soviet leaders. With the "fall" of North Vietnam to communism in 1954, the United States became committed to stopping the further spread of communism in the region.

The United States and USSR avoided fighting each other directly—and thereby the possibility of nuclear war—by fighting through proxy forces in North and South Vietnam. Unfortunately for the United States, the U.S.-backed South Vietnamese government was weak and corrupt, whereas the Soviet-backed North Vietnamese government consisted of fiercely proud and independent nationalists who were willing to fight endlessly for unification of their country. The United States further antagonized the North Vietnamese by stepping into the power void that France, the former colonial power in Vietnam, had left behind. In its zeal to battle communism, the United States essentially assumed the hated role of imperial master in Vietnam. As a result, when the United States sent troops into the territory in the mid-1960s, they suddenly faced an enemy that hated Americans. By the end of the war, American forces had dropped seven million tons of bombs on Vietnam—more than all the bombs dropped on Europe and Japan during World War II. The ultimate human cost of the Vietnam War was staggering for all sides: an estimated two million Vietnamese civilians died along with at least one million North Vietnamese soldiers, 200,000 South Vietnamese soldiers, and 58,000 American soldiers.

IMPORTANT QUOTATIONS EXPLAINED

1. *Now and then, however, there were times of panic, when they squealed . . . when they . . . flopped around on the earth and fired their weapons blindly . . . and went wild . . . hoping not to die.*

This quotation appears about halfway through the story, and it is the only passage that peels back the dispassionate surface of lists, weights, poise, bravery, and dark humor to reveal the abject terror the men truly feel during the war. If there is any morality in war, it is the men's feeling of having a moral obligation to deny cowardice and remain brave; but here we learn that all of the men succumb, at times, to panic. O'Brien's uses specific words and phrases in this passage to emphasize that panic. For example, he says that the men "squealed," a vaguely inhuman sound, more like a terrified animal than a man. Indeed, in times of extreme fear, an animal-like instinct takes over, and the men think of nothing but survival. *Flopped* is also a word that seems to describe an animal rather than a human, and O'Brien emphasizes this idea still further when he says the men "went wild." Thought processes and actions are messy, desperate, and unconscious. The sentence, appropriately, ends with the finality of the word *die.*

2. *They carried the soldier's greatest fear. . . the fear of blushing. Men killed, and died,*
because they were embarrassed not to. It was what had brought them to the war in the first
place. . . . They died so as not to die of embarrassment.

This quotation, which appears near the end of the story, reveals the men's unspoken motivation for coming to war and keeping up an appearance of detachment and strength. The exception to this idea of hidden cowardice is Ted Lavender, who was openly afraid and managed his fear not through bravado but through tranquilizers and marijuana. Before he dies, his fear is his identifying characteristic — the narrator attaches the description "who was scared" to Ted Lavender's name several times. This kind of cowardice is, for the men, taboo, and they must do whatever they can to keep up the appearance of bravery, whether it be by cutting the thumb from the gruesome dead body of an enemy or discussing a friend's death in flippant terms. There may be fear and dread beneath the surface, but their "fear of blushing" motivates them to hide those feelings.

By pointing to embarrassment as the reason why young men agreed to go to war, O'Brien debunks the notion that men go to war to be heroes. Instead, he says, they go because they are forced to: their neighbors and families expect it. Refusal or hesitation equals cowardice. By indicating that men do unspeakable things partly because of impulse but mostly because of peer pressure, O'Brien suggests that a soldier's greatest fear is not death or killing but simple embarrassment.

Twilight of the Superheroes

Deborah Eisenberg
(1945–)

CONTEXT

Deborah Eisenberg was born in 1945 to a homemaker mother and pediatrician father. She was raised outside of Chicago in the suburb of Winnetka, a place she has referred to as "hermetically sealed" and middle-class. Her parents, who are of Jewish decent, raised her as a Jew even though Winnetka was, by her own description, "anti-Semitic and restricted." A brownhaired girl, Eisenberg felt like an outcast amongst the mostly blonde children in her primarily protestant town. In addition, throughout her childhood she suffered from a serious case of scoliosis—a condition in which the spine is bent irregularly—and was therefore required to wear a full-body metal and leather brace that went from her ears almost down to her knees. Sent to boarding school to complete her early education, Eisenberg's childhood and teenage years were characterized by social and emotional distress. Always difficult, she developed a rebellious attitude, acting out and causing problems in numerous ways.

After boarding school, Eisenberg's parents wanted her to attend Marlboro College in Vermont, but she ran off with her boyfriend to New York City instead. In New York, Eisenberg acquired her undergraduate degree at the New School in downtown Manhattan. While working as a waitress, she met the man with whom she would spend most of her life, actor and playwright Wallace Shawn. She herself has described Shawn as the strangest person she'd ever met. Shawn's father, an editor at the *New Yorker*, encouraged Eisenberg to try her hand at writing, and he eventually published her first short story, "Flotsam," in the mid-1980s. Eisenberg, along with Alice Munro and Francine Prose, quickly became known as one of a select group of her generation's most important female short-fiction writers.

Eisenberg's first book-length collection of short fiction, *Transactions in a Foreign Currency*, was published in 1986, followed by *Under the 82nd Airborne* (1992), *The Stories (So Far) of Deborah Eisenberg* (1997), and *All Around Atlantis* (1997). Unlike most contemporary fiction writers, Eisenberg has continued to focus exclusively on the short-fiction form and hasn't published any novels to date. Nevertheless, critics consider her to be one of her generation's major literary masters.

"Twilight of the Superheroes" is the title story in Eisenberg's most recent collection, which deals with the psychological aftermath of the terrorist attacks on September 11, 2001. Many believe that she infused the stories with some of her own experiences after the attacks, although Eisenberg has never confirmed this. The critical reception of the work, however, has been generally positive, and she has received much praise for her ability to capture the emotional experience of the attacks without lapsing into cliché. Eisenberg currently lives in both New York City and Virginia, where she teaches writing at the University of Virginia.

PLOT OVERVIEW

Nathaniel, a twenty-eight year-old aspiring architect, reclines with his three roommates on the terrace of their thirty-first-floor sublet. He imagines himself as a grown man recounting the experience of Y2K to his grandchildren. Realizing how unimportant the event was, he laughs at his own imagined future. The idea of anyone his age actually having kids at all, let alone grandkids, seems ridiculous to him.

Nathaniel's middle-aged uncle, Lucien, meanwhile, is in his office with his assistant, Sharmila, at his art gallery on the other side of the city and is just about to close up for the evening. Lucien recalls a conversation he had earlier in the day with his client Yoshi Matsumoto, who informed Lucien that he will soon return to New York, which he claims is now "back to normal." This phrase disturbs Lucien, who recalls why Matsumoto left in the first place and how Nathaniel came to live in Matsumoto's apartment. Thinking about his nephew and family in general also prompts Lucien to think about his late wife, Charlie, who died of cancer.

Meanwhile, Nathaniel sips champagne on the balcony of Matsumoto's apartment along with his three roommates—Madison, Lyle, and Amity—and Amity's agent, Russell, to toast the end of their three-year stay in the apartment. They have lived in the apartment since Lucien helped Nathaniel settle in the city in 2000. Nathaniel and his roommates recall witnessing the terrorist attack on the World Trade Center on September 11, 2001, while eating breakfast on the terrace. The event was traumatic for all of them, and it took a long time before any of them could relax on the terrace again. Their toast marks a significant time in their lives, and Nathaniel realizes that they may all go in separate directions once Matsumoto returns.

Lucien plans to spend the evening as he usually does, alone with a glass of wine. The thought of doing so, however, makes him feel very old, and he suddenly has the desire to give Sharmila some advice about life and share some of his wisdom with her. However, realizing that she wouldn't be interested, he sends her home instead. Lucien then begins daydreaming of Charlie, which reminds him of Nathaniel and Nathaniel's parents, Isaac and Rose, who'd been Charlie's sister. They had asked Lucien and Charlie to look after their son when he'd first moved to the city, which had irritated him, not because he disliked Nathaniel but because he felt that Rose and Isaac doted on the boy too much.

Since Charlie's death, Rose and Isaac had ironically become more involved in Lucien's life, which irritated him even more. He realizes that Rose and Isaac immigrated to America from Eastern Europe, where they'd faced terrible persecution. At the same time, Lucien is grateful for Rose and Isaac because they remind him of his deceased wife. He misses Charlie very much and spends a great deal of time reminiscing about his life with her.

Nathaniel, meanwhile, recalls the time when Aunt Charlie and Uncle Lucien visited his family in the Midwest. The visit, however, was not exactly pleasant. A rivalry existed between Charlie and Rose, and Nathaniel believes that the bitterness even lasted up until Charlie's death. He finds it ironic that New York City, the place that offered his parents safe haven when they first immigrated to the country, is now his home.

Meanwhile, Lucien remembers his elementary school teacher, Miss Mueller. She was his history teacher, and he reminisces about how much of what she taught him is now considered incorrect.

Nathaniel recounts the story of his comic-book creation, Passivityman. Although his Passivityman comic is popular in the Midwest, he begins to realize that the comic doesn't hold his interest as much as it once did. He isn't sure whether that's because he's busier these days or has less drive. He looks around at his friends, those he used as models for his comic book characters, and wonders whether superpowers fade naturally as one gets older.

Lucien begins to recount the events of the morning of September 11, 2001, in his mind. He was far from the World Trade Center site that morning but headed straight to Ground Zero when he heard the news in an effort to find Nathaniel.

As Nathaniel reconstructs the day in his mind, he simultaneously recalls a fleeting affair with the girl he stayed with for a time after 9/11. The relationship didn't fulfill him in any way.

Lucien recounts the aftermath of 9/11 and the impact it had on the city. He than realizes that although most things seem to have gone back to normal, the normality is only a façade. Lucien thinks his perspective on things has changed irrevocably because of the event.

Nathaniel, on the other hand, continues drinking with his housemates, looking into the future. He realizes that his relationship with his parents has grown gentler and more mature over the years. He and his friends toast their time in Matsumoto's apartment, and Nathaniel thinks about a dream he had involving his love interest, Delphine.

Across town, Lucien toasts to the open air and thinks abstractly and pessimistically about the future.

CHARACTER LIST

Nathaniel   The story's young protagonist. Nathaniel has come to New York from his hometown in the Midwest because he's always envisioned himself living in the Big Apple. He works as an architect in the architectural division of the New York subway system but spends his free time drawing a semiautobiographical comic that dramatizes the life of his hero Passivityman. He's lived in Matsumoto's apartment with his three best friends, Lyle, Amity, and Madison, for about three years.

Lucien   The story's older main character. Lucien is an art dealer and Nathaniel's uncle, the husband of Nathaniel's mother's younger sister, Charlie. Lucien was born and bred in New York and has an intimate relationship with the city. He helped arrange for Nathaniel and his friends to live in an apartment owned by a client of his named Matsumoto. Lucien has not fully recovered from the grief of losing Charlie to cancer or from the trauma of 9/11 and feels that he's growing old.

Charlie   Lucien's wife and the sister of Nathaniel's mother. Charlie was born in America and met Lucian in New York. She was beautiful and artistic, which made her sister, Rose, jealous. Charlie died of cancer before Nathaniel moved to the city.

Lyle   Nathaniel's friend from college. Lyle sublets Matsumoto's apartment and works as a sound technician in a theater. According to Nathaniel, Lyle's "superpower" is his ability to arouse pity in anybody.

Madison   Nathaniel's friend from college. Madison sublets Matsumoto's apartment and recently quit his lucrative job working for a prestigious public relations firm. According to Nathaniel, Madison's "superpower" is level-headedness. Madison recently learned that he has a sister he never knew.

Amity   Nathaniel's friend from college. Amity sublets Matsumoto's apartment and works at a department store selling beauty products. She recently wrote a book about her experiences called *Inner Beauty Secrets*. Nathaniel believes that her special trait is exploiting the weaknesses of others.

Rose   Nathaniel's mother and the older sister of Lucien's deceased wife, Charlie. Rose emigrated from Eastern Europe when she was just a child and has never fully recovered from the experience. She lives in the Midwest and is a practicing Jew.

Isaac   Nathaniel's father and Rose's wife. Isaac immigrated to America from Eastern Europe with his family when he was a young boy and never fully recovered from the traumatic experience. He works for a company that manufactures vacuum cleaners, a financially stable occupation. He is Jewish and a member of his local temple.

Delphine   Nathaniel's older, exotic female friend. Delphine is of Armenian decent and doesn't think of herself as American. She came to New York seeking a romantic experience and dates rich, older men. She is beautiful and attends Lucien's fancy art parties.

Yoshi Matsumoto   A wealthy Japanese client of Lucien's. Matsumoto has allowed Nathaniel and his friends to sublet his apartment while he is living outside New York. The apartment is close to the site of the World Trade Center.

ANALYSIS OF MAJOR CHARACTERS

NATHANIEL   Nathaniel is part of a new generation that faces a bright future with endless possibilities but is simultaneously filled with uncertainty. Although Nathaniel has yet to accomplish anything of significance so far, his life is full of potential. He has come to New York to access the cultured, artistic, and vibrant lifestyle that his Uncle Lucien and Aunt Charlie embodied when they visited him as a child. However, his youth and inexperience, coupled with the traumatic world events he has witnessed, have stunted his personal growth and prevented him from maturing into full adulthood. After witnessing the World Trade Center collapse, he has lost his innocence without gaining an adult perspective on the world. He doesn't idealize the world but hopes to passively create an authentic space for himself and his friends, as evidenced by the hero of his own comic strip, "Passivityman." Like Passivityman, Nathaniel is trapped by the paradox of wanting to engage the world around him but also wanting to stay protected from it. Unlike Passivityman, however, Nathaniel actually does attempt to interact with others: he has a job, he has had a relationship with Delphine, and now he may need to find a place to live on his own. This final step will be an important test of Nathaniel's promise and offer him the chance to become fully independent.

LUCIEN   Spiritually and personally, Lucien is a casualty of the events of 9/11. For Lucien, it is now impossible to look even upon Nathaniel and his friends, the younger generation, with anything resembling optimism or hope. He represents a stunted old guard, jaded by world events and personal tragedies to a state most likely beyond repair. Lucien sees his own loss in the trauma of 9/11, and his inability to recover from this loss mirrors the nation's failure to recover from 9/11. Before his wife died, Lucien was proudly involved in the artistic and creative industries of New York. When he visited Nathaniel's family in the Midwest with

Charlie, he represented success and accomplishment. Since his wife's death, however, he's been unable to feel the same joy. Lucian longs for the seeming stability of the world of his childhood—a world symbolized by his schoolteacher Mrs. Mueller, whose words and image haunt him throughout the story. Nevertheless, he understands the futility of these thoughts, realizing that even in those days the stability he felt was merely a fabrication, a curtain that could be pulled back at any moment to reveal a dangerous problematic world. At the end of the story, Lucien's only comfort is in the unimportance his and Nathan's time on this planet, a wholly pessimistic and cynical perspective on the world.

THEMES, MOTIFS, AND SYMBOLS

THEMES

THE DEVALUATION OF THE AMERICAN DREAM   In the face of death, destruction, and political uncertainly, the American Dream has little value in "Twilight of the Superheroes." In many respects, Lucien has already achieved the American dream: he was born and reared in America, married the love of his life, has a successful business in a field he enjoys, and has many prosperous friends. Despite his upbringing and success, however, he is still incredibly unhappy. After the death of his wife and September 11, Lucien is unable to derive joy from any of these privileges. At the end, he remains cynical despite his achievements, and it's still unclear what could possibly breathe life or joy into him. Similarly, Nathanial's parents, Isaac and Rose, have also achieved a devalued version of the American Dream. Having come across the Atlantic as immigrants from Eastern Europe, they have acquired adequate wealth, success in business, and a large and loving family. Nevertheless, they are still haunted by an indefinable fear and live a timid, closed-off life away from other people. On paper, they have achieved the American Dream, but it fails to make them happy. Aware of his parents' unhappiness, Nathaniel rejects their path to success out of the realization that achieving the American Dream fails to offer anyone true happiness.

THE LOSS OF INNOCENCE   "Twilight of the Superheroes" documents Nathaniel and Luciens's loss of innocence as well as the national loss of innocence after September 11. Even though Nathaniel and Lucien are in different stages of their lives and have divergent perspectives on the world, 9/11 forces both of them to mature and reflect on their lives. Lucien and Nathaniel spend the story reminiscing about their naïve perspectives of the world when they were younger and contemplating the future. Lucien feels that without his wife, there is no hope for the future. Moreover, the tragedy of September 11 has prompted him to question the impact he has had on the world in general. Nathaniel, meanwhile, remembers the impact his Uncle Lucien and Aunt Charlie had on him when they visited his childhood home in the Midwest. At the time, Lucien and Charlie represented an intriguing world of glitz and glamour that Nathaniel wanted to join. Nathaniel's and Lucien's "innocent selves," however, have died and have been replaced by confused and slightly jaded adults.

MOTIFS

SEPTEMBER 11   In "Twilight of the Superheroes," the September 11 terrorist attacks highlight Nathanial and Lucien's alienation and loss of self-identity. Nathaniel and Lucien react to the fall of the twin towers in similar ways, although their experiences preceding the event differ considerably. September 11 forces them to look within themselves and question their dreams and desires, and the trauma of the terrorist attack translates into trauma in their personal lives. For Nathaniel, who actually sees the towers fall, 9/11 is a wake-up call to the harsh realities of the world. The experience helps him begin to come to terms with his passivity and complacency. For Lucien, however, 9/11 was a national trauma that mirrored his own personal tragedy—the loss of his beloved wife, Charlie—and he's better able to understand his own trauma as his fellow New Yorkers struggle with their own losses. In this way, both characters define themselves in reaction to the disaster.

FEAR   Fear is a powerful force in the lives of every character in "Twilight of the Superheroes." Fear, for example, has defined Nathaniel's parents' lives, first in Europe during World War II and then in the United States, where they live in constant fear of authority. As a result, they worry nonstop about inconsequential things and have instilled some of their paranoia and anxiety in Nathaniel. Nathaniel manages to overcome some of these fears when he moves from his college town to New York, but he grows to fear the prospect of mediocrity and failure. September 11 shakes him and brings this anxiety to the forefront of his thoughts. Lucien, on the other hand, doesn't fear for his livelihood or safety but worries for the fate of New York and the world. He has been forced to face his fear of being alone and wonders what the future will bring. September makes Nathaniel's and Lucien's fears more pronounced, and both struggle to make sense of them.

SYMBOLS

BUILDINGS AND ARCHITECTURE   Eisenberg uses buildings and architecture—traditional symbols of stability—to represent the uncertainty and frailty of life. The story begins with Nathaniel and his friends in an apartment that they never leased and can no longer call home. Their building is near the site of the former World Trade Center, itself a symbol of the vulnerability of the entire American way of life and Western culture. The terrace of the apartment, upon which Nathaniel and his friends toast their friendship and departure, even had a view of the World Trade Center. On the morning of the 9/11 attacks, the friends sat on the terrace and witnessed how fragile the world really is. In this way, the very roof under which they sought protection from the elements is irrevocably tied to the traumatic destruction of America's innocence. In addition, Nathaniel is himself an architect, a profession that his parents fear will offer him an "unreliable future." Ironically, he's even currently employed with the architectural division of the New York subway, as if, in reaction to the potential uncertainty and instability of the world, he has headed underground for protection.

SHORT STORY ANALYSIS

EISENBERG'S REVERSE EPIPHANY   Unlike many short stories, "Twilight of the Superheroes" doesn't end with an epiphany (a moment of realization); rather, it ends with just as much uncertainty and hopelessness that it began with. Because epiphanies have become so common in contemporary American short fiction, many readers expect the status quo to be overturned at the end of every short story or at least expect the protagonist's disorganized thoughts to coalesce at some new awareness. Eisenberg, however, rejects this formula as unrealistic, and she strives to write stories that maintain the confusions and uncertainty of modern life. In this way, her "reverse epiphanies," as she calls them, alter the common short story blueprint by remaining convoluted and realistically complex at they end.

"Twilight of the Superheroes" features an excellent example of a "reverse epiphany" because the story is about the inaction and uncertainty of its characters. Nathanial and his friends are stuck in one of life's ruts, while Lucien is constantly trapped in his memories of the past. A significant portion of the work is spent following Nathaniel's stationary thoughts and dwelling on the events of his past that can't be changed. When the story ends, Nathaniel still hasn't decided how to move forward, and Lucien hasn't moved beyond the confines of his memories. Instead, the story ends with one of Eisenberg's characteristic reverse epiphanies: both characters continue to dwell on the same issues that confuse them. In fact, the entire story takes place in only a matter of minutes, emphasizing Nathaniel's and Lucien's mental and emotional turmoil and keeping them stuck in time: at the end of the story, Lucien is still standing in his gallery, and Nathaniel is still reminiscing with his friends on the terrace of Matsumoto's apartment. Instead of having a revelatory moment of realization, when the lives of either character change, Eisenberg is interested merely in showing us how each character lives and thinks. She documents the status quo, leaving us with a realistic image of life to make better sense of the world.

SEPTEMBER 11 FICTION   On September 11, 2001, hijackers crashed two commercial airliners into the World Trade Center buildings in downtown Manhattan, New York City. While hijackers also crashed a plane into the Pentagon and another into a field in rural Pennsylvania, the attacks on the World Trade Center produced the most casualties and elicited the most significant public response. Published in the spring of 2006, Deborah Eisenberg's "Twilight of the Superheroes" was one of the first fictionalizations of the attacks, along with Ian McEwan's *Saturday* (2005), Jonathan Safran Foer's *Extremely Loud and Incredibly Close* (2005), Frederic Beigbeder's *Windows on the World* (2006), and *Dear Zoe* (2006) by Philip Beard. Although each of these authors interprets September 11 differently, all have found it difficult to personalize the tragedy and make sense of it. Eisenberg has tackled this issue by conveying the effects of the event on Lucien as an individual as well on Nathaniel and his friends as a group. Several of these authors have attempted to catalogue the effect of the September 11 attack on the general character of New York City too. Lucien's reminisces about the changing nature of New York, for example, is Eisenberg's attempt to explain how the attacks transformed the entire city. Eisenberg weaves Nathaniel's Armenian friend, Delphine, into her narrative, suggesting that non-Americans felt the impact of September 11 too. The body of September 11 literature is still young, and "Twilight of the Superheroes" is thus a unique contribution that will shape the way future writers and historians will interpret the event.

IMPORTANT QUOTATIONS EXPLAINED

1. *When it comes down to it, it always turns out that no one is in charge of the things that really matter.*

In this quote, at the beginning of the story, Nathaniel is imagining what he will tell his grand-children about the potential disaster that Y2K presented when many thought that the world's computers would malfunction at the dawning of the new millennium. Nathaniel remembers the anxiety surrounding Y2K because it seems pointless after the actual disaster of September 11, 2001. On the eve of the new millennium, nothing significant happened—airplanes didn't fall from the skies, stock markets didn't crash, and life continued on as normal. Even though comparing Y2K and 9/11 is futile for Nathaniel, they are inexorably tied in his mind. The fact that "we humans cannot actually think ahead" encapsulates his greatest fear in his own life. Nathaniel, in the story, is trapped in a suspended state of passivity. He is unsure of his career, unable to connect with the girl he desires, and doesn't know what he'll do without his closest friends. Anxiety about the future pervades his perspective on the world, and the futility of national and political predictions bothers his already aggravated sense of self.

A Very Old Man with Enormous Wings

Gabriel García Márquez
(1928–)

CONTEXT

Gabriel García Márquez was born in 1928 in a small village in Colombia near the Caribbean coast. His parents were poor, so his maternal grandparents raised him, and he would later claim that he drew much of his literary inspiration from his grandmother's storytelling. After attending college and law school, he began a successful career as a journalist but continued to pursue his interest in writing fiction.

García Márquez published his first collection of short stories, *Leaf Storm*, which included "A Very Old Man with Enormous Wings," in 1955. The book was an immediate success, and he consequently left journalism to devote himself to becoming "the best writer in the world," as he later told an interviewer from the *Paris Review*. García Márquez later won international acclaim for his first novel, the modern classic *One Hundred Years of Solitude*, in 1967. Subsequent novels such as *Love in the Time of Cholera* (1985) and *The General in His Labyrinth* (1989) established García Márquez as one of the most notable writers of the twentieth century. He won the Nobel Prize for Literature in 1982.

García Márquez's literary style draws heavily from European gothic writers such as Franz Kafka, who famously turned his one of his characters, Gregor Samsa, into a giant insect in "The Metamorphosis" (1915). American novelist William Faulkner has been cited as a forerunner to García Márquez as well, especially in the way Faulkner grounds his highly experimental novels in the grotesque details of a particular local culture. García Márquez's own development of the magical-realist genre has had enormous influence on writers throughout the world, especially in Central and South America. In fact, magical realism has since become one of the signature fictional genres of Latin American writers, including Argentina's Jorge Luis Borges, Chile's Isabel Allende, and Peru's Mario Vargas Llosa.

In addition to writing, García Márquez has also served as one of Latin America's most distinguished diplomats and mediators. Although he's never held any public office, he's worked tirelessly behind the scenes to mediate disputes between the government, leftist guerillas, right-wing paramilitaries, and the drug cartels during Colombia's decades-long civil war. Friends with both Cuban leader Fidel Castro and former U.S. president Bill Clinton, García Márquez also sought to bridge the gap between the two countries in the 1990s, which strengthened his reputation as a peacemaker. Many have hailed him as Colombia's only voice of reason and the country's best hope for peace.

The almost cultish reverence for "Gabo," as Colombians affectionately call him, has transformed García Márquez into both a national and Latin American icon. Also known in Colombia as *El Maestro* and *Nuestro Nobel* (our Nobel winner), he actually spends most of every year living abroad in Mexico City, Havana, Paris, Barcelona, and Los Angeles, where his son, Rodrigo Garcia, works as a Hollywood director.

PLOT OVERVIEW

One day, while killing crabs during a rainstorm that has lasted for several days, Pelayo discovers a homeless, disoriented old man in his courtyard who happens to have very large wings. The old man is filthy and apparently senile, and speaks an unintelligible language. After consulting a neighbor woman, Pelayo and his wife, Elisenda, conclude that the old man must be an angel who had tried to come and take their sick child to heaven. The neighbor woman tells Pelayo that he should club the angel to death, but Pelayo and Elisenda take pity on their visitor, especially after their child recovers.

Pelayo and Elisenda keep the old man in their chicken coop, and he soon begins to attract crowds of curious visitors. Father Gonzaga, the local priest, tells the people that the old man is probably not an angel because he's shabby and doesn't speak Latin. Father Gonzaga decides to ask his bishop for guidance.

Despite Father Gonzaga's efforts, word of the old man's existence soon spreads, and pilgrims come from all over to seek advice and healing from him. One woman comes because she'd been counting her heartbeats since childhood and couldn't continue counting. An insomniac visits because he claims that the stars in the night sky are too noisy. The crowd eventually grows so large and disorderly with the sick and curious that Elisenda begins to charge admission. For the most part, the old man ignores the people, even when they pluck his feathers and throw stones at him to make him stand up. He becomes enraged, however, when the visitors sear him with a branding iron to see whether he's still alive.

Father Gonzaga does his best to restrain the crowd, even as he waits for the Church's opinion on the old man. The crowd starts to disperse when a traveling freak show arrives in the village. People flock to hear the story of the so-called spider woman, a woman who'd been transformed into a giant tarantula with the head of a woman after she'd disobeyed her parents. The sad tale of the spider woman is so popular that people quickly forget the old man, who'd performed only a few pointless semimiracles for his pilgrims.

Pelayo and Elisenda have nevertheless grown quite wealthy from the admission fees Elisenda had charged. Pelayo quits his job and builds a new, larger house. The old man continues to stay with them, still in the chicken coop, for several years, as the little boy grows older. When the chicken coop eventually collapses, the old man moves into the adjacent shed, but he often wanders from room to room inside the house, much to Elisenda's annoyance.

Just when Pelayo and Elisenda are convinced that the old man will soon die, he begins to regain his strength. His feathers grow back and he begins to sing sea chanteys (sailors' songs) to himself at night. One day the old man stretches his wings and takes off into the air, and Elisenda watches him disappear over the horizon.

CHARACTER LIST

The Old Man   An old man with wings who appears in Pelayo and Elisenda's yard one day. Filthy and bedraggled, the old man speaks a foreign language that no one can understand. His wings and unintelligible language prompts some people to believe that he's a fallen angel and the church to believe he's a Norwegian, even though he seems oblivious to nearly everything that happens around him. By the end of the story, the old man has recovered enough to fly away, exiting Pelayo's and Elisenda's lives as suddenly as he'd entered.

Pelayo   Elisenda's husband and the discoverer of the old man. Pelayo is an ordinary villager, poor but grudgingly willing to shelter the winged old man in his chicken coop. Pelayo guards the old man from harm, humbly consults the village priest, and has the sense to resist the more extravagant advice he receives from the other villagers. Pelayo, however, does not want to take care of the man indefinitely and doesn't feel bad using the old man to get rich.

Elisenda   Pelayo's wife. Elisenda convinces Pelayo to charge villagers to see the old man but later considers him to be a nuisance. A practical woman, she primarily concerns herself with the welfare of Pelayo and their child and is therefore relieved when the old man finally leaves.

Father Gonzaga   The village priest. As an authority figure in the community, Father Gonzaga takes it upon himself to discern whether the old man is an angel as the townsfolk believe or just a mortal who just happens to have wings. Father Gonzaga is skeptical that the dirty old man could really be a messenger from heaven, but he dutifully reports the event to his superiors in the church. As he waits for the Vatican's reply, he does his best to restrain the enthusiasm and credulousness of the crowd of onlookers.

The Neighbor Woman   Pelayo and Elisenda's bossy neighbor. The supposedly wise neighbor woman actually seems more like a silly know-it-all than a true counselor and is the first to suggest that the old man is a crippled angel. She tells Pelayo to club the old man to death to prevent him from taking Pelayo and Elisenda's sick baby to heaven.

The Spider Woman   A freak-show attraction who visits the village. Punished for the sin of disobeying her parents, the spider woman now has the body of an enormous spider and the head of a sad young woman. The clear moral of the woman's story draws gawking villagers away from the old man, who is unable to offer the crowds such a compelling narrative.

ANALYSIS OF MAJOR CHARACTERS

THE OLD MAN   The old man, with his human body and unexpected wings, appears to be neither fully human nor fully surreal. On the one hand, the man seems human enough, surrounded as he is by filth, disease, infirmity, and squalor. He has a human reaction to the people who crowd around him and seek healing, remaining indifferent to their pleas and sometimes not even acknowledging their existence. When the doctor examines him, he is amazed that such an unhealthy man is still alive and is equally struck by how natural the old man's wings seem to be. Such an unsurprised reaction essentially brings the "angel" down to earth, so any heavenly qualities the old man may have are completely obscured. However, the narrator seems to take the old man's angelhood for granted, speaking of the "lunar dust" and "stellar parasites" on his wings, and the old man's "consolation miracles," such as causing sunflowers to sprout from a leper's sores, seem genuinely supernatural. In the end, the old man's true nature remains a mystery.

PELAYO Although Pelayo is kinder to the old man than the other villagers, he is certainly no paragon of compassion and charity. He doesn't club the old man as the neighbor woman suggests, but he does pen the supposed angel in his chicken coop and charge admission to the crowds of curious sightseers. Pelayo is primarily concerned with his family and sick child and is content to leave the theoretical and theological speculations to Father Gonzaga. His decision to shelter the old man and take some responsibility for him, however, suggests that he isn't as cold or heartless as he might seem. By allowing the old man to stay, Pelayo also invites mystery, wonder, and magic into his life.

ELISENDA Elisenda is a perfect match for her husband, Pelayo, being equally ordinary and concerned with practical matters. If anything, Elisenda is the more practical of the two because she suggests charging admission to see the "angel." Despite the many material advantages the old man brings, Elisenda's attitude toward him is primarily one of annoyance and exasperation. Once the old man's usefulness as a roadside attraction dwindles, Elisenda sees him only as a nuisance. Indeed, the old man becomes so troublesome to her that she even refers to her new home—purchased with proceeds from exhibiting the old man—as a "hell full of angels." The old man becomes so ordinary in Elisenda's eyes that it isn't until he finally flies away that she seems to see him for the wonder he is. Elisenda watches him fly away with wistfulness, as if finally realizing that something extraordinary has left her life forever.

THEMES, MOTIFS, AND SYMBOLS

THEMES

THE COEXISTENCE OF CRUELTY AND COMPASSION "A Very Old Man with Enormous Wings" wryly examines the human response to those who are weak, dependent, and different. There are moments of striking cruelty and callousness throughout the story. After Elisenda and Pelayo's child recovers from his illness, for example, the parents decide to put the old man to sea on a raft with provisions for three days rather than just killing him, a concession to the old man's difficult situation but hardly a kind act. Once they discover that they can profit from showcasing him, however, Pelayo and Elisenda imprison him in a chicken coop outside, where strangers pelt him with stones, gawk at him, and even burn him with a branding iron.

Amidst the callousness and exploitation, moments of compassion are few and far between, although perhaps all the more significant for being so rare. Even though he is taken in only grudgingly, the old man eventually becomes part of Pelayo and Elisenda's household. By the time the old man finally flies into the sunset, Elisenda, for all her fussing, sees him go with a twinge of regret. And it is the old man's extreme patience with the villagers that ultimately transforms Pelayo's and Elisenda's lives. Seen in this light, the old man's refusal to leave might be interpreted as an act of compassion to help the impoverished couple. García Márquez may have even intended to remind readers of the advice found in Hebrews 13:2 in the Bible: "Be not forgetful to entertain strangers: for thereby some have entertained angels unawares."

MOTIFS

PROSPERITY Pelayo and Elisenda's newfound prosperity is the physical manifestation of the magic and wonder the old man brings to their lives. As the story opens, the couple lives in an almost comical state of poverty as swarms of crabs invade their home. Even worse, their young son is deathly ill. The old man, however, brings hundreds of pilgrims who don't mind paying Pelayo and Elisenda a small fee for the privilege of seeing him. The proceeds bring Pelayo and Elisenda a new house, a new business, and more money than they know how to spend. This remarkable turn in fortune happens so gradually that Pelayo and Elisenda don't really see how remarkable it is. Elisenda even refers to her new home as a "hell full of angels" once the old man is allowed inside after the chicken coop collapses.

SYMBOLS

WINGS Wings represent power, speed, and limitless freedom of motion. In the Christian tradition, angels are often represented as beautiful winged figures, and García Márquez plays off of this cultural symbolism because, ironically, the wings of the "angel" in the story convey only a sense of age and disease. Although the old man's wings may be dirty, bedraggled, and bare, they are still magical enough to attract crowds of pilgrims and sightseers. When the village doctor examines the old man, he notices how naturally the wings fit in with the rest of his body. In fact, the doctor even wonders why everyone else doesn't have wings as well. The ultimate effect is to suggest that the old man is both natural and supernatural at once, having the wings of a heavenly messenger but all the frailties of an earthly creature.

THE SPIDER WOMAN The spider woman represents the fickleness with which many self-interested people approach their own faith. After hearing of the "angel," hundreds of villagers flock to Pelayo's house, motivated partly by faith but also to see him perform miracles—physical evidence that their faith is justified. Not surprisingly, the old man's reputation wanes when he proves capable of performing only minor "consolation miracles." Instead, the spectators flock to the spider woman, who tells a heart-wrenching story with a clear, easy-to-digest lesson in morality that contrasts sharply with the obscurity of the old man's existence and purpose. Although no less strange than the winged old man, the spider woman is easier to understand and even pity. The old man, barely conscious in his filthy chicken coop, can't match her appeal, even though some suspect that he came from the heavens. García Márquez strongly suggests that the pilgrims' result-oriented faith isn't really faith at all.

SHORT STORY ANALYSIS

MAGICAL REALISM García Márquez's literary reputation is inseparable from the term *magical realism*, a phrase that literary critics coined to describe the distinctive blend of fantasy and realism in his and many other Latin American authors' work. Magical-realist fiction consists of mostly true-to-life narrative punctuated by moments of whimsical, often symbolic, fantasy described in the same matter-of-fact tone. Magical realism has become such an established form in Latin America partly because the style is strongly connected to the folkloric storytelling that's still popular in rural communities. The genre, therefore, attempts to connect two traditions—the "low" folkloric and the "high" literary—into a seamless whole that embraces the extremes of Latin American culture. As the worldwide popularity of García Márquez's writing testifies, it is a formula that resonates well with readers around the world.

"A Very Old Man with Enormous Wings" is one of the most well-known examples of the magical realist style, combining the homely details of Pelayo and Elisenda's life with fantastic elements such as a flying man and a spider woman to create a tone of equal parts local-color story and fairy tale. From the beginning of the story, García Márquez's style comes through in his unusual, almost fairy tale–like description of the relentless rain: "The world had been sad since Tuesday." There is a mingling of the fantastic and ordinary in all the descriptions, including the swarms of crabs that invade Pelayo and Elisenda's home and the muddy sand of the beach that in the rainy grayness looks "like powdered light." It is in this strange, highly textured, dreamlike setting that the old winged man appears, a living myth, who is nevertheless covered in lice and dressed in rags.

SATIRE "A Very Old Man with Enormous Wings" functions as a satirical piece that mocks both the Catholic Church and human nature in general. García Márquez criticizes the church through Father Gonzaga's superiors in Rome, who seem to be in no hurry to discover the truth about the bedraggled, so-called angel. Instead, they ask Father Gonzaga to study the old man's unintelligible dialect to see whether it has any relation to Aramaic, the language of Jesus. They also ask Gonzaga to determine how many times the old man can fit on the head of a pin, another dig at Catholicism referencing an arcane medieval theory once thought to prove God's omnipotence. Their final conclusion that the old man with wings may in fact be a stranded Norwegian sailor only makes the church sound absurdly literal-minded and out of touch with even the most basic elements of reality. In the end, the church's wait-and-see tactic pays off when the old man simply flies away—a rib from García Márquez implying that the "wisdom" of the church has never really been needed at all.

Such criticisms of the church are only part of García Márquez's critique of human beings in general, who never seem to understand the greater significance of life. There is a narrowness of vision that afflicts everyone from the wise neighbor woman, with her unthinking know-it-all ways, to the kindly Father Gonzaga, who is desperate for a procedure to follow, to the crowds of onlookers and pilgrims with their selfish concerns. Elisenda too is more focused on keeping her kitchen and living room angel-free than on considering the odd beauty of her unwelcome guest. She, however, seems to have a moment of realization and almost of regret at the end of the story, when she watches the old man disappear from her life forever. Just as the proverbial lost hiker who can't see the wilderness for the trees, García Márquez suggests that most people live their lives unaware of their significance in the world.

IMPORTANT QUOTATION EXPLAINED

---

1. *His huge buzzard wings, dirty and half-plucked, were forever entangled in the mud. They looked at him so long and so closely that Pelayo and Elisenda very soon overcame their surprise and in the end found him familiar.*

Pelayo and Elisenda's initial impression of the old man's wings as the filthy limbs of a scavenger rather than the glorious wings of an angel is a good example of how García Márquez grounds even his most fantastic elements in the grunginess of daily life. The second sentence in particular clues readers in to one of the central elements of magical-realist fiction—re-awakening readers' sense of wonder at their own world. García Márquez suggests that if people can become inured to the presence of a winged man in a story, then they can just as easily overlook the wonders and little miracles of real life. A story such as "A Very Old Man with Enormous Wings" is meant to serve as a reminder that everyday life is filled with great mysteries and wonders that people overlook too often.

2. *What surprised him most, however, was the logic of his wings. They seemed so natural on that completely human organism that he couldn't understand why other men didn't have them too.*

When both the old man and Pelayo and Elisenda's son come down with chicken pox, the local physician takes advantage of the opportunity to examine the "angel" physically. The doctor is surprised both that the old man is still alive and that his wings seem so natural on his body. In this passage, García Márquez seems to imply that there is nothing angelic about the old man at all, although the narrator goes back to referring to him simply as "the angel" a few lines later. More important, the passage suggests that the boundary we draw between natural and supernatural is arbitrary at best. García Márquez subtly raises the question: if wings are so naturally a part of this particular man's body, then are we the freaks for not having them?

V

What We Talk About When We Talk About Love

Raymond Carver
(1938–1988)

CONTEXT

Born in 1938 in small-town Oregon and raised in the state of Washington, Raymond Carver grew up watching his father struggle with alcoholism, an affliction that proved to be hereditary and would eventually claim Carver as well. His father worked at a sawmill, and his mother worked as a waitress. When Carver was eighteen, he married his pregnant high school girlfriend, Maryann Burke, with whom he'd have a second child by the time he was twenty-one. After high school, Carver and his family moved to California, where he worked a variety of odd jobs, which would later provide inspiration for the down-and-out, blue-collar characters of his stories. In 1958, Carver discovered his interest in writing when he began taking classes at Chico State College under the instruction of writer John Gardner.

While still working odd jobs, Carver began writing poetry and short stories and published his first poetry collections, *Near Klamath* and *Winter Insomnia*, in 1968 and 1970, respectively. He published his first short-story collection, *Will You Please Be Quiet, Please?*, in 1976. The collection has since become one of his best-known works. His poetry and fiction received much critical praise, and he began teaching writing at the college level.

Carver suffered from acute alcoholism, which eventually supplanted any kind of productive work. He was hospitalized several times but failed at his attempts to quit. Finally, in 1977, he stopped drinking and took a break from writing so that he could simply work at staying sober. When he started writing again, he went on to publish several more short-story collections, including *What We Talk About When We Talk About Love* (1981), *Cathedral* (1983), and *Elephant* (published posthumously in 1988). Two compilations of Carver's stories have also been published: *Where I'm Calling From* (1988) and *Short Cuts: Selected Stories* (1993). Hollywood director Robert Altman made a film version of *Short Cuts* in 1993.

Carver is known for his minimalist approach to prose, and for this reason he's often compared to Ernest Hemingway and Anton Chekhov. His short stories focus on middle-class, often blue-collar people who are struggling with hard truths, disappointments, inertia, and small glimmers of hope in their ordinary lives. Along with writers such as Ann Beattie and Tobias Wolff, Carver is considered a writer of the "dirty-realism" school. Carver's short stories are also recognizable for their abrupt endings, sometimes called "zero endings," which do not seem to tie up the story neatly, if at all. "What We Talk About When We Talk About

Love" is one of Carver's most famous stories and often regarded as the epitome of the dirty-realism school.

Carver and his wife divorced in 1982, and Carver married his longtime girlfriend, writer Tess Gallagher, in 1988. They were married for only a few months before Carver died from lung cancer at age fifty. After his death, his editor, Gordon Lish, claimed that he edited Carver's work so heavily that he should be considered a coauthor of the stories. Carver's widow, Gallagher, similarly claimed ownership of Carver's stories and said Carver had borrowed story ideas from her own work. Such accusations, however, have not tarnished Carver's legacy, and he remains one of the most influential writers of the twentieth century.

PLOT OVERVIEW

The narrator says that his cardiologist friend, Mel McGinnis, is talking. The narrator and Mel are sitting around Mel's kitchen table in Albuquerque, New Mexico, drinking gin with their wives, Laura and Terri. They begin talking about love. Mel thinks love is spiritual and says he used to be in the seminary. Terri says that before she lived with Mel, she lived with a man named Ed who tried to kill her because he loved her so much. Mel disagrees that Ed felt any love for her, but Terri says that he did. Mel tells the narrator and Laura that Ed had also threatened him and Terri. The narrator holds Laura's hand and says that he doesn't really know whether that's love, while Laura says that you can never know about other people's situations.

Terri says Ed took rat poison when she left him but that he survived. Mel says he's dead now. Terri says he shot himself, but he "bungled it."

The narrator describes Mel. He's forty-five, and his movements are usually precise when he hasn't been drinking. The narrator asks how Ed bungled his suicide, but Mel merely replies that Ed was always threatening him and Terri. Laura asks again what happened with the suicide, and Mel says that when Ed shot himself, someone heard it and called an ambulance, and Ed lived for three days. Terri says she was with him when he died and that Ed died for love. But she admits that she and Mel were scared when Ed was threatening them and that Mel had even made a will. Mel opens another bottle of gin.

The narrator, meanwhile, describes his wife, Laura. She's a legal secretary, younger than the narrator, and seemingly very compatible with him. Laura says that she and the narrator, whose name is Nick, know all about love. Nick kisses her hand. Terri asks them how long they've been together, and Laura tells her that they've been together for about eighteen months. They all toast to love.

A dog barks outside, and the sun is bright in the kitchen. Mel says he'll give them an example of love but then says that no one knows anything about love. He says he loves Terri, but he knows he loved his first wife, Marjorie, too, even though he hates her now. He wants to know what happened to the love he felt for his first wife. He points out that Nick and Laura love each other but loved other people before they met and were each married to someone else before as well. Mel says that if something happened to him or Terri, he knows that whoever remained would find someone else to love. He admits that that's a horrible thing to say but asks the others to tell him if he's wrong. Terri asks Mel whether he's drunk, and he says he can say what he's thinking without being drunk. He says they're all just talking, and that he's not on call. He tells Laura and Nick that he loves them.

Mel says that he was trying to make a point. He tells them about an elderly couple who were nearly killed when a drunk teenager hit their camper with his car. Both of them survived but were badly injured. Mel describes how he and other surgeons operated almost all night and that afterward the couple was transferred to a private room. Mel interrupts himself to tell everyone to drink more gin so that they can all go to dinner at a new place he and Terri know about. Mel says that if he could come back in another life, he'd be a chef or a knight. Terri and Mel debate whether the correct word is *vessel* or *vassal*. Nick says that being a knight could be dangerous because of all the heavy armor.

Laura asks what happened to the old couple, then struggles to light a cigarette. Nick notes that the sun in the kitchen has changed. Mel tells Laura that if their situations were different, he'd fall in love with her. Resuming the story, Mel says that he kept checking in on the old couple, both of whom were in full-body casts. The husband was okay, and the wife was going to be okay, but the husband was depressed because he couldn't see his wife through the eyeholes in his cast. Mel says that he couldn't believe the man was depressed because he couldn't see his wife. He asks everyone whether they see the point.

Nick says they're all drunk and that the light is leaving the room. Terri says Mel is depressed and tells him to take a pill, but Mel says he's already taken everything possible. Mel says he wants to call his kids, but Terri says he'll only feel worse if Marjorie answers the phone. Terri says that Mel wishes Marjorie would remarry or die. Mel says Marjorie is allergic to bees and that he wishes he could release bees in her house to kill her. He suggests they all go out to eat, but Nick suggests they should just keep drinking. Laura remarks that she's starving, and Terri says she'll serve a snack, but she stays in her seat. Mel notices that the gin is gone, and Terri asks what they should do now. Nick says he can hear everyone's heart beating. The four friends just sit in their seats until the room is dark.

CHARACTER LIST

Mel McGinnis A cardiologist. Mel talks more than anyone else in the story. He and Terri have been married for four years. Mel has two children with his ex-wife, Marjorie, whom he now hates. Although Mel makes grand proclamations about knowing what love is, he ultimately reveals that he is confused and even alarmed by the elusiveness of love and devotion.

Nick The narrator. Nick and Laura met at work, but Nick never says exactly what he does. He is thirty-eight and has been with Laura for about eighteen months. He doesn't say much in the story, but the observations he makes about the changing light, amount of remaining gin, and sound of beating hearts gives the story its rhythm.

Laura Nick's wife. Laura, thirty-five, is a legal secretary. She barely speaks at all in the story other than to say that she and Nick understand love and, at the end, that she's hungry. But her gentle physical interactions with Nick—holding hands, touching knees—give a glimpse of what love means to her.

Terri Mel's wife. Terri used to live with an abusive boyfriend named Ed who tried to kill her. Even though Ed later threatened her and Mel before killing himself, Terri believes that Ed truly loved her. Everyone seems to disagree with how she defines love, but her ideas are clearer than anyone else's.

ANALYSIS OF MAJOR CHARACTERS

MEL MCGINNIS   The first thing we learn about Mel McGinnis is that he's a cardiologist—a heart doctor. Of the four characters in the story, Mel, by virtue of his profession, would seem to be the one most likely to have some insight into matters of the heart. Indeed, he talks more than anyone else about love and has the strongest opinions. Yet despite the fact that Mel talks a lot, he doesn't seem to know more than anyone else about love. As he keeps drinking and talking, his strong statements blur into confusing ramblings that don't seem to make much of a point. He knows the story about the elderly couple is important, but he can't explain exactly why. He knows his thoughts about past and future loves are meaningful, but the way he describes them makes him sound confused and nonsensical. And his apparent desire to kill his ex-wife with swarms of bees suggests that, far from being an expert on love, Mel knows absolutely nothing about it.

NICK   Nick, the narrator of the story, doesn't say much, but the observations and physical movements he makes are key to revealing what love means to the four friends gathered at the table. Nick speaks up only four times during most of the conversation, twice to ask questions, once to suggest that love is absolute, and finally to say that he and Laura are lucky. At the end of the story, however, his own words begin sounding as jumbled as Mel's, such as when he suggests that they either eat or keep drinking and when he makes a joke about heading "right on out into the sunset." None of Nick's comments are especially revelatory; more significant are the things he doesn't say out loud. For example, his narration includes comments on the weakening sunlight in the room, an observation that reveals how muddled the friends' ideas of love eventually become. He also touches Laura a great deal, holding and kissing her hand and touching her leg under the table. These are genuinely affectionate gestures and suggest that even though the friends may talk about love all night, their words don't really matter in the end. Finally, Nick is the only one who can "hear everyone's heart," which suggests that he may have insight into love that the others do not.

TERRI   Although no one in "What We Talk About When We Talk About Love" seems to have a firm idea of what love really is, Terri does have some extreme and somewhat disturbing opinions. One of the most detailed tales told around the table is of Terri's former lover, Ed, who was terribly abusive and threatened both her and Mel. Mel is firm in his belief that Ed was crazy, but Terri insists that Ed truly loved her. She points out that Ed tried to kill himself by swallowing rat poison when she left him and, when that didn't work, shot himself through the mouth. Although the others don't share Terri's ideas about love, she nevertheless has a more solid idea about love than anyone else in the story. While Mel talks of his hatred for his ex-wife and Nick and Laura merely touch each other softly, Terri is the only one who can genuinely say that she once experienced true love. Mel calls Terri a member of the "kick-me-so-I'll-know-you-love-me school," but no one in the story can articulate a view of love that is clearer or more convincing.

THEMES, MOTIFS, AND SYMBOLS

THEMES

THE ELUSIVE NATURE OF LOVE   The nature of love remains elusive throughout "What We Talk About When We Talk About Love," despite the characters' best efforts to define it. Mel tries again and again to pinpoint the meaning of love, but his examples never build up to any coherent conclusion. For example, he tells his friends about an elderly couple who nearly died in a car crash, but the conclusion of the story—the old man depressed by not being able to see his wife—merely confuses everyone. When he asserts that he'll tell everyone exactly what love is, he instead digresses into a muddled meditation about how strange it is that he and the others have loved more than one person. His attempts to clarify the nature of love eventually devolve into a bitter tirade against his ex-wife. He seems much more certain about what love is *not* and tells Terri several times that if abusive love is true love, then she "can have it."

Laura and Nick believe that they know what love is, but they never really provide a clear definition or explain why they're so certain in their convictions. They merely demonstrate their love for each other by blushing and holding hands, but these actions simply support the mystery of love rather than unmask it. Terri, of all the friends, seems to be most certain about the meaning of love and repeatedly claims that her abusive ex-boyfriend, Ed, truly loved her, despite his crazy way of showing it. The examples she provides of this love—beating, stalking, and threatening—are disturbing but serve as proof in her mind. Like the others, however, she cannot translate her certainty into any kind of clear explanation of the nature of love.

THE INADEQUACY OF LANGUAGE   Although the four friends talk for a while about love, the fact that they never manage to define it suggests that language can't adequately describe emotional, abstract subjects. Mel does the most talking, but his bloated stories and rambling digressions show that he has trouble conveying his thoughts and feelings, despite how much he talks. Terri speaks a great deal about her former lover Ed, but when Mel challenges her, she turns to intuition to prove her point. She believes that Ed loved her no matter what Mel or the others think, demonstrating that gut feelings about love can be more powerful and accurate than words. Laura and Nick, meanwhile, say very little about the nature of love and instead rely on physical gestures to clarify what language cannot: they hold hands, blush, and touch each other's legs. Carver indicates that words simply aren't enough when talking about love, which is probably why all four friends have fallen silent by the end of the story.

MOTIFS

DRINKING   Nick, Mel, Terri, and Laura consume copious amounts of alcohol during their discussion about the nature of love, and their increasing intoxication mirrors their growing confusion about love and inability to define it. The friends have gathered to talk and drink gin, and the pouring, stirring, and sipping of drinks punctuates their conversation. As the friends get drunk, their conversation grows blurry and incoherent and finally stops completely. Drinking also serves as a kind of ritual in the story as the friends pass the bottle of gin around the table and make toasts to love. At the end of the story, as the friends discuss going out to dinner, Mel says they must finish the gin first, as though only finishing the bottle can free them from the discussion.

SYMBOLS

THE SUN The sun in the story, which is bright at the beginning and gone by the end, represents the loss of clarity and happiness as the friends grow increasingly confused about the meaning of love. At the beginning of the story, Nick notes that the kitchen is bright and compares the friends to giddy children who have "agreed on something forbidden." The talk is light and hopeful, just a friendly conversation on a gin-soaked afternoon. However, as the conversation about love becomes increasingly dark and complex, the sun in the kitchen slips slowly away. Nick notes that the sun is "changing, getting thinner," and, not long after, that the sun is "draining out of the room." As the sun disappears completely, the conversation devolves into Mel's drunken threats against his ex-wife, including a fantasy of murdering her. At the end of the story, the friends are sitting in complete darkness. The sun has gone, as have their rosy, hopeful perceptions of love.

SHORT STORY ANALYSIS

DIALOGUE As the title suggests, "What We Talk About When We Talk About Love" is constructed almost entirely from dialogue. The story begins with the narrator, Nick, explaining who is talking and where this talking is taking place, but actual conversation soon overtakes this description. For the rest of the story, Nick interrupts the dialogue only to describe the accompanying actions, such as when someone pours a drink, sips gin, or touches someone else. Twice, Nick describes the changing sunlight, and at the end of the story, he describes them all sitting quietly as the sunlight leaves completely. Such interruptions are rare, and the ones concerning the sunlight serve as markers to lead us through the arc of the conversation. As the sun dims and the gin bottles empty, the conversation grows more confused and sometimes even hostile. The interruptions are significant, but the expanses of uninterrupted conversation are significant as well: despite the length of the discussion, the true definition or meaning of love remains elusive. These characters can talk all they want, but they'll never be able to pinpoint the nature of love.

Although Carver's dialogue seems to mimic the way people really talk, it actually reflects an effective writing technique. Carver repeats words and phrases to add rhythm to the dialogue, such as when Terri says, "But he loved me. In his own way, maybe, but he loved me. There was love there." These lines have a lilting, musical rhythm, and the repetition of "there" adds an almost poetic quality. Carver also repeats phrases for emphasis, such as when Mel twice repeats a variation of "If you call that love, you can have it." Characters sometimes echo one another, such as when Terri says, "But I love you, hon," and Mel responds, "Honey, I love you." These lines of dialogue sound natural, but at the same time Carver has not simply tried to transcribe a real-life conversation. He has focused his attention on keeping his story vibrant and compelling by subtly incorporating such literary techniques into the dialogue itself.

PLOT AND CARVER'S SLICES OF LIFE   Carver's stories are often called "slices of life" because they reveal glimpses of everyday life instead of featuring conventional plots. "What We Talk About When We Talk About Love" is indicative of this style—there is no action to speak of or change of setting, and nothing seems to really happen besides conversation over drinks. Nevertheless, such slices of life are still genuine stories because they feature clear beginnings, middles, and conclusions. More important, Carver's slice-of-life stories invariably conclude with a change in character or understanding, which is key to any piece of fiction. "What We Talk About When We Talk About Love," for example, opens in a bright room, with a full bottle of gin, and with a brand-new conversation topic: love. The middle of the story has the light fading, the gin almost gone, and a muddled, confused discussion about the true meaning of love. The story concludes with four drunken, blurry characters sitting in a dark room with no more gin, unable to continue the conversation. Although nothing has happened in the conventional sense, the discussion has made the narrator aware of his companions' humanity. Love may not have been defined, but the discussion of it—and their eventual realization that the true meaning of love will remain elusive—has brought the narrator to this pensive moment.

DIRTY REALISM   The *dirty-realism* school of writing became popular in the 1980s thanks to a group of writers who began writing about middle-class characters who faced disappointments, heartbreaks, and harsh truths in their ordinary lives. *Granta*, a highly regarded literary journal, coined the term *dirty realism* in 1983 when it published its eighth issue, which featured writers from this school. *Granta 8*, as the issue became known, included stories by Angela Carter, Bobbie Ann Mason, Richard Ford, Tobias Wolff, Raymond Carver, and many others. Although each of these dirty-realism writers has a distinctive style, they are connected by their sparse prose, simple language with few adjectives or adverbs and direct descriptions of ordinary people and events. Much of the fiction published in the *New Yorker*, where many of these writers were and are still published, is of the dirty-realism school, but today the term—as well as the practice—has somewhat fallen out of fashion. "What We Talk About When We Talk About Love" was published in 1981, at the height of the dirty-realism movement, and the story is often regarded as the prime example of the form.

IMPORTANT QUOTATIONS EXPLAINED

W

---

1. "*And the terrible thing, the terrible thing is, but the good thing too, the saving grace, you might say, is that if something happened to one of us tomorrow, I think . . . the other person, would grieve for a while, you know, but then the surviving party would go out and love again, have someone else soon enough.*"

Mel makes this comment roughly halfway through the story, after he has told everyone that he'll explain to them what love really is. Far from clarifying the matter, Mel instead points out what he considers to be love's greatest mysteries—where love goes when one person stops loving the other and how it's possible to fall in love again with someone new. Mel says that he knows he used to love Marjorie, his ex-wife, even though he hates her now, and he points out that Terri, Nick, and Laura have all loved other people in their pasts as well. Mel is genuinely disturbed by the mysteries he voices here; he doesn't even know whether what he says is "terrible" or the "saving grace." At the beginning of the story, we learn that Mel believes love is spiritual and spent five years in a seminary. His use of the phrase "saving grace" here suggests that he is invoking the divine to make sense of a difficult subject. Mel's comments also mark a turning point in the discussion about love as the discussion becomes more series and intense for him, despite the fact that he later claims that the four are all "just talking." This quotation reveals Mel's struggle to understand love and his fear that love is less permanent than he would like to believe.

W

Where Are You Going, Where Have You Been?

Joyce Carol Oates
(1938–)

CONTEXT

Born on June 16, 1938, in Lockport, New York, Joyce Carol Oates spent her childhood on her parents' farm. Lockport, a small rural town, had struggled economically since the Great Depression, but it provided Oates with a wholesome environment in which to grow up. She attended elementary school in a one-room schoolhouse, where she developed a fascination with writing. Although her parents were not highly educated, they were always supportive of her budding talents. Oates's grandmother gave her a typewriter when she was a teenager, and in high school she used it to write novels and short stories. She won a scholarship to Syracuse University, where she majored in English and graduated as valedictorian. She subsequently pursued and received a master's degree in English from the University of Wisconsin. While studying there, she met her future husband, Raymond Smith. Though she kept her maiden name, she would later publish suspense novels under the pseudonym Rosamond Smith.

After marrying Smith in 1962, Oates and her new husband relocated to Detroit, where the bleak atmosphere and social turmoil that characterized Detroit in the 1960s influenced much of Oates's writing. After securing a teaching position at the University of Windsor in 1968, she and Smith relocated to Canada for a ten-year period. In Canada, they started a small publishing house and literary magazine, the *Ontario Review*. In 1978, Oates and Smith moved to Princeton, New Jersey, where Oates is currently the Roger S. Berlind Distinguished Professor of Humanities at Princeton University.

Oates's fiction has garnered much critical acclaim. She is a three-time finalist for the Pulitzer Prize—for *Black Water* (1992), *What I Lived For* (1994), and *Blonde* (2000). In 1970, she won the National Book Award for her novel *them* (1969). Before winning, she had been a finalist three times—for *Wonderland* (1971); *Because It Is Bitter, and Because It Is My Heart* (1990); and *Blonde* (2000). She won the PEN/Faulkner Award for *What I Lived For* and a National Book Critics Circle Award for *Black Water*, among many other achievements. Many of her short stories have won the O. Henry Award, the Pushcart Prize, and inclusion in annual anthology *The Best American Short Stories*.

Aside from the merits of her fiction, Oates is perhaps equally famous for her almost unbelievably large output. After publishing her first novel, *With Shuddering Fall*, in 1964, Oates has gone on to publish close to fifty novels and novellas, close to thirty collections of short stories, eight books of poetry, eight books of plays, and many volumes of essays and criticism. In 1996, she received the PEN/Malamud Award for a lifetime of literary achievement.

"Where Are You Going, Where Have You Been?" is considered one of Oates's most famous works. First published in the literary journal *Epoch* in 1966, it was later included in the short-story collection *The Wheel of Love* (1970). Like many of Oates's short stories, it features a female protagonist struggling with adolescence who finds herself in a dangerous situation. This story was adapted for the 1988 movie *Smooth Talk*, starring Laura Dern.

PLOT OVERVIEW

Connie, fifteen, is preoccupied with her appearance. Her mother scolds her for admiring herself in the mirror, but Connie ignores her mother's criticisms. Connie's mother urges her to be neat and responsible like her older sister, June. June, who is twenty-four and still lives at home, works as a secretary at Connie's high school. She saves money, helps their parents, and receives constant praise for her maturity, whereas Connie spends her time daydreaming. Their father works a lot and rarely talks to his daughters, but their mother never stops nagging Connie. Connie is often so miserable that she wishes she and her mother were dead.

Connie is grateful for June for setting one good precedent: June goes out with her girlfriends, so their mother allows Connie to go out as well, with her best friend. Connie's friend's father drives them to a shopping plaza in town and returns later to pick them up, never asking how they spent their time. The girls often sneak across the highway to a drive-in restaurant and meet boys.

One night, a boy named Eddie invites Connie to eat dinner with him, and Connie leaves her friend at the restaurant's counter to go with him. As they walk through the parking lot, she sees a man in a gold convertible. He smiles at her and says, "Gonna get you, baby." Connie hurries away, and Eddie notices nothing. They spend three hours together, at a restaurant and then in an alley.

Connie spends the summer avoiding her mother's prying questions and dreaming about the boys she meets. One Sunday, her parents and June leave her at home alone while they go to a family barbeque. Connie washes her hair and dozes while she lets it dry in the sun. When she gets hot, she goes inside and listens to the radio. She is startled by the noise of a car coming up her driveway. From the window she sees that it's a gold convertible, and she grows afraid. She walks into the kitchen, looks out the screen door, and realizes that the driver is the man she saw in the parking lot the night she met Eddie.

The man grins and begins talking to her. Connie is careful not to show any interest and tells him several times that she does not know who he is. He gets out of the car and points to the words painted on the door. His name, Arnold Friend, is written next to a picture of a round smiling face, which Connie thinks resembles a pumpkin with sunglasses. There is another man in the car, whom Arnold introduces as his friend Ellie.

Arnold asks Connie to get in the car, but she says she has "things" to do. He laughs, and Connie notices he seems unsteady on his feet. She asks how he knows her name, and he says he knows a lot of things about her. He rattles off the names of her friends and tells her where her parents are. He demands to know what she is thinking and tells her that today she is going for a ride with him. He asks whether she saw his sign, and he draws a large X in the air. Connie thinks that she recognizes parts of him, but she does not know how or from where. When she asks him how old he is, he stops smiling and says they are the same age, or maybe he's just a little older, which she immediately knows is a lie. To distract her, he makes fun of Ellie, who is listening to music in the car. He too looks much older than Connie, which makes her feel dizzy with fear.

Connie tells Arnold he should leave, but he insists on taking her for a ride. She recognizes his voice as the voice of a man on the radio. She tells him again to leave and again grows dizzy with fear as he starts telling her what her parents are doing at that precise moment at their barbeque. She is both horrified and fascinated by his accurate descriptions. Arnold tells Connie that she is his lover and will give in to him and love him. She screams that he is crazy and begins to back away from the front door. She tells him to leave and threatens to call the police. Arnold, moving unsteadily toward the porch, tells her he will not follow her into the house—unless she touches the phone and tries to call the police. She tries to lock to door, but her fingers are shaking too much. Arnold points out that he could break down the door. She asks him what he wants, and he says he wants her, that after seeing her that night, he knew she was the one for him. He becomes more threatening, telling her that if she doesn't come out of the house, he'll do something terrible to her family when they come home.

Arnold asks Connie whether she knows one of her neighbors, a woman who owns chickens. Connie, shocked, replies that the woman is dead. Arnold says again that she should come outside or her family will get hurt.

Connie runs from the door and grabs the telephone. In a rushed, blurry scene, something happens: Connie is sweating and screaming for her mother; she can't dial the phone; and Arnold is "stabbing her . . . again and again with no tenderness." Oates does not say exactly what happens, but at the end of the scene, Connie is sitting on the floor, stunned and terrified.

From the door, Arnold tells her to put the phone back on the hook, and she obeys. He tells her quietly where they're going to go and tells her to come outside. She thinks to herself that she will never see her mother again and tries to figure out what to do. At his command, she stands up. She feels as though she is watching herself walk toward the door, open it, and walk outside toward Arnold. He comments on her blue eyes, even though she has brown eyes. Connie looks out at the vast expanses of land behind him and knows that's where she is going.

CHARACTER LIST

Connie   The fifteen-year-old protagonist of the story. Connie is in the midst of an adolescent rebellion. She argues with her mother and sister, June, and neglects family life in favor of scoping out boys at the local restaurant. She tries to appear older and wiser than she is, and her head is filled with daydreams and popular music that feed her ideas of romance and love. When Arnold Friend arrives at Connie's house, she must confront the harsh realities of adulthood, which bear little resemblance to her fantasies.

Arnold Friend   A dangerous figure who comes to Connie's house and threatens her. Arnold has pale, almost translucent skin; his hair looks like a wig; and he appears both old and young at the same time. He seems like a demonic figure, perhaps even a nightmare rather than an actual human being, but his true character is never fully clarified. He speaks calmly and quietly to Connie, which makes him seem even more threatening, and in an ambiguous scene near the end of the story, he may attack her inside her home. He ultimately convinces Connie to get in the car with him.

Ellie   A friend of Arnold's. When Arnold drives up to Connie's house, Ellie stays in the car, listening to music and watching while Arnold talks menacingly to Connie. He seems mostly indifferent to what's happening but offers to disconnect Connie's telephone, an offer Arnold refuses. His strange first name is close to the name Eddie, the name of the boy Connie was with on the night she first saw Arnold.

Connie's Mother   A near-constant source of frustration for Connie. Connie and her mother bicker constantly and disagree about almost everything. Connie's mother envies Connie's youth and beauty, which she herself has lost. At the end of the story, Connie's mother is whom Connie cries out for when she is presumably attacked by Arnold.

June   Connie's older sister. June is nearly the opposite of Connie. Twenty-four years old, overweight, and still living at home, she is a placid, dutiful daughter. She obeys her parents and does chores without complaining. Because June goes out at night with her friends, Connie is permitted to do so as well.

ANALYSIS OF MAJOR CHARACTERS

CONNIE   Connie rejects the role of daughter, sister, and "nice" girl to cultivate her sexual persona, which flourishes only when she is away from her home and family. She makes fun of her frumpy older sister, June, and is in constant conflict with her family. Her concerns are typically adolescent: she obsesses about her looks, listens to music, hangs out with her friends, flirts with boys, and explores her sexuality. She takes great pleasure in the fact that boys and even men find her attractive. Connie has cultivated a particular manner of dressing, walking, and laughing that make her sexually appealing, although these mannerisms are only temporary affectations. She behaves one way in her home and an entirely different way when she is elsewhere. Her personality is split, and when she is at home, her sexuality goes into hiding. However, Arnold Friend's arrival at her house forces her two sides to merge violently. In a way, Connie is not fully sexual until Arnold's intrusion into her home—until then, her sexuality was something outside of her "true" self, the self that she allowed her family to see.

Connie works hard to prove her maturity, but despite her efforts with clothes and boys, she is not as mature as she would like to believe she is. She desperately wants to be attractive to older men, but once an older man—Arnold—actually pays her explicit sexual attention, she is terrified. She knows little about reality or what adulthood actually entails, preferring to lose herself in the rosy ideas of romance that her beloved pop songs promote. When Arnold appears at her house, she tries to seem in control and unfazed, but she eventually breaks down and is overpowered by him. In her moments of terror, she proves herself to be child-like: she calls out for her mother.

ARNOLD FRIEND   Arnold Friend, with his suggestive name that hints at "Arch Fiend," is an ambiguous figure who may be either demon or human, fantasy or reality. Arnold makes a grand entrance at Connie's house in his gold convertible, but beyond his ostentatious car, his appearance is less than impressive. Indeed, he looks strange enough to suggest that he has mental problems or is even somehow otherworldly. He wears mirrored sunglasses, has translucent skin, and has hair that is so wild that it looks like a wig. When he walks, he wobbles, as though his shoes don't fit properly. Some critics suggest that his unsteadiness hints at the possibility that his feet are actually hooves, as the devil would have. Demon or not, however, his strangely mismatched appearance adds to the threatening quality of his calm voice and seemingly gentle coaxing as he tries to convince Connie to come outside.

Despite his strange appearance, Arnold is initially somewhat appealing to Connie in a dangerous way. He is an older, highly sexualized man who offers to take her away from her life as an unhappy teenager. He is incredibly different from Connie's family and the other boys she knows, which intrigues her. However, any appealing mystery to Arnold quickly dissipates as he begins to make threats and demands. He invites fear rather than attraction when he claims to know things about her family and neighbors that he couldn't possibly know, which calls the reality or humanness of his character into question. Although we never find out exactly who or what Arnold is, he is the catalyst that changes Connie from a child to an adult—albeit through drastic, violent means.

THEMES, MOTIFS, AND SYMBOLS

THEMES

FANTASY VERSUS REALITY   Although Connie works hard to present the appearance of being a mature woman who is experienced with men, her encounter with Arnold reveals that this is only a performance. She has created an attractive adult persona through her clothing, hairstyle, and general behavior and gets the attention she desires from boys. But Connie confuses her ability to command attention from boys with her desire to actually have them pursue her in a sexual way. The love and romance evident in songs she listens to and images of pop culture that surround her are much different from the reality of adult sexuality. Although Connie does experiment with sexuality, such as when she goes into the alley with Eddie, she is fearful of actually becoming an adult. Arnold Friend takes her by force into adulthood, but this violent act represents a shift within Connie herself: the abandoning of childlike fantasy for the realities of being a mature woman.

The line between fantasy and reality is blurred by Arnold himself, who never quite falls into one category or the other. His physical appearance makes him seem both human and less than human, and Oates never makes explicit whether he is reality or fantasy. He may be simply a strange man, he may be the devil, or he may be a nightmare that Connie is having from staying in the sun too long. In any case, whether this experience is fantasy or reality, whether Arnold is human or demon, the effect of the experience and Arnold's interaction with Connie changes the way she views the world.

THE SEARCH FOR INDEPENDENCE   Connie's conflicts with her family and efforts to make herself sexually attractive are part of her search for independence. As a teenager, she is dependent on the adults in her life for care and discipline as well as for enabling her social life. Her friend's father, for example, drives her and her friend to the movie theater. Although Connie often fights against her family, particularly her mother and sister, they constitute the only life she really knows. Her experiments with creating a sexy appearance and enticing boys in the local diner serve as her attempt to explore new worlds as well as a new side of herself. However, until Arnold Friend arrives, her explorations have always been swaddled in safety. She may go into an alley with a boy for a few hours, but no matter what happens there, she will eventually be driven back home to the familiarity of her family.

Connie's search for independence has a brutal outcome. When Arnold Friend arrives and interacts with her as the mature woman she has pretended to be, he yanks her out of her childhood adventures and places her firmly into an adult world from which no one will rescue her. The things Arnold says to Connie accurately represent the search she has undertaken as a teenager seeking maturity. For example, he says, "I'm your lover. You don't know what that is but you will" and "The place where you came from ain't there anymore, and where you had in mind to go is cancelled out." Arnold, a strange and ambiguous character, embodies all the confusions, doubts, and fears that accompany any adolescent's quest for independence. In Connie's case, her search concludes in the story on a dark, ominous note. Her search may continue, but all signs point to a more permanent end.

MOTIFS

DIZZINESS Dizziness overwhelms Connie at the moments when she realizes Arnold can and will overpower her. Initially, Arnold's presence causes Connie to feel torn between desire and fear. But as the situation progresses, fear overtakes her. When Arnold lies to Connie about his age, her heart begins to pound, and when she sees that Ellie is also a grown man, she feels "a wave of dizziness rise." Dizziness overwhelms her again when Arnold becomes impatient with her resistance. She knows that she is in over her head, and the realization makes her more vulnerable. She realizes that he is lying to her and his intentions are not necessarily good, but she cannot do anything about it. Dizziness is her fallback reaction and allows Arnold to gain an even stronger hold on her.

MUSIC Music functions as Connie's bridge from the real world to her fantasy world. Connie enjoys escaping her life by listening to music and daydreaming about boys, and she gathers her ideas about romance primarily from songs on the radio. The happiness she finds with boys is rooted in these romantic fantasies rather than in the boys themselves. When Arnold shows up at her house, she is again reveling in the music she is listening to, and it takes her a moment to realize that it is the same music that is emanating from Arnold's car. Even before Connie has noticed this similarity, she finds herself entranced by Arnold. Music relaxes Connie, and the fact that she and Arnold are listening to the same music lowers her guard just a bit. Connie has gleaned her idea of romance from her favorite music, and her encounter with Arnold reveals that the romance in her music is much more appealing than the reality of adult sexuality and seduction.

SYMBOLS

ARNOLD'S CAR Arnold Friend's flashy gold car, with its outdated phrases written on the sides, is an extension of Arnold himself: extreme and not entirely right. The car gives Connie her first clues that there might be something wrong with or dangerous about Arnold. She complains that the color of the car is so bright that it hurts her eyes, and she is puzzled by the phrase "Man the flying saucers" on the front fender, which was an expression that her peers used to use but that has fallen out of fashion. This reinforces Connie's sense that there is something not quite genuine about Arnold; he claims to be the same age as she is, but he is not entirely convincing. Not only is the car itself rather off-putting, but Arnold presents it as the vehicle that will transport Connie to her new life. Once Arnold's true, violent nature comes through, the car becomes a symbol of all that is dark and ominous about his character.

SHORT STORY ANALYSIS

THE DEDICATION AND TIME PERIOD   Joyce Carol Oates dedicated "Where Are You Going, Where Have You Been?" to Bob Dylan, and she has claimed that the story was influenced by Dylan's haunting song "It's All Over Now, Baby Blue." The story contains echoes of the song's lyrics, such as the following: "The vagabond who's rapping at your door / Is standing in the clothes that you once wore / Strike another match, go start anew / And it's all over now, Baby Blue." Many aspects of Dylan himself are mirrored in the figure of Arnold Friend. With their wild hair and short statures, Dylan and Arnold are physical doubles; but more significant is how each man is perceived. In the 1960s, Dylan was considered by many young people to be somehow otherworldly—even a sort of messiah figure. In the story, Arnold Friend is a darker version of this type of figure. He has come to take Connie away, and she is ultimately powerless to defy him. At one point, Connie observes that Arnold's voice sounds like the voice of the radio DJ, Bobby King. The DJ's first name is a link to Dylan's first name, and the DJ's involvement in the music world evokes Dylan's.

Oates's evocation of Bob Dylan is purposeful, adding richness to the story's setting, particularly the time period in which it takes place. In the 1960s, when Oates wrote "Where Are You Going . . . ," a social revolution was happening. American women were asserting their rights and independence from men, and they were claiming their sexuality in a way they had never done before. One frequently discussed topic was adolescence and the struggles and anxieties that many young girls endured as they lost their sexual innocence and became adult women. Feeling undervalued in their homes and relationships with men, women questioned their role in society and the role that sex and gender played in their lives. In "Where Are You Going . . . ," Oates explores this social upheaval in miniature: Connie, one young woman out of a country of young women, must confront her own questions and anxieties as she transitions into adulthood. Her separation from her home and family is violent, and Arnold Friend is by no means a savior. But the sense of sweeping, dramatic change taking place in 1960s America is evident in this story, from the period details to Connie's psychological terror at what lies ahead.

THE FACTS BEHIND THE FICTION   In the mid 1960s, a young man in Arizona named Charles Schmid developed a sinister reputation as "The Pied Piper of Tucson." Schmid stood out in the small town of Tucson. He was not handsome—he was short and stuffed his boots to make himself taller, and he had an eccentric appearance, with dyed black hair, makeup, and a fake mole on his upper lip—but he had a charisma and charm that made him attractive to young girls from the area. Schmid was the son of wealthy parents, and he used the trappings of wealth—a nice car, elaborate parties, gifts for his admirers—to enhance his alluring persona and lure teenagers into his realm. Unbeknownst to Tucson, Schmid was a serial killer, and three teenage girls became his victims. He buried them in the desert.

On March 4, 1966, *Life* magazine ran an article about Schmid, and Oates saw it. She sensed immediately that there was potential in the sordid story for a story of her own, and she stopped reading halfway through the article so that her imagination could take over and let the fiction develop independent of the facts. Nevertheless, many facts of the horrifying murders and Schmid are evoked in "Where Are You Going . . . ," particularly in the figure of Arnold Friend. However, the story is not meant to be a fictionalized retelling of history or recounting of actual facts. Although parallels exist between the story and real life, the facts behind the fiction should be considered as simply the seeds of inspiration. The story itself stands alone.

IMPORTANT QUOTATIONS EXPLAINED

1. *Everything about her had two sides to it, one for home and one for anywhere that was not home: her walk, which could be childlike and bobbing, or languid enough to make anyone think she was hearing music in her head; her mouth, which was pale and smirking most of the time, but bright and pink on these evenings out; her laugh, which was cynical and drawling at home . . . but high-pitched and nervous anywhere else . . .*

This quotation appears near the beginning of the story and explains the two-sidedness of Connie. At home, Connie appears childish, but away from home, she strives to appear sexy, mature, and seductive. For the most part, her two sides seem to exist in harmony. She argues with her mother and sister at home, but otherwise her transition from child to woman and back again seems to happen effortlessly. However, the fact that Connie has two sides rather than one stable, fully developed personality highlights the awkward, fearful stage she is in as an adolescent. Throughout the story, we see that she is unsure of who she really is—what is actually her and what is a fabricated image of who she wants to be. Her confident smirk and laugh at home give way to a more uncertain, giggly laugh and girly, pink mouth—which actually make her seem more immature. The gap between her former self and new, adult self is uncertain and dangerous. When Arnold Friend appears, he exploits it.

2. *She cried out, she cried for her mother, she felt her breath start jerking back and forth in her lungs as if it were something Arnold Friend was stabbing her with again and again with no tenderness.*

This quotation appears near the end of the story, after Connie has lunged for the phone and tried and failed to make a call. Arnold has repeatedly assured her that he won't come inside the house unless she touches the telephone, which, until this moment, has deterred Connie from trying to call the police. However, after Arnold's remarks become more overtly sexual and threatening, she panics and makes a move for the phone, which she is then too terrified to do anything with. These violent, explicit lines strongly suggest that Arnold has entered the house and is raping Connie—the "stabbing" and "no tenderness," as well as her extreme distress, all suggest that this violent moment is a rape.

However, Oates does not state explicitly that Arnold has raped Connie. A few lines later, it seems that Arnold is at the door again, once more trying to get her to come outside. In these lines, a literal reading reveals that it is her breath that is stabbing her lungs. Nothing in "Where Are You Going . . ." is black or white—is Arnold a dream? A demon? A psychopath?—and what actually "happens" in this scene is beside the point. The point is that Connie has faced danger and has not come away unscathed. Her life has irrevocably changed, and her future looks bleak. The menacing closing scene, with Connie opening the door to go to Arnold, strongly suggests that if bad things have happened, there are worse things to come; and if bad things have not yet happened, then they surely will.

Why I Live at the P.O.

Eudora Welty
(1909–2001)

CONTEXT

Born in Jackson, Mississippi, on April 13, 1909, Eudora Welty was a versatile artist, succeeding as both a photographer and writer. In many ways, her early work as a photographer, in which she captured the lives of the rural poor for the Works Project Administration, honed her sharp eye for detail and shaped her belief that there was an infinite number of ways of looking at a given situation. As a writer, Welty managed to step out of the shadows of William Faulkner, the esteemed writer from Mississippi, and carve a niche for herself in the writing world. She produced five novels in her lifetime: *The Robber Bridegroom* (1942), *Delta Wedding* (1946), *The Ponder Heart* (1954), *Losing Battles* (1970), and *The Optimist's Daughter* (1972), which won the Pulitzer Prize. She is generally most well known for her short stories and quickly proved herself to be a master of the form. She published her first short story, "Death of a Traveling Salesman," in 1936, eventually going on to publish four collections of stories during her lifetime.

Welty spent the vast majority of her life in Jackson, living in her childhood home, and never married or had children. Other than basic biographical information, little is known about Welty, and she deliberately kept many details of her personal life private. She believed that her work should stand on its own terms and that interpretations should not be based on her life or experiences. She did, however, publish an autobiography, *One Writer's Beginnings* (1983), in which she describes her growing-up years, her education and jobs, her photography, her family, and the people and experiences that influenced her development as a writer.

Unlike the writing of her southern contemporaries, who included Katherine Anne Porter, Flannery O'Connor, and Carson McCullers, Welty's writing is not haunted by the past or the collective guilt over the South's history of slavery, a theme that courses through much writing from southern authors in the early twentieth century. Instead, Welty focused on individual lives and families who are thrown together by circumstance and form whatever bonds they need to survive. Her work often explores the lives of people who live in stifling parochial worlds, although she also includes plenty of humor and local color. Welty believed that confined settings and suffocating circumstances were key to defining her characters. She found inspiration in the people who surrounded her while growing up in Mississippi, and the speech of the vibrant characters whom she created conveys the sly humor and idiomatic phrases of the area.

In 1941, "Why I Live at the P.O." was published in the *Atlantic Monthly* magazine and also appeared in her first story collection, *A Curtain of Green and Other Stories*. Welty was inspired to write the story after seeing an ironing board in a rural post office. Considered one of her best short stories, "Why I Live at the P.O." demonstrates typical Welty flair: quirky humor; a lonely, odd protagonist trapped in a stifling environment; and a family who provides love and alienation in equal measures.

In July 2001, at age ninety-two, Welty died at a hospital in Jackson.

PLOT OVERVIEW

On the Fourth of July, Sister's uneventful life in China Grove is interrupted by the arrival of her sister, Stella-Rondo, who has just left her husband, Mr. Whitaker, and returned to the family home in Mississippi. Sister had briefly dated Mr. Whitaker before Stella-Rondo became engaged to him. Stella-Rondo arrives from Illinois, accompanied by Shirley-T., a little girl she claims is her legally adopted daughter. The rest of the family, overjoyed at Stella-Rondo's return, does not share Sister's suspicion that Shirley-T. is actually Stella-Rondo's biological daughter. When Sister questions Shirley-T.'s dubious parentage, Stella-Rondo angrily orders Sister to never mention the matter again. In an attempt to turn Papa-Daddy against Sister, Stella-Rondo claims that Sister suggested that Papa-Daddy should trim his long, grizzled beard. Papa-Daddy believes Stella-Rondo's false claims and angrily reminds Sister that he was the one who secured her the job as the town's postmistress. Sister promptly leaves the table, while Papa-Daddy skulks outside to lie in the hammock. Uncle Rondo soon appears in the hall, dressed in Stella-Rondo's kimono. Woozy from excessive doses of a prescription medication, he heads to the yard, where Papa-Daddy relays what he believes the ungrateful Sister has said about his beard.

Sister then hears Stella-Rondo open one of the upstairs windows and goes to join her. Stella-Rondo asks Sister to look out into the yard and tell her what she sees, upset and embarrassed that Uncle Rondo has taken the kimono in which Mr. Whitaker had once photographed her. Sister defends Uncle Rondo and chastises Stella-Rondo for being overly critical, especially after suddenly appearing with an adopted daughter and imminent divorce. Stella-Rondo reminds Sister that she vowed never to speak of Shirley-T. again. Miffed, Sister goes to the kitchen to make green-tomato pickles, as the servants had been given the day off for the holiday.

Mama comes in and expresses her disapproval at Sister making a food that will not agree with Uncle Rondo and Shirley-T. Sister points out that she would have been given a much different reception if she had been the one to return home from Illinois under such questionable circumstances. Mama reminds Sister that she was spurned by Mr. Whitaker and that if she had been the one returning home, her welcome would have been no less warm. Sister disagrees and attempts to convince her mother that Shirley-T. is not adopted. Mama refuses to recognize the truth. Sister then wonders out loud whether Shirley-T. is even able to talk, and she hints that the child might have a developmental disability. Mama shouts up the stairs to relay Sister's concerns. Angered at the accusation, Stella-Rondo has Shirley-T. sing the theme song to *Popeye the Sailor Man*, a performance that is followed by the child tap-dancing loudly. Satisfied, Mama insists that Sister apologize for her accusation, but Sister refuses. Mama furiously stalks upstairs to embrace her adopted granddaughter.

Next, Stella-Rondo sees to it that Uncle Rondo, too, turns against Sister. Stella-Rondo claims that Sister has been sneering at Uncle Rondo's ridiculous appearance. Angered, Uncle Rondo strips off the kimono, throws it on the ground, and stomps on it, grinding it into the dirty floor. His anger continues to simmer that night, as he plays cards with Mama and Stella-Rondo. Then, unexpectedly, at 6:30 the next morning, he throws an entire package of lit firecrackers onto the floor of Sister's bedroom. The ensuing racket unsettles Sister's already delicate nervous condition. Sister immediately decides that it is time for her to move to the post office. Making her intentions obvious, she goes through the house collecting her belongings, including a prized possession—a radio. Mama objects to the removal of a pair of vases. Sister fires back that if Mama wishes to see them, she can always come down to the post office. The family then uniformly asserts that they will never set foot in the post office or send or receive mail.

Sister responds that, without the post office, Stella-Rondo won't be able to be in touch with Mr. Whitaker. This possibility prompts a flood of tears from Stella-Rondo. Mama expresses dismay that the joyous return of Stella-Rondo on a major holiday could turn so sour. Sister declares that it was Mr. Whitaker who left Stella-Rondo, not the other way around, and that she, Sister, had predicted exactly how things would turn out. Still crying, Stella-Rondo shuts herself in her bedroom. Sister hires a girl with a cart to haul her belongings to the post office.

Five days later, Sister has yet to hear from her family, but she convinces herself that she is happy to be alone. There is little mail to attend to, and the people in town are divided in their support of her actions. Sister asserts that if Stella-Rondo appeared at the post office and was forthcoming about the details of her life with Mr. Whitaker, Sister would plug both of her ears with her fingers and refuse to listen.

CHARACTER LIST

Sister The narrator and town's postmistress. Sister is exactly one year older than Stella-Rondo and was involved with Mr. Whitaker before Stella-Rondo became engaged to him. Sister is frank and outspoken, but her pettiness and jealousy often get the best of her, clouding her view of the world. Sister's telling of the story is full of comedy, and her humor helps her cope with stress and the hurt that her family members sometimes inflict.

Stella-Rondo Sister's rival, who returns to the family home after separating from Mr. Whitaker. Stella-Rondo relentlessly supports her own version of events, including her claim that Shirley-T. is her adopted, not biological, daughter. Hot-tempered, dramatic, and manipulative, she instigates family discord to get her family members to give her attention and emotional support.

Mama The family matriarch, who weighs 200 pounds. Gullible and self-deluded, Mama seems to believe whatever she is told, as long as it is coming from Stella-Rondo. Although she feels that she is a fair and supportive parent, her regard for Stella-Rondo, as opposed to Sister, seems abundantly clear. However, she reassures Sister that she would be treated the same way if she were to leave home and then return after a separation.

Uncle Rondo A mentally and emotionally scarred World War I veteran. Uncle Rondo wears Stella-Rondo's flesh-colored kimono and, as is his habit every Fourth of July, consumes an entire bottle of a liquid prescription medicine and all but loses consciousness for hours. Temperamental and easily provoked, he lashes out in cruel ways when he feels he is being threatened.

Papa-Daddy Sister's grandfather. With his long, shaggy beard, Papa-Daddy is the classic crotchety old man, whose deafness and salty attitude cut him off from active participation in family life. He is proud of his connections and the fact that he was able to get Sister her position at the post office, which he often lords over Sister during arguments.

Shirley-T. Stella-Rondo's supposedly adopted two-year-old daughter. Shirley-T. is mute throughout the story except for a brief moment when she loudly belts out the theme song to *Popeye the Sailor Man* and refers to Uncle Rondo as Papa.

Mr. Whitaker Stella-Rondo's estranged husband and Sister's former boyfriend. Rumored to have a drinking problem, Mr. Whitaker is a photographer who briefly opened a shop in China Grove. Although he never appears physically in the story, he is the source of the rivalry and hurt feelings between Sister and Stella-Rondo.

ANALYSIS OF MAJOR CHARACTERS

SISTER Sister, the cynical, outraged narrator of "Why I Live at the P.O.," is a complex mixture of sorely used scapegoat and self-deluded, unreliable narrator. She stands in the shadow of her younger sister, Stella-Rondo, whose return to the family home with her daughter, Shirley-T., dredges up Sister's long-simmering jealousy and resentment. Her family seems unwilling to believe her word against Stella-Rondo's, and Sister is frequently accused of saying things she did not say and doing things she did not do. When Uncle Rondo gets angry with her for making fun of his kimono, he tosses a pack of firecrackers into her bedroom. Sister's position as the much-abused daughter seems clear. However, her unrelentingly dramatic commentary and insistence on operating at a constant fever pitch undermine her justified frustration. Because Sister is the narrator, every event in the story is tinged with her outraged disbelief, and she offers no real window into how she actually feels. The extremity of Sister's narration damages her credibility.

Although no one in the family seems fully sane, Sister frequently seems as strange as the rest and participates in the criticism and alienation as much as anyone else. The jealousy that characterizes her relationship with Stella-Rondo, especially over the affections of Mr. Whitaker, brings out her own cruel streak. The fact that Stella-Rondo's marriage has failed practically delights Sister, and she even taunts Stella-Rondo about Mr. Whitaker's abandonment, saying, "I knew from the beginning he'd up and leave her." She even goes so far as to mimic Shirley-T. and suggest that her young niece has a developmental disability. Sister seems determined to prove that Stella-Rondo has lied about the parentage of Shirley-T., not letting the matter go even when it is clear that Stella-Rondo will never admit that she's right. Although from Sister's perspective it appears she was driven out of her home to the post office, the record of her own transgressions suggests she had a hand in creating her fate.

STELLA-RONDO When Stella-Rondo returns to the family fold for attention and support after the breakup of her marriage, she easily reclaims her position as the pampered favorite. Though Sister lobbies wildly for recognition and respect, Stella-Rondo is more skilled at garnering sympathy, and she easily brushes Sister aside to win the spotlight. She is used to having her own version of the truth accepted without question, and with the exception of Sister, the entire family swallows her claim that Shirley-T. is adopted. Stella-Rondo's insistence on her superiority is remarkable in light of the circumstances that brought her home. She claims that she left Mr. Whitaker, but Sister is convinced the opposite is true: "*He* left *her*— you mark my words," Sister says. Yet the truth is certainly something Stella-Rondo will do her best to conceal.

Stella-Rondo's position as the object of praise and approval has hampered her maturity and personal development. Her life has been marked by impetuousness, impatience, and a lack of commitment. Sister remembers Stella-Rondo's inability to follow through on collecting pearls for her Add-a-Pearl necklace when they were children. "She's always had anything in the world she wanted and then she'd throw it away," Sister says. Stella-Rondo's current situation with Mr. Whitaker seems to follow that pattern, although it is unclear who "threw away" whom. Stella-Rondo's spoiled position in the family and insistence on appearing perfect lead her to ignore difficult problems and deflect troubling questions. If Shirley-T. is not adopted, is Mr. Whitaker the father? Were he and Stella-Rondo intimate while he was dating Sister? Why did the family suddenly move to Illinois? No one poses these questions, although Sister surely considers them, and Stella-Rondo's stubborn avoidance is part of what drives Sister to leave home.

MAMA   Mama seems to set the precedent for the family's miscommunication, rivalry, and disagreement. The hostility between Sister and Stella-Rondo has its roots in Mama's own troubled relationships. When Stella-Rondo forbids Sister to speak Shirley-T.'s name, it echoes Mama's forbidding of anyone to speak of her cousin. Furthermore, Mama easily perpetuates lies among the family members, even though, at times, she suspects or even knows the truth. For example, she reprimands Sister for suggesting that Shirley-T. is Stella-Rondo's biological daughter, but she herself wonders how Stella-Rondo could possibly prove that Shirley-T. is adopted. Later, she links Shirley-T.'s silence and strange behavior to Mr. Whitaker's consumption of chemicals, suggesting that she knows that Mr. Whitaker is, in fact, Shirley-T.'s biological father. Rather than not understanding the split between reality and fiction, Mama merely prefers one version over the other. She would rather believe that Stella-Rondo is virtuous than believe she is a girl who has had premarital sex. Mama's desire to deny the truth ultimately proves more damaging to the family's relationships than the truth itself would have been.

THEMES, MOTIFS, AND SYMBOLS

THEMES

THE IRREVERSIBILITY OF ISOLATION   In "Why I Live at the P.O.," individuals feel isolated even within in the seemingly nurturing confines of the family, many of them taking refuge in silence. Shirley-T. is an all but mute presence; Sister accuses her of being unable to talk altogether. As on other Fourth of July holidays, Uncle Rondo has overconsumed his prescription medicine, preferring a comatose state to his shrill family. Stella-Rondo, despite the stifling heat, keeps her bedroom windows locked and shut, sealing herself off from the world around her. Sister believes that Papa-Daddy is deaf or intentionally ignoring those around him, because he removes himself from the proceedings, preferring the solitude of the hammock in the yard. When there isn't isolating silence, characters isolate themselves within flagrant lying and miscommunication. For example, Stella-Rondo convinces Papa-

Daddy that Sister insulted his beard and suggested that it be cut off, when Sister never made such assertions. The silence in the story is broken dramatically by the deafening sound of the firecrackers that Uncle Rondo throws onto the floor of Sister's bedroom.

The family's isolation gets more intense when Sister prepares to move out. The already insular group swears never to send or receive any mail, just to spite Sister. Without the radio, which Sister takes with her, the family has effectively cut off all contact with the outside world and are left with only their own dysfunctional group. Open and honest communication has proven to be an unreachable goal, so the family instead embraces an even more intense isolation. At the end of the story, when Sister announces that she'd cover her ears if Stella-Rondo tried to explain herself, she is suggesting that this trend of isolation will never reverse itself and instead get steadily worse.

THE EASY HABIT OF LYING   For all the characters in "Why I Live at the P.O.," lying and deliberate misrepresentations of the truth are easier modes of communication than honesty and openness. Rather than actually communicate, the family members lie, exaggerate, and deliberately misinterpret others' intentions and remarks. This miscommunication all takes place in the family's everyday conversations—no one needs an occasion or a reason to distort the truth. In place of rational exchanges, the family members embrace negativity, accusation, and suspicion, and such consistency suggests that this behavior has become habit.

Stella-Rondo exhibits the least amount of self-control when it comes to her need to lie, and Uncle Rondo and Papa-Daddy grow hostile to Sister because of Stella-Rondo's meddling. Stella-Rondo has mastered the art of "uncommunication." Meanwhile, Shirley-T. hovers in the gap between truth and deception. Stella-Rondo believes that if she merely states the fact that the little girl is adopted, despite her family resemblance, then it will be accepted and viewed as the truth. However, Stella-Rondo's constant lying and manipulation render her claims doubtful—especially to Sister. The family members' easy habit of lying makes every claim, no matter what it is, almost impossible to believe. However, lying is easier than communicating properly, which involves a degree of trust and honesty that proves too difficult for the family members to attain.

MOTIFS

REPETITION   Repetition appears throughout "Why I Live at the P.O.," contributing to characterization and underscoring the stasis of the family's home life. Welty uses repetition in two ways. First, there is the sense of family history repeating itself. When Sister questions the validity of Stella-Rondo's claim that Shirley-T. is adopted, Stella-Rondo forbids her from ever again mentioning Shirley-T.'s name. This gag order is mirrored later when Sister discusses the matter with Mama and makes a fleeting reference to Cousin Annie Flo, who lived in an unexplained state of denial her entire life. Upon hearing the name, Mama threatens to slap Sister for violating her order never to mention her cousin in her presence again. When confronted with difficult questions or situations, family members opt for total denial rather than attempting to sort things out.

Repetition also appears in the family's gang mentality. Both Stella-Rondo and Mama exaggerate Sister's words or claim that she's made a mean-spirited observation, when in fact she's done or said nothing wrong. Sister reacts by repeating how individual family members have "turned against" her. The family's negative and cruel mode of interacting is deeply entrenched and shows no signs of ceasing. Ultimately, Welty's repetition of actions and phrases helps dramatize the family's stasis and suggests that the family's rituals will persevere despite the grief they cause.

DENIAL   Denial is a powerful force that is deeply rooted in every member of Sister's family. Rather than face difficult truths that could tarnish their vision of themselves and their lives, the family members opt to completely deny reality. They delude themselves and willingly go along with others' self-delusions. Mama is among the most grievous offenders, willingly suspending her disbelief when Stella-Rondo claims that Shirley-T. is adopted. Determined to support whatever version of the truth is easiest or most palatable, she denies the obvious flaws in the claim—such as the fact that Shirley-T. very much resembles Stella-Rondo. The entire family exists in a state of constant denial and avoidance of the truth.

Although Sister portrays herself as the victim, she too is in denial about her own role in the family's fraught relations. She paints everyone else as being crazy and deceitful but does her part to rile up her relatives, such as by pestering Stella-Rondo about Shirley-T.'s parentage and snidely claiming that she foresaw Stella-Rondo's fate. She describes moving to the post office as a desperate move of self-preservation, but it's actually a gesture that is as childish and dramatic as anything Stella-Rondo or Papa-Daddy would do. Furthermore, no matter how certain she is that she's found happiness and peace, she is still actively involved in the family feud. She keeps track of which townspeople are with or against her, and she feels compelled to announce her happiness to the world. Sister is denying the reality that her short-term solution does nothing to resolve the problems she has with her family members.

SYMBOLS

THE RADIO   Throughout the story, the radio represents the contentious or flawed communication between the family members. The radio was once a pawn in Sister and Stella-Rondo's constant struggle to occupy the favored position in the family. When Stella-Rondo once broke a chain letter from Flanders Field, her angry uncle Rondo wrested control of the radio from her and gave it to Sister, an incident that Sister views as a major victory. When it comes time for her to move out of the house, she proudly seizes the radio, which replaces human contact when she isolates herself at the post office. By taking the radio, she also takes one of the only connections the family has to the world beyond their home. This removal represents a new low in the family's communication problems.

THE POST OFFICE   For Sister, the post office represents both independence and entrapment. On one hand, it is an escape for Sister, a haven from her family. Her job as postmistress gives her a measure of independence, and it gives her a place to go to when her family life becomes intolerable. However, it is not a total retreat, and her move reveals how trapped she truly is within the long shadow of her family. For example, Sister got the position of postmistress only because of Papa-Daddy's influence, so in one way she is escaping from her family to a place her family provided. Once settled at the post office, she is still actively involved with her family, even from afar. She monitors whose "side" other people are on and claims that she'll never listen to anything Stella-Rondo has to say. But the more adamantly Sister proclaims her independence from her family, the more mired she proves herself to be. Without her family's squabbling, Sister has nothing to rail against, and one wonders how she would identify herself apart from her family. She may long to escape her family, but the further she gets, the clearer her connection to them becomes.

SHIRLEY-T.   Shirley-T. serves as a mirror that reflects the desires and fantasies of Mama and Stella-Rondo. Named after Shirley Temple, the curly-topped singing-and-dancing child star of the 1930s and 1940s, Shirley-T. seems to take on any identity that is fashioned for her. But in addition to her doll-like presence in the story, Shirley-T. also emerges as a symbol of the family's ongoing pattern of miscommunication and animosity. After her tap-dance and vocal performance, the only other word she says, after Uncle Rondo gives her a nickel, is "Papa," mistakenly referring to him as her father. And she is already learning from those around her the dysfunctional ways of the household. As Sister is about to leave, Shirley-T. sticks her tongue out at her, showing that she has absorbed the family's mean-spirited attitude or at least become skilled at reflecting it.

SHORT STORY ANALYSIS

THE MASK OF HUMOR   Humor is woven throughout "Why I Live at the P.O.," and no character escapes Sister's appraising, comically judgmental eye. Uncle Rondo wears a kimono, and Shirley-T., like her namesake Shirley Temple, sings and dances on cue. Stella-Rondo persists in absurdly claiming that Shirley-T. is adopted, and Papa-Daddy has a beard that he claims he's been growing since he was fifteen. Sister herself is comical, hauling her belongings to the post office with the intention of living there. Even when she doesn't necessarily intend to be funny, her overly earnest and dramatic rendering of Stella-Rondo's return comes across as humorous. The relentlessness of Sister's elaborate narration, in which even small happenings become absurd, momentous events, make the story a rather wild ride through a strange world where people seem to adhere to their own set of rules.

From the beginning, however, Sister is doing more than just poking fun at her family and surroundings, and Welty employs humor to call attention to unsettling truths about her characters' lives, particularly Sister's. Sister wants to give the impression that she is not deeply affected by the family's infighting and tries to portray herself as a victim, free from any blame in the family's disintegrating relationships. Her humorous tone is a means of deflecting unpleasant realities, a mask that she can hide behind to avoid showing her true feelings. The distance she deliberately places between herself and genuine emotions becomes more apparent as the story progresses, ultimately darkening the over-the-top humor and emphasizing Sister's isolation.

WELTY'S USE OF DICTION   Welty records the unique speech patterns of Sister and the other family members to humanize her characters and situate them firmly in their local setting. She fills the lines of dialogue with idiomatic phrasing and the everyday speech of rural southerners. Instead of "must have" or "must've," for example, Welty writes "must of," a transcription that is grammatically nonstandard but true to the characters' unique self-expression. Welty also uses italics and the appearance of words themselves to add unique tones and rhythms to the characters' speech. For example, Papa-Daddy, angry at being provoked about his beard, "l-a-y-s" down his silverware. The spaced lettering emphasizes the theatrical flourish of Papa-Daddy's gesture. Words are similarly distorted during Shirley-T.'s rendition of "OE'm Pop-OE the Sailor-r-r-r Ma-a-an," in which the child's sudden outburst, peppered with a distinctive northern accent, is jarring and unexpected.

POINT OF VIEW AND THE UNRELIABLE NARRATOR The story is told exclusively from Sister's viewpoint and is thus subject to her distorting interpretations. From the story's opening paragraph, Sister is busily building her case against her family, blaming most of her discomfort and anguish on Stella-Rondo's sudden return to the family home. She recounts the injustices done to her and angles for sympathy from her audience. She is a skillful manipulator and often addresses the audience directly to call attention to particularly egregious offenses. When Stella-Rondo accuses her of scoffing at Uncle Rondo's kimono, she calls on the reader to corroborate her claim that she was actually sticking up for Uncle Rondo. When Stella-Rondo first arrives wearing an ugly hat, Sister addresses the reader, saying, "I wish you could see it." By pulling readers directly into the story, Sister attempts to garner sympathy and understanding.

Sister's manipulation ultimately makes her an unreliable narrator because she conveys her own version of the truth while failing to recognize her own pettiness and jealousy. Between her harsh, mean-spirited judgments and refusal to truly communicate or connect with others, she is guilty of the same transgressions of which she claims to be a victim. Sister believes that a change of venue is the solution to her difficult family relations, but her departure is really an act of cowardice. Instead of facing the difficulties and tensions, she is simply running away from the truth.

IMPORTANT QUOTATIONS EXPLAINED

1. *"Told him I was one-sided. Bigger on one side than the other, which is a deliberate, calculated falsehood: I'm the same."*

Sister speaks these words in the story's opening paragraph, referring to what she considers one of the lies Stella-Rondo tells to lure Mr. Whitaker away from Sister. This complaint summarizes the story's central conflict. Sister's gripe may be with her family as a whole, but the theft of Mr. Whitaker's affections proves to be the transgression she cannot get over. Welty gives a double meaning to Sister's complaint. Although Sister is talking about her physical shape, the phrase "one-sided" applies equally well to her clouded vision of herself and the world around her. Sister wishes to portray herself as a well-balanced, fair, and accurate judge of character, but her willful denial and subjectivity prove to be the source of her unhappiness. Although Sister isn't self-aware enough to understand how "one-sided" she actually is, we can see from this quotation and the rest of Sister's narration how deluded she is about herself and those around her. Sister's insistence on shunning everyone's perspective but her own emerges as the defining tragedy of the story—when Sister leaves home for the post office, she effectively refuses any possibility of expanding her view of the world.

2. *"I want the world to know I'm happy. And if Stella-Rondo should come to me this minute, on bended knees, and* attempt *to explain the incidents of her life with Mr. Whitaker, I'd simply put my fingers in both my ears and refuse to listen."*

This quotation concludes the story. Sister believes that she has triumphed over the people who have oppressed her for so long, and she wants to proclaim her victory to the world. However, Sister's announcement that she is content and satisfied does not mean that she is actually fulfilled. Ultimately, Sister is trying to convince herself that the isolation and solitude of the post office are preferable to the isolation and emotional solitude that defined her home life. However, she cannot help but confess her secret hope that Stella-Rondo will someday explain her actions and beg for Sister's forgiveness, even if Sister will refuse to listen. Despite the pride she claims to have in her escape, Sister is still mired in the rivalries that have punctuated her relationship with Stella-Rondo since the two were little girls. The story ends on a note of irony: the lack of empathy and the inability to listen, from which Sister believes she has suffered, are now being directed at Stella-Rondo by Sister herself. Sister has inherited this dysfunctional mode of communication from her family and shows no sign of breaking free of it anytime soon.

W

Winter Dreams

F. Scott Fitzgerald
(1896–1940)

CONTEXT

Francis Scott Fitzgerald was a distant cousin of his namesake, Francis Scott Key, who wrote the poem that would eventually supply the lyrics to "The Star-Spangled Banner." In naming him, Fitzgerald's parents honored their esteemed distant relative as well as the nation that had provided Fitzgerald's mother, the daughter of an Irish immigrant, with the sizable inheritance her father had amassed as a grocer. Born in Saint Paul, Minnesota, on September 24, 1896, Fitzgerald was a precocious child who published his first piece of fiction, a detective story, in his school newspaper when he was thirteen. Fitzgerald eventually attended Princeton University, where he produced musical and theatrical skits, humor pieces, and contributions to one of the university's literary magazines.

Fitzgerald favored his artistic pursuits over his academic work. In 1917, on probation and unlikely to graduate, Fitzgerald enlisted in the army, where he was eventually stationed at Alabama's Camp Sheridan. There, he fell in love with Zelda Sayre, the woman who would possess and haunt him for the rest of his life. Fitzgerald tried twice—unsuccessfully—to publish an early novel, but he still believed that the one way to gain respect from others and support and affection from Zelda and her family was to establish himself as a successful novelist.

Fitzgerald returned home to Saint Paul to pursue his ambition. In a few months, he re-worked his unsuccessful first novel, *This Side of Paradise*, and published it in 1920, to much critical praise. A week after the book's release, Fitzgerald finally married Zelda.

In the early 1920s, Fitzgerald began writing short stories, which funded his novel-writing ambitions. His reputation rose when he published his second novel, *The Beautiful and the Damned*, in 1922. Despite his growing alcoholism, he continued to write, intensifying his engagement with the ideas of idealism and success, which Fitzgerald saw as fundamental to the American character. The Fitzgeralds moved to France in 1924, where Fitzgerald wrote the novel that would prove to be his greatest accomplishment: *The Great Gatsby* (1925). The novel's publication marked the high point of Fitzgerald's career, and he was unable to reclaim his earlier momentum. His later years were marked by slow progress on his fourth novel, *Tender Is the Night* (1934); an itinerant life that saw the family shuttling between Europe and America; his failed attempt at a Hollywood screenwriting career; an increasing estrangement from Zelda; Zelda's advancing mental illness and eventual institutionalization; and Fitzgerald's mounting debts and compromised health. Fitzgerald died on December 21, 1940.

Fitzgerald is best remembered for his spoiled and conflicted Jazz Age characters, including Dexter Green from "Winter Dreams," who bears a distinct resemblance to Jay Gatsby, the protagonist of *The Great Gatsby*. Both are self-made men who are eager to rise beyond their station in life, and both find that personal fulfillment and their ideal women are ultimately elusive. "Winter Dreams" first appeared in *Metropolitan Magazine* in 1922 and later in the collection *All the Sad Young Men* (1926). The similarities between "Winter Dreams" and *The Great Gatsby* are not accidental, as Fitzgerald wrote the story while he was developing the ideas that would become the novel.

"Winter Dreams" has a distinct autobiographical bent, and the story traces Fitzgerald's experiences growing up in a middle-class family in the upper Midwest. Black Bear Lake, where the glitterati spend their summers in the story, is only a partial disguise of White Bear Lake, an exclusive resort area where Saint Paul's elite would summer. It was a place that Fitzgerald knew well. It is also arguable that Dexter Green bears a resemblance to Fitzgerald himself, a restless and talented young man desperate to advance himself in a singular pursuit of success.

PLOT OVERVIEW

In winter, Dexter Green, son of the owner of the second-best grocery store in Black Bear, Minnesota, skis across the snowed-in golf course where he caddies in the warmer months to earn his pocket money. In April, the spring thaw begins and the first golfers brave the course. Unlike the dismal spring, the autumn and winter empower Dexter and stimulate his imagination. Dexter imagines beating the golf club's most esteemed members. At work, he crosses paths with Judy Jones, who, attended by her nurse, asks Dexter to carry her clubs. Dexter can't leave his post, and Judy throws a tantrum and tries to strike her nurse with her clubs. When the caddy-master promptly returns and Dexter is free to be Judy's caddy, he quits. Hastily ending his employment as a caddie is the first in a lifelong series of impetuous acts that would be dictated to Dexter by his so-called winter dreams, which drive him to desire material success.

Dexter foregoes state school for a more esteemed eastern university, where his financial resources are stretched. He still longs for luxury, but his desires are often denied. After college, Dexter, articulate and confident, borrows $1,000 off the strength of his degree and buys a partnership in a laundry. By age twenty-seven, he owns the largest chain of laundries in the upper Midwest. He sells the business and moves to New York.

We learn more about a period of time during Dexter's rise to success. At age twenty-three, Dexter is given a weekend pass to the Sherry Island Golf Club by Mr. Hart, for whom Dexter used to caddy. Dexter feels superior to the other competitors but also that he does not belong in this world. At the fifteenth green, while the group searches for a lost ball, Mr. Hedrick is struck in the stomach by Miss Jones, who wishes to play through and doesn't realize that she has struck another player. She hits her ball and continues on, as the men alternately praise or criticize her beauty and forward behavior. Later that evening, Dexter swims out to the raft in the club's lake, stretching out on the springboard and listening to a distant piano. The sound of the tune fills him with delight at his present situation. The peaceful scene is disturbed by the roar of Judy's motorboat. She has abandoned a date who believes that she is his ideal, and she asks Dexter to drive the boat so that she can water-ski.

Waiting for Judy to arrive for their date the next evening, Dexter imagines all the successful men from esteemed backgrounds who had once loved her. He has acquired polish and sophistication despite his humble origins. Judy arrives in modest clothes, tells the maid that dinner can be served, and informs Dexter that her parents will not be in attendance, which is a relief for Dexter. After dinner, on the sun porch, Judy asks Dexter whether it is all right if she cries. A man she was dating has confessed he is poor. When she asks Dexter what his financial standing is, he tells her that he is most likely the richest young man in the entire region. They kiss, and Dexter's passion for her increases. Dexter continues his pursuit of Judy, but during a picnic she leaves with another man. She claims that nothing has happened between her and the other man, which Dexter doesn't believe.

Judy toys with the various men who seek her affections. The summer ends, and Dexter takes up residence at a club in town, showing up at the dances when Judy is in attendance. He still desires her and dreams of taking her to New York to live. He eventually forces himself to accept the fact that he will never possess her in the way he wants. He throws himself into work and becomes engaged to Irene. One night, just before the engagement is to be announced, Irene's headache forces her to cancel her plans with Dexter. He return to the University Club, where Judy, back from her travels, approaches him. They go for a drive. Judy flirts with him, telling him he should marry her, and they discuss their former passion. She asks to be taken home and begins to cry quietly. She repeats her desire to marry him. She asks him in, and he relents. Later, he does not regret that Judy's ardor cools after a month, that Irene and her family were deeply hurt by his betrayal, or that his reputation in the city has been compromised. He loves Judy above all. Leaving for the East with the intention of selling his laundries and settling in New York, the outbreak of World War I calls him back west, where he transfers management of his business to a partner. He enters basic training, welcoming the distraction of combat.

In New York seven years later, when Dexter is thirty-two, he is more successful than ever. Devlin, a business associate, informs Dexter that Judy married a friend of his, a man who cheats on her and drinks heavily while Judy stays at home with the children. She has also, according to Devlin, lost her looks. Dexter feels the loss of her beauty and spark personally, because his illusions of Judy are finally and irreparably shattered. He cries, mourning the past and his lost youth, which he will never be able to reclaim.

CHARACTER LIST

Dexter Green   A successful businessman and the story's protagonist. Dexter grew up in Keeble, a small Minnesota village, the son of a grocer and Bohemian mother. Ambitious and eager, he works hard to gain the trappings of wealth and status. Dexter both celebrates and denies his humble working-class origins. He feels like a trespasser in the halls of the affluent, but at the same time he feels superior for having worked his way into the upper ranks, a group comprising people for whom he has little respect.

Judy Jones   The daughter of the affluent Mortimer Jones. Glowing with vitality, Judy is aloof, charming, and irresistible to many men, including Dexter. She is alluring, unattainable, and whimsical, concerned only with the gratification of her desires. Judy does not seem to be fully aware of how manipulative she is toward the various suitors who pursue her—or if she is aware, she doesn't care.

Mortimer Jones   A wealthy member of the Sherry Island Gold Club and Judy's father. In one of Dexter's fantasies, Mr. Jones watches Dexter amaze the club members with his mastery of the springboard. The real Mr. Jones approaches Dexter one day, with tears in his eyes, proclaiming him the best caddy and exhorting him not to quit.

W

T. A. Hedrick   A pillar of the community. Mr. Hedrick is the man Dexter trounces in his imaginary golf tournaments. Dexter does eventually golf with Mr. Hedrick, who emerges as a bore with few skills as a player. On the course, Mr. Hedrick is hit in the stomach by an errant ball struck by Judy Jones.

Irene Scheerer   Dexter's fiancée. Irene is light-haired, sweet, and honorable. Dexter breaks her heart by cheating on her with Judy.

Mrs. Scheerer   Irene's mother. A kind presence, Mrs. Scheerer likes Dexter and the idea of him becoming her son-in-law. Dexter's betrayal of Irene hurts her deeply.

Mr. Hart   A successful man who admires young Dexter's drive and work ethic. Mr. Hart gives Dexter a weekend guest pass to the Sherry Island Golf Club.

Mr. Sandwood   A member of the Sherry Island Golf Club who golfs one day with the twenty-three-year-old Dexter. Mr. Sandwood is captivated by Judy Jones's beauty.

Devlin   A businessman from Detroit who visits Dexter in New York. Devlin informs Dexter that Judy married one of Devlin's best friends, the couple is unhappily married, and Judy has lost her legendary good looks.

ANALYSIS OF MAJOR CHARACTERS

DEXTER GREEN   Dexter is desperate to validate his existence through success and status, but he is also critical of his attempts to transcend his humble origins by blindly pursuing wealth and sophistication. Dexter both celebrates and denies his middle-class background, and he himself ultimately becomes the obstacle that stands in the way of the personal happiness he seeks. Dexter is unable to resolve this essential conflict of identity. Having finally achieved guest entrance to the country club, he feels like a trespasser, while at the same time feeling superior to the captains of industry whom he finds boring and lacking in golf skills. This inherent duality in Dexter is evident in his complex history with Judy. Although he is able to convince himself that he does not want her as a partner or wife, he cannot control the ardor her presence in his life triggers.

Dexter deliberately creates obstacles to his own happiness. Afraid of commitment, he prefers a solitary existence, hovering on the edges of a world of carousing and bachelorhood. He once coveted a life of financial ease, but when he finally reaches his goal, he feels like an outsider because he had to work hard for his money. He feels that his newly acquired status has been purchased rather than deserved. The satisfaction he feels at becoming the richest young man in the upper Midwest leads him to pursue unattainable goals, such as the possession of Judy Jones. He is blind to his emotional failings and personal shortcomings, seeing little distinction between the personal and professional. For him, love and money are inextricably linked. Dexter's fixation on the ideal proves to be the most significant obstacle to his happiness. He persists in believing that Judy is an ideal woman, when in reality she is flawed and human. Her transformation into a homely housewife ultimately shatters Dexter's illusions and ideals.

JUDY JONES   In a way, Judy Jones is shaped by men who view her as the ideal woman, as they must contort her to fit their fantasy of this vision of feminine beauty and grace. Judy depends on these suitors' attentions to give her life meaning. Just as Dexter seems out of his element when he becomes part of Judy's world, Judy too suffers from a kind of displacement. As a child, she adopts the stilted, precocious tone of a daughter of prosperity, and her self-confidence and comportment suggest a maturity beyond her years. Although she is older than Dexter, she addresses him as "Boy," which reflects not their age difference but different stations in life. When Judy enters adulthood, however, the shallow, immature, and cruel side of her nature becomes clear. Judy's selfishness, willfulness, and impulse-driven behavior are leftovers from the realm of childhood and belie the polish and sophistication that her adult beauty suggests.

Judy's lack of humility and inner reserves suggest the negative effects of an overly indulged existence in which she was sheltered from the sting of the real world. Just as Dexter equates professional success with personal validation, Judy sees her radiant beauty as a sign that she deserves great happiness. "I'm more beautiful than anybody else," she brazenly asserts, "why can't I be happy?" Judy fails to attain the happiness she seeks because she is unaware of what happiness requires and what path will lead her there. Mired in surface impressions and the flattery that her serial dating provides, she is unable to properly articulate her dissatisfaction. She uses her physical attributes as her sole means of engaging with and interpreting the world. Like Dexter's, the life she inhabits at the end of the story falls far short of the life she had expected. She is the victim of her malformed impressions of the world and inability to independently discover who she truly is.

THEMES, MOTIFS, AND SYMBOLS

THEMES

THE DARK SIDE OF THE AMERICAN DREAM The "winter dreams" of the story refer to the American Dream that Dexter comes to embody, but success brings a high cost, and social mobility restricts Dexter's capacity for happiness. Dexter is from humble origins: his mother was an immigrant who constantly struggled with the language of her adopted homeland. The central irony of the story is that realizing the American Dream yields bleak rewards. For example, when Dexter was a young caddy, he dreamed about success and wealth and the happiness they would bring. When he finally beats T. A. Hedrick in a golf tournament, however, the triumph brings him little joy. Dexter is able to transcend middle-class inertia but, despite his tireless efforts to advance his fortunes, forced to accept that money cannot buy happiness.

Dexter has an ambiguous relationship with the bluebloods and idle rich who populate his social world. On one hand, he is proud of his self-made status and has no respect for the men for whom luxury and wealth were a given. Still, the men are emblems of a world to which Dexter wants to belong. In pursuing Judy, he is attempting to validate his claim as a bonafide member of the upper class. Dexter feels that he is a newer, stronger, and more praiseworthy version of the Mortimer Joneses of the world, but he still mimics the rich in gesture and appearance. He pays meticulous attention to his appearance, concerned with small details that only an outsider who was trying to disguise himself as a man of wealth would really notice. Dexter's position in this world is precarious, and there is no room for error in appearance or etiquette. Through Dexter and the world of earned distinctions that he comes to represent, Fitzgerald exposes the hollowness that comes from the aggressive pursuit of the American

Dream. Wealth and social status substitute for strong connections to people, eclipsing the possibility of happiness of emotional fulfillment.

REALITY VERSUS IDEALISM   Reality and fantasy prove to be constantly at odds with each other as Dexter and Judy search for stability and meaning in "Winter Dreams." Dexter is the victim of his so-called winter dreams, adolescent fantasies that he is never able to fulfill. As he searches for happiness and love, he unwisely focuses his quest exclusively on Judy Jones, making her the sole object of his romantic projections. However, rather than provide fulfillment for Dexter, Judy and her displays of affection simply trigger more yearning. Dexter never sees Judy for who she really is; rather, he sees her as an ideal of womanhood and the embodiment of perfect love. Later, Judy reveals her self-serving nature when she confesses that she is breaking off relations with a man who has pursued her simply because he is not of adequate financial means. Dexter, still blinded by his idealistic view of Judy, cannot digest this information, because it suggests the reality of who Judy is.

Although Dexter recognizes the real threat of harm beneath Judy's charm and beauty and tries to convince himself that he is no longer in love with her, he cannot fully divorce himself from the romantic, uncontrollable attachment he has to her. Ultimately, Dexter becomes the victim not of Judy's fickle behavior but of his own stubborn ideals. Time and again, Dexter and Judy struggle with contradictions between reality and fantasy. On their first date, Dexter is disappointed that Judy appears in an average dress and, instead of the pomp and ritual he expected, blandly tells the maid that they are ready to eat. In their ambiguous and protracted courtship, Judy treats him with "interest . . . encouragement . . . malice . . . indifference . . . [and] contempt." The reality of this relationship is bleak, but the idealistic vision of what it could be enables it to limp along.

MOTIFS

SIMILES   Fitzgerald uses similes throughout "Winter Dreams," most notably at the beginning of the story, to make abstract notions, such as the frustrations of love and drive to succeed, more concrete. The similes also suggest the gulf that separates reality from the illusions the characters are subject to. In the first sentence of the story, we learn that, unlike Dexter, some of the caddies at the country club are "poor as sin." As winter settles on Minnesota, snow covers the golf course "like the white lid of a box," and the wind blows "cold as misery." These similes, grimly preoccupied with gloomy notions of misery and poverty, set the tone for the unhappy tale that Fitzgerald is about to convey.

Similes help clarify the abstract idea of Dexter's winter dreams. His visions of grandeur involve vague, half-formed hopes for success and wealth and the satisfaction he assumes will accompany them. Dexter is able to translate his dreams into reality. He becomes the self-professed richest young man in his part of the country and gets to face off in a round of golf with Mr. Hedrick, whom he easily beats. However, he is still dogged by the abstract—his struggle to find love and accept the responsibility of belonging to someone else. During his first fateful meeting with the adult Judy, his heart "turned over like the fly-wheel on the boat." Fitzgerald's use of simile helps provide a link between abstract and actual realms, reality and illusion, and love and its inevitable disappointments.

WINTER The title, "Winter Dreams," refers to the powerful desire for status and affluence and, with its suggestion of snowy barrenness, sets the tone for the story that unfolds. Dexter forms his greatest aspirations for his life during a season of death and dormancy, an irony that suggests that those aspirations will not be as life-affirming as Dexter imagines. Seasons in general highlight the unstoppable passage of time in the story. As Dexter gets older but no wiser, each year finds him further from the happiness he seeks. He is in many ways a misfit, his surroundings and ambitions out of synch with his humble origins. Fitzgerald highlights Dexter's unresolved, outsider status early in the story, when Dexter skis across the frozen, snowed-in golf course, using the space for something other than what it was intended. These solitary, wintry outings signal the loneliness that he will never vanquish. The fact that his dreams are born in a lifeless, stagnant season foreshadows the unhappiness and thwarted desires that await him in adulthood.

SYMBOLS

THE BOAT In the elite world of the Sherry Island Golf Club, the boat emerges not only as a symbol of luxury but also as a powerful reminder of the emptiness a life of indulgence can lead to. The boat makes a memorable entrance, with Judy at the helm, as Dexter enjoys a solitary moment on the raft anchored in the middle of the lake next to the country club. Lost in a reverie, Dexter is filled with the bliss of arrival, having finally reached the success he had long anticipated. Entertaining only the most auspicious of prospects when he looks to the future, Dexter feels at that moment a satisfaction that he may never again experience as intensely. Abruptly interrupting Dexter's musings, the whirr of the motor overpowers Dexter's thoughts about the rosy life ahead. Judy speeds across the lake in the boat, foreshadowing the profound ways that Dexter's ensuing passion for Judy will impact his future happiness.

For Judy, flying behind the boat on a surfboard, the boat is an escape from reality. Her admirers learn quickly that she is too fast to catch and lives solely for her own pleasure. Dexter obeys when she tells him to drive the boat for her, the first of an ensuing string of commands he will obey. As an object of affluence, it shows how truly divorced from reality Judy is. She tells Dexter that she is running from a man she had been dating who has begun to idealize her. The boat is her way of escaping the ways in which men try to make her fit their own dreams and reflect their idealized visions of the perfect woman. Judy hides in the boat again later, when she grows tired of the man from New York who is rumored to be her fiancé. The boat becomes Judy's haven from the oppressive affections of men who are captivated by her, an expensive toy that whisks her away from commitment or the need to accept responsibility for her actions.

GOLF BALLS Golf balls, part of the pristine world of the country club, suggest the harm that an idle life can lead to as well as the stringent requirements one must meet to belong to the upper class. Dexter, with his self-made wealth, tries desperately to blend in with this affluent world. The imagery of the golf balls emerges twice, both times reflecting the upper-class ease that the game itself embodies. First, before the spring thaw in the north country, golfers use black and red balls, which stand out better in the patches of snow that linger on the course. This reference comes early in the story, when Dexter is a young caddy, excluded from Judy Jones and her set because he is a middle-class boy of limited means. When Dexter finally gets a toehold in her world, he sacrifices his individuality for the identical white balls he uses at the club where he once caddied.

During Dexter's once anticipated but ultimately disappointing golf outing with T. A. Hedrick, golf balls, in the hands of Judy Jones, become an emblem of aggression. Judy's ball hits Mr. Hedrick in the stomach, and her obliviousness, whether feigned or genuine, serves only to further characterize her as a self-centered brat. Although there is little threat of real physical violence in this genteel, upper-class world, the incident suggests that aggression lurks just beneath the surface. Although Judy embodies the light, almost hedonist spirit that would eventually characterize the age, Fitzgerald reminds us in this episode that beneath the fun and leisure, real harm can be done. Judy's errant ball foreshadows the more potent emotional damage she imparts in trifling with Dexter's and her other admirers' affections.

SHORT STORY ANALYSIS

STRUCTURE AND NARRATIVE VOICE Fitzgerald structures and narrates "Winter Dreams" in a way that reflects his critical view of the world he depicts in the story. Like the sectional dividers in the story, Fitzgerald's characters lead fractured, incomplete existences as they search for pleasure and wealth. The story is composed of six sections of varying lengths, which suggest the many affections and betrayals that characterize Dexter and Judy's relationship. In addition, this particular structure suggests that when it comes to issues of identity and self-awareness, there is no coherent core to ground these characters in their search for stability and meaning. Indeed, a clearly defined sense of self is what Dexter lacks. Like this story, which relates aspects of his coming-of-age, he is the product of fragmentary experiences. He attempts to find in Judy the clarity and direction that his life lacks.

Fitzgerald's view of Dexter's and Judy's whirlwind lives and the ways they conduct them is apparent in the way he narrates the story. His technique of addressing the reader directly at several points in the story lends "Winter Dreams" an immediacy and underscores the fact that Fitzgerald is not only telling his story but also selecting specific details from his characters' lives for a reason. When Dexter returns to the Sherry Island Golf Club, for example, Fitzgerald writes, "But the part of his story that concerns us . . ." an address that suggests that we and Fitzgerald are complicit, looking in on Dexter's life. Direct address also takes the form of rhetorical questions, which Fitzgerald poses to us to reveal Judy's propensity for "acting" in the presence of her admirers. Ultimately, Fitzgerald's structure and narrative voice suggest a purpose to his writing of the story. In a way, he is holding up the travails of Dexter and Judy as a warning to readers who may also be caught up in decadent lives or the romantic whims of another person.

TIME AND TEMPORAL SHIFTS Fitzgerald's tale moves about in time, spanning just less than two decades in the lives of Dexter Green and Judy Jones, a structural and narrative choice that lends complexity and richness to his portrayal of the gradual wearing away of Dexter's illusions. By juxtaposing various disembodied episodes in Dexter's personal and professional lives, Fitzgerald suggests the intricate role the events play in shaping Dexter's response to Judy and setting up the high cost of his winter dreams. The past is always alive for Dexter. For example, the sting of young Judy's condescension on the golf course is a looming presence that Fitzgerald conjures to make Dexter's disillusionment at the end of the story more profound. In an aside to the reader, Fitzgerald writes, "This story is not his biography, remember . . . ." Rather, the tale serves as an emotional history of hopes that are built up and then razed.

Temporal shifts and the passage of the seasons serve as a backdrop to the romantic possession from which Dexter tries to escape over the years. The story begins when Dexter is fourteen and eventually offers a rapid summary of his rise in life—from his college years at a prestigious Eastern university to his owning and eventually selling the largest string of laundries in the upper Midwest. Although the story actually concludes when Dexter is thirty-two, the action immediately flashes back to when Dexter is twenty-three and joining the elite for a round of golf. In just a few paragraphs, Fitzgerald presents an ironic juxtaposition. Dexter goes from a being a caddy to having young caddies carry his clubs for him at the same elite country club where he had once worked. Even then, at this telling moment in his young adult life, Dexter is attempting to "lessen the gap that lay between the present and the past." Fitzgerald's fluid sense of time in the story serves to draw more attention to Dexter's lost youth and the gap that for Dexter will only widen and never close.

HISTORICAL CONTEXT "Winter Dreams" analyzes the motivations and frustrations of two young people coming of age, but it also examines the historical period that is the backdrop to the on-again, off-again relationship between Dexter and Judy. The action in "Winter Dreams" spans the early decades of the twentieth century, from the middle of the first decade to the early 1920s. The so-called Roaring Twenties, the Jazz Age was for some people a time of unchecked hedonism. Self-gratification ruled the day, and for the affluent, it was an era of opulent parties, fashionable trends, and grand social gestures. One critic intimated of the period that it was a time in which people had little concern for the past and even less regard for the future. The time period saw many young people endorse a reckless embrace of the moment, as America emerged from World War I and entered a new and unprecedented economic boom. Fitzgerald emerged as the laureate of the Jazz Age, capturing the spirit of the decade in his fiction while embodying its hedonistic, freewheeling zeal in his personal life as well.

In "Winter Dreams," as in his fiction in general, Fitzgerald avoided many of the clichéd images of the period, such as flappers, speakeasies, and gangsters. However, in his hands, a certain type of character emerged. Judy embodies all that is stereotypical of the fickle, selfish, and histrionic rich girl. She is in full possession of her beauty and thrall over men, navigating her way through her social world by the force of her charm. She is all appetite, too embroiled in the moment, with little regard for the larger implications of her changes of heart. Dexter is the convert, the middle-class imposter standing outside the dance in the gymnasium and seduced by the wealth and self-indulgence the dancing couples represent. In Fitzgerald's world, the pursuit of pleasure alienates those who are unable to indulge in escapist acts, which distract from the essential hollowness and isolation that many of his characters try to avoid. Pleasure for pleasure's sake was the unofficial motto of the flapper, the jazz babies, and the idle rich who helped the twenties achieve its mystique of hedonism and decadence in the major cities of Europe and the United States. In Dexter and Judy, Fitzgerald subtly indicts Jazz Age decadence.

IMPORTANT QUOTATIONS EXPLAINED

---

1. *Often he reached out for the best without knowing why he did it—and sometimes he ran up against the mysterious denials and prohibitions in which life indulges. It is with one of those denials and not with his career as a whole that this story deals.*

This quotation, from part II, underscores the ways in which denial informs the story, as the wealthy characters in "Winter Dreams" are forced to confront the fact that the complexities of happiness are difficult, even impossible, to master. Dexter's life, as portrayed in the story, spans his mid-teens to early thirties and is marked by a flurry of business activity but little introspection. His winter dreams of money and comfort are as insubstantial as the snow he skis across as a young man, fantasizing about a life of ease and admiration. But Dexter never pauses to examine what motives and desires actually drive his actions. Because Dexter has not analyzed his instinctive grasping for "the best," the news of Judy's unhappy marriage and compromised beauty affect him all the more profoundly.

In this quotation, Fitzgerald sets up a dichotomy between the personal realm and public arena, where Dexter makes his most profound mark. Although Fitzgerald is attempting to isolate one aspect of Dexter's varied life, he is also suggesting that the story's preoccupation with the rich is merely a ruse, meant to expose the hollow core of a world that is often too obsessed with the material trappings of success. The denial Dexter faces reverberates on many levels, referring not only to Judy's fickle affections but also to the more profound denial of happiness that emotionally cripples Dexter at the end. Finally, the quotation is noteworthy because it shows that Fitzgerald is assuming an analytical stance that his protagonist does not. Fitzgerald attempts to guide the reader to the wisdom and insight that he was hoping to convey. He acknowledges that his story is exactly that—a story—and that it serves as a cautionary tale for readers.

---

2. *"Who are you, anyhow?"*
   "I'm nobody," he announced. "My career is largely a matter of futures."

This exchange between Judy and Dexter takes place at the end of part III, when the couple is talking on the sun porch. The exchange is seemingly innocuous, but Dexter's answer reveals his essential failing and the personal obstacle he is never able to overcome as he searches for identity and meaning. As an individual, shorn of class distinction or the mark of worldly success, Dexter has a limited grasp of who he is. His winter dreams primarily concern rising above his station in life, ignoring the intangible aspects of happiness and personal development, which flounder in his drive for wealth. Dexter is a "nobody" who turns to the professional world and his own success for self-definition. However, when it comes to establishing his presence as a fully realized individual, Dexter lingers on the edge of himself, as when he hovers in the shadows of a party held at the club where he lives, watching the dancing couples. He is unable to penetrate the heart of not only this world of frivolity but of himself as well.

Happiness with Judy and then Irene eludes Dexter as he looks to these objects of his desire to define him. Judy in particular is a disastrous choice, a female complement to his persona of a lost wanderer unable to firmly root himself in his life. Judy's question reveals her often shallow way of relating to those around her. While the question smacks of abstract concerns of identity, Judy is simply slyly asking Dexter whether he is of adequate financial means. Her follow-up question of "Are you poor?" shows the true nature of her inquiry and reveals the extent to which she is interested only in a man who can provide her with material goods. If her partner is devoid of personal character, a state Dexter dangerously flirts with, she doesn't much care.

W

The Yellow Wallpaper

Charlotte Perkins Gilman
(1860–1935)

CONTEXT

Born in 1860 in Hartford, Connecticut, Charlotte Perkins Gilman became well known in her time as a crusading journalist and feminist intellectual, a follower of such pioneering women's rights advocates as Susan B. Anthony, Elizabeth Cady Stanton, and Harriet Beecher Stowe, who was Gilman's great-aunt. As a young woman, Gilman was an artist, studying at the Rhode Island School of Design and working for a short time as a greeting-card artist. In 1884, she married another artist, Charles Walter Stetson, with whom she had one daughter. She began writing and publishing in the 1890s, as her marriage with Charles was coming to an end.

Gilman was concerned with political inequality and social justice in general, but the primary focus of her writing was the unequal status of women within the institution of marriage. In such works as *Concerning Children* (1900), *The Home* (1904), and *Human Work* (1904), Gilman argued that women's obligation to remain in the domestic sphere robbed them of the expression of their full powers of creativity and intelligence, while simultaneously robbing society of women whose abilities suited them for professional and public life. An essential part of her analysis was that the traditional power structure of the family made no one happy—neither the woman who was made into an unpaid servant, the husband who was made into a master, nor the children who were subject to both. Her most ambitious work, *Women and Economics* (1898), analyzed the hidden value of women's labor within the capitalist economy and argued, as Gilman did throughout her works, that financial independence for women could only benefit society as a whole.

Today Gilman is primarily known for one remarkable story, "The Yellow Wallpaper," which was shocking for its time when it was first published in 1892. This story, which deals with an unequal marriage and a woman destroyed by her unfulfilled desire for self-expression, confronts the same concerns and ideas as Gilman's nonfiction but in a much more personal mode. Indeed, "The Yellow Wallpaper" draws heavily on a particularly painful episode in Gilman's own life.

In 1886, early in her marriage to Charles and not long after her daughter's birth, Gilman was stricken with a severe case of depression. Her condition was made worse by the presence of her husband and baby. She was referred to Dr. S. Weir Mitchell, then the country's leading specialist in nervous disorders, whose treatment in such cases was a "rest cure" of forced inactivity. Especially in the case of his female patients, Mitchell believed that depression was brought on by too much mental activity and not enough attention to domestic affairs. For Gilman, this course of treatment was a disaster. Prevented from working, she soon had a nervous breakdown. At her worst, she was reduced to crawling into closets and under beds, clutching a rag doll.

Once she abandoned Mitchell's rest cure, Gilman's condition improved, although she claimed to feel the ordeal's effects for the rest of her life. Leaving behind her husband and child, a scandalous decision, Charlotte Perkins Stetson (she took the name Gilman after a second marriage, to her cousin) embarked on a successful career as a journalist, lecturer, and publisher. In "The Yellow Wallpaper," she uses her personal experience to create a tale that is both a chilling description of one woman's fall into madness and a potent symbolic narrative of the fate of creative women stifled by a paternalistic culture. Gilman committed suicide in 1935.

PLOT OVERVIEW

In her journal, the narrator marvels at the grandeur of the house and grounds that her husband has taken for their summer vacation. She describes it as an aristocratic estate and a haunted house and wonders how they were able to afford it and why the house had been empty for so long. She discusses her "nervous depression" and marriage. She complains that her husband, John, who is also her doctor, belittles both her illness and her thoughts and concerns. Her treatment requires that she do almost nothing active, and she is especially forbidden from working and writing. She feels that activity, freedom, and interesting work would help her condition and reveals that she has begun writing in a secret journal. In an attempt to calm herself, the narrator describes the house, including details such as the "rings and things" in the bedroom walls and bars on the windows. The yellow wallpaper in the bedroom, with its strange, formless pattern, disturbs her. John approaches, so she stops writing.

In the first few weeks of the summer, the narrator becomes good at hiding her journal. She still longs for more stimulating company and activity and complains about John's patronizing, controlling ways. She keeps describing the wallpaper, which begins to seem not only ugly but menacing as well. She mentions that John is worried about her becoming fixated on it and has even refused to repaper the room so as not to give in to her neurotic worries. The narrator enjoys picturing people on the walkways around the house and says that John always discourages such fantasies. She thinks back to her childhood when she was able to work herself into a terror by imagining things in the dark. As she describes the bedroom, which she says must have been a nursery for young children, she points out that the paper is torn off the wall in spots, there are scratches and gouges in the floor, and the furniture is heavy and fixed in place. Just as she begins to see a strange subpattern behind the main design of the wallpaper, her writing is interrupted by John's sister, Jennie, who is acting as housekeeper and nurse for the narrator.

As the Fourth of July passes, the narrator reports that her family has just visited, leaving her more tired than ever. John threatens to send her to a physician named Weir Mitchell. The narrator is alone most of the time and says that she has become almost fond of the wallpaper and that attempting to figure out its pattern has become her primary entertainment. As her obsession grows, the subpattern of the wallpaper becomes clearer. It begins to resemble a woman "stooping down and creeping" behind the main pattern, which looks like the bars of a cage. Whenever the narrator tries to discuss leaving the house, John makes light of her concerns. Her fascination with the paper grows.

The wallpaper soon dominates the narrator's imagination. She becomes possessive and secretive, hiding her interest in the paper and making sure that no one else examines it. At one point, she startles Jennie, who had been touching the wallpaper and mentions that she had found yellow stains on their clothes. John thinks the narrator's health is improving, but she sleeps less and less and is convinced that she can smell the paper all over the house, even outside. She discovers a strange smudge mark on the paper that runs all around the room as if someone crawling against the wall had rubbed it.

The subpattern now clearly resembles a woman who is trying to get out from behind the main pattern. The narrator sees her shaking the bars at night and creeping around during the day, when the woman is able to escape briefly. The narrator mentions that she too creeps around at times. She suspects that John and Jennie are aware of her obsession, and she re- solves to destroy the paper once and for all, peeling much of it off during the night. The next day she manages to be alone and goes into something of a frenzy, biting and tearing at the paper to free the trapped woman, whom she sees struggling from inside the pattern.

The narrator is now insane, convinced that there are many creeping women and that she herself has come out of the wallpaper. She creeps endlessly around the room, smudging the wallpaper as she goes. When John breaks into the locked room and sees the full horror of the situation, he faints in the doorway.

CHARACTER LIST

The Narrator   A young, upper-middle-class woman, newly married and a mother, who is undergoing care for depression. The narrator—whose name may or may not be Jane—is highly imaginative and a natural storyteller, although her doctors believe that she has a "slight hysterical tendency." The story is told in the form of her secret diary, in which she records her thoughts as her obsession with the wallpaper grows.

John   The narrator's husband and physician. John restricts her behavior as part of her treat- ment. Unlike his imaginative wife, John is extremely practical, preferring facts and figures to "fancy," at which he "scoffs openly." He seems to love his wife but doesn't understand the negative effect his treatment has on her.

Jennie   John's sister. Jennie acts as the couple's housekeeper. Her presence and content- ment with a domestic role intensify the narrator's feelings of guilt about her own inability to act as a traditional wife and mother. At times, Jennie seems to suspect that the narrator is more troubled than she lets on.

ANALYSIS OF MAJOR CHARACTERS

THE NARRATOR   The narrator of "The Yellow Wallpaper" is a paradox: as she loses touch with the outer world, she comes to a greater understanding of the inner reality of her life. This inner/outer split is crucial to understanding the nature of the narrator's suffering. At every point, she is faced with relationships, objects, and situations that seem innocent and natural but are actually bizarre and even oppressive. In a sense, the plot of "The Yellow Wallpaper" is the narrator's attempt to avoid acknowledging the extent to which her external situation stifles her inner impulses. From the beginning, we see that the narrator is an imag- inative, highly expressive woman. She remembers terrifying herself with imaginary night- time monsters as a child, and she enjoys the notion that the house that they have taken is haunted. Yet as part of her "cure," her husband forbids her to exercise her imagination in any way. Both her reason and her emotions rebel at this treatment, and she turns her imagination onto seemingly neutral objects—the house and wallpaper—in an attempt to ignore her growing frustration. Her negative feelings color her description of her surroundings, making them seem uncanny and sinister, and she becomes fixated on the wallpaper.

When the narrator finally identifies herself with the woman trapped in the wallpaper, she is able to see that other women are forced to creep and hide behind the domestic "patterns" of their lives and that she herself is the one in need of rescue. The horror of this story is that the narrator must lose herself to understand herself. She has untangled the pattern of her life, but she has torn herself apart in getting free of it. An odd detail at the end of the story reveals how much the narrator has sacrificed. During her final split from reality, the narrator says, "I've got out at last, in spite of you and Jane." Who is this Jane? Some critics claim that Jane is a misprint for Jennie, the sister-in-law. It is more likely, however, that Jane is the name of the unnamed narrator, who has been a stranger to herself and her jailers. Now she is horribly "free" of the constraints of her marriage, society, and efforts to repress her mind.

JOHN Although John seems like the obvious villain of "The Yellow Wallpaper," the story doesn't allow us to see him as wholly evil. John's treatment of the narrator's depression goes terribly wrong, but in all likelihood he was trying to help her, not make her worse. The real problem with John is the all-encompassing authority he has in his combined role as the narrator's husband and doctor. John is so sure that he knows what's best for his wife that he disregards her opinion of the matter, forcing her to hide her true feelings. He consistently patronizes her. He calls her "a blessed little goose" and vetoes her smallest wishes, such as when he refuses to switch bedrooms so as not to overindulge her "fancies." Further, his dry, clinical rationality renders him uniquely unsuited to understand his imaginative wife. He does not intend to harm her, but his ignorance about what she really needs ultimately proves dangerous.

John knows his wife only superficially. He sees the "outer pattern" but misses the trapped, struggling woman inside. This ignorance is why John is no mere cardboard villain. He cares for his wife, but the unequal relationship in which they find themselves prevents him from truly understanding her and her problems. By treating her as a "case" or "wife" and not as a person with a will of her own, he helps destroy her, which is the last thing he wants. That John has been destroyed by this imprisoning relationship is made clear by the story's chilling finale. After breaking in on his insane wife, John faints in shock and goes unrecognized by his wife, who calls him "that man" and complains about having to "creep over him" as she makes her way along the wall.

THEMES, MOTIFS, AND SYMBOLS

THEMES

THE SUBORDINATION OF WOMEN IN MARRIAGE In "The Yellow Wallpaper," Gilman uses the conventions of the psychological horror tale to critique the position of women within the institution of marriage, especially as practiced by the "respectable" classes of her time. When the story was first published, most readers took it as a scary tale about a woman in an extreme state of consciousness—a gripping, disturbing entertainment, but little more. Since its rediscovery in the twentieth century, however, readings of the story have become more complex. For Gilman, the conventional nineteenth-century middle-class marriage, with its rigid distinction between the female's "domestic" functions and the male's "active" work, ensured that women remained second-class citizens. The story reveals that this gender division had the effect of keeping women in a childish state of ignorance and preventing their full development. John's assumption of his own superior wisdom and maturity leads him to misjudge, patronize, and dominate his wife, all in the name of helping her. The narrator is reduced to acting like a cross, petulant child, unable to stand up for herself without seeming unreasonable or disloyal. The narrator has no say in even the smallest details of her life, and she retreats into her obsessive fantasy, the only place in which she can retain some control and exercise the power of her mind.

THE IMPORTANCE OF SELF-EXPRESSION   The mental constraints placed on the narrator, even more so than the physical ones, are what ultimately drive her insane. She is forced to hide her anxieties and fears to preserve the façade of a happy marriage and make it seem as though she is winning the fight against her depression. From the beginning, the most intolerable aspect of her treatment is the compulsory silence and idleness of the "resting cure." She is forced to become completely passive, forbidden from exercising her mind in any way. Writing is especially off-limits, and John warns her several times that she must use her self-control to rein in her imagination, which he fears will run away with her. Of course, the narrator's eventual insanity is a product of the repression of her imaginative power, not the expression of it. She is constantly longing for an emotional and intellectual outlet, even going so far as to keep a secret journal, which she describes more than once as a "relief" to her mind. For Gilman, a mind that is kept in a state of forced inactivity is doomed to self-destruction.

THE EVILS OF THE "RESTING CURE"   As someone who was almost destroyed by S. Weir Mitchell's resting cure for depression, it is not surprising that Gilman structured her story as an attack on this ineffective and cruel course of treatment. "The Yellow Wallpaper" is an illustration of the way a mind that is already plagued with anxiety can deteriorate and begin to prey on itself when it is forced into inactivity and kept from healthy work. To his credit, Mitchell, who is mentioned by name in the story, took Gilman's criticism to heart and abandoned the resting cure. Beyond the specific technique described in the story, Gilman means to criticize any form of medical care that ignores the patient's concerns, considering her only as a passive object of treatment. The connection between a woman's subordination in the home and her subordination in a doctor/patient relationship is clear—John is, after all, the narrator's husband and doctor. Gilman implies that both forms of authority can be easily abused, even when the husband or doctor means to help. All too often, the women who are the silent subjects of this authority are infantilized and oppressed.

MOTIFS

THE JOURNAL   The narrator of "The Yellow Wallpaper" tells us her story through entries in her journal. "The Yellow Wallpaper" is a kind of epistolary story, in which the narrator writes to herself. (An "epistolary" work of fiction takes the form of letters between characters.) Gilman uses this technique to show the narrator's descent into madness both subjectively and objectively—that is, from both the inside and outside. Had Gilman told her story in traditional first-person narration, reporting events from inside the narrator's head, the reader would never know exactly what to think: a woman inside the wallpaper might seem to actually exist. Had Gilman told the story from an objective, third-person point of view, without revealing the narrator's thoughts, the social and political symbolism of the story would have been obscured. As it is, the reader must decipher the story's ambiguity, just as the narrator must attempt to decipher the bewildering story of her life and bizarre patterns of the wallpaper. Gilman also uses the journal to give the story an intense intimacy and immediacy, especially in those moments when the narrative is interrupted by the approach of John or Jennie. These interruptions perfectly illustrate the constraints placed on the narrator by authority figures who urge her not to think about her "condition."

SYMBOLS

THE WALLPAPER   "The Yellow Wallpaper" is driven by the narrator's sense that the wallpaper is a text she must interpret, and symbolizes something that affects her directly. Accordingly, the wallpaper develops its symbolism throughout the story. At first it seems merely unpleasant: it is ripped, soiled, and an "unclean yellow." The worst part is the ostensibly formless pattern, which fascinates the narrator as she attempts to figure out how it is organized. After staring at the paper for hours, she sees a ghostly subpattern behind the main pattern, visible only in certain light. Eventually, the subpattern comes into focus as a desperate woman, constantly crawling and stooping, looking for an escape from behind the main pattern, which has come to resemble the bars of a cage. The narrator sees this cage as festooned with the heads of many women, all of whom were strangled as they tried to escape. Clearly, the wallpaper represents the structure of family, medicine, and tradition in which the narrator finds herself trapped. Wallpaper is domestic and humble, and Gilman skillfully uses this nightmarish, hideous paper as a symbol of the domestic life that traps so many women.

SHORT STORY ANALYSIS

THE UNRELIABLE NARRATOR   From the beginning of the story, we are aware that the narrator has mental problems—"temporary nervous depression"—and so her narration is, from the outset, unreliable. An unreliable narrator is one whose perspectives, observations, and commentary may not be fully accurate, truthful, or even sensible. When an unreliable narrator tells a story, it's up to the readers to look further than the narrator's words to figure out what's really happening. Or readers must interpret the unreliable narrator's errors and withholdings to learn more about the narrator's motivations and feelings. In "The Yellow Wallpaper," the unreliable narrator poses a twofold problem. First, we want to take her side against John, who has locked her away, and the resting cure, which is only making her worse. Because the narrator is clearly unstable, however, we cannot align ourselves with her entirely. For instance, when John sees her crawling on the floor at the end of the story, it's difficult not to transfer our sympathies to him. This split sympathy suggests how fully cruel and ineffective this resting cure truly is, because it turns both a bright, perceptive woman and her husband into wretched figures.

The narrator is unreliable from the beginning of the story, but Gilman increases that unreliability as the narrator sinks further into her fascination with the wallpaper. As the narrator spends more time alone in the room, she becomes progressively more dissociated from the reality of day-to-day life. This process of dissociation begins when the story does: at the moment the narrator decides to keep a secret diary as "a relief to her mind." From that point, her true thoughts are hidden from the outer world, and the narrator begins to slip into a fantasy world in which the nature of her situation is made clear only in symbolic terms. Gilman shows us this division in the narrator's consciousness by having the narrator puzzle over effects in the world that she herself has caused. For example, the narrator doesn't immediately understand that the yellow stains on her clothing and long "smooch" on the wallpaper are connected. Similarly, the narrator fights the realization that the predicament of the woman in the wallpaper is a symbolic version of her own situation. At first she even disapproves of the woman's efforts to escape and intends to "tie her up." The narrator's delusions and misperceptions intensify until she has lost her hold on reality altogether.

IRONY Almost every aspect of "The Yellow Wallpaper" is ironic in some way. *Irony* is a way of using words to convey multiple levels of meaning that contrast with or complicate one another. There are three types of irony: verbal, dramatic, and situational. In *verbal irony*, words are frequently used to convey the exact opposite of their literal meaning, such as when one person responds to another's mistake by saying "nice work." (Sarcasm—which this example embodies—is a form of verbal irony.) In her journal, the narrator uses verbal irony often, especially in reference to her husband: "John laughs at me, of course, but one expects that in marriage." Obviously, one expects no such thing, at least not in a healthy marriage. Later, she says, "I am glad my case is not serious," at a point when it is clear that she is concerned that her case is very serious indeed.

Dramatic irony occurs when there is a contrast between the reader's knowledge and the knowledge of the characters in the work. Gilman uses dramatic irony extensively in "The Yellow Wallpaper." For example, when the narrator first describes the bedroom that John has chosen for them, she attributes the room's bizarre features—the "rings and things" in the walls, the nailed-down furniture, the bars on the windows, and the torn wallpaper—to the fact that it must once have been used as a nursery. Even this early in the story, the reader sees that there is an equally plausible explanation for these details: the room had been used to house an insane person. Another example is when the narrator assumes that Jennie shares her interest in the wallpaper, although it is clear that Jennie is only now noticing the source of the yellow stains on their clothing. The effect intensifies toward the end of the story, as the narrator sinks further into her fantasy and the reader remains able to see her actions from the outside. By the time the narrator fully identifies with the trapped woman whom she sees in the wallpaper, the reader can appreciate the narrator's experience from her point of view as well as John's shock at what he sees when he breaks down the door to the bedroom.

Situational irony refers to moments when a character's actions have the opposite of their intended effect. For example, John's course of treatment backfires, worsening the depression he was trying to cure and actually driving his wife insane. Similarly, there is a deep irony in the way the narrator's fate develops. She gains a kind of power and insight only by losing her self-control and rationality.

GENRE "The Yellow Wallpaper" is nestled among several genres. First, Gilman points back to the tradition of the psychological horror tale as practiced by Edgar Allan Poe. A psychological horror tale focuses on the interior life of a character or characters, portrays the character's perception or misperception of reality, and is mostly concerned with action that takes place within the mind. Poe, for example, employs an insane narrator to tell the story of "The Tell-Tale Heart," much as Gilman does for "The Yellow Wallpaper." Going further back, Gilman draws on the tradition of the Gothic romances of the late eighteenth century, which often featured spooky old mansions and young heroines determined to uncover their secrets. Gilman's story is also forward-looking, however, and her moment-by-moment reporting of the narrator's thoughts is clearly a move in the direction of the sort of stream-of-consciousness narration used by such twentieth-century writers as Virginia Woolf, James Joyce, and William Faulkner.

IMPORTANT QUOTATIONS EXPLAINED

1. *If a physician of high standing, and one's own husband, assures friends and relatives that there is really nothing the matter with one but temporary nervous depression—a slight hysterical tendency—what is one to do? . . .*
    So I take phosphates or phosphites—whichever it is, and tonics, and journeys, and air, and exercise, and am absolutely forbidden to "work" until I am well again.
    Personally, I disagree with their ideas . . .

This passage, which appears near the beginning of the story, introduces the main elements of the narrator's dilemma. The powerful, authoritative voices of her husband, her family, and the medical establishment urge her to be passive. Her conviction, however, is that what she needs is precisely the opposite—activity and stimulation. From the outset, her opinions carry little weight. "Personally," she disagrees with her treatment but has no power to change the situation. Gilman also begins to characterize the narrator here. The confusion over "phosphates or phosphites" is in character for someone who is not particularly interested in factual accuracy. And the choppy rhythm of the sentences, often broken into one-line paragraphs, helps evoke the narrator's hurried writing in her secret journal as well as the agitated state of her mind.

2. *I sometimes fancy that in my condition if I had less opposition and more society and stimulus—but John says the very worst thing I can do is think about my condition, and I confess it always makes me feel bad. So I will let it alone and talk about the house.*

This excerpt appears near the beginning of the story and helps characterize both the narrator's dilemma and the narrator herself. Notably, the narrator interrupts her own train of thought by recalling John's instructions. Gilman shows how the narrator has internalized her husband's authority to the point that she practically hears his voice in her head, telling her what to think. Even so, she cannot help but feel the way she does, so the move she makes at the end—focusing on the house instead of her situation—marks the beginning of her slide into obsession and madness. This mental struggle, this desperate attempt not to think about her unhappiness, makes her project her feelings onto her surroundings, especially the wallpaper, which becomes a symbolic image of "her condition." The play on words here is typical of Gilman's consistent use of irony throughout the story. She feels bad whenever she thinks about her "condition"—that is, about both her depression and her condition in general within her oppressive marriage.

3. *I don't like to* look *out of the windows even — there are so many of those creeping women, and they creep so fast. I wonder if they all come out of that wall-paper as I did?*

In the story's final scene, just before John finally breaks into her room, the narrator has finished tearing off enough of the wallpaper so that the woman she saw inside is now free — and the two women have become one. This passage is the exact moment of full identification, when the narrator finally makes the connection that she has been avoiding, a connection that the reader has made already. The woman behind the pattern was an image of herself — she has been the one "stooping and creeping." Further, she knows that there are many women just like her, so many that she is afraid to look at them. The questions she asks is poignant and complex: Did they all have to struggle the way I did? Were they trapped within homes that were really prisons? Did they all have to tear their lives up at the roots to be free? The narrator, unable to answer these questions, leaves them for another woman — or the reader — to ponder.

Young Goodman Brown

Nathaniel Hawthorne
(1804–1864)

CONTEXT

Nathaniel Hawthorne was born in 1804 in Salem, Massachusetts, and raised by a widowed mother. His ancestors were some of the earliest settlers of the Massachusetts Bay Colony. John Hathorne (the original spelling of the family name), one of his great-grandfathers, had served as a judge at the Salem witch trials of 1692 and condemned twenty-five women to death. Hawthorne felt both fascination with and shame for his family's complicity in the witch trials and incorporated those feelings into his fiction, much of which explores the social history of New England and the Puritans.

Hawthorne attended Bowdoin College in Maine, where he met Henry Wadsworth Longfellow, who would go on to become a famous poet, and Franklin Pierce, who would become president of the United States. After college, he also met several other important New England writers of the early nineteenth century, including Ralph Waldo Emerson, Herman Melville, and Henry David Thoreau. Melville dedicated his masterpiece *Moby-Dick* (1851) to Hawthorne in appreciation for the help Hawthorne gave him in writing it. Emerson and Thoreau were active in transcendentalism, a religious and philosophical movement of the early nineteenth century that was dedicated to the belief that divinity manifests itself everywhere, particularly in the natural world. It also advocated a personalized, direct relationship with the divine in place of formalized, structured religion. Hawthorne incorporated many elements of transcendentalism into his writing, including the belief in free will as opposed to divine intervention. In 1842, he married a fellow transcendentalist, Sophia Peabody.

Hawthorne held a variety of jobs after college, including editor and customs surveyor, while he began developing his writing. Hawthorne first published "Young Goodman Brown" anonymously in *New England* magazine in 1835 and again under his own name in his short-story collection *Mosses from an Old Manse* in 1846. Like most of the stories in *Mosses*, "Young Goodman Brown" examines Hawthorne's favorite themes: the loss of religious faith, presence of temptation, and social ills of Puritan communities. These themes, along with the story's dark, surreal ending, make "Young Goodman Brown" one of the Hawthorne's most popular short stories. The story is often seen as a precursor to the novels Hawthorne wrote later in his life, including *The Scarlet Letter* (1850), *The House of the Seven Gables* (1851), *The Blithedale Romance* (1852), and *The Marble Faun* (1860).

In 1853, Pierce, Hawthorne's college friend, became president and appointed Hawthorne a United States consul. Hawthorne moved to Europe for six years and died in 1864, shortly after returning to America.

PLOT OVERVIEW

Goodman Brown says goodbye to his wife, Faith, outside of his house in Salem Village. Faith, wearing pink ribbons in her cap, asks him to stay with her, saying that she feels scared when she is by herself and free to think troubling thoughts. Goodman Brown tells her that he must travel for one night only and reminds her to say her prayers and go to bed early. He reassures her that if she does this, she will come to no harm. Goodman Brown takes final leave of Faith, thinking to himself that she might have guessed the evil purpose of his trip and promising to be a better person after this one night.

Goodman Brown sets off on a road through a gloomy forest. He looks around, afraid of what might be behind each tree, thinking that there might be Indians or the devil himself lurking there. He soon comes upon a man in the road who greets Goodman Brown as though he had been expecting him. The man is dressed in regular clothing and looks normal except for a walking stick he carries. This walking stick features a carved serpent, which is so lifelike it seems to move.

The man offers Goodman Brown the staff, saying that it might help him walk faster, but Goodman Brown refuses. He says that he showed up for their meeting because he promised to do so but does not wish to touch the staff and wants to return to the village. Goodman Brown tells the man that his family members have been Christians and good people for generations and that he feels ashamed to associate with him. The man replies that he knew Goodman Brown's father and grandfather, as well as other members of churches in New England, and even the governor of the state.

The man's words confuse Goodman Brown, who says that even if this is so, he wants to return to the village for Faith's sake. At that moment, the two come upon an old woman hobbling through the woods, and Goodman Brown recognizes Goody Cloyse, who he knows to be a pious, respected woman from the village. He hides, embarrassed to be seen with the man, and the man taps Goody Cloyse on the shoulder. She identifies him as the devil and reveals herself to be a witch, on her way to the devil's evil forest ceremony.

Despite this revelation, Goodman Brown tells the man that he still intends to turn back, for Faith's sake. The man says that Goodman Brown should rest. Before disappearing, he gives Goodman Brown his staff, telling him that he can use it for transport to the ceremony if he changes his mind. As he sits and gathers himself, Goodman Brown hears horses traveling along the road and hides once again.

Soon he hears the voices of the minister of the church and Deacon Gookin, who are also apparently on their way to the ceremony. Shocked, Goodman Brown swears that even though everyone else in the world has gone to the devil, for Faith's sake he will stay true to God. However, he soon hears voices coming from the ceremony and thinks he recognizes Faith's voice. He screams her name, and a pink ribbon from her cap flutters down from the sky.

Certain that there is no good in the world because Faith has turned to evil, Goodman Brown grabs the staff, which pulls him quickly through the forest toward the ceremony. When he reaches the clearing where the ceremony is taking place, the trees around it are on fire, and he can see in the firelight the faces of various respected members of the community, along with more disreputable men and women and Indian priests. But he doesn't see Faith, and he starts to hope once again that she might not be there.

A figure appears on a rock and tells the congregation to present the converts. Goodman Brown thinks he sees his father beckoning him forward and his mother trying to hold him back. Before he can rethink his decision, the minister and Deacon Gookin drag him forward. Goody Cloyse and Martha Carrier bring forth another person, robed and covered so that her identity is unknown. After telling the two that they have made a decision that will reveal all the wickedness of the world to them, the figure tells them to show themselves to each other. Goodman Brown sees that the other convert is Faith. Goodman Brown tells Faith to look up to heaven and resist the devil, then suddenly finds himself alone in the forest.

The next morning Goodman Brown returns to Salem Village, and every person he passes seems evil to him. He sees the minister, who blesses him, and hears Deacon Gookin praying, but he refuses to accept the blessing and calls Deacon Gookin a wizard. He sees Goody Cloyse quizzing a young girl on Bible verses and snatches the girl away. Finally, he sees Faith at his own house and refuses to greet her. It's unclear whether the encounter in the forest was a dream, but for the rest of his life, Goodman Brown is changed. He doesn't trust anyone in his village, can't believe the words of the minister, and doesn't fully love his wife. He lives the remainder of his life in gloom and fear.

CHARACTER LIST

Goodman Brown   A young resident of Salem and the story's protagonist. Goodman Brown is a good Christian who has recently married Faith. He takes pride in his family's history of piety and their reputation in the community as godly men. His curiosity, however, leads him to accept an invitation from a mysterious traveler to observe an evil ceremony in middle of the forest, one that shocks and disillusions him.

Faith   Goodman Brown's wife. Faith is young, beautiful, and trusting, and Goodman Brown sees her as the embodiment of virtue. Although Goodman Brown initially ignores Faith's claims to have had disturbing nightmares, seeing her at the evil ceremony in the forest prompts him to question his wife's righteousness.

The Old Man/Devil   The man, possibly the devil, who tempts Goodman Brown into attending the ceremony in the forest. The man intercepts Goodman Brown in the middle of the dark road, then presides over the ceremony. He sees through the Salem villagers' charade of Christian piety and prides himself on the godly men he has been able to turn to evil.

Goody Cloyse   A citizen of Salem Village who reveals herself to be a witch. Goody Cloyse is a Christian woman who helps young people learn the Bible, but in secret she performs magic ceremonies and attends witch meetings in the forest. Goody Cloyse was the name of an actual woman who was tried and convicted of witchcraft during the historical Salem Witch Trials of 1692; Hawthorne borrows her name for this character.

The Minister   The minister of Salem. The minister, a respectable pillar of the community, appears to be a follower of the devil.

Deacon Gookin   A member of the clergy in Salem who appears to be a follower of the devil. The deacon is an important man in the church of Salem, and Goodman Brown thinks of him as very religious.

ANALYSIS OF MAJOR CHARACTERS

GOODMAN BROWN   Goodman Brown shows both innocence and corruptibility as he vacillates between believing in the inherent goodness of the people around him and believing that the devil has taken over the minds of all the people he loves. At the beginning of the story, Goodman Brown believes in the goodness of his father and grandfather, until the old man, likely the devil, tells him that he knew them both. Goodman Brown believes in the Christian nature of Goody Cloyse, the minister, and Deacon Gookin, until the devil shows him that Goody Cloyse is a witch and the other two are his followers. Finally, he believes that Faith is pure and good, until the devil reveals at the ceremony that Faith, too, is corruptible. This vacillation reveals Goodman Brown's lack of true religion—his belief is easy to shake—as well as of the good and evil sides of human nature.

Through Goodman Brown's awakening to the evil nature of those around him, Hawthorne comments on what he sees as the hidden corruption of Puritan society. Goodman Brown believes in the public professions of faith made by his father and the elders of his church and in the societal structures that are built upon that faith. Hawthorne suggests, however, that behind the public face of godliness, the Puritans' actions were not always Christian. The devil in the story says that he was present when Brown's father and grandfather whipped Quakers and set fire to Indian villages, making it clear that the story of the founding of New England has a dark side that religion fails to explain. The very fact that Goodman Brown is willing to visit the forest when he has an idea of what will happen there is an indication of the corruptibility and evil at the heart of even the most faithful Puritan.

FAITH   Faith represents the stability of the home and the domestic sphere in the Puritan worldview. Faith, as her name suggests, appears to be the most pure-hearted person in the story and serves as a stand-in of sorts for all religious feeling. Goodman Brown clings to her when he questions the goodness of the people around him, assuring himself that if Faith remains godly, then his own faith is worth fighting temptation to maintain. When he sees that Faith has been corrupted, he believes in the absolute evil at the heart of man. His estrangement from Faith at the end of the story is the worst consequence of his change of heart. If he is able to be suspicious of Faith, Hawthorne suggests, then he has truly become estranged from the goodness of God.

THE OLD MAN/DEVIL   In "Young Goodman Brown," the devil appears to be an ordinary man, which suggests that every person, including Goodman Brown, has the capacity for evil. When the devil appears to Goodman Brown in the forest, he wears decent clothes and appears to be like any other man in Salem Village, but Goodman Brown learns that the devil can appear in any context and not appear out of place. By emphasizing the devil's chameleon nature, Hawthorne suggests that the devil is simply an embodiment of all of the worst parts of man. By saying that the devil looks as though he could be Goodman Brown's father, Hawthorne creates a link between them, raising the questions of whether the devil and Goodman Brown might be related or the devil might be an embodiment of Goodman Brown's dark side. Later in the story, Goodman Brown, flying along with the devil's staff on his way to the ceremony, appears to be a much more frightening apparition than any devil could be by himself. Although it is never fully clear whether the old man and Goodman Brown's experiences in the forest were a dream or reality, the consequences of Goodman Brown's interaction with the old man stay with him for the rest of his life.

THEMES, MOTIFS, AND SYMBOLS

THEMES

THE WEAKNESS OF PUBLIC MORALITY In "Young Goodman Brown," Hawthorne reveals what he sees as the corruptibility that results from Puritan society's emphasis on public morality, which often weakens private religious faith. Although Goodman Brown has decided to come into the forest and meet with the devil, he still hides when he sees Goody Cloyse and hears the minister and Deacon Gookin. He seems more concerned with how his faith appears to other people than with the fact that he has decided to meet with the devil. Goodman Brown's religious convictions are rooted in his belief that those around him are also religious. This kind of faith, which depends so much on other people's views, is easily weakened. When Goodman Brown discovers that his father, grandfather, Goody Cloyse, the minister, Deacon Gookin, and Faith are all in league with the devil, Goodman Brown quickly decides that he might as well do the same. Hawthorne seems to suggest that the danger of basing a society on moral principles and religious faith lies in the fact that members of the society do not arrive at their own moral decisions. When they copy the beliefs of the people around them, their faith becomes weak and rootless.

THE INEVITABLE LOSS OF INNOCENCE Goodman Brown loses his innocence because of his inherent corruptibility, which suggests that whether the events in the forest were a dream or reality, the loss of his innocence was inevitable. Instead of being corrupted by some outside force, Goodman Brown makes a personal choice to go into the forest and meet with the devil; the choice was the true danger, and the devil only facilitates Goodman Brown's fall. Goodman Brown is never certain whether the evil events of the night are real, but it does not matter. If they are a dream, then they come completely from Goodman Brown's head—a clear indication of his inherent dark side. If they are real, then Goodman Brown has truly seen that everyone around him is corrupt, and he brought this realization upon himself through his excessive curiosity. Goodman Brown's loss of innocence was inevitable, whether the events of the night were real or a dream.

THE FEAR OF THE WILDERNESS From the moment he steps into the forest, Goodman Brown voices his fear of the wilderness, seeing the forest as a place where no good is possible. In this he echoes the dominant point of view of seventeenth-century Puritans, who believed that the wild New World was something to fear and then dominate. Goodman Brown, like other Puritans, associates the forest with the wild "Indians" and sees one hiding behind every tree. He believes that the devil could easily be present in such a place—and he eventually sees the devil himself, just as he had expected. He considers it a matter of family honor that his forefathers would never have walked in the forest for pleasure, and he is upset when the devil tells him that this was not the case. He himself is ashamed to be seen walking in the forest and hides when Goody Cloyse, the minister, and Deacon Gookin pass. The forest is characterized as devilish, frightening, and dark, and Goodman Brown is comfortable in it only after he has given in to evil.

MOTIFS

FEMALE PURITY   Female purity, a favorite concept of Americans in the nineteenth century, is the steadying force for Goodman Brown as he wonders whether to renounce his religion and join the devil. When he takes leave of Faith at the beginning of the story, he swears that after this one night of evildoing, he will hold onto her skirts and ascend to heaven. This idea, that a man's wife or mother will redeem him and do the work of true religious belief for the whole family, was popular during Hawthorne's time. Goodman Brown clings to the idea of Faith's purity throughout his trials in the forest, swearing that as long as Faith remains holy, he can find it in himself to resist the devil. When Goodman Brown finds that Faith is present at the ceremony, it changes all his ideas about what is good or bad in the world, taking away his strength and ability to resist. Female purity was such a powerful idea in Puritan New England that men relied on women's faith to shore up their own. When even Faith's purity dissolves, Goodman Brown loses any chance to resist the devil and redeem his faith.

SYMBOLS

THE STAFF   The devil's staff, which is encircled by a carved serpent, draws from the biblical symbol of the serpent as an evil demon. In the Book of Genesis, the serpent tempts Eve to taste the fruit from the forbidden tree, defying God's will and bringing his wrath upon humanity. When the devil tells Goodman Brown to use the staff to travel faster, Goodman Brown takes him up on the offer and, like Eve, is ultimately condemned for his weakness by losing his innocence. Besides representing Eve's temptation, the serpent represents her curiosity, which leads her into that temptation. Goodman Brown's decision to come into the forest is motivated by curiosity, as was Eve's decision to eat the forbidden fruit. The staff makes clear that the old man is more demon than human and that Goodman Brown, when he takes the staff for himself, is on the path toward evil as well.

FAITH'S PINK RIBBONS   The pink ribbons that Faith puts in her cap represent her purity. The color pink is associated with innocence and gaiety, and ribbons themselves are a modest, innocent decoration. Hawthorne mentions Faith's pink ribbons several times at the beginning of the story, imbuing her character with youthfulness and happiness. He reintroduces the ribbons when Goodman Brown is in the forest, struggling with his doubts about the goodness of the people he knows. When the pink ribbon flutters down from the sky, Goodman Brown perceives it as a sign that Faith has definitely fallen into the realm of the devil—she has shed this sign of her purity and innocence. At the end of the story, when Faith greets Goodman Brown as he returns from the forest, she is wearing her pink ribbons again, suggesting her return to the figure of innocence she presented at the beginning of the story and casting doubts on the veracity of Goodman Brown's experiences.

SHORT STORY ANALYSIS

HISTORICAL CONTEXT   In "Young Goodman Brown," Hawthorne references three dark events from the Puritans' history: the Salem Witch Trials of 1692, the Puritan intolerance of the Quakers, and King Philip's War. During the Salem Witch Trials, one of the most nightmarish episodes in Puritan history, the villagers of Salem killed twenty-five innocent people who were accused of being witches. The witch hunts often involved accusations based on revenge, jealousy, botched child delivery, and other reasons that had little to do with perceived witchcraft. The Puritan intolerance of Quakers occurred during the second half of the seventeenth century. Puritans and Quakers both settled in America, hoping to find religious freedom and start their own colonies where they could believe what they wanted to. However, Puritans began forbidding Quakers from settling in their towns and made it illegal to be a Quaker; their intolerance soon led to imprisonments and hangings. King Philip's War, the final event referenced in Hawthorne's story, took place from 1675 to 1676 and was actually a series of small skirmishes between Indians and colonists. Indians attacked colonists at frontier towns in western Massachusetts, and colonists retaliated by raiding Indian villages. When the colonists won the war, the balance of power in the colonies finally tipped completely toward the Puritans.

These historical events are not at the center of "Young Goodman Brown," which takes place after they occur, but they do inform the action. For example, Hawthorne appropriates the names of Goody Cloyse and Martha Carrier, two of the "witches" killed at Salem, for townspeople in his story. The devil refers to seeing Goodman Brown's grandfather whipping a Quaker in the streets and handing Goodman Brown's father a flaming torch so that he could set fire to an Indian village during King Philip's War. By including these references, Hawthorne reminds the reader of the dubious history of Salem Village and the legacy of the Puritans and emphasizes the historical roots of Goodman Brown's fascination with the devil and the dark side.

THE DARK ROMANTICS In the nineteenth century, American writers, including Nathaniel Hawthorne, were influenced by the European Romantic movement but added their own nationalistic twist. The most famous European Romantics included William Wordsworth, Samuel Taylor Coleridge, and William Blake. The characteristics of the movement, which began in Germany at the beginning of the eighteenth century, included an interest in the power of the individual; an obsession with extreme experiences, including fear, love, and horror; an interest in nature and natural landscapes; and an emphasis on the importance of everyday events. Some writers in America who drew from the Romantic tradition were James Fenimore Cooper, Washington Irving, and the transcendentalists Henry David Thoreau and Ralph Waldo Emerson. American Romantics in the early nineteenth century tended to celebrate the American landscape and emphasize the idea of the sublime, which glorified their beautiful home country. They also created the concept of an American Romantic hero, who often lived alone in the wilderness, close to the land, such as Cooper's Leatherstocking or Thoreau himself at Walden Pond.

"Young Goodman Brown" fits into a subgenre of American Romanticism: the gothic or dark romance. Novels and stories of this type feature vivid descriptions of morbid or gloomy events, coupled with emotional or psychological torment. The dark Romantics joined the Romantic movement's emphasis on emotion and extremity with a gothic sensibility, hoping to create stories that would move readers to fear and question their surroundings. Edgar Allen Poe, who wrote "The Fall of the House of Usher" (1839) and "The Tell-Tale Heart" (1843), was probably the most famous of the writers to work in the American dark Romantic genre. Goodman Brown's encounter with the devil and battle with the evil within himself are both classic elements of a dark Romance.

THE FALL OF MAN "Young Goodman Brown" functions as an allegory of the fall of man, from which Hawthorne draws to illustrate what he sees as the inherent fallibility and hypocrisy in American religion. Hawthorne sets up a story of a man who is tempted by the devil and succumbs because of his curiosity and the weakness of his faith. Like Eve in the book of Genesis, Goodman Brown cannot help himself from wanting to know what lies behind the mystery of the forest. And like Eve, Goodman Brown is rewarded for his curiosity with information that changes his life for the worse. In the course of the ceremony in the forest, the devil tells Goodman Brown and Faith that their eyes will now be opened to the wickedness of themselves and those around them. Adam and Eve were exiled from the Garden of Eden and forced to undergo all the trials and tribulations of being human, and Goodman Brown returns from the forest to find that the joy in life has been taken away from him. He has become suspicious of those around him, even the woman he once loved.

IMPORTANT QUOTATIONS EXPLAINED

1. *On he flew among the black pines, brandishing his staff with frenzied gestures, now giving vent to an inspiration of horrid blasphemy, and now shouting forth such laughter as set all the echoes of the forest laughing like demons around him. The fiend in his own shape is less hideous than when he rages in the breast of man.*

This passage, in which Goodman Brown gives up on trying to resist the devil's temptations, takes up the devil's staff, and makes his way toward the ceremony, appears about a third of the way into the story. It suggests that some of the shame and horror Goodman Brown feels when he returns to Salem Village may come from his feeling of weakness at having succumbed to evil. Goodman Brown resists the devil while he still believes that various members of his family and community are godly, but when he is shown, one by one, that they are all servants of the devil, he gives in to his dark side completely and grabs the devil's staff. The change that comes over him after either waking up from his dream or returning from the ceremony can be explained partially by his shame at having fallen so quickly and dramatically into evil.

2. *But, irreverently consorting with these grave, reputable, and pious people, these elders of the church, these chaste dames and dewy virgins, there were men of dissolute lives and women of spotted fame, wretches given over to all mean and filthy vice, and suspected even of horrid crimes. It was strange to see that the good shrank not from the wicked, nor were the sinners abashed by the saints.*

In this passage, which appears halfway through the story, Goodman Brown sees the ceremony and the dark side of Salem Village. The transgression of social boundaries is one of the most confusing and upsetting aspects of the ceremony. The Puritans had made a society that was very much based on morality and religion, in which status came from having a high standing in the church and a high moral reputation among other townspeople. When Goodman Brown tells the devil at the beginning of the story that he is proud of his father and grandfather's high morals and religious convictions, he is describing how the society in which he lives values these traits above all others. When Goodman Brown sees the mingling of these two different types of people at the ceremony, he is horrified: the ceremony reveals the breakdown of the social order, which he believed was ironclad. Hawthorne is pointing out the hypocrisy of a society that prides itself on its moral standing and makes outcasts of people who do not live up to its standards.

---

3. *"By the sympathy of your human hearts for sin ye shall scent out all the places—whether in church, bedchamber, street, field, or forest—where crime has been committed, and shall exult to behold the whole earth one stain of guilt, one mighty blood spot."*

Near the end of the story, the devil promises Goodman Brown and Faith that they'll have a new outlook on life, one that emphasizes the sinning nature of all humanity, and condemns Goodman Brown to a life of fear and outrage at the doings of his fellow man. This dark view of life is a complete turnaround from the ideas that Goodman Brown had held at the beginning of the story. Then, he thought of his family as godly; Faith as perfectly pure; and the Reverend, Deacon, and Goody Cloyse as models of morality. The devil ultimately shows him that his views are naïve and gives him the ability to see the dark side in any human context. When Goodman Brown returns to the village, he trusts no one. As the devil's speech suggests, Goodman Brown has seen the evil in every human, and once he has started seeing it, he cannot stop.

A+ Student Essays

1. In what ways do Richard Wright's "The Man Who Was Almost a Man" and Alice Walker's "Everyday Use" reflect and comment on the black American experience and the struggle for greater equality and civil rights?

The main characters in "The Man Who Was Almost a Man" and "Everyday Use" each represent a different facet of the black American experience and struggle for greater equality, recognition, and inclusion. Wright's protagonist, Dave, and the three women who reunite in Walker's story all face personal conflicts. Their struggles for independence, connection, and a greater understanding of the past are separate from their historical context of slavery, segregation, and second-class status, but they are not entirely free of that context. The eradication of slavery triggered more than a century of struggle and progress on the part of former slaves and the succeeding generations, as they strived to achieve equality and greater economic power and establish their voice as a viable presence in American society. The characters in these two stories are clearly emblems of their times.

In "The Man Who . . . ," Dave is a typical teenager, restless and unhappy with his lack of economic and personal power. He longs for the freedom to make his own decisions and be the master of his own fate. When Dave acquires a gun and accidentally shoots a mule, he looks to his future and sees nothing but toil and poverty, with no hope for escape. His hasty decision to board the train and head to the presumed paradise of life in the North is his renunciation of what are to him unacceptable conditions. Although on one level Dave's flight is the act of an individual desperate to assert his independence and maturity, on another, it gestures to the more general social unrest of the time, specifically the mass exodus of black Americans attempting to sever their ties with an oppressive sharecropping system and the poverty that came with it. Dave's conclusive gesture of running away represents a powerful rejection of this dehumanizing system, mirroring the similar journey made by countless waves of blacks, many former slaves or the children of former slaves as they headed to the industrial centers of the North in search of greater economic opportunity.

In "Everyday Use," Dee expresses her racial identity differently—rather than trying to flee her past to establish a new life, she attempts to swallow it whole. She has adopted the African name Wangero Leewanika Kemanjo, an identity she believes connects her more deeply to her African past. By looking to the continent of her ancestors for inspiration, however, her sudden embrace of her African roots blinds her to the living heritage inherent in the family heirlooms that she sees only as quaint reminders of a bygone era. Her ancestors lived in a world much like Dave's, living off the land and scraping by through strenuous labor and the survival skills passed on from generation to generation. It is a proud tradition that Dee cannot understand or appreciate. The personal rivalries that divide Dee from her mother and sister take on a larger social meaning in this story, because the characters represent two particular facets of black life in the late 1960s and early 1970s. The respective camps—the radical and politicized Dee and the more passive, accepting Maggie and Mama—reflect differences in ideology and awareness that divided the black community in its attempt to seize its rightful place in American history and society.

2. Compare and contrast the protagonists' experience of adolescence in "Where Are You Going, Where Have You Been?" by Joyce Carol Oates and "A&P" by John Updike.

The protagonists of Joyce Carol Oates's "Where Are You Going, Where Have You Been?" and John Updike's "A&P," Connie and Sammy, respectively, are both teenagers in the midst of naïve adolescence who come face to face with an incident that pushes them dramatically into adulthood. For Connie, the incident is a threat to her personal safety; for Sammy, it is a confrontation with authority. In both cases, each teenager is given a sudden push into adult life, with very different consequences.

At the beginning of "A&P" and "Where Are You Going . . . ," Sammy and Connie are average teenagers taking part in unremarkable activities. Sammy works a summer job at a local grocery store, and Connie spends time with her friends without adult supervision. Although these activities are common for teenagers, both Sammy and Connie find the activities liberating. Sammy feels like an adult because he is on equal footing with Stokesie, his twenty-two-year-old coworker, who is "married, with two babies" and has already passed from adolescence into adulthood. Connie, likewise, is constantly annoyed by her mother's criticisms but experiences "the pure pleasure of being alive" when she is hanging out with the boy she likes named Eddie—a time when she is completely independent and does not have to answer to any adults.

The perceived maturity that Connie and Sammy get from their activities is enhanced by the fact that both experience a type of sexual awakening. Sammy's attraction to the three bikini-clad girls who enter the A&P grocery store and the fact that he shares this attraction with Stokesie allow him to see himself as Stokesie's peer and consequently as an adult. When the bikini-clad girls enter the store, Sammy states that Stokesie's family-man status is "the only difference" between them. Similarly, it is Connie's stolen time at the drive-in restaurant "where the older kids hang out" that inspires in her the resolution that "she was pretty and that was everything." At the drive-in, because more than one boy approaches her, Connie feels more mature than even her plain older sister, June.

This budding sexuality and a growing awareness of it offer Sammy and Connie their first feelings of adult empowerment. When Sammy witnesses his manager, Mr. Lengel, speak rudely to the bikini-clad girls, he quits on the spot, partly because he's offended by the manager's attitude and partly because he wants to impress the girls. This response is both irresponsible and independent, immature and mature. His actions have placed him in a precarious situation, and he understands that the world may not always treat him kindly. But most important, he finds power in his actions: the power to act on his beliefs. Connie also begins to feel independent and strong because of her activities away from adult supervision, but her independence leads to truly dangerous consequences. When she opts to stay home alone while her parents go to a barbecue, she is confronted with the aggressive advances of a threatening figure whom she may have seen at the drive-in. Because Connie is aware of her sexuality but not yet mature enough to understand its power, she becomes a victim of this man's aggression and is plunged violently into adulthood. The ambiguous ending of the story suggests that her entry into adulthood may in fact mark the end of her life.

3.   Explain the effect of magical realism in "A Very Old Man
     with Enormous Wings" by Gabriel García Márquez and
     "Super-Frog Saves Tokyo" by Haruki Murakami.

In both "A Very Old Man with Enormous Wings" by Gabriel García Márquez
and "Super-Frog Saves Tokyo" by Haruki Murakami, a supernatural stranger
arrives in a realistic world whose inhabitants struggle to make sense of the
newcomer. The magical creatures remain mysteries, as neither story clearly
explains the strangers' true natures. Although both stories end on an ambiguous note, Murakami's story provides an emotional satisfaction that García
Márquez's intentionally avoids.

    In both stories, characters try to evaluate the creatures by using logical
analysis. At their first meeting, Frog tells Katagiri that he is "a real frog" and
proves it by croaking. Frog looks and sounds like a frog, and Katagiri's powers
of observation and analysis confirm that the creature fits into the category of
"frog," despite the fact that Frog can shrink and disappear at will, speak, and
battle with deadly subterranean worms. Father Gonzaga attempts to apply
a similar test of logic, with the opposite outcome. When the townspeople attempt to discern whether the old man is "a flesh-and-blood angel," he argues
that "if wings were not the essential element in determining the difference
between a hawk and an airplane, they were even less so in the recognition of
angels." Although the bedraggled old man may not look like anyone's notion of
an angel, he is undoubtedly otherworldly. In both stories, intellectual catego-
rization of the creatures seems incomplete, as characters struggle to reconcile observable facts with undeniable evidence of magic. The observers keep
collecting evidence about the strangers but grow no closer to determining
whether Frog is "a real frog" or the old man is "a real angel."

    The supernatural event remains mysterious and open-ended in both
stories, but the event becomes truly magical and transcendent only in the
Murakami story. In "A Very Old Man . . . ," the magic of the story seems pointless. We have no sense of why the old man has come to the village. He might
have been washed in by the sea or summoned by the sick child, but in the
end, he doesn't seem to effect any change, other than raising enough money
for Pelayo and Elisenda to build a fancy house. When he grows back his wings
and flies off, it seems to be a natural act, as if he were a bird that instinctively

knew to fly south for the winter. The old man has taught the villagers nothing. This may be a condemnation of the townspeople's inability to recognize magic when they see it, but in the end, the old man's appearance on earth is a wholly unsatisfying experience.

"Super-Frog," on the other hand, strongly suggests several reasons for Frog's presence in 1995 Tokyo, and because he seems to fulfill these tasks, the tale becomes emotionally satisfying. Frog has ostensibly come to battle Worm and save the city, a mission he completes. But there is also the sense that Frog has been summoned for Katagiri's benefit to bring a magical experience to the life of a humdrum, ignored, but entirely deserving human. Magic doesn't seem pointless in this story but rather seems to rectify situations that have been neglected by "real" existence. Finally, Frog serves a comforting role for readers. The stories in Murakami's collection *after the quake* take place during a fraught period of Japanese history, after the 1995 Kobe earthquake and before the gas attacks on the Tokyo subway, two events that were unfathomably destructive. Murakami's story suggests that there may have been equally unfathomable reasons behind them. If a massive earthquake could be caused by the spasms of a giant worm, perhaps there were similarly mythical reasons behind the other tragedies—reasons beyond our ability to understand. "Super-Frog" offers traumatized readers a measure of consolation by suggesting that somewhere, without our knowing it, there are magical creatures dedicated to our well-being.

4.   How is the notion of community developed in "A Rose for
      Emily" by William Faulkner and "The Lottery" by Shirley
      Jackson?

William Faulkner's "A Rose for Emily" and Shirley Jackson's "The Lottery,"
two classics of Southern Gothic literature, both depict quiet, conservative
towns whose genteel exteriors belie a grotesque secret, the nature of which
is revealed to the reader through a shocking surprise ending. Faulkner and
Jackson both depict communities with a highly developed collective identity
that is strengthened by the presence of a clearly marked outsider. The horror
the reader feels at the conclusion of "A Rose for Emily," however, is expressed
very differently from the horror stirred by "The Lottery," and that crucial difference ultimately determines the definition of community in each story.

The unnamed towns in these stories both foster strong bonds among the
inhabitants. In "The Lottery," ritual group activities—the lottery in particular, but also "the square dances, the teen club, [and] the Halloween program"—bond the townspeople by creating a series of collective social rhythms,
encouraging a sense of shared tradition. In the opening paragraphs, the village seems to move as a collective organism. The villagers filter into the town
square in specific subgroupings: first the children, who separate into boys and
girls; then the men; then the women. During the process of the lottery, we
learn how these strict communitywide rules dictate how individual members
are ranked within specific family units. The communal nature of life in this
town is highlighted by the fact that the entire story takes place in the town
square, the village's most public location.

In "A Rose for Emily," the distinction between public and private space also
helps create strong bonds among townspeople. Emily Grierson's grand house
is the ultimate private space, because virtually no one knows what happens
behind its closed doors. Faulkner makes it seem as if the entire town is trying
to peer into the shuttered windows, drawing them together in the process. He
heightens this feeling by having the townspeople narrate the story collective-
ly, as if the entire town shared a single consciousness.

In both stories, there is one person who stands outside the community,
whose separation strengthens the collective identity of the remaining townspeople. In Faulkner's story, the townspeople come together via their shared

feelings of fascination, pity, and eventually revulsion toward Miss Emily. Her imposing house provides a symbol they can rally around: it is a secret that none of them can crack, and they are all equally powerless before it. In Jackson's story, it is the outsider Tessie Hutchinson who is the powerless one. She becomes the scapegoat, an individual arbitrarily chosen to bear the burdens of the community. She must die, the tradition holds, so that the rest of the village can enjoy a good harvest and continued healthy existence. The village completes the ritual and asserts its collective strength by joining together to stone her to death, and we can see that group bonds even trump family bonds when little Davy Hutchinson accepts from a villager a handful of pebbles to cast at his mother.

In Faulkner's story, the town shares the reader's astonishment at the discovery that Miss Emily has been sleeping next to the corpse of her former lover, Homer Barron, for so many years. In Jackson's story, on the other hand, the entire community is revealed to be complicit in the grim ritual. Whereas our horror is reserved for a single, sick-minded woman in "A Rose for Emily," "The Lottery" proves far more chilling when we realize that the sickness is widespread and therefore much harder to deny or disavow. Community offers the promise of reprieve and comfort in Faulkner—we can withdraw back into society and be thankful that we don't share Emily's disease. Jackson's story, however, offers no such relief, as we become disgusted at the community itself and its ability to commit horrible crimes in the name of the greater good.

5.   Compare and contrast how Ernest Hemingway and Ray-
     mond Carver develop their characters through the use
     of dialogue in the stories "Hills Like White Elephants" and
     "What We Talk About When We Talk About Love."

Ernest Hemingway pioneered a minimalist prose style that profoundly influenced American fiction. Raymond Carver, in his story "What We Talk About
When We Talk About Love," utilizes the minimalist style Hemingway made
famous in such stories as "Hills Like White Elephants." Yet, even though both
stories rely heavily on the use of dialogue, Carver's characters are voluble and
expansive whereas Hemingway's characters are laconic, even cryptic. By the
end of both stories, however, we know just as much about Hemingway's characters and their future as we do about Carver's characters and theirs, despite
this extreme difference in length and the authors' use of dialogue.

"What We Talk About When We Talk About Love" is a story about storytelling, and Carver's characters talk at length about the meaning of love. To put
their various definitions in context, the characters provide specific examples,
turning much of the story into a fluid conversation. Mel, for example, tells the
story of an elderly man injured in an accident who was distraught because he
could no longer see his wife's face, and Terri talks about a former boyfriend
who threatened to kill her. The storytelling is explicit and the dialogue easily
understandable, even if the drunken characters never truly succeed in pin-
ning down an indisputable definition of love.

Hemingway's characters in "Hills Like White Elephants," on the other
hand, tell no stories and say little. In fact, much of their conversation is cryptic and seemingly unimportant if not nonsensical: they talk about the scenery,
touch on their history together, and order a lot of drinks. Worse, Hemingway
never even uses dialogue tags to clarify which character is speaking. The
result is slightly confusing, misleading many first-time readers to think the
story has no real point. Whereas we know exactly what Carver's characters
are talking about, it's possible to read "Hills Like White Elephants" for the first
time without ever realizing that the couple is debating whether the woman
should have an abortion.

Remarkably, however, we understand the personalities of Hemingway's
characters just as precisely as we understand those of Carver's, despite the

fact that "Hills Like White Elephants" is only half the length of "What We Talk About . . . " Because Carver's dialogue is so straightforward, his characters' personalities are easily distinguishable. Mel's frustration with his ex-wife makes him cynical and somewhat of a skeptic, whereas Terri is more of a hopeless romantic. The narrator, Nick, meanwhile, seems to be more of a realist, knowing that love is too difficult to define in words and therefore preferring to hold his wife, Laura's, hand in silence. Hemingway manages to convey just as much characterization in fewer pages, however, by glossing over the surface and allowing us to read deeper into the characters on our own. The woman's wistful comments about the hills and her readiness to change her opinions suggest that she's torn and confused, whereas the man's terse remarks reveal him to be insensitive and unsympathetic. Their mutual fixation on alcohol also allows them to fill the awkward silences and thus becomes a major component of the story, despite the fact that it initially seems inconsequential. With tiny brushstrokes, Hemingway achieves the same effect as Carver with fewer than half of the words.

6.   To what extent is "The Yellow Wallpaper" a feminist story?

Charlotte Perkins Gilman's "The Yellow Wallpaper" is often characterized as a feminist tale, a vivid example of the disaster that can result when a smart woman is prevented from working and made a prisoner in her own home. But if Gilman's protagonist and narrator is clearly a victim of a misogynist world, she is at the same time, more subtly, a feminist in her own right. She may be a housewife under her husband's thumb, but her insistence on writing, sneaky attempts at enacting revenge, and madness itself make her a feminist character.

The narrator's refusal to stop writing is a striking act of independence. Her husband has the patriarchal conviction that it is inappropriate for women to work and furthermore that physical and mental harm may come from working. When he forbids his wife from writing, he forbids her from doing what she enjoys and values. The fact that the narrator continues to write, taking great pains to hide her work from John and his sister, Jennie, shows grit and strong character. The narrator says, "I *must* say what I feel and think in some way—it is such a relief!" The existence of the story itself, which takes the form of her secretive journal entries, is physical evidence of the narrator's rebelliousness.

The narrator's descent into madness, meanwhile, is self-destructive but also satisfyingly vengeful. Her husband has refused her every request, from sleeping in a different room, to being allowed to write, to leaving the cottage a little early. He has further refused to listen to her when she hints that her mind is deteriorating despite her physical improvement. By going mad, she proves that he was wrong to believe that the illness was simply hysteria, wrong to condescend to her, and wrong to refuse to listen to her. Her insanity hurts her the most, but it also hurts him, both by undermining his total confidence in himself and depriving him of the cheery housewife he wants. The narrator's spiral into madness also allows her to slip out of her husband's grasp. He has made her a physical prisoner in the house, but she manages to mentally escape by going insane. Gilman stresses this painful victory in the final lines of the story, in which the narrator says, "'I've got out at last . . . in spite of you and Jane. And I've pulled off most of the paper, so you can't put me back!'" The narrator is crazed as she speaks these lines, but she is also triumphant.

In the grip of madness, the narrator begins to forge a strong feminist identity. Paradoxically, it is when her hold on reality begins to loosen that she sees the world as it really is. As insanity grips her, the narrator looks at John and sees not a loving husband but a threatening, scary oppressor, and she decides it is necessary to deceive Jennie, who has been acting as her jailor. The metaphors she creates also demonstrate an accurate understanding of her situation. She envisions a woman caught behind the wallpaper who shakes the bars that fence her in. As time goes on, this woman becomes her twin, and eventually the narrator imagines that she has become the trapped woman. This progression suggests that, little by little, the narrator comes to understand that she is a captive. "The Yellow Wallpaper" is not an uplifting tale of a woman who manages to overcome oppression and misogyny. Nevertheless, its miserable and misunderstood protagonist displays an inspiring and fiery feminist spirit.

7. Compare and contrast the protagonists of D. H. Lawrence's "Odour of Chrysanthemums" and John Steinbeck's "The Chrysanthemums." What do their lives, and the portrayals of their lives, say about the problems faced by women in the early- to mid-twentieth century?

John Steinbeck's short story "The Chrysanthemums" pays homage to D. H. Lawrence's story "Odour of Chrysanthemums," and Steinbeck draws parallels between his story and Lawrence's. The similarities and differences between the lives of Lawrence's protagonist, Elizabeth, and Steinbeck's protagonist, Elisa, suggest that women suffer most not from contending with family problems or economic difficulties but simply from being forced to live life in misogynist societies.

Steinbeck echoes many aspects of Lawrence's story to underscore how little the world had changed for women between 1909, when Lawrence wrote his story, and 1938, when Steinbeck wrote his. Some of the similarities are simple, but striking. For example, the protagonist of Lawrence's story is named Elizabeth, a name quite similar to that of Elisa, Steinbeck's protagonist. Both stories begin with descriptions of claustrophobic landscapes that foreshadow the stormy and repressed emotional states of their main characters. Both stories also use chrysanthemums to symbolize these women and their unhappiness. Elisa's and Elizabeth's personalities are very similar too: both women are proud, attractive, and understimulated. They live in places and times where their talents are not appreciated or used. Moreover, both women exist only as wives, not individuals, and are defined by their relationship to men. By creating strong similarities to Lawrence's story in plot, structure, and character, Steinbeck points out how closely Elisa's restrictive, repressive society resembles Elizabeth's.

Steinbeck's protagonist has a much less difficult life than does Lawrence's, yet the two women suffer equally from the misogynistic sentiment that surrounds them. When "Odour of Chrysanthemums" begins, Elizabeth is mired in poverty, and when it ends, it seems clear that she will suffer even worse deprivations in the future. Her mother-in-law is an addle-brained, querulous woman. Her husband is an irresponsible drunk who dies during the course of the story, leaving Elizabeth with the burden of providing for their children.

In contrast, Elisa is childless, which means that she has fewer demands on her time. Her husband is a dense man, but also a kind one and good provider, and Elisa is financially comfortable. Yet despite the significant differences between Elizabeth's and Elisa's life, both women are equally unhappy, primarily because their societies allow them no scope to exercise their gifts. Because Elizabeth can never apply her intelligence, she'll never escape the poverty she lives in or achieve any kind of personal fulfillment. Elisa is a passionate woman who longs to see the world and discuss important ideas but is similarly confined to gardening and housekeeping.

The key differences between the two women highlight the tragedy of Elisa's life. The lack of melodrama in Elisa's life makes her situation both devastating for her and revealing for us. She cannot blame her misery on anything tangible, yet her misery is just as overwhelming as Elizabeth's. Steinbeck gives Elisa advantages that Elizabeth doesn't have and then shows us that these advantages mean nothing at all. He contends that deep unhappiness is not caused by poverty, betrayal, or death. Rather, Lawrence's and Steinbeck's stories suggest that no matter what their economic or family situations, women confined by archaic social standards will inevitably lead unhappy lives.

8. Ambrose Bierce's "An Occurrence at Owl Creek Bridge" and Tim O'Brien's "The Things They Carried" use misdirection and evasion as narrative techniques. Why? What do the writers accomplish with these techniques?

Ambrose Bierce's "An Occurrence at Owl Creek Bridge" and Tim O'Brien's "The Things They Carried" dance around the edges of their actual subjects. Both stories direct our attention to plotlines or details that turn out to be diversions from the true focus of the narratives. These diversions suggest Bierce's and O'Brien's belief that the truth, particularly the truth about war, cannot be conveyed by direct, straightforward accounts.

On first glance, both stories seem to be earnest war tales characterized by plain talking and direct narration. "An Occurrence at Owl Creek Bridge," which purports to be about a prisoner's escape from certain death, chronicles every physical pain and mental agony suffered by the prisoner, Peyton Farquhar. The narrator offers a minute account of Farquhar's actions and thoughts and a wealth of convincing details. "The Things They Carried" offers an insider's look at what American soldiers carried as they fought in Vietnam, from flak jackets and radios to photos and letters. The title itself underlines the supposedly listlike focus of O'Brien's story, and the details, like those in Bierce's story, convince us of the story's realism. Both stories provide a first layer that is almost stereotypically soldierly: masculine, restrained, and slightly sentimental. The stories' clear narrations, details that give us the sensation of being there with the soldiers, and tendency to impose order on war and war experiences by making lists all conspire to distract us and make us believe that this first layer is the one we should pay attention to, the one that captures the so-called reality of war.

Yet it is the second, less obvious layer that is more important in both stories. At the end of "An Occurrence at Owl Creek Bridge," we discover that all the events previously narrated happened in Farquhar's mind, rather than in reality. Bierce's aim is not simply to mislead. He is trying to accomplish something important by narrating not what happened, but what *didn't* happen. He is interested in exploring the psychology of a dying man and intends to capture the incredibly detailed thoughts, fantasies, desires, and fears that flash through his protagonist's mind in the seconds before he dies. His true subject is not Farquhar's death, but rather Farquhar's mental state in the moments before his death. Similarly, O'Brien's story is about far weightier subjects that the physical objects the men carry. The items carried are not important in and of themselves, but because they turn out to be ways of understanding the psychology of each man as an individual and of the men as a group. O'Brien's true subject is what war does to men. The things carried are simply his window into the way the soldiers deal with death, the fear of embarrassment that motivates all acts of bravery, the irrational guilt that plagues those in command, the thoughts of those at home that lift up the men and distract them from the task at hand, and the savage violence that they endure and inflict.

Both Bierce and O'Brien believe that the truth can be captured most accurately and fully not when it is tackled head-on but when it is approached obliquely. Their stories suggest a paradox: for O'Brien and Bierce, misdirection and even deception, rather than plain facts, are what enable us to understand the reality of soldiers' existences.

9. Discuss the role of horror in Nathaniel Hawthorne's "Young Goodman Brown" and Edgar Allen Poe's "The Tell-Tale Heart."

Both Hawthorne's "Young Goodman Brown" and Poe's "The Tell-Tale Heart" are notable for the atmosphere of terror and dread that pervades each story. The two stories use horror to highlight the viciousness inherent in the supposedly civilized world of everyday life. Hawthorne and Poe differ, however, in their understanding of the origins of the evil they recognize in the world.

"Young Goodman Brown" takes place in Salem, Massachusetts, infamous for its witch trials. By setting his story here, Hawthorne draws attention to how civilization occasionally tips over into madness. The fine line between order and chaos is reinforced by the fact that Goodman Brown steps from the streets of the town into the frightening darkness of the forest in almost a single moment. Brown himself recognizes that evil lurks just below the surface of everyday life, noting that murderous Indians or even the devil could be lurking unseen in the woods. The latter remark is deeply ironic, because the old man that Brown goes into the woods to meet quite obviously *is* the devil. The fact that the old man looks just like Brown's grandfather underscores Hawthorne's idea that the benign appearance of the world masks sinister and disturbing truths.

Poe's story also deals with the presence of evil in everyday life, although Poe explores this idea differently. In contrast to the precise setting of Hawthorne's story, "The Tell-Tale Heart" depicts an entirely generic situation: the nameless narrator says nothing about where he lives or what his relationship is to his victim. By setting his story in no particular place and giving his murderer no identity at all, Poe makes it universal—this horrible murder could be happening anywhere. Poe compounds the ordinariness of evil by having the murderer matter-of-factly describe how he killed the old man, cut up his body, and buried it in the floor. Although the narrator is somewhat frantic at the outset, insisting that he is not mad but just diseased, the fact that he knows that he needs a sane-sounding explanation for his crime shows that he is not irrational. Rather, he is simply an ordinary person who has committed a horrible deed.

Although both stories depict evil in the everyday world, Hawthorne's tale provides a complex explanation for the presence of evil, whereas Poe offers the potentially less comforting suggestion that ordinary evil has no explanation at all. As Goodman Brown travels through the woods, he meets people whom he believes to be upstanding citizens, only to learn that in the heart of each individual rests a sinister nature. Brown returns to his aptly named wife, Faith, but cannot embrace social life again because he is convinced that people are inherently evil, even though his adventure may have just been a dream. Hawthorne's story shows that evil comes into the world when we believe other people to be evil, even though we might be right in our beliefs. Thinking people to be evil is, in and of itself, evil. Poe, on the other hand, offers no explanation for evil. Poe's narrator claims that his heightened sense of hearing allowed him to hear things in heaven and hell, which sounds like a potential explanation for (or sign of) his madness, but then claims that the look of the old man's eye is what drove him to murder. The disconnection between the senses of hearing and sight acts a reminder of the futility of seeking causal explanations for the horror inherent in everyday life. For Poe, the question of what causes evil is unanswerable—it is enough merely to recognize that irrational evil is a central part of human life.

10. Discuss the use of symbols in Raymond Carver's "Cathedral" and Annie Proulx's "Brokeback Mountain." How do the symbols demonstrate the main characters' masculinity?

Raymond Carver's "Cathedral" and Annie Proulx's "Brokeback Mountain" challenge conventional notions of masculinity, and these challenges are reinforced by the symbols used in the stories.

As "Cathedral" begins, the narrator anxiously waits for the blind man, an old friend of the narrator's wife, to arrive. The narrator feels threatened by the blind man, even though he knows that his wife and the blind man are just friends. When he first sees Robert, the narrator, the narrator is shocked that the blind man has a beard, and throughout the story, the narrator describes Robert picking up his beard and sniffing it. He is similarly shocked to discover that Robert has been married, and the narrator wonders how Robert could be married to and have sex with someone he's never seen. The beard symbolizes Robert's masculine virility. He expected the blind man to be rendered incapacitated by his blindness, unable to be sexual or masculine. Later in the story, the narrator tries to explain to Robert what a cathedral looks like. Unable to articulate the structure's majestic beauty, the narrator must find another way to convey the meaning of the word *cathedral* to the blind man. Robert suggests that they draw it together, an intimate gesture that requires Robert to hold the narrator's hand as he draws the cathedral. In this way, the cathedral symbolizes the breakdown of the narrator's masculine posturing. As the narrator draws, he not only feels Robert's hand around his own, but he also shuts his eyes to simulate the experience of being blind. This experience teaches the narrator to recognize not only the masculinity in another being but also that person's fundamental humanity.

When Ennis del Mar and Jack Twist first meet in Proulx's "Brokeback Mountain," they display stereotypical masculine traits. Both have been raised as ranchers; both are "rough- mannered, rough-spoken, inured to the stoic life." On Brokeback Mountain, the two fall in love and begin a decades-long sexual relationship. Isolated from civilization, Ennis and Jack experience the opportunity to be who they truly are without being judged or condemned by society. At the end of the summer, they leave mountain and begin lives of marriage, fatherhood, and work. They meet occasionally, once or twice a year. As they age, these meetings are increasingly characterized by bitterness over what might have been, particularly for Jack. To Ennis and Jack who asks to have his ashes scattered there, the mountain symbolizes freedom, first love, and the life they were not able to live. After Jack's death, Ennis discovers that Jack had saved two shirts from that summer, carefully tucking Ennis's shirt inside his own. Ennis buys a postcard photo of Brokeback Mountain, which he hangs above his nesting shirts. The shirts symbolize the closeness of the two men, the deep soulful bond between them that they were unable to display in life. But the shirts and mountains also remind readers that the men's sexual orientation has rendered them no less masculine than they were at the beginning of the story. On the mountain, Ennis and Jack discovered a new part of their masculine selves, a part that lets them feel loved and give love in return.

By the end of "Cathedral," Carver's narrator has overcome his isolation and learned to accept other people as people. Similarly, by the end of "Brokeback Mountain," Proulx's main character, Ennis, has learned to accept parts of himself that might not fit with his ideas of how men should behave.

Appendix: Titles Listed by Author

Sherwood Anderson	A Death in the Woods
James Baldwin	Sonny's Blues
Ambrose Bierce	An Occurrence at Owl Creek Bridge
Raymond Carver	Cathedral
	What We Talk About When We Talk About Love
Willa Cather	Paul's Case: A Study in Temperament
John Cheever	The Swimmer
Anton Chekhov	The Lady with the Pet Dog
Kate Chopin	The Story of an Hour
Richard Connell	The Most Dangerous Game
Julio Cortázar	A Continuity of Parks
Stephen Crane	The Open Boat
Arthur Conan Doyle	The Red-Headed League
Deborah Eisenberg	Twilight of the Superheroes
William Faulkner	A Rose for Emily
	Barn Burning
F. Scott Fitzgerald	Babylon Revisited
	Winter Dreams
Charlotte Perkins Gilman	The Yellow Wallpaper
Nathaniel Hawthorne	The Birthmark
	Young Goodman Brown
Ernest Hemingway	A Clean, Well-Lighted Place
	Hills Like White Elephants
Shirley Jackson	The Lottery
W. W. Jacobs	The Monkey's Paw
James Joyce	Araby
	The Dead
Franz Kafka	A Hunger Artist
	The Metamorphosis
Jamaica Kincaid	Girl
Stephen King	Rita Hayworth and the Shawshank Redemption
Jhumpa Lahiri	Interpreter of Maladies
D. H. Lawrence	Odour of Chrysanthemums
Gabriel García Márquez	A Very Old Man with Enormous Wings
Bobbie Ann Mason	Shiloh
Guy de Maupassant	The Necklace
Herman Melville	Bartleby the Scrivener
Haruki Murakami	Super-Frog Saves Tokyo
Joyce Carol Oates	Where Are You Going, Where Have You Been?

Tim O'Brien	The Things They Carried
Flannery O'Connor	A Good Man Is Hard to Find
	Everything That Rises Must Converge
Tillie Olsen	I Stand Here Ironing
Edgar Allen Poe	The Fall of the House of Usher
	The Tell-Tale Heart
Katherine Anne Porter	The Jilting of Granny Weatherall
Annie Proulx	Brokeback Mountain
J. D. Salinger	A Perfect Day for Bananafish
John Steinbeck	The Chrysanthemums
Leo Tolstoy	The Death of Ivan Ilych
John Updike	A & P
Kurt Vonnegut	Harrison Bergeron
Alice Walker	Everyday Use
Eudora Welty	Why I Live at the P. O.
Richard Wright	The Man Who Was Almost a Man